THE TEMPLE OF NINGIRSU

VOLUME 1

The Temple of Ningirsu

The Culture of the Sacred in Mesopotamia

PUBLISHED BY
EISENBRAUNS AND THE BRITISH MUSEUM

University Park, PA & London

SÉBASTIEN REY

*With contributions from
Angelo Di Michele, Elisa Girotto,
Holger Gzella, Fatma Husain,
Ashley Pooley, Jon Taylor and
Paul Williamson.*

Library of Congress Cataloging-in-Publication Data

Names: Rey, Sébastien, 1981– author.
Title: The temple of Ningirsu : the culture of the sacred in Mesopotamia / Sébastien Rey ; with contributions from Angelo di Michele, Elisa Girotto, Holger Gzella, Fatma Husain, Ashley Pooley, Jon Taylor and Paul Williamson.
Other titles: Culture of the sacred in Mesopotamia
Description: University Park, PA : Eisenbrauns ; London : The British Museum, [2024] | Includes bibliographical references and index.
Summary: "A comprehensive re-examination of the history of the temple site in the sacred Sumerian city of Girsu through modern excavations and the re-evaluation of earlier archaeological discoveries. Examines the role of rescue and preventative excavations as a way to stabilise and preserve exposed but inadequately recorded archaeological sites"—Provided by publisher.
Identifiers: LCCN 2023040167 | ISBN 9781646022649 (v. 1 ; hardback) | ISBN 9781646022649 (v. 2 ; hardback)
Subjects: LCSH: Excavations (Archaeology)—Iraq—Girsu (Extinct city) | Sumerians—Religion. | Temples—Iraq—Girsu (Extinct city) | Girsu (Extinct city) | Iraq—Antiquities.
Classification: LCC DS70.5.G57 R494 2024 | DDC 935—dc23/eng/20231208
LC record available at https://lccn.loc.gov/2023040167

Copyright © 2024 The British Museum and Sébastien Rey
All rights reserved
Printed in China
Published by The Pennsylvania State University Press,
University Park, PA 16802-1003

Eisenbrauns is an imprint of The Pennsylvania State University Press.

The Pennsylvania State University Press is a member of the Association of University Presses.

It is the policy of The Pennsylvania State University Press to use acid-free paper. Publications on uncoated stock satisfy the minimum requirements of American National Standard for Information Sciences—Permanence of Paper for Printed Library Material, ANSI Z39.48–1992.

Cover illustrations: (*slip case*) reconstruction of the Ur-Bau plaza (digital model by Sandra Grabowski © The Girsu Project and artefacts-berlin.de); (*vol. 1 front*) the Thunderbird Mace Head, British Museum 23287 (photo by Dani Tagen © The Girsu Project); (*vol. 1 back*) reconstruction of the Early Dynastic Temple of Ningirsu (digital model by Sandra Grabowski © The Girsu Project and artefacts-berlin.de); (*vol. 2 front*) copper foundation peg from Gudea's New Eninnu, British Museum 96566 (photo by Dani Tagen © The Girsu Project); (*vol. 2 back*) reconstruction of the Ur-Bau plaza (digital model by Sandra Grabowski © The Girsu Project and artefacts-berlin.de).

CONTENTS

List of Illustrations | ix
List of Abbreviations | xvii

Part 1: General Introduction

CHAPTER 1 The Temple of Ningirsu from Its Origins to the Present Day | 3

CHAPTER 2 The Rediscovery of Ancient Girsu | 28

CHAPTER 3 A Contextualised Chronology of Ancient Girsu | 42

Part 2: The Mound of the House of the Fruits

CHAPTER 4 Introduction to the French Excavations on Tell K | 53

CHAPTER 5 The French Excavations on Tell K: Sarzec and Heuzey in Detail | 56

CHAPTER 6 After Sarzec: Cros in Detail | 71

CHAPTER 7 The Great Rift of Girsu: Genouillac and Parrot | 80

CHAPTER 8 Tell K: Plans and Sections | 91

CHAPTER 9 Photographs of Tell K, 1888–1931 | 107

CHAPTER 10 Tell K: A New History of the Temple of Ningirsu | 135

CHAPTER 11 The Origins and Early Historical Significance of the Temple of Ningirsu | 145

CHAPTER 12 The Lower Construction | 157

CHAPTER 13 The Objects from the Lower Construction | 174

CHAPTER 14 The Tessellated Earth | 193

CHAPTER 15 The Outer Block (P'Q'R'S') and Associated Finds | 203

CHAPTER 16 The New Sanctuary: The Ur-Nanshe Building | 212

CHAPTER 17 The Eanatum Extension Phase | 237

CHAPTER 18　The Stele of the Vultures | 243

CHAPTER 19　The Enmetena Restoration | 259

CHAPTER 20　From Enmetena to the Destruction of the Early Dynastic Complex | 290

CHAPTER 21　Darkness and Renaissance: Tell K in the Akkad, Lagash II and Ur III Eras | 307

Part 3: The Mound of the Palace

CHAPTER 22　An Overview of the French Excavations on Tell A | 325

CHAPTER 23　The French Pioneers on Tell A: An In-Depth Account of Their Findings | 328

CHAPTER 24　Plans of the French Excavations and a Plaster Maquette | 344

CHAPTER 25　Photographs of the Early French Excavations | 356

CHAPTER 26　The French Legacy: Challenges and Preserved Treasures | 380

CHAPTER 27　The Mound of the Palace Today: A Landscape of Trenches and Spoils | 385

CHAPTER 28　First Excavation Results: The French Historical Phase (1877–1930) | 394

CHAPTER 29　The Effects of Modern Looting | 408

CHAPTER 30　Coda: Objects from the Spolia of Tell A | 412

CHAPTER 31　Before the Big Move: The Early Dynastic and Akkad Temple Complex | 416

CHAPTER 32　The Early Dynastic Sanctuary of the Goddess Bau | 444

CHAPTER 33　The Ur-Bau Complex: The Relocated Ningirsu Temple and the Restored Temple to Bau | 458

CHAPTER 34　The Gudea Sanctuary of Ningirsu: The New Eninnu | 467

CHAPTER 35　The Historical Significance of the New Eninnu from Lagash II Times to the Old Babylonian Period | 502

CHAPTER 36　The New Eninnu from Lagash II Times to the Old Babylonian Period | 519

CHAPTER 37　The Statues of Gudea from the New Eninnu | 547

CHAPTER 38　Gudea's Temple Plan and the Physical Remains | 570

CHAPTER 39　The Metrology of Statue B | 581

CHAPTER 40　The Gates of the New Eninnu and the Monuments to the Slain Heroes | 591

CHAPTER 41　The Steles of Gudea | 608

CHAPTER 42　The Bricks of the New Eninnu | 630

CHAPTER 43　The Inscribed Clay Nails of the New Eninnu | 643

CHAPTER 44　The Foundation Deposits of the New Eninnu | 658

Part 4: The Ningirsu Temple in the Hellenistic Era

CHAPTER 45 The Renaissance of the Eninnu | 673

CHAPTER 46 The Stratigraphy of the Hellenistic Shrine | 687

CHAPTER 47 The Meaning and Purpose of the Hellenistic Eninnu | 724

CHAPTER 48 The End of the Hellenistic Eninnu | 744

Acknowledgements | 753
Table of Correspondences | 755
References | 759
Illustration Credits | 765
Index | 769

ILLUSTRATIONS

1. Statue of Gudea. British Museum 122910   4
2. City-states of Sumer in the third millennium BCE   7
3. The Thunderbird Mace Head. British Museum 23287   8
4. Reconstruction of the Early Dynastic Temple of Ningirsu   9
5. Artist's impression of a Sumerian temple   11
6. The Feathered Figure. Musée du Louvre AO221   12
7. The Mace of Mesilim. Musée du Louvre AO2349   13
8. Tablet containing the Hymn to the Reeds. Musée du Louvre AO3866   15
9. The Cylinders of Gudea. Musée du Louvre MNB1512 and MNB1511   17
10. Gudea as the Architect with a Plan (Statue B). Musée du Louvre AO2   18
11. Reconstruction of Gudea's New Eninnu   19
12. South-facing view of the sacred precinct of Girsu (the Urukug) in 2017   20
13. A copper foundation peg from Gudea's New Eninnu. British Museum 96566   21
14. The Temple of Ningirsu on Tell A: a view of the British Museum team's excavations in 2017   22
15. Plan of the British Museum team's excavation trenches on Tell A   24
16. Plan of the sacred precinct of Girsu (the Urukug), showing the reconstructed Lagash II and Early Dynastic shrines on Tells A and K, respectively   26
17. Ernest de Sarzec (front row, centre) with his escort in Tello   29
18. General Plan of the Mounds of Tello (Plan B), Sarzec and Heuzey 1912   30
19. Seated statue of Gudea: the Colossus (Statue D). Musée du Louvre AO1   31
20. Pencil sketches, made in 1850 by H. A. Churchill, of a statue of Gudea from Tell Hamman. British Museum 92988 / ME Ar. 184.9   32
21. British Museum keeper R. D. Barnett refitting the hands of the Gudea Colossus to the other preserved parts of the statue at a ceremony in the Louvre in 1958   33
22. Ur-Nanshe Plaque A. Musée du Louvre AO2344   36
23. The Silver Vase of Enmetena. Musée du Louvre AO2674   37
24. Gaston Cros with a group of tribespeople   38
25. Henri de Genouillac's excavations on Tell K, c.1930   40
26. The Early Dynastic inscribed stone Plaque of Enanatum. British Museum 130828   47
27. Objects associated with the Ur-Nanshe Building   59
28. Objects associated with the Lower Construction   62
29. Early Dynastic relief of a nude man carrying fish. Musée du Louvre AO4110   78
30. Pottery from Tell K I   83
31. Pottery from Tell K II   84
32. Pottery from Tell K III   85
33. Sarzec and Heuzey 1912, Plan C (1): The Ur-Nanshe Building. Plan C (2): Plan and Elevation of the Lower Construction, and a Cross-Section of the Central Area of Tell K   93
34. Sarzec and Heuzey 1912, Plan D: General Plan of Tell K   97
35. Cros 1910, Plan A: The Principal Excavation Area of Tello   100
36. Cros 1910, Plan B: Excavations in the Vicinity of the House of the Fruits   102
37. Cros 1910, SW and NE Sections of Tell K   103

x   Illustrations

38. Cros 1910, Plan C: Stairways and Water Supply Network   105
39. Sarzec and Heuzey 1912, Pl. 54 (1): The SE Façade of the Ur-Nanshe Building   108
40. Sarzec and Heuzey 1912, Pl. 54 (2): The S Corner of the Ur-Nanshe Building   109
41. Sarzec and Heuzey 1912, Pl. 55 (1): The Enmetena Block   110
42. Sarzec and Heuzey 1912, Pl. 55 (2): The Oval Reservoir   112
43. Sarzec and Heuzey 1912, Pl. 56 (1): The Lower Construction   113
44. Sarzec and Heuzey 1912, Pl. 56 (2): The Stele of the Captives   114
45. Sarzec and Heuzey 1912, Pl. 57 (1): The Ring Post from pavement F   115
46. Sarzec and Heuzey 1912, Pl. 57 (2): The Well of Eanatum   116
47. Sarzec and Heuzey 1912, Pl. 57 bis (2): Stack of planoconvex bricks   118
48. Sarzec and Heuzey 1912, Pl. 58 (1): View from the top of the Large Stairway   119
49. Sarzec and Heuzey 1912, Pl. 58 (2): View from the bottom of the Large Stairway   120
50. Sarzec and Heuzey 1912, Pl. 58 bis (2): The curved channel on the edge of Tell K   122
51. Sarzec and Heuzey 1912, Pl. 52 (1): First view of the Pillar of Gudea   124
52. Sarzec and Heuzey 1912, Pl. 52 (2): Second view of the Pillar of Gudea   125
53. Diagram showing the construction of the Pillar of Gudea   126
54. Sarzec and Heuzey 1912, Pl. 53 (2): The Pillar of Gudea completely exposed   128
55. Cros 1910, View No. 1: Stairways and Water Supply Network   130
56. Cros 1910, View No. 2: Stairways and Water Supply Network   131
57. Genouillac 1934, Pl. 1 (2): Excavations on Tell K   132
58. Genouillac 1934, Pl. 46 (1): The Well of Eanatum   133
59. Comprehensive plan of Tell K   138
60. The Stratigraphy of Tell K from Early Dynastic times to the reigns of Gudea and Shulgi   140
61. Plan showing the principal constructions and notable objects excavated on Tell K, dating from Early Dynastic times to the reigns of Gudea and Shulgi   142
62. The Circular Bas-Relief. Musée du Louvre AO2350   149
63. Ur-Nanshe Plaque B. Musée du Louvre AO2345   152
64. An Ur-Nanshe copper foundation peg with a copper collar. British Museum 96565   153
65. Early Dynastic lapis lazuli cylinder seal, with motifs probably relating to Ningirsu's cosmic battle with the Slain Heroes. British Museum 22962   155
66. Reconstruction of the layout of the subterranean rooms and corridors of the Lower Construction   158
67. Reconstruction of the Lower Construction, showing its subterranean areas and above-ground walls   159
68. A foundation peg from the Lower Construction. British Museum 108980   160
69. Detail of a foundation peg from the Lower Construction. British Museum 108980   161
70. Reconstruction of the antecella in the Lower Construction   163
71. Late Uruk cylinder seal   167
72. Reconstruction of the Lower Construction's antecella and cella   170
73. The Thunderbird Mace Head. British Museum 23287   176
74. Presargonic shell plaque, showing Ningirsu with a horned crown fighting a seven-headed monster   180
75. Reconstruction of the Girsu Land Stele   182
76. Reconstruction of the Stele of the Captives   184
77. Reconstruction of the Circular Bas-Relief   186
78. Akkad cylinder seal from Nippur that shows a sandal attached to the shaft of a standard featuring a ceremonial mace head   188
79. A courtier at the court of Narmer of Egypt holding a pair of sandals belonging to the king. From the Palette of Narmer, c.3200 BCE   189
80. The Standard of Ur (detail of the war panel). British Museum 121201   190
81. Diagrams showing the way in which Sumerian temples were laid out with respect to the cardinal points   194
82. Evolution of the sign é, meaning 'house' or 'temple'   200

83. Three Sumerian signs: é ('house'); kid ('reed mat'); gan₂ ('field')   201
84. Reconstruction of the Ur-Nanshe Building on the summit of Tell K   213
85. Close-up of the massive platforms of Tell K   214
86. A two-part copper foundation deposit from the reign of Ur-Nanshe. British Museum 96565   216
87. An inscribed door socket of Ur-Nanshe. Musée du Louvre AO252   218
88. Four reconstructed views of the Ur-Nanshe Building   224
89. The Genealogical Plaques of Ur-Nanshe (Plaques A, B, C and D)   231
90. The Ur-Nanshe Building in the reign of Eanatum   241
91. The Thunderbird Mace Head. British Museum 23287   242
92. Reconstruction of the Stele of the Vultures   244
93. Two possible views of Ningirsu's divine chariot   247
94. Reconstruction of the obverse and reverse of the Stele of the Vultures   252
95. Reconstruction of Tell K in the reign of Enmetena   260
96. A view of the hanging gardens planted on Tell K by Enmetena   266
97. An Enmetena foundation deposit. Musée du Louvre AO2353   268
98. Reconstruction of the brewhouse   270
99. A cutaway view of the reconstructed brewhouse   271
100. A view of the interior of the brewhouse   272
101. Reconstruction of a bull lyre from Girsu   280
102. Detail of a lyre player and a singer on the peace panel of the Standard of Ur. British Museum 121201   282
103. The Plaque of Dudu. Musée du Louvre AO2354   294
104. Tablet containing the Lament over the Destruction of Lagash. Musée du Louvre AO4162   300
105. Fragment of a vase dedicated to Ningirsu by the Akkad king Rimush (TG3545)   309
106. Fragment of the Akkad Stele from Girsu. Musée du Louvre AO2678   311
107. Reconstruction of the Akkad Stele   312
108. Carved limestone basin inscribed in the name of Gudea   330
109. Objects from Tell A dating from the reign of Gudea   332
110. A selection of the fragments of the Gudea Steles recovered by Cros   336
111. Sarzec and Heuzey 1912, Plan A: Ground plan of the so-called Palace, with underlying Sumerian remains   345
112. Plaster Maquette of Sarzec's excavations on Tell A. Musée du Louvre AOmg246   348
113. Cros 1910, Plan H: The shrine and stone stairway on the NE side of Tell A   349
114. Sarzec and Heuzey 1912, Ground plan of the Hellenistic walls and underlying Sumerian remains (Heuzey's New Plan)   351
115. Genouillac 1936, Elevation and plan of the excavations on the Mound of the Palace   353
116. Sarzec and Heuzey 1912, Pl. 49 (1): The NE façade of the so-called Palace   357
117. Sarzec and Heuzey 1912, Pl. 49 (2): Close-up of the NE façade   358
118. Sarzec and Heuzey 1912, Pl. 50 (1): The Gate of Gudea (1888)   359
119. Sarzec and Heuzey 1912, Pl. 50 (2): A second view of the Gate of Gudea (1888)   361
120. Sarzec and Heuzey 1912, Pl. 51 (1): The external face of the Ur-Bau wall   362
121. Sarzec and Heuzey 1912, Pl. 51 (2): The inside face of the Ur-Bau wall   364
122. Sarzec and Heuzey 1912, Pl. 53 (1): The Gate of Gudea (1889)   365
123. Sarzec and Heuzey 1912, Pl. 53 bis (1): The Gate of Gudea completely exposed (1895)   366
124. Sarzec and Heuzey 1912, Pl. 53 bis (2): The continuation of the Hellenistic NW façade (OP)   367
125. Sarzec and Heuzey 1912, Pl. 61 (top): The exedra   368
126. Sarzec and Heuzey 1912, Pl. 61 (bottom): The cistern block   369
127. Sarzec and Heuzey 1912, Pl. 61 bis (top): The cistern block and the base of the Ur-Bau wall   370
128. Sarzec and Heuzey 1912, Pl. 61 bis (bottom): A second view of the cistern block and the base of the Ur-Bau wall   371
129. Cros, unpublished photo of the Gate of Gudea   372

xii   Illustrations

130. Cros, unpublished photo of the trench at the base of the Gate of Gudea   373
131. Cros 1910, View No. 11: The area of the Gudea Steles between Tells A and B   374
132. Cros 1910, View No. 12: Drainage channel close to the area of the Gudea Steles between Tells A and B   375
133. Genouillac 1936, Pl. 72 (2): The Gate of Gudea, seen from inside Court A   376
134. Genouillac 1936, Pl. 72 (1): Close-up of the foundation deposit uncovered on the SE side of the Gate of Gudea   377
135. Genouillac 1936, Pl. 73 (1): The well inside Court C   378
136. Heuzey's New Plan and Genouillac's plan of Tell A superimposed   383
137. Aerial view of Tell A   386
138. Plan of the Spoil Heaps of Tell A   367
139. Plan of the British Museum team's excavation trenches on Tell A   392
140. Aerial view of the central area of Tell A, showing the British Museum team's excavations and the surrounding French spoil heaps   395
141. Mount Sarzec (SH1)   396
142. Impressions of cylinder seals found on Tell A by the British Museum team   397
143. Aerial view of the French excavations on Tell A   401
144. Fragment of a Lagash II stone statue, showing two hands clasped in prayer (TG3067)   406
145. An oval looting pit cutting through the mud-brick walls of the New Eninnu   409
146. Objects discarded by looters   410
147. Plan showing the distribution of Lagash II and Ur III inscribed clay nails in the British Museum team's trenches   414
148. The sequence of mud-brick platforms excavated by the British Museum team on Tell A   418
149. The principal sections recorded by the British Museum team in Area B1   420
150. The two-step red platform and white platform, excavated by the British Museum team on Tell A   421
151. Detail of the stepped red platform in Area B1   421
152. The white platform in Area B1, showing the truncation caused by French excavation trenches   423
153. Early Dynastic ceremonial vessels from Tell A   425
154. Pottery from the Temple Platforms I   430
155. Pottery from the Temple Platforms II   431
156. Pottery from the Temple Platforms III   432
157. Pottery from the Temple Platforms IV   433
158. Pottery from the Temple Platforms V   434
159. Pottery from the Temple Building I   438
160. Pottery from the Temple Building II   439
161. Pottery from the Temple Building III   440
162. Pottery from the Temple Building IV   441
163. Pottery from the Temple Building V   442
164. Pottery from the Temple Building VI   443
165. Fragment of an Early Dynastic relief excavated by Sarzec between Tells J and K. Musée du Louvre AO48   445
166. Reattached fragments of an inscribed bowl dedicated to the goddess Bau. British Museum 90902   446
167. Plan of the Early Dynastic Urukug, showing the reconstructed shrines on Tells A and K   450
168. Statue of Ur-Bau from Tell A. Musée du Louvre AO9   459
169. Inscribed copper foundation peg and inscribed stone tablet from the reign of Ur-Bau, together with the clay pot in which the objects were supposedly found by Sarzec. Musée du Louvre AO311, AO261 and AO451   462
170. A cutaway reconstruction of Gudea's New Eninnu   472
171. Close-up of the reconstruction of the Ur-Bau plaza   475
172. The NE façade of the Ningirsu temple on the SE side of Gudea's New Eninnu   479
173. The inscribed stone door socket found by the British Museum team inside the main entrance in the NE façade of the Ningirsu temple   481
174. Section of the SE façade of the Ningirsu temple (wall 2139), showing the brickwork and the positions of the *in situ* clay nails   482
175. Section of the SW façade of the Ningirsu temple (wall 2159), with two *in situ* clay nails   483
176. The inscribed stone door socket and copper pivot found by the British Museum team inside the entrance to the cella of the Ningirsu temple   484
177. Artist's impression of the cella in the Temple of Ningirsu at the heart of Gudea's New Eninnu   487

178. Artist's impression of the antecella in Gudea's Temple of Ningirsu   488
179. The remains of the well (M) in the antecella of Gudea's Ningirsu temple   489
180. The podium, presumably for the Gudea Statues, on the SE wall of the antecella inside the Ningirsu temple   490
181. The internal walkway on the SW side of the Ningirsu temple   491
182. Section of the NE façade of the inner envelope wall (3049 and 2032) on the SW side of the Ningirsu temple, showing the positions of the *in situ* clay nails   493
183. Section of the continuation of the façade of the inner envelope wall (2031), showing a single *in situ* clay nail   494
184. Reconstruction of the central courtyard inside Gudea's New Eninnu, looking towards the south-east   495
185. Reconstruction of the central courtyard inside Gudea's New Eninnu, looking towards the north-west   496
186. Artist's impression of a gate in the external façade of the New Eninnu   497
187. Section of the NE wall (2059) inside the SW gateway passage in the temenos wall of the New Eninnu, showing four *in situ* clay nails   498
188. One of the oversized fired bricks that formed the cover of the foundation box (2092) installed in the E corner of the tower on the SE side of the SW gateway that gave access to Gudea's New Eninnu   500
189. The stone foundation tablet (TG1501) seen *in situ* inside the rectangular foundation box (2092)   500
190. Reconstruction of a cylinder seal belonging to Gudea. Musée du Louvre AO3541   503
191. Reconstruction of a cylinder seal belonging to Ur-Sharura, a servant of the deified Gudea   508
192. Reconstruction of a cylinder seal belonging to Lu-Dumuzi, a cupbearer to the deified Gudea   508
193. Inscribed fragments from Girsu unearthed by the British Museum team   510
194. The Stratigraphy of Tell A from Early Dynastic times to the Hellenistic era   520
195. Section of the SW ambulatory of the Ningirsu temple, showing a sequence of fills deposited from the Lagash II period through to Old Babylonian times   525
196. Section of the SE ambulatory of the Ningirsu temple, showing the early sequence of fills capped with Hellenistic foundation fill 2136   525
197. Repairs and fills inside the New Eninnu's SW gate   528
198. Impression of a Lagash II cylinder seal found inside the layer of burnt materials that were ritually deposited in the stairwell chamber of the Ningirsu temple   533
199. Pottery from the New Eninnu I   538
200. Pottery from the New Eninnu II   539
201. Pottery from the New Eninnu III   540
202. Pottery from the New Eninnu IV   541
203. Pottery from the New Eninnu V   542
204. Pottery from the New Eninnu VI   543
205. Pottery from the New Eninnu VII   544
206. Pottery from the New Eninnu VIII   545
207. The diorite statues of Tell A, including Statues A–F of Gudea and the portrait of Ur-Bau. Musée du Louvre, AO8 (A), AO2 (B), AO5 (C), AO1 (D), AO6 (E), AO3 (F) and AO9 (Ur-Bau)   549
208. Statues of the Akkad rulers Manishtusu (standing and seated) and Naram-Sin. Musée du Louvre, SB48, SB49 and SB53   550
209. Areas of damage on the diorite statues of Tell A   560
210. Areas of damage on the diorite statues of Tell A   561
211. Statue B. Musée du Louvre AO2   571
212. Close-up of the tablet on Statue B. Musée du Louvre AO2   573
213. The ground plan from Statue B superimposed on the plan of the British Museum team's excavations and Heuzey's New Plan   575
214. Old Babylonian tablet demonstrating a method for working out the square root of two. Yale University YBC7289   582
215. The standard unit on Gudea's measuring rod expressed as fractions of sixty and as a table of reciprocals   584
216. The ground plan from Statue B correlated with the standard units on the adjacent measuring rod   586
217. A two-stage geometrical method for constructing the ground plan on Statue B   589
218. The Ur-Nanshe Building on Tell K, showing its position with respect to the cardinal points and the path taken by the sun as it passes over Tello in the course of a year   593

219. The New Eninnu of Gudea on Tell A, showing its position with respect to the cardinal points and the annual path of the sun   596
220. Reconstruction of the Gudea Stele devoted to Enki   617
221. Reconstruction of the Gudea Stele to Ningirsu and Bau   619
222. Reconstruction of the Gudea Stele with the seven-headed mace   621
223. Reconstruction of the Gudea Stele devoted to Bau and Gatumdug   622
224. Reconstruction of the Gudea Stele referred to as the sunrise relief   624
225. Reconstruction of the Gudea Stele referred to as the relief of abundance   625
226. Reconstruction of a two-sided Gudea Stele   627
227. Reconstruction of the Gudea Stele referred to as the music stele   628
228. The rectangular Thunderbird bricks found by the British Museum team   632
229. Models of structures built with square bricks (red) and rectangular half-bricks (pink)   638
230. A clay nail inscribed in the name of Gudea, seen *in situ* in the inner envelope wall (2031)   644
231. Diagrams showing the placement of Gudea's Standard Inscription on a clay nail   649
232. Close-up views of the Standard Inscription on the stem of a single clay nail   652
233. A typology of the clay nails found on Tell A   653
234. The inscribed stone tablet (TG1501) found *in situ* in its foundation box (2092) by the British Museum team   659
235. Inscribed stone tablet from the reign of Gudea. British Museum 91008   660
236. Four views of a copper foundation peg inscribed in the name of Gudea. British Museum 96566   661
237. Three copper foundation pegs from Girsu   666
238. A Hellenistic brick stamped in the name of Adadnadinakhe, found *in situ* by the British Museum team on Tell A   674
239. Sherd of a Hellenistic glazed tile found by the British Museum team on Tell A   675
240. Reconstruction of the Hellenistic shrine on Tell A, after it was enlarged around 250 BCE, showing the N corner and the articulated NE façade   680
241. Close-up of the reconstruction of the Hellenistic shrine's NE façade   681
242. Plan of the British Museum team's Area B12   684
243. Excavated section of the SW façade of the original Hellenistic shrine, constructed shortly after 331 BCE   688
244. Section of the NW façade of the enlarged Hellenistic shrine, showing the underlying mud-brick temenos of Adadnadinakhe   694
245. The W section of the British Museum team's Area B10   695
246. The E section of Area B10   696
247. Sumerian stone demon amulets   697
248. Pottery from the Hellenistic shrine I   706
249. Pottery from the Hellenistic shrine II   707
250. Pottery from the Hellenistic shrine III   708
251. Pottery from the Hellenistic shrine IV   709
252. Pottery from the Hellenistic shrine V   710
253. Pottery from the Hellenistic shrine VI   711
254. Hellenistic storage jar with a vertical neck and a band rim, dating from the late fourth century or early third century BCE   712
255. Aramaic inscriptions excavated by the British Museum team   713
256. Sumerian terracotta figurines found by the British Museum team   716
257. Terracotta figurines of riders on horseback from the Hellenistic shrine   717
258. Nude female terracotta figurines from the Hellenistic shrine   718
259. Terracotta heads of deities and presumed royal figures from the Hellenistic shrine   719
260. Terracotta plaque showing a goddess wearing a mural crown   721
261. Close-up of the point of impact on a Hellenistic-era terracotta fertility goddess (TG4293) that was possibly broken intentionally   722
262. Second close-up of the lower edge of the break on the same terracotta fertility goddess (TG4293)   723
263. Terracotta of a figure wearing a diadem (TG4436), showing possible intentional damage or decapitation   723
264. Reconstruction of Court A inside the Hellenistic shrine   725
265. Close-up of the reconstruction of Court A   726

266. Reconstruction of a niche inside the Hellenistic shrine, containing Statue A, a standing portrait of Gudea   727
267. Artist's impression of the bronze statue of Heracles (AO2890) found on Tell A by Sarzec   728
268. Sherd of a ceramic vessel decorated with a portrait of Alexander the Great   729
269. A silver coin struck in Babylon shortly after the arrival of Alexander the Great in 331 BCE   730
270. Sumerian terracotta figurine of a horned nude goddess (TG3842), retrieved by the British Museum team from the Hellenistic strata of Tell A   731
271. Corner of a limestone basin with a lion's head (part of a Thunderbird motif), inscribed in the name of Gudea. Musée du Louvre AO73   732
272. A selection of the Hellenistic spindle whorls unearthed by the British Museum team on Tell A   736
273. Some of the Hellenistic loom weights unearthed by the British Museum team on Tell A   737
274. Partly reconstructed drawings of the Alexander coin found on Tell A by the British Museum team   740
275. Terracotta showing a crowned head (TG2123)   742
276. Partly reconstructed drawings of the coin from the reign of Antiochus III found on Tell A by the British Museum team   746

ABBREVIATIONS

AO	*Antiquités Orientales* (Musée du Louvre)
Ashm	Ashmolean Museum, Oxford
BM	British Museum, London
CAD	The Assyrian Dictionary of the University of Chicago
CT	Cuneiform Texts from Babylonian Tablets in the British Museum
CUSAS	Cornell University Studies in Assyriology and Sumerology
DP	Documents présargoniques
DUROM	Durham Oriental Museum
EŞEM	Eski Şark Eserleri Müzesi, Istanbul
ETCSL	The Electronic Text Corpus of Sumerian Literature
FAOS	Freiburger Altorientalische Studien
HMA	Hearst Museum of Anthropology
IM	Iraq Museum, Bagdhad
NAMN	National Archaeological Museum of Naples
RIME	The Royal Inscriptions of Mesopotamia, Early Periods
ROM	Royal Ontario Museum
RTC	Recueil de tablettes chaldéennes
SB	*Suse Bis* (Musée du Louvre)
TG	Tello/Girsu
U	Ur
UET	Ur Excavations. Texts
VA	Vorderasiatisches Museum, Berlin
YBC	Yale Babylonian Collection

PART 1 General Introduction

CHAPTER 1

The Temple of Ningirsu from Its Origins to the Present Day

Gudea's Dream and the French Rediscovery

More than 4,000 years ago, Gudea, the ruler of the Sumerian city of Girsu, had a dream in which he was visited by a supernatural being whose awe-inspiring presence, which took the form of a raging deluge, filled the entire cosmos (Fig. 1). The unearthly colossus wore the horned crown of a god and had the wings of the fabled Thunderbird. He was flanked by ferocious lions, who lay on the ground beside him, and he uttered some obscure words about the building of a house. Day seemed to break on the horizon. Then there was a woman, perhaps a high priestess, who placed a stylus of shining silver on a tablet that contained a chart of propitious stars, which she proceeded to consult, while a warrior outlined the plan of a building on a tablet of lapis lazuli. There was a basket and a brick mould, and birds twittered ceaselessly in a poplar tree. A stallion pawed at the ground.

Perplexed by his night vision, which is recorded at the beginning of the long narrative inscribed on the Cylinders of Gudea, the ruler set out on a mystic journey by sacred barge down the ancient canal that connected Girsu with the temple of Nanshe, a goddess known to interpret the dreams that were sent by other deities. She explained what he had seen: the divine being with the eagle-like wings of the Thunderbird and the body of a flood storm was Nanshe's brother Ningirsu, the supreme god of Girsu, who had commanded Gudea to build a magnificent temple in his honour. The dawning of day was a sign that Gudea's personal god, Ningishzida, would offer his assistance in the endeavour. The woman with the divinatory tablet was the goddess Nisaba, bringing a bright star that augured well for the endeavour, while the mighty warrior was the god Ninduba, who was laying out the temple's design. The basket was ready to hold the first brick that would be made with the holy brick mould, and the noisy birds were a sign that the ruler would not be able to sleep until he had completed the project. Finally, the stallion was Gudea himself, eager to get on with the task. In a second oracular dream that was activated by an incubation ritual the god Ningirsu spoke directly to Gudea (A11):

> Laying the foundations of my temple will bring immediate abundance. The great fields will grow rich for you: the levees and ditches will be full to the brim for you, and the water will rise for you to heights never reached by the water before. Under your rule, more oil than ever will be poured and more wool than ever will be weighed in Sumer.

Upon waking, Gudea mobilised the entire populace of Girsu to build Ningirsu's temple, and he dispatched heralds to the four corners of the earth to procure precious materials worthy of the god. While sacred hymns were sung and incantations were being recited, the ruler and a cohort of high priests performed consecration rituals and purifying rites in order to sanctify the sacred ground on which the temple was to stand. Among his numerous preparatory actions, Gudea cleansed the city, banishing ritually unclean and unpleasant-looking people, and he forbade debt collection and the burial of bodies. From far-off places, including Elam, Susa in Iran, Magan in Oman, the cedar mountains of Lebanon,

FIGURE 1. Statue of Gudea. British Museum 122910.

and Meluhha in the Indus Valley, he procured an impressive array of expensive materials: cedar, ebony, gypsum, carnelian, diorite and alabaster, together with copper, silver and gold. The ruler's reach appeared boundless. When the work began, he consulted the heavens and precisely laid out the walls of the temple with pegs and ropes, as he had been instructed, and he performed the holiest construction rituals, notably the fabrication and consecration of the first brick, imbued with apotropaic properties, for which he solemnly moulded the clay. When the 'good brick' turned out to be the 'most beautiful' that could be imagined, as it is described in the Cylinder Inscriptions (A18), the entire state of Lagash spent the day celebrating. Then, as the construction of the temple proceeded, Gudea worked as a hands-on overseer, enthusiastically assisting the skilled craftsmen who were commissioned to create a building befitting Ningirsu's power and grandeur.

Foremost among the temple's features was the god's inner sanctum, made up of a sleeping chamber and a grand dining hall. Accompanying this inner space was a series of ancillary structures, including a room hung with Ningirsu's godly weapons, a gem storehouse, a wine cellar, a brewery, a chapel for commemorative offerings and a courtyard that echoed constantly with the sounds of prayers and kettle-drums. Bau, Ningirsu's wife, had her own private quarters in the form of a splendid personal shrine. Upon completion, the divine abode appeared both magnificent and formidable, like Imdugud (or Anzu), the radiant Thunderbird himself, as he appeared when he attacked the ill-fated mountain at the end of the world, striking from the sky with his fearsome, outstretched wings. After Gudea had introduced Ningirsu and Bau into the temple, substantially present in their carved representations, he commanded the entire population of Lagash to kneel and prostrate themselves. The Heroic God then made himself manifest, entering the temple complex as a terrible storm thundering into battle and subsequently emerging like the sun god rising over Lagash. The goddess Bau crossed the threshold of her sacred enclave like a respectable woman taking possession of her well-ordered household, and she emerged like the Tigris at high water when it benignly irrigates a verdant, fruitful garden. As a reward for his efforts, Gudea was showered with acclaim, and his land became marvellously fertile.

Four thousand years later, in 1877, Ernest de Sarzec, a French diplomat turned archaeologist, was posted to Basra in the south-east corner of present-day Iraq, which at that time was part of the Ottoman Empire. He had long nurtured an interest in archaeology, and he soon began to excavate at the site of Tello. Over the next half-century, Sarzec and his successors, led by Gaston Cros, Henri de Genouillac and André Parrot, unearthed fabulous hoards of inscribed clay tablets, archaic statues, bas-reliefs, votive artefacts and significant archaeological fragments of buildings, including some almost complete structures, that dated from the very distant past. They had discovered ancient Girsu, one of the major sacred centres of a bygone Mesopotamian civilisation that thrived in the third millennium BCE.

Most of the very early statues unearthed in Tello depicted the ruler Gudea, who reigned from around 2125 to 2100 BCE, and they all show him with his hands interlocked in a gesture of devout prayer. The inscriptions, set down in wedge-shaped cuneiform characters, were entrusted to two French philologists and epigraphers, Arthur Amiaud and François Thureau-Dangin, who soon discovered that the texts were in Sumerian, the world's oldest known written language. It has since been established that the cuneiform system of writing was developed in Sumer around 3200 BCE, but the very existence of Sumerian was first postulated by the Assyriologist Jules Oppert only in 1869, less than a decade before Sarzec first visited Tello.

The recovery of the Sumerian legacy was made possible by a remarkable series of archaeological achievements that produced extraordinary results, notwithstanding the inevitable missteps and regrettable losses. The pioneering explorers who worked among the ruins of crumbled mud-brick architecture were assisted from afar by linguistic scholars and historians, notably the Louvre curator Léon Heuzey, who pored over repositories of evidence, including objects, fragments of clay tablets and stone sculptures engraved with a largely unreadable script, together with the notes, sketches, plans and photos that were sent back from Iraq to Paris by the excavators. With great persistence, they jointly succeeded in shedding light on a forgotten world of archaic temples, palaces and concealed cities that had lain buried beneath the sands and alluvial silt of the Mesopotamian flood plain for thousands of years. Girsu, along with Lagash, its civic sibling and coequal in an overarching statehood that joined the two ancient cities and their associated territories in a single political structure, was one of a number of Sumerian urban centres, including Uruk, Eridu, Nippur and Ur, that were built on the arid land between the Tigris and the Euphrates, where they prospered thanks to the life-giving waters of those two mighty rivers. In the century and a half since these sites first came to the attention of archaeologists, they have come to be recognised as some of the world's first cities.

Ningirsu and the Thunderbird

From the flourishing of the early proto-urban religious centres, through the more familiar historical cycle of rising and falling imperial powers, to the collapse of Seleucid rule in Babylonia in 150 BCE, Mesopotamia see-sawed dramatically between fragmentation and unification. From the outset, rival Sumerian cities rose to become seats of regional power or provincial satellites of hegemonic authorities (Akkad, Ur III and Babylon I, for example), striving for and sometimes achieving independence, before being subjugated once again. The pattern was repeated many times.

For much of the third millennium BCE, Sumer was a protean mosaic of rival city-states (notably Ur, Uruk, Lagash and Umma), each made up of one or more urban, political and religious centre(s) that were surrounded by a rural area containing a relatively dense network of settlements and a variety of other habitations. Economic and social activities were entirely dependent on the success of artificial irrigation that delivered water from the Tigris and the Euphrates via elaborate systems of canals and waterways. Cities crystallised around immemorial cult centres and charismatic proto-urban sanctuaries—the Ekur of Nippur, the Eanna of Uruk and the Eabzu of Eridu, to name just a few (Fig. 2).

The Sumerians believed that cities and their rural hinterlands were the property of divine overlords. Human rulers acted as the earthly representatives of the gods, stewarding their estates and striving conscientiously to promote the well-being of the land and its inhabitants by following divine instructions that were communicated in signs and portents that could be interpreted by schools of learned priests. The sky god, An, who was the founding ancestor of the celestial ruling dynasty and the ultimate source and guarantor of power both in heaven and on earth, resided at Uruk in the Eanna (or 'temple of heaven'), where he lived with Inanna (the 'lady of heaven'), the goddess of carnal love and warfare. Enki, the water god, who was the creator of all technical know-how and the foremost expert in magic, reigned in Eridu, where he had his royal seat at the Eabzu (the 'temple of the watery deep', or the 'abyss'). Ur belonged to the moon god, Nanna (a male deity in Sumer), Larsa to Utu, the sun god, and so forth. Established on the basis of cultic allegiance to one or other of the major deities in the pantheon, Sumerian cities formed an amphictyony, or league of neighbouring states, that was centred around the great cult of Enlil at Nippur. Revered as the sovereign god of the cosmos and the pantheon's supreme divinity, Enlil was worshiped in the Ekur (the 'temple of the mountain'), where he presided over the plenary assembly of gods. The sign of his unsurpassed authority was the Tablet of Destinies, a supernatural object that was the emblem and talisman of his cosmic power.

Girsu belonged to Ningirsu (literally, the 'lord of Girsu'), Enlil's son and his most intrepid and warlike courtier—known as the Heroic God, he was tasked with combating demonic forces and maintaining cosmic order. His shrine was honoured as the sacred centre of the city-state of Lagash (later an extended consolidated territory) that lay in the south-easternmost part of the Mesopotamian alluvium, overlooking the storied shoreline of the Gulf, which in those days was situated a mere 30 km away from the city. Girsu looked north as well as south, however, for many of the chaos-inducing supernatural creatures that Ningirsu fought were believed to have their origins in the legendary Great Mountain in the northern reaches of the Sumerian world—the Taurus Mountains in present-day Turkey, where the Tigris and Euphrates rise. Overcoming the forces of disorder, the fearsome combatant god of Girsu harnessed the rampaging rivers and their tributaries, allowing the inhabitants of Sumer to create a network of canals that brought irrigation waters into Mesopotamia's agricultural floodplain.

Consequently, Ningirsu acquired a dual aspect: originally envisioned as a thundercloud, he was worshipped as the god of thunderstorms and floods, either fructifying or devastating. Sumerian myths depicted his warlike prowess in extravagant detail, sometimes focusing on his better-known hypostasis, Ninurta of Nippur. In the epic poem Lugale ('O king!'), Ningirsu, in his guise as the Heroic God, slays the malevolent archdemon Asag and vanquishes the villain's army of stone warriors with the help of his divine weapon—the magic mace, Mow-down-a-myriad, which is Ningirsu's Excalibur. Lugale is probably a condensed recasting of an archaic precursor poem, referred to under the title of the 'Myth of the Slain Heroes', which seems to have extoled

FIGURE 2. City-states of Sumer in the third millennium BCE.

Ningirsu's valiant exploits and glorious feasts. No longer extant, this earlier epic is alluded to in the inscriptions preserved on the Cylinders of Gudea, where it is said to describe the supernatural beings that Ningirsu captured as trophies, together with the legendary beasts defeated by the Heroic God, who is there referred to as the God of Wrath.

The most prominent of the fabulous beasts vanquished by Ningirsu—a feat that brought him eternal acclaim—was the demigod Imdugud, the mythical Thunderbird, which was a gigantic lion-headed eagle, with a body that flashed lightning and a roar that sounded like thunder (Fig. 3). Renowned for stealing the Tablet of Destinies—the symbol and guarantor

FIGURE 3. The Thunderbird Mace Head. British Museum 23287.

of Enlil's pre-eminence—this supernatural creature became Ningirsu's avatar and the emblem of Girsu. It was originally visualised as an enormous thundercloud in the shape of a bird, but was also considered to be the personification of the fabled South Wind—still recognised today in Iraq as the harbinger of devastating storms. In the myth entitled 'Anzu-bird and the Tablet of Destinies', the Heroic God—the chosen champion of the divine assembly—takes on the impetuous Thunderbird, who has stolen Enlil's potent tablet. Aided by the resourceful god, Enki, Ningirsu subdues the creature with his cohort of winds, re-establishing Enlil's divine authority and restoring equilibrium to the cosmic order ordained by the gods. Crucially, however, he doesn't slay the hybrid bird, but rather tames it, making it his heraldic symbol, and also his avatar or alter ego, such that the god and the Thunderbird were believed to have been mystically conjoined as one being. That is why Ningirsu is very often pictured with an emblematic Thunderbird, or even symbolised by an image of the supernatural creature, who appears as a representative aspect of his divinity. Invoking the myth that unites the god and the fabulous bird, Imdugud's outstretched wings and irresistible talons, which are capable of seizing the fiercest predators, act in large part as a metaphor for the god's taming of the Mesopotamian wilderness.

The Meaning of the Temple

The crux of Sumerian polytheism can be described as a twofold response, articulated verbally in myths and hymns, and enacted in the rituals of cultic worship, to the particular experience of immanent confrontation with the supernatural that Rudolf Otto (1917) called a *mysterium tremendum et fascinans*. The sense of terror could range from demonic fear through awe to a terrified awareness of sublime magnificence; fascination extended to an irresistible magnetism that demanded unconditional allegiance to the divine. Accordingly, the temple of the patron god was the most important and prominent landmark in every Sumerian city (Fig. 4). As was first clarified many years ago in the work of Jean

FIGURE 4. Reconstruction of the Early Dynastic Temple of Ningirsu.

Bottéro and Samuel Noah Kramer (1989), the theocentric liturgy in ancient Mesopotamia revolved around serving the gods—providing for their divine needs through sacrifice, libation and ritual, and constructing their magnificent abodes, which represented the pinnacle of sacred art and architecture. Revered as the actual house of the deity to which it was dedicated, the temple was, in the revealing phrase of Titus Burckhardt, a *sacratum*, where humans might experience with the utmost intensity the reality of the pattern that was imbued into the seeming indeterminacy of space and time. For whereas, in the contingent universe of unfolding events, time might take precedence over space, in the construction of the temple, time and space were conceptually intertwined as a continuum that expressed the order that was infused into the cosmos when the world was created. The site of the temple, thought of as a holy space or *locus sanctus*, was divinely ordained and remained sacred in perpetuity, so that any changes to its structure, including the raising of its foundations to a new level, or its removal to another site (an extremely rare occurrence that is perhaps uniquely represented by the transfer of the Temple of Ningirsu in Girsu from Tell K to Tell A), were matters of the utmost seriousness that had to be duly consecrated and divinely approved. The Sumerians believed that the very idea of the temple, along with the principles of its design and attendant construction rituals, had been instituted by Enki, the most ingenious of the gods, and vouchsafed by him to the first rulers of Sumer.

A key organising principle of the temple's sacred space was the horizontal plane of the sanctified ground, where its base was established, added to which was the vertical dimension that was brought into being by the architectural structure. Through its design, scale and proportions, and most importantly on account of the way it was laid out, the building spatially encoded key elements of Sumerian cosmology in a material form, and so gave expression to the structured arrangement of nature. The temple was the mooring rope that exhibited and safeguarded the stable order of things, and its architectural principles were an expression of the divine assurance that the earth would remain productive because natural processes were dependable. It was the place where humans could interact with, and be confronted by, the sublime tethering of nature's three principal realms, governed by their respective deities: An, the god of the celestial heavens; Enlil, the god of the earth and the air (what would now be called the atmosphere); and Enki, the water god. The temple's chief podium, considered as a metaphorical substitute for the sacred mountain, which, as Enlil's estate, was the supreme locus of divinity, symbolised strength and permanence. There was also a set of meanings based on the cardinal directions, because one absolute constant in the construction of a Sumerian temple was that its corners were aligned with the four cardinal points, marking their positions like a sacred compass. The image of the compass should not be misunderstood, however, because (as is discussed in Chapter 14) the presiding concept bears no resemblance to the modern notion of a circular device with a magnetic needle that turns on a central pivot. For ancient Sumerians the earth was laid out as a grid pattern, with a primary, north–south axis (or series of parallel axes, to be more precise), from which the other cardinal points were derived. To a greater or lesser degree the arrangement was reflected in the marking out not only of temples, but also of fields and plots of lands, with surveyors' pegs and ropes. This foundational action is referenced repeatedly in the texts and images that provide the most profound insights into the Sumerian system of the world as it is demonstrated in their temple architecture. The holiest buildings did not therefore reveal the structure of the cosmos in a merely allegorical or symbolic way. Instead, they gave actual physical form to principles that were woven into the texture of reality, rendering them more apparent and allowing them to be more intensely experienced, such that the difference between the sacred space of the temple and the outside world was a matter only of degree, and not one of quality. Consequently, the temple was the real embodiment and confirmation of the universal order that had been established when the heavens and the earth were formed from chaos.

The sacred character of the spaces within Sumerian sanctuaries was graded and differentiated to create a sacral hierarchy, with the innermost sanctum—the meeting point of terrestrial and divine realms—at its core. Moving away from the centre towards the periphery, successive zones became less profoundly sacred. There were certain necessary, permanent features that Sumerian temples had to have (see Chanteau 2017). These included the enclosing temenos wall (whose precise form changed over time) that separated the holy interior of the sacred precinct from the less sacred or secular exterior, an altar for sacrifices and libations, and a podium on which stood the material incarnation of the deity—the divine cult statue. This holiest of platforms was, in the purest sense, the locus of the divine: the point that anchored the earth amid the billowing cosmic waters, with the immeasurable reservoir of sweet water below and the limitless oceans of salt waves all around. The way in which the sacred walls and installations expressed these beliefs meant that temple architecture was performative, not contemplative, and its sanctity was affirmed in ceremonial events: the rituals of consecration and activation rites.

The temple was a local instantiation of the cosmic order—the place where the ruler and higher clergy could implement awe-inspiring interactions with the god (Fig. 5). This reflected the political realities of the state, but these were inextricably linked to deeply held religious beliefs. In the ground beneath the building, temple guardians in the form of horned deities that supported, held or embodied foundation pegs were solemnly entombed in symbolic deposits, often together with dedicatory tablets that were commissioned by the presiding Sumerian ruler, and in later times they were also inscribed in his name. Inside, the sanctuary paid homage to a panoply of lesser divinities, and it was furnished with a set of occult objects that facilitated the performance of the cosmic offices of its chief god. At certain periods, the council of supernatural beings was enshrined in a series of ancillary chapels and banqueting halls, while sacred objects were at all times housed in treasuries belonging to the deity. The holy building's elaborate construction featured transitional, or locular spaces to support and enhance religious practices. They included ceremonial stairways and gateways, open-air ambulatories, processional routes and sacred courtyards, along with a range of service rooms that contained cultic appurtenances and equipment associated with offering rituals.

The Origins and Evolution of the Ningirsu Temple

In their pioneering excavations of Girsu, Sarzec and his successors exhumed rich archaeological remains in an area that they called the Mound of the House of the Fruits (*La Maison des fruits*), or Tell K. This turned out to be a series of shrines containing abundant religious accessories dedicated

FIGURE 5. Artist's impression of a Sumerian temple, showing the temple façade (right) and the enclosing temenos wall.

to Ningirsu that dated from around 3000 BCE to 2300 BCE. The first explorers had brought to light parts of the earliest temple complex devoted to the tutelary deity of Girsu, who was the divine proprietor of Lagash. Instituted in the Early Dynastic I epoch (3000–2600 BCE), well before the reign of Ur-Nanshe (c.2450 BCE), the founder of the First Dynasty of Lagash, the ancient temple establishment was developed by successive rulers in the course of the entire Early Dynastic period. In essence, it was an expansive religious precinct, which was constructed on a large artificial mound made of mud-bricks that was significantly raised above the surrounding flood plain. It was accessed by ceremonial stairways, as well as by some more utilitarian ascents. From at least the time of Ur-Nanshe, the elevated sacred summit was surrounded by an oval-shaped temenos, or bounding wall that was fitted with a monumental gatehouse and subsidiary entrances, and throughout its entire history the temple's inner sanctum was made up of an enclosed rectangular shrine that housed two rooms: the cella, where the statue of the divinity was displayed, and the antecella, which was a treasury or trophy room. Fronted by a ceremonial approach that included a gentle slope or stairway, the holiest rooms of the earliest Ningirsu temple were situated underground, but subsequent temples stood on the top of the mound, and at certain periods in its later history the temple building was raised on a podium that elevated it above the rest of the sacred summit.

As was standard in Sumerian sacred architecture, the corners of the temple's bipartite core were meticulously oriented to the cardinal points (although, for reasons that are discussed in Chapter 12, the placement of the Lower Construction, the earliest of the Tell K Ningirsu shrines, was slightly anomalous), and this vitally important fact might have affected the placement of the neighbouring structures. Around the main building were the temple annexes: offices, service apartments and other facilities needed for religious practices.

A wealth of cuneiform inscriptions recovered from in and around the House of the Fruits on Tell K sheds some light on how the early temple developed. Among them are an exceptional archaic plaque known as the Feathered Figure (the *Figure aux plumes*; Fig. 6), a beautifully carved mace head donated to the temple by Mesalim of Kish (Fig. 7), who was a contemporary of Lugalshaengur of Lagash, together with dedicatory and commemorative artefacts commissioned by later rulers, notably Ur-Nanshe, Eanatum, Enmetena and Urukagina. These indicate that, as successive rulers raised and enlarged the shrine over many generations, the form of the earliest version of the temple gradually evolved to incorporate an expanded area with a network of buildings, including an area known as the 'broad' courtyard (kisal-daĝal), a sacred well (pú.šeg$_{12}$), a brewery (é.bappir) and a coach house for the god (é.^{ĝeš}gigír.ra).

The last manifestation of the sequence of Ningirsu temples that were constructed on Tell K between the time of the Lower Construction and the reign of Urukagina was razed to the ground towards the end of the Early Dynastic III period (*c.*2300 BCE), when Girsu was finally conquered by Lugalzagesi, the ruler of Umma (and Uruk). This catastrophic event left behind an identifiable destruction horizon that included the defaced and smashed remains of highly significant cult objects that were removed from their sacred settings and deliberately desecrated. More generally, the French pioneers unearthed numerous sacred treasures dating from about 3000 BCE to around 2350 BCE on the Mound of the House of the Fruits, but they found no traces there of the later temple

FIGURE 6. The Feathered Figure. Musée du Louvre AO221.

FIGURE 7. The Mace of Mesilim. Musée du Louvre AO2349.

to Ningirsu that was thought to have been built by Gudea sometime between 2125 BCE and 2100 BCE. Consequently, the inferred New Eninnu dating to the time of Gudea, which could not be found on the site of previous temples to Ningirsu, soon became one of the most sought-after archaeological structures in all of Mesopotamia. The history that gradually emerged, and which has now been rewritten in the comprehensive reinterpretation of the archaeology of Tell K outlined in Part 2 of this book, together with the results of the British Museum team's re-excavation of Tell A that are recorded in Part 3, shows that the early quest for the Gudea temple was hindered by some severe misunderstandings. First, because the sequence postulated by Sarzec, Heuzey and their early successors for constructions that are now known to have been built after the time of Ur-Nanshe was disastrously oversimplified and therefore categorically mistaken in some critical respects; and secondly, because the Gudea temple that the early explorers expected to find on Tell K was actually the New Eninnu that Gudea constructed on Tell A.

The sequence of temples that were built on Tell K, followed by Gudea's New Eninnu on Tell A, were known by a succession of different appellations, while particular instantiations were often given more than one name. This was in accord with the practice in ancient Sumer more generally, where temples were regularly known by several names—official and ceremonial, ordinary or popular—as well as by other epithets and by-names that were brought into being for specific reasons (George 1993, pp. 59–63). Not all of the preserved titles for a particular temple were in constant use, and a selection of names was drawn upon at different periods, with the shifting nomenclature reflecting historical changes in the temple's architecture and also in contemporary religious practices, which did not remain static over time. Some names expressed new beliefs (or newly emphasised strands of belief) about the functions and particular powers of the temple's divine occupant, condensing particular aspects of the mythology surrounding the god into compound appellations. Special epithets were sometimes applied to mark important construction or refurbishment projects that were carried out by named rulers who wished to associate their own pious legacies as caretakers of the temple with the crowning achievement of their reigns. New titles given to temples might also reflect the changing conception of the relationship between the temple and the polis, and the developing sociopolitical order.

The name of the first Ningirsu temple on Tell K, dating back to the Early Dynastic I period and now known as the Lower Construction (following Sarzec's usage), is preserved on the Feathered Figure—the small, but extraordinarily significant stone monument, carved with words and images, that shows Ningirsu taking possession of his new residence. The temple is there referred to as é.^{d}Nin.ğír.su, which literally means the 'house of Ningirsu', and its elemental signification was doubtless intended to have a specially powerful and immediate impact. With the ascent to the throne of Ur-Nanshe, some 500 years after the epoch of the Lower Construction, the politico-religious landscape of Girsu–Lagash underwent numerous profound changes. In this context, the Tell K temple, in the iteration now referred to as the Ur-Nanshe Building (again following Sarzec), was entirely redesigned and rebuilt on a freshly raised sacred summit (thereby contrasting markedly with its subterranean predecessor), and the entire sacred complex was enlarged and replanned. To reflect these changes in the territory's political and religious organisation, Ur-Nanshe added a new name to the time-honoured epithet (é.^{d}Nin.ğír.su) recorded on the Feathered Figure, and the complex was now also known as èš.ğír.sú, meaning the 'sanctuary of Girsu'. This stressed the role of the god's sacred city (the extensive area of more and less substantial sacred mounds and buildings of which Girsu was formed) as the religious centre of Ur-Nanshe's enlarged and re-established state: the tripolis that united Girsu, Lagash and Ur-Nanshe's native home of Nigin as a single political entity. It is important to note that the earlier and later terms, the 'house of Ningirsu' and the 'sanctuary of Girsu', were alternates that were never used together in a single Ur-Nanshe inscription. Accordingly, although their specific connotations were different, with one epithet stressing the temple's age-old primal sanctity and the other highlighting the new order ushered in by Ur-Nanshe, they were considered to be equivalents, and both could be used to designate the Ur-Nanshe religious complex on Tell K (Falkenstein 1966, p. 117).

After the reign of Ur-Nanshe, these two names were replaced in royal inscriptions by titles that were probably coined to describe the various expansions and reorganisations of the state's cult centre that took place under subsequent rulers, and also to fulfil some of the more general purposes outlined above. The most famous name of the Ningirsu temple, é.ninnu, meaning 'house fifty', which was a specially auspicious choice, and its equally illustrious counterpart, anzu^{mušen}.bábbar, referring to Imdugud, the White Thunderbird, are relative latecomers in the temple's long history. The seminal term é.ninnu is first attested during the reign of Enanatum I (Falkenstein 1966, p. 117) on a superb white mace head dedicated to Ningirsu by one of the king's legates, on which the god Ningirsu is integrated with his avatar—the Thunderbird or lion-headed eagle. The assimilation was by no means new, of course. Indeed, it is attested on the Ningirsu temple's foundational document, the Feathered Figure, where the plumes that adorn the god's crown represent the wings of Imdugud. Similarly, some rare archaic bricks survive that are stamped with images of the Thunderbird with outstretched wings, and these doubtless originate from one of the temple's ancient iterations. Unfortunately, none were found *in situ*, but they testify to the antiquity of the fusion of the god and the mythical hybrid bird. The term Eninnu ('house fifty') refers to the fifty divine powers of Enlil, which he granted to his filial champion, Ningirsu. In this context, where 'fifty' stands for an infinite plenitude, the word Eninnu is perhaps best translated as the 'house of the almighty'.

Like that of Ur-Nanshe, the reign of Enmetena also saw a consolidation and reshaping of the territory of Ningirsu. Under Enmetena the state of Lagash as a whole was expanded significantly, and this was accompanied by a major renovation of the god's sanctuary on Tell K. To mark these events the ruler furnished the sacred precinct with a new epithet, èš.gi.^{d}Nin.ğír.su.ka (the 'reed sanctuary of Ningirsu'), which was also used in the form of a by-name, èš.gi.gi.gù.na, meaning the 'reed sanctuary of the giguna', or the 'multi-coloured reeds'. Crucially, the term èš.gi.gi.gù.na did not replace the word Eninnu, which was still the undisputed official ceremonial name for the temple in other Enmetena royal inscriptions. As in the time of Ur-Nanshe, when the older and newer titles (the 'house of Ningirsu' and the 'sanctuary of Girsu') were used concurrently, here too 'house fifty' and the 'multi-coloured reeds' were clearly equivalent ways of referring to the temple in its setting (Falkenstein 1966, p. 135; and Selz 1995, p. 228).

As evidenced by the inscriptions on the Feathered Figure, the relationship between sacred reeds and Ningirsu, like the association between the god and the Thunderbird, was also extremely ancient. The connection is found again in the beautiful Hymn to the Reeds (Fig. 8) from the time of Ur-Nanshe, a paean to the god's potent generative power (RIME 1.9.1.32):

> O shining reed!
> O reed of the canebrake of the fresh water source!
> O reed, you whose branches grow luxuriantly.
> After the god Enki set your roots in the (post) hole,
> your branches greet the day (or the sun god).
> Your 'beard' (is made of) of lapis-lazuli.
> O reed that comes forth (from) the shining mountain,
> O reed, may the Earth lords and the Earth princes
>   bow down (before you).
> May the god Enki pronounce a (favourable) omen
>   (for your construction).
> Its shining renowned standard(?)
> The god Enki cast it (with?) his (magic) loop.
> Praise (be to) Ningirsu!
> Šul-MUŠ×PA, the personal god of the king,
> carried the shining work basket.
> Ur-Nanshe, king of Lagash, son of Gunidu,
> (he was) 'son' of Gursar, built the
> 'Shrine-Girsu'.

The fame of the name é.ninnu.anzu^{mušen}.bábbar, meaning 'house fifty: the White Thunderbird', which was known throughout Mesopotamia, was a later phenomenon that can be attributed to Ur-Bau, from whom it was adopted by Gudea. It was used in every Gudea inscription, including the Cylinder Inscriptions, where it was chosen to designate the massively enlarged temple complex built by Gudea on Tell A, which combined the many buildings and

FIGURE 8. Tablet containing the Hymn to the Reeds. Musée du Louvre AO3866.

installations that had been gradually added to the evolving ancient precinct over many centuries into a centrally planned totality. Encapsulating the new sense of grandeur, Gudea's novel term, é.ninnu.anzu^{mušen}.bábbar, crystallised numerous meanings associated with the succession of Ningirsu temples on Tells K and A, and also with Sumerian temples at large. In this context it is worth recalling the point made long ago by Thorkild Jacobsen (1976), that the special sanctity of the temple derived from the fact that it was perceived not only as the abode of the god but also as the principal medium through which the deity exercised his or her cosmic functions. The temple and the god could therefore be conceived of almost as one and the same thing. Much more than a theatrical backdrop for religious ceremonies, the sacred space channelled the deity's sublime energy, thereby playing a performative role in the divine offices that were carried out within its walls. Similarly, Ningirsu's power was made vividly manifest in the form of thunderclouds and thunderstorms, and this is one of the several meanings that come together in the Gudea epithet, é.ninnu.anzu^{mušen}.bábbar. It was used to express the belief that the almighty power of Ningirsu (invested in him by Enlil) was instilled into the very fabric of the building, with the further addition of the image of the white flashing, or radiant Thunderbird to signify the god in his pre-anthropomorphic shape as a lion-headed eagle, recalling the fact that he tamed the wilderness and therefore invoking Ningirsu in his dual aspect as the god of the storm, and also as the god of irrigation and agricultural abundance. Although the expressive term was used alongside other epithets and by-names, it gradually eclipsed its counterparts, acquiring a charisma that ensured it remained current after the later renovations of the Gudea temple by the kings of the Third Dynasty of Ur, and the further refurbishments that were subsequently carried out in the Isin-Larsa and Old Babylonian periods.

Gudea the Architect: The New Ningirsu Temple

The design of the temple built by Gudea was revealed to Sarzec and Thureau-Dangin in exquisite detail after the deciphering of two extraordinarily important monuments from ancient Girsu—the Cylinder Inscriptions of Gudea and a statue, known as the Architect with a Plan (Statue B), that shows Gudea at prayer, supporting a tablet on his lap, on which is drawn the plan of the outer wall of a sacred complex dedicated to Ningirsu. Dating from around 2120 BCE, these two treasures of Sumerian culture were unearthed by Sarzec in 1877 and 1880, soon after he first started work on the site. They came to the attention of an international public when they were shown at the 1889 *Exposition Universelle* in Paris and they have never since ceased to inspire a long list of artists and intellectuals. The two masterworks were unearthed along with a plethora of dedicatory artefacts, among which were inscribed cones, ritual tablets, foundation pegs, door sockets, temple plaques, votive steles, mace heads and dedicatory vases, all commemorating in abridged and standardised form Gudea's construction of the magnificent enlarged Ningirsu sanctuary. Like a performative mantra the same formula is repeated on these objects over and over again: 'For the god Ningirsu, Enlil's mighty hero, Gudea, the ruler of Lagash, has made everything function as it should and built for him his Eninnu, house fifty: the White Thunderbird, restoring it to its proper place'.

The celebrated Cylinder Inscriptions, which form the longest literary work that survives from ancient Sumer, were inscribed on the Cylinders of Gudea: two hollow terracotta cylinders that were filled with a substance described by Sarzec as 'plaster' and finished at each end with specially made conical plugs (Fig. 9). Remarkably, despite their inherent fragility, the two preserved cylinders were found intact at the base of Tell K on a low hillock or monticule labelled by Sarzec as Tell I' (also known as the Mound of the Turning Path). The text they contain is made up of a hymn to the god and a royal chronicle that celebrates Gudea's huge building project, the crowning event of his reign. The preserved cylinders, A and B, were originally two parts of a trilogy, entitled 'Ningirsu's House Having Been Built', that was completed with an inferred Lost Cylinder. Cylinder A narrates the epiphany described above, when Ningirsu appears to Gudea in a dream and gives enigmatic instructions for the building of his new dwelling. This is followed by Gudea's visit to the goddess Nanshe, who interprets the dream narrative, and then comes the description of the long series of events that culminate in the construction of the glorious new place of worship. Cylinder B describes the introduction into the sanctuary of the Heroic God and his consort, the goddess Bau, together with Ningirsu's divine household—the company of lesser divinities that attend the divine couple. It also records the rituals

FIGURE 9. The Cylinders of Gudea: Cylinder A (left) and B (right). Musée du Louvre MNB1512 and MNB1511.

of consecration and inauguration that were carried out in order to make the holy buildings ready to accommodate the divinities. The Lost Cylinder, which is known only from a few cuneiform fragments, probably contained the prologue to the temple hymn, and a narrative of Ningirsu's famous exploits, most importantly his subduing of the Thunderbird. Acting as an *imago mundi*, the Cylinder Inscriptions encapsulate all the essential particulars of the sacred world of the Sumerians, dividing them thematically into two principal components: metaphors of power, expressing authority (the assembly of the gods and kingship), productivity and righteousness; and ideograms of the cosmos, expressing order and chaos, primordial combat and the divine temple.

The portrait of Gudea as the Architect with a Plan (Statue B; Fig. 10), which was found on the Mound of the Palace (Tell A), is a miracle of archaic statuary. Carved in the round from a large piece of diorite, which is a hard and durable stone that is not easy to work, but which is capable of expressing fine details and taking a high polish, the statue's material substance was intended as a symbol of permanence. On his lap the seated ruler holds a tablet that features the precisely incised blueprint of a religious precinct, together with a surveyor's measuring rod and peg (used to establish the ground plans of buildings), and a symbolic altar displaying the divine horns that are in this case probably an attribute of Ningirsu. The plan itself is a clear orthogonal projection

FIGURE 10. Gudea as the Architect with a Plan (Statue B). Musée du Louvre AO2.

that depicts the outlines of the extremely thick containing wall that demarcates the boundary between areas that were held to be merely, or ordinarily sacred and the holiest inner sanctum. The *enceinte* or main enclosure of the entire complex is reinforced by external buttresses and pierced by monumental gates that are decorated with recesses and pilasters, and flanked by large towers (Fig. 11).

Some of the incised marks on Statue B encode what is apparently the world's first scientific measuring system, based on a standard unit that is divided into fractions. In this context, it should be recalled that metrology, or the art of measurement, was believed by the Sumerians to be the mother of all languages—the language of the gods—and when, in the Cylinder Inscriptions, Gudea lays out the temple walls he is compared to the goddess Nisaba, who knows and safeguards the 'inmost secrets of numbers' (A19). The dream narrative recorded on the Cylinder Inscriptions includes the designing of Ningirsu's temple by the god Ninduba, who draws on a tablet of lapis lazuli, and the plan that rests on Gudea's lap has therefore tentatively been thought to be a carved representation of that divinely ordained and inspired blueprint. This can now be confirmed because the British Museum team's excavations show that the design documented on the statue does indeed represent the actual layout of Gudea's New Eninnu, the latest iteration of the shrine to Ningirsu, which came to be regarded in Sumerian times as one of the most sacred places in all of Mesopotamia. The sanctuary was praised from the earliest times for its splendour and magnificence, and as the Cylinder Inscriptions relate, its construction required social organisation, human and economic resources, on a previously unheard-of scale.

The performative role of the temple was expressed through the careful placement in its walls of ritual cones, the display of votive artefacts and the formation of liminal spaces that were marked by the symbolic thresholds and exceptionally thick walls that are shown on the blueprint on Statue B. Combined with incantations, prayers and offerings, these emblematic features were intended to capture, contain and channel the awesome, impetuous aura of the Heroic God, conceived of as an imposing radiance—a 'numinous power', to use Rudolf Otto's phrase. The belief that divine forces could be harnessed by means of the temple lies at the heart of Sumerian religion, and it is against this doctrinal background that Gudea's architectural programme should be understood. In accordance with the god's own plan, he not only built a dramatically updated version of the original temple and its successors that had stood on Tell K for centuries, he also consciously reshaped the newly instituted sacred space as a conduit for the god's energy and functions. These beliefs were enacted in every detail of the building's construction. Horned deities holding ritual foundation pegs delineated the hallowed ground and symbolically stabilised the religious complex between the earth and the sky, like a huge ship at anchor. Temple cones, or clay nails, acted like lightning rods, channelling the god's sublime aura, which was then contained inside the massive walls. As they brought offerings, passing through a portal embellished with inscribed stones, worshippers and the clergy entered the temple's *sanctum*

FIGURE 11. Reconstruction of Gudea's New Eninnu on the summit of Tell A, showing the enormous temenos walls (in grey) and the massive ascending platforms on which the complex was built. The model gives visual form to the text of the Cylinder Inscriptions and the information recorded on Statue B.

sanctorum at right angles to the divine cult statue so that they could avoid facing it directly, shielding their eyes, as it were, to protect themselves from the formidable power of the god's gaze and radiance.

The Big Move and the Hellenistic Complex

The Architect with a Plan is part of an abundant set of stunning finds made by Sarzec on the Mound of the Palace (Tell A) that included other Lagash II inscribed sculptures portraying Gudea and his immediate predecessor, Ur-Bau, in similarly devout attitudes that are signalled by their interlocked hands (Fig. 12). Of extreme significance, however, is the fact that the Lagash II statuary from Tell A was found not in a Sumerian setting, but among Hellenistic archaeological remains dating from the late fourth to the third century BCE—the epoch of Alexandrian and Seleucid Babylonia

that was inaugurated after the arrival in Babylon of Alexander the Great, some 2,000 years after Girsu flourished under Gudea. Accordingly, the first architectural structures that the French pioneers unearthed on the Mound of the Palace turned out to be the ruins of a Hellenistic complex that was constructed by an enigmatic figure named Adadnadinakhe, who was long thought to have been the local ruler of a principality in the fading Seleucid kingdom. It was conjectured that this provincial governor, who seemingly cultivated a taste for antiquities, must have collected ancient statues as relics to display in his palatine complex. The palace, it was further supposed, was intended to be the epicentre of an emerging regional power until Adadnadinakhe's ambitions were crushed by the arrival of the Parthians, sometime around the middle of the second century BCE. Partly contradicting this narrative, it has subsequently been thought more likely that Adadnadinakhe was a local dignitary, possibly a high priest or a chief scribe, who operated under Seleucid tutelage, and that

FIGURE 12. South-facing view of the sacred precinct of Girsu (the Urukug) in 2017, showing Tell A in the foreground and Tell K in the distance. The British Museum team's main excavation area can be seen in the centre of Tell A; the irregular mounds dotted around Tells A and K are the spoil heaps left by the French excavators.

he built and furnished a memorial shrine in honour of the ancestral rulers of Mesopotamia. The ancient artefacts that he collected were therefore displayed not in a working palace or administrative centre but in a temple or place of remembrance and worship that was erected by Adadnadinakhe above the ravaged remains of the sacred metropolis of Girsu on Tell A, probably with the consent of the Seleucids.

As is detailed in Part 4 below, the findings of the British Museum team mean that both of these narratives can be superseded by a much more complete historical account of the origins and development of the Hellenistic shrine. Adadnadinakhe perpetuated the immemorial Sumerian rituals of burying foundation deposits and stamping bricks with his theophoric name in both Aramaic and Greek characters, and he unearthed the famous statues of Gudea, which were displayed alongside a range of other ancient and contemporary artefacts in a temple that combined aspects of Mesopotamian and Hellenistic worship. The updated shrine was purposefully and carefully built on the fragmentary remains of the Sumerian religious platforms that were buried in the Mound of the Palace. Thanks to his diligence, Adadnadinakhe's archaising Babylonian name (literally meaning 'Adad the god, the giver of brothers'), which was recorded on the Hellenistic-era bricks that were laid under his authority on Tell A, became inextricably connected with what is now known to be the final flowering of the extended series of temples devoted to Ningirsu that date back to the time of the Lower Construction on Tell K.

Two thousand years later, when the French pioneers of the late nineteenth century and early twentieth century CE explored Tell A, they found an array of disconnected items, including Hellenistic remains, that were all thought at first to have formed parts of the structure of the new sanctuary that was believed to have been built by Gudea. Gradually, the Sumerian archaeology was disentangled from the much later strata. The former included ritual deposits that took the form of stone tablets inscribed in the names of Gudea and his immediate forerunner, Ur-Bau, together with copper figurines of deities shaped into (or holding) inscribed foundation pegs (Fig. 13). Additional confusion was caused by the fact that quantities of Sumerian inscribed and stamped bricks, dedicated to Ningirsu and deriving from Tell A, were later used by the French archaeologists to build dig houses on the site. Considered in conjunction with the history of the early shrines found on the Mound of the House of the Fruits, however, the rich assemblage of deposits found on Tell A suggested that the sacred nucleus on Tell K, around which the sacred city of Girsu developed over centuries, was transferred to the Mound of the Palace in the Lagash II period. The relocation, which was carried out by Ur-Bau, profoundly contradicted the timeless Sumerian tradition of constructing temple after temple to a particular god on the same spot. It therefore represented a radical disruption of the spatio-temporal continuity that was believed by the Sumerians to be absolutely fundamental to the maintenance of social and cosmic order. Such an extraordinary break with a pattern of belief that had, in effect, the force of a sacred natural law had to be justified by a complex apparatus of theological reasoning and explanation, and broader ideological discourse. Above all, it had to be authorised by a command issuing from the god Ningirsu himself. No explanatory documents from the reign of Ur-Bau have survived, but with regard to the New Eninnu of Gudea, these conditions were fulfilled by the cumulative effect of the fabulous objects previously described. More explicitly, the Cylinder Inscriptions, which chronicle the god's theophany and his command that Gudea should build a new temple, were publicly displayed in a purpose-built shrine on Tell K, while the divine blueprint was carved in hard diorite for all time on the tablet on Statue B. In addition, a myriad votive objects were commissioned that restate the Gudea mantra, largely borrowed from his predecessor, Ur-Bau, that echoes ad infinitum the status of the god, the power of the temple and the legacy of the ruler.

The proclamations provide the theological grounds for the grand reconstruction of the temple on its new site on Tell A, following the epoch-making transfer of the locus of worship by Gudea's father-in-law, Ur-Bau—a change that was crowned by the construction of Gudea's New Eninnu. The audacious development was perhaps partly caused and made easier by the series of tumultuous upheavals that had taken place in Lagash over the preceding century. They began

FIGURE 13. A copper foundation peg from Gudea's New Eninnu; the object is shaped as a kneeling horned deity supporting an oversized peg (here seen from above). British Museum 96566.

around 2300 BCE with the devastating invasion led by Lugalzagesi, who conducted a widespread campaign of destruction that laid waste to urban and rural places of worship, obliterating the state's most important sanctuary on Tell K. The disruption continued with the advent of the Akkad conquerors, led by Sargon of Akkad, who took control of the entire region, including Lagash, from about 2300 BCE to 2250 BCE. With the liberation of Lagash after the downfall of the Akkad regime, the state of Lagash enjoyed a new lease of life, but the ancient shrine to its tutelary god on Tell K in the sacred city of Girsu was undoubtedly little more than a grotesque shadow of its former self. Ur-Bau and Gudea therefore ushered in a new era—a social, cultural and economic renaissance—that was expressed first in Ur-Bau's renewal of the territory's principal temple in its changed location on Tell A, and subsequently by Gudea's construction of the New Eninnu.

A Summary of the British Museum Team's Research

Once a radiant centre that was renowned throughout Mesopotamia, Girsu was forgotten for millennia, when it lay buried in the life-sustaining flood plain of the Fertile Crescent. Released from the interred ruins, but weathered beyond recognition by centuries of wind and rain, some votive artefacts dedicated to the Sumerian deities Ningirsu, Bau, Nanshe and the rest of the pantheon occasionally surfaced to provide an obscure glimpse of the antique sacredness of Girsu, a city that was shaped for the gods from its inception. In the late third millennium BCE, when Gudea built his new temple, Girsu was a bustling megapolis that covered hundreds of hectares. As the sacred civic hub of the state of Lagash, it was serviced (together with Girsu's political and more overtly secular counterpart, the city of Lagash itself) by a network of waterways and irrigation canals. The splendid Sumerian urban centre was long ago reduced to a vast area of weathered hillocks that are now pockmarked with large excavation pits and the many holes dug by looters, and further disfigured by giant spoil heaps and the parched lines of ancient watercourses. Any remaining exposed fragments of sacred and quasi-sacred architecture from the series of magnificent buildings that were constructed between the earliest times and the much later Hellenistic era of Adadnadinakhe have

FIGURE 14. The Temple of Ningirsu on Tell A: a view of the British Museum team's excavations in 2017.

been so eroded by the remorseless march of time that they are featureless and nondescript. In addition, the central area of Tell K in particular was dramatically reduced by the successive efforts of the French pioneers from its original height of about 14 m above the surrounding flood plain almost down to sea level, leaving nothing of note behind except for a series of spoil heaps and the remnants of excavation trenches. The situation on Tell A, where the French pioneers did not attempt to dig below the level of the Gudea walls, was fortunately somewhat less catastrophic.

Returning to Tello after a period of some eighty years during which no systematic fieldwork was carried out on the site, the British Museum team initially observed very little of immediate import on the Mound of the Palace—a few inscribed and stamped pieces of broken bricks, produced under Gudea, Ur-Bau and Adadnadinakhe, that lay scattered around on the heaps of spolia that form the sad legacy of the French expeditions. Yet, in this desecrated landscape, which was little more than a wasteland of rubble, the team's salvage excavations soon uncovered extensive mud-brick walls—some ornamented with inscribed clay cones—that belonged to the long-lost Ningirsu temple that lay at the heart of the Gudea's New Eninnu complex, which was renovated several times in the Ur III, Isin-Larsa and Old Babylonian periods (Fig. 14). The wealth of momentous discoveries, which are laid out in detail in Part 3 of this book, followed long periods of conflict in the region in the twentieth and twenty-first centuries CE. They represent a significant milestone in the renewed archaeological research that is a feature of modern Iraq.

The first aim of the British Museum team's new fieldwork on Tell A was to try to resolve the pandemonium that was caused by the digs that were carried out before the Second World War. Matching ancient inscriptions with physical remains, the team was able to offer new insights into the principles that underlay the sanctuary's design and to describe the functions of its main parts (Fig. 15). As the work progressed, the renowned sanctuary emerged in ever-increasing detail. The retrieval works showed that Gudea's Temple of Ningirsu, which was situated at the heart of the vast complex, was organised on the indirect-approach principle, such that supplicants did not immediately face the god as they entered his chapel, and that the entrance portals to the *sanctum sanctorum* were marked with inscribed stones. The temple itself was made up of a cella (or sanctuary chamber) that housed the sacrificial altar and the podium on which Ningirsu's statue was displayed. This was the focal point of the cult, and it was accompanied by a vestibule or antecella that contained ritual basins for ablutions, together with a libation well and a wide, low display platform that was used to exhibit votive artefacts and (presumably) the statues of worshipping rulers. A lengthy stairwell chamber gave access to the roof. The inner area was surrounded by a network of peripheral open-air ambulatories (all enclosed within the sanctuary's massive walls) that were studded with numerous inscribed cones, while in front of the Ningirsu temple was a forecourt that housed the earlier religious platform created by Ur-Bau. Also identified was a large ceremonial court that separated the shrine presumed to be dedicated to the goddess Bau from the Ningirsu temple, which was fronted by a gated inner wall that was built on a stepped support decorated with recessed niche panelling. The entire religious complex, which was built on a series of enormous ascending terraces, was enclosed by an impressive temenos wall that was strengthened with buttresses and pierced with monumental towered gateways. Significant remains of the enclosing wall were exposed during the British Museum team's work.

Ever since Sarzec discovered the divine blueprint carved on the statue of Gudea as the Architect with a Plan, scholars have debated whether the inscribed design represented the generic layout of a temple complex or the actual footprint of Gudea's New Eninnu. One key reason for this was that the accompanying numerical signs that were also included on the statue could not be deciphered with any degree of certainty. The British Museum team's decoding of the vitally important measuring system that was used by Gudea when the New Eninnu was conceived sheds light on the procedures that were followed by the ruler and his attendants as they planned the large-scale structure, and this in turn helped to clarify the phases of construction. Remarkably, when the carved blueprint was compared with the sacred complex itself, it was discovered that the massive walls of the temenos that are carved on Statue B overlap perfectly with parts of the enclosure wall and gateways that were exposed during the British Museum team's excavations on Tell A. The extremely attractive assumption that the plan recorded on the statue was in fact an exact copy of the actual blueprint for the sanctuary could therefore be confirmed.

Further excavations were carried out on Tell A beneath the Lagash II Ningirsu temple to probe the deepest layers in

24　General Introduction

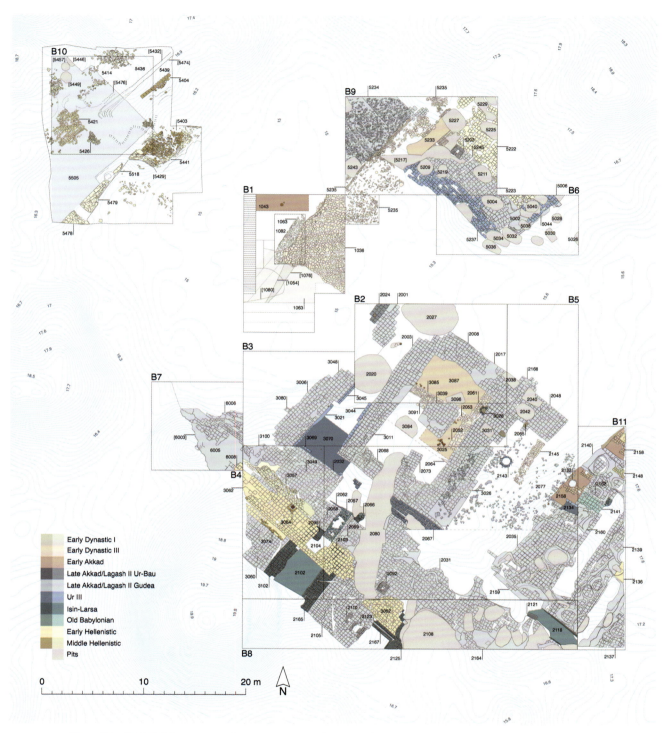

FIGURE 15. Plan of the British Museum team's excavation trenches on Tell A.

the archaeological history of Tell A, dating back to the origins of the sacred mound. This work led to the discovery of an archaic sanctuary that was in use during the Early Dynastic I–III and Sargonic periods (3000–2250 BCE), prior to the era of Ur-Bau and Gudea. The exposed remains include a number of lower-lying superimposed religious platforms and an associated series of temple rooms and annexes that were dedicated, as is argued in Chapter 32, to the great goddess Bau, the consort of Ningirsu. The structural layout, architectural design and accompanying ceremonial altar, together with some of the accessories used for offerings and sacrifices, that have so far been found in the layers belonging to the earlier sequence of shrines recall features seen at other major temple sites in Presargonic Sumer, above all the Lagash I Ningirsu temples on Tell K, which the Bau shrine found below the New Eninnu on Tell A mirrored in scale and orientation. These potent indicators of the structure's religious significance dovetailed with the results of the team's concurrent research into the religious landscape of the expansive sacred precinct of Girsu, the Urukug (Irikug or iri.kù in Sumerian), in particular the identification and excavation of a substantial section of the Early Dynastic temenos wall to the north-west of Tell A (Fig. 16). In consequence, it became increasingly clear that the early cult platforms on Tell A, which were built and redeveloped in the site's second most commanding location from at least the beginning of the third millennium BCE, were devoted to Bau. The further fascinating conclusion is that the Ningirsu temple at the heart of Gudea's New Eninnu was built on top of earlier temple buildings that were dedicated to Ningirsu's wife, Bau, the 'beloved lady of Girsu'.

Gudea's New Eninnu, which in scale and splendour eclipsed its forebears, remained in use as the centre of worship in Girsu for about 400 years, down to the Old Babylonian period. Restored on several occasions, first by Shulgi in Ur III times, then far more extensively in the Isin-Larsa period, it was finally deconsecrated and ritually buried, probably at the time of the abandonment of Girsu around 1750 BCE. That was not the end of the sanctuary's history, however. At the more recent end of the time spectrum, in several areas of Tell A the British Museum team also uncovered significant traces of the Hellenistic complex that was commissioned by Adadnadinakhe. A careful reappraisal of the French excavations carried out before the Second World War, combined with the results of the new fieldwork, enabled a redating of Girsu's Graeco-Babylonian resurgence, represented by the work of Adadnadinakhe, to the late fourth century BCE. The Hellenistic shrine flourished when the Seleucids were at the height of their power in Babylonia, rather than in the dying days of the empire—a revised time frame that necessitates a complete reinterpretation of Adadnadinakhe's ideological programme as a syncretising endeavour that fused Mesopotamian and Hellenistic modes of worship. Adadnadinakhe's shrine, together with all its contents, including the Sumerian statues that he unearthed, was desecrated and destroyed in the mid-second century BCE, but the revised chronology sheds a great deal of light on Hellenistic Girsu in the hoary heartland of the long-dead Sumerian civilisation.

The British Museum team's renewed fieldwork on Tell A revealed a palimpsest of archaeological layers that encompasses a period of some 3,000 years—a vertiginous *mise en abîme* or infinite regress that articulates the superimposed destinies of gods, idols and ancestors, all of whom were interlinked parts of the powerful sacred nexus that found its fullest Sumerian expression in the New Eninnu of Gudea. As is also now clear, that history was by no means self-contained. It evolved from—and was in many ways the fulfilment of—the earlier sequence of shrines to Ningirsu that were built on Tell K. Part 2 of this book re-examines the published French results to reassess the archaeological remains that were found on Tell K by Sarzec and his successors, using a wealth of innovative clarifications and a vividly reconceived theoretical framework to present an exhaustive revised interpretation of the series of temples to Ningirsu that were built on Tell K from around 3000 BCE to about 2250 BCE. Part 3, which is devoted to Tell A, also reviews the results that were published by the French explorers before laying out the pivotal findings of the British Museum team's fieldwork, which was carried out between 2016 and 2022. This includes analyses of the Early Dynastic I–III and Sargonic sacred complexes—the cultic counterparts of the Ningirsu temple on Tell K—that were dedicated in all likelihood to the goddess Bau. It goes on to present an extended reassessment of the history of the shrine after the principal sacred building was transferred to Tell A by Ur-Bau, followed by the construction of Gudea's New Eninnu. Part 3 also includes an account of the shrine's later refurbishments in Ur III and Isin-Larsa times, and its deconsecration in the Old Babylonian period. Finally, Part 4 examines the temple's reincarnation in Hellenistic Girsu from the late fourth century BCE, when Adadnadinakhe rebuilt the Eninnu and unearthed numerous

26 General Introduction

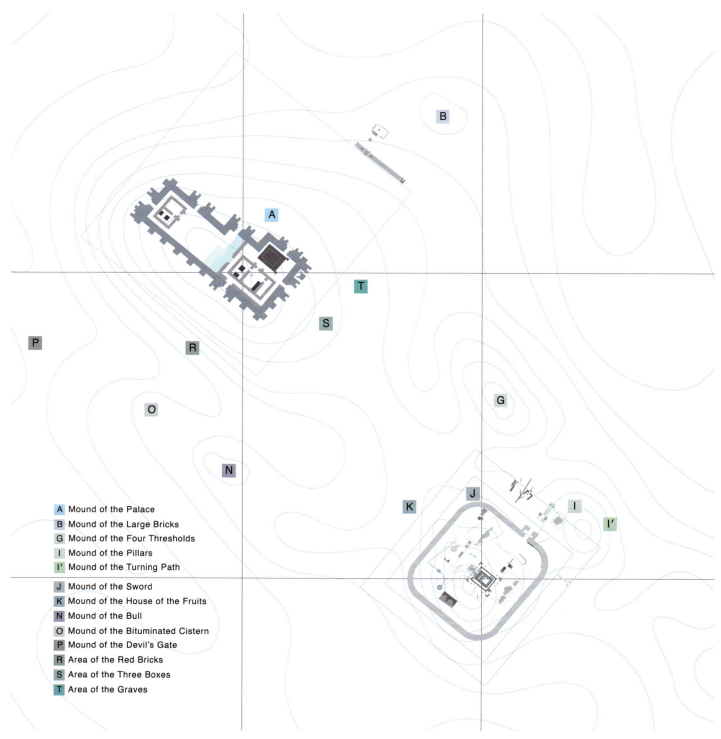

FIGURE 16. Plan of the sacred precinct of Girsu (the Urukug), showing the reconstructed Lagash II and Early Dynastic shrines on Tells A and K, respectively. The contour lines, taken from Sarzec's Plan B, show the site as it was before the French excavations began; the letters A to T indicate mounds and areas named by Sarzec. The N–S axes extend through the N corners of the earlier and later Ningirsu temples.

artefacts deriving from the time of Ur-Bau and Gudea. The Babylonian–Hellenistic temple (as it is described below), which thrived under the Seleucids, was destroyed in the mid-second century BCE, when the last chapter in the long history of Girsu as an active centre of worship was finally closed.

For clarity's sake, the methodology of the British Museum team's procedures, including the painstaking reanalysis of the French results, the salvage excavations and the subsequent reinterpretations, can be expressed in the following schedule of work:

1. Systematically analyse and reorganise historic data sets (Tells K and A). Where new excavations are undertaken (Tell A), continue to stage 2; in the absence of new excavations, proceed to stage 6 (Tell K).
2. Correlate existing data sets with key features of the site.
3. Define one or more fixed points of reference in order to establish the most potentially fruitful targets.
4. Excavate and record the new findings, plotting them on a stratigraphic grid and noting archaeological contexts.
5. Organise, tabulate and interpret the new findings.
6. Re-examine historic data sets, applying modern stratigraphic methods and noting any conspicuous absences (for example, pottery, fired-brick rubble and other small finds that are not mentioned). Scrutinise recorded find heights and related information to produce a revised stratigraphy for the site (Tells A and K).
7. Where new fieldwork has been carried out, incorporate the new finds and adjust the stratigraphic interpretations from stage 6 accordingly (Tell A); cross-reference the stratigraphy with reanalysed data from the whole site, including areas where no new fieldwork has been carried out (Tells A and K).
8. Present consolidated new interpretations (Tells A and K).
9. In the context of the updated understanding of the site, develop and present any arising conceptual interpretations—historical, religious and social, for example (Tells A and K).

CHAPTER 2

The Rediscovery of Ancient Girsu

The Impact of Sarzec

It was in 1880, three years after his epoch-making first finds in Tello, that Ernest Chocquin, as he was then styled, formally adopted the patronymic De Sarzec, the name he took when he purchased the Chateau de Sarzec near Poitiers that had previously belonged to his father and grandfather. Registered as a civil engineer from 1864 to 1868 (according to a note at the Ministry of Foreign Affairs), in the 1860s he was based in Alexandria, working as a director in the gas department at Lebon & Cie., a French lighting firm that in 1865 won the franchise to supply Egypt with electricity and to provide lighting in Cairo and Alexandria powered by natural gas (Pillet 1958, p. 53). In the aftermath of the calamitous French defeat in the Franco-Prussian War (1870–1), a decree of 1872 appointed Sarzec consular officer of the French Republic in the port city of Massawa (in present-day Eritrea), which was then in one of the African provinces of the Ottoman Empire (also known as the Sublime Porte). He worked in Massawa for four years, witnessing the failure of the expansionist ambitions of Isma'il Pasha, khedive of Egypt, whose attempts to annex the Nile basin were successfully resisted by Yohannes IV, the Ethiopian Neguse Negest or king of kings. Having established friendly relations with Yohannes on behalf of France, Sarzec earned the enmity of Isma'il, which made it impossible for him to carry out his duties, and in 1875 he was posted to Basra. As is shown by archival consular and political correspondence, his interest in archaeology had taken root before his departure for the flood plains of southern Iraq. In 1875, for example, he commented on ancient and forgotten ruins 'of the type found in Gondar and Aksum' (Pillet 1958, pp. 52–66), going on to add: 'One may still see there the fine ruins of several Greek temples [actually Aksumite], along with the perfectly preserved remains of a splendid palace, also in the Greek style, that was once an imperial residence'.

The huge impact that Sarzec had on the recovery of the archaeological remains of ancient Girsu that lay under the ground in Tello began with his work on Tell A, or the Mound of the Palace, as it quickly became known (Fig. 17). This was his principal focus when he arrived at the site in 1877, and it remained of primary interest during several subsequent seasons. Also known by its French name, the *Grand tell*, Tell A was (and still is, despite the ravages wrought by time and previous excavations) the archaeological megasite's largest and tallest mound (Fig. 18). Located on the site's northern perimeter, the rise acquired its familiar name, the Mound of the Palace, on account of the imposing prestige architecture that was uncovered there, which was at first thought to be a palatial royal residence (Sarzec and Heuzey 1912, pp. 3–7).

The first phase of Sarzec's excavations (Season 1) ran from 5 March to 11 June 1877, immediately after he had taken up his post as French vice consul in Basra, and it yielded a huge fragment of splendid figurative statuary, with a cuneiform inscription on its shoulder. It proved to be the harbinger of an extraordinary number of spectacular finds. The fragmentary Gudea Colossus (as it is referred to here), part of an exceptional cache of artefacts that soon came to light, was a momentous discovery that announced the very existence of Sumerian civilisation to the world at large (Fig. 19). It became the first object to be accessioned into the collections that

FIGURE 17. Ernest de Sarzec (front row, centre) with his escort in Tello.

form the Louvre's Department of Near Eastern Antiquities, which was founded in August 1881 as a direct result of Sarzec's work. The Gudea Colossus (Statue D) therefore has the distinction of being numbered AO1 (AO referring to the museum's Register of Oriental Antiquities). According to the French explorer's own account in *Discoveries in Chaldea* (Sarzec and Heuzey 1912, p. 4) the upper part of the statue was found on the ground in a ravine running along the northeastern slope of Tell A:

> During my first tour on horseback, I encountered at ground level, at the foot of the principal mound, a magnificent fragment of a colossal statue, with an inscription on the shoulder. It had rolled down from the neighbouring rise, which certainly contained the ruins of a large building. It was, so to speak, the starting point for my discoveries and the first milestone that showed me the direction that my research should take.

Several scholars, including Sarzec's successors Genouillac and Parrot, have expressed doubts about the veracity of his rather romanticised narrative, according to which the explorer casually stumbled across this magnificent relic of the forgotten world of ancient Sumer, as though by accident, on his very first outing at the site. On the contrary, they correctly maintain that Statue D, and in particular its upper portion, together with other archaic sculptures from Tell A, had been unearthed before Sarzec's preliminary investigations in 1877 (see Genouillac 1936, p. 13). Parrot's *Tello: Twenty Seasons of Excavations* (1948, pp. 15–16) includes the text of a letter dated 17 March 1942 that seems unequivocally to confirm that Sarzec was alerted to the existence of ancient treasures in Tello when he heard that a number of statues had previously been found there. Addressed to Thureau-Dangin by Ibrahim Élias Géjou, a minor consular official and a prolific dealer in Mesopotamian antiques, the letter gives a vivid account of an evening party in Basra that Sarzec attended shortly after his arrival in the city:

> In 1877 M. de Sarzec was appointed consular agent of France in Basra and was the guest of M. Gabriel Asfar, when one evening M. Gilliotti, director of postal and

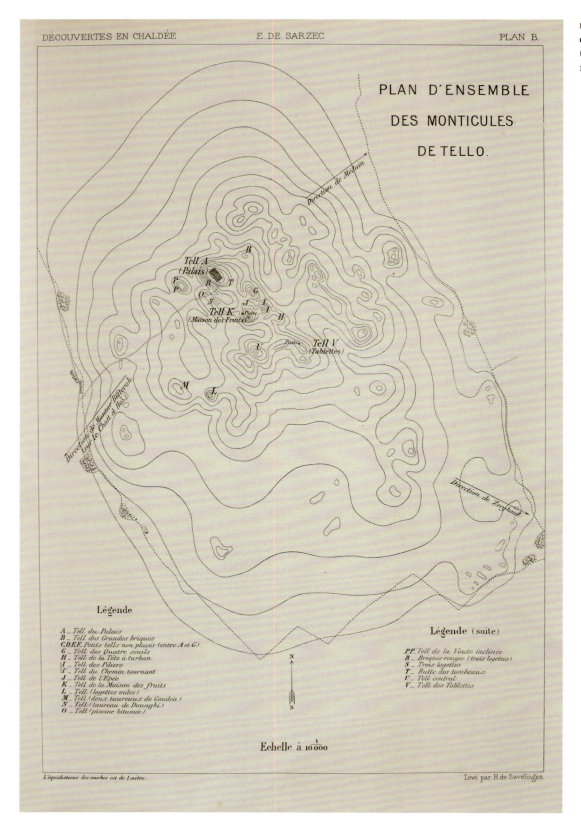

FIGURE 18. General Plan of the Mounds of Tello (Plan B), Sarzec and Heuzey 1912.

FIGURE 19. Seated statue of Gudea: the Colossus (Statue D). Musée du Louvre AO1.

telegraphic services in Baghdad, returning from an inspection of the telegraph lines that the Arabs were constantly tearing down, told these gentlemen that on his trip he had seen some statues strewn along the banks of the Chatt-El-Haï. Hearing these words, De Sarzec decides to go immediately to the place and asks M. Asfar to recommend him to the notable of the area: M. Naoum Serkis. He finds the statues in question, and just as he is loading them onto his barge, the Turkish vali [civil governor] at that time, Takk-El-Dine Pasha, keeps one of his statues back to offer to the Sultan, but which in fact he keeps for himself. It is this statue that

M. Platt and I bought from the vali's heirs, and that you saw with me at M. Platt's house. I heard this story from the very mouth of M. Asfar, who repeated it to me several times, and it was in 1880 that I got to know M. de Sarzec, when I joined the French Consulate in Baghdad as a chancellery clerk. That's all I know about this subject.

As this implies, there is little doubt that the torso of the Gudea Colossus together with other sculptural remains had already been exposed before Sarzec first visited Tello in 1877, and that many pieces were readily accessible to him when he arrived there. It is also unquestionably the case that other important objects originating in Tello were recovered before his excavations began. They include a cuneiform tablet from Gudea's archive that entered the Louvre in 1873 (Parrot 1948, p. 16) and a statue of Gudea at prayer that was acquired for the British Museum in 1851, a quarter of a century before Sarzec began work at the site. The fragmentary and rather battered statue, carved from dolerite, which is the earliest object in the British Museum collections that can be attributed to the reign of Gudea, was one of the first Sumerian artefacts to reach Europe (Fig. 20). It was found in 1850 at the site of Tell Hamman, some 40 km from Tello, by the archaeologist William Kennet Loftus, who was then employed as a surveyor for the Turco-Persian Boundary Commission. Inscribed with cuneiform text and showing Gudea with characteristic interlocked hands, the statue was possibly transported to Tell Hammam in antiquity, either from Tello or perhaps from Zurghul (ancient Nigin).

Of much greater relevance to the present discussion is the pair of hands from the Gudea Colossus that was bought for the British Museum by George Smith, the renowned British Museum philologist, who achieved international fame in 1872 when he deciphered the eleventh tablet of the Gilgamesh epic, including the Mesopotamian story of the Great Flood from which the later Old Testament narrative of Noah's flood was derived. After his recovery of the flood narrative, which understandably captured the public imagination, Smith travelled to the region three times between 1873 and 1876, and the sculpted hands were sold to him on his last expedition in 1876, the year in which he died of dysentery in Aleppo at the age of just thirty-six. The hands of the Gudea Colossus were eventually reunited with the other preserved remains of the statue (including, by that time, the lower

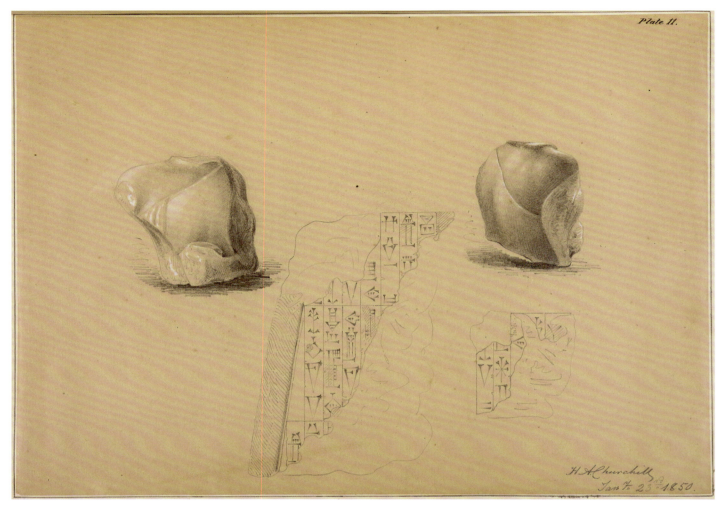

FIGURE 20. Pencil sketches, made in 1850 by H. A. Churchill, of a statue of Gudea from Tell Hamman, showing details of the cuneiform inscription. British Museum 92988 / ME Ar. 184.9.

part, as described immediately below) in May 1958, after prolonged negotiations between the Trustees of the British Museum and the authorities at the Louvre that resulted in an agreement to transfer the interlocked hands to Paris, where they were reattached to the torso (Fig. 21).

Sarzec returned to Tello the year after the recovery of the upper part of the Colossus. Excavating on Tell A from 18 February to 9 June 1878 (Season 2), he uncovered numerous treasures *in situ*, among which were the lower portion of Statue D, along with inscribed door sockets and foundation deposits. Significantly, on Tell I', known as the Mound of the Turning Path (the *Chemin tournant*), at the base of Tell K, he discovered the intact Cylinders of Gudea, with their celebrated inscriptions that narrate and commemorate the ruler's momentous construction on Tell A of the New Eninnu (as outlined above). Sarzec arranged to have his first finds from Tello sent back to France in July 1878, in a shipment that included artefacts excavated in 1877 and 1878, together with other objects acquired on these trips. The entire assemblage was then purchased by the Louvre with funds provided by the French government.

The important object that was not sent back to Paris in the first shipment was the bottom part of the Gudea Colossus. Too heavy to transport, it was reinterred in the ground at the site for safekeeping. The subsequent history of the enormous piece of statuary provides a vignette that illustrates the scramble for treasure that was engaged in by two venerable institutions, the Louvre and the British Museum,

FIGURE 21. British Museum keeper R. D. Barnett refitting the hands of the Gudea Colossus to the other preserved parts of the statue at a ceremony in the Louvre in 1958.

as they competed for cultural dominance in the nineteenth century. The lower part of the Colossus was still buried where it had been left by Sarzec, when Hormuzd Rassam briefly visited Tello on behalf of the British Museum in March 1879. The details of his visit are described in *Asshur and the Land of Nimrod* (1897), where he records that, although he did not remove the massive fragment, he uncovered it in order to take a cast or 'squeeze' of the inscriptions. He goes on to remark that, if he had continued his work on the site for even 'one day longer', he would doubtless have come across the 'nest of black statues' that lay 'within a few feet' of the Colossus—referring to the cache of diorite statues of Gudea (and one of Ur-Bau) that Sarzec subsequently excavated and sent back to the Louvre. The difficulties faced by the competing archaeologists were exacerbated by the need to obtain imperial Ottoman excavation permits, known as firmans, that were issued by the Ottoman Sublime Porte in Constantinople. As Rassam ruefully noted, Sarzec began working at the site without a permit, and in point of fact the French pioneer undertook his first two seasons in a private capacity, funding the work with his own money, without the support or official backing of the French authorities. For his part, Rassam had a wide-ranging firman that was obtained through Rassam's good friend Austen Henry Layard, who was then the British ambassador in Constantinople. It authorised him freely to explore large areas of Mesopotamia, but it did not extend to the district that included Tello, which was controlled by the powerful Muntefik tribe, who were part of a semi-independent state, or pashalic, under Nasir Pasha. Despite the lack of formal authorisation, Rassam remained at the site from 2 March to 5 March 1879, when he opened some soundings in Tell A, and he subsequently sent a collection of objects back to London (discussed further in Chapter 32).

Sarzec resumed his work in Tello in January 1880 (Season 3), now in possession of the coveted Ottoman permit. With the financial backing of the French government and the enthusiastic support of the Louvre, he concentrated his large-scale excavations at the heart of the Mound of the Palace. The ruins of the monumental edifice were found to be made of reused archaic spolia and ex-votos, together with bricks bearing an inscription in Aramaic and Greek characters. Sarzec also unearthed the host of Lagash II headless sculptures mentioned by Rassam, as well as other fragments of Sumerian statuary and a plethora of Sumerian and Hellenistic antiquities. From 12 November 1880 to 15 March 1881 (Season 4), Sarzec continued to explore the Palace complex, opening a series of deep trenches that revealed archaic constructions bearing Sumerian cuneiform signs and royal cartouches that were found to be distinct from, and situated below, the so-called Palace. It now became evident that the readily detectable architectural structures on the mound's highest levels, which were until then thought to have been parts of a royal building dating from the time of Gudea, had in fact been constructed nearly two thousand years later, in the Hellenistic era, by the enigmatic Graeco-Babylonian figure, Adadnadinakhe.

Sarzec's fieldwork in Tello was undertaken during a period of relative lawlessness in the region that was caused by the revolts of Arab tribes against the Ottomans, who controlled Babylonia. Performed under Ottoman imperial auspices, the Frenchman's operations were therefore regularly targeted by raids, and the site was often caught in no man's land. A long-lasting legacy of those troubled times—one that continues in one form or another to the present day—were the lootings that took place between the successive pioneering French excavations (1877–1933), and ever-increasingly in the wake of the Gulf Wars at the end of the twentieth century CE. The recurring violence and thefts were mentioned by Sarzec in his early correspondence with Heuzey at the Louvre. In a letter dated 17 March 1881, for example (published in Parrot 1948, p. 19), the vice consul informed his colleague in Paris that bandits regularly raided the site, and went on to say that: 'most of the works or fragments that I send back have first been stolen from me, and I have had to buy them back afterwards'. The extent of the looting and of Sarzec's enforced repurchasing is unknown, but it raises important questions about how many stolen artefacts were lost in the process, and what exactly might have gone missing.

During a long interruption to the fieldwork between 1881 and 1888, Sarzec spent time in France and doubtless also in Baghdad, where he was promoted to the post of French Consul in 1883. In terms of the progress of his research, the period was by no means wasted because it enabled Sarzec and Heuzey to collaborate on written accounts of the exceptional discoveries that had already been made at the Tello site, beginning with 'Chaldean Excavations', a paper read by Heuzey in 1881 at the *Académie des Inscriptions et Belles-Lettres*. Three years later there followed a longer report on the excavations that was published in 1884 as the first instalment of Sarzec and Heuzey's *Discoveries in Chaldea*. At the same time, the editing of the cuneiform inscriptions found in Girsu was entrusted to Julius Oppert, Arthur Amiaud and later to Thureau-Dangin. Beginning in 1882, they produced a regular stream of facsimiles, followed by transcriptions and translations of the inscriptions found on the Gudea Statues and the Cylinders, along with other Sumerian cuneiform tablets and archaic votive objects (see, for example, Oppert 1882, pp. 28–40; and Amiaud 1887, pp. 287–98). Amiaud made pioneering contributions to the deciphering of the Tello inscriptions until his premature death in 1889, when Thureau-Dangin continued his work, going on to lay the foundations of Sumerology. His landmark publication of the royal inscriptions of Sumer and Akkad (1905) enabled a more authentic chronology of events in the third millennium BCE than had been possible until then.

By the last quarter of the nineteenth century, linguistic scholars were relatively familiar with cuneiform documents deriving from the Assyrian period, but the texts that were discovered by Sarzec opened a window onto much older cultures. Although the Sumerian inscriptions from Tello were written in cuneiform script, the fact that the script itself was not standardised and that it underwent significant changes over the centuries created a host of problems, beginning with the difficulty of recognising the ancient shapes of characters that were known from later Assyrian sources. In other cases older habits persisted, however. For example, while it was possible to use syllables to write the Sumerian words ensi (ensí), meaning 'ruler', and Lagash, the name of the city and the state, the traditional spellings, PA.TE.SI and SHIR.BUR.LA^{ki}, were nonetheless retained. Accordingly, early translations of Gudea's inscriptions routinely refer to him as the 'patesi of Shirpourla'. The correct reading of the key word Lagash was soon established, but it was decades before scholars began to refer to Sumerian rulers as ensis. Further confusion resulted from the fact that the way Gudea was styled in such inscriptions was itself an archaism because the centre of power had been transferred from Lagash to Girsu long before his ascent to the throne.

The linguistic identity of Sumerian also caused confusion. As early as the 1850s, there was evidence to suggest that cuneiform had not been created to serve the needs of a Semitic language such as Akkadian. Henry Rawlinson incorrectly believed that it had been borrowed from Egyptian, but texts had already been found that showed Sumerian was an agglutinating language, in which meanings are formed by grouping semantic units, rather than by applying patterned changes to consonantal roots, as is the practice in Semitic languages. When its character was slowly brought to light, the emerging language was first classified as Scythic or Turanian, and was often referred to as (Old) Chaldean. Most confusingly for later scholars, it was even called Akkadian. The term Sumerian—the name by which it is now universally known—was proposed by Oppert in 1869, but it was many years before it gained wide acceptance.

In tandem with the problems caused by local uprisings against the Ottomans, Sarzec's work in Tello was also repeatedly suspended by the Ottoman Sublime Porte, who demanded a share of the fabulous Sumerian treasures that were being unearthed. Long and arduous negotiations between the Ottoman Porte and French diplomats in Constantinople eventually led to an agreement, after which Sarzec returned to Tello in 1888 (Season 5), when he opened further trenches in the Mound of the Palace, particularly in the central and northern parts of Tell A, and he attempted with little success to disentangle the complex stratigraphic relationship between the Hellenistic and Sumerian ruins. His main focus in 1888–9 (Season 6) now shifted elsewhere, however, as he turned his attention to Tell K (and also to nearby Tell I, referred to as the Mound of the Pillars). Of great significance is the fact that, in 1888, Sarzec commissioned the surveyor and field photographer Henri de Sevelinges to work on topographical maps and architectural plans of the area. The first of these, Sarzec's Plan A, which is described in detail below, was later finalised by Sarzec and Paul Murcier. Sevelinges also sketched the archaeological ruins that had been previously exposed, including the reattributed architecture on Tell A, and he took the first photographs of the site (see Chapters 22 and 25). In 1889, while Sarzec was busy on Tell K, Gudea himself became an international phenomenon at the *Exposition Universelle* in Paris, where he was celebrated as a significant royal architect (*roi-bâtisseur*) in a series of exhibits dedicated to the history of labour. This was the event that first alerted the public at large to the very existence of Sumer, and it made Sarzec a figure of some renown.

After a further interruption (1890–3), Sarzec launched a new series of large-scale excavations in Tello that ran from 1893 to 1895 (Seasons 7–9), in the course of which he dispatched legions of workmen to another giant mound, Tell V, also-known as Tablet Hill, which was the political and administrative centre of ancient Girsu. Unfortunately, his work was marred by the terrible looting of tens of thousands of clay tablets from palatial and temple archives dating from the Presargonic, Akkad, Lagash II and Ur III periods. From 1893 to 1894 (Seasons 7 and 8) Sarzec also renewed his efforts on the Mound of the Palace, exploring the substructure of the south-eastern part of the Hellenistic complex, where he uncovered more of the Sumerian sacred architecture (dedicated to Ningirsu) that was built under Gudea's Lagash II predecessor, Ur-Bau. In 1895 (Season 9), Sarzec undertook a significant operation in the central area of Tell A, where he completely exposed the structure known as the Gate of Gudea and revealed further traces of the Hellenistic complex.

No works were carried out between 1895 and 1898, but negotiations with the Sublime Porte in Constantinople led to the Louvre's reacquisition of some of the great treasures that had previously been found by Sarzec in Tello, including the Mesilim mace head, the Ur-Nanshe genealogical relief plaques, fragments of the Stele of the Vultures and the silver Vase of Enmetena, all of which came from Tell K (Figs. 22 and 23). Subsequently, in March 1899 (Season 10), Sarzec went back to Tello, hoping to complete his work on Tablet Hill (Tell V) and Tell K. Finally, after briefly returning to France, he descended the Tigris for the last time in February 1900, when his river barge passed the flotilla of the German Assyriologist Herman Hilprecht, the epigrapher with the American team at Nippur (present-day Nuffar), who was on his way to Baghdad. Hilprecht (1903, p. 258) recalled the encounter in picturesque style:

> A heavy thunderstorm was raging over the barren plains of 'Irâq, and the muddy waters of the Tigris began

FIGURE 22. Ur-Nanshe Plaque A. Musée du Louvre AO2344.

suddenly to rise, greatly interfering with my progress, when the two steamers came in sight of each other. I stood on the bridge of the English 'Khalîfa', intently looking at the approaching Turkish vessel which flew the French colours from the top of its mast. A tall figure could be faintly distinguished on the passing boat, leaning against its iron railing and eagerly scanning the horizon with a field-glass. A flash of light separated the thick black clouds which had changed day into twilight, and illuminated the two steamers for a moment. I recognised the features of de Sarzec, the newly (1899) appointed minister plenipotentiary of France, who in an instant had drawn a handkerchief, which he waved lustily on his fast disappearing boat as a greeting of welcome to the representative of the Philadelphia expedition. A month later a cordial and urgent invitation was received from the French camp near Tellô. I still regret that at that moment my own pressing duties at the ruins of Nuffar did not allow of an even short visit to Southern Babylonia, and that consequently I missed my last chance of seeing de Sarzec in the midst of his trenches and directing his famous excavations in person.

Sarzec's last excavations in Tello took place from February to May 1900 (Season 11), when he resumed work at the House of the Fruits (Tell K) and Tablet Hill. Coming full circle, he also returned to the supposed Palace on Tell A, reopening deep trenches at the heart of the complex in search of more examples of the praying statues of Gudea that had first made his name. With his health failing, he subsequently returned to France and died shortly afterwards in Poitiers in May 1901.

After Sarzec: Cros, Genouillac and Parrot

After Sarzec's death, the archaeological site was placed under the direction of the French army officer Gaston Cros (Fig. 24). Excused from his military duties in 1902,

FIGURE 23. The Silver Vase of Enmetena. Musée du Louvre AO2674.

he travelled to the Mesopotamian flood plain via Palmyra, reaching Tello in 1903. Cros was the first archaeologist to undertake scientific surveys of a site's environs and to study its geographical setting, and the prospections that he performed on horseback after 1903 are the forerunners of the seminal regional surveys undertaken by Robert McC. Adams and Hans Nissen in the 1960s and 1970s (Adams and Nissen 1972; and Adams 1981). He also foreshadowed the work done in the 1960s by Jacobsen, which fundamentally re-evaluated the conceptual model of the 'hydraulic society' proposed by Karl Wittfogel in his magnus opus, *Oriental Despotism* (1957). After his eventual departure from the region in 1909, Cros was first reassigned to the French expeditionary corps in Mandate Morocco. Subsequently promoted to the rank of lieutenant colonel in 1912, he was transferred to a regiment in Africa, where he took part in the French expedition, led by Hubert Lyautey, the first resident-general of the French protectorate in Morocco, against the Zaian confederation of Berber tribes. After the outbreak of the First World War, Cros returned to metropolitan France, fighting in defence of Paris at the First Battle of the Marne (1914), before being promoted to the rank of colonel and placed in command of the Moroccan brigade, which was composed of Tirailleurs and Zouaves, on the Yser. He was killed at the front in Artois in 1915.

Cros took a number of published photos of Tells A and K during his excavations in Tello, all of which are considered in detail below (Chapters 9 and 25). In addition, a remarkable album resurfaced in 2019, when it was offered to the British Museum by a French art collector and scholar, who chanced

FIGURE 24. Gaston Cros (centre, facing the camera) with a group of tribespeople. Unpublished photo from Cros's album, probably taken in Tello in 1903.

upon it in a rare book store in Strasbourg. Cros's personal photographic journal, which contains 104 annotated views and an attached envelope of fifteen unmounted prints, documents his journey from the Mediterranean Sea to the marshlands of Iraq, via Baalbek and the Syrian Desert, along the caravan route running through Palmyra, and then southwards down the Euphrates River. It also contains views taken on his return voyage across the Persian Gulf and the Indian Ocean. The highlight of the entire set, however, is the series of some eighty photographic prints of his excavations in Girsu, two of which, showing some of the work he undertook on Tell A, are published here for the first time. The British Museum acquired this exceptional archive in September 2019, a week before the team left for Iraq to continue in Cros's footsteps, renewing the excavations at the temple site where he had left off more than a century earlier.

Whereas Sarzec had directed operations and organised logistics from a redoubt on the banks of the Gharraf (or Shatt el-Haï) at Mantar-Qaraghol, the ancient canal connecting the Tigris and the Euphrates, Cros set up camp directly on site. Since Sarzec's departure in 1900, Tello had been left unguarded, and Tablet Hill in particular had been subjected to numerous raids by gangs of looters, who notably stole an exceptional hoard of Presargonic tablets (mentioned in Chapter 2) that derived from the administrative archives of the Early Dynastic queens of Girsu, who oversaw the temple household of the goddess Bau.

Armed with instructions from Heuzey and aided by a cohort of 250 workers, from 1 January to 31 May 1903 (Season 12) Cros opened a series of new soundings across the site on the Mound of the Palace (Tell A), Tablet Hill (Tell V) and the Mound of the House of the Fruits (Tell K), including its environs, where he exposed a temple fishery and a stairway. In addition, he dug new trenches on the rise known as the Central Hill (Tell U). Some unique masterpieces of Sumerian art and culture came to light, notably a headless statue of Gudea that, almost incredibly, turned out to be the torso belonging to a head previously exhumed by Sarzec on Tell V. Among Cros's other magnificent finds was the Presargonic clay tablet on which is inscribed the remarkable lament of Urukagina (the Lamentation over the Destruction of Lagash), which chronicles the conquest of Lagash by Lugalzagesi. On Tell A, Cros concentrated his labours in the area of the Gate of Gudea, where a deep opening into the depths of the mound revealed fragments of sacred temple architecture dating back to Early Dynastic times. Significantly, Cros introduced new methods of identifying architectural features made of fragile sun-dried mud-bricks—a critically important material that Sarzec had generally overlooked.

The following year (1904, Season 13), Cros converted his temporary encampment on the site into a more permanent dig house, using inscribed bricks, mainly from the Mound of the Palace, that were found on scattered heaps of discarded spoils. The spoil heaps had steadily increased since Sarzec's first excavations in the late 1870s and 1880s, while the excavators had also unfortunately left the Hellenistic complex open and exposed to looters, vandals and impoverished locals from the deprived marshlands, who ransacked the site in search of valuables and building materials. From his new headquarters, Cros worked on several areas simultaneously, managing large-scale digs on Tablet Hill, the area of the House of the Fruits, the newly discovered Devil's Gate (Tell P, or the *Tell de la Porte-du-diable*) and in the mound known as Necropolis Hill (Tell H). At the same time, he undertook a remarkably comprehensive topographical survey of Tello and its hinterland, studying and accurately plotting the subsurface relics of ancient walls and canals.

In 1905 (Season 14), now promoted to the rank of commandant, Cros enthusiastically pursued his stratagem of exploring the site on multiple fronts, including the Mound of the House of the Fruits, Tablet Hill and the Mound of the Necropolis (Tell H), while also opening broad new trenches in Tells I and B. Additionally, in the area between the Mound of the Palace and the rise referred to as the Mound of the Large Bricks (Tell B), he exposed well-preserved parts of the richly decorated fired-brick façades that fronted the huge mud-brick platforms that were established by Gudea to raise the overall height of the mound's uppermost terrace on which the New Eninnu was built. In the same area he found a stone stairway that gave access to the upper levels of the mound and a small sanctuary that was fitted with three external pedestals that were associated with the exceptional Steles of Gudea, created to commemorate Gudea's construction of the new sacred complex. Fragments of the Gudea Steles were found between the shrine and the stairway.

The work was interrupted between 1905 and 1909, when isolated and sporadic Arab raids on armed Ottoman positions in the region escalated into an all-out revolt that led to lethal clashes in Nasiriya and Shatra. In 1909 Cros returned to Tello for his last campaign (Season 15), when he discovered new fragments of the Gudea Steles in the area between the Mound of the Large Bricks (Tell B) and Tell A; working on Tell I, he also deployed his exceptional skills in the uncovering of the Sacred Enclosure of Gudea. After Cros's departure from Babylonia in 1909, there followed a twenty-year hiatus (1909–29), during which no methodical fieldwork was carried out in Tello, but in 1910, in collaboration with Heuzey and Thureau-Dangin, Cros published his *New Excavations at Tello*. Some of Cros's findings were also incorporated into the final section of the monumental *Discoveries in Chaldea* (1912), which was written by Heuzey, but intended principally to present the later work done by Sarzec and to interpret his findings.

The First World War inevitably extended into the region, with the Allied forces led by the British on one side and the Central Powers represented by the Ottoman Empire on the other. Although the Mesopotamian theatre of conflict included the Iraqi marshlands, and pitched battles and sieges took place in Nasiriya and especially at Kut, the archaeological site in Tello was fortunately left relatively unscathed. Less fortunate was the fact that it had become famous for its rich pickings among the many bands of looters that were active in the area and ready to strike whenever the site was left unguarded. A notorious raid took place in 1924, in a new locale later identified as the Temple of Ningishzida, when a number of presumed Lagash II statues of Gudea and Ur-Ningirsu were dug up and stolen, though their authenticity has been questioned.

Twenty years after Cros left Tello in 1909, work at the site was resumed under the direction of Henri de Genouillac, who arrived early in 1929. By this time the archaeological landscape had changed considerably on account of the huge spoil heaps left by Sarzec and Cros, and the pits dug by looters. Genouillac, who had difficulty establishing the precise locations of previous excavations, opened trenches through the existing spoil and rubbish heaps to make way for the small-gauge railway tracks and mine-cars that he used to remove his own spolia. Vast quantities of bricks had been stolen, and many walls had collapsed, but Genouillac nevertheless also took the decision to build a new dig house on the site, using the remaining bricks from Tell A—a step that accelerated the rapid disintegration of extremely significant layers of architecture on the mound.

From 18 January to 15 April 1929 (Season 16), Genouillac followed Cros's lead by reopening a series of trenches across the site, starting with the Mound of the Palace. In particular, he targeted the northern half of the Hellenistic structure, carving out deep trenches and notably exposing Lagash II foundation boxes containing ritual tablets and statues of divinities from Gudea's reign. Excavations on the so-called Eastern Tells, the Sacred City, Tablet Hill (Tell V) and the Temple Mound of Ningishzida disclosed significant archaeological structures and ruins dating from the Lagash II and Ur III eras, and from the Larsa period through to Old Babylonian (Babylon I) times.

In his next campaign, conducted between 27 November 1929 and 27 February 1930 (Season 17), Genouillac extended his multifaceted digging plan by simultaneously opening a total of ten areas, running north to south from the Mound of the Palace to the Temple of Ningishzida, and east to west from the Temple of Nanshe to the Eastern Tells. He completed this phase of the work on Tell A by uncovering more sculptural debris from the Lagash II period, along with the remains of Sumerian paved floors and drains or wells. These operations, which were carried out in January 1930, were the last systematic excavations on the Mound of the Palace in the period before the Second World War.

Although Genouillac should be credited with the introduction of some new archaeological methods at the site, including more precise approaches to the dating of ceramics, his fieldwork remained poor and outdated, even by the standards of the time. To take one glaring example, he dug giant pits without paying proper attention to the vitally important sequence of layers of occupation (Fig. 25). By contrast with the rare talents of Cros, vividly attested in the superior systematic records that Cros kept, Genouillac's bleak legacy highlights the scientific chasm that separated the two pioneers.

FIGURE 25. Henri de Genouillac's excavations on Tell K, c.1930.

From 17 November 1930 to 22 February 1931 (Season 18), Genouillac was joined by Parrot, and they concentrated their efforts on a giant stratigraphic pit in the Mound of the House of the Fruits, reaching supposed Ubaid deposits from prehistoric times. Exploration of the Eastern Tells led to the discovery of a spectacular landmark of Sumerian engineering, known as the Enigmatic Construction, which has only recently been identified as the oldest bridge yet brought to light anywhere in the world. Having replaced Genouillac as site director in 1931, Parrot expended most of his archaeological energies in the Eastern Tells, where he completely exposed the Enigmatic Construction. This work was carried out between 27 November 1931 and 12 March 1932 (Season 19), and from 22 November 1932 to 23 January 1933 (Season 20).

In February 1933, in response to shifting political circumstances, France and the Louvre Museum voluntarily relinquished the legal right to renew fieldwork at the Tello site. As a symbol of the changed situation, they ordered Parrot to lower the French tricolour and to dismantle the dig house that was made of inscribed bricks dating from the time of Gudea, mostly originating from Tell A. In 1934 and 1936 Genouillac published his *Excavations at Telloh* in two volumes: the first dedicated to the Presargonic period, the second to Ur III and Larsa times. Finally, the year 1948 saw the release of Parrot's comprehensive overview, *Tello: Twenty Seasons of Excavations*.

Disentangling the French Legacy

As is observed repeatedly in this book, it is widely acknowledged that the large-scale excavations undertaken by the French pioneers and first explorers of Babylonia were generally marred by the lack of an overall methodological approach to archaeological fieldwork and to recording techniques in particular. With regard to Tello, the partial exception to this is Cros, whose fieldwork methods and record keeping systems have been sadly overlooked by more recent scholars. Carried out in the heroic age of Mesopotamian flood plain archaeology, the efforts of the first French explorers opened up previously non-existent areas of study, but they did so using untried and unscientific techniques that clearly and permanently left behind the imprints of the norms current at the time. In terms of archaeological methods and logistics, they adopted approaches related to the ongoing Industrial Revolution that were frankly calamitous when compared with present-day standards. Although their efforts played an important role in the formation of Sumerian archaeology, therefore, the contributions of the pioneers to Mesopotamian scholarship cannot be isolated from the many problems inherent in their work, not least its destructive effects.

To take one important example, the pioneers excavated speedily and voluminously, destroying large swathes of the archaeological record and failing to document much of what they uncovered as they worked. This left an unfortunate legacy, but also caused them much confusion at the time. After the first four seasons at the Mound of the Palace, for instance, Sarzec, acting on the advice of Heuzey, subsequently went back to the tell over and over again to try to make sense of what had already been excavated, trying to clarify the stratigraphy of the intricate layers of architectural remains. More problematic still, Sarzec failed to identify the fundamental fact that the main building materials used on the site were not fired bricks, but huge numbers of sun-dried mud-bricks. He therefore only unearthed hard-baked or kiln-fired mud-brick structures, neglecting some of the most revealing sources of information.

Scholars of ancient Iraq have made valiant attempts to elucidate the stratigraphic layers that the nineteenth- and early twentieth-century French teams too hastily exposed in the Mound of the Palace and the Mound of the House of the Fruits. Unfortunately, it appears extremely unlikely that it will ever be possible to use the imperfect records they kept to correlate the archaeological sequence of events with associated material deposits in order to facilitate the kind of detailed stratigraphic analysis that would nowadays provide the basis for any historical interpretation. Despite that, and as is laid out in great detail below, a careful reassessment of the French results reveals that there is still much to be learned from their work. These interpretations, relating to Tells K and A, are laid out in Parts 2 and 3 below. Similarly, as confirmed by the British Museum team's fieldwork on the site, and as is considered exhaustively below, the commonly shared criticism that the French archaeologists indiscriminately razed the mounds of Tello to the ground is quite wrong and should be abandoned.

CHAPTER 3

A Contextualised Chronology of Ancient Girsu

Defining the Timeline

The relative chronology of Mesopotamia is organised into a scheme that subdivides into two different terminological strands. Whereas successive pre- and proto-historic cultures are categorised according to the names of the sites where they were first identified (Ubaid and Uruk, for example), the classification of later periods is based on the identification of historical phases (for example, the Early Dynastic and the Third Dynasty of Ur, which is usually written as Ur III). The break in the naming conventions, which signals a change in methodology as well as in terminology, is founded on the appearance and development of the first written texts. The advent of the textual, or historical era in southern Mesopotamia is represented by the phases called Uruk IV (or Late Uruk) and the earlier Uruk III periods, the latter of which is coeval with the Jemdet Nasr epoch, as classified in the periodisation based on site names, while in the central part of Mesopotamia the historical sequence associated with the appearance of writing in the Diyala region (a series of sites along the Diyala river—a tributary of the Tigris) is known as the Protoliterate era.

The historical periodisation that is derived from textual sources was developed by scholars between the late 1920s and the early 1930s, when the earlier terminology based on site names was already well established. Accordingly, there is some overlap between the Uruk IV and Uruk III periods on the one hand, and the Jemdet Nasr (or Protoliterate) eras on the other, because the latest prehistoric phases (named after sites) coincide with the emerging historical phases in the textual era. The earliest historical phases, when writing was not yet fully formed, is also known as the proto-historic period, but apart from the specific connection with Diyala, the term Protoliterate has never gained universal currency among scholars, who prefer to speak of the Late Uruk or Jemdet Nasr eras. In terms of absolute chronology, whether it is known as proto-historic, Late Uruk or Jemdet Nasr, the period during which writing emerged can be dated to the end of the fourth and the beginning of the third millennium BCE. The third millennium, after the appearance of more developed textual sources, is then divided into three main parts: the Early Dynastic (or Protodynastic) period (which is further categorised as Early Dynastic I, II and III), followed by the Akkad (or Sargonic) period, and finally the era of the Third Dynasty of Ur (Ur III), which is also referred to as the Neo-Sumerian period.

The almost bewildering complexity of the terminology and periodisation of Mesopotamia, especially in the third millennium BCE, is further complicated by the fact that almost all the names used to describe the historical subdivisions in the textual era have been, and still are in many cases, the subject of heated scholarly debates. An important part of the discussion revolves around the transition phase, the Jemdet Nasr period, and its overlap with the Early Dynastic era (see Finkbeiner and Röllig 1986). The term Early Dynastic was coined by archaeologists from the Oriental Institute of the University of Chicago, who investigated numerous sites in the Diyala valley in central Iraq during the 1930s. It was first used as a catch-all to designate the interval between the Jemdet Nasr and the Akkad phases, but later refined to connote three successive periods: Early Dynastic I–III (Frankfort 1936, pp. 35–59). Initially, the term Early Dynastic, with its threefold subdivision, was based on artistic styles, and in particular it reflected the discovery of geometric-style sculptures in which human forms were considered to have been rendered with an emphasis on abstract shapes. The chronological sequence, which was drawn up with reference to historical developments, was later adopted by archaeologists and scholars working on a range of sites in central and southern Mesopotamia.

Although the research carried out by the Chicago archaeologists who worked on the Diyala project was of fundamental importance in laying the chronological foundations for the archaeology of Mesopotamia in the third millennium BCE, the threefold sequence that they formulated for the Early Dynastic period engendered a thorny archaeological problem with respect to the definition of the Early Dynastic II period (see Nissen 2015). As has been demonstrated by a critical rereading of the excavation reports, the Early Dynastic II phase was determined on the basis of flexible, even mercurial criteria that were applied to aspects of excavated material culture (see Evans 2007), and it was employed especially in the sequence associated with the Inanna temple in Nippur. Consequently, it can perhaps be regarded as a back-formation, with the outline of a tripartite division arbitrarily generating the need to identify an Early Dynastic II ceramic horizon in various Mesopotamian sites in order to fill the schematic gap between Early Dynastic I and III. Scholars therefore soon raised doubts about whether an Early Dynastic II phase could in fact be verified, and when the periodisation of the Diyala sites was eventually revised, the cultural traits that were previously invoked to distinguish the Early Dynastic II period were cast into doubt. This resulted in a proposal, advanced above all by American scholars, that the Early Dynastic II period should be redefined as Late Early Dynastic I (see Zettler 1989).

What is not in doubt is the overall continuity between the Jemdet Nasr phase (referred to as the Proto-literate era by archaeologists of the Diyala project) and the Early Dynastic I period, even though the picture is a little more complicated than that straightforward statement suggests. Recent reconsiderations of the archaeological data deriving from a number of excavations carried out in central and southern Iraq have highlighted the continuity, but also shown that the Early Dynastic I period was not simply a transitional phase that led to the appearance of a mature culture of writing. It was itself a long and complex time of interrelated historical changes, many aspects of which still lack clarity and definition.

The Early Dynastic III period is conventionally divided into Early Dynastic IIIa and IIIb—historical subcategories that are based on written evidence. The Early Dynastic IIIa era is associated with texts from Fara and Tell Abu Salabikh (the time frame is therefore also known as the Fara period), while the Early Dynastic IIIb era (also referred to as the Presargonic period) is connected with the First Dynasty of Lagash (see Sallaberger and Schrakamp 2015). The subdivision has been confirmed by the discovery of elements of contemporary material culture at many sites, and it can therefore be regarded as secure.

By contrast, the transition between the Early Dynastic IIIb and the Akkad phases, which is much more problematic, is the subject of considerable scholarly debate. Part of the difficulty can again be attributed to ideas and terminology introduced by the Diyala project archaeologists, who identified a proto-imperial Akkad phase that was thought to have intervened between the Early Dynastic IIIb period and the Akkad phase proper. The Diyala project hypothesis was reassessed following subsequent reinvestigations of the Diyala sites that were carried out over an extended period by another team from the Oriental Institute of Chicago (see Gibson 1982; and Gibson 2011). This led to a revision of the Diyala stratigraphic sequence and a reinterpretation of its material culture, rendering the idea of a proto-imperial phase obsolete and correspondingly placing more attention on the transition phase between the Early Dynastic IIIb and Early Akkad eras. This is a crucial issue for any understanding of the chronology relating to the Akkad expansion that took place under Sargon of Akkad and his successors. Historical judgements about the length of the Early Dynastic IIIb period, together with the transition from Early Dynastic IIIb to the subsequent Early Akkad and Akkad phases, are closely linked to inscriptions deriving from the reigns of successive Akkad rulers, but some important overlaps between archaeological finds relating to the reigns of the Early Dynastic IIIb rulers Urukagina of Lagash and Lugalzagesi of Umma, on the one hand, and to that of Sargon of Akkad on the other, have caused confusion (see Sallaberger and Schrakamp 2015, pp. 85–104) because the textual and archaeological evidence is somewhat contradictory. In consequence, certain artefacts and objects can be dated to the Early Dynastic IIIb period when they are linked with epigraphic documents deriving from the reigns of Urukagina and Lugalzagesi, but they can also be defined as Early Akkad when they are connected with texts that mention Sargon. It is an impasse that cannot currently be resolved due to the paucity of data from stratigraphically investigated sites. The upshot is that it is extremely difficult to determine the exact length of the Early Dynastic IIIb period, as well as the onset and duration of the transition phase between the Early Dynastic IIIb and Early Akkad eras, and the exact point at which the transition produced a material culture that can be identified as distinctively Early Akkad.

The critical reconsideration of the postulated protoimperial period was stimulated by finds representative of Akkad material culture that corroborated the existence of evident Akkad phases. The main data set relating to the chronology resulted from a programme of research known as the WF Area excavations that were carried out in Nippur (Gibson and McMahon 1995; and McMahon 2006). The finds deriving from the WF Area soundings provided evidence of an interesting, and currently unique transition sequence between the Early Dynastic III period and the Akkad phase that has not so far been replicated elsewhere and has not conclusively resolved the debate about the dividing line between Early Dynastic IIIb and Early Akkad times. Nor has it enabled the definitive attribution of many unearthed pottery forms to the Akkad period (see Matthews 1997; Gibson and McMahon 1997; Roaf 2001; and Gruber 2015).

Whereas the history of the Akkad supremacy, including the Early Akkad epoch, is reasonably well defined by the succession of recognised rulers, the post-Akkad period is particularly complicated and confused due to problems arising from the postulated Gutean period (see Sallaberger and Schrakamp 2015, pp. 113–17). One problem is that data sets obtained from Late Akkad pottery assemblages are not only limited in number, they also originate from the same sites as the data relating to the Early Dynastic IIIb and Early Akkad periods, and on this basis the definition of the Late Akkad era currently conflicts with the periodisation that is attested by epigraphic texts linked to successive rulers. The Late Akkad time frame also includes the Lagash II dynasty, which arose in the twilight of Akkad dominance (see Sallaberger and Schrakamp 2015, pp. 119–22). The Ur III phase that follows, which is again determined on the basis of historical data deriving from inscriptions, continues through to the second millennium BCE. At this point in the chronology the terminology begins ever more closely to reflect historical events. The term Isin-Larsa, for example, highlights the antagonism between two competing dynasties in the central part of southern Iraq, while the definition of the Old Babylonian period reflects the hegemony enjoyed by the first dynasty of Babylon. The big change reflected in these later times is the greater abundance of data sets deriving from pottery assemblages found at numerous sites. The pottery corroborates the distinctiveness of a series of well-investigated chronological periods that are attested by inscriptions. A wealth of data has been assembled that relates to the Ur III period and more especially the subsequent Isin-Larsa and Old Babylonian phases. Indeed, the identification of a further subdivision—Early and Late Isin-Larsa—was made many decades ago in Delougaz's pioneering work on ceramics (Delougaz 1952). Though the term Old Babylonian has generated a number of misunderstandings (and is sometimes considered to include the Isin-Larsa period), it is generally taken to represent a time span that starts with the first dynasty of Babylon and ends with the fall of Babylon in the sixteenth century BCE. Importantly, the ceramic repertoires of the second millennium BCE are the subject of a pivotal work of synthesis and synchronisation that deals with pottery remains from all the main archaeological sites in the Mesopotamian area (Armstrong and Gasche 2014).

After the Old Babylonian phase, Girsu seems to have been largely abandoned for about a thousand years from which no archaeological traces of activity have emerged. The site was then reoccupied in Hellenistic times (in the late fourth century BCE, as detailed in Part 4 below), and the chronology of the period from Alexander the Great's conquest of the Achaemenid Empire through to the end of Graeco-Macedonian rule in Iraq in the mid-second century BCE is solidly established. The sequence of rulers in the Seleucid period is well documented, though the details of the regional archaeological sequence in the territories of the central part of southern Iraq is vaguer and requires further research.

Problems of Terminology and Absolute vs Relative Chronology

One principal reason why the chronology of the third millennium BCE remains a hotly debated archaeological topic is because the terminology used to describe it reflects the preserved historical or textual sources rather than the excavated cultural remains. As has been remarked, the use of a mainly historical terminology inevitably creates some chronological dissonance because the invoked historical time frames do not always apply to the geographical regions that they are taken to cover (see Sallaberger and Schrakamp 2015). The adoption of a historical terminology also tended to influence the way generations of researchers viewed elements of material culture that were found at Iraqi sites, where developments were too often interpreted as linear and substantially homogeneous. The simplification meant that the special character of local areas and regional differentiations were regularly overlooked. The situation is analogous to the way in which the relative chronology of ancient Egypt was interpreted before it was transformed into a Roman province by Augustus. Happily, in more recent times the flawed picture has been redrawn to accommodate the unmistakable signs of regional variations and distinctive local cultures, while new lines of research have produced extremely interesting results that rightly portray the third millennium as a period of political and territorial fragmentation—developments that are striking in the central part of southern Mesopotamia. The political fragmentation and the associated particularity of everyday political reality in the Early Dynastic IIIb era are well attested in the numerous terminological variants that are used to designate the holders of power in the various political entities that existed before the Akkad period (see Marchesi 2015).

A further compelling difficulty arises with regard to the connections between the relative chronology of ancient Mesopotamia (the sequence of named periods and their associated subdivisions) and the absolute chronology of specific dates and events. In terms of dates, the relative chronology of Mesopotamia is anchored in the time line attributed to the first dynasty of Babylon (Babylon I), which is defined by researchers in different ways, depending on the dates they assign to the reign of Hammurabi of Babylon at one end of the range and to the end of the first dynasty of Babylon at the other (Sallaberger and Schrakamp 2015, pp. 5–6). The hypothesis that currently enjoys the most credit among scholars, and which seems to be consistent with the greatest weight of evidence, is the Middle Chronology II (abbreviated as MC II), which dates the reign of Hammurabi to between 1784 BCE and 1742 BCE, and places the fall of Babylon I in the year 1587 BCE (Sallaberger and Schrakamp 2015, p. 11).

The dates postulated in the construction of an absolute chronology have undoubtedly had an impact on the understanding of the development of material culture within the relative framework, but the actual dating of events is nonetheless the subject of intense debate. Accordingly, although the proposed adoption of the Middle Chronology II as the marker that defines the absolute time line of ancient Mesopotamia was the result of an enormous effort of data revision (Sallaberger and Schrakamp 2015), the sequence is far from definitive, and it has by no means been accepted by all scholars. Indeed, the seminal study of ceramic repertoires mentioned above (Armstrong and Gasche 2014) takes the alternative New Low Chronology as its frame of reference. Proposed by Cole (2014), the New Low Chronology brings the key dates adduced by the Middle Chronology II forward by about a century, dating the reign of Hammurabi to between 1696 BCE and 1654 BCE, and the end of Babylon I to 1499 BCE.

A Suggested Periodisation for the Archaeology of Ancient Girsu

With regard to periodisation, this book adopts the established terminology, identifying the Jemdet Nasr period as the transitional phase between the end of the fourth and the beginning of the third millennium (3100 BCE to 2900 BCE). This is followed by the Early Dynastic period (2900 BCE to 2300 BCE), with the Early Dynastic II era being considered as part of the Early Dynastic I period. The subdivision of the Early Dynastic III period into Early Dynastic IIIa and IIIb is retained, while Early Dynastic IIIb incorporates parts of the internal sequence found at Girsu, notably the epoch of the Lagash I dynasty. For the subsequent Akkad period (2300 BCE to 2100 BCE) it is preferable in the case of Girsu to distinguish two subphases: Early Akkad and Late Akkad. The former roughly corresponds to the period of Akkad supremacy, from 2300 BCE to 2200 BCE, while the latter, which ranges from 2200 BCE to 2100 BCE, includes the transition period that is defined in some chronologies, again based on textual, or historical data, as Gutean. With respect to the internal sequence of Girsu, the Late Akkad period corresponds with the epoch of the Lagash II dynasty. The Ur III period (2100 BCE to 2000 BCE) and the Isin-Larsa period (2000 BCE to 1800 BCE) are used to define the last century of the third millennium and the first two centuries of the second millennium. Finally, the Old Babylonian period, which is considered to extend from 1800 BCE to 1600 BCE, is marked by a break in the occupation sequence of Girsu that probably affected the entire site. It is also generally accepted that the tenth or twelfth regnal year of Samsuiluna was the moment when Old Babylonian dominance came to an end in Girsu and in other parts of southern Mesopotamia (see Armstrong and Gasche 2014, pp. 1–2).

The Chronology of the Rulers of Lagash I

Beginning with Ur-Nanshe, the founder of the First Dynasty, and ending with Urukagina, the Lagash I era, which included at least nine rulers from seven successive generations (not all from the same family), lasted for approximately 150 years (Sallaberger and Schrakamp 2015, pp. 81–4). The series of rulers and their lineages are presented in Table 1 below. Of the nine Lagash I rulers whose names are known, only two—Enentarzi and Urukagina—have no identifiable genealogical links with their respective predecessors. While the sequence is securely established, the reign durations and absolute dates of individual rulers are estimates. The exceptions are Enentarzi and Lugalanda, whose reign durations can be determined by using the dating formulae recorded on administrative tablets.

Table 2 (below) contains a suggested chronology for the series of Lagash I rulers that is based on the regnal dates of the dynasty's last ruler, Urukagina (c.2316 BCE to 2307 BCE), as estimated in the Middle Chronology II. Although the time line is expressed in terms of absolute dates, the chronology uses round numbers to reflect the fact that they are estimates.

TABLE 1. Genealogical links between Lagash I rulers: sons are represented by a vertical bar (|); brothers are represented by an em dash (—); a question mark (?) indicates an unknown descent or transition.

Generations	
1	Ur-Nanshe
2	Akurgal
3	Eanatum — Enanatum I
4	Enmetena
5	Enanatum II (?)— Enentarzi
6	Lugalanda
7	(?) Urukagina

TABLE 2. A reconstructed chronology for the rulers of Lagash I.

Generation	Ruler	Length of Reign (+/− 5 years)	Dates
1	Ur-Nanshe	35	c.2460–2425 BCE
2	Akurgal	5	c.2425–2420 BCE
3	Eanatum	30	c.2420–2390 BCE
	Enanatum I	20	c.2390–2370 BCE
4	Enmetena	35	c.2370–2335 BCE
5	Enanatum II	8	c.2335–2327 BCE
	Enentarzi	5	c.2327–2322 BCE
6	Lugalanda	6	c.2322–2316 BCE
7	Urukagina	9	c.2316–2307 BCE

FIGURE 26. The Early Dynastic inscribed stone Plaque of Enanatum, showing the ruler of Lagash with his hands clasped in an attitude of worship. British Museum 130828.

In terms of the average length of the reigns of successive rulers, thirty years represents a long reign, twenty years a reign of medium length, and ten or fewer years a short reign.

With the exception of Enentarzi and Lugalanda, for whom precise information exists, the rulers' estimated reign durations are based on the actions and events mentioned in their respective royal inscriptions, and the number of children they are known to have had, with further weight being given to their generational relationships. The six reigns that span the period from Eanatum to Enentarzi include three generations, and the preserved inscriptions from the successive periods in office indicate that two of the rulers enjoyed long reigns. Since Enentarzi is also known to have served as the temple administrator (sanga) of Ningirsu under Enmetena, his predecessor Enanatum II must have been on the throne for a relatively short period—a theory that is further confirmed by the scarcity of inscriptions in his name (Fig. 26). The surviving inscriptions in the names of Eanatum and Enanatum I would suggest that they enjoyed long and medium reigns, respectively. Since the two rulers were brothers, the duration of their successive reigns has been conservatively estimated to give a plausible combined figure of fifty years in office for a single generation. The fact that little is known about Akurgal suggests that he ruled for a short time, and this is corroborated not only by the extended reign of his father, Ur-Nanshe, but also by the combined length of the period in office that was enjoyed by his two sons, Eanatum and Enanatum I. In total, the Lagash I dynasty is estimated to have lasted for around 153 years, from approximately 2460 BCE to 2307 BCE.

The Chronology of the Rulers of Lagash II

According to recent reconstructions, the Lagash II period, which probably lasted for about eighty years, spanned four

TABLE 3. The sequence of Lagash II rulers according to the lists of offerings recorded on the Maeda Tablet and the Perlov Tablet.

Maeda Tablet	Perlov Tablet	
	Gudea	Gudea is named first on the Perlov Tablet as the recipient of a different offering (perfumed oil) than the other listed rulers, who receive sheep fat.
Ur-Ningirsu I	Ur-Ningirsu I	Ur-Ningirsu I is listed as Ur-Ningirsu ugula on the Maeda Tablet, while the Perlov Tablet refers to him simply as Ur-Ningirsu.
Pirigme	Pirigme	
Ur-Bau	Ur-Bau	
Gudea	[Gudea]	
Ur-Ningirsu II	Ur-Ningirsu II	Ur-Ningirsu II is listed as Ur-Ningirsu dumu Gudea on the Maeda Tablet, while the Perlov Tablet refers to him only as Ur-Ningirsu.
UrGAR		
Urabba		
Urmama		
Nammahni	Nammahni	Nammahni's name is spelt nam.ha.ni on the Maeda Tablet, but the spelling on the Perlov Tablet is nam.mah.ni.

or five generations from Puzurmama to Nammahni (Sallaberger and Schrakamp 2015, p. 122). It is not, strictly speaking, a dynasty because power was not systematically transferred between blood relatives, but as extended family ties can be reconstructed for some Lagash II rulers, and given that the rules of succession in this period are unknown, the term 'dynasty' can reasonably be used in its broader sense to mean a more or less consecutive series of rulers who all form part of a politically continuous regime. Also of note is the fact that, by contrast with the practice of their Lagash I predecessors, rulers in the Lagash II period rarely mention their filiations in their inscriptions, and this has further hindered the reconstruction of a possible dynastic sequence based on genealogical descent. As opposed to the rulers of Lagash I, who styled themselves as either ensi or lugal, the rulers of Lagash II all adopted the title ensi.

Like their predecessors in the Lagash I era, the Lagash II rulers are not mentioned in the renowned Sumerian King List (the oldest preserved version of which dates to the Ur III era), which purports to detail every pre-eminent ruler in history, all the way back beyond the Great Flood to the time when kingship was first handed down from the gods. As the selective nature of the list suggests (and it is interesting to note that the neighbouring rival state of Umma was also left out), it was probably intended to legitimise the hegemonic dominance of particular city-states. Three Lagash II sovereigns (Ur-Ningirsu, Ur-Bau and Gudea) do appear in a later composition known as the Rulers of Lagash, which dates to the middle of the Old Babylonian period. The text, which also chronicles a succession of monarchs from antediluvian times to the reign of Gudea, follows the pattern set by the Sumerian King List, but it is generally deemed fanciful and regarded as a work of political satire that was written by a Lagash scribe to ridicule the compilers of the Sumerian King List, who chose to omit the rulers of Lagash (Sollberger 1967, p. 279). This idea, which is reconsidered below in Chapter 35, was formulated to account for the appearance in the Rulers of Lagash of kings who are not attested elsewhere, and also to make sense of the extremely long reigns (in excess of 100 years) that are said to have been enjoyed by all the monarchs included in the text.

Despite the various problems, the Lagash II sequence of rulers can be partly reconstructed with reference to two lists of offerings preserved in two sets of inscriptions known as the Maeda Tablet (BM18474) and the Perlov Tablet (Pushkin GMII 1.2.b.38), the contents of which were analysed by Tohru Maeda (1988) and Boris Perlov (1980), respectively (see also Sallaberger 1993, pp. 281–3). The two texts present a similar sequence of rulers from Ur-Ningirsu I to Ur-Ningirsu II, after which they differ, as can be seen in Table 3 below.

Absent from both tablets are three additional monarchs who must have ruled Lagash in the post-Sargonic period: Kaku, Lu-Bau and Lugula. Although the order of their reigns is uncertain, they are listed elsewhere on administrative tablets that bear the names of the respective rulers' first year in office, using the formula: [year] PN ensi. Kaku is named

TABLE 4. A partially reconstructed chronology of the rulers of Lagash II.

Ruler	Estimated reign	Estimated dates with reference to MC II	
(Ur-Ningirsu I, Pirigme)	—	—	
Ur-Bau	25 years	c.2150–2125 BCE	
Gudea	25 years	c.2125–2100 BCE	**Urnamma of Ur** c.2102–2085 BCE
Ur-Ningirsu II	5 years	c.2100–2095 BCE	
(UrGAR, Urabba, Urmama)	—	—	
Nammahni	5 years	c.2090–2085 BCE	

on AO3310 (RTC188); Lubaba on AO3327 (RTC189); and Lugula on AO3328 (RTC190). A prosopographic study of the occurrence of the names found in the surviving documents indicates that the three were related and that they were linked to Urmama, suggesting that they were active in the latter part of the reign of Urnamma of Ur (Sallaberger and Schrakamp 2015, p. 12). Since, according to the Maeda Tablet, Urmama preceded Nammahni, the reigns of Kaku, Lubaba and Lugula may be dated to the later Lagash II period, after the time of Ur-Ningirsu II. This raises frequently debated questions concerning the synchronism and relative periodisations of Lagash II and Ur III—in particular, whether Gudea and Urnamma were contemporaries, and the circumstances in which Girsu was annexed by Ur. Another Lagash II ruler named Lumma is attested in a list of offerings that has also been dated to the Ur III period, and he may safely be added to the series of Lagash monarchs, even though his place in the sequence is unknown. Setting aside the several uncertainties, the Maeda Tablet and the Perlov Tablet both state that Ur-Ningirsu I was the first ruler of the Lagash II dynasty, and both name Nammahni as the last in the sequence. These starting and finishing points have gained wide acceptance. The rest of the established sequence is traditionally based on the Maeda Tablet and therefore includes UrGAR, Urabba and Urmama—three monarchs who do not appear on the Perlov list.

In sum, the available evidence provides an imperfect and incomplete picture of the Lagash II chronology, in which regard it is important to stress not only that no reconstruction can accommodate all the currently known data, but also that the many imponderables make it impossible to formulate a clear idea of the period's historical setting. Despite that, a rather scattered sequence can be proposed that has two attested lines of filiation: first, Ur-Ningirsu I and Pirigme, who were father and son; secondly, the line initiated by Ur-Bau that includes Gudea (Ur-Bau's son-in-law), Ur-Ningirsu II and Nammahni. The dates of the monarchs in the Ur-Bau line can be estimated using the surviving sources, which are plentiful and informative, in combination with the chronological anchor point that is provided by the more secure dating of contemporary Ur III rulers. In view of the brief overlap between the regnal years of Gudea and Urnamma of Ur, Gudea's reign is judged to have ended around 2100 BCE, and this lays down a marker from which the dates of his predecessor, Ur-Bau, and two of his successors, Ur-Ningirsu II and Nammahni, can be deduced. The chronology shown in Table 4 is based on the assumption (derived from the preserved sources) that Ur-Bau and Gudea both enjoyed rather long periods in office of about twenty-five years, and that the reigns of the monarchs who came after them (from Ur-Ningirsu II to Nammahni) were much shorter.

PART 2 The Mound of the House of the Fruits

CHAPTER 4

Introduction to the French Excavations on Tell K

TELL K, KNOWN AS THE MOUND OF THE HOUSE OF the Fruits (*La Maison des fruits*), is a large rise on the south side of the sacred precinct of Girsu (approximately 200 m south-east of the Mound of the Palace (Tell A)), where the French pioneers explored an intricate sequence of structures and installations dating back to Early Dynastic times. These turned out to be the remains of successive iterations of the principal sanctuary of the god Ningirsu before the temple was eventually transferred to Tell A around the end of the third millennium BCE. The first extensive excavations on Tell K were undertaken by Sarzec, who focused his attention there in 1888 and 1889 (Seasons 5 and 6), after his long absence from Tello, and again in 1899 and 1900 (Seasons 10 and 11). Following Sarzec's death, Cros reopened a series of trenches in and around the mound between 1903 and 1905 (Seasons 12, 13 and 14). Finally, nearly thirty years later, Genouillac and Parrot returned to Tell K between 1930 and 1931 (Season 18), when they dug a colossal pit that largely devastated what was left of the mound.

The buccaneering fieldwork begun by Sarzec and in a sense completed by Cros provided some key archaeological information that is still of value despite being fragmentary and problematic. There is no doubt that when Sarzec started work on Tell K he expected to find more of the spectacular, well-preserved treasures that had first attracted him to Tello, and which he unearthed on the Mound of the Palace during his early seasons on the site after 1877. This perhaps explains why, on Tell K even more than elsewhere, he paid little or no attention to mud-brick remains, concerning himself almost exclusively with building materials that were considered more prestigious, notably baked bricks and stone, which in fact represented only a tiny part of the ruins. The challenge of using the French results to help to clarify the relationships between the various remains found on Tell K is further complicated by the fact that Sarzec and his successors did not install grids on the site, while stratigraphic analysis, which was then still in its infancy, was unknown to them. Their excavation results (as is also seen when their work on Tell A is examined in detail), which were poorly recorded and sometimes not documented at all, present later researchers with an extremely inadequate and problem-ridden interpretative framework. In consequence, any attempt to recontextualise the recorded archaeological finds and architectural features by rationalising the hurriedly exposed stratigraphic layers is an almost Heraclean task. Despite all of these drawbacks, not least the fact that Tell K was exposed at lightning speed and with scant attention to crucially important details, the first French explorers produced published reports and some usable (if relatively unsystematic) data sets, including plans, sections and photographs, that can be used as the basis of a reinterpretation of the archaeological remains.

Sarzec's field observations on Tell K gave rise to two reports that were both produced after his earlier work (Seasons 1–4) had been written up in collaboration with Heuzey in the first instalment of *Discoveries in Chaldea* (1884). The first of these, Heuzey's stand-alone volume entitled *A Chaldean Royal Villa Dating Back to 4000 BCE* (*Une villa royale chaldéenne vers l'an 4000 avant notre ère, d'après les levés et les notes de M. de Sarzec*), published in 1900, was followed in 1912 by the concluding volume of *Discoveries in Chaldea*, which was formed of texts that had previously been published as a series of instalments. As the title of the 1900 publication suggests, both of these reports are principally the work of Heuzey, with the second being completed more than ten years after Sarzec's death (and four years after Heuzey had given up his post at the Louvre in 1908). While he worked on these publications, Heuzey had access to all of Sarzec's papers and other materials, including excavation notes, photographs and plans drawn up in the field, supplemented by letters and telegrams describing the progress of the work, and he also conducted frequent interviews with Sarzec prior to Sarzec's passing (Heuzey 1900, p. vi). Nevertheless, he was writing at a great distance, thousands of miles from the site, and he was not present during any of the excavations, so his view of the work that was carried out there was derived entirely from what he could learn at one or more removes. To highlight what this means, the difficulty of assimilating the fragmentary data was compounded by the fact that Heuzey could not fall back on his own recollections of the excavations to help him fill any gaps. Accordingly, the two publications, which are often mutually contradictory, tend to be vague, with thin, undeveloped descriptions, either because Heuzey chose not to elaborate or because he lacked the necessary information.

An important problem concerns the precise locations of excavated architectural remains and recovered objects, particularly the depths at which they were found. In the best cases, depth is measured with respect either to the top of Tell K or in relation to intermediate landmarks (the floor level established by Ur-Nanshe for example). But the usual practice followed by Sarzec and Heuzey is to give stratigraphic coordinates relative to the deepest level down to which Sarzec excavated, so that the find locations of objects and structures are measured as heights above that lowest point. When Sarzec arrived at the site, the top of the mound lay 14 m above the surrounding plain (the measurement given in Sarzec and Heuzey 1912, p. 406), while the bottom of the deepest sounding dug by Sarzec was 17 m below that topmost point (as noted in Heuzey 1900, p. 2; and Sarzec and Heuzey 1912, p. 415; see Plan C (2); Fig. 33 below). The figure of 17 m, measuring from the original top of the mound to the floor of the deepest excavation pit, was used by Sarzec and Heuzey as a scale on which to plot the locations of objects and architectural features inside the tell. What it means is that, for example, an object that was uncovered at a depth of 4 m below the mound's summit was logged as lying 13 m above the bottom of the deepest excavation point—at a 'Sarzec height' of 13 m. To avoid adding to this confusing situation, and also because the maximum height of the summit of Tell K as measured by Sarzec cannot now be verified because the mound was subsequently dramatically truncated, Sarzec heights have been retained in the descriptions and analyses that follow. Sarzec's scale is included on the section (Plan C (2)) that he drew up to plot the positions of the buildings and some of the objects that were found within Tell K, though the diagram cannot be entirely relied upon, as it was made a posteriori from the plans, as was the usual practice at the time. The Sarzec scale was also included by Cros on his complementary NE and SW sections (1910, pp. 70–1; Fig. 37 below) that provide a wide-screen view (so to speak) of the mound's interior.

The publications that were based on the information collected by Sarzec present other difficulties. Sketches were included of a few details (presumably selected from many other drawings that must have been made over the years), and the published plans present the principal remains and occasional objects, but the locations and often also the dimensions marked on the plans do not always correspond with the data given in the accompanying texts. It is not clear how exactly Sarzec carried out his measurements and surveys (a question mentioned only in passing by Heuzey (1900, p. vi)), but in some cases it is necessary to treat them with caution. It is also clear that special attention was paid by Sarzec and Heuzey to a select number of star artefacts, giving the false impression that a diverse corpus of inscribed votive objects, varying in age, was produced by a small group of rulers. When finds are not marked on the plans, which is the case with most of the cultic appurtenances, for example, the corresponding descriptions provide only a very rough idea of their positions. In the absence of clear reference points, as would have been provided by a grid, all that remain are stated distances (sometimes accurately measured, and sometimes only estimated) and a vague orientation with respect to features of the site that happened to be visible at the time (the corner of a building for example). Overall, the graphic information on the plans is insufficient, while the photographic record is sparse, and the written descriptions in the reports are often inadequate to compensate for these shortcomings. When making such a judgement, however, it should not be forgotten that Sarzec and Heuzey had no previously established frames of reference to fall back on, but were rather defining a field of study that in almost every important respect was new.

When Cros undertook investigations on Tell K three times between 1903 and 1905, he did manage to solve some outstanding problems, and his work yielded important new data, even though his procedures also caused fresh difficulties. His results, which were eventually published in 1910, again contain curtailed descriptions and imprecise plans that are rather sketchily drawn. Cros paid more attention to mud-brick architecture than his predecessor, and he took a great deal of personal responsibility for the written reports that were produced in his name, but these strengths were offset by his relative lack of archaeological experience. This highlights the positive aspect of Heuzey's contribution to all subsequent attempts to understand Tell K: although he never saw the site with his own eyes, he was an accomplished scholar, motivated by academic, historical and archaeological concerns, and these factors made him sensitive to the need for a systematic approach based on accurate data, even if he was sometimes unable to provide it. Finally, the later explorations of Tell K that were undertaken by Genouillac and Parrot provide scant additional information.

Taken as a whole, Sarzec's excavations on Tell K gave rise to little more than a collection of objects, with only a few morsels of baked-brick and stone structures escaping the destructive fate that befell more fragile remains. Added to the generally unsatisfactory quality of the data as it was recorded and presented by him, these flaws would seem to make any attempt to reinterpret (or often to interpret for the first time) the archaeology of the site almost impossible. Parrot suggested as much in 1948 when he outlined his own extremely modest and mostly unsuccessful explanation of the walls forming the Lower Construction (Parrot 1948, p. 58). After taking charge of the site, Parrot tried to summarise the available data, but his presentation is marred by a multitude of errors, and his proposed update to the minimal analysis offered by Heuzey is finally inconclusive. Thereafter, it is undoubtedly true to say that most of the more recent specialists who have studied Tell K have been deterred by the haphazard character of the information bequeathed by the French excavators. Accordingly, in his 1984 study, Tunca (1984, p. XXI) synthesises what was known about protodynastic religious architecture in Mesopotamia, but expressly rejects the French data because he considers it unusable. The buildings of Tell K are occasionally mentioned by other scholars, notably Heinrich and Seidl (1982, pp. 134–6) and Crawford (1987), but these papers eschew systematic analysis. A thorough study of Tell K was published by Jean-Daniel Forest in 1999, and though some of his interpretations have many times been questioned, his approach provides an important and comprehensive contribution to an understanding of the Mound of the House of the Fruits. Forest's work inspired some briefer pieces, notably those by Huh (2008) and Marchesi and Marchetti (2011).

In order to reassess the situation, and to provide an inclusive historical and archaeological frame of reference for the presentation of the new investigations detailed in this book, the following chapters present an in-depth summary of the French excavation results in chronological order, together with the associated plans, sections and photographic data sets. For Tell K (as also for Tell A), a methodical understanding of the work done by Sarzec and his successors is the necessary precondition for a meticulous reconstruction of the stratigraphy and architecture of the Ningirsu sanctuary and its associated artefacts.

CHAPTER 5

The French Excavations on Tell K: Sarzec and Heuzey in Detail

THIS CHAPTER LAYS OUT THE RESULTS OF SARZEC'S work on Tell K as reported in the two principal publications: Heuzey's *A Chaldean Royal Villa Dating Back to 4000 BCE* (1900) and the collected volume of Sarzec and Heuzey's *Discoveries in Chaldea*, which appeared in 1912, eleven years after Sarzec's death. They detail the discovery of the Early Dynastic IIIb structure, dating from the time of Ur-Nanshe (*c*.2460–2425 BCE), otherwise known as the House of the Fruits or the Ur-Nanshe Building, along with later features there and elsewhere on the site from the times of Eanatum and his successors (*c*.2420–2300 BCE), the Akkad interval (*c*.2300–2180 BCE), the Lagash II period (*c*.2180–2085 BCE) and the Third Dynasty of Ur (*c*.2085–1995 BCE). Beneath the Ur-Nanshe Building was found an older, Early Dynastic I–IIIa structure, known as the Lower Construction (*La Construction inférieure*), which presented some complicated problems of interpretation. After this had been levelled, Sarzec opened a limited sounding that descended a further 8 m (or slightly more) until he reached the water table 17 m below the original summit of the tell. As noted above, this was the measure against which Sarzec heights were plotted. On the way down he recovered a number of fragmentary objects dating back to the fifth and fourth millennia that are unfortunately impossible to contextualise. The French reports, plans and photos are first described systematically, without detailed exegesis, to give a narrative account of the materials that form the basis of the comprehensive reinterpretation of the archaeology of Tell K that follows.

The Ur-Nanshe Building, or the House of the Fruits

When Sarzec returned to Tello in 1888, following his seven-year absence, he decided to make Tell K the focus of his new excavations. The artificial hill, which rose to a height of approximately 14 m above the surrounding flood plain, was the second highest and second most extensive rise on the site, after the Mound of the Palace (Tell A), which lies approximately 200 m north-west of it. At the highest point of Tell K, at a depth of around 2.5 m, or perhaps a little less, in the layer of mud-bricks that formed the summit of the mound, Sarzec unearthed the last traces of the foundations of a fired-brick construction, judged to date from the time of Gudea, which is marked on Plan C (1) (Fig. 33 below) as wall O. A short distance away was found a door socket bearing the name of Gudea, and almost at the same level were two foundation boxes, each containing a copper foundation figurine and a stone tablet dedicated to Ningirsu (Sarzec and Heuzey 1912, p. 407). The boxes are shown on the section on Sarzec's Plan C (2) (Fig. 33), where they are both labelled *Logette*. The deposits in the W box were found to be inscribed in the name of Shulgi, while the other box was installed in Gudea's name. Two large stone discs and the fragments of a third votive disc were found grouped at a depth of 1.4 m, all inscribed and dedicated to Ningirsu in the names of three governors of Lagash: Nammahni, Lugirizal and Ur-Ninsun, who were contemporaries of kings of the Third Dynasty of Ur.

56

Slightly lower down in the mound, at a Sarzec height of about 14.5 m, the shattered corner of a wall was excavated (marked *Mur* on Plan C (2)). It is not otherwise described, except in passing, when Heuzey (1900, p. 3) mentions that it was made of square bricks. Heuzey attributes no architectural structures on Tell K to the Sargonids, but wall *Mur* can now be dated to the Akkad period, and more Sargonic remains were found by Sarzec on the Mound of the Pillars (Tell I, as detailed in Parrot 1948, pp. 133–4), including a fragment of an Akkad stele and another inscribed stone fragment that are both discussed below. A composite pillar was found on Tell I that is referred to, in the singular, as the Pillar of Gudea, though it was actually made up of four columns. That is presumably why Sarzec, rather confusingly, called Tell I the Mound of the Pillars (*Tell des piliers* in French), using the plural.

It is worth noting at this point, albeit in passing, that Sarzec reported no finds between the bottom of wall *Mur*, at a Sarzec height of about 14.5 m, and the sealed construction that he found about 0.55 m below it. As is explained in Chapter 16, however, the time frame represented by this gap in the record, which is referred to for simplicity's sake as the Sarzec gap, included a sequence of highly consequential events, including two reconstructions of the Ur-Nanshe temple and the final razing of the mound by hostile invaders at the end of the Early Dynastic period. Partly because Sarzec simply consolidated all mud-brick remains into the homogeneous mass marked *Brique crue* on the section on Plan C (2), and partly because any walls that were built in the years represented by the Sarzec gap were violently and comprehensively destroyed, no structural deposits whatsoever were recorded in this layer by Sarzec. Nonetheless, since there can be no doubt that inclusions of pottery sherds, residues of organic matter, pieces of stone, fired-brick rubble and other seemingly insignificant scraps must have existed in these occupation strata, the conspicuous lack of any mention of anything apart from amorphous 'mud-brick' in the opening section of the report can probably be further accounted for by Sarzec's expectations and relative inexperience. His four seasons on Tell A, which, it should be stressed, were the first systematic archaeological excavations he had ever undertaken, must presumably have prepared him for the discovery of built structures and broken, but in many instances relatively intact, artefacts that represented the splendid remains of a lost culture. Similar kinds of materials were soon also found a little lower down in the body of Tell K—discoveries that surely confirmed the very particular and personal approach to archaeology that he had formed while working on Tell A. At this stage of his career, therefore, he was in no way sensitised to the numerous tiny morsels of archaeological remains that are of extreme value in the reconstruction of historical sequences—precisely the kinds of materials that the British Museum team found discarded in great quantities on the spoil heaps of Tell A—all of which were unfortunately resolved by Sarzec into consolidated *Brique crue* when he began operations on Tell K in 1888.

Accordingly, the next finds described by Heuzey (1900, p. 5), which were also uncovered in 1888, were a little deeper down in the mound, at a depth of about 3 m from the original summit of the tell (at about 14 m on the Sarzec scale), where Sarzec discovered the remains of a 'carefully levelled' construction that was sealed with a layer of bitumen, 0.05 m thick, that covered a flat bed of planoconvex fired bricks (not shown on the section on Plan C (2)). Bonded with more bitumen, the bricks mostly measured 0.27–0.28 m × 0.14–0.15 m × 0.05 m (t), and their convex faces were marked with a thumbprint (Heuzey 1900, pp. 5 and 11). Seven bricks found in the levelled walls were a little larger, with measurements of 0.29–0.3 m × 0.2 m × 0.05 m, discounting the additional thickness of the convex curvature, which measured 0.02 m (Heuzey 1900, p. 6; the figures are simplified in Sarzec and Heuzey 1912, p. 407, where they are given as 0.29 m × 0.2 m × 0.07 m). These seven anomalous bricks were systematically aligned at the top of the levelling, at the W corner of the building, in line with the facings: four on the SW side, and three turning back towards the north-west. All seven were inscribed in the name of Ur-Nanshe, and Heuzey considers it highly likely that they had been reused, though this is reconsidered below (Heuzey 1900, p. 6; see also Sarzec and Heuzey 1912, p. 408).

Heuzey states that the truncated building was preserved to a height of more than 1.12 m, made up of fourteen courses of brickwork. Taking the convex curvature of the bricks into account, each course would have been 0.08 m thick, including mortar. Rectangular in plan, with the long wall running northwest–south-east, the building measured 10.6 m × 7.3 m (Heuzey 1900, p. 5; though 10.5 m × 7.3 m according to Sarzec and Heuzey 1912, p. 407), and its corners were accurately oriented to the cardinal points. As Heuzey describes them, the exterior walls, which were 0.6 m thick with no openings, enclosed narrower fired-brick walls, with a width of 0.3 m and possibly preserved to a height of three or four courses, that were also built without openings. In Heuzey's view, the narrower walls formed the outer walls of two disconnected rooms that were separated by a void (0.8 m wide) that Heuzey describes as 'corridor'. The larger, SE room (A on Plan C (1)) was practically square, with sides measuring 4.1 m; the NW room (B on Plan C (1)) was shallower, measuring approximately 4 m × 1.9 m, and indented in the middle on the corridor side, as Heuzey interprets it, to form what is said to be a small recess or niche that Heuzey (1900, p. 10) says was 1.2 m (w) × 1 m (deep), though it measures 1.6 m × 0.8 m on Plan C (1).

The internal and external walls of the main building were all apparently plastered with bitumen (which is not visible in Sarzec's photo (Pl. 54 (1); Fig. 39 below), and the entire structure rested on a bed made of three courses of flat bricks (not clearly marked on Plan C (2)), the top of which formed a paved floor, coated with bitumen, that lay slightly more than 4 m below the surface of the tell (Heuzey 1900, p. 8), at a Sarzec height of approximately 13 m. The bottom of the three-course base, which was not sunk into the ground, was found at the same level as the surface of an exterior pavement (Heuzey 1900, p. 7). At the same height as the top of the walls, which Heuzey says had been deliberately levelled, were found two small attached protrusions (marked D and E on Plan C (1)), each made of fired bricks. The SW protrusion (D) measured 0.3 m × 1.4 m (but 0.5 m × 1.6 m on Plan C (1)); the NE one (E) measured 2.2 m × 1.65 m. Heuzey (1900, pp. 8–9) suggests that they were later additions that were constructed when the foot of the building lay buried almost a metre below the surface of the ground.

Various objects were discovered at several locations around the outside of the building, at the same height as its levelled walls, and in some cases slightly above them, as detailed below (Fig. 27). Of these, the most important were considered to be:

The Stone Monument of Eanatum (No. 12 on Plan C (1)), found at the levelling height (Heuzey 1900, p. 22; Heuzey's Fig. 13), at a Sarzec height of 14 m above the bottom of the lowest sounding.

The Mortar of Enanatum I (No. 13 on Plan C (1)), also found at the levelling height (Heuzey 1900, p. 22; Heuzey's Fig. 14), at a Sarzec height of 14 m.

Three fragments of the Stele of the Vultures of Eanatum (Nos. 9–11 on Plan C (1)), found a little above the height of the levelled walls (Heuzey 1900, p. 20; Heuzey's Fig. 12), so slightly above the Sarzec height of 14 m.

Heuzey states that the building was destroyed by a fire, traces of which, he says, were everywhere apparent, but while ashes, molten bitumen and charred bricks had accumulated in the levelled rooms, the spaces that Heuzey describes as corridors were filled with mud-bricks placed edgewise at a slight angle to each other to create a zigzag or herringbone effect. This prompts Heuzey to wonder whether the mud-bricks were a filling or a deliberate arrangement that dated back to Ur-Nanshe's original construction (Heuzey 1900, p. 11). He then connects the remains that are interpreted as signs of a catastrophic fire (1910, p. 11) with finds made by Sarzec outside the building and further afield on the mound that seemed to him to reveal a widespread destruction horizon. In consequence, he assumes that the building and the rest of the tell were levelled at the same time in the course of a single destructive event.

Approximately 1 m below the height of the levelled walls, at a Sarzec height of about 13 m, more objects were uncovered beneath the ash and rubble that filled the inside of the building, including a number of items that were found inside rooms A and B. Among them were:

Two door sockets (Nos. 1 and 2 on Plan C (1)) found in the E (1) and S (2) corners of the large room A, fixed to the bitumen base, 4 m apart (Heuzey 1900, p. 11; but 3 m apart on the plan), which Heuzey (1900, pp. 11 and 13) thinks had been moved from their original locations. No. 1 was a kind of vertical boundary stone in the shape of a truncated cone that was carved from grey limestone and laterally inscribed in the name of Ur-Nanshe. Quite different in form, No. 2 was hemispherical and carved from yellowish stone. An exact replica of No. 2 (labelled No. 3) was discovered at an unspecified height some distance from the building. On their upper circular faces Nos. 2 and 3 both bore Ur-Nanshe inscriptions that radiated out from a central cavity towards their circumferences.

In the narrower room B, under 'the layer of ash' (Heuzey 1900, p. 13), a set of copper blades was found towards

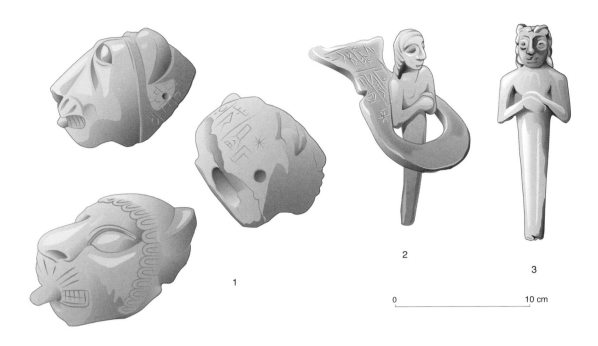
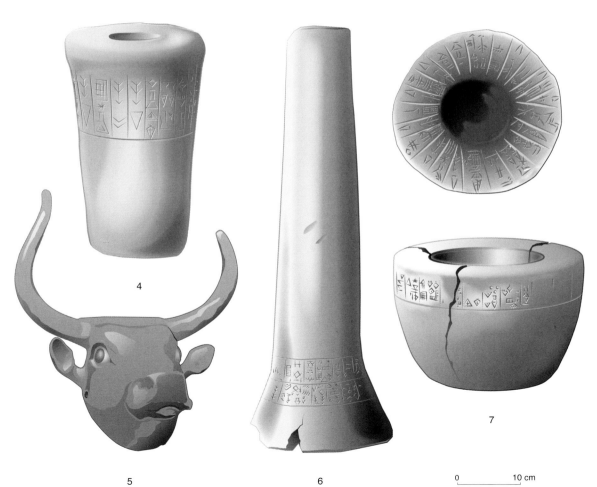

FIGURE 27. Objects associated with the Ur-Nanshe Building: 1. the Stone Heads of Lions; 2. an Ur-Nanshe foundation peg with a copper collar; 3. an Enmetena foundation peg; 4. the Ur-Nanshe door socket in the shape of a vertical boundary stone; 5. a Copper Bull's Head; 6. the Stone Monument of Eanatum; 7. the Mortar of Enanatum I.

the W corner and on the paving; the remains of similar implements were found scattered in the mud-bricks that filled the so-called corridor and in the neighbouring parts of the building, one of which was a blade with an illegible inscription.

Outside the building was a spacious planned area, which Heuzey calls the Ur-Nanshe *sol* (meaning 'ground' or 'level'), which was uncovered at the same Sarzec height of about 13 m, with its base at the same level as the base of the Ur-Nanshe Building. On Plan C (2) this is marked as precisely 12.83 m on the Sarzec scale—a measurement that provides a key reference point on the plan and throughout the discussion. In addition to some minor appurtenances, the extended Ur-Nanshe ground (to use Heuzey's term) exhibited two significant features. First, a NW pavement (F on Plan C (1), uncovered in 1889), which was the same width as the building, extended out from the temple's NW face to a distance of 10 m (9 m on Plan C (1)). Its top surface was found at almost the same level as the building's interior floor, placing it at a Sarzec height of 12.98 m (calculated by adding the Sarzec height of the Ur-Nanshe base (12.83 m) to the thickness of the floor (0.15 m, or three courses of bricks)). Pavement F, which was in poor condition, was made of square bricks in two sizes, with sides of 0.3 m and 0.25 m, respectively, that were laid with the same NW–SE alignment as the building itself.

Also found were the square bases of eight pillars or columns (all labelled H on Plan C (1)), each with sides measuring 0.6 m, that were carefully positioned around the outside of the temple. Each pillar base was made of four square fired bricks with sides of 0.3 m (therefore different from the rectangular bricks used to construct the walls of the Ur-Nanshe Building) that were laid flat on a bed of bitumen. The bases were arranged in four pairs, respectively facing the building's short NW and SE façades and its long NE and SW façades. The centres of the individual bases were aligned with the building's corners (as can be seen on Plan C (1)), and they were placed at a distance of about 4 m (3.7–3.8 m according to Plan C (1)) from the walls. When the H–H lines are diagramatically extended, parallel to the sides of the building, a spacious quadrilateral is created that measures approximately 16 m × 19 m. Fragments of charred wood that were found in the bases showed that they had held square wooden posts with sides of 0.45 m (as Heuzey describes them), one of which, identified as cedar, had been 'spared by the flames'

(Heuzey 1900, p. 14) to a height of 0.17 m. The drawings of the posts on the section on Plan C (2) show them as round, and this is perhaps more likely, in which case the recorded dimension would presumably refer to their diameter. Heuzey supposes that the burnt remains of the wooden pillars, which he interprets as supports for a covered gallery, again showed that the temple had been destroyed by a major fire.

Several other objects were recovered outside the building, some of which were above and some below the Ur-Nanshe base level (12.83 m), though Heuzey is sometimes unclear about the exact heights. Notable among them were:

Three perforated plaques (Nos. 4–6 on Plan C (1)) that are vaguely described by Heuzey (1900, p. 18) as having been found 'a few decimetres above or below' the building's lower level. Showing Ur-Nanshe and his relatives, these were probably not decorative supports for other artefacts, but rather originally displayed on the walls of the building (Heuzey 1900, p. 19). A fourth relief of the same type, portraying the ruler as a builder with a basket of hallowed bricks on his head, was subsequently found elsewhere on the site, though Heuzey (1900, p. 18) does not say where.

A number of lions' heads carved in stone, all between 0.07 m and 0.16 m tall (see Sarzec and Heuzey 1912, p. 227), five of which (No. 7 on Plan C (1)) were found together on same level as the top of the Ur-Nanshe pavement (at a Sarzec height of 13 m), adjacent to pavement F and close to the square base (H) that lay to the north-west of the building's W corner. Heuzey (1900, p. 19) remarks that several appeared to have been made as pairs, and all were hollowed out behind (to create a mortise) and pierced with a hole designed to hold a dowel pin (*cheville d'arrêt*). At least two were inscribed in the name of Ur-Nanshe (see Heuzey 1900, p. 19). Heuzey compares them to the protome of a lion in translucent green alabaster, also with an Ur-Nanshe inscription, that was found in 1898 at an unknown height 10 m north-east of the building, in the cavity of a door socket commissioned by Enmetena (see Sarzec and Heuzey 1912, pp. 350 and 414).

Eight clay tablets (No. 15 on Plan C (1)), dating to the Early Dynastic IIIa period, that were found about 0.1 m under the SW side of the Ur-Nanshe base (12.83 m on the Sarzec scale).

The archaic relief known as the Feathered Figure, which was uncovered approximately 8 m north of the W corner of the Ur-Nanshe Building (Heuzey 1900, p. 24), and above the level of the Ur-Nanshe floor.

A giant copper spear head (No. 16 on Plan C (1)), apparently found 0.15 m above the Ur-Nanshe base level (12.83 m), though this must be mistaken, as is explained below; it was inscribed in the name of Lugalnamnirshumma, a king of Kish.

Two bulls' heads made of copper (0.14 m tall) and a copper vase (No. 18 on Plan C (1)), unearthed 0.25 m above the Ur-Nanshe base level (Heuzey 1900, pp. 37–8).

A large ring post (3.27 m long), discovered on pavement F in front of the building's NW façade (No. 17 on Plan C (1)).

The Lower Construction

Beneath the Ur-Nanshe Building, which was dismantled in the course of the excavations, Sarzec encountered a layer of mud-bricks (recorded as being 0.7 m thick) in which some elaborate foundation deposits were found. They included at least five stone tablets and associated archaic figurines that were made of copper and supplied with hooks and ringed supports. The latter, which are described by Heuzey as 'easels', were used as stands for the tablets (see Sarzec and Heuzey 1912, p. 408; and Heuzey 1900, p. 28). Four of the deposits are noted on the left side of Plan C (1): the first (a), which was found 11 m from the building's SW façade (marked as 13–14 m on the plan); the second (b), found 11 m to the north-west of the W corner, beyond pavement F (marked as 12.5 m on the plan); the third (c), found 14 m from the NW façade, also beyond pavement F (marked as 17.5 m on the plan); and the fourth (d), found 24 m from the E corner of the building (though considerably more distant on the plan). The fifth, which was found 20 m from building's S corner, was too far away to appear on Plan C (1). The three labelled a, b, c and the fifth (not shown on the plan) were found at depths of between 0.3 m and 0.5 m below the Ur-Nanshe base level (at Sarzec heights ranging between 12.53 m and 12.33 m), while figurine d was found deeper down in the mound, 1.7 m below the Ur-Nanshe base level (at a Sarzec height of 11.13 m). The tablets bore a lengthy inscription, while the figurines and their ringed supports were more briefly inscribed (Heuzey 1900, p. 28).

Immediately below the initially recorded layer of mud-bricks, 0.7 m beneath the Ur-Nanshe base level, Sarzec found a 'subfloor' (as it is described by Heuzey), which was made of three courses of fired bricks that were bonded with bitumen and coated on top with bitumen. The brickwork was placed on a course of thick gypsum slabs that were laid on a bitumen base. This intricate subfloor (for which Heuzey's term is provisionally retained), with a total thickness of about 0.55 m, had been installed on top of an earlier temple that lay deeper in the mound, and the entire structure had also been surrounded by a mass of mud-bricks (marked *Briques crues* on the section on Plan C (2)) that merged with the mud-bricks in which the foundation tablets and copper figurines were found (above the subfloor) to form a homogeneous matrix. Sarzec and Heuzey do not usually note differences between mud-brick deposits, but in this case they make a distinction between the initial layer of mud-bricks that were found between the Ur-Nanshe base and the subfloor, and the surrounding mass, all of which they attribute to Ur-Nanshe. It may be that the discovery of the foundation deposits in the intervening mud-brick layer helped to set it apart from the amorphous mass. In any case, the slight differentiation yielded valuable information because some significant finds were made in the enveloping layers of mud-bricks associated with the subfloor, but placed around the outsides of the older buried structure (Fig. 28). They included:

The Mace of Mesilim, king of Kish, with a dedication to Lugalshaengur, that was found 1.15 m below the Ur-Nanshe base level, in the uppermost layers of the mud-brick mass that surrounded the buried walls (Heuzey 1900, pp. 23–4). Marked as No. 14 on Plan C (1), it is shown 11 m from the Ur-Nanshe Building, in line with the middle of the temple's long SW façade (though, as with the other two objects listed immediately below, it was unearthed at a depth of more than 1 m below the bottom of the Ur-Nanshe Building's walls).

A fragment of an onyx bowl that was found 1.25 m below the Ur-Nanshe base level, also in the mass of

62 The Mound of the House of the Fruits

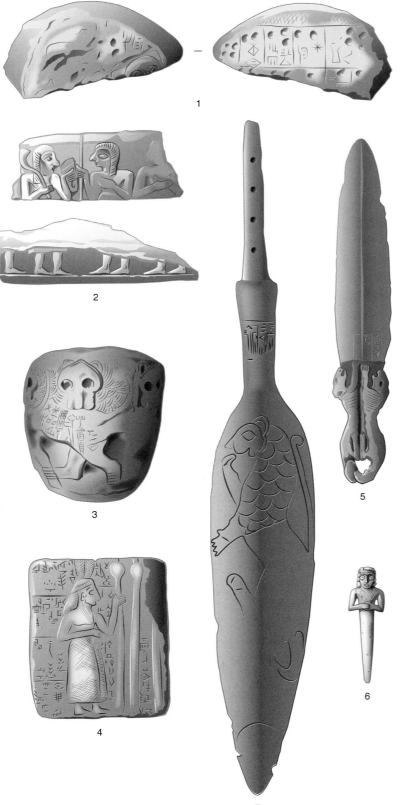

FIGURE 28. Objects associated with the Lower Construction: 1. the Girsu Land Stele; 2. the Circular Bas-Relief; 3. the Mace of Mesilim; 4. the Feathered Figure; 5. the copper dagger inscribed with lion motifs; 6. a foundation peg from the Lower Construction; 7. the Colossal Spear Head.

mud-bricks. Inscribed in the name of Ur-Nanshe, it is marked as No. 8 on Plan C (1), where it is shown 8 m from the E corner of the Ur-Nanshe Building.

A superb inscribed dagger with an ornate handle that was found in the mud-brick mass at a depth of 1.3 m below the Ur-Nanshe base level. Not marked on the plan, it is described in the text as having been discovered 25 m north-east of the Ur-Nanshe Building (see Sarzec and Heuzey 1912, p. 415).

The composite layer of bricks, gypsum and bitumen (Heuzey's subfloor) was precisely placed on top of the walls of the two-room core of the Lower Construction, which was preserved to a height of more than 2.85 m and built of planoconvex bricks measuring 0.22 m × 0.13 m × 0.05 m (t), according to Heuzey (1900, p. 47), but 0.2 m × 0.13 m × 0.05 m according to the later report (Sarzec and Heuzey 1912, p. 411). No information is recorded about the medium with which the bricks were bonded, but they were not signed with thumbprints (as the upper, Ur-Nanshe bricks were), and nothing is said about the radius of curvature or the number of courses, though the section (Plan C (2)) shows thirty courses. If it is assumed that the maximum thickness of the bricks was 0.07 m, as for the Ur-Nanshe bricks, then 30 courses × 0.07 m = 2.1 m, leaving 0.75 m for the mortar, or approximately 0.025 m of mortar per course, which is perhaps conceivable.

Rectangular in plan, and measuring 8.2 m × 6.2 m, the Lower Construction had a similar layout to the Ur-Nanshe Building. It was made up of two unequally sized rooms: one to the NW measuring 4.5 m × 1.4 m, and one to the SE measuring 4.3 m × 4.1 m (3.5 m × 3.3 m in Heuzey 1900, p. 51). Separated from each other by a blank partition wall, each of the rooms had its own doorway (about 1.5 m wide), on their NW and SE sides, respectively. The walls of the Lower Construction, which were nearly 0.8 m thick, are described as resting directly on a paving of large gypsum slabs that each measured 1–1.2 m × 0.5–0.6 m × 0.15–0.2 m (t). The paving extended beyond the building's walls, but was apparently only preserved on the NE side, where it is described by Heuzey as a 'veritable esplanade' that was found to extend 12 m and in places as far as 17 m out from the NE façade (Heuzey 1900, pp. 47–8). The gypsum paving stones were (partly or wholly) differently aligned inside and outside the building, as is illustrated on Plan C (2), where the interior of room T on the SE side can be seen, though no information is recorded about the layout of the pavement in the NE room U. To calculate the height of the pavement more precisely: the initially identified layer of mud-bricks below the Ur-Nanshe base level was 0.7 m thick; the composite layer of fired bricks, gypsum slabs and bitumen on top of the Lower Construction was approximately 0.55 m thick; and the walls of the two-room core of the Lower Construction were 2.85 m high. Subtracting these numbers from 12.83 m (the Sarzec height of the Ur-Nanshe base level) gives a Sarzec height of 8.73 m for the top of the gypsum pavement (12.83 m − 0.7 m − 2.85 m = 8.73 m). Since the base of the Lower Construction was placed by Sarzec at a height of 8.48 m, that suggests that the installed paving was 0.25 m thick, which correlates well with the thickness of the slabs as noted by Heuzey.

In the larger of the two rooms, offset towards its N corner, Sarzec found a cruciform pillar, 1.3 m × 1.05 m × 1.8 m (h), made of four blocks of bricks arranged around a central vertical cavity that was perhaps designed to hold the shaft of a weapon, a statue, a stele or a plaque. Heuzey says that the brick pillar was discovered in the room's E corner, but this may be confusion or just a matter of imprecise nomenclature, as can be seen by comparing Plan C (2), where it is drawn in the room's N corner (labelled 1). Also on the floor of the larger room, 0.6 m inside the doorway and situated along the axis of the opening, was found part of the base of a large limestone stele measuring 2 m × 0.8 m. It depicted a line of figures, of which the bottom halves of six survived: three soldiers and three naked prisoners of war. Heuzey notes that the subject suggests it might have been a victory stele (Sarzec and Heuzey 1912, p. 413). Other movable remains excavated in the room (some on the paving) included a rounded fragment of a small decorated limestone stele (referred to below as the Girsu Land Stele), together with a fragment of a circular bas-relief, other pieces of which had already been recovered outside the building, but always 'in very deep soundings' (Heuzey 1900, p. 53; another fragment of it was unearthed in 1897, again probably outside the building). Also outside the walls, to the north-east of the structure and 4 m from its E corner, the excavators uncovered the opening of a well, or perhaps rather a pit that was walled with mud-bricks to a thickness of 0.8 m (Heuzey 1900, p. 48). Heuzey remarks that it was filled with ashes, which perhaps prompted Parrot (1948, p. 59) to suggest that it might have been a hearth, even though it was excavated to a depth of 4 m.

Part of the paving on the floor of the large room, in front of the cruciform pillar, was laid in an unusual way. A pattern was formed of one slab that had been cut into eight triangular pieces that were placed in the shape of a star, as can be seen on Plan C (2). Buried underneath it was an unspecified number of uninscribed copper foundation figurines, whose bottom halves were shaped into long rounded points. They were arranged in concentric circles in the underlying mass of mud-bricks, and more of the same type of figures were subsequently discovered under the W corner of the building, bundled together 'like bunches of asparagus' (Heuzey 1900, p. 57, quoting Sarzec).

While clearing the top surface of the walls, Sarzec identified fifteen circular holes (0.15 m in diameter) that opened out below into vertical ovoid cavities, shaped like vases, with maximum diameters of 0.3 m and total heights (or depths) of 0.8 m (0.6 m in the later text, but that is probably a mistake; see Sarzec and Heuzey 1912, p. 413). Surrounded by the courses of fired bricks, they were lined with the same bitumen coating as was used on the walls themselves, but the bitumen inside the cavities was marked with deep grooves, prompting Heuzey later to suggest that the vase-like forms had been shaped on frames or templates made of reeds (Sarzec and Heuzey 1912, p. 413). There were fifteen cavities in the walls of the two rooms, fairly regularly spaced at intervals of about 1.5 m: five in each of the long side walls, including in the N and W corners of the NW façade (but not in the building's S and E corners), with four more on each side of the two entranceways, and one in the centre of the partition wall between the two rooms, all of which are marked on Plan C (2). Heuzey's first thought was that the cavities might have been designed to hold wooden poles (possibly coated with bitumen) that were secured with ropes, but he later revised this for structural reasons, suggesting instead that they were accessible hiding or storage places for choice delicacies, especially fermented liquids (Heuzey 1900, pp. 58–61; and Sarzec and Heuzey 1912, p. 413). The idea that they might have been structural supports for a roof or a screen was not entirely abandoned, however, particularly as more of the same kind of openings were found in later surveys of the structure (as many as twenty-two altogether, as detailed in Sarzec and Heuzey 1912, p. 413; see also Cros 1910, p. 76; and Heuzey 1900, pp. 59 and 61), irregularly placed at different levels.

A second phase of construction was identified in which a considerable section of the two-room building was embedded in a larger masonry rectangle, measuring 8.4 m × 11.6 m, that rested on the gypsum pavement and rose to a height of 2.15 m. The entire block, whose corners are labelled P'Q'R'S' on Sarzec's Plan C (2), was curiously not centred around the walls of the old building. Instead, its orientation was adjusted by about three degrees, such that, as is shown on Plan C (2), the surrounding block followed the lines of the gypsum pavement (V). Heuzey (1900, p. 51) suggests that the walls of the two-room Lower Construction (PQRS) had been carefully positioned to create a space by the S corner (marked R) that could accommodate a 'religious obstacle', meaning a sacred artefact or natural object that was considered to be immovable. He speculates, incidentally, that this might have been a sacred boundary, a pathway, an altar, a border stone or a sacred tree. Drawing on his classical background, he quotes the examples of the Erechtheion on the Acropolis, which was positioned to accommodate Athena's sacred olive tree, and the temple of Jupiter on the Capitol, which had to house a boundary stone dedicated to Terminus because the augurs would not allow it to be displaced. The distances between the two-room building and the new outer walls ranged between 2.4 m and 2.7 m on the SE side; 1.6 m and 2.1 m on the NE side; 0.8 m and 1.1 m on the NW side; and on the SW side gradually decreasing from 0.4 m at the S corner down to nothing at all where the two walls met towards the W corner.

The newer structure was made of courses of fired bricks similar to those used in the original building, alternating with courses of gypsum slabs like the ones found on pavement V, except on the SW side, where the gradual narrowing towards the W corner was effected with brick and gypsum fragments; everything was bonded with bitumen. Heuzey (1900, p. 49) suggests that the internal floor of the original building's smaller NW room (U on Plan C (2)) must have been raised to the same level as the external block (which probably also explains why Parrot (1948, p. 55) added a layer of tiles to his section) and he therefore infers that it must have been made of fired bricks. In fact, the outer masonry was extended to fill the interior of the smaller room entirely, and the supposed brick paving was actually the top course of the infill produced by extending the block into the room, as Plan C (2) clearly shows. In consequence, no conclusive information was recorded about the original materials that were used to cover the floor of room U, in particular whether it was tiled with gypsum slabs from pavement V, as room T was, or whether it had a brick floor as Heuzey surmises (without offering any evidence). By contrast with room U, the SE room T, remained accessible, though it was enclosed to the height of the new surrounding block, and probably, in Heuzey's view (1900, p. 51), reduced to little more than a basement or cellar that he thinks could have been entered through an upper opening via a ladder. Its doorway was filled, and the entire SW face inside the room was also lined to a height of 2.15 m (perhaps even a little more on the section on Plan C (2)) with a wall of fired bricks that was 0.4 m thick. New bitumen cavities (similar to the ones mentioned above) were found in the surrounding block: four in the new NW façade, and three in the masonry that filled the adjacent small room, all of which are shown on Plan C (2).

In Heuzey's view, the entire arrangement was executed by Ur-Nanshe, who wished to create a solid foundation for his upper building. Preparatory work for that new temple was also manifest in the levelled top (or subfloor, as he describes it) of the Lower Construction and the thick layer of mud-bricks that had been laid down above that to form a substantial new base that was altogether 1.25 m thick. In addition, as previously discussed, a very considerable mass of mud-bricks had been laid all around the lower walls, consolidating the extended area occupied by the Ur-Nanshe Building and its associated installations.

Heuzey then explains (Sarzec and Heuzey 1912, p. 415) that Sarzec extended his excavations to a depth of more than 1.5 m, without giving more precise details. If this is taken to mean 1.5 m below the Lower Construction, that would suggest that he dug down to a Sarzec height of 6.98 m (8.48 m − 1.5 m, measuring from the level of the base of the Lower Construction's gypsum pavement, as indicated on Plan C (2)). Having levelled the ground completely, he then conducted a sounding in the middle of this area that descended a further 8 m to a depth of a little more than 17 m below the original summit of the tell (as indicated on Plan C (2)), where he reached the water table.

Temple Annexes on Tell K

Around the Ur-Nanshe Building, at a variety of distances and at very different heights, Sarzec unearthed numerous installations, the functions and dates of which were (and in some instances still are) often difficult to determine. The most important ones are detailed below.

The Double Cistern (G)

Close to the Ur-Nanshe Building's S corner, inside the area marked out by the pillar bases (H on Plan C (1)) that Heuzey suggests held wooden posts that were supports for a covered gallery, was found a small double cistern (G), measuring 1.6 m × 1.7 m and divided into two rectangular containers lined with bitumen. It was made of bricks, probably planoconvex, that measured 0.22 m × 0.13 m and were signed with thumbprints. This construction is not illustrated on the section on Plan C (2), but it is recorded in a photo (in the right foreground of Sarzec and Heuzey 1912, Pl. 54 (2); Fig. 40 below) that seems to confirm that its uppermost surface was either a little lower than, or perhaps the same height as, the lowest course of baked bricks in the wall of the Ur-Nanshe Building's adjacent S corner. This is also confirmed by Heuzey (1900, p. 16), who describes cistern G as lying lower than the nearby installations described below. The probable conclusion is that the double cistern G was built at the same level as the top of pavement F, on top of the extended Ur-Nanshe ground.

Two Cistern Blocks (IJ, KL)

About 8 m east of the building's NE wall were found two installations made of planoconvex fired bricks (0.3 m × 0.2 m) that were bonded with bitumen and marked with thumbprints (IJ and KL on Plan C (1)). Each of the installations was formed of a solid block, the upper surface of which was coated with bitumen, and they both included an integrated basin or water container that was also lined with bitumen (Heuzey 1900, p. 16). The tops of the structures were found at a height of about 1 m above the Ur-Nanshe base level, at approximately the same height as the bottom of the fired-brick floor of the upper building (as is confirmed on Plan C (2)). The one nearest to the building (IJ, on the W side of the two) was oriented north-east–south-west (with the flat bituminated top to the north-east), and it measured approximately 4.4 m × 2.2 m × 0.95 m (h), though its height is a little less on the section. The second (KL), oriented northwest–south-east and positioned 2 m east of IJ, measured approximately 3 m × 1.8 m, and its height, although not specified, can be estimated as 0.95 m, the same as IJ. The water container on the larger structure (I on IJ) had square sides of 1.95 m and was 0.95 m deep; the adjoined surface, at the same height as the top sides of the cavity, was 2.35 m long. The long side of the rectangular cavity (K on KL) was about 1.55 m (allowing 0.25 m for the width of the brick surround, the same as for IJ), while its short side, as measured on the plan, was about 0.9 m. Its adjoined flat surface (L) measured approximately 1.8 m × 1.7 m (w).

Channels M and N

The more easterly of the two cistern blocks (KL) was considered to be somehow associated with a drain, gutter or channel (M) that extended out to the north-east (the direction of flow indicated by an arrow on Plan C (1)), but the exact relationship between cistern KL and the channel was not established. At its W end, nearest the building, channel M was 0.25 m wide, from where it rapidly widened to 0.35 m at its E outlet. Although its manner of construction is not clearly described, it seems to have been made up of a bed of bitumen enclosed in four rows of stepped bricks (two rows on each side) towards its W end, followed by two narrow walls for two-thirds of its length towards the E outlet, while the S containing wall was pierced with an opening about halfway along its surviving length. The bricks were probably rectangular, planoconvex and signed with thumbprints (Heuzey 1900, p. 6), and they seem to have been altogether unlike those used on the second water-management installation (N), which is discussed immediately below.

In Heuzey's view, channel M must have stretched for more than 14 m before joining the transverse duct marked as N on Plan C (1), but its length on the plan is only about 5 m, and a further 9 m (to make Heuzey's 14 m) would reach well beyond channel N (on the far right of Plan C (1)). Furthermore, channel N was made in a completely different way, with the conduit resting on a low wall of square bricks (Heuzey 1900, p. 16). Finally, while Heuzey says that the NW–SE stretch of channel N was 13 m long (discounting the hook-shaped section that turned south then west), the NW–SE stretch appears on Plan C (1) to have been 8 m, or slightly more. Nevertheless, the length of the entire structure, including the hook-shaped end, does add up to almost exactly 13 m (8.2 m + 2.3 m + 2.6 m = 13.1 m).

The history and function of channel N, which is said to have been found at the same height as the 'Ur-Nanshe constructions' (Sarzec and Heuzey 1912, p. 423) are all the more difficult to interpret because Heuzey goes on immediately to say that Sarzec 'exaggerated' the channel in the hatched lines (*la ligne brisée*) that he used to depict its hooked form on Plan C (1). To prove this he refers to a photo of it (Sarzec and Heuzey 1912, Pl. 58 bis (2); Fig. 50 below), captioned *Caniveau coudé de Tell K*, that shows a beautifully made waterway shaped into a smooth ninety-degree bend around two sides of a fired-brick mass. The fact that this in no way corresponds with the description in the text or channel N as it is drawn on Plan C (1) makes Heuzey's remark extremely hard to comprehend, though he does insist that the rounded bend of the channel in the photo and the hooked end of channel N on Plan C (1) are one and the same thing.

Finally, a little further towards the east, the excavators discovered another 'narrow base' made of fired bricks that was possibly the bottom of a wall or another conduit. Apparently visible on the surface 'before the first excavations', it took a curving path in order to skirt the base of the tell (Sarzec and Heuzey 1912, p. 423). It was presumably found some distance from the main structures on the tell, including channels M and N, and probably situated at a lower topographical level than the other installations described.

The Well of Eanatum

Expanding the scope of his excavations to the edges of the tell, Sarzec found a well made of baked bricks, more or less at surface level (as it is described), about 25 m west of the Ur-Nanshe Building. The first traces of the structure came in the form of a few scattered planoconvex bricks that were marked on top with both a thumbprint and the print of an index finger, and some of them bore a long inscription in the name of Eanatum. Also found were some inscribed sacred stones or pebbles from a river (*galets sacrés*), together with decorative items, notably 'some reliefs'. In addition, there were fragments of shell inlays—some engraved, some cut and unfinished—and a number of them were trapezoidal and convex (Heuzey 1900, pp. 70–1).

The well itself was built as a double column of planoconvex bricks that were laid in an alternating pattern of courses of bricks laid flat to form horizontal beds, as well as courses laid sideways, on their narrow edges. All bonded with clay, the bricks measured 0.32–0.29 m × 0.21–0.2 m × 0.05–0.04 m (or 0.3 m × 0.2 m × 0.05 m 'on average' according to Sarzec and Heuzey 1912, p. 417), and some of them were also inscribed with brief texts dedicating the well to Ningirsu. The well's orifice, which is described as standing about 0.5 m above the Ur-Nanshe base level, was protected by a corbelled dome, 0.6 m high (0.3 m on the sketch in Heuzey 1900, p. 73, though 0.9 m when the coping is added). The dome rested on a circular coping that was 0.6 m (h) × 0.75 m (w), and its internal and external diameters were 2.8 m and 4.25 m, respectively. By contrast, the internal diameter of the well shaft itself was only 1.6 m, while its external diameter was 2.8 m (the two-brick thickness of the walls was 0.6 m).

A bitumen conduit supported on walls made of square bricks extended out from the E side of the well at an unstated height before bending ninety degrees to the north-west, where it joined a small circular cistern (1.7 m in diameter), similarly constructed of bitumen and bricks, that was placed on or adjacent to a brick pavement. From there the channel continued out to the edge of the upper part of the tell in the north-west, meeting a walled channel with a height of 0.9 m that is described by Heuzey (1900, p. 75) as a type of aqueduct that ran from the north-east to the south-west (the direction of flow is indicated by the arrow on Sarzec's Plan D). Heuzey (1900, p. 75) suggests that this NE–SW channel on the edge of the tell might have been a later addition to the nearby principal installations built by Eanatum. The well was first excavated to a depth of about 4 m without yielding anything of interest. When the excavators pressed on with the work (presumably meaning they dug deeper) they found a stray fragment of a limestone relief from the time of Gudea and a small rectangular piece of gold leaf, with holes in its corners, that might once have covered a cylindrical object, perhaps a mace handle. The surface of the gold leaf was smooth, apart from some scored lines that could have been the dividers that separated parts of a lost inscription, and Heuzey notes its exceptional interest as one of the very few items made of gold found on the site (Sarzec and Heuzey 1912, pp. 418–19).

The Enmetena Block

To the south-east of the well, at a distance of 2.7 m and close to the surface, Sarzec uncovered a very large rectangular fired-brick block (*massif* in French) that measured 18.7 m × 6.9 m (Heuzey 1900, p. 77). The length is elsewhere noted as 17.7 m (Sarzec and Heuzey 1912, p. 419), reducing to just 12 m on Plan D. The block's NE side (facing the tell) was preserved to a height of about twenty courses (1.7 m), but only a few courses remained of its outer, SW side. Situated on the outskirts of Tell K's principal construction area, it is described as leaning inwards towards the slope of the mound, and perhaps even embedded in its sloping side. Heuzey says that the block was found at a very low altitude, about the same as the base of the floor of the Lower Construction, at a Sarzec height of 8.5 m, or almost exactly halfway between the bottom of the deepest sounding and the original summit of the tell, but the information he gives is incorrect. As is discussed below, and as the photos confirm, the block was found at a much higher level than Heuzey suggests, perhaps because he did not correctly interpret Sarzec's notes or because he was simply mistaken. Cros later followed Heuzey in assuming that the block was placed lower than it in fact was. The bricks used to build the block, which were flat and not marked with thumbprints or fingerprints, measured 0.33 m × 0.24 m × 0.06 m, meaning that the height of approximately twenty courses amounted to 20 × 0.06 m = 1.2 m, leaving a total thickness of 0.5 m for the mortar, or 0.025 m of mortar per course. Some of the bricks, particularly those laid at the corners, bore a brief inscription in the name of Enmetena (the nephew of Eanatum).

Among the finds made in the vicinity of the Enmetena Block was a perforated plaque in the name of Dudu, the high priest (sanga) of Ningirsu under Enmetena, which was discovered near the block's S corner (Heuzey 1900, p. 79). A little further to the east, not far below the surface of the ground, in a trench that Heuzey describes as descending from the House of the Fruits (the Ur-Nanshe Building) towards the Enmetena block, which at that time (1888) had 'not yet been cleared', the excavators found the famous silver Vase of Enmetena, dedicated to Ningirsu (see Sarzec and Heuzey 1912, pp. 419–20). Heuzey (1900, p. 81) also records information given to Sarzec by his local workers about some finds made in the same area, south of the Enmetena block, during Sarzec's long absence from Tello (1881–8). Among them were a stone tablet inscribed by Urukagina and an associated diorite statue of a ruler that were both sold in Baghdad but subsequently turned up in a private collection in Paris from where they were eventually transferred to the Louvre.

The Enmetena Esplanade

Sarzec and Heuzey's further descriptions of the N area of Tell K, which are laid out piecemeal in the two texts, are increasingly confusing. Starting closest to the well,

Heuzey notes a stone door socket that was found 4.7 m away (described as 4 m north-east of the well in Sarzec and Heuzey 1912, p. 420), which was apparently stuck to a piece of paving made of square fired bricks and might therefore still have been in its original setting. A second similar socket was found further away in the same direction (recorded as 19 m north-east of the well in Sarzec and Heuzey 1912, p. 420) in the vicinity of a gate. They bore the same inscriptions and are compared by Heuzey with another socket in the name of Enmetena that was uncovered at an undetermined depth on the upper level of the mound, 10.3 m north-east of the Ur-Nanshe Building (Sarzec and Heuzey 1912, p. 414).

The gate, which was probably 17 m from the well (Heuzey (1900, p. 82) gives the distance without mentioning the point of origin) was made of two unequally sized masonry piers—the remains of the gateposts—that were built of square bricks of unspecified dimensions that were bonded with bitumen. Preserved 'to the height of a man' (Heuzey 1900, p. 82; cf. the photos, Pl. 55 (1 and 2), in Sarzec and Heuzey 1912, Figs. 41 and 42 below), they framed a threshold of eight courses that was 1.7 m wide. The gate led north-eastwards, opening out into another *enceinte* or enclosure, which Heuzey (1900, p. 82) describes as a terrace or esplanade that ran between the centre of the tell and the 'wall of the plain'. He assumes that this 'new area', as he calls it, was walled off with mud-bricks and delimited by the placement of the large copper foundation figures that are mentioned below.

The remains of a pavement or esplanade made of square fired bricks are mentioned repeatedly but briefly and unsystematically by Heuzey in connection with all of these finds. Initial traces of it were apparently found close to the first door socket (4.7 m from the well), suggesting that it probably covered the ground in the area of the well. It is also mentioned in connection with the small circular cistern that was found to the north-west of the well, either adjacent to the pavement or possibly even built on it (Sarzec and Heuzey 1912, pp. 412 and 418). The pavement also extended out to the north-east, beyond the gate with its eight-course threshold, and beyond the NE–SW walled channel (0.9 m high, as described earlier), as far as the 'wall of the plain', which perhaps means the NE edge of the tell (cf. Plan D), though this is not clearly stated.

The 'new area' to the north-east of the gate was delimited by two pairs (described as 'a double series') of large copper figurines that were accompanied by stone tablets. They were found buried under the pavement at a depth of 0.8 m, together with a fifth deposit that was found on its own at the same depth. All five were found *in situ* (Heuzey 1900, p. 86): two to the north-west of the NW gatepost, one by the gate and the other near the Oval Reservoir (described below); while three were found to the south-east of the SE gatepost, two of them in the large, empty space associated with three 'small cisterns' (*bassins*, also described below), with the third 'in the same row' being placed some considerable distance away, below the pavement that led to the 'door itself' (*la porte même*) of the new enclosure, as Heuzey (1900, pp. 86–7) vaguely puts it.

The Oval Reservoir

The middle of the Enmetena Esplanade that was more or less defined by the copper and stone foundation deposits was occupied by a very large oval pool or reservoir that measured 5.1 m × 4.6 m, though it was irregularly shaped, with a short curve sharply resolving into a straight line on the side towards the edge of the tell, and a pronounced belly on the other side (as can be seen on Plan D). The bottom of the Oval Reservoir sloped down towards its NE end, where its two sides approached each other and formed what is described as a short 'canal' or weir (0.8 m long, according to the lengthy note from Sarzec that Heuzey (1900, p. 83) quotes verbatim) that issued into a transverse waterway, creating a T-shaped junction that extended in two directions: towards the centre of the tell and out towards the plain (Heuzey 1900, pp. 82–3). Near the Oval Reservoir, towards the south-east (the centre of the tell), were three smaller cisterns or containers built of fired bricks (measuring 0.3 m × 0.25 m), each of which included two or three bitumen-lined compartments. As mentioned above, two of the new enclosure's foundation deposits were found in the spaces between these smaller containers.

The bottom or base (*fond*) of the Oval Reservoir was built of large square bricks (0.44 m × 0.44 m × 0.1 m), which Sarzec says (in the note quoted by Heuzey) were beautifully made and carefully grouted with bitumen. Those on the periphery had been cut to match the installation's curves (Heuzey 1900, p. 83), and the structure was edged with a low coping made of three courses of 'oblong' bricks that measured 0.32 m × 0.25 m × 0.05 m. The Oval Reservoir's internal curving surface (*fond*) was found at a level 1.7 m higher than the base level of the Ur-Nanshe Building (Heuzey 1900, p. 82), indicating a Sarzec height of 14.53 m. Taking into account its SW–NE slope, however, the installation itself was between 1.5 m and 1.9 m tall (as described below), which gives a Sarzec height of between 14.33 m and 14.73 m, meaning that the topmost level lay approximately 2.3 m below the summit of the tell, which is the figure given by Heuzey. It is also mentioned that the Oval Reservoir was found standing on a pavement that must have been situated underneath the entire structure, including the coping and the internal brickwork bed, presumably also at a Sarzec height of around 14.33 m. Taking the bottom of the Oval Reservoir to be some 1.7 m above the base of the Ur-Nanshe Building, and therefore 2.3 m below the top of the tell, Heuzey (1900, p. 86) wonders whether it might be attributed to Gudea or to Shulgi. Elsewhere, however, he says that it was 1.5 m higher than the opening of the Well of Eanatum and the floor of the Ur-Nanshe Building, which would also indicate a Sarzec height of 14.33 m (12.83 m + 1.5 m), and this is doubtless the correct figure. The potential confusion is indicative of the difficulties caused by taking multiple points of reference for height measurements. From the point of view of later researchers, the most helpful reference value for heights on the upper part of the tell is the Ur-Nanshe base level because unlike brickwork structures that might have had courses removed from them, for example, the Ur-Nanshe base was treated as fixed.

The Oval Reservoir, Sarzec reports in the note quoted by Heuzey (1900, p. 83), was mostly demolished in 1895 'by the Arabs', and when he cleared the last remnants of it in 1899, he found underneath it a layer of earth mixed with ash, fragments of bitumen and potsherds, which was 0.7 m thick to the south-west, reducing to 0.3 m in the north-east (possibly because of the sloping nature of the construction). Below that was a further course of fired bricks (measuring 0.31 m × 0.27 m × 0.07 m) that were laid flat and found to be marked across their entire length with a deep groove made with a finger. This intermediate platform rested on some elaborately laid courses of mud-bricks (0.21 m × 0.14 m × 0.05 m or 0.06 m) that are described as being extremely homogeneous (*d'une très grande consistence*). In the note quoted by Heuzey, Sarzec begins by saying there were 'four' courses, but he then goes on to describe six. The top two courses were laid upright on their long sides at a slight W–E angle, with each course supported by a band (*cordon*) of the same bricks laid flat. The two lower courses were again placed vertically on their long sides in a herringbone pattern, but without intervening flat courses. Underneath the courses of mud-bricks was a final layer of fired bricks (0.31 m × 0.23 m × 0.07 m), and beneath that was found a single brick (0.32 m × 0.22 m × 0.06 m) that was deeply inscribed with a two-barred cross ('similar to the Lorraine cross', as Heuzey says), except that the bars were placed at upward-pointing angles on both sides of the stem. Sarzec adds that the entire multi-layered block was the same approximately ovoid shape as the Oval Reservoir, and it was plastered with clay to a thickness of 0.3 m. He then goes on to state that 'the construction' ranged in height between 1.9 m on its SW side to 1.5 m on the NE side, which refers the overall height of the entire sequence of layers that Sarzec interprets as a single entity composed of the topmost installation together with all the associated underlying supports.

When the area around the Oval Reservoir was cleared, Sarzec discovered parts of an extended pavement of fired bricks measuring 0.32 m × 0.22 m × 0.05 m that were carefully made, being flat on both sides and uninscribed, but bearing a lengthways stripe made with a finger on their upper faces, which were also fringed or hemmed with a groove or recess that is described as 'regular' (Heuzey 1900, p. 84). This tiling, remnants of which were found around the installation up to 'a certain distance', was laid at the level of the lowest course of bricks that formed the threshold of the gate (described above) that was situated to the south-west of the Oval Reservoir.

North and East of the Oval Reservoir

To the north-east of the Ur-Nanshe Building, at a distance of 22 m from the temple's N corner, Sarzec noted a 'curious' small rectangular block made of several courses of unbonded Ur-Nanshe bricks that were carefully stacked: two courses of bricks laid flat, followed by two courses standing on their narrow edges, and finally two more courses laid flat, with their concave faces uppermost, to form the top of the block (see the photo in Sarzec and Heuzey 1912, Pl. 57 bis (2); Fig. 47 below). Measuring 1.65 m × 1.05 m × 0.5 m (h), the block's upper surface lay just 0.25 m below the level of the Ur-Nanshe base (at a Sarzec height of 12.58 m). Describing it as a depot or brick stack, Heuzey (Sarzec and Heuzey 1912, p. 410) suggests that the cavity in which the bricks were found had been specially dug as a storage area.

Towards its NE corner the original surface of Tell K fell away noticeably. Abutting onto its NE slope was a small rise, referred to as the Mound of the Sword (*Tell de l'épée*) or Tell J (Heuzey 1900, p. 90), where, 'flush with the ground' (Sarzec and Heuzey 1912, pp. 67–8), Sarzec found another reservoir (described as a *piscine*) that measured 6.5 m × 3 m and was coated on the inside with bitumen. This very large container is said to have been situated 1.2 m below the Ur-Nanshe base level at a Sarzec height of 11.63 m (12.83 m – 1.2 m) and 3 m below the Oval Reservoir, at a Sarzec height of 11.53 m (14.53 m – 3 m), which means that the two figures are broadly consistent (see Sarzec and Heuzey 1912, pp. 67 and 422). In the area of the Tell J reservoir, specifically in the valley that lay between Tell J and two other small mounds, Tells I and I', which were connected at the base and known jointly as the Mound of the Pillars (the *Tell des piliers*), a number of interesting objects were discovered. In particular, very close to the Tell J reservoir, were found two fragments of the Stele of the Vultures (Sarzec and Heuzey 1912, pp. 114–15, 406; and Heuzey 1900, p. 21) and at least one door socket in the name of Enanatum II. In total, four examples of the socket were discovered, and although it is not clear where exactly they were found, they are all described as having been unearthed in the same locality (Sarzec and Heuzey 1912, p. 68).

The Stairways of Tell K

When Sarzec extended the trenches on Tell K beyond its outskirts on its SE and E sides, he discovered an array of lower terraces and two flights of steps that led up towards the main surface of the mound. The Small Stairway, which was found on the SE side of Tell K and described as 'narrow', was 1.4 m wide and composed of eighteen steps, each constructed of two courses of square Gudea bricks. It was approached via a paved walkway that ran between two foundation boxes, all inscribed in the name of Gudea. Its preserved height is difficult to establish, since no indication is given of the relative heights of the lower terraces and the Ur-Nanshe base level on the upper part of the tell, but the top of the Small Stairway might conceivably have been about 11 m below the original summit of the tell (giving a Sarzec height of about 6 m for the recorded flight of steps). If it is assumed that the indicative height of the preserved stairs was around 2.7 m (18 steps × 0.15 m per two-brick step would make 2.7 m, if the bricks were the standard Gudea thickness, though that is not mentioned in the text), that would presumably place the bottom of the steps at an elevation of about 14 m below the tell's original summit (at a Sarzec height of around 3 m), which would mean that the bottommost step was plausibly laid at the level of the surrounding plain. It should be stressed that it is not clear how much of the original stairway was preserved (as can also be seen in Sarzec's photo (Pl. 58 (2)); Fig. 49 below).

The Large Stairway, which was excavated about 35 m north-east of the upper level of Tell K, was judged to date back to the Early Dynastic period, but later refitted in the reign of Gudea. It ascended in a south-westerly direction towards the middle of the NE side of the tell, and was also composed of about eighteen steps, of which sixteen were well preserved. It was built of rectangular bricks for which no measurements are given, but many of them were marked with a single stroke of a finger and are described as being comparable to the bricks found around the Oval Reservoir, near the votive tablets inscribed in the name of Enmetena (Sarzec and Heuzey 1912, pp. 424–5), by which are presumably meant the foundation deposits that delimited the Enmetena Esplanade. The steps were made of single courses of bricks, creating a very gentle ascent that led to a landing or platform that was supported by a substructure of two matching blocks, placed side by side, that are described as being 'of the same construction', which presumably means they were made of the same bricks. Of great interest is the fact that the two underlying blocks were apparently each fitted with bitumen-lined vase-shaped cavities, similar to those found on the walls associated with the Lower Construction, though the ones on the stairway had wider bellies (*panses*). Two Gudea-inscribed foundation boxes that were placed on top of the landing confirmed the subsequent refitting (Sarzec and Heuzey 1912, p. 424). The top of the Large Stairway was at about the same level as the base of the floor of the Lower Construction (at a Sarzec height of 8.48 m). Finally, a little further to the west, at a distance of 15 m, lying between the Large Stairway and Tell K, the excavators uncovered traces of a rectangular room, together with some scattered bricks that measured 0.34 m × 0.25 m. These, along with other bricks found in the vicinity, were inscribed in the name of Enanatum I.

CHAPTER 6

After Sarzec: Cros in Detail

Cros's Excavations Reconsidered

When Cros began work on Tell K in 1903, the only feature still visible on the mound's significantly lowered and reshaped summit was the uppermost section of the deep Well of Eanatum, which was preserved above the surface of the ground to a height of 1.5 m. He therefore started by reopening some of his predecessor's trenches in and around the tell, following this up in 1904 and 1905 by digging deeper and also by excavating new trenches in areas that Sarzec had left largely untouched. The topography of Tell K had changed considerably by this time. The huge spoil heaps left by Sarzec were dotted around, while the deepest sounding under the Ur-Nanshe Building had been backfilled, and a massive spoil heap, 9 m high, stood in the centre of the mound. Despite these disfigurements, there were other areas of the site where Sarzec's trenches and pits were at relatively high altitudes, and some of Cros's trenches revealed previously undiscovered archaeological remains from the times of Ur-Nanshe and his successors. In addition, particularly on the tell's N side, some sectors had not been touched by Sarzec, and this was also true on both the W side and towards the south, where Sarzec had prepared the ground by carving a network of fairly shallow trenches between which lay a series of untouched rectangular blocks of earth.

Sarzec had made very deep openings around the Ur-Nanshe Building (which Cros consistently refers to by its familiar name, the House of the Fruits), in a zone measuring 31 m × 40 m. This was where he excavated his deepest sounding, descending to groundwater level at a depth of 17 m below the original height of the tell. More generally, however, Sarzec did not dig much deeper than the Lower Construction, the base of which lay at a Sarzec height of 8.48 m (marked on the section on Plan C (2); Fig. 33 below). Sarzec had more or less levelled the upper part of the tell to this height, or perhaps on average even a little lower, creating a surface or trenching horizon that Cros refers to as the Sarzec Esplanade (see Cros's SW and NE Sections; Fig. 37 below). Sloping slightly down from the south-west to the north-east, the esplanade measured 120 m × 60 m, with its long side on the tell's principal SW–NE axis. The height differential along that axis was very approximately 1 m, with the ground level falling away to the north-east.

In general terms, the Sarzec Esplanade was the starting point for Cros's excavations, and in his text he very often defines depths with respect to this reference level. It is important to understand precisely what this means, however, because previous scholars have generally supposed that Sarzec removed the summit of Tell K comprehensively down to the base of the Lower Construction, taking more than 8 m off the top of the entire mound to establish a kind of plateau at a Sarzec height of between approximately 8 m and 8.5 m above the deepest sounding. On the contrary, as Cros mentions from time to time in his book, there were many places where the Sarzec Esplanade was significantly higher or lower than this average value, either because Sarzec's work was inevitably inconsistent or because of the natural slope of the tell. Furthermore, there were other places around the tell where Cros started digging at levels noticeably above or below the height of the esplanade because Sarzec had not excavated systematically in these areas. It is unfortunate that Cros's published information on these points is ad hoc and patchy, and that he did not establish a system of explaining fully and in detail the situation as he found it for each and every square metre of the new excavations he undertook. He also occasionally says that 5 m or 6 m should be added to the depths he gives for excavated objects and structures, because this represented the amount that had been removed from the top of the tell by his predecessor before he arrived (Cros 1910, p. 73). This was true in some places, but not in others. In particular, as noted many times previously, the base of the Lower Construction (at a Sarzec height of 8.48 m) was approximately 8.5 m below the original summit of the tell (which lay at 17 m on the Sarzec scale).

For these reasons, Cros's descriptions have too often been neglected in studies of the Early Dynastic architecture found on Tell K. It has usually been thought that the starting level of his excavations was below the Lower Construction, defined as the extensive trenching horizon left behind by Sarzec, and that the horizon was more or less flat across its entire extent. Had this in fact been the case then Cros's finds would all date to earlier epochs, before the Lower Construction was built— the Jemdet Nasr, Uruk and Ubaid periods, for example—but as is clarified below, this was not at all the situation that Cros had to deal with. In consequence, many of his discoveries actually date from the time of Ur-Nanshe and his successors, but this fact only becomes apparent when Cros's figures for the depths at which objects and structures were found are subjected to minute scrutiny.

These arguments are considered in detail below, but one example serves to illustrate their significance. In Trenches 9 and 10, on the S side of Tell K (marked on Cros's Plan B; Fig. 36 below), Cros dug down to a depth of more than 9 m. If the height of the Sarzec Esplanade were taken to be his starting point, that would place the bottom of his trenches at a depth of between 0.5 m and 1 m below the level of Sarzec's deepest sounding, which would mean he dug down below groundwater level (the figure is calculated by subtracting 9 m from the base height of 8 m or 8.5 m for the esplanade). But even on Cros's SW Section, which is relatively approximate in the way it is drawn, the bottom of the South Trenches (as they are labelled on Cros's Plan B) lies at a Sarzec height of 4 m. When this figure is considered in conjunction with the depth of the trenches, then a total Sarzec height of 4 m + 9 m = 13 m can be calculated for the uppermost surface level of Trenches 9 and 10, which is very slightly higher than the level of the base of the Ur-Nanshe Building (at a Sarzec height of 12.83 m). This also corresponds approximately with the indication Cros gives elsewhere in his text about the depths of these excavations, namely that he dug about 5 m below the Lower Construction, which would give a maximum Sarzec height of about 8.48 m − 5 m = 3.48 m for the bottom of Trenches 9 and 10.

This understanding does not by any means solve every problem of depths or dating on Tell K because Cros is often vague and surprisingly unsystematic, and there are several places where the levels at which he started digging are not at all clear. Despite that, when Cros's descriptions, plans and sections are carefully compared with the records left by Sarzec, and especially when the depths of his trenches are calculated on the Sarzec scale, much new information is revealed. With those caveats stated, the account of his work that follows is taken from his *New Excavations at Tello*, published in 1910.

The Trench by the Well (1903)

Cros (1910, p. 16) states that the Trench by the Well, which measured 10 m × 13 m (overall), was dug down to a depth of 2.5 m below the Sarzec Esplanade. His Plan B shows an irregular excavation on the E side of the Well of Eanatum, with its main body running east–west, connected via a narrow arm in its SW corner with the well itself, which the trench partly encircles. The depth of 2.5 m below the esplanade given by Cros seems at first glance to suggest that he dug down to a Sarzec height of approximately 8 m − 2.5 m = 5.5 m, but this is incorrect for a number of possible reasons. First (as previously noted), Cros himself occasionally says that the depths measured in the vicinity of the well should be adjusted upwards by 5 m or even 6 m to take account of the fact that the Sarzec Esplanade was that much higher on this side of the tell. This would imply that the Trench by the Well might have descended to a depth of either 7.5 m or 8.5 m (instead of 2.5 m) below the surface of the ground, suggesting maximum Sarzec heights of 9.5 m or 8.5 m, respectively. A further complication is that Cros (1910, p. 72) also mentions that when he arrived on Tell K, the Well of Eanatum, from which (he says) hardly even the topmost courses of brickwork had been removed, rose 1.5 m above the Sarzec Esplanade, and was a prominent landmark on the site that provided an invaluable fixed point when it came to assessing the altitudes of other structures. If this was taken as the starting point for the depth given for the Trench by the Well, it is possible that the excavation was begun at a Sarzec height of 8 m + 1.5 m = 9.5 m, level with the top of the well, and that would mean that the trench descended to a maximum Sarzec height of 7 m.

Cros found that the cut that the Sumerian builders had dug to accommodate the well had been filled with sand around the brickwork, but this perhaps applied only to the top layers that he excavated. A photo taken in 1934 by Genouillac (Pl. 46 (1); Fig. 58 below) confirms the account given by Parrot (1948, pp. 65 and 122), who uncovered a lower backfill of potsherds, together with some exceptional 'incised supports' (discussed below). The platform itself, including the surrounding area, was made up of a mass of mud-bricks, but unfortunately Cros does not give their dimensions.

West of the House of the Fruits: Trench 8 (1905)

In the space between the Ur-Nanshe Building and the Enmetena Block, 19 m south-east of the well and 4 m west (or south-west) of the building, Cros dug Trench 8, which measured 8.5 m × 10.5 m (Cros 1900, p. 75). No depth is given, but the list of finds made in the trench provides some further information. At a depth of 0.3 m Cros uncovered a layer of small-format planoconvex mud-bricks that were covered with a horizon of overburden composed of black soil that Cros identifies as rubble from previous excavations. Beneath that was a platform, 0.7 m thick, of planoconvex mud-bricks that were laid on a bed of sand, and it is worth noting that this compares with the layer of mud-bricks, also 0.7 m thick, that was found beneath the Ur-Nanshe Building (discussed above).

At a depth of 1.7 m was found a section of a low, open waterway (probably originally covered and buried in the mud-brick platform) that was made of fired planoconvex bricks marked with a thumbprint, which Cros identifies as being of the Ur-Nanshe type. It was built with three flat bricks across its width, on top of which were two laid on their edges, all bonded with bitumen. According to Cros, this channel probably flowed from the Well of Eanatum, running first from the north-west to the south-east and then turning south-west, from where it descended steeply upon reaching one of the former slopes of the tell (Cros 1910, p. 75).

Cros's Plan K (an overview of the entire site that is not reproduced here) indicates that a wide Presargonic wall was also found in Trench 8. It was situated about 5 m west (or south-west) of the Ur-Nanshe Building, running parallel to the building on one side and to the Enmetena Block on the other. This wall probably joined another one that was found in Trenches 9 and 10 to form a corner, but there is little or no further information about either of them. It is nevertheless likely that both of these structures were parts of the mud-brick mass that formed the principal terrace at this level.

The depths given for the finds made in Trench 8 suggest that it was about 1.7 m deep. The problem is that no figure is given for its height with respect to the surface of the tell, and specifically whether the excavations were begun at 8 m, the reference height of the Sarzec Esplanade, or possibly higher. The Ur-Nanshe bricks signed with thumbprints that were used on the channel found at the bottom of the trench might imply that the channel was built around the time when the 0.7 m layer of mud-bricks was deposited between the Ur-Nanshe Building and the Lower Construction, though the bricks used to build that foundation layer were not marked with thumbprints. Nevertheless, this could mean that the channel was placed at a Sarzec height of around 12.83 m, which would begin to make sense if the Sarzec Esplanade was again 5 m or 6 m higher at this point than the reference value of 8 m. If that were the case, it would mean that the area had been left undisturbed by Sarzec, and that there might have been layers above the base level of the Ur-Nanshe Building that Sarzec either did not find or did not report.

The South Trenches: Trenches 9 and 10 (1905)

Trenches 9 and 10, with a combined area of 34 m × 13 m, were dug 31 m south-east of the Well of Eanatum and 6 m from the SE corner of the Ur-Nanshe Building, with the long side of the trenches running parallel to the building's SE façade. Along the SE flank of the rectangular pit formed by the two trenches was found a compact platform of mud-bricks that was exposed laterally to a thickness of 3 m, though this was not the platform's full extent as shown by the fact that the excavations did not reach its external face. Cros (1910, p. 75) has no doubt that this was a retaining wall or block that was built to stabilise the side of the artificial rise that supported the upper terrace. He says explicitly that the retaining block was as high as the depth of the trenches, and seems to imply that their long wall abutted onto it for its entire length, meaning that the exposed part of the block was 34 m long, more than 3 m thick (between its inner and outer faces) and at least as high as the depth of the trenches, which is later given as 6 m.

When the ground was excavated immediately below the level of the Sarzec Esplanade, a layer of debris was exposed that was made up of mud-bricks, black earth, rubble and some fired planoconvex bricks marked with thumbprints that were judged to be of the Ur-Nanshe type. Digging down a further 0.3 m in the area of the trenches that was closest to the Ur-Nanshe Building (approximately 6 m to the south-east), Cros found a burnt floor that had been reddened with heat, and it is noteworthy that the deposits found in Trenches 9 and 10 were extremely similar to those found in Trench 8. Cros noted that the depth of the trenches at this point, including the layer of debris and the fire-damaged floor, was 6.3 m lower than the original summit of the tell. The best way to judge what that means relative to the Sarzec scale is to look at Cros's SW Section (Fig. 37 below), where Trenches 9 and 10 are called the South Trenches (*Tranchées Sud*). The Sarzec height of the part of the tell's original summit that lies above them, as marked on the section, is between 15 m and 16 m, while the Sarzec height of the esplanade on either side of the trenches is 9 m. This is in accord with Cros's comment (1910, p. 76) that in this area 6 m should be added to the depths he gives in order to calculate their position with respect to the former top of the tell (9 m + 6 m = 15 m, which correlates with the Sarzec height of the original top of the tell above Trenches 9 and 10). This suggests that the depth given for the burnt floor should be interpreted as meaning 0.3 m below the local height of the Sarzec Esplanade (9 m, as previously indicated), which would place the floor at a Sarzec height of 8.7 m.

A number of objects were uncovered in the double trench, the most important of which were the remnants of more bituminated capsules. At a Sarzec height of 8.1 m, and at a distance of 12 m from the Ur-Nanshe Building, the openings of two broken vase-shaped bituminated cavities were discovered that were similar to the ones that Sarzec found elsewhere on the site, in particular in the walls of the Lower Construction and its surrounding masonry block. The Sarzec height of 8.1 m would place these bitumen vases (to use Cros's term) just below the level of pavement V, on which the Lower Construction was built, and this would suggest that they either predated the pavement or were possibly associated with it and therefore dated back to the Jemdet Nasr period. Cros says that they were placed in the building's subsoil or *sous-sol* (1910, p. 76). In any case, their presence strongly indicates that these fittings were continuously installed in such sacred spaces over a long period, and this might be further confirmed by the discovery in Trench 9, at a Sarzec height of 7.4 m, of part of a third broken bitumen capsule dating back to the Uruk period that Cros associated with some other small finds from the same epoch.

Irrespective of the heights at which they were excavated, Cros remarks, these capsules were all 'the same' as the ones found by Sarzec in the walls of the Lower Construction, but his diagram (1910, p. 76) indicates that the lowest of the three that he unearthed was 0.6 m tall and about 0.55 m wide at its widest point. These measurements differ from the ones given by Sarzec and Heuzey (1912, p. 413), where the illustrated capsule is 0.8 m tall and has a maximum width of 0.3 m. The lengthways difference can almost certainly be explained by the fact that the capsule shown in Cros's diagram is broken, so that its slender curving neck has partly fallen inside the wider cavity below, thus reducing its original overall length or tallness. Its broad cavity is undoubtedly significantly wider than the one illustrated by Sarzec and Heuzey, but in this respect it was perhaps comparable to the ones that Sarzec found embedded in the two blocks that formed the substructure of the landing on the Large Stairway (discussed above), which are described as having wider 'bellies' than the ones found in the walls of the Lower Construction (Sarzec and Heuzey 1912, p. 424). The opening in the narrow neck at the top of Cros's illustrated capsule (measuring about 0.18 m or perhaps a little more at its narrowest point) would also appear to have been somewhat wider than the openings on the ones found by Sarzec in the walls of the Lower Construction, which had a maximum recorded diameter of 0.15 m.

Also of particular interest were frequent layers of fish deposits, especially on the E side of the trenches, the first of which were discovered at the same Sarzec height (8.1 m) as the first two bitumen capsules listed above (see Cros 1910, pp. 81–3). The black earth at this level was interspersed with large yellowish horizontal patches, 0.04–0.05 m thick, in which Cros was surprised to find the remains of pressed fish (with their skeletons and parts of their skin and scales still discernible) that he describes as provisions rather than kitchen refuse: salted or sun-dried fish, most likely preserved for eating, but they might also perhaps have been used as sacred offerings. Similar deposits (forming the same yellow 'patches') were found on the E side of the trench at Sarzec heights of 8.2 m, 7.6 m and 7.5 m, respectively, and another thick deposit was found 0.6 m directly below the first two bitumen capsules, at a Sarzec height of around 7 m. More layers of preserved fish came to light on the W side of the trenches at very considerable depths that would date them back to Uruk and possibly even Ubaid times, though the stratigraphy is complicated by the need to keep such comestibles in controlled conditions, meaning that at any era they might have been stored in underground larders or cellars.

Interestingly, Cros makes special mention of some larger kinds of preserved fish: for example, tuna and the 'fish of Tobias', as he calls them (referring to the story of the huge fish caught in the Tigris by Tobias that is found in the Apocryphal Book of Tobit), which might have been carp or perhaps the species known as king barbus or barbel (*luciobarbus esocinus*), often called mangar. He also notes that cuttlefish bones were occasionally found in the same layers, and these might have been from the large variety known as pharaoh cuttlefish. Sea fish such as tuna and cuttlefish that were brought from the Gulf (which in those times lay only 30 km or 35 km south-east of Girsu, even though it is now 350 km away) might usually have been preserved, but local freshwater fish from the nearby rivers or marshes could either have been preserved or cooked shortly after being caught, or perhaps brought from one of the many tanks that were found to the north of Tell K (see Cros 1910, pp. 100–19). Otherwise, they might have been pressed for oil or used to make a version of garum, a fermented liquid made from fish that was extremely popular as a sauce or flavouring ingredient (comparable with modern fish sauces), but was also used medicinally.

The North Trench: Trench 5 (1903)

The North Trench, which measured 15 m × 25 m, was excavated to a depth of more than 3.5 m beneath the Oval Reservoir, 20 m north-east of the N corner of the Ur-Nanshe Building and 37 m north-west of the Well of Eanatum. Cros's description of the trench again presents problems with respect to the height of the Sarzec Esplanade, which he says descended to 'a certain' depth below the Oval Reservoir. This would place it significantly higher than the reference value of 8 m or 9 m relied upon elsewhere because the bottom of the uppermost reservoir was found approximately 1.7 m above the base level of the Ur-Nanshe floor (placing it at 14.53 m on the Sarzec scale). According to Sarzec's own account (detailed above), however, when he uncovered the reservoir's manifold substructure he found beneath it a brick pavement that was at approximately the same level as the Ur-Nanshe base, and that would place the Sarzec Esplanade at a Sarzec height of approximately 12.83 m, meaning it was 4 m or so higher than the paving of the Lower Construction, which is the usual reference height attributed to the esplanade. Accordingly, if the North Trench was 3.5 m deep, it was probably excavated to a Sarzec height of 12.83 m − 3.5 m = 9.33 m (approximately).

The first thing Cros found in the trench was a compact mass of mud-bricks, about 1.7 m thick, from which several small objects were recovered. Most importantly, at a depth of 0.25 m, the workmen found two gypsum slabs (0.18 m × 0.22 m) that were the same as the slabs from pavement V that were also found in the masonry that encased the walls of the Lower Construction, along with a fragment of circular bas-relief, other parts of which were found associated with the Lower Construction and in very deep soundings elsewhere (mentioned above and in Heuzey 1900, pp. 53–6). It is noteworthy that the broken piece of relief was found at a Sarzec height of 12.83 m − 0.25 m = 12.58 m, meaning it was only slightly deeper than the base of the Ur-Nanshe Building.

At a depth of 1.7 m (a Sarzec height of 11.13 m) the composition of the ground changed, and Cros found numerous planoconvex bricks, all of the same type, both fired and unfired. On the SE side of the trench the bricks formed a very gently rising slope, which Cros (almost certainly incorrectly) identified as a narrow stairway, 0.6 m wide and oriented towards the Ur-Nanshe Building, of which three supposed steps were preserved. Cros (1910, pp. 84–5) notes that as he dug deeper he found the same fired and unfired bricks in increasing numbers, and they formed a homogeneous block that was coextensive with the trench. Many more small objects were uncovered down to a depth of 2.2 m (a Sarzec height of 10.63 m), while the trench itself descended a further 1.3 m to a Sarzec height of about 9.33 m (as noted above).

South-East of Tell K: The Rectangular Blocks of Earth (1904)

The area to the east of the Ur-Nanshe Building (in the vicinity of the hooked channel N marked on Sarzec's Plan C (1); Fig. 33 below), which was higher than the level of the esplanade, had been left largely untouched by Sarzec. He had, however, prepared the ground by excavating a network of shallow trenches that intersected at right angles to demarcate a set of low rectangular blocks of earth. He intended to examine this part of the tell systematically at some later date, but did not live to do so. A total of thirteen blocks of earth can be seen on Cros's Plan A (produced in 1903; Fig. 35 below), where they are criss-crossed by two or possibly three trenches running south-west–north-east and four running south-east–north-west. One of the blocks illustrated on the SW side of the group is triangular, probably to keep the way clear towards the passage through the spoil heaps just below it (to the south or south-south-east), and the southernmost one of the whole group is much bigger than the others: at least twice as wide and significantly longer on its NW–SE axis. In 1904 Cros excavated the block that originally lay closest to the SE corner of the Ur-Nanshe Building, noting (1910, p. 86) that its top surface was 1.6 m above the height of the Sarzec Esplanade (at a Sarzec height of 8.5 m + 1.6 m = 10.1 m). By the time his Plan B was drawn, after the 1905 campaign (Season 14), only eight remained. His excavations in and around the first block revealed another long brick drain or waterway that sloped down towards the east or south-east; it is marked *Caniveau* on Plan B, where the direction of flow is indicated by an arrow. Made of archaic fired bricks in a range of measurements (0.20 m × 0.17 m, 0.22 m × 0.17 m and 0.27 m × 0.2 m), it sloped very gently eastwards for a distance of 14 m, reaching a depth of 0.35 m lower than the Sarzec Esplanade and therefore descending by 1.95 m over its 14-m length.

To investigate further, Cros excavated the adjacent rectangular block of earth, which was at least 22 m long and extended as far as the Pillar of Gudea, and there found another 1 m of the channel in the form of a terracotta pipe that had a diameter of 0.33 m. He then enlarged the trench, following a line that was approximately parallel to the Large Stairway, noting that the summit of the tell in the area of the SE rectangular blocks would have been 2.1 m above the Sarzec Esplanade, which was here 1 m lower than it was around the Ur-Nanshe Building (Cros 1910, p. 87). If the esplanade was at a Sarzec height of between 9 m and 8.5 m around the Ur-Nanshe Building, therefore, it would have been between 8 m and 7.5 m around the SE rectangular blocks, while the upper edge of the tell would have risen to a Sarzec height of just 10.1 m or 9.6 m (8 m or 7.5 m + 2.1 m), considerably lower than in the central area above the Ur-Nanshe Building.

In the enlarged trench, at a depth of 1.1 m (about 1 m above the level of the Sarzec Esplanade, so at a Sarzec height of 9 m or 8.5 m), an empty foundation box made of square bricks was found. The bricks, one of which was stamped in the name of Gudea, were bonded with bitumen, which was also used to coat the interior surface of the box. A Gudea foundation tablet was uncovered a little below the box, together with remains of ash and molten copper. Digging deeper, 0.5 m below the Sarzec Esplanade (at a Sarzec height of 7.5 m or 7 m), the excavators found two elongated planoconvex bricks inscribed in the name of Eanatum. At a depth of 0.9 m (presumably relative to the esplanade, and so at a Sarzec height of 7.1 m or 6.6 m) a layer of mud-bricks was recorded with a thickness of 0.6 m, under which was a layer of grey mud-bricks, 0.5 m thick, and beneath that there was a compacted floor that reached a depth of 2 m below the Sarzec Esplanade (a Sarzec height of 6 m or 5.5 m). Finally, when Cros returned to this SE area in 1905, he excavated at a distance of 4 m from the Pillar of Gudea, uncovering the foundations of a construction that he judged possibly to have been associated with the pillar (Cros 1910, p. 87).

North-East of Tell K: Trenches 6 and 7 (1903)

Believing that the Large Stairway that had been uncovered by Sarzec was a principal access point to the upper levels of the mound, Cros opened two adjoining trenches in its vicinity in 1903. Trenches 6 and 7, with a combined area of 30 m × 23 m, were excavated to a depth of 3.5 m in the NE face of the tell, starting at a distance of 7 m from the Large Stairway. Almost as soon as he started digging in Trench 6, Cros came across the remains of some walls that signalled the existence of a series of structures, all with a similar NE–SW orientation, that seemed to extend the slope of the tell to form a new level below the base of the Large Stairway. Three main structures were subsequently uncovered in and around the two trenches, all of which are described in the subsections below: the Rectangular Construction, which was a cistern or reservoir designed to collect water; some bituminated waterways (that Cros calls 'ramps'), which were part of a water supply and drainage system; and a collection of stairways, particularly in Trench 7.

The Stairways

In Trench 7 Cros uncovered the largest of three new stairways, twenty-five steps of which were preserved, including a number of double treads in the lower section. Resting on a bed of fired bricks and a mass of mud-bricks, the base of the first new stairway was 2.17 m wide, and it led up towards the Enmetena Esplanade. Immediately to the north-west, parallel and adjacent to it, and separated by a gap of just 0.4 m, was a narrower flight of thirteen steps that were 1.1 m wide and made of two types of fired bricks. Both kinds measured 0.32 m × 0.21 m, and all were laid lengthways and bonded with clay. The first kind, erroneously described as post-Enmetena, were flat and marked with a lengthways groove; the others, attributed to Eanatum, were gently planoconvex and marked with two fingerprints. The longer flight of twenty-five stairs was seemingly made of the same bricks, except for the bottom three steps, on which the treads were wider (0.4 m) and made of more substantial bricks that measured 0.42 m × 0.27 m × 0.065 m. Below this Double Stairway, as Cros calls it, were found two or three similar flights of stairs from earlier epochs that were separated from the Double Stairway by a layer described as compacted earth (*terre battue*). A third flight of stairs, 2.05 m wide, was found 0.56 m away, perpendicular to the Double Stairway, and ascending towards the north-west. Made of the same bricks, it originally had eight steps, of which Cros found six preserved (though seven are shown on Cros's Plan C; Fig. 38 below). Fragmentary structures (marked E and F on Cros's Plan C) were recorded in the space bounded by the Double Stairway and its perpendicular counterpart. Made of poorly laid planoconvex bricks, these walls enclosed an area in which, among other things, were found two terracotta drainage shafts.

The Double Stairway's shorter flight of thirteen steps led up to an intermediate landing, beneath which Cros detected an irregular pavement made of small planoconvex Ur-Nanshe bricks that were marked with a thumbprint. The pavement, which sloped slightly to the east, was found at a depth of 1.9 m (probably below the landing, though Cros does not explicitly say so), but according to his calculations it was 7 m above the water table and therefore at a Sarzec height of 7 m. This means it was 1.48 m deeper than the Lower Construction, which lay at 8.48 m, placing the pavement about 6 m below the level of the base of the Ur-Nanshe Building, which lay at a Sarzec height of 12.83 m. This computes very well because 12.83 m − 6 m = 6.83 m for the Sarzec height of the pavement, calculated with respect to the Ur-Nanshe base.

If Cros does indeed mean to say that the irregular pavement was found 1.9 m below the upper landing on the shorter flight of stairs, that would place the top of the shorter flight at a Sarzec height of 7 m + 1.9 m = 8.9 m. The pavement's location is perhaps confirmed by Cros's photo (View No. 2; Fig. 56 below) that seems to show that a deep void was dug immediately adjacent to the top of the shorter flight. The irregular pavement was therefore presumably at the bottom of that pit, which was narrower than the width of the shorter flight. Cros (1910, p. 99) notes that the pavement lay at a depth of 3.1 m below the level at which the trenches were opened, and he records elsewhere (1910, p. 96) that the pavement extended under the base of the Double Stairway (at a Sarzec height of 7 m).

The uppermost step of the longer flight of twenty-five steps on the Double Stairway was (Cros says) found at a Sarzec height of at least 10 m (or 10 m above groundwater level, as he puts it). But this, he goes on to note, was only the height to which it had been preserved, and it must originally have had an upper section that perhaps took it up as far as the level of the Ur-Nanshe base at a Sarzec height of 12.83 m. The heights of these installations can also be confirmed by considering the upper surface of the water distribution head on the water supply network (described below), which was found beneath the starting point of the excavations at a depth of 0.6 m. This equates to a depth of 2.9 m below the Ur-Nanshe base, placing the distribution head and starting level of the excavations at Sarzec heights of 9.33 m and 9.99 m, respectively. These heights should, of course, be treated with caution.

A few finds were recorded in the vicinity of the new stairways and the NE area, including some fish skeletons at a depth of 0.25 m in the Rectangular Construction (which Cros says was not surprising if it was indeed a reservoir). Perhaps the most interesting discovery was made 1.5 m towards the south-west, at a depth of 1.8 m in the rectangular blocks of earth behind the largest stairway. This was a stone bas-relief (Fig. 29), measuring 0.17 m × 0.20 m × 0.35 m, that showed a broad-shouldered naked man carrying some heavy loads of

FIGURE 29. Early Dynastic relief of a nude man carrying fish. Musée du Louvre AO 4110.

fish hanging from rings. Cros notes that the way in which it was carved recalled the style of the figures on the Stele of the Vultures.

The Water Supply Network

The bituminated ramps, as Cros calls them, formed a multi-phase system of water channels, including a circular distribution head, that were excavated to the south-east of the Large Stairway. They were oriented north-east–south-west, with the distribution head towards the south-west. The network was found 7 m to the south-east of the collection of stairways in Trench 7, running parallel to its principal NE–SW axis. The distributor, which was 2 m in diameter and found at a depth of 0.6 m (at a possible Sarzec height of 9.33 m, as calculated above), was built of a double layer of fired planoconvex bricks that were bonded with bitumen and laid on a bitumen bed. They were marked with two fingerprints, like the bricks used on the Well of Eanatum, as Cros remarks (1910, p. 93), but slightly larger, measuring between 0.27 m × 0.2 m and 0.4 m × 0.21 m. The main conduit that led into the distributor was a channel built on a platform, with a width of 1 m, that sloped from the south-west towards the north-east. It was made of planoconvex bricks in two sizes (0.27 m × 0.2 m and 0.4 m × 0.21 m) that were bonded with bitumen.

Three more channels (marked BBB on Cros's Plan C) branched off from the distributor in different directions: north, north-north-east and east. The central one (heading north-east), which Cros says was the most important of the three, was 0.94 m wide and excavated over a length of 16 m; it was made of planoconvex bricks (0.27 m × 0.2 m) that were again marked with two fingerprints and bonded with bitumen. After emerging more or less horizontally from the distributor, it descended north-north-east by a total of 2.8 m along its 16-m length until it disappeared under the rubble of previous excavations at a depth of 3.5 m. Cros does not specify what this 3.5 m depth is relative to, but if he is thinking of the starting level of the excavations, that gives a Sarzec height of 9.9 m − 3.5 m = 6.4 m for the low NNE end of this central channel (based on the calculations performed above). The fact that it dropped by a total of 2.8 m gives a Sarzec height of 6.4 m + 2.8 m = 9.2 m for its upper end (the one joined to the distributor), which correlates well with the overall Sarzec height of 9.33 m for the distribution head.

The channel that branched off to the north, which was preserved to a length of 11 m, forked off from the distributor at a distance of 0.5 m and then descended sharply before levelling off until it was almost horizontal. It was built of three courses of planoconvex bricks measuring 0.40 m × 0.21 m that were marked with two fingerprints. Finally, all that was left of the distributor's E outlet (listed first in Cros's text) was a very badly damaged section that branched off to the east (or north-east) towards the Rectangular Construction, which was judged to be a reservoir (as detailed immediately below).

The Rectangular Construction

The Rectangular Construction (marked A on Cros's Plan C) was a large cistern or reservoir that was doubtless associated with the adjacent water supply network. It was found at a depth of 0.25 m in Trench 6, preserved to a height of 0.5 m, with the Sarzec height of its uppermost surface being 9.99 m − 0.25 m = 9.75 m. It stood on a bed that is described as compacted clay (*terre battue*), 0.6 m thick, beneath which was a layer of potsherds and fragments of fired bricks, 0.3 m thick, that was placed on the underlying mass of mud-bricks. It must originally have been rectangular or square in shape, since the preserved walls formed a semi-rectangle that was oriented towards the north-east, with an opening almost in the middle of the NE wall that had been blocked with a minor internal wall. The surviving parts of the construction measured 4.3 m × 5.6 m (overall), and the thickness of the walls ranged between 1.1 m and 0.9 m. Inside the principal walls, behind the blocked opening, was found a small squarish installation measuring 1.85 m × 1.8 m that was slightly misaligned with the main walls. All the structures were made with flat rectangular fired bricks that were marked with a line made with a finger, and the bricks were bonded with clay. They were found in three similar sizes, and Cros (perhaps not entirely reliably) suggests they were of the type used by the successors of Enmetena. Measuring 0.3 m × 0.22 m, 0.3 m × 0.25 m and 0.34 m × 0.25 m, all were 0.05 m thick. The minor internal wall that blocked the opening was made of a single row of fired bricks laid lengthways, with measurements of 0.3 m × 0.22 m.

The long SE wall, which was rough and irregular on the outside, probably because the entire construction had been partly or fully embedded into and so surrounded by the mud-brick mass of the platform (Cros 1910, p. 92), was fitted on its smoothly finished internal wall with a bench that was 0.3 m wide. Below the structure, 0.5 m in front of the doorway in the NE façade, but not aligned on the same axis, Cros discovered another conduit at a depth of 0.5 m (at a Sarzec height of 8.75 m, which is calculated by subtracting the preserved height of the building (0.5 m) and the depth at which the new channel was found (also 0.5 m) from the Sarzec height of 9.75 for the construction's uppermost surface). For a distance of 2.9 m it rested on a fired-brick bed or paving measuring 2.9 m × 2.2 m; it then continued for a further 2 m, where it was protected with a cover, before it finally disappeared under the remains of a more recent channel that lay 0.8 m above it. The fired-brick paving and channel were made of the same rectangular bricks as the rest of the structures uncovered. Cros describes these as post-Enmetena, but as with the bricks found on the Double Stairway, this might well be mistaken.

CHAPTER 7

The Great Rift of Girsu: Genouillac and Parrot

IT IS COMMON IN THE SCHOLARLY WORLD OF RESEARCH into the history of Mesopotamia for the early founders of the discipline to be subjected to some especially harsh criticism. While some of this is doubtless justified, it is also important to remember the particular contexts in which the pioneers and explorers operated in the territories of ancient Sumer when the region was under Ottoman rule and in the era of Mandate Iraq. They faced difficulties of many kinds: political obstacles, problems of access and transportation, and extreme physical hardships to name just a few. In addition, they lacked the appropriate methodological tools and scientific frameworks that have since been developed to aid the monumentally complex task of understanding Sumerian sites—never forgetting that Sumerian archaeology is quite different from that of Assyria, with its abundance of documentation and rich networks of historically attested associations. For these reasons, the achievements of the pioneers should also be acknowledged, as should their legacy. Despite his faults and flaws, Sarzec was an adventurer worthy of the pages of Victor Hugo. For better or for worse, he was infused with a pure romantic spirit that drove him to give everything for the sake of Tello, including finally his own life. Nonetheless, Sarzec could not have become the Sarzec of archaeological legend, so to speak, without Heuzey, his *éminence grise*. Working at his desk in Paris, Heuzey, the deus ex machina of Tello, undertook a practically incomparable effort of interpretation that continues to yield significant insights. As for Cros, he was blessed with the charisma and panache almost of a Homeric hero, who attempted to tame the historical and geographical wilderness of ancient Sumer before eventually losing his life on the battlefields of Flanders in World War I.

After what might be conceived of as a heroic age of trailblazing exploration in Girsu, followed by the lengthy hiatus that was precipitated by the Great War, came the era of academic (some might say professional) archaeology that was personified by the Assyriologist Henri de Genouillac and his deputy and successor, the Louvre curator André Parrot. Both men were trained scholars, and they arrived at the site armed with updated methodological approaches that enabled them to formulate new ideas about its history, and especially its material culture. Genouillac was a gifted philologist, while Parrot was a remarkable art historian, but neither of them was an experienced archaeologist, and this unfortunately led to what was arguably one of the most disastrous undertakings in modern archaeology anywhere in the world—the opening of the Great Pit in Tell K, which was dug between 1930 and 1931 (Season 18). Seeking to emulate the impressive results produced by the deep stratigraphic explorations that had been carried out in Ur, Genouillac and Parrot embarked on a gargantuan effort to bring to light the whole history of the site by excavating an enormous double trench (*Chantiers* I and II), with a surface area of 800 square metres, on the western slope of Tell K, where they aimed to reveal the totality of the site's superimposed archaeological layers, all the way down to the pre-anthropic geological horizon. A pit of that size is gigantic by any standards, but Genouillac and Parrot compounded the catastrophe by employing an army of workers to excavate it to a depth of 14 m in just three months (November 1930 to February 1931). The chaotic, unimaginable scale of the work, and the hundreds of workmen who were let loose on the mound can be seen in the photos that were subsequently published by Genouillac, some of which are reprinted here (Figs. 25 and 57). The staggering volume of the disaster represents no less than 11,200 cubic metres of dispersed archaeological deposits, without a single plan, cross-section or even a sketch to document the titanic operation. The effects of this debacle are felt on the archaeological site to the present day: the Great Pit has been left open since 1931, exposing its interior to constant erosion and creating an enormous rift at the heart of the tell. After every thunderstorm, water runs through the wide ravines that lacerate the pit's sides, ravaging and destroying neighbouring archaeological layers, and causing huge portions of deposits to collapse every year. The Great Pit is nothing less than a shameful open scar on the face of Girsu.

For a Few Pots More

Only one relative positive emerges from this deplorable mess—and even that comes fraught with an abundance of issues. Among the other objects that they unearthed, Genouillac and Parrot collected large numbers of potsherds. It is perhaps unsurprising to learn that, in the extensive digs that were carried out between 1877 and 1909 by Sarzec and Cros, very little attention was paid to the largest corpus of archaeological finds that a site such as Girsu would usually produce, namely the pottery remains. Ceramology, including ceramic dating based on typologies, was not developed as a tool of Mesopotamian archaeology until long after the Great War, while the method of using of pottery assemblages to assist in the construction of robust comparative chronological sequences was still in its infancy when Genouillac and Parrot resumed fieldwork at the site between 1929 and 1933. Genouillac, who was especially conscious of the potential importance of such previously overlooked and seemingly rather ignoble artefacts, creditably attempted in the two volumes of his *Excavations of Telloh* (1934 and 1936) to rationalise and bring some order to the enormous number of potsherds that had been found at the site. Although the text contains some important new insights, his guiding methodological principles and approach lacked serious scientific scope. For example, his selection of what were considered to be third-millennium diagnostic ceramic types was not based on criteria that can be defined as truly typological because his benchmarks were functional.

He focused on the possible reconstructed uses of the vessels in question rather than on their shapes and sizes. The ceramics presented by Genouillac do not therefore represent specific historical periodisations or occupation phases, and his publication of diagnostic pottery types was essentially and mainly limited to an examination of pots that were found undamaged, or at least more or less intact, together with brief notes on the dating of other fragments according to a chronology that was derived from ancient inscriptions. Furthermore, Genouillac's study provides no quantitative information about the retrieved pottery assemblages from which the vessels discussed and published in a series of illustrative plates were selected. Most problematic of all is the fact that the examined pottery is generally dissociated from its archaeological context. The stratigraphic provenances of finds in particular excavated areas are not well recorded, and in a large number of cases Genouillac does not even provide the general find location of the published examples—often failing to mention the trench from which items originated. In consequence, Genouillac's third-millennium diagrammatic plates of diagnostic potsherds are a miscellany taken from the entire corpus of sherds that were found in several trenches at a range of locations across the site. Only in a very few instances is it possible—with a great deal of painstaking effort—to reconstruct the archaeological contexts of some individual types.

The starting point for Genouillac and Parrot's destructive excavation of Tell K is also obscure, and although the deeper, proto- and prehistoric deposits from the Uruk and Ubaid periods (beneath the Lower Construction) and their associated pots seemed to have held a special interest for Genouillac (1934, pp. 1–68; Pls. II–VII), very little is noted about the Early Dynastic archaeological layers that were exhumed in the topmost layers of the Great Pit. Genouillac (1934, p. 3) reports that he started digging at the topographical level of the Enmetena Esplanade (therefore at a Sarzec height of around 13.63 m, as is explained in Chapter 19 below; see Fig. 60), which is a surprisingly exact indication that was probably not based on direct observation. This becomes apparent when it is considered that, following the departure of Cros, there was a twenty-year interruption to the fieldwork in Tello, and as Genouillac himself remarked, the topography of Tell K had changed significantly during this time. Equipped as he was with adequate surveying tools, it would presumably have been possible for Genouillac to recalculate the level of the Enmetena Esplanade, but there is no indication that he did so. Nor should it be forgotten that some landmarks had (perhaps miraculously) survived: for instance, although the uppermost section of the Well of Eanatum had eroded and partially collapsed by the time Genouillac arrived, the structure was still largely intact and must have served as a height marker for Genouillac, as it did for Cros when he started his own work on Tell K some twenty-seven years earlier. Nonetheless, Genouillac's records with regard to the opening of the Great Pit appear to be flawed.

The confusion, which is embedded in the text (Genouillac 1934, p. 3, n. 1), is that Genouillac defines the starting height for his excavations (the Enmetena Esplanade) as being 8 m below the original summit of the mound, by which he means the height of Tell K when Sarzec began to dig there in the late nineteenth century. This would place the Enmetena Esplanade at a Sarzec height of around 9 m, only slightly higher than the Sarzec height (8.48 m) of the base of the Lower Construction—a figure that does not correlate with the heights given by Sarzec and subsequently confirmed by Cros, albeit somewhat problematically. Furthermore, with no indication of the methodology he might have employed, it is difficult to see how Genouillac could have calculated his point of origin with respect to the initial summit of Tell K, which had many decades previously been dramatically truncated by Sarzec. Genouillac also says, however, that he dug down as far as the water table (as Sarzec had also done in a limited way to establish the base point for his calculations), noting that he reached it at a depth of around 14 m. Remarkably, that figure tallies reasonably well with an assumed starting point of approximately 13.63 m, that being the Sarzec height of the Enmetena Esplanade (again, as calculated in Chapter 19 below), so it would seem likely that this was indeed close to the topographical level at which he started to dig the Great Pit.

As already intimated, Genouillac's accounts of his excavation results, especially the pottery contained in the uppermost deposits, at depths of a little more than 5 m below his starting point (therefore at a presumed Sarzec height of around 8.6 m), are concluded at great speed in a few comments that are spread out unsystematically throughout his book. Sometimes the information he gives is very general, and at other times it is more specific, as in the following examples (1934, pp. 4, 22–3 and 23–4):

Here are the results for painted ceramics (usually painted in black on yellow terracotta, sometimes brown on worked pink clay) ... *b*) two thick polychrome sherds, found at 5.25 m [at a Sarzec height of *c.*8.35 m], related to the ceramics of the Jemdet Nasr period (TG.5093, TG.5094: AO14298 (A and B), reproduced on pl. 34); *c*) two monochrome vases of a similar date (TG.5190, TG.5397: AO14280, AO14279, pl. 34) ...

In the south corner of Trench II (*Chantier* II) we found a cache of goblets and bowls from the era of the First Dynasty of Ur; despite the poor condition of some, these are later pieces that were buried in the ground for unknown reasons at depths of up to 3 m [at a lowest Sarzec height of about 10.6 m] ... and again at depths of 1.5 m and 2 m [down to a Sarzec height of about 8.6 m] were found more bowls and goblets, conical and vase-like, some of them quite tall.

Between 6 m and 10 m [at Sarzec heights of between 7.6 m and 3.6 m] signs of the Warka V period appear routinely, with bone points and bitumen handles. Incised pottery—combed, printed and marked with fingernails—is characteristic of this level (9 m) [4.6 m Sarzec]; pottery mosaics. But the types that persist through to Warka IV are already apparent (coarse bowls, animal figurines, treasure boxes), indicating the unity of this civilisation ... At 13.5 m [0.1 m Sarzec], close to the water table, spouted cups recalling Ubaid forms, and at the same time bowls inscribed with fingernails. Sherds of painted pottery and fired clay sickles.

The resulting schematised typology is laid out in a series of plates at the back of the book, where numerous simplified diagrams display the various kinds of ceramics as Genouillac interprets them. Pls. II–VII present pottery types dating back to Ubaid and Uruk times; Pl. VIII describes pots that are dated to the Jemdet Nasr and Early Dynastic I periods; while Pls. XI–XIII sketch examples that range from Early Dynastic IIIb times through to the Early and Late Akkad eras. The entire third millennium is condensed into four plates that are supplemented with a few illustrations, and it should be stressed again that the plates provide no information about where the examples were found. Despite the sketchiness of the data, it has nevertheless been possible to try to salvage a workable chronology, isolating third-millennium potsherds that might well have come from Tell K (Figs. 30–2). Needless

The Great Rift of Girsu: Genouillac and Parrot   83

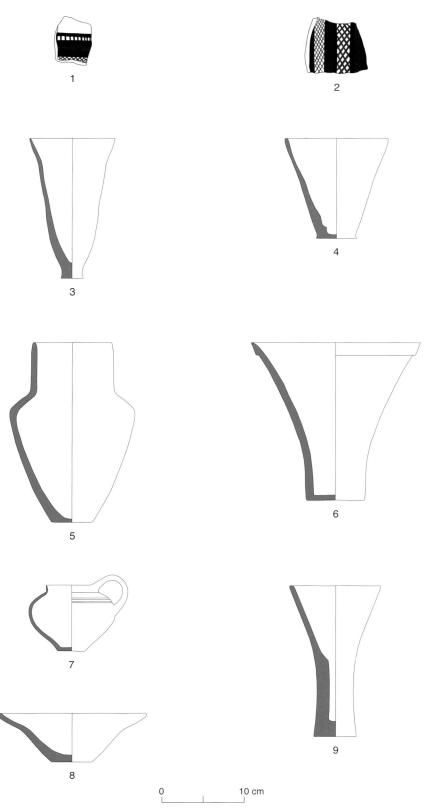

FIGURE 30. Pottery from Tell K I.

84 The Mound of the House of the Fruits

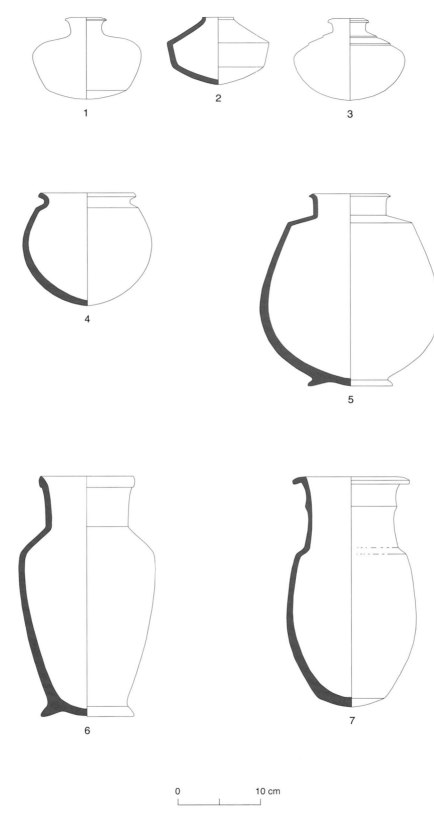

FIGURE 31. Pottery from Tell K II.

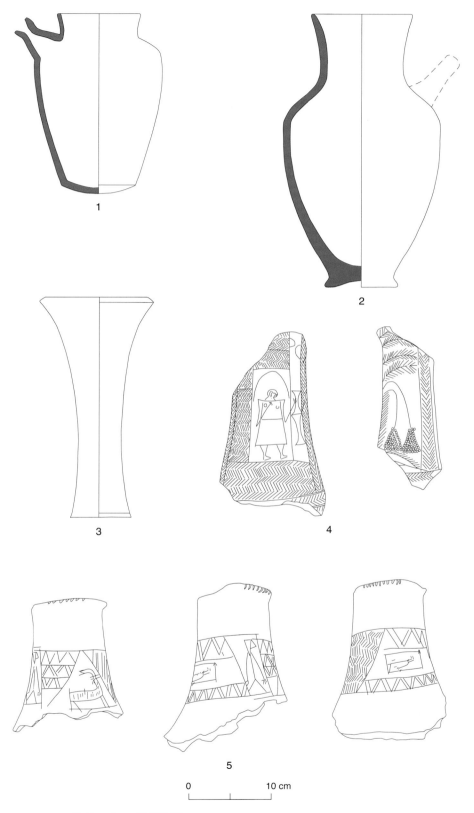

FIGURE 32. Pottery from Tell K III.

to say, the results, which must be considered with a high degree of caution, are tentative at best.

Based on the excavation reports produced by Genouillac and later by Parrot (1948), it seems that a large number of potsherds dating back to the third millennium were retrieved in the Great Pit of Tell K between 1930 and 1931 (Season 18). A few other areas of the site (listed in Parrot 1948, pp. 29–32) also yielded Early Dynastic and Akkad pottery, including the Trench of the Dig Headquarters (Genouillac's Site IX, southeast of Tell L), excavated in 1929 (Season 16), and Site III, excavated between 1929 and 1930 (Season 17), which revealed possible residential quarters from the Late Early Dynastic period; but also the area of the Devil's Gate (*Porte du Diable*) in the vicinity of Tells P and P' that was excavated between 1930 and 1931 (Season 18), where Early Dynastic IIIb remains from one of the sacred precinct's monumental gates were found, together with parts of the associated temenos wall. Even on the basis of the very limited amount of archaeological information that pertains to these excavation areas, therefore, it is probably safe to say that only on Tell K did the later French archaeologists reach exceptionally deep layers that contained remains dating back to times earlier than the Early Dynastic IIIb era. It follows that most, if not all, of the other Jemdet Nasr and Early Dynastic I to Early Dynastic IIIa potsherds illustrated in Genouillac's plates must have originated from Tell K.

Parrot, who assisted Genouillac in the field when the Great Pit of Tell K was dug, provides some context for the provenances of the published pottery assemblages in his *Tello: Twenty Seasons of Excavations* (1948), which is illuminating in some respects, despite presenting difficulties of its own. There are also moments when Parrot plainly contradicts Genouillac, and in these admittedly rare instances the reader is left guessing as to who is right and who is wrong. Parrot, who includes sketches of some of the ceramics he discusses, specifies just two archaeological contexts on Tell K that are associated with pottery illustrated in Genouillac's plates: the first (1948, p. 77) is a deposit 2 m beneath the Ur-Nanshe horizon (indicating a Sarzec height of 12.83 m – 2 m = 10.83); and the second (1948, pp. 121–2) is the large packing around the Well of Eanatum. With respect to the first, Parrot (1948, Fig. 18 (d and e)) presents rather basic diagrams of two vessels, seemingly from a pre-Ur-Nanshe epoch, that were found 'under a layer of packed earth, two meters thick, almost devoid of finds, representing the foundations of monuments built by rulers of the lineage of Ur-Nanshe'. The two vases (here relabelled Fig. 30.9 and Fig. 32.3) are clearly not contemporaries, however, and it may be that Genouillac's schematic drawings led Parrot to commit this error. Furthermore, Parrot's Fig. 18 misrepresents the vessels' proportions, even though the Genouillac typological diagrams, which are clearly labelled, indicate the dimensions of the pots. Different scales are sometimes adopted depending on the varying vessel types, however, and this can generate misunderstandings, as probably happened in this instance. The conclusion is that while the conical beaker (Fig. 30.9; Parrot 1948, Fig. 18 (d)) could certainly have been found in a layer that was either contemporary with or predated the Ur-Nanshe phase, the other tall vase (Fig. 32.3; Parrot 1948, Fig. 18 (e)), with its flaring triangular rim, curvilinear body and flat base, can be securely dated to the Late Akkad or Ur III period, as confirmed by numerous comparisons.

The second archaeological context, the packing around the Well of Eanatum, is seemingly less contentious because it was found to contain a particular type of pottery known as cylindrical stands or stemmed dishes (1948, pp. 121–2). That said, it should be noted that the two examples of this type that are presented by Parrot (1948, Fig. 29 (a and b)), who considers them to be representative of the ceramics of this kind that were found on Tell K, actually originated in the vicinity of the Devil's Gate (Tells P and P'). Genouillac (1934, Pl. 64 (2)) includes numerous fragments of stemmed dishes with incised decorations of both the simpler type and the type with geometric patterns, together with more elaborately decorated ceramics that exhibit floral motifs and representations of animal and human figures alongside geometric patterns. Unfortunately, it is impossible to know where they were all found: some presumably came from Tells P and P', while others were in all likelihood found on Tell K, probably in the area of the Well of Eanatum. The incised decorations on the illustrated examples are characterised by deeply engraved lines and markedly stylised representations of chosen subjects—characteristics that carry over into the details of, for example, the textures that are used to fill the subjects' outlines. Where horned animals (1934, Pl. B (TG.1800); Pl. 64 (3): TG.5630) or fish scales (Pl. 63 (4)) are concerned, patterns of deeply incised lines are used to make the representations more realistic. For instance, in the small fragment depicting two fish (Pl. 63 (4)), only a fraction of which is preserved, the prevailing incised line is used alongside other stylistic solutions, notably the roughly semicircular indentations (possibly made with a fingernail or the obliquely applied end of a cylindrical stick), to enhance the visual impact.

Lacking their upper and lower parts, two stems of dishes with more elaborate representations were found by the Devil's Gate (Tells P and P′). Photos of both are shown in Genouillac (1934, Pls. 63 and 64), while Parrot reproduces simplified sketches of them (1934, Fig. 29 (a and b)). The stem of one of the vessels (Fig. 32.4 above) exhibits a dense geometric decoration of zigzags that frames two rectangular areas, in the first of which (Genouillac 1934, Pl. 63 (1); Parrot 1934, Fig. 29 (a)) a human figure is depicted under an arched vault. The human form is rendered extremely schematically, with geometric lines. The rounded forms of the head and profile are abstract and simplified, such that both eyes are shown on the same side of the nose, and the figure has a long ear, almost like that of a sheep or a goat. The body is formed of a broad irregular quadrilateral, with a gently concave top from which the hourglass form of the neck emerges. The arms are made with single lines, sharply pointed at the elbows, that frame spaces next to the figure's torso to suggest their upper parts; the hands are reduced to nothing more than the fingers, which are represented like the simplified vein structure of a leaf, with no attempt at realism. The male figure, who is bald, is shown wearing a classic kaunakes skirt that is decorated with the same pattern of zigzags as is seen on the framing rectangles, while below the skirt his stumpy, almost triangular legs converge at thin ankles that are joined to quasi-triangular feet. Facing to the right, the figure has his right hand placed on his chest, just below the centre of his neck, while his left arm reaches up from the acute angle of the elbow to indicate, or take hold of, a tall cylindrical object like a spool that flares out at the top and bottom. The spool-like shape that the figure points at or holds is shown standing on a counterpart that is slightly taller but otherwise identical. The base of the superimposed objects is not placed on the ground but at the same level as the hem of the figure's skirt, and there is seemingly no indication of a third element might have supported the two just described. Above them, at the top of the long panel in which they are inscribed, are two irregular half-circles or half-ellipses that are extremely difficult to interpret. Interestingly, a pronounced line emerges from the bottom of the upper spool (pointing away from the figure) that is at almost exactly the same angle as the figure's left forearm, and the fact that his two forearms are parallel makes a threefold pattern of parallel lines, with the one extending out from the base of the upper spool serving a highly uncertain representational purpose. The second rectangular area (Genouillac 1934, Pl. 63 (3); Parrot 1934, Fig. 29 (a′)) is only partially preserved. On the left is a portion of a palm trunk that shows the pattern of the bark, but with no outlines, together with part of its crown of pinnate leaves, below which, on two long stalks, hang two stylised clusters of dates. To the right of that is a tall, slender slightly curving cylinder or quadrilateral that is covered in broken downward-pointing chevrons. It looks very much like a second, more clearly defined palm trunk, but the fact that a similar form can be seen to the right of the scene with the figure and the spool-like objects suggests that in this case the tree-like designs were used as fillers to separate representational decorative elements. In any event, this trunk-like form cannot have been intended to be the source of the palm fronds to the left of it because the chevrons formed by their leaflets face the wrong way.

The other vessel (Fig. 32.5 above) has more sober decorations that are developed in a rectangular band that takes up only a part of the surface of the preserved stem. A zigzag filler seemingly occupies the space between a series of triangular and trapezoidal forms containing different subjects that might be read, from left to right, as: a supine human figure that is depicted extremely schematically, with bare incised lines; another very abstract human shape that is upright, as though walking, and made up of simple lines like a matchstick man; and a horned animal against a large blank triangle. Parrot (1948, p. 122) interprets the stretched-out figure as a funerary scene that shows a body lying in a rectangular 'chamber', and he suggests that the animal is an ibex. The stylised creature, which is depicted with its horns curving backwards behind its head, certainly looks like a mountain goat, and it is apparently shown against an equally stylised mountain landscape that is represented principally by the large framing triangle. In addition to their function as decorative fillers, the smaller triangles to the animal's left might be read as more mountainous forms, while the sequence of plain uprights on the right might be read as trees or tree trunks. To the right of the presumably dead figure, whose 'chamber' might more accurately be interpreted as an interred coffin or sarcophagus, the outsized figure (who might reasonably be taken to be a man) faces away from the feet of the body behind him and towards the panel with the ibex. Putting these scenes together, the stem of the vessel seems to be decorated with the narrative of a death and a burial, accompanied by a gigantic or heroic victor or survivor, in a setting of mountains and forests, as symbolised by the horned animal. Perhaps the most likely candidates for the story shown are episodes from the Gilgamesh legend, possibly the death of Enkidu or of the hero himself, but that cannot be verified. Nonetheless, the fact that the shapes are so simplified, even to the point that representation and pure decoration seem nearly indistinguishable, would imply that the narrative (if that is indeed what is intended) was extremely familiar to those who viewed and used the vessel, and that they were expected to read the scenes with a high degree of visual literacy.

In the end, it is impossible to be sure what the imagery on the two pots was designed to show, or for whom these particular vessels were made, but such stemmed dishes represent a type of vessel that was characteristic of the pottery production of southern Iraq over a long period. Characterised by a complexity of manufacture, they exhibit engraved decorations that take a primarily geometric approach, sometimes adding more elaborate patterns that include floral and animal subjects. Chronologically, they have certainly been recorded in strata relating to the Early Dynastic IIIa and IIIb periods, but more ancient specimens have been found at numerous sites (see Moon 1982). The Tello specimens show a rather elaborate decoration, seemingly with narrative, or quasi-narrative interpolations, but it is currently impossible to correlate figurative trends with samples from other sites. It should be noted, however, that the palm tree motif has interesting similarities with examples found in and around Adab (Wilson 2012, Pl. 91a) and especially in Nippur (McMahon 2006, Pl. 80.5).

If this attempt to disentangle Genouillac's hugely problematic sequence is anywhere close to correct then it should provide a reasonably secure context for the crucially important earlier period represented on Tell K by the pre-Lower Construction horizon characterised by pavement V (Jemdet Nasr) and its subsequent phase, represented by the building of the Lower Construction itself (Early Dynastic I). It must be acknowledged, however, that the proposed sequence rests entirely on the above-mentioned supposition, derived from the few examples recorded by Genouillac and further discussed by Parrot, that polychrome sherds and monochrome pots were found at a topographical height of approximately 8.35 m (measured on the Sarzec scale).

With respect to Girsu more generally, only a relatively small amount of pottery from the Jemdet Nasr and Early Dynastic I periods has been published. The fragments of polychrome pottery mentioned earlier (Fig. 30.1 and 30.2) were found in strata that Genouillac defined as Warka IV. They have geometric decorations consisting of vertical bands and cross-hatched fillings. Other fragments pertinent to this phase are the conical vase with a band rim (TG.5613: Genouillac 1934, pp. 25–8, Pl. II; here labelled Fig. 30.6) that shows parallels with specimens found in Level XIV of the Temple of Inanna in Nippur that have been dated to the Jemdet Nasr period (Wilson 1986, p. 60, Figs. 5.3 and 5.4). Among closed shapes can be included a kind of jar with a plain vertical rim, a strap handle and a large shoulder with combed horizontal lines and a flat, narrow base (TG.4304: Genouillac 1934, Pl. VI; here Fig. 30.7). This type of vessel exhibits precise parallels with items found in contexts dated to the Jemdet Nasr period in Shuruppak and Ur (Martin 1988, p. 175 (12); Sürenhagen 1999, Pl. 53 (14)).

Examples of pottery shapes that remained in use through the Jemdet Nasr and Early Dynastic I periods include mass-produced types, together with other pottery shapes that display features distinctive of this chronological period, namely solid-footed goblets (TG.4332: Genouillac 1934, Pl. VIII; here Fig. 30.3), conical beakers (TG.4242: Genouillac 1934, Pl. VIII; and also TG.5610 (AO14389 (A and B); here Fig. 30.4) and jars with plain rims (Fig. 30.5). It is important to note that the attribution of the reserved slipware found by Genouillac to this chronological period is more complex. The fragment in question is briefly described in a note by Genouillac (1934, p. 36, n. 3: TG.4837 (AO14312 (A))). The upper shoulder of the vase is decorated with brown fan lines that originate close to the neck of the vase. The Uruk site provides parallels for this decorative pattern that date from both the Jemdet Nasr and Early Dynastic I periods (Pongratz-Leisten 1988, pp. 294–5, Nos. 140, 175, 191 and 210). Based on the description provided by Genouillac, however, this specimen seems to exhibit undeniable similarities with two sherds of large reserved slip jars found in Late Early Dynastic I contexts during the British Museum team's recent excavations on Tell A (Area B1; see Chapter 31 below), though the pattern of decoration on the Genouillac find seems to suggest that it is older than the examples found in Area B1.

Generally in the third millennium BCE, the most common diagnostic sherds include two types of mass-produced pottery: the bowl and the goblet. The conical bowl (Fig. 30.8) is one of the most distinctive chronological markers of the period, and one of the most quantitatively attested forms in the pottery assemblages of the third millennium BCE that have been found in sites in the south of Iraq. Typological examples from Tello include TG.4182 (Genouillac 1934, Pl. VIII), and two other conical bowls that were found on Tell K in the area of the Enmetena Esplanade: TG.4243 and TG.4698 (AO25120). Regarding the latter, Genouillac notes that TG.4698 was found at a depth of 3 m (a Sarzec height of 10.60 m). The other common pottery shape, the goblet or conical beaker (Fig. 30.9), is attested from Early Dynastic IIIa–b times through to the Late Akkad period. Unfortunately, the schematic drawings in Genouillac's plates of the vessels of this type that were found on Tell K make it impossible to define their features with any precision—an inadequacy that also rules out a more accurate dating.

More interesting is the data that can be deduced from ceramics with closed shapes. For example, Genouillac's plates illustrate some short bottles, three of which can be considered to be representative types on account of their distinctive characteristics. The first (Fig. 31.1 above) has an everted rim, a large shoulder, a low carination and a rounded base; another specimen (Fig. 31.2) has an everted rim, a ridged shoulder and a rounded base; and the last one (Fig. 31.3) has a plain rim, a double-carinated body and a rounded base. The kinds of short bottles just described are characteristic of the Early Dynastic IIIb and Early to Late Akkad periods, and comparative data from other sites might help to construct a sequence for them. The specimen with the ridged shoulder (Fig. 31.2) and the one with the double-carinated body (Fig. 31.3) can accordingly be dated to the Early and Late Akkad periods with a reasonable degree of certainty.

The collection of jars published by Genouillac is particularly varied. Though they are all of medium size, they each have distinctive features, and the list includes a range of discrete types: a jar with a globular body, an everted rim, a well-marked shoulder and a rounded base (Fig. 31.4); a necked jar with a triangular rim, a stepped shoulder, an ovoid body and a ring base (Fig. 31.5); a high-necked jar with a thickened rounded rim, an ovoid body and a ring base (Fig. 31.6); a high-necked, double-ridged rim jar with a well-marked shoulder and a rounded base (Fig. 31.7). In addition, a fragment of a spouted jar with a plain rim, an ovoid body and a rounded base (Fig. 32.1) should be noted. Finally among the closed forms is a spouted jar with a plain rim, a slightly flared neck, an ovoid body and a ring base (Fig. 32.2) that can also be considered as representative.

The repertoire of jars can be securely dated to the Early and Late Akkad periods. Only the type with a globular body, an everted rim, a well-marked shoulder and a rounded base (Fig. 31.4) could perhaps also have been produced during the Early Dynastic IIIb period, although the well-marked shoulder seems again to date it to Akkad times. The interpretation of the spouted jar types (Fig. 32.1 and 32.2) is somewhat different. The latter type (Fig. 32.2), which represents one of the few vases from its established chronological phase that has been found on Tell K, has parallels from sites including Shuruppak (Martin 1988, p. 185 (96 and 97)) and Larsa (Thalmann 2003, Fig. 38.1), where it was found in contexts dated respectively to the Early Dynastic IIIa and the Early Dynastic IIIb eras. The other type of spouted jar (Fig. 32.1), which has been excavated in Abu Salabikh, has been found mainly in Early Dynastic IIIa contexts; with respect to the internal sequence of Abu Salabikh, it seems to disappear abruptly in the subsequent Early Dynastic IIIb period (Moon 1987, p. 128). In Nippur this type of vase was found in burials that date to a post-Early Dynastic IIIa phase, though the Nippur data suggests that this type of vessel was in use in the early part of the post-Early Dynastic IIIa period.

Notwithstanding the many caveats and unresolved issues, the revised analysis of the third-millennium BCE pottery assemblage found on Tell K, based on the data published by Genouillac, is of great interest. Comparisons with the ceramics found during the British Museum team's excavations on Tell A also provide fresh insights. It must be stressed again, however, that the pottery repertoire published by Genouillac did not derive exclusively from Tell K, and even the examples that are attributed to Tell K might in reality have been found elsewhere. The sequencing is therefore affected by a degree of uncertainty that is further compounded by the sparsity of types. Even when a collage of third-millennium ceramic forms from various excavation areas, including Tell K, is taken into account, the resulting assemblage and categorisation of third-millennium pottery shapes that derive from Tello is based on an extremely small number of different types of vessels.

If a chronological analysis of third-millennium BCE activity in Girsu were to be based exclusively on the published findings of Genouillac, the conclusion would be that the occupation of the site from the Jemdet Nasr and Early Dynastic I periods was characterised by the presence of high-quality ware, including polychrome pottery and reserved slipware, together with common ware. A rather evanescent Early Dynastic IIIa period would follow that cannot clearly be defined by ceramic forms, apart from mass-produced pottery and probably a type of spouted jar, since there is nothing in Genouillac's plates that would relate exclusively to this chronological horizon. This is interesting in itself, however, because the Early Dynastic IIIa phase is very well attested in the British Museum team's recent finds from Tell A. As represented in Genouillac's plates, the following Early Dynastic IIIb and Early and Late Akkad periods are quantitatively and consistently characterised by a coherent repertoire that also exhibits the greatest variety of shapes.

The analysis of the pottery assemblages carried out above highlights the predominant role played in the third millennium BCE by mass-produced types, including solid-footed goblets, conical beakers and conical bowls. A comparison of the assemblages also offers a clearer impression of the high-quality ceramics that distinguish the pottery originating from Girsu in the third millennium. Indeed, although prestige pottery makes up only a minimal proportion of the totality when compared with the predominating common ware, it was nevertheless represented both in the Jemdet Nasr and Early Dynastic I periods (as attested by examples of polychrome ceramics and reserved slipware), and in the Early Dynastic IIIa–b and Akkad eras (as attested by the stemmed dishes decorated with schematic and stylised features discussed above), suggesting a rich figurative repertoire. There can be no doubt that the continuity thus evinced suggests a long-standing and enduring manufacturing culture that produced decorated ceramics of exceptional quality, including a wide range of types of pots and offering stands that were mass-produced to be used at ritual offerings and ceremonial feasts. The quality and variety was surely maintained over a long period because the vessels were made to supply the needs of one of ancient Sumer's most important sacred centres, with its significant temple complexes and annexes.

CHAPTER 8

Tell K: Plans and Sections

DESCRIBED BELOW ARE THE PUBLISHED PLANS AND sections of Tell K. Two plans were included in the instalments of Sarzec and Heuzey's *Discoveries in Chaldea* that were issued prior to the appearance of the complete edition in 1912: Plan C (1) shows the Ur-Nanshe Building with some of its immediately surrounding features and installations, while Plan C (2) shows the Lower Construction, both in plan and as a separate elevation, together with the section that details the stratigraphic context of the principal superimposed structures and a few associated deposits. Both printed on the same page, these drawings were made after Sarzec's excavations in 1888 and 1889 (Seasons 5 and 6) and also after his later work in 1899 and 1900 (Seasons 10 and 11). A variant of Plan C (1) appears as Plate 1 in Heuzey's *Chaldean Royal Villa* (1900), where it differs in a number of superficial but noticeable ways from the one in *Discoveries in Chaldea*—for example, the shading is different and in places less informative, and the lettering is not the same. For whatever reason, the version in Heuzey's *Chaldean Royal Villa* was clearly printed from a different original plate. Plan C (2) is also included as Plate 2 in Heuzey's 1900 publication, and in this case the two sets of diagrams are identical and manifestly printed from the same printer's plate, though the title below the frame of the diagram is slightly, but trivially different in Heuzey's *Chaldean Royal Villa*. Also included in Heuzey's earlier book (1900, p. 76) is a supplement (*Plan complémentaire*) to Pls. 1 and 2 that shows the W side of Tell K (specifically the Well of Eanatum, the Enmetena Block and the Enmetena Esplanade). The information contained on Heuzey's Complementary Plan was incorporated into a fuller and more complete overview of the tell that was first published in the final volume of *Discoveries in Chaldea* in 1912 as Plan D. It shows the large, central terrace complex and its environs, paying particular attention to the Ur-Nanshe Building and its related features, as well as the peripheral temple annexes of Eanatum and Enmetena, and the outlying Large and Small Stairways. The discussions below refer to Plan C (1 and 2) and Plan D as published in the 1912 edition of Sarzec and Heuzey's *Discoveries in Chaldea*.

In his *New Excavations at Tello* (1910) Cros published four diagrams, mainly recording the work he carried out in different parts of the mound: a detailed topographical sketch of the whole of Tell K (Cros's Plan B); NE and SW cross-sections of the whole of the mound on two facing pages that together show the relative locations and depths of all the main features, including the two superimposed temples, the Well of Eanatum, the South Trenches (Trenches 9 and 10) and Sarzec's deepest sounding (the reference point for the Sarzec scale of heights that is also included on the sections); and a detailed plan of Cros's excavations on the NE slope of the tell (Trenches 6 and 7), showing the Rectangular Construction, the layout of the Double Stairway in relation to the nearby perpendicular stairway, and the disposition of the water supply network with its circular distribution head. In addition, following his first campaign of 1903, Cros compiled Plan A (1910, p. 4), which shows a topographical overview of Tell K in relation to the surrounding mounds. Finally, Genouillac and Parrot added no new plans to their summarising overview of work carried out at the site.

Sarzec and Heuzey 1912, Plan C (1): The Ur-Nanshe Building

Plan C (1) (Fig. 33) shows the plan of the Ur-Nanshe Building and the finds and structures uncovered around it. Entitled 'Plan of the Ur-Nanshe Building' (*Plan de la construction d'Our-Nina*), it includes a scale bar towards the bottom left, a north-pointing arrow (top centre) and a legend in the bottom right corner. The main temple is illustrated on the left (with some smaller finds to its left); to the right are the building's annexes and some minor additional finds. Built architectural structures (meaning brick-built structures) are indicated with upper-case letters; found objects are labelled with arabic numerals; and lower-case letters are used to mark the find locations of copper figurines and tablets. The principal Ur-Nanshe architectural remains (walls, block-like installations and column bases) are outlined and shaded with diagonal lines. Dotted lines are used to represent dismantled structures, as well as more recent and anomalous remains. Also shown is the brick pavement (F) that abuts onto the NW façade of the building. Devoted exclusively to archaeological discoveries, the plan shows no topographical or other local features.

As described on Plan C (1), the Ur-Nanshe Building is a rectangular structure with no openings that measures 11.1 m × 7.6 m (according to the scale), inside which are two walled rooms (A and B), again with no openings, measuring 4.8 m × 4.8 m (A), and 4.8 m × 2.6 m (B, overall). The unshaded areas inside the building indicate empty spaces in the two rooms, but also around them, as well as in the unshaded SW–NE area between them that, according to the plan, includes a niche, marked C. It should be stressed that when Sarzec excavated the interior areas around and between the two rooms they were actually filled with mud-bricks laid in a herringbone pattern (as detailed above). This is noted explicitly in the text, and the fact that the mud-bricks are replaced on the plan by unshaded empty spaces reflects Heuzey's (and perhaps also Sarzec's) interpretation that rooms A and B were surrounded by corridors.

The inner walls as they appear on the plan are 0.3 m thick and therefore noticeably thinner than the outer ones, which are 0.58 m thick. A shape that is interpreted as a recess or niche (C), measuring 1.47 m × 0.88 m, is depicted along the SE wall of room B. Outside the building on the SW wall, protrusion D, which measures 0.9 m × 0.58 m, is represented by dotted outlines; opposite D, on the NE wall, is another rectangular protrusion (E), also drawn with dotted lines, that measures 1.9 m × 2.3 m. Pavement F extends outwards from the NW façade of the Ur-Nanshe Building for a distance of 9.4 m, and it is the same width as the building (7.5 m). Although it is noted in the text that the pavement was made of square bricks or tiles, that is not clear on the plan, where the tiles appear to be rectangular. South-east of the temple, 2 m from its S corner and 0.58 m to the east, can be seen structure G, referred to as a split basin (*Bassin à refend*) or double cistern, that measures 1.6 m × 1.7 m and is drawn with the same hatched lines as the main constructions. Symmetrically placed, two associated with each of the building's four corners, are eight small squares (H), marked with outlines and hatched interiors, that are identified in the legend as the remains of eight wooden pillars (*Piliers en bois*), though the detailed text confirms that they were in fact brick bases in which some residues of charred wood were found. It is worth pointing out that the lines of the building's façades, if extended, would meet the centres of these square bases rather than their outside edges, and that the bases are all placed at a distance of approximately 4 m from the building, though the precise distances vary slightly, and the pillars aligned with the E and S corners (on the NE and SW sides) are perhaps a little closer.

To the east or north-east of the Ur-Nanshe Building, Plan C (1) shows four structures, all marked with the same hatched lines. Structure I (8.23 m north-east of the NE wall) illustrates a small reservoir or container (also called *Bassin*) that has an attached bitumen-coated platform (J); the joined features are oriented south-west–north-east, with their SE side in line with the SE façade of the building. Further to the east, structure K (15 m north-east and 1.47 m south-east of the building's NE wall) is a second, smaller container that is also attached to a bituminated platform (L) to form another joint structure that is placed on a SE–NW axis (perpendicular to IJ). North-east of the N corner of platform L is a gutter or conduit (M) that is 5.29 m long and situated 16.75 m north-east of the building's NE wall. An arrow drawn along the outside of the NW wall of channel M points out to the north-east to indicate the direction of flow. To the east of channel M there is another gutter or conduit (N) whose N end is 26.5 m north-east of the NE wall of the Ur-Nanshe Building. Channel N is differently oriented from the other water installations in this area, running north-north-west to

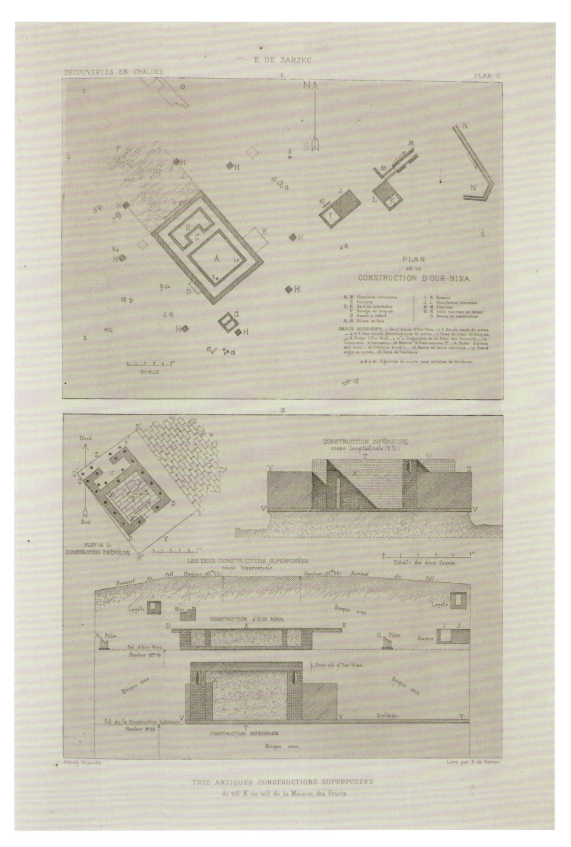

FIGURE 33. Sarzec and Heuzey 1912, Plan C (1): The Ur-Nanshe Building (top). Plan C (2): Plan and Elevation of the Lower Construction, and a Cross-Section of the Central Area of Tell K (bottom).

south-south-east, a direction of flow that is also indicated by a small arrow.

North of pavement F, at the very top of the plan and cut off by its border, is structure O. Drawn with dotted lines, it represents the remains of a construction. On either side of the Ur-Nanshe Building, in line with its NW façade, are two small squarish structures (0.9 m × 1 m), both drawn with dotted lines. The one nearest to the building's SW side is a little more than 1 m away from it (inside the line of the square pillar bases, H–H); the one on the NE side is about 7.5 m away from the building (beyond the H–H line). These structures are not identified on the plan or in the legend, but the section on Plan C (2) suggests that they might be two foundation boxes, marked *Logette* on the left and right sides of the Ur-Nanshe Building, towards the top of the section, just below the summit of the tell. Paired foundation figurines and tablets (a, b, c, d) are indicated around the building near the edges of Plan C (1), where they are shown towards the south-west (a), the north-west (b and c) and the east (d). Details of the locations of finds and foundation figurines and tablets, marked on Plan C (1) relative to the Ur-Nanshe Building are as follows:

Finds
1. 0.3 m north-west of the SE wall
2. 0.3 m north-west of the SE wall
3. 10.3 m north-east of the NE wall
4. 4.11 m south-west of the SW wall
5. 4.11 m south-west and 0.9 m north-west of the SW wall
6. 5.9 m north-west and 2.35 m south-west of the NW wall
7. 3.8 m north-west and 1.17 m south-west of the NW wall
8. 7.9 m north-east and 4.4 m south-east of the NE wall
9. 2.35 m south-west of the SW wall
10. 7.35 m north-east of the NE wall
11. 7.35 m north-east of the NE wall
12. 4.11 m south-east and 3.5 m south-west of the SE wall (5.88 m south of the S corner)
13. 5.3 m south-east and 2.35 m south-west of the SE wall
14. 11.17 m south-west of the SW wall
15. 6.8 m south-west of the SW wall
16. 9.4 m north-east of the NE wall
17. 0.3 m north-west of the NW wall
18. 16.75 m south-east of the SE wall

Figurines and Tablets
a. 13.8 m south-west of the SW wall
b. 12.9 m north-west and 1.14 m south-west of the NW wall
c. 17.6 m north-west of the NW wall
d. 25.3 m east and 3.23 m north of the E corner

Sarzec and Heuzey 1912, Plan C (2): Plan and Elevation of the Lower Construction; Cross-Section of the Central Area of Tell K

Plan C (2) (Fig. 33), which is printed under Plan C (1) on the same page, is in three parts that show a plan of the Lower Construction (top left), a reconstructed elevation of the Lower Construction (top right), and below them, filling the bottom half of the plate, a cross-section of the tell that details the stratigraphic positions of the two main buildings and selected remains. This cross-section is the most important guide to the stratigraphy of the tell as Sarzec excavated and interpreted it.

Plan C (2): Plan of the Lower Construction

The small plan of the Lower Construction in the top left corner of Plan C (2) features a north-pointing arrow along the left side of the diagram, the title of the drawing in the lower left-hand corner and a scale bar to the right, below the illustration. Salient details are marked with capital letters, while arabic numerals are used to label three structures inside the larger of the building's two rooms. The walls are outlined and shaded with hatched lines, while the pavements are outlined and left unshaded. Inside the larger SE room (T) is a wall (XX') that is outlined without shading, as is the rectangular structure or platform P'Q'R'S', measuring 16.8 m × 12.20 m, that runs around the walls; the principal NW and SE sides of this outer platform are marked Z (on the NW side) and Y (on the SE side), respectively. Lines Y and Z demarcate the width of the pavement that extends underneath the block, as can also be seen on the elevation to the right of the plan, where the pavement is marked V–V.

Placed within the perimeter of the platform defined by the outer block and the pavement, but with a slightly different orientation, the building itself is labelled at its corners, PQRS. The distances between the corners of the building and the labelled NW and SE faces (Z, Y) of the lines of the outer block and pavement are variable: 1.17 m from Q to the nearest point on the NW (Z) end of the platform; 0.88 m from P to the NW (Z) end; 2.65 m from corner S to the SE (Y) end of the block; and 2.35 m from R to the SE (Y) end. Whereas the platform is placed on a NW–SE axis, the building deviates by about three degrees from that, creating the gap that can be seen between its S corner (R) and the Q'R' line of the platform.

The rectangular building PQRS measures 11.66 m × 9.16 m (according to the scale), and it is oriented approximately north-west–south-east, but just off axis in relation to the platform indicated by the outer block P'Q'R'S', as noted. It contains a NW room (U) and a SE room (T) that measure 4.4 m × 1.47 m and 4.7 m × 4.4 m, respectively. Both rooms have an opening or doorway that is 2.1 m wide, and the building's walls are 1.26 m thick. Equally distributed inside the hatched outlines of the walls are fifteen small black dots that represent bitumen pockets that were found set vertically into the brickwork, and it is noteworthy that no bitumen pockets are located in the building's S and E corners (labelled R and S). Four additional black dots can be seen in the unshaded area of the outer block in front of room U (between U and the platform's NW side, Z), and three more are placed inside room U: two against the SE wall, approximately in line with the ones in the walls on the two sides of the door, and a third approximately in the middle of room U's SW wall. Inside room T there is a pavement that is laid along the building's NE–SW axis, and another substantial pavement (marked V on the plan) is shown extending out to the north-east, away from the NE edge of the outer platform (P'S'). The slabs that make up pavement V are laid along the same NW–SE axis as the outer block, and it extends 5.88 m out to the north-east, where the label V is marked on its broken NE edge. Inside the building, room T contains four structures: the wall (XX') that is mentioned above; a cross-shaped element (labelled 1) towards the N corner; a star-shaped constellation of triangular bricks (2) to the south-east of the cross; and a stele (3) that screens the inside opening of the door.

Plan C (2): Elevation of the Lower Construction

The elevation of the Lower Construction is shown to the right of the plan just discussed. Below it, again to the right, is a scale bar that defines the ratio for both this elevation and the cross-section below. The elevation is drawn looking towards the south-west: the NW (Z) end of platform P'Q'R'S' is on the right-hand side; the SE (Y) end is on the left. The pavement that extends out from the NE face of the building is indicated by the two Vs on either side of the floor. Diagonal hatched shading is used to pick out the placement of P'Q'R'S' around the building, and the height of this external structure can now be seen. The deposits below the Lower Construction (and below the pavement) are marked with looser hatched lines that are broken and intermittent. The walls of the building are shown to be made of thirty courses of brickwork, while the deposits that were found covering the building are not illustrated in this reconstruction. Inside room T there is a narrow structure to the left (with its top surface angled down from right to left) that represents a side view of the stele (No. 3 on the plan). Embedded in the partition wall that divides the two rooms (T and U) can be seen the vase-shaped bituminated capsule that is shown on the plan as a centrally placed black dot. Here drawn to scale, it descends to a depth of 0.84 m inside the wall, while its maximum width is 0.28 m, and the opening at the top is 0.14 m. These measurements differ very slightly from those given in the text.

Plan C (2): Cross-Section of the Central Area of Tell K

At the bottom of Plan C (2) is the cross-section of Tell K that details the superimposition of the two buildings: the Ur-Nanshe Building above and the Lower Construction underneath. The scale bar for this section and the elevation just discussed is shown on the top right. Drawn looking towards the north-west, the section outlines the top of the tell (*Sommet du Tell*), which is highest in the centre, and slopes down gently towards the north-east (on the right) and slightly more sharply towards the south-west (on the left). The undifferentiated deposits above the building in the uppermost part of the tell are described with the same loosely broken hatched lines as are used to show comparable material in the elevation. The buildings and installations found within the tell are shaded with much tighter diagonal hatching that produces a dark grey effect. In some instances details of the courses of brickwork or other coverings are indicated, while the wooden remains that were found in the pillars (H) are shaded with vertical lines, and the mass of ash and burnt material found inside the two buildings is rendered with an irregular texture of fine dots. The areas inside the building between the outer and inner walls are filled with the same textured markings as the rooms, suggesting that they were also filled with ashy deposits. As also noted at the beginning of this chapter, however, this reflects Heuzey's idea that those supposed volumes were corridors that ran around and between the two rooms, even though they were in fact filled with mud-bricks that were laid in a zigzag pattern.

Lines of dashes demarcate the limits of the excavation (or perhaps just the limits of the section) on both sides of the diagram, and the same lines are used to note the two vitally important base levels below the Ur-Nanshe Building and the Lower Construction. The reference heights of these base levels as well as the height of the top of the tell are logged and highlighted with vertical arrows (two for the summit, and one for each of the levels beneath the buildings). The height given for the top of the tell (17 m) is measured with respect to the depth of the deepest sounding excavated by Sarzec: the point below the tell at which he reached the water table, which is suggested here by the framing line at the bottom of the plan, from where an arrow points upwards to the base of the Lower Construction. This is the baseline from which the heights given for levels of the two buildings (12.83 m and 8.48 m, respectively) are measured. Five annotations, which are sporadically placed alongside and beneath each of the two buildings, inform the reader that the tell was made of mud-bricks (*Brique crue*).

The section records the locations and stratigraphic positions of a few significant items. First, are the two foundation boxes (*Logettes*) that are placed under the summit to the left and right. Although they are not specifically marked as such on Plan C (1), they are probably the two unlabelled square structures, drawn with dotted lines, that are shown on Plan C (1) to the north-east and south-west of the Ur-Nanshe Building. Just below and to the right of the base of the SW foundation box (which is slightly lower than its NE counterpart) can be seen the stepped fragment of a wall (*Mur*), which is referred to in passing in the text as an isolated corner. Its SW face is closely aligned with the SW face of the SW wall of the Ur-Nanshe Building, which is situated about 0.4 m beneath it and 3 m below the top of the tell. As the section clearly illustrates, the Ur-Nanshe Building was levelled and covered with a bitumen layer, which is also shown covering protrusions D and E that jut out on the building's two sides. On top of the bitumen layer Sarzec also found a bed of fired bricks, but they are not shown on the section. The fact that protrusions D and E seem to be floating, with nothing to support them, shows that their base was significantly higher than the reference height of the base of the building (12.83 m), but also that they were installed just below the levelling horizon. This would suggest that they were associated with a new floor level that was part of a reconstruction phase, though Sarzec and Heuzey do not say that. As can be seen in the photo of protrusion D (Pl. 54 (2); Fig. 40 below), the protrusions were not found to be coated with bitumen. Combined with the fact that the bed of bricks on the levelling above the temple's principal walls was not recorded, this indicates some inaccuracy in the way the data was translated into the section in this area.

Twelve preserved courses of brickwork are marked on the section below the bituminated level, and the building is placed on a floor or pavement that (measured by the scale on the plan) is another two courses thick, though no bricks are illustrated. Nevertheless, this seems to be in accord with the text, which notes that the levelled building was made up of fourteen courses. The section indicates that the levelled walls are 1.12 m high, which is also the figure noted in the report. The base of the floor on which the building rests is shown to be 4.1 m below the top of the tell, and at this level two of the pillars (H) are shown, including some more substantial wooden remains. Although, as noted above, Heuzey explicitly says that the wooden pillars were square, the drawing seems to indicate that they might in fact have been round, which would also seem logical, though whether enough of their charred remains survived to confirm their actual shape is questionable. On the right of the section, to the north-east, the consolidated cistern and bituminated platform (IJ) can be seen, with its joint base shown slightly higher (0.3 m) than the bottoms of the pillars and the base level of the Ur-Nanshe Building.

Further down, 0.7 m under the Ur-Nanshe Building and 4.8 m below the top of the tell, is a series of six superimposed layers that are illustrated with horizontal lines. They record two extremely thin deposits, one on the top and another at the bottom, perhaps representing bitumen, together with a noticeably thicker line second from the bottom, and three others. These layers seal off the Lower Construction directly below it. Vase-shaped bitumen capsules are shown vertically in the SW and NE walls of room T, and the walls themselves are 2.85 m high, with thirty courses of bricks illustrated between the layers that cap the top of the Lower Construction and the pavement (*Dallage*) on which it stands, which is pavement V, as noted on the section. The enveloping outer structure (P′Q′R′S′ on the plan of the Lower Construction on Plan C (2)) is shown outside the two principal walls to a height of 2.13 m; also shown is wall XX′, inside room T, which reaches a height of 2.27 m, made up of twenty-three courses of bricks. Under the Lower Construction is pavement V, which is labelled on both sides of the building. It extends out on the right (to the north-east), where it is cut off by the line of dashes that frames the section. Pavement V rests on the mud-brick ground 8.48 m above the bottom of the deepest sounding and 8.52 m below the top of the tell.

Sarzec and Heuzey 1912, Plan D: General Plan of Tell K

Plan D (Fig. 34), which presents a more extensive picture of Tell K, including, as its title announces, structures relating to the time of Ur-Nanshe and 'his dynasty' (*Le Tell de la Maison-des-Fruits à l'époque d'Our-Nina et de sa dynastie*), is the only plan made from the information collected by Sarzec that offers such a detailed wider view. It features a north-pointing arrow in the upper left-hand corner and a scale bar at the bottom, left of centre, where the main terrace is cut off by the edge of the drawing. The landscape around the excavations is shaded with grey watercolour, which contrasts with

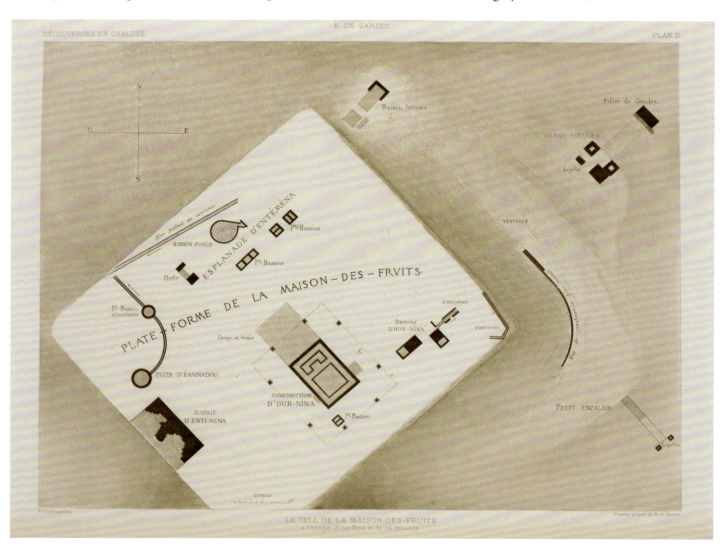

FIGURE 34. Sarzec and Heuzey 1912, Plan D: General Plan of Tell K.

the large squarish unshaded area that contains the principal buildings and installations. Oriented north-east–south-west, and showing the Ur-Nanshe Building, the Enmetena Block, the Well of Eanatum and other installations, this unshaded square represents the part of the mound that was judged to be the upper platform of the tell. As is discussed with respect to one of Sarzec's photos (Pl. 58 bis (2); Fig. 50 below), Heuzey compiled this plan from excavation notes after Sarzec's death (Sarzec and Heuzey 1912, p. 423), and it contains some inaccuracies, seemingly limited to some of the peripheral structures shown in the photo.

The carefully applied descriptive shading at the edges of the Ur-Nanshe platform is noticeably darker around the arc of the E corner, but much lighter between the nearby 'more recent' wall (*Mur de construction plus récente*) and the Small Stairway with its two foundation boxes (*Logettes*). The band of lighter grey continues up and around to encompass a large bituminated cistern or reservoir (*Bassin bitumé*) in the north, labelled J (not to be confused with the double installation IJ on Plan C (1)), which is very lightly shaded indeed, and the lighter grey band bulges out to the north-east to take in the top of the Large Stairway. Otherwise, the differentiations in shading, which are slight but nevertheless expressive, describe some of the tell's topographic characteristics, though they were in fact reconstructed later, not recorded at the time. They show the Large Stairway ascending the side of a slope, where it reaches a landing, while the Small Stairway, which climbs the continuation of the same slope, leads up to the lightly shaded level that arcs around the tell's E corner. Cistern J is also located on a rise that is separated from the main upper platform by a narrow depression that is illustrated with heavier shading; similar darker shading suggests relief all around the main platform, but less prominently towards the north-west and the south-west.

The walls on Plan D are shown in black and also in dark grey watercolour shading. In a few instances further details are illustrated, among which are the paving on the floor of the Oval Reservoir, the flights of steps on the Large and Small Stairways, some texture inside the Well of Eanatum (though it is not clear what this represents) and a thick, irregular mass of bricks on the SW side of the Enmetena Block. The eight wooden pillars (H) around the Ur-Nanshe Building are joined with dotted lines to indicate a consolidated structure, doubtless suggestive of the covered walkway hypothesised by Heuzey. As gauged by the scale on Plan D, the Ur-Nanshe Building measures 10.6 m × 7.5 m, while the surrounding area demarcated by the eight pillars measures 20 m × 16.9 m. The pillars themselves are placed between 4 m and 4.6 m from the building's corners (distances that again vary slightly from those given elsewhere). The pavement (F on Plan C (1)) extends 8.75 m out to the north-west, and its edges are shown as though the brickwork formed an unbroken rectangle.

Standing 21.25 m south-west of the Ur-Nanshe Building, the Enmetena Block measures 11.9 m × 6.9 m, while just to the north-west of it, at a distance of 2.5 m, is the Well of Eanatum, which has an outer diameter of 3.75 m, as it appears on the plan. A narrow gutter or channel emerges from the well's NE side, heading out to the north-east before curving to the north-west, where it meets a small circular cistern or tank (*Bassin circulaire*), with an outer diameter of 2.5 m. Issuing from the NW side of the circular cistern, the channel continues out towards the north-west (the direction of flow indicated by an arrow), where it almost meets a wall that supports a markedly wider conduit that was perhaps interpreted as an aqueduct (*Mur portant un caniveau*) that runs east-north-east–west-south-west (with the direction of flow again expressly indicated). The length of this wider supporting wall and waterway is 28 m. As noted above, on Heuzey's Complementary Plan (1900, p. 76), where the installations are labelled with the same wording, the narrow channel issuing from the small circular tank is shown meeting the aqueduct.

A series of installations can be seen on the SE side of the wider wall and channel, at a distance of 18.75 m north-west of the Ur-Nanshe Building. On the left of this ensemble, as we look at the plan, there is a gate measuring 4 m × 1.9 m, with an opening that is 1.7 m wide; and to the north-east of the gate is the Oval Reservoir, measuring 5.9 m × 4.4 m (overall), with three smaller containers or cisterns to the south-east of it (below it on the plan). To the south-west (on the left as we look), the longest of the three smaller containers, which has three compartments (or open tanks), measures 4.4 m × 1.25 m (overall). The other two both measure 1.87 m × 1.87 m, and they both have two compartments, which are, however, differently aligned in the two structures: the two compartments in the cistern on the south-west (on the left as we look) are oriented north-east–south-west, while the compartments in the one to the north-east of that are oriented north-west–south-east.

Two more water installations (*Bassins d'Our-Nina*: IJ and KL on Plan C (1)) can be seen on the unshaded upper platform, 8.1 m north-east of the E corner of the Ur-Nanshe Building, and both are made up of a cistern (a container or cavity) that is joined to a solid block with a flat top surface coated with bitumen. Solid black and dark grey watercolouring are used to show their component parts. The installation closest to the building (IJ on Plan C (1)), which measures 4.4 m × 1.87 m, is oriented north-east–south-west; the other one (KL on Plan C (1)), which measures 3.1 m × 1.87 m, is oriented north-west–south-east. To the north-west of them, and apparently connected to the latter (KL on Plan C (1)), there is a gutter or conduit (labelled *caniveau*), 5 m long, that flows towards the north-east, as indicated by an arrow. To the north-east and east of this, on the edge of the upper terrace, is another, three-part waterway (also labelled *caniveau*) that runs north-west–south-east then north-north-east–south-south-west, before finally heading west. The three parts measure 7.5 m, 2.5 m and 2.5 m, respectively, giving a total length of 12.5 m.

Adjacent to the three-part channel is the darker band of shading that illustrates the slope around the E corner of the upper terrace. On the E fringe of that darker band are the remains of the wall described as 'more recent' (*Mur de construction plus récente*) that apparently follows the line of the slope. Starting at the top (as we look), it runs 12.5 m in a south-easterly direction, before bending towards the south and then continuing towards the south-west in a long curve that also measures 12.5 m (or a little more). As is clarified below with reference to Sarzec's photo of this curving construction (Pl. 58 bis (2); Fig. 50 below), which confirms that it is incorrectly drawn and labelled, it should be stressed that Plan D does not present this structure accurately. To the south-east of the wall referred to as 'more recent', on the other side of the adjacent band of lighter shading, is the Small Stairway, with the flight of steps closest to the tell measuring 5 m in length, and the pavement to the south-east that leads to the steps shown as being 5.6 m long. On the SE edge of the approach to the Small Stairway, flanking it on its two sides, are two square foundation boxes (*Logettes*), each measuring 0.6 m × 0.6 m. The top of the flight of steps on the Small Stairway is situated 46.25 m east of the E corner of the Ur-Nanshe Building.

The architectural features associated with the Large Stairway lie 56.25 m north-east of the Ur-Nanshe Building. Closest to the building are two brick structures, probably foundation boxes, labelled *Logettes*: the larger one to the south-east measuring 3.1 m × 2.5 m, and the smaller one to the north-west of that measuring 1.87 m × 0.93 m. Just to the north-east of these boxes are two squarish structures, each measuring 2.2 m × 1.87 m (overall, according to the scale bar), with lightly watercoloured squares in their centres. The flight of stairs itself, which numbers eighteen steps, is 7.5 m long and 3.1 m wide. At the base of the stairs stands the Pillar of Gudea, flanked by a narrow wall that abuts onto its SW face; shaded dark grey, the wall is 5 m (l) × 0.6 m (t), while the composite pillar, which is shown as a black rectangle, measures 4 m × 1.87 m. South-west of the two foundation boxes, at a distance of 12 m, where the continuation of the Large Stairway might have ended in the band of lighter shading along the NE side of the tell, can be seen a faintly outlined structure that is drawn as a rectangle of narrow doubled lines and labelled 'traces' (*Vestiges*). It measures 3.1 m × 3.1 m, although its NW façade is not illustrated and was probably not preserved.

Finally, in the N corner of the tell are three grey-shaded structures, all with the same NE–SW orientation, that are placed 39.3 m north-north-east of the N corner of the Ur-Nanshe Building. Furthest to the north (towards the top of the plan) is a bituminated cistern or tank (*Bassin bitumé*), labelled J, that measures 5 m × 2.2 m. Its NE face is edged with a wall (or a similar structure) that is coloured black on the plan and wraps around the cistern's N and NE corners. South-west of this bitumen-coated cistern are two similarly shaded blocks that are adjacent but not aligned: one is square and measures 2.2 m × 2.2 m, while the other, which is rectangular, measures 2.2 m × 0.6 m.

Cros 1910, Plan A: Plan of the Principal Excavation Area of Tello (Campaign of 1903)

Cros's Plan A (Fig. 35) provides an overview of the site that includes the main areas that Cros excavated in the first half of 1903 (Season 12). The plan, which was drawn by Cros himself (as confirmed by the caption on the bottom right), has no north-pointing arrow, but instead has 'North' and 'South' (*Nord, Sud*) printed in brackets centrally above and below. On the top left, outside the plan's frame, are the words 'Chaldean Mission' (*Mission de Chaldée*), presumably indicating the official nature of Cros's work, and on the top right is the

100 The Mound of the House of the Fruits

FIGURE 35. Cros 1910, Plan A: The Principal Excavation Area of Tello.

label, Plan A. Centrally, below the frame at the bottom of the plan is the title: *Plan de la Partie Principale des Fouilles de Tello (Campagne de 1903)*. Perhaps surprisingly, Plan A does not contain a scale bar, though Cros must surely have drawn it to scale. The general topography of the entire area is described with widely spaced contour lines, amid which are four mounds: the Mound of the Palace (*Tell du Palais*) to the north-west (top left), which is depicted without any archaeological details; the Mound of the Tablets (*Tell des Tablettes*) to the south-east (bottom right); the Great Tell (*Grand Tell*) to the south; and spreading out over most of the central area, especially towards the west (on the left), is the Mound of the House of the Fruits (*Tell de la Maison des fruits*), or Tell K.

Tell K is very elaborately drawn, with detailed contour lines recording the shapes of the sides of the raised areas. The central terrace shows the Well of Eanatum (*Puits d'Eannadou*) on the W side (to the left); to the east of that is a neat-looking, steep-sided rectangular rise that is presumably the spoil heap that occupied the location of the dismantled Ur-Nanshe Building and Lower Construction, neither of which are marked. Just to the north of the steep rectangle is Cros's Trench 5, and to the north-east of that are his Trenches 6 and 7. To the north of Trenches 6 and 7, embedded in the sides of the mound, are Trenches 2 and 4, and still further to the north of them are Trenches 1 and 3, which are close to the Mound of the Palace. A tiny fringe inside the border of the trenches shows the boundaries within which they were dug, but no depths are indicated. Despite that, Cros's meticulous approach is especially apparent in the way the trenches are drawn because particular installations are illustrated, for example in Trenches 6 and 7, where the water supply network and newly uncovered stairways can be seen. The unshaded expanse in the central area of the mound (around the well, the steep spoil heap and Trench 5) presumably indicates the general height of the tell as Cros found it in 1903: the level defined by him as the Sarzec Esplanade. Also in the central area (on the Sarzec Esplanade) can be seen four of the archaeological witnesses (*Témoins*) that were left unexcavated by Sarzec to provide height indicators. Three are on the NE side of the rectangular crater and the fourth is to the east or north-east of that, close to Trench 6.

Two features of interest on Plan A are the rectangular blocks of earth (fringed with outer lines to show that they are elevations rather than trenches) on the SE side of the principal area, and the elongated strips to the south of the main area. Thirteen of the rectangular blocks that were prepared by Sarzec but not excavated by him (as discussed above) can be seen to the east of the E corner of the main spoil heap, including one triangular one that has seemingly been reshaped to allow the removal of spoil through the access point beneath it (to the south-east), and one extremely large one at the bottom of the set. The long strips and the steep, irregular mound to the south and south-west of the rectangular blocks are presumably more spoil heaps that had perhaps had openings cut through them after they were deposited. It is probable that they were partly formed of spoils removed from the unshaded central area of the Sarzec Esplanade, which had been dramatically truncated before Cros's arrival, and by this date the removed piles of earth were significant features of the landscape, as the plan shows. When Plan A was drawn, the ground forming the Sarzec Esplanade between the SE side of the steep spoil heap in the centre of the mound and the elongated strips to the south of it (below it on the plan) had not yet been excavated by Cros.

Cros 1910, Plan B: Plan of the Excavations in the Vicinity of the Mound of the House of the Fruits

Cros's detailed plan (Fig. 36) of the excavations that targeted Tell K features a north-pointing arrow in the top right corner and a scale bar at the bottom on the right. Extending the view significantly beyond the Ur-Nanshe Building, it shows the location of Cros's excavation trenches, which are numbered and mostly also named, together with the spoil heaps (*Terres provenant des fouilles*), which are drawn with loose but informative contour lines. Towards the north and north-west (at the top of the plan, in the middle and on the left) two large spoil heaps are separated by an excavated area, Trenches 2 and 4. The S edge of the NW heap (the left one of the two) marks the N or NW limit of the excavation area around the Ur-Nanshe Building; it is bounded on its SW and SSW edges by a collection of smaller heaps, and on its S, SE and E edges by a cluster of four heaps. The elongated heap to the south is curiously dissected into six parts, divided by neat-looking cuts. Within the centrally excavated area, where the Ur-Nanshe Building is prominently labelled (*Maison des Fruits*), there are two spoil heaps: a rectangular one oriented south-west–north-east that incorporates the building (which by this time had been dismantled, though its location is indicated by dashed lines), and a smaller one to the north-east, between Trench 5 (the North Trench) and Trenches 6 and 7, which together form the N corner of the excavation area. As just noted, lines of double dashes show the original position of the building below the rectangular heap. South and south-west of the Ur-Nanshe Building are Trenches 9 and 10 (the South Trenches) and Trench 8 (the West Trench), while the unnumbered trench around and adjacent to the Well of Eanatum (*Puits d'Eannandou*) is named the Trench by the Well (*Tranchée près du Puits*).

Between the spoil heaps to the east and south-east are eight of the rectangular blocks of earth that were formed by the shallow preparatory trenches excavated by Sarzec in his final season on the tell (as discussed above). Oriented northeast–south-west, and drawn with lines of dashes (partly contoured to indicate their heights), they are identified as 'Rectangles left by the previous excavations' (*Rectangles laissés par les anciennes fouilles*). To the north and west of the rectangular blocks of earth are the remains of the Large Stairway (*Large Escalier (Vestiges)*), the Pillar of Gudea (*Pilier de Goudéa*) and a foundation box (*Logette*), all drawn with lines of dashes. An adjacent mud-brick block (labelled *Briques crues*) is rendered in more detail. To the south-west of this group, next to the westernmost rectangular block, can be seen a gutter or channel (*Caniveau*), oriented approximately west–east, with an arrow to show the direction of flow. West of this, along the edge of the central spoil heap that stands above the rectangles that indicate the Ur-Nanshe Building, are three small unidentified circular structures that indicate the locations of *Témoins* or archaeological witnesses, as confirmed by comparison with Cros's Plan A (above).

The remains uncovered by Cros in the NE Trenches 6 and 7 are also illustrated. They include the Double Stairway (*Double Escalier*), the water supply and drainage network

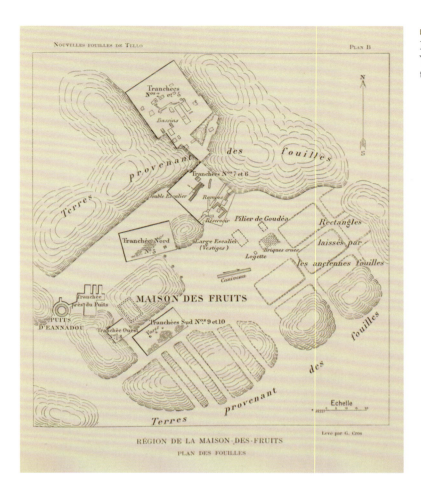

FIGURE 36. Cros 1910, Plan B: Excavations in the Vicinity of the House of the Fruits.

with its circular distribution head and associated water channels (*Rampes*, as Cros labels them), and the rectangular water collection point (*Réservoir*) with its missing SW wall. Mudbrick tiling is shown on the floors of the North Trenches (Trench 5) and the South Trenches (Trenches 9 and 10), where three *Vases* are marked. These are the bituminated cavities (described above) that Cros discovered: two at a Sarzec height of 8.1 m, and the third at 7.4 m.

Cros 1910: The SW and NE Sections of Tell K

Cros produced two main cross-sections of Tell K (Fig. 37): a SW Section showing the principal Mound of the House of the Fruits (as Cros consistently calls it), and a NE Section showing the area around the Large Staircase and the Pillar of Gudea, entitled the Tell of the Pillars (*Tell des Piliers*).

Printed across a double-page spread (pp. 70–1), they form two sides of a single view, intended to be stitched together, so to speak, to provide a panoramic record of the tell's interior. When the sections are correlated with Cros's Plan B, they plot a continuous diagonal line from the plan's SW corner (a little above the spoil heap on the bottom left of Plan B) that runs up through the principal remains towards the top right (NE) corner, approximately meeting the bottom (S) end of the north-pointing arrow on Plan B. Both sections therefore look from the south-east (the bottom right of Plan B) towards the north-west (the top left of Plan B). Scale bars showing proportionate lengths in metres are printed at the bottom of each section (the ratio is, of course, the same on both), while the vertical bars on the extreme left and right edges of the SW and NE Sections, respectively, indicate Sarzec heights from point zero at the bottom of Sarzec's deepest sounding. The original undulating top of the tell, which

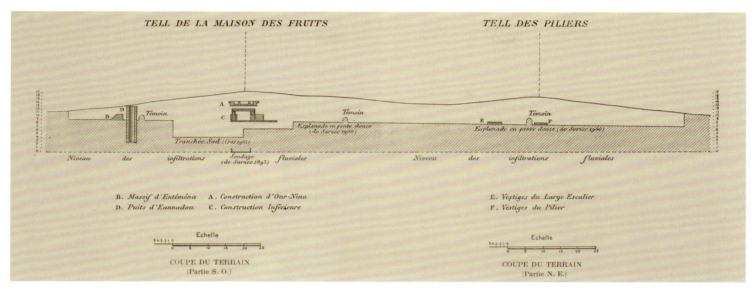

FIGURE 37. Cros 1910, SW and NE Sections of Tell K.

by Sarzec's final season (1900) had been drastically reduced to the levels indicated on the plan by the Sarzec Esplanade (labelled *Esplanade en pente douce (de Sarzec 1900)*), is drawn with a clean curving line; the architectural remains of the two buildings (previously dismantled by Sarzec) are shown floating, as it were, inside the tell on the SW Section, leaving their former positions and stratigraphic relationships to be inferred from the vertical scale bar on the left. The profiles of the deeper excavation horizons represented by the Sarzec Esplanade are rendered diagrammatically with rectilinear lines, below which unexcavated deposits are shaded with diagonal hatching. Lines of dashes at the bases of the two sections show the depth at which the water table was reached (*Niveau des infiltrations fluviales*), while the position of the deepest trench dug by Sarzec, labelled *Sondage (de Sarzec 1893)*, is noted beneath the two buildings on the main part of the tell on the SW Section.

The SW Section confirms that the tell's highest point was originally above the Ur-Nanshe Building, 17 m above the water table. The top surface of the tell on this SW Section is shown sloping away to the south-west (on the left), where it is cut off at a Sarzec height of a little more than 11 m. To the north-east (on the right of the same section), where the gradient is less pronounced, the original summit of the tell is cut off by the edge of the diagram at a Sarzec height of 13.5 m. It can be seen from the continuation of the summit's outline on the NE Section, however, that it formerly rose to a height of 15.5 m above the Pillar of Gudea before falling away again to 10 m on the NE side (on the extreme right of the NE Section). Prominent in the upper, central part of the SW Section is the Ur-Nanshe Building (A), with its base just below 13 m. To the left of this is the Well of Eanatum (D), the top of which is drawn just below the original surface of the mound at a height of 13 m. As depicted on the section, the well descends to a Sarzec height of 2.5 m, and it is shown to be made up of twenty-four courses. To the left of the well is the Enmetena Block (B), with its top at 10.5 m and its base at 9 m, which is the cut-off point for Sarzec's excavations in this area; the damaged, crumbling SW façade of the block is represented by the angled wall on the left. As considered in detail below with respect to the Enmetena Block, the SW Section gives a misleading and inaccurate impression of the height of the well as it was in 1903, when Cros first saw the site, and also of the relative heights of the well and the adjacent block, both of which rose to about the same Sarzec height of 10.5 m, though the well was probably a little higher. To the right of the well is one of Sarzec's height markers (*Témoin*), three of which are shown on the two sections. As for the *Témoins* noted on Plan B (above), these archaeological witnesses or baulks (essentially undisturbed piles of earth) were purposely left unexcavated to establish height benchmarks across the tell (see Cros 1910, pp. 71–2).

The Lower Construction (C) is shown below the Ur-Nanshe Building on the SW Section, with its base at a depicted height of about 8.5 m and its uppermost surface levelled and capped at 12 m. Below that, the trenching horizon descends to two different depths: the higher of the two trenches lies at 7 m, which accords with Sarzec and Heuzey's statement (1912, p. 415) that Sarzec extended his principal trench to a depth of 1.5 m below the Lower Construction; the deeper trench to the left of that indicates the South Trenches (*Tranchées Sud*, or Trenches 9 and 10) that are labelled on the section as having been dug by Cros in 1905, and they descend to a Sarzec height of 4 m. In the centre, beneath the two buildings at the bottom of the SW Section, is Sarzec's deepest sounding, which was dug in 1893 and extended down to the water table. To the right of the buildings (also on the SW Section), at a height of 9 m, is the gently sloping Sarzec Esplanade (excavated in 1900), above which can be seen another of Sarzec's height markers (*Témoin*). The NE Section shows the continuation of the Sarzec Esplanade, and in particular how it gradually fell away to a height of 7 m on the NE edge of the tell (the right-hand side of the NE Section). This section also shows the remains (*Vestiges*) of the Large Stairway (E) and of the Pillar of Gudea (F), which are both recorded at a height of 7.5 m. Between them stands the third of Sarzec's three height markers (*Témoin*), which is also marked on Cros's Plan A, but not on Plan B. The witnesses to the right of the main structures on the SW Section might perhaps be associated with one of three marked on the NE side of the main part of Tell K on Cros's Plan A, but the viewpoint makes this difficult to establish. The one on the left of the structures on the NE Section is perhaps the mound seen in Sarzec's photo, Pl. 54 (1) (Fig. 39 below).

Cros 1910, Plan C: The Double Stairway and the Water Supply Network

Cros's Plan C (Fig. 38), which is a detailed overview of the excavations around the Double Stairway and water supply network (called 'bituminated ramps', or *Rampes bitumées*), features a scale bar in the bottom right-hand corner, a legend to explain the labelled installations (bottom left) and a north-pointing arrow at the top on the left, though as the plan is south-facing, the arrow actually points downwards. On the more general plan of Tell K (Cros's Plan B) these excavations, which are to the north-east of the Ur-Nanshe Building, are called Trenches 6 and 7.

The limits of the excavations are demarcated by a wavy, perhaps scalloped border that is elaborated with radiating sets of short dashes on the curves to illustrate the slopes. Similar sets of short, straight lines are used on the outlines of the excavated architectural remains, probably to suggest that deeper excavations were carried out in their immediate vicinity. In the NW area of the plan (bottom right) can be seen two parallel flights of stairs (C and C'): the more extended one (C) featuring twenty-five steps; the shorter one (C') showing thirteen steps leading up to a brick pavement (E) that is described in the legend as an 'underground pavement' (*Pavage souterrain*). A narrow gap between the paired flights of stairs seems to be filled with a course of bricks that follows the angle of ascent and, according to the plan, is not stepped, though Cros's photo contradicts this (View No. 1; Fig. 55 below). Perpendicular to the Double Stairway is another wide, but short flight of stairs (D) that contains seven steps. On the SW side of the brick pavement (E) are some narrow walls (F), judged to be the remains of dwellings; some short lines of wall on the NW side of the pavement might be intended to form parts of the same ensemble.

The principal arteries (B) of the elaborate construction of bituminated channels (*Rampes bitumées*) that form the water supply and drainage network are situated on the SE side of the stairways and illustrated in such detail that the individual bricks are clearly visible. The network is made up of a long, well-preserved central channel oriented towards the north-east; the broken remains (below) of a channel facing north, another short stretch of which can be seen on the NE side of the Double Stairway; and the scant remains of what appears to be a channel facing east towards the top of the diagram. These three waterways meet at a round structure (the circular distribution head) at the S end of the excavations, and from there a fourth channel extends out towards the south-west. The explanatory note and arrow on the plan indicate the direction of the Well of Eanatum, but whether this channel was actually associated with the well is doubtful.

On the SE side of the set of channels that make up the water supply network is the Rectangular Construction (A), here described as a 'reservoir' (*Réservoir*), with three substantial walls forming all or part of three sides of a slightly oblique rectangle that is oriented north-east–south-west. Its NE wall is pierced with an opening (offset towards the partial rectangle's N corner) that is blocked inside the structure by a narrow wall, directly behind which can be seen a slightly

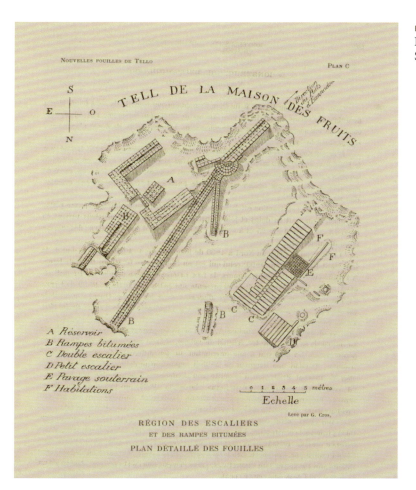

FIGURE 38. Cros 1910, Plan C: Stairways and Water Supply Network.

misaligned rectangular block (5 bricks × 4 bricks) that is oriented north-north-east–south-south-west. Outside the reservoir, on its NE side, are some parts of another bituminated channel (B), also oriented north-north-east–south-south-west, which has a squarish block at its SW end (closest to the opening in the NE wall of the reservoir), one corner of which branches out along the channel's SE wall. On the plan the installation seems to finish with a shallow curved wall at its NE end, but the text confirms that at this point it was covered with a domed top as it disappeared below the remains of yet another channel that was situated above it. The relative position of this final channel is not entirely clear on the plan, but the text confirms that it was higher and more recent than the domed end of the one below. The two have the same orientation, but the water-carrying bed of the higher, narrower channel, which is placed a little to the south-east, is not aligned with the water-carrying part of the wider channel beneath it.

Cros 1910, Cross-Section of the Double Stairway and the Older Stairways Below

Cros produced a schematic representation of the Double Stairway (slightly misleadingly called the *Grand Escalier* on the cross-section) and three older flights of stairs that were uncovered at different levels beneath it (not reproduced here). This is the flight of stairs close to the water supply network on Cros's Plan B, and it should not be confused with the Large Stairway uncovered near the Pillar of Gudea by Sarzec. The Double Stairway on the top of the slope contains twenty-five steps, of which the bottom three (which are a little wider as we look at them) have slightly deeper treads than the ones above. The stairway below that includes eighteen steps, several of which are two or three bricks deep.

The deepest flight of stairs is made up of two distinct tiers that probably represent two phases of construction. The top tier of the two contains ten steps, the eighth of which (counting from top to bottom) is five bricks deep, with the larger drop possibly signalling that there is a step missing at this point. There is a gap below the tenth step, and below that is an additional step made of three bricks that seems to float independently, but that is perhaps because an intermediate step that connected it with the rest of the flight above is missing.

The tier below that, which is the deepest flight shown on the section, numbers nine steps, with the top step of this tier placed immediately below the top step of the tier just above it. The eighth step (again counting down from the top) on this bottommost tier is made up of two bricks, making it approximately the same thickness as the corresponding step on the middle of the three principal superimposed stairways (discounting the upper tier of this bottom set). No scale bar is included on the section, but if it is assumed that the riser on each step of the Double Stairway was roughly 0.075 m (the thickness of one brick plus mortar), that would mean that the uppermost flight of steps rose by 0.075 m × 25 steps = 1.875 m.

CHAPTER 9

Photographs of Tell K, 1888–1931

IT IS EXTREMELY FORTUNATE THAT WHEN SARZEC began his large-scale excavations on Tell K in 1888 he had a camera with him because it means that there are photos documenting the work from the outset, which was sadly not the case for Tell A, where there are no photos of the first four seasons. Sarzec's photos of Tell K were mostly taken in 1888 and 1889, though he did take further shots when he returned to Tello in 1889 and 1900. The two photos that Sarzec took of the Pillar of Gudea—remains that are not discussed in great detail elsewhere—are included at the end of the descriptions of his published views because the accompanying texts (in Sarzec and Heuzey 1912) are further illustrated with diagrams that provide detailed analyses of how the structures were built. There are regrettably no published photos of the trenches Cros opened in the central area of Tell K, but there are two good views of the excavations he carried out around the Double Stairway and water supply network in the NE part of the tell. Finally, there are a few photos taken by Genouillac and Parrot between 1930 and 1931.

Sarzec, The SE Façade of the Ur-Nanshe Building. Sarzec and Heuzey 1912, Pl. 54 (1)

This photo (Fig. 39), taken looking north, shows the SW façade of the Ur-Nanshe Building (not the SE façade as stated in the published title), which runs diagonally from the bottom right-hand corner of the image up towards the centre foreground, spanning about two-thirds of the photo's width. Immediately in front of the viewer, at the bottom on the right, with a stretch of extremely dark shadow running vertically down its SE (right-hand) edge, is protrusion D, the remaining top of which abuts onto the uppermost course of the building's wall. Nine or ten courses of bricks can be counted at the building's S corner (bottom right), and there are also nine on both sides of protrusion D, but as the wall extends towards the W corner (on the left) it is generally increasingly damaged and only a few courses are preserved. This is also the case for the central part of the NW wall (where the tent's long guy rope stretches down towards it), which is much reduced, a fact that contradicts the written report, where it states that the NW wall was found intact to a height of fourteen courses, or 1.12 m. The text also notes that the building was sealed off with a layer of bitumen and a bed of bricks, neither of which is visible in the photo, suggesting that the bitumen and brick capping layers had already been removed when it was taken. Perhaps more informatively, the section on Sarzec's Plan C (2) (Fig. 33) shows the walls made up of twelve courses, beneath which is a floor that is two courses thick, altogether making fourteen courses, as described in the text. The sealing layer of bricks is not noted on the section, however, though the bitumen coating is.

A single course of bricks can probably just about be seen along the top edge of protrusion D, which appears in the section on Plan C (2) to be the same thickness as two bricks. Below the wall is a homogeneous mass of mud-bricks that shows the grooved traces of the workers' picks. In the photo's bottom left corner a fairly even scattering of rectangular bricks seem almost to form a pavement, which, if this is indeed the case, is situated about half a metre below the

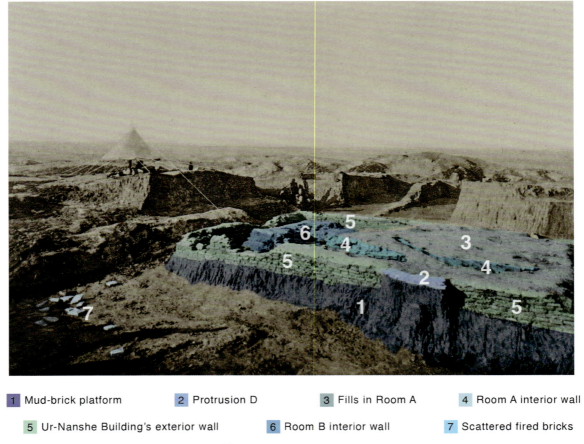

| 1 Mud-brick platform | 2 Protrusion D | 3 Fills in Room A | 4 Room A interior wall |
| 5 Ur-Nanshe Building's exterior wall | | 6 Room B interior wall | 7 Scattered fired bricks |

FIGURE 39. Sarzec and Heuzey 1912, Pl. 54 (1): The SE Façade of the Ur-Nanshe Building.

bottom of the walls of the Ur-Nanshe Building. Alternatively, they could be bricks that were once part of the damaged W end of the building's SW façade. The tops of the walls on all sides of the building have been truncated, and inside the building, behind the SW wall, a little to the right of centre, two courses of the SW side of room A (the larger of the two internal rooms) are visible. Behind that, more centrally still, and away from the viewer towards the picture's middle ground, can be seen six courses of the inside face of the NE wall of the Ur-Nanshe Building. Closer to the viewer, in front of and perpendicular to the inside of the NW wall, on the left of the structure, are the remains of a thick wall that is part of the smaller of the building's two internal rooms (B), with six courses of bricks discernible in its W corner (the side nearest to the camera). To the right of the photo, the SE half of the building is filled with diverse materials to the top of the truncated walls; on the NW side, and in the area between the preserved wall of room A and the SW façade, the fill had apparently been partly excavated before the photo was taken.

Behind the building and to the north-west of it, centrally as we look and oriented south-west–north-east, can be seen the neatly cut sides and levelled horizon of one of Sarzec's wide trenches, in the middle of which is a long, narrow block (sloped like a mound on the side nearest to the camera) that has been left standing. This may be one of Sarzec's unexcavated witnesses (*Témoins*), or height markers (perhaps the one that is marked on the left of the main structures on Cros's SW Section; Fig. 37). In the middle of the photo is a group of four figures, partly in shadow, and to their right (as we look), towards the horizon, can be seen a squarish structure; though hard to identify, a comparison with Plan C (1) (Fig. 33) suggests that this might be associated with structure O. To the left of the workmen (again as we look), outside the building's NW wall and parallel to it, more of Sarzec's excavation cuts can be seen, situated below his tent on the truncated summit of the tell. Beneath this, closer to the front of the picture, there is a baulk (the deliberately unexcavated edge of a trench) that stands between the side of Sarzec's trench and the NW façade of the building. Pavement F should be to the left of the structure, extending out from the NW façade towards the baulk, and the fact that it is not visible would suggest that the photo was taken before the paving was excavated.

Sarzec, The S Corner of the Ur-Nanshe Building. Sarzec and Heuzey 1912, Pl. 54 (2)

Taken looking towards the north-east, this photo (Fig. 40) shows the S corner of the Ur-Nanshe Building, directly in front of the viewer, with the SW façade and protrusion D (with a similar dark shadow on its right-hand edge as in the previous photo) in the immediate foreground, slightly to the left of centre. The courses of bricks (laid flat) are here clearly visible, and ten can be counted on and around the S corner, though they seem perhaps to be reduced on the left, towards where the SW façade is cut off by the left-hand edge of the photo. The numbers of courses are less clear on the two sides of protrusion D, but eight can still be made out. Below the brickwork that makes up the wall, and also below the top surface of D, which is the only part of the protrusion that abuts onto the building, can be seen the homogeneous mass of mud-bricks on which the building stands.

Inside the building (as can also be seen in the previous photo) the SE area is filled with a heterogeneous material, which, towards the north-west as we look, might already have been partly excavated. At this point, to the left of and behind protrusion D, the SW wall of room A is visible, and behind that, towards the photo's middle ground, is the inside face of the Ur-Nanshe Building's NE wall. On the far side of the NE wall, a little further into the distance and on the left side of the picture as we look, the sharp cut and level floor of Sarzec's trench can be seen, including the long line of

FIGURE 40. Sarzec and Heuzey 1912, Pl. 54 (2): The S Corner of the Ur-Nanshe Building.

1 Mud-brick platform   2 Protrusion D   3 Ur-Nanshe Building's exterior wall
4 Double Cistern G   5 Room A interior façade wall   6 Fills in Room A

earth in the middle that might be a witness or height marker. In the middle of the photo, behind the S corner and the shady line of the SE wall of the Ur-Nanshe Building, is a squarish block of homogeneous mud-brick remains that is scarred with the vertical pick marks typically produced when excavating this relatively soft substance. This confirms the note on the section (Plan C (2)) that the entire mound around the upper building and the Lower Construction was made of mud-bricks (*Brique crue*). A comparison of the photo with Plan C (1) suggests that the two cisterns with attached blocks and bituminated surfaces (IJ and KL) should be located in the area occupied by the squarish mud-brick mass and the ground to the right side of it as we look, near the three most distant workers.

In the foreground, at the bottom of the photo, to the right of the Ur-Nanshe Building's S corner, is the double cistern labelled G on Plan C (1). The dark patches that can be made out on the upper surface of the walls, which appear to be truncated, are remnants of the bitumen that was used to bond the bricks, while the very dark areas (much darker than the shadows) on the bottoms of the two troughs might also be bitumen residues. The top of the double cistern seems to be approximately in line with the base of the Ur-Nanshe Building, as also stated by Heuzey (1900, p. 16). This double cistern is not illustrated in the section on Plan C (2).

Sarzec, The Foundation of the Enmetena Block. Sarzec and Heuzey 1912, Pl. 55 (1)

This photo (Fig. 41) shows the base of the Enmetena Block, viewed looking towards the north-east. Central in the foreground of the picture is the block's S corner, with the clean line of the well-preserved SW façade extending out towards the left side of the image; though the lower lines of brickwork are partly obscured by a coating of mud or rubble that adheres to its front face, the top course is consistently visible. Details of the brickwork are much clearer in the SE façade,

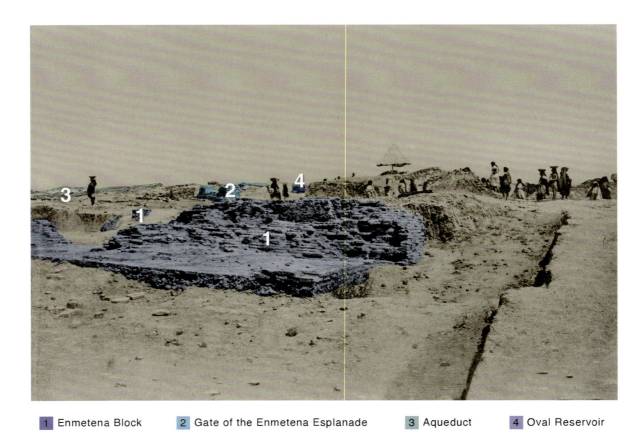

| 1 Enmetena Block | 2 Gate of the Enmetena Esplanade | 3 Aqueduct | 4 Oval Reservoir |

FIGURE 41. Sarzec and Heuzey 1912, Pl. 55 (1): The Enmetena Block.

which runs at a slight diagonal away from the viewer and a little to the right, from the S corner towards the group of figures (two in profile clearly carrying loads on their heads) who are standing on the gentle undulation in front of the horizon line on the right. Four courses of bricks (laid flat) can be made out on the section of the SE façade that is closest to the S corner, behind the spindly bush that sits in a hollow next to the wall, but further to the right (towards the E corner) a large chunk of the façade has disappeared. Behind the relatively even section in the foreground, more of the block is sporadically preserved, rising in places to a height of twenty-three courses. This part of the block, which extends towards the north-west on the left, where there is a single standing figure, seems to form its back wall. A smooth, upward-sloping ramp to the left of the higher parts of the structure is possibly an access route for the excavators, and beyond that, on the extreme left of the photo, are thirteen preserved courses of bricks that might be the continuation of the block.

Two dark, squarish mounds in the middle distance, left of centre, between the single standing figure on the far left and the two figures (one of whom might be riding a pack animal) in the centre, are the gateposts belonging to the gate that stood at the entrance of the area described on Sarzec's Plan D as the Enmetena Esplanade. Beyond that, the structures behind and slightly to the right of the gate are probably the Oval Reservoir and one of its associated cisterns. The Ur-Nanshe Building must be situated to the right of that area, in and around the mound (which is either the top of the tell or a spoil heap) where the local people are gathered. Sarzec's tent is prominent behind.

This photo confirms that the Enmetena Block was found close to the surface of the tell, which slopes gently upwards in this peripheral SW area, from the south-west towards the north-east. The fact that the damaged tops of the block's walls follow this upward slope suggests that the brickwork might have been partly exposed on the surface of the tell and that some of the bricks might have been removed or that the tops of the walls might have been eroded. As is illustrated on Cros's NE Section and as can also be seen on the next photo (Pl. 55 (2); Fig. 42), the top of the block was discovered at a lower level than the base of the Ur-Nanshe Building, though that is difficult to make out in this photo on account of the viewpoint. The higher walls that make up the back of the block (more distant as we look), which are better preserved, might have been embedded in the adjacent mud-brick mass that fills the ground between the block and the Ur-Nanshe Building.

Sarzec, The Large Oval Reservoir. Sarzec and Heuzey 1912, Pl. 55 (2)

Taken looking south, this photo (Fig. 42) shows the Oval Reservoir in the foreground, situated in the Enmetena Esplanade, with the gateway on the right (as we look), and the largest of the three smaller cisterns found in the enclosure visible to the left of the gate on the other side of the large reservoir. The straight line of bricks in the immediate foreground, heading diagonally away from the viewer into the picture, slightly towards the left, is the mouth of the Oval Reservoir, in which the SE outlet of the T-shaped junction can be seen on the far side of the installation, while the junction's NW conduit is visible on the side nearest to the front of the image. A single course of bricks can be made out at the top of the wall that forms this end of the reservoir, with the bricks on the right towards the front of the picture seemingly forming a base or corner that could be as many as five bricks high. The subfloor packing is visible in the section below the reservoir.

The single containing course of bricks on top of the main crossbar of the T-shaped junction forms an edge, within which, stretching out to cover the reservoir's oval floor, is a smooth pavement of square bricks that are laid in long lines extending from the mouth (nearest to the viewer) out to the rounded back of the container on the right. The orientation of these long lines that span the full length of the reservoir is north-east–south-west, while the bricks are laid so that the joint between two bricks in any one of the long NE–SW lines meets the middle of each of the two bricks on either side of it in the adjacent long lines, so that the lines of grouting are continuous one way, but staggered the other. This is the same pattern as is illustrated on Sarzec's Plan D, but the orientation there is different because the plan shows the long lines of grout running north-west–south-east. This tiling is surrounded by the curving edge of the reservoir that is three courses of bricks high all the way round. A few loose bricks can be seen lying on the pavement inside the reservoir at its SW end, and just to the right of them the interior floor of the reservoir seems to rise abruptly, either because the slope is steeper at that point, or perhaps because the floor is stepped.

| 1 | Subfloor packing | 2 | Oval Reservoir | 3 | Gateway | 4 | Cisterns | 5 | Well of Eanatum |

FIGURE 42. Sarzec and Heuzey 1912, Pl. 55 (2): The Oval Reservoir.

On the other side of the Oval Reservoir, in the middle ground of the photo and on the right as we look, can be seen the two jambs of the gate that gave access to the Enmetena Esplanade, with a high threshold between them. The gateway seems to be much closer to the Oval Reservoir than it appears to be on Plan D. Ten or eleven courses of bricks can be counted in both gateposts, while the one to the north-west (on the right) seems noticeably narrower, as it also appears to be on the plan; three courses of bricks can be made out in the threshold, though Heuzey (1900, p. 82) says there were eight. Remnants of another structure can be seen behind and to the right of the narrower gatepost, and behind that again, much lower than the structures just discussed and probably running along the ground, is a line (or lines) of bricks running south-east–north-west that probably form part of the waterway that connected the Well of Eanatum, which is behind the gateway as we look, with the small circular cistern (probably situated towards the right edge of the photo). From there it flowed out of the small cistern towards the north-west (on the right). The Well of Eanatum appears lower in the photo than might be indicated by Cros's NE Section, but that is perhaps because of the falling slope of the tell. The low brickwork structure to the left of the well, with two silhouetted figures standing on the slope of the mound above it on the left, is probably the Enmetena Block.

The top of the small cistern with three cavities, which is prominent in the middle ground of the photo, is lower (perhaps considerably so) than the NE end of the Oval Reservoir. Its NE and NW walls are preserved to a height of ten courses of bricks, but part of the NW wall of the NE compartment has collapsed. Behind it can be seen the section of one of Sarzec's trenches, with some steps carved into it to give access to the tent on the top of the tell. The Ur-Nanshe Building is located on the other side of the tent.

Especially noteworthy in this photo is the slope of the tell, which falls away markedly from the summit, where the tent has been pitched, to the Enmetena Block on the right, which is considerably lower. This confirms why the Oval Reservoir, which was logged as having been found 2.3 m below the summit of the mound, could nevertheless have lain just below the surface of the ground. In cases such as this, the published statements about heights below the summit of the mound take the highest part of the tell, where Sarzec erected his tent, as their point of reference.

Sarzec, The Building below the Ur-Nanshe Building. Sarzec and Heuzey 1912, Pl. 56 (1)

This photo (Fig. 43), taken looking west, presents the Lower Construction and the added external block that ran around and partly inside it (P'Q'R'S' on Sarzec's Plan C (2)). The sharply defined corner in the immediate foreground is corner S' of the surrounding block. Above that, behind the standing figure dressed in white, is the E corner of the Lower Construction (corner S on Sarzec's Plan C (2)). The SE wall of the temple's two-room core, with the opening that leads into room T, runs diagonally into the middle ground of the photo on the left (the walls of the inner rooms being higher than the surrounding block) to where the man on the left side of the opening into room T (as we look) seems to be communicating with the man in white in the foreground. The prominent figure who is visible inside the Lower Construction, through the opening that leads into room T, from where he seems to be looking out at the camera, has his back against the inside face of the Lower Construction's inner SW wall.

Alternating layers of fired bricks and gypsum can be seen in the SE façade of the external block (to the left of corner S'). The detailed text says that the block rose to a height of 2.15 m, but that is clearly not the case here, which probably means that the photo was taken before the lower parts of the structure had been excavated. The report and Plan C (2) both record that the encircling block and the inner walls of the Lower Construction were differently oriented, with the block at its widest on the SE side, and that is clearly confirmed in the photo. The report also states, however, that the NE side of the external block (extending upwards from corner S' towards the middle of the picture's right margin) was

FIGURE 43. Sarzec and Heuzey 1912, Pl. 56 (1): The Lower Construction.

1 Outer Block 2 Room T 3 Room U 4 Brick construction

114   The Mound of the House of the Fruits

between 1.6 m and 2.1 m thick. This does not correspond with the picture, where the block on the NE side seems much narrower than that. There are no signs of the bituminated capsules that were found in the tops of the walls around room T, including on either side of the entrance and along the NE wall.

A trench that has been dug behind the entire composite structure follows the overall NW–SE orientation of the two sets of walls. Two people can be seen standing in this cut, on the extreme left of the photo, from where it can be followed to the right, along the back of the two-part building to a point roughly outside the E corners (Q and Q' on Sarzec's Plan C (2)), where it turns towards the photo's right margin, following the NW façades. In the background, some distance behind the four people on the photo's right-hand edge, can be seen the remains of a brick construction that is difficult to identify.

Sarzec, Stele Found in the Lower Construction. Sarzec and Heuzey 1912, Pl. 56 (2)

The stele found inside the opening of room T in the Lower Construction (No. 3 on Sarzec's Plan C (2)) stands in the middle foreground of this photo (Fig. 44). Though it is not clear where the photo was taken, it is apparent that the object has been removed from its original location. It stands in front of a more or less homogeneous mud-brick section, where it seems to be placed on a slope, with the left side of its base resting on some semicircular objects. It is not easy to say what they are, but they look as though they might have been formed of clay. The labourers directly behind, all of whom have turned to look at the camera, are working on a structure that might be the Lower Construction, in which case the gap in the wall behind on the right might perhaps be the opening of room T, though this is by no means certain.

FIGURE 44.   Sarzec and Heuzey 1912, Pl. 56 (2): The Stele of the Captives.

Sarzec, Large Copper Implement Found near the Ur-Nanshe Building. Sarzec and Heuzey 1912, Pl. 57 (1)

This photo (Fig. 45) presents the imposing copper ring post that was found outside the NW façade of the Ur-Nanshe Building on pavement F. It is marked as No. 17 on Plan C (1), where it is shown to be straight and undivided. As it is seen in the photo, however, it is in two parts that are laid side by side: the upper section, including the semicircular ring, having been detached from the lower section. The plan also records that the object was found on pavement F on the NW side of the temple, but the photo shows it on a floor of plain mud-bricks. Sarzec and Heuzey state that it was broken, but whether the two parts were found placed end to end in a long, straight line or whether they were found side by side as in the photo is not clear. If the photo was taken when the post was still *in situ* outside the building, that would also cast a little doubt on the exact formation of pavement F, though it seems far more likely that the object had been moved from its find location before being photographed. The long, thin strip next to the ring post (on the left) is a tape measure or perhaps a jointed wooden measuring rod.

If it is correct to assume that the dark marks on the measure are placed at intervals of a tenth of a metre then the length from the bottom of the post up to the end of the ruler in the middle of the photo is approximately 0.9 m (or perhaps a little more). The section of the post next to the ruler (starting at the bottom on the left) is the long, lower part; the upper section with the half-ring lies next to it on the right, with the protruding circular band on the end furthest away from the viewer indicating the top of the pole (as illustrated on Plan C (1)). The two parts were therefore probably joined where the copper casing below the half-ring (on the

FIGURE 45. Sarzec and Heuzey 1912, Pl. 57 (1): The Ring Post from pavement F.

upper part of the post that is closest to the front of the image) met the casing on the narrower end of the bottom part of the post (in the top right corner of the photo). If the lengths of the pieces are compared with the measuring rule, it can be estimated that the post as seen in the photo is about 3 m long (on the plan it is 3.25 m). It is widest at the foot in the photo's bottom left corner. That being the case, the post was not folded, but rather purposely or accidentally broken into two parts that were then laid down next to each other, with the tops of each part both pointing in the same direction. The remains of the post seem to be hollow, which suggests it was made from an organic core that was probably formed of bundled reeds that were wrapped in sheets of thinly beaten copper. The inner core of organic material having decayed and disintegrated over time, the sections of copper casings were all that survived. It is possible roughly to estimate the pole's original diameter. If the rather flattened copper end closest to the picture's bottom left corner, which was about 22 mm wide and 5 mm tall (as measured against the ruler), is treated as an ellipse, that would equate to a circle with a diameter of about 210 mm, which would be the approximate thickness of the base of the pole, including the copper casing.

Sarzec, The Well of Eanatum. Sarzec and Heuzey 1912, Pl. 57 (2)

Taken looking north-east, this photo (Fig. 46) shows the Well of Eanatum, which has been excavated to produce a clear section. Above the well shaft, the top of the structure is made of six or seven courses of bricks that are laid flat to form the base of a dome that is wider than the shaft itself and may represent a later phase of construction. The lower part of the structure, where the brickwork is noticeably different, is built with smaller bricks that are marked with a thumbprint and a fingerprint, as can be seen on the convex surfaces of the ones facing the viewer, particularly towards the top on the right but also at the top on the left. The report states that one of the two marks was made with an index finger, but that is not clear in the photo. The bricks in the shaft are laid in alternating

FIGURE 46. Sarzec and Heuzey 1912, Pl. 57 (2): The Well of Eanatum.

1 Well of Eanatum   2 Coping of the well and the dome of Enmetena   3 Gateway of Esplanade

courses, horizontally and vertically, with the vertical bricks placed as slightly opposed diagonals to form a herringbone pattern. Each course is made up of two rows, giving a thickness for the walls of 0.6 m (2 bricks × 0.3 m), as is also noted in the detailed text. Nineteen courses can be seen in this section: ten laid vertically in an overall herringbone pattern, and nine laid flat.

Directly behind and above the well, centrally and a little to the left, can be seen the two gateposts from the entrance to the Enmetena Esplanade. About eight courses of bricks can be made out on the narrower jamb on the left, while only three courses are visible on the one on the right (centrally as we look). About halfway between the right-hand gatepost and the tent in the photo's top right corner (just above the right side of the well) are two or three courses of bricks, but it is extremely difficult to see what they relate to.

Sarzec, Small Ogival Vault Found near the Ur-Nanshe Building. Sarzec and Heuzey 1912, Pl. 57 bis (1)

This photo (not reproduced here) documents a small ogival (arch-shaped) vault that was found in the vicinity of the Ur-Nanshe Building, though its exact whereabouts cannot be ascertained as no structure of this kind is marked on any of the plans or sections and no mention of it is made in the accompanying reports. The only clues as to its location are the combination of the long, narrow shallow trench that runs from the bottom left of the photo up to the top right, where it meets (or perhaps extends past) a brick structure, seven courses high, that stretches more or less horizontally across the back of the photo, including a more elevated, but randomly heaped up pile of bricks towards the right. Apparently rising above the surface of the tell, this background wall could perhaps be part of one of the later construction phases found in the tell's SE corner, possibly associated with Gudea, but this is hardly more than a guess, and it would tend to contradict the title of the photo, which states that the arched brick dome was found near the Ur-Nanshe Building. Cros (1910, p. 93) describes a vaulted waterway found by the Rectangular Construction and water supply network to the north-east of the Ur-Nanshe Building, but that one, which had another water-carrying ramp above it, ran underground and cannot, therefore, be identical with the one in the photo. In any case, the structure in this photo would almost certainly have been dismantled during Sarzec's excavations.

The vault photographed by Sarzec is made of rectangular bricks that are laid flat, but gradually angled down and inwards towards the central void as the walls get higher so that the bricks lean on each other (so to speak) to render the structure self-supporting. A pair of bricks creates a V shape at the apex of the arch, and the bottom of the V descends a little below the curve, possibly forming a two-part keystone, but this might also be due to subsidence.

Sarzec, Small Block of Planoconvex Bricks Found near the Same Construction. Sarzec and Heuzey 1912, Pl. 57 bis (2)

This photo (Fig. 47) presents a small block of curved or planocovex bricks (*Briques bombées*) that was found close to the 'same construction', by which is meant the Ur-Nanshe Building, referred to in the title of Pl. 57 bis (1), discussed immediately above. The view is focused on one of the block's corners, where the dark shadow suggests that this is likely to be the N corner (the further implication being that the block presumably has the same NW–SE orientation as many of the important structures on Tell K). It is built of gently curved, rectangular bricks that are marked centrally with a thumbprint and fingerprints. This probably means that it is the small block that was found by Sarzec about 24.5 m east of the Oval Reservoir, even though the dimensions given for it in the detailed text (1.95 m × 1.75 m × 0.65 m) do not tally precisely with calculations based on the photo (presented below).

The bricks on the top surface of the block are laid flat, with their long sides running from the bottom left to the top right of the photo (presumably north-east–south-west), except for four bricks in the first row up from the bottom left, which are oriented the other way (top left to bottom right), as are the bricks in the first row of the layer below. Beneath the two uppermost courses of bricks that are laid horizontally are two courses laid vertically and diagonally to create a herringbone effect. The base of the block is made of two courses of bricks laid horizontally. As this photo of a brick stack suggests, the zigzag pattern, alternating with layers of bricks placed flat, undoubtedly gave added stability to such unbonded blocks of planoconvex bricks while they were in a holding location, before they were used on actual walls.

FIGURE 47. Sarzec and Heuzey 1912, Pl. 57 bis (2): Stack of planoconvex bricks.

Centrally, the widest part of the top surface numbers nine flat bricks, counting from the top left to the bottom right of the photo as we look. Sarzec notes that the bricks measured 0.29 m × 0.2 m × 0.05 m, which means that the width of the block along this line amounts to 1.8 m (9 brick widths × 0.2 m). This is a little at variance with the width of the similarly oriented face of the block at the bottom left of the photo, when that is calculated based on the lengths of the six bricks laid vertically on their long sides that are clearly visible in the middle two courses, where 6 brick lengths × 0.29 m = 1.74 m. In the other direction, from the bottom left to the top right of the photo, the measurement for the top surface of the block is based on five bricks that are laid with their long sides oriented along the diagonal running from bottom left to top right, plus the width of one brick laid the other way, as is seen in the course below, which works out at 1.65 m (5 brick lengths × 0.29 m = 1.45 m + 0.2 m). The height as calculated from the photo includes four flat courses (two at the top, and two at the bottom) plus two vertical courses in the middle, which gives a total of (4 flat courses × 0.05 m) + (2 vertical courses × 0.2 m) = 0.6 m. The fact that the bricks are laid in different directions means the block is not perfectly rectangular, and this probably accounts for the discrepancy in the measurements given by Sarzec and those calculated from the photo. It should be noted that the block stands on a mud or mud-brick foundation and that the heterogeneous section behind it and to the right seems to show evidence of rubble deposits.

Sarzec, The Large Stairway in the North-East: The View from the Top, Showing the Pillar of Gudea and the Large Foundation Box. Sarzec and Heuzey 1912, Pl. 58 (1)

Taken looking towards the north-east, this panoramic photo (Fig. 48) presents the view from the top of the Large Stairway, giving a perspective, as Sarzec comments in the title, on the Pillar of Gudea and the associated large foundation

FIGURE 48. Sarzec and Heuzey 1912, Pl. 58 (1): View from the top of the Large Stairway.

1 Large square block 2 Brick pavement 3 Foundation boxes
4 Large Stairway 5 Pillar of Gudea

box (*vue d'en-haut avec perspective sur le pilier et sur la grande logette*). In the foreground on the right, beyond the sloping path down which the labourer is walking, can be seen parts of the SW and NW faces of a large square block that is preserved to a height of about nine courses of bricks that are laid horizontally. It is eight bricks wide (from left to right across the picture plane) and seven or eight bricks long. To the left of it, in the immediate foreground, partly hidden by the shrubs that are growing on the far side of the sloping path, is another brick structure that is higher than the one just described, but mostly obscured from sight.

Behind these, on the left and right sides of the broad central trench that leads out into the distance, are two rectangular brick platforms or pavements, one on each side of the stairway, oriented left to right as we look, that measure twelve bricks long by five bricks wide. In the middle of each pavement there is a square box made of bricks, and both boxes are similarly preserved to a height of six courses. The Large Stairway descends between the two pavements towards the Pillar of Gudea, which is the large brick structure in the middle of the photo. The pillar is about twenty-two courses high, and along the base of its SW wall (closest to the viewer) can be seen a low bordering ledge or wall, five courses high, that extends out beyond the base of the pillar to the south-east (on the right of the photo). Immediately to the south-east of the pillar and the low ledge (just to the right as we look), there is the flat top (with a dark rectangular patch in the middle) of a small brick box that has been sunk into the ground. This is not marked on Sarzec's Plan D; nor is it shown on Cros's Plan B. Directly behind the Pillar of Gudea is another square structure made of bricks that is also absent from Sarzec's Plan D. Twelve courses of bricks can be made out in its SW face (closest to the viewer), and it has a smaller flat square of bricks on top, in the middle. Since the photo was taken looking down the slope of the tell, it can be assumed that it is situated at the level of the pillar.

As well as providing a marvellous view of these significant structures, this photo also records Sarzec's excavation strategy. Broad straight trenches can be seen running north-east–south-west and north-west–south-east, and to the right are the rectangular blocks of earth illustrated by Cros on his Plans A and B. As this photo clearly shows, the trenches defining the blocks of earth were not as shallow as might be suggested by Cros's plans, but were in fact significant cuts. In addition, the photo confirms the steepness of the slope of the tell in this NE area.

Sarzec, The Large Stairway in the North-East: The View from the Bottom, Including the Base of the Pillar with Four Columns. Sarzec and Heuzey 1912, Pl. 58 (2)

This image (Fig. 49) records a view of the Large Stairway that is diametrically opposed to the one captured in the previous photo. Taken looking south-west, it shows the steps from below, along with the base of the Pillar of Gudea (the *Pilier aux quatre colonnes*, as it is referred to in the title), the NE face of which is in shadow immediately in front of the viewer in the photo's bottom right corner. Like the other side of the pillar, seen in the preceding photo, this side also has an adjoining ledge or low wall, but unlike the one on the SW face this one is not shown on Sarzec's Plan D. Four courses of the lower NE wall are visible in the photo's bottom right-hand corner, and fourteen courses of the NE face of the pillar can be made out above it. These walls are smooth and well made when compared with the SE wall (to the left as we look), in which the courses of bricks are irregularly stepped, possibly due to erosion or other damage (the opposite, NW side, as seen in the previous photo, is fairly regular and vertical). The top of the pillar is smooth and flat, except for a few loose bricks.

Beyond the pillar, the Large Stairway leads up to the two brick platforms, each fitted with one of the two brickwork boxes that were seen in the previous photo. Seventeen steps are visible, of which the bottom one is partly obscured towards the right of the photo, where it disappears behind the ledge on the pillar's SW side (the other side as we look). The steps are fourteen bricks wide, and the risers are one

FIGURE 49. Sarzec and Heuzey 1912, Pl. 58 (2): View from the bottom of the Large Stairway.

1 Pillar of Gudea   2 Large Stairway   3 Brick pavement
4 Foundation boxes   5 Large square block

brick high. The three bricks on the left that jut out beyond the main flight indicate either that more bricks lie beneath it, or that it is built on top of an earlier stairway.

From this viewpoint it can be seen that the brick platforms flanking the top of the stairway are indeed twelve bricks wide, and though they are shown as nearly square on Sarzec's Plan D they are in fact more elongated, north-west to south-east, parallel with the picture plane in both photos. Seen from this angle, the top of the brick block on the other side of the stairs (as we look) seems to be about the same height as the pavements, but the deeper trench beyond it provides a view of the block's NE wall, and this demonstrates that its base was considerably lower than the top of the stairs and the two pavements. The top of the other brick structure on the right, which was obscured by vegetation in the previous photo, can here be seen just beyond the right-hand platform, and from this vantage point it does indeed appear to rise a little higher than the top of the adjacent brick block on the left. No lower courses of bricks can be made out on the right-hand structure, but it might be built on a mud-brick or packed-mud floor.

Sarzec, The Small Stairway in the South. Sarzec and Heuzey 1912, Pl. 58 bis (1)

The subject of this photo (not reproduced here) is the Small Stairway on the SE side of the tell, viewed from the bottom of the steps, looking up towards the north-west. In the immediate foreground, to the right of the walkway that precedes the bottom step, is a very damaged brick box that is identified as a foundation box on Sarzec's Plan D, where a counterpart is shown opposite on the left that is not visible in the photo. Stretching away from the viewer, the pavement that leads to the stairs (which Plan D shows to be more than 5 m long) is smooth and well plastered. Sixteen steps are visible in the photo, which also shows that the risers are two bricks high, making the Small Stairway considerably steeper than the larger one, where the steps are just one brick high.

Sarzec, The Curved Channel of Tell K. Sarzec and Heuzey 1912, Pl. 58 bis (2)

Writing in *Discoveries in Chaldea* (Sarzec and Heuzey 1912, p. 421), Heuzey states that this photo (Fig. 50) shows the curving waterway on the E corner of the lower part of Tell K that is labelled on Sarzec's Plan D as a 'more recent' construction (*Mur de construction plus récente*), though he does temper that judgement a little by saying that Sarzec exaggerated the lines of some of the conduits in this area. As indicated in Chapter 5 above, Heuzey's statement conceals several inaccuracies that are addressed below, but for the moment it can provisionally be taken at face value. In the foreground of the photo, on the other side of the narrow trench, a straight section of the channel runs from right to left. On the SE side (the left as we look), it bends away from the viewer towards the south-west, forming a smooth ninety-degree curve. The conduit is constructed of rectangular bricks that are probably flat: the ones in the foreground (parallel with the picture plane) are laid so that their short edges follow the line of flow, but just before the channel starts to turn, the orientation seems to change so that the bricks are laid lengthways with respect to the flow. Along the channel's NE side, nearest to the viewer, in the foreground, the water-carrying hollow is flanked by a wall that is four rows of bricks thick, with the bricks mostly laid so that their long sides are parallel to the line of flow. It is also possible to make out traces of levelled mud-bricks in front of this fired-brick wall (towards the bottom of the photo), and these could mark the battered remains of a large mud-brick *enceinte*.

The SW arm of the channel is bordered on both sides by a deep excavation, on top of which, on the SE side (to the left), can be seen a row of bricks that seem almost as though they might be about to fall into the trench. It is not clear whether this is another structure or whether these are bricks that have been removed in the course of the excavations. On the far left edge of the photo, about halfway up, there is a stack of bricks that might have been put there by the excavators. To the west of the waterway, on the right of it as we look, and on the right-hand side of the deep excavation, is a large brickwork block with façades that seem to follow the lines of the channel. Its NE side (closest to us) is at least eight bricks high, and the long SE side, which extends away from the viewer into the distance, seems to be preserved to a greater extent. Unlike the channel, which is built with rectangular bricks, the block is made of square bricks. The irregular appearance of the top of the block, where the square bricks can clearly be seen, suggests that multiple layers of bricks have been sporadically removed, while the NW side (on the right) is greatly reduced, and the contour of that wall is extremely irregular.

FIGURE 50. Sarzec and Heuzey 1912, Pl. 58 bis (2): The curved channel on the edge of Tell K.

1 Mud-brick wall   2 Large brickwork block   3 Curving channel   4 Fired-brick wall

The SW corner (in the distance) seems to curve around towards the right of the photo, following the line of the excavations just beyond it.

A principal reason why this structure should indeed be identified as the curving brickwork construction in the SE corner of the lower part of the tell is the fact that the wider, reinforced section of the NE wall in the immediate foreground resembles the wider part of the 'more recent' wall (*Mur de construction plus récente*), as it is marked on Plan D; furthermore, the line of the curve of the structure in the photo does not seem to resemble anything else on any of the plans or in any of the reports. There are several problems with this straightforward conclusion, however. One issue is that the plan refers to this structure only as a 'wall', while the title of the photo unequivocally says it is a waterway or channel (*caniveau*), as in fact it clearly is. In addition, the brickwork block inside the curve does not appear on Plan D, and there is nothing else around the plan's 'more recent' wall that represents the other features seen in the photo. More importantly, what does 'more recent' mean? Since the bricks used to build the channel are rectangular, they cannot be attributed to Gudea or any Sumerian rulers from the post-Akkad period. In any event, there would have been no reason for Gudea to construct such an elaborate water installation on a mound that was taken out of active religious service (as discussed in great detail in later chapters) after the Temple of Ningirsu was moved to Tell A. It is possible, however, to give a very rough estimate of the dimensions of the rectangular bricks. The only available benchmark for their size is the silhouetted worker (in all likelihood a man) who is walking along the top of the wall in the foreground of the photo. If it is assumed that he is of average height for the period, say about 168 cm (or 5 ft 5 in.), and that he has an average shoe size for his height of US size 7, that would make his foot approximately 23.5 cm long, and the photo seems to indicate that his foot is about the same length as the width of a brick (as can just about be made out for his trailing foot). When that brick width is compared with the numerous sizes used on Tell K, it seems most closely to correlate with the fired bricks used on the Enmetena Block, which were rectangular and flat (rather than planoconvex) and measured 0.33 m × 0.24 m × 0.06 m: a rather broad, almost squarish ratio (1:1.375) that seems comparable with the large bricks visible on the wall in the foreground. Numerous caveats notwithstanding, all of this strongly suggests that the curving construction in the photo was not 'more recent' but was built in Early Dynastic times, and can plausibly be dated to the reign of Enmetena.

The channel therefore shows a marked contrast with the substantial block, which is built of square bricks and can therefore probably be attributed to Gudea. Ur-Bau also built with square bricks, but there is no evidence to suggest that he carried out any significant work on Tell K. This is perhaps the source of some of the confusion about the photo and the plan. Heuzey (Sarzec and Heuzey 1912, p. 423) mentions the difficulties he had interpreting the terrain when compiling Plan D, presumably with Sarzec's notes and sketches, but some years after Sarzec's death. Compared with the Early Dynastic waterway, the block could certainly be described as a 'more recent wall', but the description seems to have been mistakenly attached to the channel, while the wall or block was erroneously omitted altogether from Plan D, as was the smaller block in the photo's middle ground, to the right of centre. These errors presumably crept in while Heuzey was trying to decode Sarzec's notes and diagrams without the advantage of being able to consult the man himself. At the risk of pre-empting arguments that are laid out later in this book, the block built of square bricks that is seen in the photo must surely be the remains of the outer wall of the extended platform terrace that Gudea built after the Akkad interval to reinforce and support the upper part of the mound, which by that time had become a memorial shrine to the ancient Eninnu of Tell K (the working Temple of Ningirsu having been moved to Tell A).

Potentially even more problematic than the admittedly somewhat speculative data about the size of the rectangular bricks and the confusion about the conduit and the block is the photo's viewpoint. If, as Heuzey suggests, the photo was taken looking over the thicker end of the misnamed 'more recent' wall as it appears on Plan D, then the viewer should be looking south-westwards towards the central part of the mound, where the remains of the SE side of the main part of Tell K should be. In the distance, therefore, should be seen whatever was left of the area originally containing the Ur-Nanshe Building and the Lower Construction (with the Pillar of Gudea and the Large Stairway behind the camera to the right). In fact, the camera is placed on a rather high rise, looking down over the brickwork remains and out to the surrounding plain, which is even lower than the structures in the foreground, and this is not at all in accord with the viewpoint suggested by Heuzey, as described at the beginning of this paragraph.

It does, nonetheless, make sense in terms of the downward slope of the channel, which, as stated at the outset, runs from right to left across the front of the photo and then continues downwards after the smooth curve, with the water flowing out towards the lower alluvial plain in the distance (perhaps following the line of the excavated trench on the left as we look). This means that the higher ground must be on the right, beyond the right-hand edge of the photo and out of sight (the beginning of the sloping side of the upper terrace might be the well-excavated mud-brick platform about halfway up the photo's right margin), and what is seen in the picture must be the extreme SE edge of the lower part of the mound. Consequently, the right-angled bend seen in the photo was situated much further to the south-east than it appears on Plan D. Indeed, the beginning of the wider part of the channel must in reality have been approximately in line with the E corner of the upper platform (all as seen on Plan D), with the camera pointing in a SW direction, out towards the plain, and the main archaeological area of Tell K (the area of the Ningirsu temple) out of sight on the right, beyond the confines of the picture. This means that Plan D probably contains three important inaccuracies: first, the Gudea block is omitted (as is the smaller block-like installation); secondly, the channel is misnamed as a 'more recent wall', a term that Sarzec probably used to describe the Gudea block; and thirdly, the bending channel, which is placed too far towards the north-west, should have been drawn further down (towards the Small Stairway) so that the beginning of the wider section that is seen at the front of the photo was roughly aligned with the E corner of the main area of Tell K.

Sarzec, The Pillar of Bricks: Two Aspects. Sarzec and Heuzey 1912, Pl. 52 (1) and Pl. 52 (2)

The first two photos of the structure known as the Pillar (or Pillars) of Gudea (Pl. 52 (1) and Pl. 52 (2)); Figs. 51 and 52) show the state of the brickwork mass from two contrary viewpoints (*aspects* in French) shortly after it was first uncovered. Probably taken looking north, Pl. 52 (1) shows the four adjacent pillars slightly below the level of the ground on the

124 The Mound of the House of the Fruits

FIGURE 51. Sarzec and Heuzey 1912, Pl. 52 (1): First view of the Pillar of Gudea.

far side of the image, where the earth has been dug away from around the front of the two circular forms that are furthest away from the viewer. On the surface of the ground, behind the hollow that has been cut to expose the pillars' rounded fronts, can be seen a pick that has been left by the side of the shallow pit by one of the workers. The four pillars are surrounded by a brickwork enclosure on three sides (on the left, on the right and closest to the near edge of the image). On the right of the photo, rising above the tops of the pillars themselves, can be seen some cylindrical remains of the layer of thick plaster or cement with which the composite shape was coated, and more of the plaster or cement coating can be seen rising above the surface of the pillars at the front of the image.

On the left of the picture eleven courses of bricks can be seen. They are square bricks, said by Heuzey to be the 'usual' Gudea type, with sides of 0.32 m. Their thickness is not mentioned in the text, but Gudea bricks with thicknesses of 0.09 m and 0.07 m were recorded on the site, and the approximate height of 0.84 m given by Heuzey for the base of the block (Sarzec and Heuzey 1912, p. 424) suggests that he understood these to be the thinner type. The upper eight courses of the left-hand wall, which are one and a half bricks wide, are bonded by the simple method of alternating the positions of the whole and half-bricks in successive courses (see Chapter 42 below). The bottom three courses of the same wall are wider, protruding out to the left by about the width of a brick, though the bonding pattern in these lower courses is less clear, and the bricks perhaps look less well preserved, but this might be due to the fact that they have not yet been fully excavated. The courses of bricks in the middle of the fairly irregular wall closest to the front of the picture, which again appear to be more damaged, are about one and a half or two bricks wide. The wall on the right of the pillars extends out beyond their cylindrical sides by about the width of two bricks, while the brickwork towards the bottom right of the image (pointing towards the bottom right-hand corner) seems to be about a brick wider than the rest of the wall to the left of it.

FIGURE 52. Sarzec and Heuzey 1912, Pl. 52 (2): Second view of the Pillar of Gudea.

The elaborate way in which the pillars were made of five different kinds of specially shaped bricks can be partly seen in Pl. 52 (1), as can the way in which successive layers were made in two different shapes: a rosette with a circular centre surrounded by eight radiating truncated sectors or petals, and a starlike arrangement of eight sectors surrounded by an outer concentric band known as an annulus (also shown in Heuzey's diagrams; Fig. 53). The banded star shape is much clearer in Pl. 52 (2), where the eight sectors are visible in the slice of pillar that is closest to the front of the picture, and it is apparent that each is capped with a piece of the concentric band. The four-pointed (or four-cusped) central space with convex sides between the four pillars is filled with two very precisely made bricks that can be seen most clearly in the first photo. As is discussed below, the two images give an excellent insight into the way the pillars were made.

Capturing a diametrically opposed view and therefore probably taken looking south, Pl. 52 (2) shows the construction at a slightly later stage in the excavations. The surrounding pit has now been significantly enlarged in all directions, though it is not yet much deeper. Sarzec can be seen sitting on the ridge in the top left corner of the image, shaded by a parasol, with a saddled horse and six seated workers next to him (on the right as we look). Further to the right and further into the background are two more saddled horses, while a small group of standing workers and the head of another horse can be seen towards the right margin. It is interesting to note that Sarzec is looking intently at the group of standing workers, who are seemingly examining something on the ground. This might be part of the upper section of the Large Stairway, which should be in this general direction, and it is worth recalling that the total height of the four pillars and their brickwork base was estimated by Heuzey as 1.68 m (to be discussed further below) so the original ground level of the base of the block was significantly lower than the surface of the ground as it is seen in the photo. At this stage of the excavations the trench around the pillars looks rather untidy. In the shade, below where Sarzec is seated, there is a

126   The Mound of the House of the Fruits

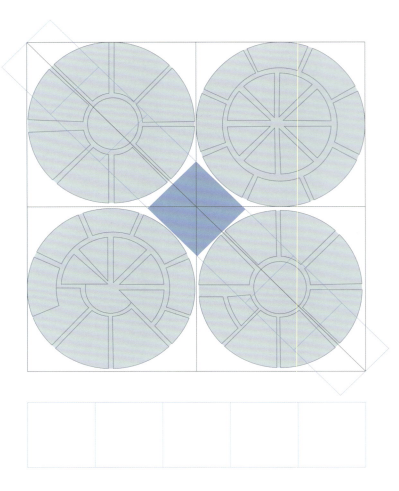

FIGURE 53. Diagram showing the construction of the Pillar of Gudea, based on the drawing in Sarzec and Heuzey 1912, p. 425.

bundle of objects that appears to include some cloth sheets or items of clothing and perhaps some stray bricks, together with a circular implement on the left that looks like a flat sieve (with one of its string or wire handles visible) for sifting removed earth.

In Pl. 52 (2) the wall behind and to the left of the pillars (as we look) appears to be two bricks thick, and its lower section apparently extends further out towards the photo's left margin, though the underlying courses have not yet been exposed. The wall to the right is one and a half bricks thick, and parts of the cylindrical cement casing with which the pillars were coated can perhaps be made out against that far wall, but it is much more clearly visible at the very front of the image, where the coating appears to be about the thickness of a square brick (0.07 m). The starlike form and the rosette of which successive courses of the brickwork in the pillars were made can be seen clearly in Pl. 52 (2). The two shapes alternated course by course to establish a bond pattern, which was further strengthened by rotating successive courses so that the middle of one sector meets the joins between those above and below. Since the central angle of each of the eight sectors is forty-five degrees, the rotation amounted to twenty-two and a half degrees. Heuzey suggests that the roseate and starlike patterns had a shared symbolic meaning relating to Sumerian ideograms of divinity (Sarzec and Heuzey 1912, pp. 431–2), and this is of course an extremely attractive idea, but the two shapes were probably also employed in combination with the rotation in order to spread the downward-bearing weight of the structure. For example, if the dead centre of every pillar had been occupied by the central angles of eight sectors, that would presumably have created a weak spot, but that potential deficiency was offset by alternating the two patterns, with the small circle at the centre of the rosette spreading the load. Further bonding and load spreading was created by the alternation between the concentric band (the annulus) of the starlike pattern and the petal (or curving-angled sector) of the rosette.

It can clearly be seen in all three photos (including Pl. 53 (2)) that the bricks used to construct the pillars were manufactured with great precision and know-how, and also that they were laid with extreme care. Heuzey says that they were bonded with bitumen, and though that is not obvious in the photos it is apparent that the joints between the multiform bricks in each course were very regular and also rather narrow, perhaps as little as 0.01 m. The sizes of the differently shaped bricks that make up the four circles of the pillars can be fairly accurately estimated. Heuzey says the square occupied by the four pillars had sides of 1.54 m (based on measurements he took of the brickwork that was transported back to the Louvre), but if that figure is compared with Pl. 53 (2), which is discussed in more detail below, it seems that the four circular pillars occupied a square that was five bricks wide (as also assumed by Heuzey), meaning the sides of the square were probably closer to 1.6 m (a figure that would accommodate the joins between the component pieces that formed each circular course of the pillars but not necessarily the cement coating, which was no doubt in any case a later addition). This would make the diameter of the individual pillars or circles 0.8 m, and their radii 0.4 m. The diameter of the small circle at the centre of the rosette, which occupies about 20% of the total diameter of the pillar, was therefore about 0.16 m, with the radii of the curving-angled sectors (cut off at their central angles by the small inner circle) measuring about 0.32 m. The outer arcs of the curving-angled sectors each measured about 0.3 m (calculated as $2\pi r \div 8$, where $r = 0.4$ m). As can be shown, these figures all correlate extremely well with the estimated sizes of the pieces that formed the starlike pattern. Measured as the extension of the radius of the overall circle of the pillar, the width of the encircling annulus occupied about 10% of the overall diameter, meaning each annular sector had a radius of about 0.08 m. Since the diameter of the large circle included two annular sectors (one at each end), that means the radii of the pointed sectors also measured 0.32 m ((0.8 m − 0.16 m) ÷ 2), the same as the radii of the rosette petals. The precision with which the size and placement of the pillars' component parts was worked out strongly confirms Heuzey's comment (Sarzec and Heuzey 1912, p. 424) that they were eruditely fashioned (*savamment agencées*).

The most interesting of the brick shapes used to make the composite block of four pillars are the ones that can be seen filling the gap in the middle of the structure that is created by the arcs of the four touching circles (where, incidentally, no cement coating can be seen, as is visible in Pl. 52 (1)). The shape of the gap between the four circles looks like a square turned through forty-five degrees (Fig. 53), but with concave sides, all of which have the same regular curvature. The named geometrical figure that most closely corresponds with this would be a hypocycloid, which is created by rolling a smaller circle around the inside of the circumference of a bigger one and recording the outline traced by a single point on the circumference of the smaller, rolling circle. In order to create a four-sided hypocycloid, however, the ratio of the radii of the bigger and smaller circles has to be 4:1, and in this case the smaller circles represented by the pillars are proportionally much larger when compared with that of an imagined bigger concentric circle whose circumference would touch the circumferences of all four pillars. The actual ratio is about 2.4:1, with the radius of the imagined larger concentric circle calculated as 0.96 m (the diameters of two pillars) plus the length of the line that dissects the concave-sided diamond (for want of a better term) through the middles of its concave sides.

This means that the length of the sides of a smaller square that would fit perfectly into that concave-sided diamond, touching the circumferences of all four pillars, would be very close to 0.32 m (Fig. 53). Even when a margin of error is factored in, that figure is clearly so close to the size of the standard Gudea brick (0.32 m × 0.32 m) that it becomes reasonable to suppose that the entire construction was derived from the proportions of a single brick. Indeed, the diagonal of the larger square (with sides of five bricks) in which the four pillars were contained was almost exactly seven brick lengths long (worked out in purely geometrical terms as the square root of fifty, or 7.071), and this surely suggests an applied, real-world understanding of the proportional relationships between the sides and diagonals of squares with sides of certain sizes. As is indicated by the way in which the four circles of the pillars relate to the square in which they all fit rather than to the larger concentric circle that could contain them all, the builders seem fundamentally to have accommodated circles to squares—to have derived circles from squares, so to speak, rather than the other way round,

128 The Mound of the House of the Fruits

as later Greek or Renaissance builders (for example) might have approached the problem. They seem also to have had a precursory understanding of some of the geometrical principles that would very much later be crystallised by Pythagoras, but which were seemingly used for practical purposes by Mesopotamian builders in the late third millennium BCE, as is further discussed with regard to the metrology of the plan of Gudea's New Eninnu on Statue B in Chapter 39 below.

As is also clear in Pl. 52 (1), the concave-sided diamond that filled the central gap was formed in two halves (with the straight side the same length as the side of the square just mentioned that would fit inside the diamond), and this was no doubt so that successive courses of that two-part filler shape could also be rotated through forty-five degrees, again creating stability by ensuring that the superimposed joins were placed diagonally across each other rather than one on top of another. The series of concave-sided diamonds was not bonded with the surrounding pillars, however, so they were not structural. Instead they formed a long plug that filled the gap in the middle of the construction, presumably with the primary purpose of stopping water and other unwanted materials from getting inside it.

Sarzec, The Pillar Completely Cleared. Sarzec and Heuzey 1912, Pl. 53 (2)

This photo (Fig. 54) gives an excellent view of the block of four pillars after they had been excavated, with the ground around the base of the block cleared away and cut into a clean-sided trench on the left, where a small group of workers can be seen sitting on the levelled earth above the excavation. The ground inside the trench on the right is more uneven than the rest, and there are some tools on top of the low ridge behind, close to the photo's right margin, perhaps suggesting that the work in this area was ongoing when the picture was taken. One of the implements is a circular container that looks like a shallow metal pan that might have been used to carry portable remains. Plan D shows that the corners of the block were oriented towards the cardinal points, and if that was indeed the case then the picture probably shows the N corner, which

FIGURE 54. Sarzec and Heuzey 1912, Pl. 53 (2): The Pillar of Gudea completely exposed.

is seen looking southwards. Sarzec's dig tent can be seen on the top of the mound behind, however, and if the corner closest to the camera really is the N corner, that would mean that the tent, which was presumably pitched in the central area at the top of Tell K, lay due south along that axis. Yet this is not how the relationship appears on Plan D, and this suggests either that the plan is slightly inaccurate in this instance, as it also is with respect to the location and labelling of the curving channel that is erroneously marked as a 'more recent' wall, or perhaps that Sarzec's tent is not in the expected position.

The base of the block (the stylobate as Heuzey calls it) is made up of eleven courses. If the bricks were 0.07 m thick and tightly laid, with just 0.01 m of bonding material between the courses, for example, that would indicate a height for the base of about 0.88 m, which is a little more than Heuzey's estimate of 0.84 m. He also suggests (as noted above) that the bricks were probably bonded with bitumen, but that is not readily apparent. The brickwork in the N corner (closest to the camera) is extremely neat and well preserved, while the bricks on the left end of the NE wall, especially towards the E corner (on the left as we look) are increasingly irregular. The way the bricks are laid along the NE wall, with courses of full bricks alternating with courses that begin and end with half-bricks, suggests that the wall below the pillars was probably created as a single entity, and the same can be said of the clearly visible part of the wall that forms the NW base below the pillars. It is extremely difficult to make out the exact dimensions of the base, but the NE and NW walls both seem to be about eight bricks wide, equating to about 2.56 m, which is also the figure calculated by Heuzey for what he refers to as the 'short side'. As previously noted, the width of two pillars spans about five bricks, so that the square occupied by all four of them has sides of about 1.6 m. The adjacent wall above the base to the left of the pillars seems to be twelve (or thirteen) courses of bricks tall (approximately 0.96 m for twelve courses, including thin layers of bonding material), which is again more than Heuzey calculates, though the damage affecting the top three or possibly four courses makes it difficult to be categorical about this. The maximum height of the base plus the upper wall as seen in the photo would therefore amount to about 1.8 m. On the SW wall (behind the pillars as we look) the upper part of the wall above the base rises to about nine courses.

The front two pillars (closest to the camera) are very well preserved to a height of nine courses. Behind that, the remains of four further courses can be made out, making thirteen in total. This is about the same number of courses as in the E corner, but since the pillars are evidently lower than the adjacent wall, the comparison would confirm that the specially manufactured bricks used to build the pillars were not as thick as the standard Gudea bricks. This is perhaps clearest in the seventh and eighth courses of the pillar on the left of the two at the front of the picture, particularly where the side of the pillar meets the E end of the NE wall, where the bricks used to build the pillars are noticeably thinner. If it is correct to assume that seven courses of standard bricks rise to about the same height as nine courses of pillar bricks, as seems to be the case where the left-hand one of the two front pillars meets the NE wall, that would give a thickness of about 0.06 m for the pillar bricks (which correlates well with the published thickness of 0.058 m for the examples in the Louvre (AO388)). That being the case, the total height of thirteen courses of pillar bricks would be approximately 0.78 m (or a little more). The rotation of successive pillar courses to create a stable bonding pattern (as described above) is extremely clear in the front two pillars.

At the back of the block on the right (in the W corner) the wall seems to project out slightly towards the right margin of the picture, especially close to the level of the ground, where two or three courses can be seen in the shadows. According to the plan, the SE end of the SW wall protruded beyond the block's S corner, but this is not visible in the photo, though that may be because the angle from which the photo was taken meant the lower projecting wall was hidden from view behind the block. Sections of the pillars' thickish cement casing can be seen, especially on the sides and extending in between the upper parts of the arcs of the two pillars that are above the NW wall of the base.

Cros, Stairways and Bituminated Ramps: The NE Slopes of Tell K (1). Cros 1910, Topographic Views, No. 1

This photo (Fig. 55), taken looking south-west, shows the Double Stairway and the water supply and drainage system, which Cros refers to as 'bituminated ramps' (*Rampes bituminées*). The Double Stairway is visible on the right-hand side of the photo, where twelve steps of the shorter flight and twenty-four of the longer one can be counted. Between the

130 The Mound of the House of the Fruits

| 1 Mud-brick platform | 2 Stairway of Ur-Nanshe | 3 Stairway of Eanatum | 4 Double Stairway of Enmetena |
| 5 Water supply network | 6 Rectangular Construction | 7 Cistern | 8 Blocking wall |

FIGURE 55. Cros 1910, View No. 1: Stairways and Water Supply Network.

two flights of steps is a narrow stepped slope that might be a drain or gutter with a ledge at the bottom. This is also illustrated on Cros's Plan C (Fig. 38), which provides a detailed sketch of these installations, though on the plan it does not appear to be stepped. The photo seems to show a similar slope running down the left side of the longer flight of steps, but this is not marked on the plan. Directly behind the stairs is the vertical back wall of Cros's Trenches 6 and 7. In the middle distance, under the pointed mound, to the left of the higher flight of stairs and at the same level as its top step, a horizontal waterway extends out towards the north-east, in the direction of the viewer. It reaches the circular distribution head at the point where a figure (the highest of the people under the pointed mound) can be seen standing on it, and from there, at a lower level, two channels branch out towards the viewer: the one on the right (as we look) heads towards the north, while the one on the left heads north-east.

The structure to the left of the distribution head is the reservoir (A on Cros's Plan C), otherwise referred to as the Rectangular Construction. Its NE wall and N corner face the viewer; to the left is the E corner, and behind that, stretching out towards the back of the trench in the middle distance, is the inside face of its SE wall. The opening in the NE wall, close to the N corner, can be seen behind the standing silhouetted figure in the foreground. On the far side of the opening, inside the reservoir, is a narrow blocking wall, behind which, inside the main walls, was found a smaller rectangular block that does not seem to be visible. The reservoir is oriented slightly more towards the east-north-east than the main arteries of the water supply network. In front of the NE wall, towards the photo's bottom left corner, can be seen another structure, which must be the other water-carrying channel (also labelled B) that is marked on Plan C.

This photo shows very clearly how the N and NE extensions of the water supply network, in particular, were built on bases made of mud-bricks. It also reveals that the heights of several of the features recorded in the photo are closely comparable: the foot of the Double Stairway is at the same height as the lower waterways on the right of the reservoir; the sloping angle of the branching channels in the middle foreground compares with the slope of the flights of steps; and the top of the Double Stairway is at about the same height as the upper part of the water installations (close to the back of the trench, under the pointed mound). These congruities signal that the features seen in the photo were built at around the time, as part of the same programme of works. Furthermore, it looks very much as though the stairway ascended to a platform that was at the same level as the higher parts of the water supply and drainage system, implying that the top of the steps and the upper part of the water system were embedded in the same section of earthwork.

Cros, Stairways and Bituminated Ramps: The NE Slopes of Tell K (2). Cros 1910, Topographic Views, No. 2

This superb photo (Fig. 56) of the Double Stairway and the water supply and drainage system, which is taken looking south-east towards the rectangular blocks of earth, shows the two adjoining flights of stairs running across the foreground, with the water supply network and reservoir just beyond. In the bottom left-hand corner, cut off by the edges of the picture, can be seen a small but significant portion of the other flight of stairs that was found close to the Double Stairway; it is marked on Cros's Plan C, where it runs perpendicularly away from the bottom of the Double Stairway up towards the north-west. The section below the Double Stairway in the photo shows how it was built on a fine homogenous compound of mud-bricks. At the top of the Double Stairway's shorter flight of stairs, extending out towards the right edge of the photo, are three horizontal courses of bricks at a slightly lower level than the top of the shorter flight, while above that, ascending the slope at about the same angle as the main stairways, is a flight of steps made with single bricks. Additionally, on the fourth step down from the top of the longer of the two flights on the Double Stairway, there is a block that seems to take up about three-quarters of the width of the step, though it does not fill the depth of the tread from front to back, as it is noticeably shallower.

The photo shows how the Double Stairway was situated in Trenches 6 and 7, with the surrounding earth having been thoroughly and carefully removed to leave the well-cut trenches clear of rubble. The soft deposits of the mud-brick platform have been taken away from around the stairway, leaving the fired-brick superstructure floating (as it were),

FIGURE 56. Cros 1910, View No. 2: Stairways and Water Supply Network.

1 Mud-brick platform   2 Stairway of Enmetena   3 Stairway of Eanatum
4 Stairway of Ur-Nanshe   5 Water reservoir   6 Water channels

while the lines made by the workers' picks can be seen in the soft mass of mud-bricks below the steps. This reveals the way the stairway was built into the sloping side of the mound, and that the higher, more or less horizontal part of the main conduit leading down into the water supply network (on the right of the photo, apparently at about the same overall elevation as the top of the stairway) was built on top of the platform.

The water supply network lies immediately beyond the stairs, with the circular distribution head on the right, while two of the conduits are also clearly visible: the longer, best-preserved one slightly further away from the viewer and the one of intermediate length stretching out towards the stairs and the front of the photo. The brick structure adjacent to and on the far side of the circular distribution head is the third of the three conduits (the shortest and least well preserved of the three) that seems, when the photo is compared with the plan, possibly to have connected with the Rectangular Construction. From the vantage point of the photo, that shorter conduit appears to be at a slightly higher level than the circular distribution head, and this might suggest that it supplied water to the distributor, though if the photo is again compared with Plan C it seems more probable that the channel leading into the reservoir and the distributor were both supplied by the main conduit that descended from higher up the slope on the right of the photo. On the left of the photo, in the middle ground, is the Rectangular Construction. The neat brickwork on the inside face of its SE wall can clearly be seen, as can the narrow blocking wall inside the entrance on the NE side (on the left). The smallish brickwork block that is shown inside the reservoir on Plan C is again not visible, even from this higher viewpoint. In the far distance are some of the rectangular blocks of earth that were laid out by Sarzec and later excavated by Cros, as discussed above (the relationship between the stairway and the rectangular blocks is best seen on Cros's Plan B; Fig. 36).

Genouillac, Three Untitled Photos (1930–1). Genouillac 1934, Pl. 1 (2)

Of the first three photos taken by Genouillac when he worked on Tell K from 1930 to 1931 (Season 18), printed as

FIGURE 57. Genouillac 1934, Pl. 1 (2): Excavations on Tell K.

Pls. 1 and 2 in *Excavations at Telloh*, only one is included here (Fig. 57), primarily for the sake of completeness. As in seen in this example (Pl. 2.3), the three photos show the devastating scale on which Genouillac excavated the remains of the mound, employing numerous labourers who seem to be working in unsupervised groups.

Genouillac, Untitled (1930–1). Genouillac 1934, Pl. 46 (1)

It is difficult to know the direction in which this interesting photo (Fig. 58) was taken, but it shows the external face of the shaft of the Well of Eanatum, with a boy or young man standing at the bottom to give a sense of scale. In the middle of the photo, at the top, the upper part of the wall of the shaft is visible on the right-hand side of the structure, about half a metre below the top of the section, where the alternating courses of bricks are placed vertically and horizontally (six courses of each in this truncated section), and the wall is two bricks thick. Below that is the outer convex surface of the well shaft, with a total of forty-five courses of bricks, alternately vertical and horizontal, descending almost to the base of the trench. The courses of vertically placed bricks are slightly inclined, generally in opposed directions from course to course, to create a pattern that can loosely be described as herringbone, even though the bricks are not as systematically arranged as the term herringbone might

1 Mud-brick platform

2 Well of Eanatum

3 Filling of shards

4 Upper part of the Well

FIGURE 58. Genouillac 1934, Pl. 46 (1): The Well of Eanatum.

suggest, with several consecutive courses leaning in the same direction, and bricks within the same course sometimes leaning in different directions.

The bell-shaped cut around the well can be seen in the section. Surrounding both sides of the base of the well shaft is a filling of sherds that rises to a height of twenty courses of bricks. Above that, the space around the shaft is filled with a fine homogeneous material that must presumably be sand, as described by Cros (1910, p. 73). A series of horizontal lines can be seen running across the section on the left of the well; these are some of the layers of mud-bricks of which the mound was formed.

CHAPTER 10

Tell K: A New History of the Temple of Ningirsu

THE FRENCH PIONEERS LEFT BEHIND A MASS OF DATA pertaining to one of the most important Sumerian temple sites of the Early Dynastic period. How can it best be analysed and exploited to achieve a fuller understanding of the archaeology of Tell K? There is no doubt that the data was inadequately recorded, and that the excavations were in some important ways badly executed. Despite that, when the work is viewed in context, and when the general state of the archaeology of the time is taken into account, there are numerous positives. The investigations were carried out methodically, with a sense of scientific purpose and within evolving historical and procedural frameworks. They resulted in voluminous published reports, plans, sections and photos (all detailed above) that remain usable and contain a lot of valuable information, and for these reasons the commonly accepted scholarly view that this whole body of work should simply be excluded from studies of Sumerian temple architecture must be rejected. The systematic re-examination and recontextualisation of the material presented in this book suggests that this is an unnecessarily defeatist conclusion and that, on the contrary, the work of the French explorers gives rise to a number of possibilities that deserve serious consideration.

There are nevertheless some formidable challenges that should not be minimised. First and foremost, as repeatedly noted in a range of contexts, Sarzec failed to recognise the importance of mud-bricks until much of his work had been completed, by which time the evidence had been destroyed. This fact is apparent from the outset in Heuzey's initial account of Tell K, where mud-bricks are treated as an amorphous aggregate, and little or no attention is paid to their systematic architectural use. As a result, especially in the earlier reports, Heuzey tends not to distinguish between mud-brick walls, platforms and other structures, all of which are lumped together as a consolidated mud-brick compound. But the almost exclusive focus on remains made of fired bricks or stone transformed the temple complex into the disconnected parts of a skeleton without a skin, as it were. To change the metaphor, it is the archaeological equivalent of the aftermath of a shipwreck, with a few surviving objects floating on the waves, divested of meaning and structural purpose. Here too, however, it is important not to dismiss the French legacy too hastily because the large quantity of documented information, combined with remains that survived *in situ*, as especially revealed in the underlying parts of Tell A that were the focus of the British Museum team's excavations, allow for plausible reconstructions based on a solid methodology and a systematic review of the data. The approach includes recontextualising the provenance of objects and structures, and assessing their intrinsic character (as well as where and when they were found, and in what state of preservation); noting how finds were handled by the excavators and treated subsequently; cross-checking recorded stratigraphic information against a calibrated interpretation of the whole mound from which the data was gathered; and comparing all of these analysed findings with the significant benchmarks derived from the British Museum team's work on Tell A.

The problem created by Sarzec's failure to distinguish mud-bricks was clearly recognised by Cros when he began work on Tell K in 1903, picking up where his lately deceased predecessor had left off and in some senses trying to salvage what was left of the mound. It must be acknowledged that Cros achieved a great deal. The topography of Tell K had been transformed into a landscape of enormous trenches and spoil heaps by the time he arrived there, but Cros's understanding of what he found, and his determination to document and describe it as accurately as he could, made it possible for him to resolve some problems and begin to put some flesh back on the bones—or, to pursue Forest's metaphor (Forest 1999, p. 21), to anchor the wreck in some fairly solid ground. He also demonstrated in practice some of the inferences that had been partially drawn by Heuzey, namely that Tell K was composed of a series of huge superimposed terrace platforms that had been built at different periods, but that remains from any one period could be found at different levels within the mound, in large part because of its overall sloping profile. In particular, the height differential between the centre and the periphery meant that there was no straightforward, one-to-one correlation between the depth at which objects and buildings were excavated and the date at which they had been made or constructed. Cros was aided in his efforts by his grasp of Sarzec's system of recording the location of finds on Tell K, not by measuring their depth beneath the top surface of the tell (which in any case had long since been truncated by as much as 5 m or 6 m in many places, and by a much greater amount in limited areas), but by noting their height above the water table at the bottom of Sarzec's deepest sounding: point zero on Sarzec's scale.

In addition, Cros rationalised the data by identifying a typology of bricks based on their size, characteristics and stratigraphic provenance, and their associations with other materials, especially objects that were inscribed. This enabled him to postulate a chronological sequence for all of the structures on Tell K, based on a few key reference points that were derived from a classification of the numerous brick types used on the mound. Though it cannot, of course, be relied upon entirely, the rationalised data remains extremely useful, especially when it is supplemented with the bricks that Cros omitted, as in the following list:

> The fired bricks on the Lower Construction, which were small-format, planoconvex and without marks (measuring 0.22 m × 0.13 m × 0.05 m), were similar to the mud-bricks found in the associated platform in Trench 5.

> The fired bricks used on the Ur-Nanshe Building, which were slightly larger (measuring 0.28 m × 0.15 m × 0.05 m), were mostly planoconvex and marked with a single thumbprint. Again, they were similar in size and shape to their mud-brick counterparts found in the Ur-Nanshe platform across the whole of Tell K, notably in the Trench of the Well, the West Trench (No. 8) and the South Trenches (Nos. 9 and 10).

> The Ur-Nanshe fired bricks marked with a thumbprint (above) were a slightly different size from the ones inscribed in his name. The inscribed Ur-Nanshe bricks measured 0.3 m × 0.2 m × 0.05 m.

> The preceding types of Ur-Nanshe bricks differed markedly from the square fired bricks used on pavement F on the NW side of the Ur-Nanshe Building (marked on Sarzec's Plan C (1); Fig. 33) on the NW side of the building, and the square fired bricks used on the bases of the wooden columns (H) that demarcated the larger area around the temple. These square bricks, which were all flat, were found in two sizes, with sides measuring 0.25 m and 0.3 m. Pavement F was laid using bricks of both sizes, while the column bases (H) were made only of the larger size. In common with the Early Dynastic square bricks from later periods that were found elsewhere on Tell K, including the ones used on the Enmetena Esplanade, these square bricks were perhaps used principally as floor tiles. The square shape became standard in Girsu after the Akkad interval, when it was the primary form for Ur-Bau and Gudea.

> The fired bricks used to line the shaft of the Well of Eanatum, which were found to be rectangular, planoconvex and marked with a thumbprint and a fingerprint, measured 0.32 m × 0.21 m × 0.05 m, though a number of slightly variant sizes were found. According to Sarzec their average dimensions were 0.3 m × 0.2 m × 0.05 m.

> The fired bricks used for the pavement in the area of the Enmetena Esplanade and the associated Oval Reservoir, which were approximately the same size as those used on the Well of Eanatum, were flat and marked with a longitudinal groove made with a finger, and they measured about 0.32 m × 0.21 m × 0.05 m.

The fired bricks used to build the Enmetena Block, which were rectangular, flat and unmarked, measured 0.33 m × 0.24 m × 0.06 m.

For several reasons any such typochronology is not without its problems, for example because bricks were reused, and successive builders sometimes used the same types, and also because certain kinds of bricks (such as some of the ones found by Sarzec below the Oval Reservoir) seem only to have been employed in extremely limited contexts. Similarly, the same ruler occasionally made use of different types, while similar marks were applied to bricks from different periods. Nevertheless, it provides a good idea of the general and relative chronologies of the different structures and associated brick types, and although the details are sometimes confusing and even contradictory (notably when it comes to the Sarzec Esplanade), it is a pity that more attention has not been paid to Cros's creditable work because it sheds light on the mound's buildings and infrastructure, in particular the colossal mud-brick terrace platforms. Crucially, it also addresses previously unconsidered stratigraphic factors that are of considerable importance.

As Heuzey, Cros and more recently Forest have all understood, the temple architecture on Tell K can only be interpreted if it is considered as a whole, with respect to the entire mound (Fig. 59). The approach has to be comprehensive and total because the remains represent a very large complex made up of distinct structures that were all established on superimposed platforms and therefore archaeologically interconnected. The stratigraphy of Tell K as a whole is therefore relevant to any individual part of it, and this means that particular details cannot be approached in isolation. In consequence, local stratigraphic sequences must be collated to reconstruct a general chronological sequence that works on the scale of the entire mound, using comparisons of finds made in different parts of the site to fill gaps in what is known about the various construction phases. The interacting sequences help to establish the contemporaneity of different structures, and also to understand the chronological development of the complex (Fig. 60).

This approach—a total archaeology, to borrow the concept of 'total history' from the French historian Marc Bloch—is the best, if not the only way to make sense of the huge amount of problematic data that has been inherited from Sarzec and his successors, not least because it compensates for some significant lacunae in the published material. More importantly, it is a safeguard against the dangers of overinterpretation that can arise when particular sequences (notably, in this case, the central part of Tell K) are treated in isolation, and discontinuities in the data are filled with local interpolations, for instance by adding invisible layers or transitional phases for which there is no evidence, and which, when collated with finds made in other areas of the mound, can turn out to be little more than pure inventions. This has become a trend in the discipline of archaeology over the past few decades: bending archaeological data to fit an overcomplicated stratigraphy, with the justification that some or all of the evidence was collected a long time ago and must therefore be faulty. Any such interpolations have to be introduced with extreme caution (never forgetting that errors can be made even in the present age of digital archaeology), and only after the most minute cross-examination of the complete data set, including published reports, graphic representations and especially photographs. Otherwise, there is a risk of opening a Pandora's box of infinitely variable stratigraphic permutations—realigning structures and features, moving layers and adjusting measurements to make them fit a predetermined theory. As can be seen in the recontextualisation of the archaeology of Tell K presented below, a total and systematic approach mitigates these issues.

The increasing overinterpretation of the phasing or sequencing of the central section of Tell K is so flagrant in the bibliographic record that the following list speaks for itself: there are two phases in Heuzey, three in Parrot, four in Forest and six in Marchetti and Marchesi. As the present study lays out in detail, there are good reasons why the original sequence proposed by Heuzey should be reconsidered, but it is worth pausing for a moment to reflect on the general principle on which the ever-increasing succession of phases is based. In approaching the Lower Construction and the Ur-Nanshe Building, together with their associated deposits and artefacts, the proposed sequencings all assume that successive building phases should be defined from scratch. Depending on the number of phases identified, scholars have therefore assumed that two, three, four or six temples were built one on top of the other during the Early Dynastic period. But this fails to take account of the full spectrum of events that might have affected these religious buildings and their associated installations. In addition to their construction and reconstruction, the buildings might have been

138 The Mound of the House of the Fruits

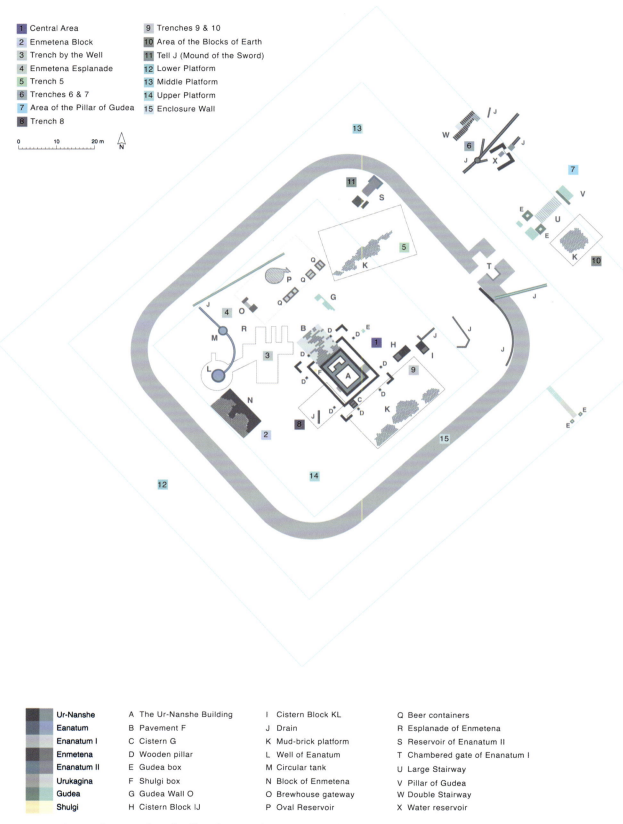

FIGURE 59. Comprehensive plan of Tell K, showing the monumental platforms, the temenos wall and other remains dating from Early Dynastic times to the reigns of Gudea and Shulgi. The named and numbered trenches refer to Cros's Plans A and B.

renovated, destroyed or abandoned. Crucially, they could also be decommissioned: closed and ritually interred prior to the construction of a new building or temple on the same spot, often at an elevated level. It is particularly noteworthy that the desacralisation phases have been completely overlooked on Tell K. The decommissioning of temples, which entailed considerable work that involved numerous rites and left behind significant traces, is vividly described in ancient inscriptions and attested by other temple excavations, including the British Museum team's work on Tell A. It should therefore come as no surprise that evidence of such procedures can also be identified on Tell K.

Another misleading idea is that Tell K contains a sequence of temples that were built in rapid succession, with each new iteration connected to a new ruler or overlord (Mesilim, for example) who might have left behind just one or two ex-votos. On the contrary, the buildings unearthed on Tell K seem to have been marked by a particular longevity, evidenced by renovations and repairs that were recorded on bricks, door sockets, foundation pegs and so forth. These actions and objects do not by any means necessarily signal the construction of an entirely new complex—a fact that is corroborated by the British Museum team's excavations of the contemporaneous Early Dynastic platforms on Tell A. It is also vividly attested by Gudea's New Eninnu, which was still in use on Tell A 400 years after its completion, having been renovated in the Ur III and Isin-Larsa periods.

The archaeological contexts of the diverse hoard of cultic objects found on Tell K present a further difficulty, but also an opportunity, because the provenances of the recovered artefacts, and especially their stratigraphic locations, provide vital clues that aid an understanding of the history of the mound's sanctuaries (Fig. 61). Countless studies have been devoted to a constellation of star objects, stressing their individual interest and worth, but far too little has been said about their broader archaeological characteristics and settings. These include, for example: first, for broken objects, whether or not they were ritually fractured prior to being buried, smashed as an act of desecration, broken accidentally or were simply subject to the passage of time; secondly, a detailed consideration of the archaeological horizon in which objects were found, and whether they were abandoned, caught up in a more general structural collapse, damaged by fire, or ritually interred; thirdly, whether particular items were found singly, as part of a loose scattering, or grouped (randomly or on purpose) with other similar or dissimilar objects; and finally whether the precise features of the find locations of objects were arbitrary, or perhaps of greater significance, as with objects that were unearthed, for instance, near thresholds and corners, next to walls and so forth.

Another critically important problem that has previously received scant attention is the difference between the kinds of damage that can be observed on sacred artefacts. As detailed on several occasions in the course of this study, there is a categorical difference between the desacralisation or deconsecration of sacred objects, on the one hand, and their malign defacement on the other. As is described below with respect to a number of key artefacts from Tell K, and also with regard to some of the Gudea statues found on Tell A, the pivotal question of whether such highly symbolic objects were damaged when they were ritually decommissioned, or whether they were profanely violated by antagonistic hands, is difficult to answer. The main reason for the quandary is that, although the intentions of the two actions were diametrically opposed, their results can appear very similar, making it extremely hard to judge whether a cult object was piously deconsecrated or symbolically defiled. The problem is further confounded by the fact that occasionally an object or a group of objects might show traces of having been first desacralised and later defaced (as is argued for some of the Gudea statues from Tell A). The key point to consider is that in all such cases (excluding instances where sacred artefacts were mindlessly smashed), both acts were deliberate, controlled and carried out by operatives who understood the religious significance of what they were doing. Clearly, the straightforward assessment of an object's condition might not be sufficient to determine beyond reasonable doubt whether an apparently intentional breakage—an impact, a crack or any other disfigurements—resulted from acts of planned deconsecration or were consequences of premeditated defilement or desecration. As regards figurative representations, both types of action targeted the same attributes: first and foremost, the facial features, notably the forehead, eyes, nose and ears (and sometimes also the fingertips and the tips of the toes). In acts of ritual desacralisation, the power or sacred essence of the representation was deactivated by symbolically vitiating parts of the anatomy and sensory centres before the image was interred. The aim was to nullify the eyesight, the intellect and the senses of smell, hearing and touch of figurative representations that

140　The Mound of the House of the Fruits

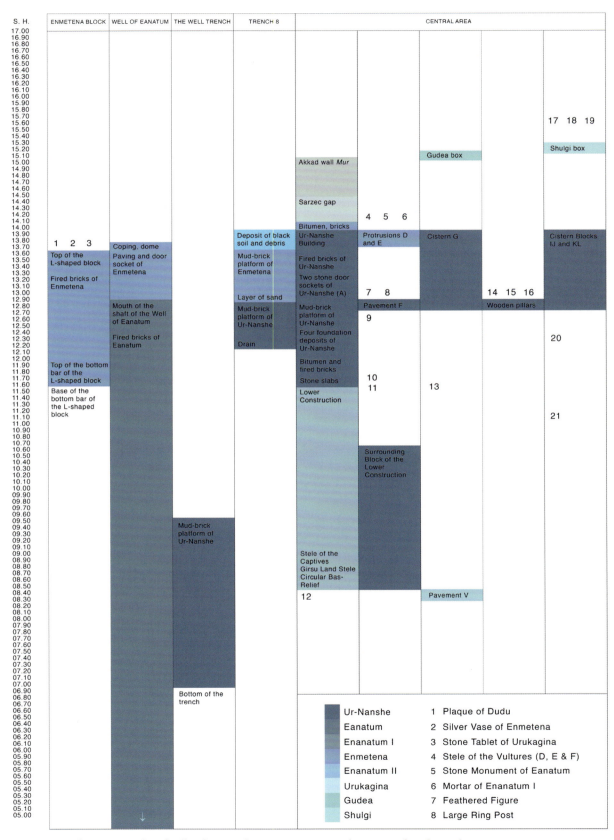

FIGURE 60. The Stratigraphy of Tell K from Early Dynastic times to the reigns of Gudea and Shulgi.

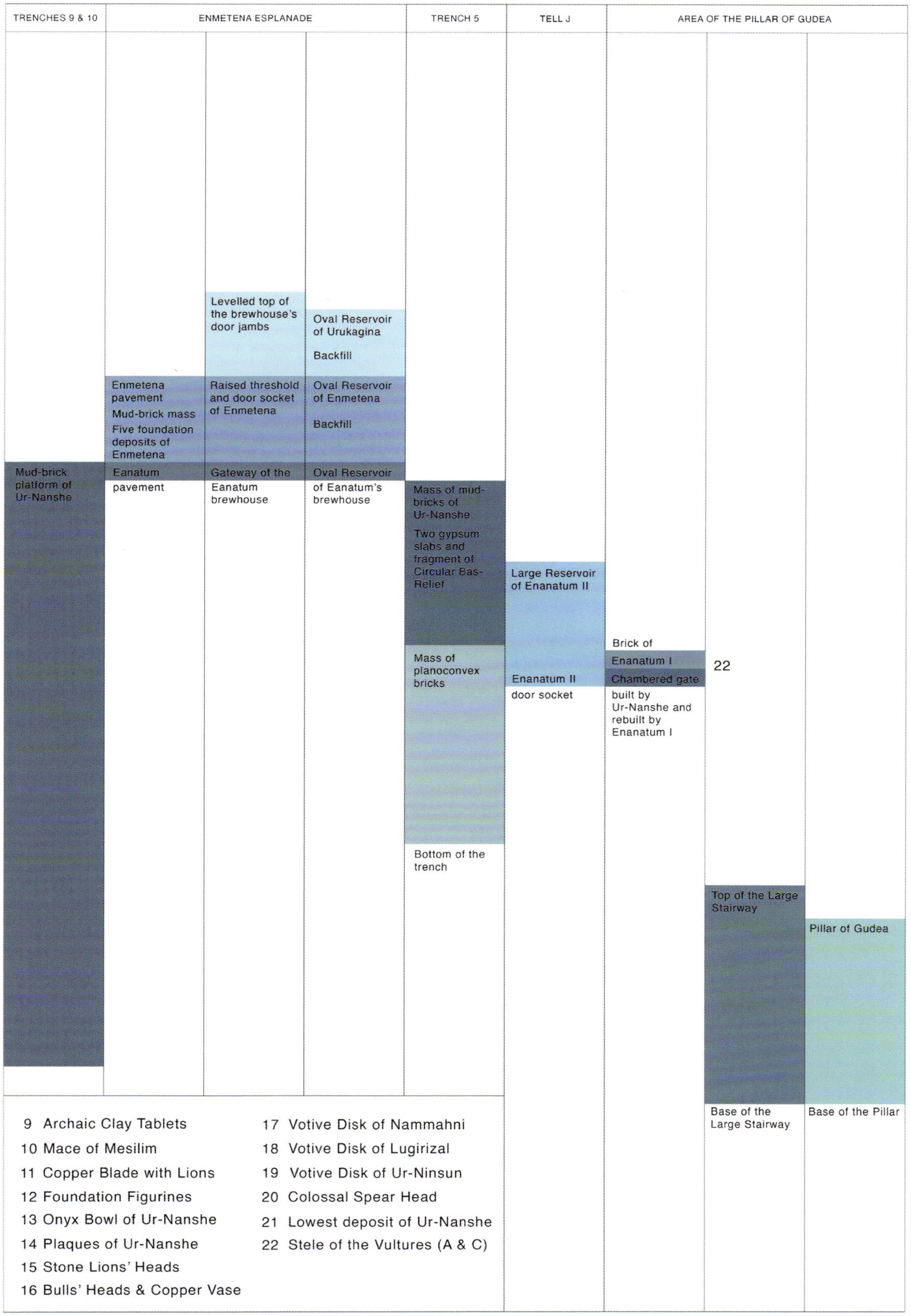

TRENCHES 9 & 10	ENMETENA ESPLANADE		TRENCH 5	TELL J	AREA OF THE PILLAR OF GUDEA	
		Levelled top of the brewhouse's door jambs	Oval Reservoir of Urukagina Backfill			
	Enmetena pavement Mud-brick mass Five foundation deposits of Enmetena	Raised threshold and door socket of Enmetena	Oval Reservoir of Enmetena Backfill			
Mud-brick platform of Ur-Nanshe	Eanatum pavement	Gateway of the Eanatum brewhouse	Oval Reservoir of Eanatum's brewhouse			
			Mass of mud-bricks of Ur-Nanshe Two gypsum slabs and fragment of Circular Bas-Relief	Large Reservoir of Enanatum II		
			Mass of planoconvex bricks	Enanatum II door socket	Brick of Enanatum I Chambered gate built by Ur-Nanshe and rebuilt by Enanatum I	22
			Bottom of the trench		Top of the Large Stairway	Pillar of Gudea
					Base of the Large Stairway	Base of the Pillar

9 Archaic Clay Tablets
10 Mace of Mesilim
11 Copper Blade with Lions
12 Foundation Figurines
13 Onyx Bowl of Ur-Nanshe
14 Plaques of Ur-Nanshe
15 Stone Lions' Heads
16 Bulls' Heads & Copper Vase
17 Votive Disk of Nammahni
18 Votive Disk of Lugirizal
19 Votive Disk of Ur-Ninsun
20 Colossal Spear Head
21 Lowest deposit of Ur-Nanshe
22 Stele of the Vultures (A & C)

142 The Mound of the House of the Fruits

FIGURE 61. Plan showing the principal constructions and notable objects excavated on Tell K, dating from Early Dynastic times to the reigns of Gudea and Shulgi.

had previously been transubstantiated and invested with a real spiritual presence by animation rituals. Similar elements were damaged in controlled acts of desecration or defilement that often also focused on emblems of power, but the motive in such instances was to abase and erase the religious and dedicatory force of images in acts of *damnatio memoriae* that conceptually obliterated them from existence. Since the condition of a particular object or set of objects does not necessarily confirm their ultimate fate, the analysis of condition must be supplemented by a close consideration of the objects' archaeological provenances, never forgetting that deconsecrated artefacts were solemnly buried in favissas or ritual pits in specially selected locations within a temple site. Condition is therefore important, but context is crucial.

Following on from that, the specific question of whether objects were found *in situ* or not is extremely problematic, partly because the definition of *in situ* is often somewhat loose, and the criteria (positive and negative) are applied indiscriminately. If an object was not found in what is presumed to have been its original location, should it therefore simply be regarded as a stray, or can a more exact judgement usefully be made about why it was no longer *in situ*—whether, for example, it was dislodged because of an architectural collapse? In order to avoid such interpretative generalisations, a threefold system of contextualisation is adopted in the present study: primary, for objects definitively found *in situ*—for example a paired foundation peg and tablet found in a platform, or an inscribed brick that was part of a built structure; secondary, for objects displaced by destructive events, for example a dislodged votive plaque that can be associated with a collapsed wall, or a deliberately defaced and displaced stele that was scattered in a destruction horizon; and tertiary for decontextualised objects, such as a fragment of a relief that was found in the packing of a sub-floor, or an isolated object found in a pit. As regards Tell K, a systematic discussion of the stratigraphic provenances of recovered artefacts, based on the system of contextualisation just outlined, is vital for the interpretation of the complex as a whole. Furthermore, just as some of the principal buildings on the mound remained in use for long periods, sometimes for several centuries, so objects invested with particular symbolic significance could also enjoy extended longevity. This adds a further layer of complexity to the discussion because artefacts produced under the authority of one ruler could be retained by his successors—one example being the Gudea door sockets from his Lagash II New Eninnu. As the British Museum team's investigations on Tell A have shown, these were still operational in the Isin-Larsa period, 400 years later.

Finally, an issue that has strangely never been addressed is the fact that the established corpus of finds from Tell K, which is made up almost exclusively of artefacts that were considered by the French pioneers to be of special interest, represents no more than a tiny portion of the totality. This means that the whole complex has been interpreted, and inevitably in many cases misinterpreted, on the basis of a relatively tiny number of supposedly representative items.

It is evident, of course, that hundreds or even thousands of apparently trivial potsherds were not recorded by Sarzec and his successors, but this is equally the case for a huge number of other finds that were not regarded as important. The truth of this is sadly evident in the enormous spoil heaps that are spread out across Tell K today, in which a plethora of discarded finds lie buried. There is no doubt that some of them contain important information about the history of the site, and that a fuller picture of the range of activities that took place there over many centuries can only emerge when the surviving objects and fragments, no matter how large or small, have been studied systematically. One consequence of the approach based on a small selection of star artefacts—an issue that crops up repeatedly in the bibliography—is that the focus of interest is narrowed to include only isolated areas or trenches, or particular data sets. In practice, such constricted viewpoints are governed by the choices Sarzec and Heuzey made when they drew Plan C (1 and 2) (Fig. 33), pinpointing a limited set of numbered items that were found in the vicinity of the Ur-Nanshe Building. Objects found just outside the boundaries demarcated by the plans (the Enmetena Vase, for example) are consequently all too often overlooked, even if their archaeological contexts are similar to items marked on the plans. This again means that the established range of sources is not actually representative.

In sum, in close collaboration with Sarzec, Heuzey compiled and interpreted the mass of first-hand data from Tell K that Sarzec gathered. The task was made more complicated by the fact that Sarzec was in Iraq for long periods, while Heuzey was in Paris, and that after Sarzec's death in 1902 Heuzey was left to make sense of Sarzec's notes on his own. Nonetheless, the resulting publications are the primary sources of information available to later researchers. Added to that are any further judgements that can be made about the actual excavations that Sarzec carried out on the tell. Finally, there are the published accounts of the work undertaken by Cros (often closely guided by Heuzey), not neglecting the fact that Cros's particular set of skills was rather different from that of Sarzec. The historical foundation provided by all of this material is that Tell K contained two important Early Dynastic sanctuaries, each centred around a core building: the earlier Lower Construction and the superimposed Ur-Nanshe Building. Both religious centres had associated annexes, and both enjoyed long lifespans, including several subphases of construction that were marked by specific building events, renovations, deliberate deconsecrations or malign acts of destruction, as well as ritual interments. This is the archaeological context for the detailed analyses of the stratigraphic relationships between the structures uncovered on Tell K that are laid out in the following chapters, preceded by an overview of the history of Girsu against the broad backdrop of changing political, social and religious trends in Sumer in the fourth and third millennia BCE.

CHAPTER 11

The Origins and Early Historical Significance of the Temple of Ningirsu

Prolegomenon: The Pre-Eminence of Uruk and the Role of Inanna

The history of Girsu at the beginning of the third millennium BCE is shrouded in a seemingly impenetrable fog of obscurity, such that the origins of the Temple of Ningirsu lie buried in the darkness of proto-historic times. The problem is a general one that affects the whole history of Sumer in the early third millennium. After the exceptional richness and sunlike radiance of the previous period, known as the Late Uruk era (c.3400–3100 BCE), which witnessed, among other things, the birth of cuneiform writing, the centuries that followed left behind very little evidence of the events and historical personalities that shaped them. The long epoch of uncertainty is conventionally divided into two periods, known as Jemdet Nasr (c.3100–2900 BCE) and Early Dynastic I (c.2900–2600 BCE). The latter, which was formerly considered to have an early and a late phase (labelled Early Dynastic I and II), is also referred to as the heroic age because, according to the later chronicle known as the Sumerian King List, this is when most of the semi-legendary heroes of Sumer were believed to have lived—Enmerkar, Lugalbanda, Gilgamesh and Agga, for example. The main difficulty that impedes an understanding of what was happening in ancient Sumer between about 3400 BCE and 2900 BCE is the absence of explicit testimony from appropriate sources. Very little documentation has survived, apart from some extremely early proto-cuneiform texts that are mostly administrative records, lexical lists and school exercises, while the task of establishing the context and significance of the documents that have been preserved is made all the more difficult by their scarcity and also by the lack of complementary supporting evidence.

Despite these evident stumbling-blocks, archaeologists and Assyriologists have sketched out the broad outlines of a much-debated political and religious evolution that is tentatively thought to have taken place during the period. One basis of this theory is the phenomenon known as the Uruk expansion, which refers to the appearance and subsequent collapse of identifiable cultural colonies or centres of Uruk influence (sometimes called 'emporia') that spread out beyond the Mesopotamian heartland in southern Iraq to encompass a vast territorial zone in which Uruk values and practices predominated. The dynamic engine that powered the expansion was the sustained urban growth and development of Uruk itself. And yet, while there can be no doubt that Uruk played a crucial, dominant role in Babylonia and beyond from around 3400 to 2900 BCE, it should also be recalled that the main sources that confirm the city-state's power and prestige also originate in Uruk. It is therefore vital to remain cautious about the effects of Uruk's own propaganda and self-promotion, and to be aware that the shape of the historical model may not therefore be representative for the whole of Sumer. Those caveats aside, with its charismatic social, religious and aesthetic standards, Uruk certainly played a key role in the history of the region during the late fourth and early third millennia BCE, especially in the territories that were controlled by the principal Mesopotamian cities. Uruk influence can be seen above all in the widespread cult of the state's great goddess, Inanna, as witnessed by the multiplication of shrines dedicated to her in places well beyond the confines of the city and its surrounding countryside. More specifically, the administrative or political control that Uruk must have exercised over Babylonia is attested by texts from Jemdet Nasr (perhaps NI.RU) and Uqair (Urum), for instance, that record the dispatch of special deliveries of goods that were owed or pledged to the goddess Inanna in Uruk (see Szarzyńska 1993, pp. 7–26).

It is not possible to say with certainty whether the proliferating cult of Inanna that was exported from Uruk reached Girsu and its environs at this very early period. The fact that Girsu and neighbouring Nigin had definite connections with Uruk is probably confirmed by their appearance in an archaic source known as the Uruk List of Cities, though it should be stressed that the ability of scholars to read and understand this archaic material is limited, while the process of correlating information derived from such archaic texts with what is known from later sources is far from straightforward (see Lecompte 2009). In consequence, most entries in the Uruk List of Cities are simply unintelligible, but Girsu and Nigin seem to be included as GÍR$_a$ SU$_a$ (59) and NANŠE$_b$ (18) in the original, and as ĝír.su (60) and ^{d}nanše (18) in the edited Early Dynastic version. Lagash is markedly absent from the list, however, though it might of course have appeared in a lost section, or lie hidden in the preserved text, masked by unfamiliar spelling or indecipherable characters. In any event, though the origins of her cult remain obscure, there is no doubt that Inanna became an important deity later on in the history of Girsu and Lagash. In the reign of Gudea she was a member of the Lagash pantheon that revolved around Ningirsu, taking her place alongside the local goddesses Bau, Gatumdug (perhaps originally a hypostasis of Bau whose distinct identity had again become merged with that of Bau by that date) and Nanshe. Inanna was manifestly venerated in Girsu from the time of the First Dynasty founded by Ur-Nanshe in the Early Dynastic IIIb period through to the abandonment of the city in Old Babylonian times (c.1750 BCE), but whether Inanna worship in the area began centuries earlier, during the period of Uruk ascendancy in the early third millennium, is unknown. The picture is further complicated by the profound reshaping of the religious setting of the entire state of Lagash that took place in the reign of Ur-Nanshe, who might have inducted Inanna into the local pantheon.

The leading role that Inanna played in the dominant religious practices in a large area of southern Mesopotamia in the age of state formation in the late fourth and early third millennia BCE seems to be corroborated by the first written administrative records from Uruk, though these are slightly at odds with the evidence provided by the Uruk List of Cities. The list opens with an incipit that successively enumerates Ur, Nippur, Larsa and Uruk, an order that has been interpreted in a theological sense as a repertoire of sacred places that reflects a religious hierarchy, beginning with the household of the moon god Nanna, followed by that of the god Enlil, the sun god Utu and so on. The clear implication is that Nanna, Enlil, Utu and Inanna were all members of the primordial pantheon of Uruk (Englund 1998, p. 92). That being the case, however, why was Inanna not listed first, especially as her paramount importance is indicated by other relevant archaeological and epigraphical evidence? Much remains unclear, but the crux of the matter lies in identifying some continuous lines that run through the thinking of the period, even if it is finally impossible to go beyond a fairly rudimentary stage of reconstruction. Nonetheless, it seems likely that the scribes and thinkers who produced these archaic documents were imbued with beliefs that led them to identify particular territories with the gods who protected them. Classifying the enumerated cities and their environs according to doctrinal criteria, the first scribes thus left behind implicit testimonies of how geographical settings were perceived in sacred contexts. Although no archaic catalogue of the gods has survived, the Uruk List of Cities seems to be guided by a framework of theological assumptions (see Lecompte 2009).

The Emergence of Girsu and Lagash after the Uruk Ascendancy

Following the collapse of the networks of influence associated with Uruk, a pan-Babylonian league or federation of cities emerged. The first of several such organisations, it developed particularly during the Jemdet Nasr period, and some key evidence for its emergence is contained in another major archaic source: the City Seal, also known as the City Seal Impressions, referring to the proto-cuneiform symbols made by the seal on a number of preserved clay sealings that probably record the names of cities. It is generally accepted that there was some form of cooperation between the cities named in the City Seal Impressions, even though not all of the urban centres have yet been identified (see Matthews 1993, pp. 33–40). The names that have been deciphered include Ur, Larsa, Nippur, Uruk, Kesh, Zabala(m) (?) and possibly Ku'ara (Urum?) and Cutha (?). In addition, several archaic texts from the city of Jemdet Nasr form a corpus that indicates possible connections between the cities of Uruk and Jemdet Nasr, though this depends on whether the characters transcribed as NI_A + RU (NI.RU) have been correctly understood as referring to Jemdet Nasr (Steinkeller 2002, p. 253). A further complication is that, although the Uruk expansion abated in the late fourth millennium, the state of Uruk itself nevertheless continued to flourish and grow through the Jemdet Nasr and Early Dynastic I periods, when the city reached the peak of its size and prosperity. It has therefore been suggested that Uruk might have maintained its central, commanding role in the region even after its cultural values and practices had ceased to predominate. Adding to these difficulties is the fact that the written records from these early periods do not provide a reliable definition of the territories and political spheres of influence that served as the basis of emerging cities or states in the wider Mesopotamian floodplain.

A few key hypotheses have been formulated to explain the regional political structures of the early third millennium BCE, though the absence of reliable epigraphic documentation makes it finally impossible to confirm whether any of them accurately describe the actual historical circumstances that prevailed: a) the City Seal confirms the existence of independent states that were comparable in size and structure to the documented city-states of the subsequent Early Dynastic period; b) while maintaining their independence and local autonomy, the cities represented in the City Seal Impressions were all members of a common league with an unknown centre; or c) the listed cities all acknowledged the overriding supremacy of Uruk. The likelihood of the last argument is probably reduced because (as noted above) Uruk does not figure first on the list, and that might point to the existence of a league of states rather than to a group of subordinates that owed allegiance to a dominant regional power. It is nevertheless conceivable that Uruk administrators held sway over relatively limited parts of Sumer and exercised direct rule over cities such as Larsa. Conversely, the purported league of cities might have been principally a religious rather than a political organisation (assuming those two things were at least partially separable at that period), and might perhaps best be regarded as a religious amphictyony or association of states. Amidst the dizzying range of possibilities, one thing that can currently be said with some degree of certainty is that (unless their names are present but indecipherable) neither Girsu nor Lagash are listed in the City Seal Impressions, and they were not therefore part of any league of cities or religious association of states that might have existed during Jemdet Nasr and Early Dynastic I times.

More illuminating information can be derived from some exceptional documents that have strangely been ignored in the quest to construct a picture of Girsu in the early third millennium. They include four foundational artefacts that were all intimately connected with the Lower Construction, the earliest-known iteration of the Temple of Ningirsu on Tell K. They are the relief plaque known as the Feathered Figure; the so-called archaic Lagash *kudurru* or border stone, here referred to as the Girsu Land Stele; the Circular Bas-Relief; and the archaic victory stele, which is here titled the Stele of the Captives. As is demonstrated in the following chapters, a thorough re-examination and recontextualisation of these important objects helps to elucidate the period of obscurity, suggesting a plausible historical framework for the origins of the Ningirsu temple, as well as a more precise answer than has previously been found to another vital question: the date of the union between Girsu and Lagash. Surprisingly, this key issue has rarely been addressed, the general consensus being that the fusion of Girsu and Lagash into a single state that also included Nigin (forming the tripolis or triad of the territory of Lagash) was the masterstroke of Ur-Nanshe. While there is no doubt that Ur-Nanshe initiated changes that amounted to a politico-religious earthquake, or that he was the originator of the recognised Presargonic city-state of Lagash that established a widely adopted pattern of organisation and governance, this does not mean that an antecedent union between Girsu and Lagash could not have existed, even if the details and characteristics of the alliance are largely unknown.

Dating back to Early Dynastic I times, the earliest historical and archaeological evidence from Girsu paints a picture of a pre-eminent archaic city whose distinction and prestige were inextricably bound up with its tutelary god, Ningirsu, and his temple on Tell K. In this respect, the Feathered Figure (discussed in detail in Chapter 13 below), which is rightly perceived as an extraordinary object today, was also viewed as such for many centuries after it was created in the Early Dynastic I period, down to the reign of Enmetena in

Early Dynastic IIIb times. Throughout the first part of the third millennium BCE, as a foundational artefact that was preserved as a precious relic by successive rulers of the First Dynasty established by Ur-Nanshe, the sculpture was held to be imbued with a special content and potent significance. It features the earliest representation of the mighty Ningirsu taking procession of his temple, which is referred to in the Sumerian text inscribed on the relief as his house (é.Ningirsu) and symbolised graphically by two tall posts that are crowned with his emblem—the mace head that is his divine weapon. The work incorporates a hymn to the god (^{d}Nin-ĝír-su zà-mì) that is written in archaic cuneiform script, and just as importantly an inventory of some now obscure, but precisely measured and demarcated plots of land that are identified with ceremonial names, all of which are recorded as belonging to Ningirsu. With its remarkable combination of imagery and texts, the Feathered Figure appears to have signified the synthesis of a primordial legal, religious and social order that was based on the link forged between the heroic god and the city at the precise moment when he took possession of his house and lands. It was a relationship that extended to include the ruling class and the citizenry who served Ningirsu by maintaining his dwelling, working his lands and administering the state on his behalf.

Girsu's identity as a sacred centre of the first order was crystallised in the cardinal connections between the god and the state that were communicated by the makers of the Feathered Figure, and the same nexus is commemorated on another seminal object that dates from about the same period. The usual name given to the Lagash *kudurru* is extremely misleading. The word *kudurru* relates to the Akkadian term for a Mesopotamian (specifically Babylonian) symbolic boundary stone on which were inscribed the records of land grants (or documents pertaining to the sales of land) at a much later period in the region's history, long after the date of the Early Dynastic I carved stone excavated on Tell K that is here referred to as the Girsu Land Stele (detailed in Chapter 13). Though fragmentary and difficult to read, the Girsu Land Stele lists huge tracts of land, amounting in total to some 4,666 km², that presumably denoted the extent of Ningirsu's domain, and which, by direct extension, was also the territory ruled on the god's behalf by archaic Girsu. The sheer size of the lands controlled by Girsu is staggering. As a point of comparison, the agrarian area administered by Presargonic Lagash when it was still part of the tripolis has

been estimated at about 3,000 km². Carved in stone instead of being inscribed on inexpensive clay, the Feathered Figure and the Girsu Land Stele were both presumably intended to be permanent and enduring records of the foundational covenant between the god and the state that had a multi-layered significance: religious, political, legal and archival. The durability of the materials of which the artefacts were made was no doubt symbolic of the enduring nature of the contract between the people and the god, and of Ningirsu's undying sovereignty over the land—and it would perhaps come as little surprise to the designers and fabricators of those objects that they are still in existence some 5,000 years later. In terms of the history of Mesopotamia in the early third millennium BCE, these two exceptional documents leave little doubt that Girsu in the Early Dynastic I period was an important political centre in Sumer and that it exercised control over a very large area of land that probably extended far beyond its immediately surrounding countryside.

The question of whether Girsu was an independent city-state in the strictest sense of the word, or whether it had already formed a strong bond with Lagash, is difficult to answer. The earliest preserved occurrence of the word Lagash ([GA]L.LU$_2$ LA.BUR.NU$_{11}$) is found on an Early Dynastic I tablet from the city of Ur that slightly predates the Feathered Figure (see Glassner 2000, p. 47; and Lecompte 2020, p. 432). Remarkably, the word also incorporates the first-known instance of the use of the Sumerian term lugal to signify something close to the modern idea of a 'king' or a 'lord'. Though the precise meaning of lugal in this context is uncertain, it undoubtedly represents something quite different from the raft of titles that had been used to designate the holders of power since Late Uruk times. These include: en, meaning 'eminent one', or 'priest'; ensi (ensí), literally meaning 'lord of the grain', and denoting 'governor' or 'city ruler'; sanga (saĝĝa), the word used to refer to a 'temple administrator'; and possibly also nám.šità (or namešda), literally meaning 'lord of the mace' (see Steinkeller 2017, pp. 96–100 and 103–4). This small scrap of evidence deriving from a broken archaic tablet from Ur comes fraught with caveats, however. It surely does not imply that, since there was apparently no lugal in Ur, the ruler of Lagash was also the overlord of Ur; and it is quite possible that the use of the word might not originally have meant 'king' at all, but perhaps denoted something entirely different—a person's name, for example. Similarly, taken as a whole, the remains of the archaic archives of Ur are too small and cryptic to give a truly reliable insight into the territorial formations that existed at the period, though the mention of Lagash is without doubt unusual because foreign places are not commonly mentioned in such Ur documents. All things considered, the possibility remains that the appearance of Lagash on the archaic Ur tablet, in a compound word that includes the term lugal, signals the existence of a greater regional power, with its centre in Lagash, that presided over a federation or league of cities that was a rival to the alliance led by Uruk or Ur. The corollary to this is that, by this date, Ur had probably become the de facto replacement for the defunct central administration of the previous Uruk regime, whose influence had been decisive in the preceding centuries (see Sallaberger et al. 2015, p. 58).

Do these admittedly conjectural possibilities imply that Girsu and Lagash had developed into autonomous neighbouring regional superpowers by the early third millennium, or were they already very closely allied? The answer to that tantalising question might be finally unknowable, but further clues can be gleaned from the contemporary Circular Bas-Relief and the Stele of the Captives from Tell K (see Chapter 13). The two objects have been the subjects of important exegeses, but they have not been scrutinised with a view to resolving the problem of whether a powerful union between Girsu and Lagash existed during Early Dynastic I times. The fragmentary condition of the Stele of the Captives (not to mention the fact that is was reprehensibly discarded by Sarzec and subsequently lost or destroyed) means that its testimony must inevitably be rather limited and generalised, though it does clearly signify the apparent might of Girsu in a rare monumental portrayal of some Girsu soldiers in charge of a group of defeated and shackled prisoners of war. The Circular Bas-Relief (Fig. 62) tells a much richer and more cogent story. It depicts what was in all likelihood a ceremonial

FIGURE 62. The Circular Bas-Relief. Musée du Louvre AO2350.

pact between two rulers, each holding insignias of power, as they head their respective cohorts of prominent followers. Beyond the fact that one of the principal protagonists must surely have been a ruler of Girsu, the people and events that the carving commemorates cannot be known with certainty. Nevertheless, as is argued in greater detail in Chapter 13, it is tempting to connect the carved scene with an epoch-making agreement between Girsu and Lagash that essentially united the two domains. Furthermore, it is surely of the utmost importance that these four archaic objects—the Circular Bas-Relief (a carved altar podium that held another cult object), the Stele of the Captives, the inscribed Girsu Land Stele and the Feathered Figure—were all housed in the most sacred space at the heart of the earliest known Temple of Ningirsu on Tell K. Taken together, they document the theological and political rationale of a developing, but already pre-eminent regional power, noting the extent of the land that it controlled, and commemorating the state's supreme divine overlord, Ningirsu.

Whether this theory is right or wrong, it is probable that an alliance between Girsu and Lagash had already been formed before Ur-Nanshe ascended to the throne in about 2460 BCE. This is proven by archaeological and epigraphic evidence that dates back to the preceding Early Dynastic IIIa period, also referred to as the Fara epoch, after the name of the ancient Sumerian site of Shuruppak. A fairly significant amount of historical data has survived from Fara times, including cuneiform tablets, temple hymns (known as zà-mì) from Abu Salabikh and the first royal inscriptions, all of which provide solid foundations for the construction of a historical narrative. One striking fact that immediately jumps out from these texts is that, even in the very first written accounts from the period, the union between Girsu and Lagash is referred to as an established reality, as though the close alliance had been in place for centuries. The first named ruler who can be identified was a certain Lugalshaengur about whom nothing is known apart from his title: ensi of Lagash (with Girsu notable by its absence). Lugalshaengur's name and office were found carved alongside that of Mesilim king of Kish, who was in effect a foreign overlord, on the superb votive mace head dedicated to Ningirsu that was found by Sarzec (discussed further in Chapter 15). The juxtaposition indicates that by the time the mace was inscribed and placed in the Temple of Ningirsu on Tell K (possibly sometime between 2600 BCE and 2500 BCE, though the exact date is unknown) the state of Lagash—presumably including Girsu, since that was Ningirsu's primary abode—had already lost some of its previous eminence and become subservient to Kish, the rising great power of central Mesopotamia. Despite that, the charisma of the Ningirsu temple continued to exert its influence to the extent that Mesilim, who was at that moment one of the most powerful kings in the region, and a figure who went on to achieve legendary status during the whole of the subsequent Presargonic era, honoured it with an exceptional token of respect. Intriguingly though rather vaguely, the inscription on the splendid mace head, which refers to the donor as a 'temple builder for the god Ningirsu', intimates that Mesilim might even have left his architectural mark on the temple itself.

Signs of the new order that emerged with the rise of Kish have come to light in other parts of Sumer, probably in association with the Hexapolis (also known as the Kiengir League or Regio), which was another confederation of cities that cooperated on a supraregional level. The alliance included Shuruppak, Umma, Uruk, Nippur, Adab and (this time) Lagash, all under the dominance or hegemony of Kish. Nothing is known about the precise nature of the new league, including its manner of organisation and the extent of Kish's authority, but it is safe to say that, unlike Uruk in its glorious heyday, Kish's influence was not maintained on account of the magnetic allure of its religious practices. That role appears to have been taken up by Nippur, which was on the way to becoming the undisputed cult centre of the Sumerian world, most importantly because it was the home of Enlil, the supreme deity of the Sumerian pantheon. This is reflected in the exceptional Praise Be hymns from modern-day Abu Salabikh (perhaps ancient Kesh or Eresh), which take the form of verses that all follow exactly the same pattern of naming a city and praising its god, before going on to celebrate more of the city's fine qualities (see Biggs 1974, pp. 45–56). The entire series begins with Nippur and Enlil: 'In the city of Nippur, praise to [the] god Enlil'. Lagash, Nigin (which is referred to as Sirara, the name of its sacred precinct) and Girsu are included in the sequence, together with a host of cities representing all parts of Babylonia. The verses celebrating Lagash allude to its 'sweet clay', whatever that might mean, and then pay homage to the goddess Gatumdug (Lagaš im.ku₇ ᵈGá.tùm.dùg zà-mì). The Nigin section extols Nanshe, while Girsu is described as the 'Girnun house', and praise is offered to Ningirsu (Gír.su é.gír.nun ᵈNin. ğír.su zà-mì). The pan-Babylonian scope of the Praise Be hymns clearly reflects a shared cultural identity that was based on common religious beliefs, with Enlil of Nippur at the head of the canonical pantheon. Indeed, the intention behind the hymns seems to have been to crystallise a generally acknowledged theological creed and to consolidate Enlil's authority (Selz 1997, p. 170).

As for the Hexapolis, some Early Dynastic IIIa tablets from Shuruppak record that the federation, referred to as ki.en.gi, jointly conscripted a body of corvée troops (guruš) to fight an adversary whose identity is unknown, though it could presumably have been Ur, a city-state that is hardly mentioned in the Shuruppak texts. It seems that Kish might well have been the hegemonic guardian of this new world order, and the possibility of some form of overlordship is intimated by the fact that Mesilim of Kish acted as the arbitrator in resolving the border dispute between Lagash and neighbouring Umma. The problem of assessing the true power of Kish is made more complicated by the city's prominence in the Sumerian King List, which contains a supposedly unbroken series of dynasties and kings (nonetheless excluding Lagash altogether) that extends from the mythical beginnings of kingship down to the times in which the preserved manuscripts were composed. In one recension, starting with the first dynasty of Kish, the sequence encompasses the Ur III epoch and the period after the fall of Isin; a second version begins with the kings who ruled before the flood, before going on to itemise the sequence of postdiluvian rulers, again beginning with the first dynasty of Kish and finishing with the first dynasty of Isin. As this suggests, Kish generally looms large in Sumerian semi-legendary historiography, although its pre-eminence in factual historical sources is more nuanced—it receives little attention in the surviving lexical lists of geographical locations, for example. But the kingship of Kish held an irresistible fascination for other Sumerian cities (and for the Akkad rulers who came to power much later), such that the title of lugal Kish was regularly adopted by strong, or would-be omnipotent rulers as an honorific and a mark of power. Accordingly, in an inscription from Presargonic Girsu, the epithet is said to have been bestowed upon Eanatum (the grandson of Ur-Nanshe) by Inanna (RIME 1.9.3.5): 'With the rulership of Lagash, she [Inanna] gave him [Eanatum] the kingship of Kish'. Later on, the title lugal Kish was used by Sargonic rulers as a synonym for 'king of the world', a meaning that was reinforced by a play on words between the Sumerian word KIŠ and the Akkadian *kiššatum*, connoting a 'totality'. Kish was clearly a cultural and political centre at the heart of a network of connected Sumerian cities that reached out to include the much wider Mesopotamian sphere of influence (or koine) that took in Mari and Ebla, though the often-invoked idea of a Kish civilisation (Gelb 1982, pp. 121–202) is probably an overstatement. Perhaps the overriding conclusion is that an extensive area of Mesopotamia that stretched out beyond the Sumerian heartlands was composed of a large number of separate city-states that increasingly had a common character and shared core values: political, religious (both institutional and territorial) and linguistic features including a shared language, writing conventions, numbering and dating systems.

The Influence of Ur-Nanshe

The reign of Ur-Nanshe of Lagash (Fig. 63) ushered in a new era known as the Early Dynastic IIIb or Presargonic period, comprising the succession of rulers who governed Lagash between about 2460 and 2300 BCE. After Ur-Nanshe himself, notable rulers include his grandson Eanatum, his great grandson Enmetena and the final Presargonic ruler, Urukagina, whose reign came to an end when the consolidated state of Girsu and Lagash was finally and decisively overrun by the neighbouring state of Umma, led by Lugalzagesi. Preserved historical sources increase exponentially during the reigns of Ur-Nanshe and his successors. Comprising royal inscriptions and administrative documents, they form a corpus of texts that includes about 120 royal inscriptions and some 2,000 administrative tablets from the households of the last queens of Lagash (the é.mí or 'house of the women', later renamed by Urukagina as the é.Bau (é.^{d}ba-ba$_6$), or 'house of the goddess Bau') that date to the last three reigns of the First Dynasty (Enentarzi to Urukagina, c.2327–2307 BCE). These documents help to provide a richer and more reliable picture of the Ningirsu temple's historical context in the period, and they contribute greatly to the archaeological understanding of how the temple developed and changed under successive rulers.

Royal titles including ensi and lugal were generally used on inscriptions in Girsu and Lagash throughout the period, as they were in Sumer as a whole, but they seem to have been less closely bound up with straightforward notions of hierarchical status than they had been in the preceding centuries.

152 The Mound of the House of the Fruits

FIGURE 63. Ur-Nanshe Plaque B. Musée du Louvre AO2345.

Local customs and the precise historical conditions or circumstances of the merged domain seem to have determined the use of such appellations, and a close attention to such specifics is an important guide to the evolution of the state's political and territorial structures (see Marchetti and Marchesi 2011, pp. 110–13). The complexity of the territorial formations that characterised the Early Dynastic IIIb period in southern Mesopotamia is illuminated by a consideration of the region's intertwined political and religious history. Certain cities that demonstrated enhanced religious and cultural charisma constituted centres of influence that enabled them to cut through the intricacies of local politics and assume the role of overarching regional entities. This was certainly the case with Nippur (see Selz 1990, p. 180). As in previous eras, states seem to have formed changing alliances or federations that were overseen by a dominant member, whose authority was consequently magnified, with the autonomy of the subordinate cities being proportionally diminished.

As suggested above, Ur-Nanshe, who came from Gursar, which was probably in the vicinity of Nigin, appears to have consolidated the already close association—one that should probably be referred to as an existing union—between Lagash and Girsu. He did not usher in a new state *ex novo*, but rather turned the already settled alliance into a more formal and widely acknowledged national entity, if that term can be admitted. As his inscriptions proclaim, he achieved this in geographical terms by unifying the entire territory of Girsu–Lagash from the Gu'edena borderlands that demarcated the state's inland boundaries to the coastal areas known as the Gu'abba (the district of the sea). Perhaps even more importantly, he created a new religious framework for the merged state that was absolutely crucial for its survival and sustainability (Fig. 64). Ur-Nanshe's reformed religious structure was centred around the pantheon that was headed by Girsu's chief god, Ningirsu, while the associated infrastructure of sacred places and ritual practices was the foundation upon

FIGURE 64. An Ur-Nanshe copper foundation peg with a copper collar (both inscribed). British Museum 96565.

which the whole state, with its diverse urban and rural centres, together with its rulers, priests and citizenry more generally, was built. At first glance, the new formation might seem unwieldy compared to other contemporary states of the time, but in terms of size it was probably smaller than the Hexapolis previously controlled by Kish. Such extended unified territories were therefore not unknown, even if the state ruled by Ur-Nanshe was more homogeneous than previous looser confederations. As also noted above, Nigin was absorbed into Ur-Nanshe's unified territory, though the triad of cities (Girsu, Lagash and Nigin) seem each to have maintained their own traditions and local social systems. This might similarly have been the case for less prominent districts, but the reconstituted religious substructure that Ur-Nanshe instituted provided the fixative that held the compound together. The metaphor of fixing probably understates the case, however, and it would perhaps be better to say the spiritual dynamics of the worship of Ningirsu and the Girsu pantheon provided the positive energy that fused the state's disparate parts into a single whole. Rulers of the First Dynasty accordingly strove to maintain the bonds of solidarity among its multiple urban and regional members through the mediation of religion. This was the practical effect of the various city and rural cults, ritual processions in honour of the state's foremost deities, together with sacred festivals and the formal reverence paid to former rulers and priestly officials, who were known as the 'sleeping lords or en(s)' (see Rosengarten 1960, pp. 249–302; Selz 1995; and Steinkeller 2017, pp. 30–1).

The idea that, in the greater part of the third millennium BCE, southern Mesopotamia was the scene of ceaseless competition for ascendancy between a relatively small group of city-states seems generally to hold true. Such conflicts were probably settled—or perhaps extremely well contained—inside the borders of the formally combined territory of Girsu, Lagash and Nigin, though the only evidence that survives is circumstantial. With the apparent weakening of Kish, perhaps in the late Early Dynastic IIIa period, the Hexapolis presumably collapsed, and that is why Lagash and Umma, both now freed from the overarching constraints imposed by the alliance, could dispense with the resolution of their long-standing disagreement that had been negotiated by Kish and renew hostilities over control of their shared border—a conflict that was prolonged throughout most of the Early Dynastic IIIb era. Other connections were maintained, however. For example, Umma, which continued to cooperate with Uruk, even sustained links with the slightly more distant region of Nippur. Viewed in this light, the attempt at unifying the entire region by military means that was undertaken by Lugalzagesi (the eventual conqueror of Lagash in the reign of Urukagina) at the very end of the Presargonic era could possibly be seen as an outgrowth or even a late survival of the old Hexapolis. As previously indicated, it is also striking that the rulers of Uruk (in common with powerful states at other periods) adopted the title of king of Kish to cement their desired supremacy, even though the two cities were long-standing rivals.

Unfortunately, the details of the many city alliances that must have existed in the Early Dynastic IIIb period are not known, but it is on record that the rulers of the extended state of Lagash regularly and independently opposed other cities without forging agreements with potential allies. Under Eanatum, for instance, Lagash apparently clashed with the combined forces of Umma, Uruk, Ur, Kish and Akshak. By contrast, although Enmetena seems once again to have subdued the state of Umma, he also apparently made a pact with Lugalkineshdudu, the king of Uruk, with whom he established a bond that was referred to as a 'brotherhood'. What lies behind the epithet is an open question, but it might indicate an attempt to resolve some sort of intervention in the affairs of Lagash that had been attempted by the king of Uruk, or perhaps it was simply an attempt on the part of Enmetena to attract a desirable ally. A further suggestion is that the pact might have been a response to the control exercised by Lagash during the reign of Enmetena over the venerable city of Badtibira (entered in the Sumerian King List as the second antediluvian locus of kingship): perhaps the 'brotherhood' between Lagash and Uruk therefore signalled the king of Uruk's acceptance of the state of affairs as a fait accompli. It is also noteworthy that, under Enmetena, a decision was taken to cancel debts owed to Lagash by citizens of Uruk, Larsa and Badtibira. As has been suggested elsewhere (Selz 1995, p. 150), the debt-relief programme, which might have been instituted for commercial reasons, was perhaps a way of restoring financial independence to groups of citizens who could then have helped to supply Lagash with new labour forces. Despite the speculative nature of the narrative, which is impeded by a frustrating lack of further details, a complex picture can be sketched out of the changing relative situations of a close-knit group of states during Early Dynastic IIIb times.

A further question concerns the reign of Lugalzagesi, and especially his ability to establish a reasonably unified political entity in the vast territory that he aspired to govern. Apart from the state of Lagash, which Lugalzagesi spectacularly obliterated at the end of Urukagina's reign, his inscriptions boast of the extensive terrain that he subdued and ruled, including the cities of Uruk, Umma (the state from which he launched his programme of expansion), Ur and Larsa. Despite this, certain Mesopotamian cities that were governed by renowned individuals who possessed outstanding abilities and exceptional personal appeal were able to resist being incorporated into Lugalzagesi's proto-imperial realm because their rulers were capable of forging alliances and expedient unifications that, to a greater or lesser degree, preserved their political independence. Coupling his military might with a good understanding of regional politics, Lugalzagesi succeeded in bringing together Uruk and Umma, despite their very distinct identities, before extending his sphere of influence over the whole of Babylonia. His imperialist aims notwithstanding, the reign of Lugalzagesi in a sense represented a final outburst of the immemorial tendency of Sumerian cities to group themselves in changing political formations. Lugalzagesi, who probably came from the city of Eresh, which was perhaps in central Mesopotamia, initially relied on support from the region of Nippur (Steinkeller 2003, pp. 621–37). He was promoted or appointed to be the ruler or ensi of Umma before becoming lugal (king) of Uruk, and in the process he assembled forces that even the consolidated might of Lagash, with its well-coordinated politico-religious ethos, was unable to resist.

As is described in detail in subsequent chapters, Lugalzagesi razed the Temple of Ningirsu on Tell K to the ground in an act of desecration that signalled the end of Early Dynastic Girsu and Early Dynastic Lagash as a whole. With its triad of cities, its vast land area and its integrational system of civic and religious practices, the state of Lagash as it had been redefined by Ur-Nanshe, flourished for some 150 years. It thus represented an original and enduring attempt to bring disparate regions together as a coherent national entity, and as its longevity confirms, Lagash was a much more successful model for a federal alliance than the preceding series of hegemonic leagues in which one city dominated the rest. The Lagash system was the legacy of Ur-Nanshe, who astutely founded the state on a comprehensive religious vision in which politics and spiritual matters were inextricably intertwined, and at the very heart of the restructured polis was the redesigned and newly elevated Temple of Ningirsu on Tell K (see Selz 1995, pp. 291–304).

Whatever form the precursor association between Girsu and Lagash might have taken (and the situation with respect to Nigin is less well known), it seems clear that the two cities each maintained their own age-old sacred and cultural traditions, together with their respective regional networks of power and influence (see Selz 1990, pp. 111–42). Based on the prominence of particular deities, each had ancient links with other Sumerian cities: Girsu gravitated in the orbit of Nippur because of the close kinship between Ningirsu and Enlil (Fig. 65); Lagash, where Inanna seems to have been worshipped with more zeal than Gatumdug, was in a zone of influence that also included Uruk; while Nigin, where Nanshe presided, was presumably linked to Eridu, the home of Enki, since he controlled the divine circle to which Nanshe belonged. Ur-Nanshe's unification of the three cities therefore had huge theological consequences. In some instances the single identity of a deity who was designated by different names in different places was split to form distinct parts (so to speak), as was the case for Gatumdug and Bau, who, as noted above, were probably re-syncretised under Gudea. In other cases local gods who did not formerly enjoy close relations were henceforth believed to be connected. It has been argued, for instance, that the bond between Ningirsu and Nanshe, which was a primary influence on the evolution of the Early Dynastic pantheon, was an artificial creation brought into being by Ur-Nanshe to serve his political aims (Selz 1995, p. 298). Religious processions in honour of Ningirsu, Bau and Nanshe confirmed the unity in diversity of the single state, composed of three principal cities with their respective outlying areas, knitting the state together in the same way as the deities were united in the pantheon. It is recorded that the ritual processions that were organised to

FIGURE 65. Early Dynastic lapis lazuli cylinder seal, with motifs probably relating to Ningirsu's cosmic battle with the Slain Heroes, undertaken at the behest of his father, Enlil: above are two human-headed bulls or bison being attacked by lion-headed Thunderbirds; below is a bird hovering between two bulls, behind which are a mountain goat, a stag and another bird. British Museum 22962.

celebrate the feast days of the city deities of Girsu and Nigin extended out into the countryside, bringing the cities, villages and rural areas together under the same religious and cultural aegis.

As his name seems to confirm, Ur-Nanshe came from Gursar, which was probably in the vicinity of Nigin, the cult centre of Nanshe. This fact perhaps increased his sensitivity to the importance of distinct local traditions, making him alert to the need to combine differences without obliterating them. That is surely why the unification of the three cities went hand in hand with the evolution of religious practices, including the alterations made to the Lagash pantheon by Ur-Nanshe and the later rulers of the First Dynasty. The theological reformation seems to have been pursued as a revised administrative system, complementing and perhaps to some extent eclipsing the importance of merely personal links between the heads of the local ruling clans that had contributed to ongoing cohesion among the disparate political groups. The harmony of the state's pantheon also strengthened the image of the tripartite state of Lagash in its relations with other city-states. The display of theological unity conferred an integrity on the state that, for a century and a half at least, allowed it to sustain its autonomy and prosperity. At the centre of the national organisation was the Temple of Ningirsu on Tell K, which was the fixed point around which the state revolved.

CHAPTER 12

The Lower Construction

THE OLDEST EARLY DYNASTIC RELIGIOUS COMPLEX dedicated to Ningirsu that was found on Tell K, and for which there is systematically recorded data, was the Lower Construction. The building itself should not be conceived of as an insular unit. It was rather the core feature of a composite whole that included a number of associated archaeological structures and objects in its immediate vicinity in the central area of the tell, together with a series of other deposits, notably the large mud-brick terrace platform for which evidence was found in Cros's Trench 5 (the North Trench), situated about 20 m to the north-east. Significantly, the excavated structure was composed of two elements that were built at different times: the inner walls and the outer block. As is further detailed below, these were curiously situated on a gypsum pavement (pavement V) that had been partially dismantled.

The Two-Room Core (PQRS)

At the heart of the original building was a bipartite fired-brick structure, the corners of which are marked PQRS on Sarzec's Plan C (2) (Fig. 33), that was shown to be a cella (room U), that held the cult image, and a trophy room (room T). As notably proposed by Forest (1999) and corroborated below, there is little doubt that this twofold space was partially or wholly situated underground, where it was furnished with surrounding walkways that were walled with mud-bricks (Figs. 66 and 67). The possible presence of enclosing mud-brick walls was considered at an early stage by Heuzey and later rather ambiguously noted on the section on Plan C (2), which was drawn long after Sarzec started work on Tell K in 1888. It is clear (as previously mentioned) that Sarzec dug through this soft material (*Brique crue* on Plan C (2)) at great speed, not just around the Lower Construction, but over a large area (estimated by Cros to have measured in total 31 m × 40 m = 1,240 m²). In consequence, little or no distinction was made between the seemingly formless mass of compacted mud-bricks in which the Lower Construction was found enveloped and the planned mud-brick architecture that must have stood around the innermost fired-brick walls. Sarzec's haste also made it extremely difficult to distinguish between layers of the solid mud-brick foundation platform that was laid at a much later date by Ur-Nanshe in order to raise the mound and the mud-brickwork associated with the earlier temple. Nor was it possible to identify traces of any mud-brick superstructures that might have stood above the two-room core.

Sarzec was not necessarily solely responsible for these losses. As discussed below, it is possible that large swathes of any mud-brick walls that might have surrounded the central fired-brick structure were deliberately demolished when (as is also argued below) the sanctuary was decommissioned, and that portions of the surrounding mud-brick walls were incorporated into the compact layer of foundation fill that was intended to support overlying walls that were built after the Lower Construction had been taken out of service. Accordingly, even if Sarzec had paid proper attention to this material, the task of identifying mud-brick formations that might have surrounded the Lower Construction would

158   The Mound of the House of the Fruits

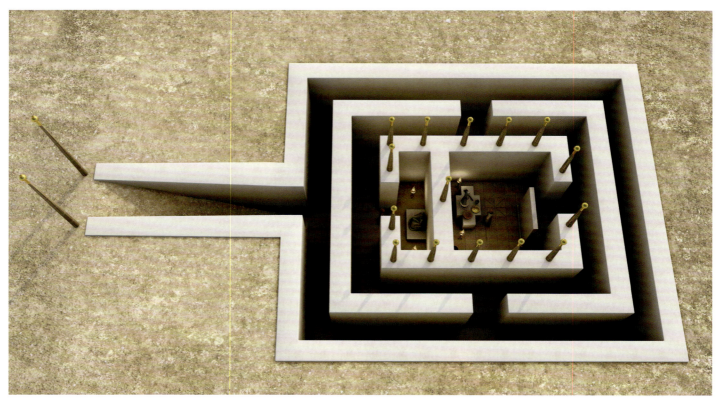

FIGURE 66. Reconstruction of the layout of the subterranean rooms and corridors of the Lower Construction.

probably in any event have been extremely difficult, if not impossible.

The parallel drawn by Forest (1999, pp. 13–14) and others between the original Lower Construction and the semi-subterranean Stone Building in Uruk is extremely persuasive, despite the fact that the Stone Building (dating to the Late Uruk period, c.3400–3100 BCE) was both much earlier and served a different purpose, being a sacred storehouse rather than the major temple dedicated to the supreme local deity. The casing of mud-brick walls that probably originally surrounded the fired-brick walls of the Lower Construction suggest that it too was a semi-subterranean structure in which the buried cella and trophy room were placed below an overlying temple terrace that lay at ground level, on the top of the mound, where it extended out on all four sides of the open parts of the temple below. As with the Uruk Stone Building, therefore, it is highly likely that viewers (perhaps high-standing members of the congregations who witnessed liturgical rites) could look down into the interiors of the two most important sacred rooms from that viewing terrace on the top surface of the tell. The discovery of doorways in the Lower Construction's two sunken main rooms would confirm that the extended subterranean platform around it was indeed perforated with voids: underground walkways ('covered peripheral corridors', as Forest describes them) that ran through the mass of mud-bricks to allow for circulation around the main building and access to inferred suites of rooms. The floor of the viewing gallery that was situated around the tops of the walls of the buried cella and trophy room would have been on top of that mud-brick mass, such that the entire arrangement again invites comparison with the Uruk Stone Building.

The comparison with the Uruk edifice is architecturally and historically persuasive, but there is also a clinching stratigraphic reason why the main rooms of the Lower Construction must have been placed underground. A benchmark moment in the entire archaeological sequence of Tell K is Ur-Nanshe's raising of the floor of the temple from 8.48 m (the base of the Lower Construction) to 12.83 m (the base of the Ur-Nanshe Building). At first glance this might suggest

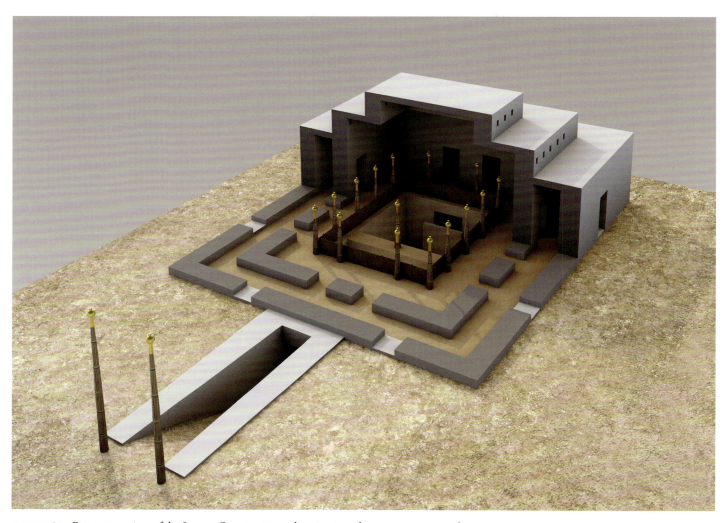

FIGURE 67. Reconstruction of the Lower Construction, showing its subterranean areas and above-ground walls.

that Ur-Nanshe added 4.35 m to the top of the tell, but as is indicated above and further detailed in Chapter 16 that was not the case. Without pre-empting later discussions, the evidence shows that Ur-Nanshe generally added about 0.7 m of mud-bricks across the central area of the mound, including above the sealed walls of the Lower Construction. What this means is that, in the epoch of the Lower Construction, the central part of the upper surface of the tell—the ground level from which visitors to the temple could look down into its sacred rooms—must already have been situated at a Sarzec height of between 11.58 m (the base height of the Lower Construction plus the combined height of pavement V and its main walls) and 12.13 m (the base height of the Ur-Nanshe building minus the 0.7 m of mud-bricks that

Ur-Nanshe added). Conversely, if the Lower Construction had been open and generally accessible at the base level of 8.48 m, Ur-Nanshe would have had to add 4.35 m across the entire top of the mound, and there is no evidence whatsoever to suggest that this is what he did.

Traces of the Lower Construction's extended base platform, which was made of small-format planoconvex mud-bricks, were unearthed by Cros in Trench 5, some 20 m to the north-east of the Lower Construction's N corner, suggesting that it might have occupied an area measuring as much as 40 m × 35 m = 1,400 m². It is important to note, moreover, that the hollow spaces that formed rooms and corridors inside the mud-brick mound were presumably not only built to facilitate the way the building was used. They also solved a problem of structural engineering by reducing the weight, which might otherwise have been too great, of the mass of mud-bricks that bore down on the Lower Construction's main subterranean walls. Again comparing it with the Uruk Stone Building, Forest (1999, pp. 13–14) postulates that the Lower Construction was surrounded by not one but two underground peripheral corridors, meaning there would have been two principal voids and a second line of mud-brick walls around it. Access was probably via a single gently inclined ramp (or stepped slope) that descended from the top surface of the tell on the NW side of the temple (again as for the Uruk Stone Building) down through the mud-brick mass to meet the below-ground circulation corridors. If there were two rings of peripheral walkways, as Forest supposes, then the approach to the holy rooms would have been through a maze-like arrangement of twofold concentric spaces.

The identification of the two rooms inside the fired-brick walls (PQRS) as the cella and the trophy room was aided by the discovery, *in situ*, under the paved floor of room T on the SE side, of a number of well-preserved foundation pegs. Made of copper, they take the form of uninscribed figures that are shaped from the waists down into elongated rounded points (Fig. 68). Their hands are held in front of their chests in attitudes of prayer, and they have long hair dressed in horizontal waves (Fig. 69). The exact number was not recorded, but several figures were found arranged in concentric circles in the mud-bricks that lay beneath the paved floor of room T, and more were found in the mud-brick mass under the W corner of the building (marked Q on the plan) and possibly elsewhere, though this might not have been the case. The report distinctly states that a number of circles of foundation figures were placed vertically in the ground below the floor of the room, but the exact position of the groups with respect to the building above them is subject to some slight uncertainty in the text because Heuzey contradicts himself about their placement. In his 1912 interpretations (Sarzec and Heuzey 1912, p. 239), he first suggests that they were found under the pavement and generally under the four corners of the building, and that in all cases they were laid in concentric circles, but later on (p. 414) he says that circular groups were excavated under the pavement and the W corner only, in order to protect that corner in particular (*les unes dans l'angle Ouest, comme pour le protéger plus particulièrement*). Surely more reliable is his previously published account (Heuzey 1900, pp. 56–7), which was almost certainly written with Sarzec's notes in front of him, as were other parts of the same text, where Sarzec's own written reports are quoted verbatim. In this instance he says that the figures were found under the pavement inside the building, in front of the pillar in room T (No. 2 on Sarzec's Plan C (2)), and under the W corner, where they were arranged, as he says: 'in a round, like "bunches of asparagus", following M. de Sarzec's expressive comparison, in order to protect the building' (*en rond, 'comme des bottes d'asperges' suivant la comparaison expressive de M. de Sarzec, achevaient de protéger l'édifice*). This being so, it seems that one or more groups of figurines were buried in front of the cross-shaped brick pedestal (probably a support for a standard, a cult statue or perhaps more likely

FIGURE 68. A foundation peg from the Lower Construction. British Museum 108980.

FIGURE 69. Detail of a foundation peg from the Lower Construction. British Museum 108980.

a stele) that was located in the centre of room T, while a second group (also arranged in a circle or a 'round') was found under the W corner (Q) of the building (the 'edifice'), where they were laid in bundles. Interestingly, Heuzey (1900, p. 57) goes on in his earlier text to speculate that the buried figures were intended to defend the building 'without doubt against the particularly harmful demons that predominated on this side of the horizon'. The invocation of demons is questionable, but the W corner surely had special significance for the builders of the temple, as is discussed below.

Like the earliest phase of the Lower Construction, the associated figures must also date from the Early Dynastic I period. Foundation figurines such as these were cast in solid copper, using the direct process of lost-wax casting. Accordingly, each figure was made from a different mould, and each was individually crafted during the production process, when the bronzes were worked to remove marks left by the casting. The figurines range in height between about 0.07 m and 0.17 m, and typically feature well-modelled heads with sharp, prominent noses, flat button-like eyes, small mouths with pursed lips and occasionally also a recessed jaw. Thick gatherings of hair are conventionally styled into furrowed horizontal bands to give the impression of cascading waves or curls that hang down to the shoulders. The arms are carefully sculpted, with some separated from the sides of the body, and the hands are clasped at the chest, with the left hand wrapped around the right and supporting it from below. The torsos taper down to a narrow point that forms the peg or stake that can be inserted into the ground. The presence of shapes interpreted as breasts previously led scholars (notably Heuzey 1900, p. 56) to suggest that the statuettes might be intended to portray females. In general, however, such figurines are not usually given expressly identifiable attributes of gender, and there is no special reason to think that the examples found by Sarzec were exceptional in this respect.

The symbolism of the figurines and their specific placement is dealt with in a later subsection, but it should be stressed here that these objects could in principle have functioned as the real surveying pegs that were used for the laying out of the temple (as described below), a process that was accompanied by an array of religious ceremonies. Perhaps more likely, however, is that the lines of the temple walls were established using wooden pegs and ropes, and the elaborate figurines were then ritually interred. Like the ones placed under the W corner, the pegs found under the floor of room T could also have been buried as part of these preliminaries because the outlines of the room would have been defined when the walls were pegged out. Additionally, in the case of the Lower Construction, it should be noted that the temple was built on a pre-existing floor (pavement V), as argued below, and this is suggestive of the fact that pegs could be used to reconsecrate sacred domains when they were renovated or, as in this instance, radically repurposed. One essential, overriding significance of the pegs, which is stressed in key passages from the inscriptions on the Gudea Cylinders (see Chapters 43 and 44), was to define the hallowed space and also to moor the temple symbolically to the earth, like a ship at anchor, thereby protecting it from the cosmic forces of chaos that had been suppressed when the world was created, but which were always liable to disrupt the orderly processes of nature on which humans rely. Unlike sacrificial hoards or offerings in other parts of the ancient world, where sets of artefacts or arrays of substances were removed from general circulation and placed in spiritually charged contexts as gifts for the gods, the foundation deposits of Mesopotamia usually comprised an assemblage of objects that marked out a sanctified area, expressed the piety of a ruler and enabled the temple building to 'function' properly—a much-used phrase, particularly in the inscriptions of Ur-Bau and Gudea (see Chapter 42), whose precise meaning derives from the rituals that accompanied the planning of the temple, together with the procedures by which it was laid out, and the significance of its orientation (all considered below).

The pegs associated with the Lower Construction differ in at least one important respect from those that were used at subsequent periods. The way they were manufactured meant that each figurine was essentially unique, and this might testify to the fact that they were deposited on behalf of the whole community by a corporate body of representatives: the college of clerics who were responsible for laying out the temple and sanctifying the space. A similar meaning might be expressed by the relatively large number of pegs that were interred, and the way they were placed in bundles, as Sarzec noted. Unlike later Lagash foundation pegs from the time of Ur-Nanshe through to the reign of Gudea, which were limited in number and inscribed with the names of individual rulers, the figurines found under the Lower Construction were anonymous, and conceivably therefore deposited on behalf of the state of Lagash at large. Such an intention would compare well with the dedicatory inscriptions on the Feathered Figure and several other objects especially associated with the Lower Construction (all described below), where personal names are only recorded in one instance. In particular, the pegs evoke the imagery of the Circular Bas-Relief (Fig. 62), where the ruler is accompanied by named followers (who are not members of his family, as in the later Ur-Nanshe Genealogical Plaques), all of whom (apart from the musical trio) have the same crossed hands, and many of them are portrayed according to the same aesthetic conventions as were used to shape the foundation figurines. None of this should be taken to suggest that Early Dynastic I Lagash was not ruled by particular individuals, but it perhaps demonstrates the changing nature of authority or kingship between the era of the Lower Construction and the new modes of government ushered in by Ur-Nanshe.

Finally, Heuzey surmises that the hollow cruciform pillar found in room T (Fig. 70) might have held a long-handled weapon or a statue (though, as noted above, a stele is perhaps the likeliest object). In front of it, an area of paving on the floor had been cut into eight triangles that were laid like a diamond or a star (No. 2 inside room T on Plan C (2)). Other movable objects deposited in this room are discussed in detail later, but this was the trophy room, and room U to the north-west was the cella.

Pavement V

Alluding to the approach to cultic architecture previously taken by the builders of Uruk, the idea that the two-room Lower Construction (PQRS) was a subterranean fabrication built into a platform that contained underground passageways and subsidiary rooms is attractive, and might be still more so if the vexed question of the relationship between the Lower Construction and pavement V, which was found on its NE side, could be conclusively resolved. Heuzey's description of pavement V (as labelled on Sarzec's Plan C (2)) is decidedly unclear. The original building was placed on this paving of gypsum slabs (made of material that Heuzey (Sarzec and Heuzey 1912, p. 412) suggests was brought from the region of present-day Mosul), though apparently offset towards pavement V's NW edge, and all or partly angled a little (as is detailed further below) so that the SW face of the building gradually diverged from the SW side of the pavement, from the W corner (Q), where the two coincided, to the S corner (R), where there was a gap of 0.4 m between

FIGURE 70. Reconstruction of the antecella in the Lower Construction, including the possible arrangement of the cult objects; the door in the SE façade is at the bottom.

the wall of the building and the edge of the pavement, as can be seen on Plan C (2). The pavement stretched out towards the north-east, though the slabs were differently aligned from the ones found inside the building in room T, and there is no information about how the pavement was laid under the rest of PQRS. Heuzey (1900, pp. 47–8) refers to the NE remnant as a 'veritable esplanade', which also begs the question of its relationship with any mud-brick walkways that ran around the other sides of the building's two sunken holy rooms. No evidence of pavement V was recorded elsewhere, and no sign whatsoever of it having existed on other sides of the building appears on Plan C (2).

The NE sector of the pavement seems to have been exactly the same width as wall P′S′ of the Lower Construction's outer block, as is evident where the pavement met P′S′. From there, it extended continuously for 12 m towards the north-east, with other patches being found sporadically at a distance of up to 17 m, beyond which no more traces were recorded. The plans suggest that the pavement was coextensive with width of the outer block on the NW and SE sides (Y and Z on Plan C (2)), and in particular the section on Plan C (2) shows that its SW side was exactly aligned with the SW wall of the outer block (Q′R′). The surviving parts that remained were unquestionably fragments of a greater whole that extended out to the NE, with some of the losses doubtless being due to the fact that slabs were reused in the surrounding block and in the layer that was later built to seal the top of the Lower Construction.

The sketchy nature of the information makes it difficult to determine the function of pavement V with respect to the two-room subterranean nucleus of the Lower Construction and the presumed mud-brick walls that formed underground corridors and rooms around it. Was it part of the floor of one or more passageways that allowed people to circulate around the building, part of a more open esplanade (as Heuzey seems to suggest, though this idea supposes that the cella and trophy room were situated at ground level rather than being underground), or a main artery leading out to the north-east? Alternatively, was it built on the underlying mud-brick platform expressly to provide the substructure or foundation base of the inner, two-room shrine? The placement of the building as well as its orientation (the reason for the manifest gap between the pavement and the building by the Lower Construction's S corner) militate against this last suggestion, as perhaps does the changed alignment of the paving slabs in room T, where they were laid along a NE–SW axis, by contrast with the extended area to the north-east, where the individual slabs were laid on a NW–SE axis. The lack of clear continuity between the two elements makes it possible—though highly unlikely—that the internal and external pavements were stratigraphically discontinuous. For example, the external NE section of pavement V, which could have been laid first, might have been partly dismantled to furnish the slabs supposedly used later inside room T. The corollary to this, as developed by Forest (1999, pp. 12–15), is that the dismantling of pavement V must have started before the fired-brick walls of the original, two-room Lower Construction were incorporated into the latest iteration of the surrounding underground mud-brick formations. But this presupposes a laborious set of procedures that would have involved cutting through any original subterranean mud-brick walls that surrounded the space to be occupied by the Lower Construction's two-room core to allow slabs from the NE part of pavement V to be collected, transported and laid inside room T before it was built, and then rebuilding the outer mud-brick walls in order to surround the space to be occupied by the open-roofed, buried shrine, all of which seems improbably overcomplicated.

The most likely explanation of the relationship between pavement V, the Lower Construction's two-room core and the surrounding block (P'Q'R'S') is that the pavement pre-dated both of the structures that were built on it. This would also almost certainly imply (though the argument does not depend on it) that the pavement's orientation was primary, such that any rectangular building erected on it, whose sides were parallel to its edges, would have been correctly aligned with the cardinal points—an essential, unchanging feature of all Sumerian temples. This would further suggest that pavement V was associated with an earlier building that came before the Lower Construction, and although this idea is necessarily fraught with uncertainty there can be little or no doubt that the Lower Construction was not the first, but the latest in a series of structures that were built on the same spot. This is presumably confirmed by Sarzec's discovery of courses of mud-bricks with embedded bitumen-lined vases at significant but unspecified depths below the Lower Construction, while Cros found Middle Uruk objects and bitumen-lined capsules down to a Sarzec height of 7.4 m (for the top of the lowest capsule that was inserted vertically into the mound), providing evidence of meaningful activities that were carried out in excess of 1 m lower than the base of pavement V, which lay at the Sarzec reference height of 8.48 m. The difference between the Lower Construction and whatever came before it is that the Lower Construction surely represents a new phase of religious worship in which Tell K was rededicated as the divine preserve of Ningirsu. This is confirmed by both its scale and the radical, even revolutionary nature of its design, as well as by the richly evocative meanings that were expressed in the assemblage of objects that were found associated with it, all of which are thoroughly considered in Chapter 13. Without pre-empting those arguments, it is highly probable that the moment captured on the Feathered Figure, which shows Ningirsu taking possession of his house and lands, indicates the fact that the Lower Construction was the foundational edifice of a new development in the sacred history of Tell K.

To all intents and purposes, the striking form taken by the Lower Construction rendered pavement V obsolete. The original reason for fitting expensive paving slabs to create the ceremonial approach to an inferred earlier religious building was invalidated by the fact that the Lower Construction was an underground temple that was approached from above via a slope or stairway, probably on the NW side (as mentioned previously), that ran down through the mud-brick mass that enclosed the outer walls of the building's two holiest sunken spaces. It is presumed that the access route was on the NW side partly because of the analogy with the Uruk Stone Building, but two local factors add further circumstantial confirmation: first, the fact that pavement V was made redundant and covered by bands of mud-brick walling indicates that the new approach was surely not on the NE side; and secondly, that being the case, it seems fair to assume that the new walkway acted as the precedent for the access paving (pavement F) that was fitted on the NW side of the later Ur-Nanshe Building, which closely followed the ground plan of the Lower Construction in other respects. Containing below-ground corridors and rooms, the mud-brick mass that surrounded the Lower Construction extended out on all sides of the cella and trophy room, so that only the interiors of the two buried rooms were visible from the upper terrace that was formed by the top surface of the mound. The subterranean floors that ran around the outsides of the interred rooms must also have been mostly made of mud-bricks, and, like the NE extension of pavement V, they would all have been invisible from the viewing gallery. In addition, the NE extension of pavement V must have been overlaid with thick bands of the mud-brick walls that had been erected to create underground corridors and rooms. Parts of the NE part of the paving could still have been used as a serviceable floor, but it was certainly no longer a main ceremonial artery, and the fact that it was made of a prestige material was surely rendered largely irrelevant by the purely functional purpose it served in the architectural context of the Lower Construction. The only places where it could still be clearly seen and appreciated were in the trophy room and no doubt also in the cella (though that was not explicitly recorded by Sarzec), where it was visible from the upper viewing platform, but in these spaces (again, the situation in the cella was not recorded) it had been taken up and relaid so its placement was not continuous with the remains of the paving that were preserved outside the walls of the two rooms, and its original and later uses had been differentiated. Furthermore, some of the paving slabs inside room T had been carefully cut to form the intricate star shape noted by Sarzec, and this added decisively to the distinction between the old and the new.

The Lower Construction was therefore presumably built on the pre-existing pavement, but slightly offset towards its NW end, and with the previously noted gap of 0.4 m between the building's S corner (R) and the SW edge of the pavement (Q'R'). As Heuzey (1900, p. 51) adroitly observes, the offset and the apparent slight rotation of the building that created the gap in the S corner might readily be explained by the existence of a sacred feature or 'obstacle' in that area, extending into the 0.4 m space between R and Q'R', that was considered to be immovable when the Lower Construction's two-room core was being built: perhaps a pathway, an altar, a boundary stone, or even a tree. As Heuzey recalls, similar planning conundrums were well documented with respect to later temples elsewhere, notably in ancient Greece and Rome. Moreover, though Heuzey does not say this, it can be assumed that if an object (or even an augural event) such as those listed was the reason why the building was offset and turned, then any such sacred object or event must surely have become evident on top of the pavement after it had been installed, otherwise it would also have interfered with the laying of the pavement itself. Though the idea cannot be confirmed, it is tempting to link the advent of an inferred divine impediment to the cardinal placement of the Lower Construction with the establishment of the new religious phase on Tell K that the building represents. In conjunction with its design, as well as the significance of its associated foundational objects and its changed approach axis (from north-east to north-west), this would add a further strand to the overall sense that the commissioning of the temple and the architectural form that it took were consequences of a revolutionary change that took place in the religious practices of Girsu at a particular moment in time. It is a thesis that must be treated with an extremely high degree of caution, but further circumstantial evidence might tend to support it— namely the fact that the later block (P'Q'R'S') reverted to the orientation of pavement V when it was built around the main inner walls (PQRS). This doubtless confirms that the cardinal orientation of the pavement was correct, but also that the pressing reason (whatever it was) why walls PQRS had to be displaced with respect to the pavement when they were built was no longer valid. If that was on account of the presence of an immovable sacred entity, as Heuzey suggests, then the obstacle either did not any longer exist when P'Q'R'S' was built (for example, because it had been broken if it was an artefact, or it had died if it was alive), or it was no longer considered to be sacred, and the most likely explanation for the last possibility (as is explored more fully below) is that the supposed entity might have been deconsecrated. Tentatively adding to the idea that the divine impediment was a meaningful factor in the ushering in of a new phase in the religious history of Girsu, the surmised moment of radical change gave way to a new status quo.

The assumption that the pavement predated the building helps to explain how and when the slabs inside room T (and perhaps also in room U) came to be laid differently. Key parts of the pre-existing pavement must have been lifted prior to the construction of the main inner walls, PQRS, to allow for the ritual interment of the building's foundation figurines in their allotted places under the floor of room T, and also under the temple's W corner, adjacent to room U. This would have provided an opportunity for these parts of the pavement to be relaid with the changed alignment recorded on Plan C (2). Unfortunately, as repeatedly noted, the extent of the realignment—whether it was just under room T or whether it continued under the whole area of PQRS—was not recorded, but the fact that foundation figurines were discovered under the temple's W corner strongly suggests that the slabs were lifted and relaid under much of the building and almost certainly in the two principal rooms.

The Orientation of the Lower Construction

The conclusion that might loosely be drawn on the basis of Sarzec and Heuzey's rather vague description is that the two-room core of the Lower Construction was rotated by three degrees in an anticlockwise direction (so to speak) with respect to the pavement. The idea of rotating the structure, even as a metaphor, is potentially extremely misleading, however, because there is a categorical difference between turning the entire building by three degrees around a central point, like a wheel around its axle, and adjusting the angle of the N–S line that ran through the building from its N corner, so that the changed orientation began at that fixed point of origin, and the effect of the change was realised gradually along the entire length of the N–S axis to create the 0.4 m gap between the S corner (R) and the Q'R' façade of the outer block. As is discussed in Chapter 14, the former idea would have been inconsistent with the principles that informed Sumerian temple architecture, which was demonstrably based on treating the N corner as primary.

To visualise the process, it should be imagined that a correct N–S axis was established by astronomical observation, as it would have been for navigational purposes, for example, by using the north star as the fixed point of reference. A foundation peg was hammered into the ground at the point on that axis where the N corner of the building was going to be built, and a cord was then fixed to the N peg and pulled taut, stretching due south, to mark the N–S line. If the temple was to be built around this cardinal axis then the rest of the walls could be pegged out by creating a bisected right angle at the north peg to establish the lines of the NW wall, perhaps followed by the NE wall; the W and E corners could then be pegged at points on these NW and NE lines, depending on the desired lengths of the respective walls; and further bisected right angles could be created at the now defined W and E corners to establish the lines of the SW and SE walls, which would meet to form a right angle at the S corner. In the case of the Lower Construction the S end of the cord that marked the N–S axis, pegged at the point where the building's N corner was going to be built, must have been moved by three degrees towards the east to create the necessary 0.4 m gap. (In practice, the angle would perhaps have been determined by the size of the gap rather than the other way round.) The corners and walls would then have been pegged out in the usual way.

This would have meant that the N corner was pegged at a point on the established N–S axis, but the rest of the corners (and walls) would have deviated slightly from the cardinal alignment. With reference to Plan C (2), therefore, the N corner (P) was probably pegged on the N–S line, but the three-degree shift applied to the S peg would have meant that Q deviated by three degrees away from the west towards the south-west, while the S corner (R) pointed slightly towards the south-east, and the E corner (S) pointed slightly towards the north-east. The deviation would have been imperceptible to the naked eye, but the exact observation and recording of such details in the natural world and in human affairs were seemingly rudimentary components of Sumerian culture, and the principle that sacred temples had to be built with their corners facing the cardinal points was consistently applied. The ruler, the high priests and other officials who oversaw the layout would have known it was incorrect, as would the builders, and if it was generally known that pavement V had been built to accommodate an earlier, properly aligned temple then the deviation would have been visible to anyone who had access to the subterranean outer walls of the building's two main rooms.

The idea that a mistake was made with the placement of the Lower Construction is hardly credible because the astronomical observations that were used to establish the cardinal axis of a Sumerian temple were not one-off procedures. The general principles that underlay the observational processes are sketched out below, but they must have been tried and tested for practical purposes, including navigation, which no doubt depended on a longstanding familiarity with some key celestial motions. In addition, there was a panoply of religious associations between stars and planets and the gods. Though compilations of data from this very early period are sadly lacking, the Sumerian sign for god or deity, DINGIR, which also meant the 'sky' or 'heavens', and was a cognomen of the supreme deity, An, was a schematic rendering of a star. One particular celestial association between a deity and a heavenly body that is attested from late fourth millennium is the identification of Inanna with the planet Venus in its two

FIGURE 71. Late Uruk cylinder seal (location unknown).

aspects as the morning and evening star. A surviving Late Uruk cylinder seal (Fig. 71) depicts a standing bull accompanied by five pictographs, UD, SIG, DINGIR, MUŠ₃ and EZEN, that can almost certainly be translated as: 'the festival [EZEN] of the morning [HUD₂] and evening [SIG] goddess [DINGIR] Inanna [MUŠ₃]'. Administrative tablets from the same period refer specifically to festivals that were held to celebrate these two manifestations of the goddess (Szarzyńska 1993).

As regards the positioning of a temple—a matter of the utmost seriousness—the necessary decisions would assuredly have been the outcome of a sophisticated scholarly culture that was administered by experts who conceivably spent their lives pondering over such minutiae, so that any proposed alteration to a given orientation would have been rigorously scrutinised and debated, and further contextualised with respect to previously recorded data. A similar rebuttal applies to the idea that the differently angled temples might have resulted from observed movements in the fixed stars that determined the cardinal points at successive building phases. First, the movements of the so-called fixed stars over the time frames in question (even if a century elapsed between the Lower Construction and its surmised precursor) would have been vanishingly small compared to the documented three-degree shift just discussed; and secondly, any such supposed observed movements, no matter how small, could have been rigorously scrutinised with respect to established points of reference. Finally, one pragmatic way of resolving the issue would have been to reduce the angle of the S corner (R) from ninety degrees to eighty-seven, which would have meant that the thick SW wall (QR) narrowed very gradually along its length towards the S corner. Nothing of the sort was recorded by Sarzec or shown on the plan, however.

The way in which temples were pegged out starting with the N corner, which was defined with respect to the north star, helps to explain the placement of the foundation figurines under the Lower Construction's W corner, and probably also those buried under the floor of room T. Unlike the initial N–S axis, the temple's S, E and W corners were not derived from astronomical observation, but were rather geometrical constructs that were generated with respect to the pegged-out N–S line. On a properly aligned temple the E and W corners therefore pointed due east and west, meaning that if a line bisecting the W corner were extended to meet the N–S axis the size of the angle at the point where the two lines meet would be ninety degrees. The W corner should probably be conceived of as dominant because, as demonstrated by the layout of the temples, that was the one that was firstly and most closely linked to the already established N corner. As specified in Chapter 14, which deals with the Sumerian concept of the tessellated earth, the S and E corners were derived geometrically from the prior placement of the N and W angles, and since Sumerian temples were not square but rectangular, the construction of the S corner also implied the existence of a second N–S axis (and thereafter a potentially infinite number of parallel axes). There is no logical reason why the W corner was laid out first after the principal N–S axis and the N corner were marked out. It could just as well have been the E corner, and then the temple's orientation might have been flipped, as it were, so that the long walls ran north-east–south-west instead of north-west–south-east, but as a matter of historical fact this is not how it was done on Tell K, where the Lower Construction appears to have been placed in accordance with a practice that was standard throughout ancient Sumer. This suggests some important features of the way Sumerian culture conceived of time, the seasons and the annual cycle.

Generally speaking, the sun rises in the east and sets in the west, but in reality it only rises due east and sets due west twice a year, at the spring and autumn equinoxes, around 20 March and 20 September, respectively (a fuller discussion of these matters is contained in Chapter 40 below). These are the only occasions on which the sun would have risen and set along the extensions of the lines that bisected a temple's E and W corners and met its N–S axis (or axes to speak more precisely) at ninety degrees. The exact orientation of the E and W corners was therefore closely connected with the agricultural cycle, particularly with the planting, growth and harvesting of the two main crops of grain (predominantly barley) that were successively harvested and sown biannually in autumn and spring, roughly coinciding with the equinoxes. Sarzec, being no doubt a French gourmet to his fingertips, and perhaps indulging in a little homesickness for some of his native cuisine, wonderfully describes the sets of foundation pegs found under the Lower Construction's W corner as being like 'bunches of asparagus'. If he had said sheaves of barley, he might have hit the nail on the head. This does not mean to say that the pegs themselves were intended to look like barley stalks, or that the particular way in which they were interred under the Lower Construction negated their other symbolic meanings, above all the belief that they acted like mooring posts that anchored the temple to the earth (as is discussed further in the context of the tessellated earth). Rather, they were metaphorically or even poetically bundled together (to paraphrase Sarzec) in a manner comparable with sheaves of grain. In this regard, it should be recalled that, in addition to his role as a warrior god, Ningirsu was also closely associated with agriculture and irrigation. His identity as a deity of planting, growth and harvest is amply attested in the inscriptions on the Feathered Figure, as is examined further in Chapter 13, but with this in mind it is reasonable to assume that the pegs buried under the W corner might have been akin to harvest offerings, the key difference being that the foundation 'bunches' were intended to give thanks for and protect the produce of the land not on one specific occasion but in perpetuity. The deposited pegs, which were apparently laid in a 'round', were intended to celebrate and perhaps also (especially in this case, where the precise placement of the temple's corners was compromised) to ensure the dependability of the agricultural cycle.

The fact that they were placed under the W corner (and indeed that the W corner was seemingly considered dominant when the temple was laid out) offers another insight into Sumerian thinking. The vital equinoctial moment was not the rising of the sun in the east but its westerly setting, which must therefore have been intimately linked with life-giving themes of growth, fruition and reaping. The priority accorded to the W corner might also show that any associated festivals were evening events that began as the sun sank below the horizon, but this is difficult to corroborate. The elaborate nature of the harvest or fertility deposit under the W corner of the Lower Construction, and the particular care with which the bundled pegs were handled, could well have been an acknowledgement of the temple's overall slight but significant misalignment that meant that its function as a seasonal clock was potentially compromised. The impressive offering was perhaps intended to make amends for that acknowledged inaccuracy.

More generally, the westerly direction (including the W corner and the W side of the temple overall) has another celestial association that is also discussed in detail in Chapter 40 below. In lunar calendars the beginning of each month is marked by the appearance of the new moon, when it can be seen above the horizon, looking westwards, shortly after sunset. The regular observation of the crescent new moon, which is the chief natural indicator in the functioning of the lunar calendar and the reckoning of time, must unquestionably have been an event of considerable importance, but it is not exclusively associated with due west because the moon also rises and sets at a range of places on the westerly and easterly horizons, depending on the time of year, as defined by the corresponding position of the sun, whose light renders the moon visible. Incidentally, the new moon appears and sets only in the west because it crosses the sky from east to west during the daytime, with its shadowy side pointing to the earth, making it invisible until evening, when the sun descends below the horizon. These issues are addressed more fully in Chapter 40, but the placement of the bundled foundation deposits especially under the temple's W corner would appear to place particular stress on the equinoxes—seasonal events that depend on solar motions.

Despite the contradictions contained in Heuzey's accounts of the foundation pegs found in the mud-brick mass beneath the Lower Construction, more pegs were indubitably found under the pavement of room T, where they appear to have been arranged in concentric circles below the exceptional starlike pattern of tiling found on the floor. How might the pegs discovered under room T have related to the ones found under the W corner? If, as seems conceivable, the pegs under room T also related to Ningirsu's identity as an agricultural deity, then the answer perhaps lies in a connection that was made between the agricultural cycle and the concentric circles. It is a universal commonplace to conceive of the passing of the year in terms of cycles that are identified with circular motions, but the image of the circle as it is used in this way is a complex abstraction that has developed over millennia. It cannot derive from the motions of the sun and the moon, which observably do not follow circular paths, but there are demonstrable astronomical connections between circularity and seasonal recurrence that have guided human actions since time immemorial. Accordingly, as can be seen in many readily available photos taken with extremely long exposures, the stars in the night sky manifestly appear to rotate around the fixed point that is defined in the northern hemisphere by the north star. The stars that are closer to that celestial pole (in this case the north star) than they are to the geographical latitude of the observer never drop below the horizon, which means that they trace complete circles in any twenty-four-hour period, though an inferable arc of all the circles remains invisible during daylight hours. These stellar circles suggest a general pattern of celestial concentricity that can be seen most clearly from either of the poles, but which would presumably have been visible to attentive astronomers gazing up at the clear night skies over ancient Girsu, at a latitude of approximately thirty-one degrees north. Furthermore, in the context of such observations, different stars and (more importantly) constellations come and go seasonally, and the overall annual pattern of movement is again circular. The exact make-up of the stars that are held to belong to defined constellations at any epoch is another cultural construct, and with a few exceptions the compositions and names of the constellations recognised in Mesopotamia around 3000 BCE are uncertain (see Rogers 1998), though it seems that constellations named Taurus, Leo and Scorpio were already defined (Britton and Walker 1996, p. 42). The apparent diurnal and annual motions of the stars were used by all ancient peoples as temporal and seasonal indicators, not least in ancient Sumer, where the relationship between the fixed star, conceived of as a divine yoke or anchor, and the rest of the moving heavens was enshrined in the foundational Mesopotamian myths of creation and the ordering of the cosmos. These potential links between celestial observations, cyclical seasonal patterns and harvest or fertility might account for the deposition of the pegs under room T of the Lower Construction. The conclusion is necessarily speculative, but with particular reference to the slightly misaligned temple, it seems plausible to suggest that the circles of extra pegs buried under room T were intended as another ritually sanctioned offering that was designed to protect and secure the agricultural cycle.

The Bitumen-Coated Cavities

Of extreme interest are the vase-like bituminated cavities that were inserted vertically down into the tops of the fired-brick walls: fifteen in the two-room building (PQRS) and a further seven on the NW side of the surrounding block (P′Q′R′S′), of which three were inside room U, while four were outside room U's external wall (PQ). As regards their purpose, Heuzey's first hypothesis is surely the correct one. They were probably housings for relatively lightweight posts or poles, the bottoms of which were swaddled with balls of rope that pressed against the sides of the deeper, ovoid sections of the openings, where rope imprints were found. The poles themselves could not have had diameters greater than approximately 0.15 m, which was the width of the narrow mouth at the top of the walls (as marked on the section in Heuzey 1900, p. 57); the egg-shaped or spherical plug of rope that held them must have had a maximum diameter of about 0.3 m (the maximum width of the ovoid section below); and the rope-secured bases of the poles could not have been longer than 0.8 m (the maximum depth of the bituminated cavity as measured from the top of the wall).

Stabilised in this way, the poles were perhaps used to anchor light reed screens that were mounted on the tops of the walls (Fig. 72)—a similar arrangement to that which has been proposed for the Uruk Stone Building. Ropes were probably the material of choice for the anchoring plugs because they provided elasticity: absorbing the stresses caused by the weight and movement of the reed screens and thus preventing the foundational bitumen surround from cracking. Forest's alternative suggestion, which is treated in more detail below, is that the projecting poles (made of wood or bundled reeds) provided the framework for a coating of adobe that formed superstructures on top of the fired-brick walls of the Lower Construction (PQRS) and then later on the outer block.

At first glance all of this seems straightforward enough, but the assumption that the cavities were the anchor points for vertical poles that were held in place by rope plugs raises some questions that are not easy to answer. First, how and when could the rope plugs, which were twice as wide as the openings, have been inserted into the cavities? Heuzey postulates that the bitumen vases (as he calls them) were formed on reed frames, which is doubtless why the diagram drawn to illustrate them (Sarzec and Heuzey 1912, p. 413) exhibits a regular pattern of notches on the inside surface of the bitumen. That would imply that the reed frames (essentially reed basketwork) were woven around the bottoms of poles that had already been fitted with rope plugs that had a maximum

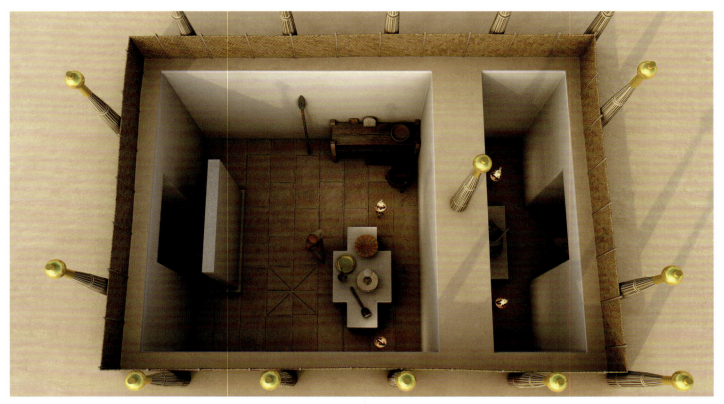

FIGURE 72. Reconstruction of the Lower Construction's antecella (left) and cella (right), showing the poles housed by the bitumen-coated cavities embedded in the tops of the walls.

diameter of about 0.3 m. The bitumen would then have been applied to the outside of the reed frame, and the assemblage would have been left to set before being fitted into the walls.

This is plausible, and it means that the reed frames must have formed a layer between the balls of rope and the bitumen coatings, which might perhaps have been desirable, depending on how flexible the bitumen was when it set. Nonetheless, it would surely also have meant that, even if some relatively elastic substance (perhaps more bitumen) was poured into the cavities to fill the spaces around the plugs and poles (probably once they were *in situ* in the walls), there would inevitably have been some movement in the bases of the poles, making them inherently slightly unstable. This would strongly militate against Forest's idea that the poles were used to secure rigid, but relatively brittle adobe walls that might have been susceptible to cracking. Sarzec seems to have recorded no trace whatsoever of any remnants of the reed frames or poles, but that is understandable since reeds are organic and perishable and so would not have survived. Also, the poles themselves were conceivably not single pieces of wood, as might

be imagined, but bundles of reeds with individual diameters of between about 40 mm and 45 mm. The estimate is derived from Wilfred Thesiger's observation (1964, p. 92) that the poles utilised by the inhabitants of the Iraqi marshlands to build reed houses were the same as the reed punt-poles used to propel canoes, while the frames of local reed houses photographed by Sarzec (Pl. 62 (2)) were made of bundles of similarly slender stalks. This being the case, a bunch of nine thin reed poles would have been needed to create a single post with a diameter of 0.15 m. Finally, the bundled poles with their rope plugs and bituminated reeded anchors must have been manufactured as units (on site or in the environs of Girsu), which were then transported to their installation points. How practical that was would have depended upon a number of factors, including the exact nature of the bitumen mix, but there can be little doubt that the assemblages must have been awkward to handle and potentially rather fragile. In this context, it is worth mentioning that bitumen was universally used in the form of mastic (as it is referred to by today's builders, who take advantage of a version based on silicone). In ancient

Sumer the compound was made of bitumen mixed with sand, loam or limestone fillers and fibrous materials, including significant amounts of vegetable matter.

A further interesting question is, how were the bituminated fittings incorporated into the walls of the building? Two possibilities seem highly improbable: a) contrary to the argument made above, the fittings were not manufactured as assembled units, but instead the shapes were cut into the finished walls then lined with bitumen and the ropes and plugs were (somehow) inserted later; or b) the finished walls were cut open to accommodate the vase-shaped bases of the poles and later rebuilt around them. The first of these suggestions fails to deal with the problem of inserting the rope plugs into openings that were too small for them; the second might perhaps have happened as an afterthought or a repair, but surely not as a planned procedure. It is therefore far more likely that the assembled fittings were built into the brickwork as it was being laid. This is the supposition that is represented in Heuzey's diagram, where the bricks (bonded with bitumen and perhaps drawn a little thicker than they really were) are neatly cut to accommodate the bituminated vase. The diagram also shows a thick deposit of bitumen (about the thickness of one brick) underneath the cavity. Was that part of the manufacturing process or was it a variable addition that was deployed while the bricks were being laid? Probably the latter.

It is also worth recalling at this point that bitumen-coated cavities, all displaying similar vase-like shapes, were found at several locations on Tell K and at a range of Sarzec heights that represent an extremely long timespan. Of most immediate relevance to the ones found in the tops of the walls of the Lower Construction are the two discovered by Sarzec at the Sarzec height of 8.48 m: one in each of the two blocks that formed the substructure of the landing at the top of the Large Stairway. He notes that they had larger 'bellies' than the ones in the walls of the Lower Construction, and while no other explicit information is given, the two sets of examples seem otherwise to have been very much the same. The stairway is the subject of two of Sarzec's photos (Pl. 58 (1 and 2); Figs. 48 and 49), but the blocks are not visible there because the Early Dynastic stairs were refitted by Gudea, whose foundation boxes and bricks were still in place when the photos were taken. One thing that seems unambiguously clear about the cavities that were placed at the top of the Large Stairway is that they were embedded at ground level in their surrounds. This seems to distinguish them markedly from those found in the walls of the Lower Construction, but the difference may be more apparent than real, as is discussed at the beginning of this chapter, because for viewers of the rites that were performed in the Lower Construction's subterranean holy rooms, the tops of the walls were effectively situated at, or very close to, what was then the uppermost surface of the mound (at a Sarzec height of about 11.58 m). It could therefore be the case that the capsules used to support poles and probably also reed screens above the sacred rooms of the Lower Construction expressed a continuity with capsules at other periods that were used at floor level (possibly including some of the ones beneath pavement V, though their extreme age makes that a highly uncertain matter). In particular, it is perhaps reasonable to suppose that the capsules fitted at the sides of the landing at the top of the Large Stairway could have been used as the supports for a pair of standards that were raised on poles at one of the entrances to the sacred precinct.

The only practical benchmark that might help to confirm whether bituminated capsules were capable of being used in this way is the large ring post that lay in two pieces on the ground on pavement F outside the Ur-Nanshe Building. The probable reasons why and when the post was deposited there are considered in Chapter 19, but on a functional level, the question can be asked: how did a post of this kind stand up, and could it conceivably have been supported in a cavity in the same way as the presumed light poles were on the walls of the Lower Construction? The first thing to note about the ring post is that it was large and heavy. With a total base diameter of about 210 mm (including the copper casing), it was almost certainly formed of bundles of lighter reed poles. In consequence, if it is again assumed that the big post was made of a bundle of smaller poles with base diameters of between about 40 mm and 45 mm, approximately nineteen poles would have been needed to create a large post with a thickness of roughly 200 mm (not counting the copper casing). It can be estimated that the lighter component poles would perhaps have weighed about 0.6 kg per metre on average (taking into account their natural taper), and the ring post was about 3 m tall, meaning the total weight of the bundled poles would have been about 3 m × 0.6 kg × 19 poles = 34.2 kg. For simplicity's sake the post has been treated as though it were a cylinder, though in reality it also narrowed along its length. The thick post was then covered with thin copper sheeting, the surface area of which can be worked out by multiplying the circumference of the base ($2\pi \times 0.105$ m) by its height, which gives 0.65 m $\times 3$ m $= 1.95$ m^2. To account approximately for the copper needed to cover the half-ring and the protruding band at the top of the ring post, this figure can be neatly rounded up to 2 m^2. The weight of copper sheeting, which is commonly publicised by commercial suppliers, can be estimated as approximately 18 kg and 27 kg per square metre for sheets of copper with thicknesses of 2 mm and 3 mm, respectively. Depending on the thickness of the copper sheet, therefore, the overall weight of the post would have been somewhere between 70 kg and 90 kg, and in all likelihood the hand-beaten copper would have been rather thick, meaning the 3-m ring post was probably at least 90 kg in weight, though its tapering form might have reduced this somewhat.

A post of this height and weight, which was doubtless made still heavier and placed under more structural stress by the addition of a flag or streamers, or some other sacred emblem, would have needed a substantial base to support it. No actual dimensions were recorded for the wide-bellied cavities found at the top of the Large Stairway, but a comparison might tentatively be drawn with one found by Cros in Trenches 9 and 10 that was 0.55 m wide at its widest point (1910, p. 76), and therefore considerably fatter than the ones in the Lower Construction that had a maximum width of 0.3 m. The capsules in the walls of the Lower Construction were 0.8 m tall, and this seems generally to have been true of the other examples, including the ones on the Large Stairway. This gives surmised overall measurements for the wide-bellied cavities at the top of the Large Stairway of 0.8 m (h) × 0.55 m (maximum width). That being the case, it might be further supposed that the total length of the bundled reeds that made up the ring post was 3.8 m, the bottom 0.8 m of which was not cased in copper but fitted with a rope plug and a bitumen surround before being buried in the mud-brick platform, with the result that about 21% of the post's entire length (0.8 m of 3.8 m) was set into the ground. The extra length would have added about 9 kg to the total weight of the pole (ignoring the weight of the rope or any associated ballast), with the additional weight all lying underground. The proposed diameter of the uncased bottom end of the post (200 mm) could be slightly varied because, as the presumed manufacturing process explained above would confirm, the bitumen enclosures were constructed around the already prepared bundles of poles and their previously attached rope plugs so the absolute diameter of the bottom of the post was not critical. It would also make sense to suggest that the lower section of the exposed (above-ground) part of the post might have had its copper casing fitted, or at least finished, after the feature was installed in the platform. This would have allowed it to be applied so that the post's copper bottom was flush with the level of the ground, no doubt covering the underlying opening of the cavity, which would presumably also have been sealed with bitumen to prevent water seeping in and damaging the uncased subterranean section of the post and its rope plug. Though the comparison should not be taken too literally, this is in fact how the ring posts appear on the uppermost register of the famous Uruk Vase, for example, where the substantial posts seem to sit on the ground without extraneous support.

Could a bitumen cavity of the shape and dimensions described really have supported a ring post of about this size and weight? That basic fact is not proven by the preceding calculations, but if the question could be answered in terms of physical loads and stresses, not neglecting the effects of wind on a post installed outdoors, it would go a long way towards confirming whether bitumen cavities might indeed have been used as foundations for such tall uprights. The other point to address is that no bituminated capsules were found that might be associated with Ur-Nanshe so the data derived from the ring post found outside the Ur-Nanshe Building is only a case study relating to the kind of object that might have been installed in such fittings. Significantly, the cavities uncovered in the blocks on the landing at the top of the Large Stairway might have been installed several decades after Ur-Nanshe's reign because (as noted above) the Early Dynastic bricks used to build the steps were signed with the single finger stroke that was the regnal marking of Enmetena. The expansive character of the works carried out by Enmetena, as well as the fact that he tirelessly trumpeted his achievements far and wide, make it eminently plausible to think that he might have installed two standard-bearing posts at the top of the Large Stairway on either side of a monumental entranceway, and it would not be surprising to discover that such standards were a common feature of the sacred precinct throughout its history, though no evidence has survived to confirm this. It should also be stressed that Sarzec was only alerted to the existence of these bituminated fixtures when, to his great surprise, he discovered them embedded in the walls of the Lower Construction, where they were unmissable. After that, he noted several more of them, including in the ancient layers of mud-bricks that he found in his deep sounding, but it is perhaps conceivable that any ground-based capsules that were possibly lodged in the mud-brick platform higher up in the mound, particularly around the level of the Ur-Nanshe Building, could have been overlooked. Finally, bearing all of this in mind, it is worth recalling that, in the Hymn to the Reeds from the reign of Ur-Nanshe (quoted in Chapter 1 above), the construction of the Ningirsu temple is associated with the erection of a post made of reeds that is inserted into a hole in the ground and fitted with a 'beard' of lapis lazuli as well as a 'standard' and a 'loop'. The deity who is said to preside over the construction is Enki, who included technical skills among his many powers.

CHAPTER 13

The Objects from the Lower Construction

SOME OF THE MOST INTRINSICALLY INTERESTING and archaeologically significant objects found on Tell K were closely associated with the Lower Construction. The religious and cultural meanings that they express, which are vital components of the history of the mound, are discussed in the following sections. Taken together, they confirm that the Lower Construction was an epoch-making building that almost certainly ushered in a new era of worship in Girsu.

The Feathered Figure

The Feathered Figure (Fig. 6) is a rectangular limestone bas-relief that measures 0.18 m (h) × 0.15 m (w) × 0.04 m (t) and is worked on both sides. The obverse shows a clear figurative image in shallow relief, with incised details, around which there is an inscription that fills most of the flat background space, apart from the long, narrow gap between the two post-like features immediately to the right of the figure. The reverse is entirely filled with writing, but whereas the inscribed characters on the front are divided only with horizontal lines, the inscription on the back is separated into boxes formed of five fairly evenly spaced horizontal lines running all the way across the surface of the stone, together with short, less regularly spaced vertical lines that look as though they might have been placed along the horizontal dividers to accommodate units of text.

The scene on the front consists of two main elements: a figure on the left, with two rather narrow uprights to the right, each of which is fitted with an ovoid that is placed near the top. The figure, who is facing the two tapering posts or poles, reaches towards and possibly holds the nearest one of the two with his left hand. If he were indeed holding the post, however, then the fact that his hand and fingers are obscuring its vertical lines would mean that it is the back of his hand that is visible, and the sculptors must have endowed him with two right hands. Similarly, if he were grasping the pole in his left hand, the left-hand fingers would be behind the upright, while his thumb would be wrapped around the front, but they are not. The idea that the object is actually in his hand derives from Heuzey, who later said that this was a mistake, and that the hand is open (see Sarzec and Heuzey 1912, pp. 165 and 302, n. 4). This is surely correct, and the corollary is that the figure's left hand is situated in the gap between the two poles, in front of the one that is nearest to him, with his open palm facing the viewer and his outstretched fingers extending through the gap, and that he is therefore using his left hand to gesture towards the space that the two posts frame and lead into.

In terms of composition, if the front of the stone is notionally divided vertically into fifths then the fifth on the extreme left (to the left of the figure) has no representational content and is filled only with writing. At first glance, it appears that the fifth on the extreme right is similarly empty of imagery, so that the central scene might be framed symmetrically on both sides by vertical margins, but on closer inspection the remains of a third upright can be seen towards the sculpture's extreme right edge, and particularly towards its bottom right corner. From there, two roughly parallel lines rise above the halfway point of the image (above the horizon line, as it were, which coincides more or less exactly with the horizontal line that runs across the middle of the picture, approximately at the level of the figure's waist). The top right-hand corner of the carving is damaged, and the missing portion makes it impossible to see whether the third upright was another ovoid-topped post or something else, but it can perhaps be observed that the third one is noticeably flatter than the other two in the way it is carved, being defined only by its inscribed outlines, whereas the others are modelled in relief so that they stand out sculpturally from the plane surface. Though the bases of all three uprights have been eroded, the faint traces of a horizontal line can perhaps be made out at the bottom of the post that is closest to the figure, and this might indicate that it was depicted as though it was standing on the same ground surface as his feet. It should also be pointed out, albeit with a degree of caution, that the damage in the top right-hand corner looks deliberate. This is particularly true of the straightish diagonal incision that runs from the middle of the carving's right edge upwards and inwards towards the preserved post that is furthest away from the figure. This does not look like erosion or an accidental break. On the contrary, it appears that the stone has been cut with a chisel, and there are lines at the base of the diagonal cut (where the incision meets the raw interior of the stone) that seem to show the effect of a sharp, flat blade that has been hammered down vertically into the stone's surface. From there, the mutilated area arcs round and upwards, becoming less regular towards the top of the plaque. The damaged portion is also very shallow, perhaps 0.01 m or less. The exact depth is difficult to gauge, but certainly the reverse shows no signs of a break running all the way through the stone. None of this is consistent with the idea that it might have been dropped on a hard surface, for example. On the contrary, the defacement appears to have deliberately targeted the upper right-hand corner: the area that contained the top half of the third post.

The standing figure occupies the entire height of the carving. He is barefooted, and his head is shown in profile as he looks towards the two poles on the right. His feet are also turned towards the uprights, but his torso is shown frontally. His clothing is limited to a long skirt that is secured at the waist with a waistband or perhaps a belt, and a headdress that takes the form of a circlet with two tall, elaborate protrusions behind. The skirt is decorated with three areas of slightly varied cross-hatching: along the waistband or belt, down a narrow strip on the right, and filling the broad main area of the skirt below the waistband and to the left of the vertical strip. It is difficult to say what the vertical line on the skirt is intended to represent, though it is tempting to imagine that it might be some kind of split or pleat to facilitate walking. The pectoral muscles in the figure's bare chest are indicated in shallow relief. His long hair is pulled back neatly behind his head, and his face, which is hairless, seems almost to rest on a diagonally incised mass that must be a long, pointed beard that covers his neck below the jawline, extending down over the left part of his chest (as we look). It is worth pointing out that the beard of the principal figure on the front of the Stele of the Vultures (on Fragment D) is depicted in exactly the same way, leaving the facial features uncovered.

As soon as the carving was discovered, the figure's headdress was interpreted by Sarzec and Heuzey as a crown with two large feathers attached vertically behind the head, and that is why they gave it the plaque the name by which it is still known, the *Figure aux plumes*, meaning 'figure with feathers' or Feathered Figure as it is referred to here (Sarzec and Heuzey 1912, p. 164). Although this interpretation has been questioned, and other ideas have been advanced, notably that the feathers might be ears of barley (Marchesi and Marchetti 2011, p. 195) or spikes of wheat (Dolce 1997, pp. 1–5), the original identification is almost certainly the right one. Recent detailed re-examinations point to notable similarities between the headdress and representations of the wings of the Imdugud or Thunderbird on archaic monuments from Girsu (Lecompte 2020, p. 435), and a particularly apt and direct comparison can be made with the image of the lion-headed eagle on the much later Mace of Mesilim (Fig. 7). The similarity between the chevron-like form of the hybrid bird's feathers on the top surface of the mace head and the decorative features of the headdress in the Feathered Figure is particularly striking (to the point that both might equally be taken for ears of wheat, if the image on the mace head did not tend to confirm that they are feathers). In addition, feathers are a key symbolic and ornamental component of the Imdugud crown that is worn by the goddess Ninhursag, the mother of Ningirsu, on the front of the Stele of the Vultures (Romano 2008, pp. 41–57), and there too they are carved in the same chevron-like way. One other carving should be mentioned in passing: the Early Dynastic fragmentary relief (AO48; Fig. 165), which features a seated female figure, presumably the goddess Bau, who has long feather-like extensions falling down from the back of her crown. In his early catalogue of

Sumerian finds Heuzey (1902, No. 2) describes the piece as a 'mythological fragment', and he refers to the feathery forms as the goddess's hair, but this is far from certain. Unfortunately, little or no information was recorded about the preserved remnant, which measures 0.185 m (h) × 0.259 m (w) × 0.078 m (t), except that it was found in the environs of Tell K (Heuzey 1902, p. 80).

It is, of course, no surprise that the sculptors drew on the inextricable link between Ningirsu and Imdugud that went back to the most archaic times. The same connection was invoked by the makers of the Stele of the Vultures when they showed Ninhursag wearing the Imdugud crown in her son's honour. As is clear from the iconography on the Mace of Mesilim, which was dedicated to Ningirsu, the use of the Thunderbird as a chief emblem of the god was well established in the age of Kish, and the association was fundamental in Presargonic times, as witnessed by a second mace head—dedicated to Ningirsu by Barakisumun, a legate of Enanatum I—that shows offerings being brought to the Imdugud bird, who acts as the god's avatar (Fig. 73). As these examples indicate, the same traditional way of depicting the feathers was seemingly the norm over a very long period. Nor can it be accidental that in two instances the imagery was found preserved on mace heads because the weapon was the chief symbol of Ningirsu in his guise as the heroic god of combat. As is argued in more detail below therefore, the Feathered Figure depicts Ningirsu himself, largely by making use of an iconographic triad that was a core component of the god's cult in the city of Girsu from as far back as it is possible to go: Ningirsu, wearing a crown decorated with the feathers of the Thunderbird, is shown in association with two (or perhaps originally three, though the third one is more precisely considered below) monumental maces with ovoid heads fixed on long shafts.

The archaic inscription, which presents a host of philological difficulties, has been the subject of some remarkable studies and editions, notably the first copy made by Thureau-Dangin (Sarzec and Heuzey 1912, p. XXXIV), the masterful interpretation of Wilcke (1995, pp. 669–74) and more recently the illuminating recension by Lecompte (2020). It is a composite text that contains, on the stone's figurative obverse, a hymnlike literary composition that draws on a creation myth relating to a divine mace, the building of a temple and the birth of grazing animals. The text-only reverse is filled with an inventory of plots of land that is intertwined with a doxology in praise of Ningirsu and his temple. The following translation of the two sides is based on a synthesis of Wilcke's transliteration and Lecompte's philological revision, with the latter's more recent interpretation being generally preferred. Some obscure expressions have been rendered in more readable English, but it should be made clear that several terms remain extremely difficult to decipher. The text on the obverse reads:

> The mace head of lapis lazuli is brought to the gateway. It is not built of wood, and it is not built of reeds. The lord created it. The fitting ornament with neither branch nor head is placed on a foundation. The lord created it. Amidst the meadows, the lord created the bison, and the gazelle is born. The long rope on the banks of

FIGURE 73. The Thunderbird Mace Head, showing offerings being brought to Ningirsu in the guise of his avatar, the lion-headed eagle. British Museum 23287.

the river is brought by the prince. The bison is born, and the gazelle is born. Amidst the grasses, the master created them.

And on the reverse is the inventory of plots of land (with measurements of areas converted into hectares preceding the names of the lands) together with the doxology:

25.92 ha: I$_3$-ŠUM$_2$
64.8 ha (or 388.8 ha): the orchard of the SANGA$_x$ canal
32.4 ha from the deity Me-dar
19.44 ha along the A-suḫur canal
194.4 ha or 1166.4 ha: NI-DU$_6$
6.48 ha: the BAD marsh

Ningirsu, you are the god of Girsu. You are a raven, you are the E$_2$-TAB. Ningirsu, you are the god of Girsu. The field in the SANGA$_x$ orchard is laid out. You are a raven, you are the E$_2$-TAB su$_3$. The KALAM GI$_4$ field is laid out: the splendid temple of Ningirsu. The lord created it. The field is laid out... admirable... Lamma. The throne of the temple, overlooking 6.48 ha (or 8.28 ha)... the annuity [to] the one who is greatly praised. Glory to Ningirsu, the lord who places the crown on the lowered head. Glory to Ningirsu.

This is a simply extraordinary and unique text that is one of the oldest-recorded literary compositions in human history. Falling into no known or clearly defined generic category, it is, at one and the same time: a sacred temple hymn, a creation myth, a song of praise, an inventory of the god's fields, orchards and pasture lands, and a document relating to the distribution of the wealth that the estates produce. At its heart is the god Ningirsu and his house (é.Ningirsu), which clearly connotes the temple as well as his institution at large. No mention is made of the personal name of any individual human or other major deity, and the only indication of a household or servant comes with the image of the god placing a crown on the bowed head of an obedient follower, though this might surely be taken as a symbolic reference to the god's multitude of human worshippers (the citizenry of Girsu), represented by their nominee. Finally, a distinction might also be drawn between the pastures, orchards and other lands devoted to agriculture on the one hand, and the area that is either occupied by the temple, or overlooked by it on the other: 'The throne of the temple, overlooking 6.48 ha...'

The hymn begins with the image of a lapis lazuli mace or mace head, which is invoked as Ningirsu's supernatural weapon and one of his divine emblems. The mace is associated with a threshold, and something is referred to that is not made either of reeds or wood. The latter statement might be intended to stand in apposition to the lapis mace, thereby emphasising the rarity of the material of which the weapon is made, but that makes little sense because it would surely have been taken for granted that a monumental mace head in the doorway of a temple would be made of something intrinsically weightier and more precious than mere wood or reeds (as indeed it is in the hymn), and by the same token it is hardly conceivable that the long shaft of the mace could have been made from anything but wood or reeds. It is therefore more likely that the construction that is not built of wood or reeds is the god's temple, which is introduced explicitly later in the text, and that this is the edifice (presumably made of bricks and stone) that is entered via the gateway that is related to the mace. Next follows a construction ritual during which an appropriate headless and branchless emblem of power and authority is installed on a foundation of some kind. It is impossible to know what this means with any certainty (and since the Sumerian term used for the item could be a plural, the words might signify more than one symbolic object). The allusion might be to the deposition of some sacred objects on a display base in the finished temple, or it perhaps indicates something analogous to the burying of foundation deposits. The fact that the offering (or offerings) was headless and branchless surely rules out the mace, except on the highly unlikely assumption that the mace head was not thought of as being in any way like a head. It would also preclude figurative statues, as well as any treelike or vegetative forms with branches or leaves, and perhaps, by extension, the representation of any creatures with limbs. What remains? One possibility that might relate specifically to the Lower Construction on Tell K, which was made of fired bricks and mud-bricks like the building in the text, are the poles (made of wood or bundled reeds) that were inserted into the bitumen cavities in the temple walls. This would depend on whether the word is singular or plural, but as the Lower Construction was subterranean, the tops of the walls acted like a foundation for the protruding posts, which in effect took the form of headless and branchless trees (with invisible roots), and analogous posts on another temple would presumably have created the same impression.

Despite the many insoluble difficulties associated with the opening lines of the text, there is little doubt that the figure around which it was inscribed should be identified as Ningirsu, and that the long poles fitted with mace heads are doorpost emblems that mark the threshold of his temple. The fact that the uprights in the carving are actually monumental maces is attested by the horizontal strokes at the tops of the shafts, just below the mace heads, which probably indicate sections of the coiled rope or twine that was used to help to secure real mace heads in place, perhaps as extensions of a rope wrapping that was fitted around the top end of the pole before it was inserted into the hole in the bottom of the stone. It is noteworthy, by the way, that the heads of the monumental maces depicted on the relief seem to have been carved as though they have vertical holes running all the way through them because the continuations of the shafts can be seen sticking out above the mace heads near the carving's top edge.

The fact that the upper half of the third pole on the right of the sculpture, furthest away from the god, has been badly broken makes it initially difficult to judge whether it was also shown fitted with a pyriform mace head or perhaps another divine totem instead, but there are three reasons why it was probably not simply a third mace: first, as previously mentioned, it is differentiated from the other two posts and the figure of the god, which are sculpturally modelled and lie noticeably proud of the plaque's surface, because it is rather flat and seemingly defined only by outlines; secondly, the paired maces are associated with the two sides of a doorway, so there is no reason for there to be a third one; lastly and most importantly, the third post is decisively separated from the other two, at least up to the middle horizontal line that runs across the carving, by parts of the inscription. It cannot be known whether words were also inscribed between the third pole and the two paired maces above the level of that horizontal divider, but even the partial presence of cuneiform signs in that area is highly significant, because it seems to confirm that the long space between the twinned maces is the only continuous portion of the background on either the front or the back of the carving that has been left intentionally blank and free of writing. The other possibly uninscribed area is the thin strip to the right of the third post, at the carving's extreme right edge, and although this looks as though it might also have been left empty, the mutilated area towards the top right corner and the lighter damage that runs vertically along the right side of the bottom half of the stone make it impossible to be sure. Especially when interpreted in the context provided by the inscription, the ensemble of poles that forms the opening that is being entered by the god seems clearly to have been meant to portray a sacred space that is somehow separate from ordinary reality. It might be thought of as a liminal dimension that is framed by the doorpost emblems and consequently revealed as a locus of interaction with the divine. But the depiction is perhaps even more specific. The blank space between the two maces seems graphically to form a portal that leads into a domain that is set apart from the busy visual activity of words and imagery that fills the rest of the relief. With his head and feet facing that empty area between the twinned poles therefore, the god is probably portrayed just as he is about to grace the sacred region with his presence: gesturing with his left hand through the opening between the two maces, he is apparently on the point of entering the temple. The fact that he is pictured walking (if that word can be admitted) from the left to the right also adds to the sense that he is heading towards an exceptionally sacred realm because conceptually he is moving against the flow of the text, which reads from right to left (and from bottom to top, though whether it should be read laterally across the carving or column by column is a moot point). This stresses the idea that he is proceeding in the direction of a space that is distinct from that shown on the rest of the carving, and the fact that it was left empty of text doubles down on that symbolism.

The implication is that the symbolic threshold was probably specifically intended to represent the entrance to the temple's cella, the sanctum sanctorum, with the god about to take up residence. How, in that case, should the third post be interpreted? One possibility is that it was conceived of as being placed inside the sacred space as the divine standard that is thought to have occupied the cella of Sumerian temples, where it stood between the doorway and the statue of the god on its podium. This is how Heuzey interpreted the third post, which he called the 'principal cult object' (Sarzec and Heuzey 1912, p. 302). How it might be conceived of spatially in the relief with respect to the entranceway formed by the maces is unclear, though it is important to stress that the image was designed symbolically, so the sculptors were not constrained by uninvented perspectival norms, and sacred meanings were presumably intended to trump all other considerations. In this respect, perhaps the most intriguing point is whether the third post in the Feathered Figure should be identified as the 'fitting ornament' or emblem of divinity that is described in the inscription as branchless and headless. This would entirely depend upon the nature of the divine standard that was associated with Ningirsu, but if the damage in the plaque's top right corner was indeed deliberate, that might indicate that the god's symbol was intentionally effaced and desacralised before the carving was eventually ritually interred as part of the decommissioning rites that were carried out long after it was made (as is discussed further below).

Another detail worth mentioning is that the fact that the cella is approached from left to right in the Feathered Figure might have a particular significance. When it is recalled that Sumerian temples were always positioned so that their corners faced the cardinal points, it becomes clear that a Sumerian viewer of the Feathered Figure would very easily have been able to work out that the left to right direction almost certainly correlates with a NW–SE axis of approach, which is the same principal axis as was established for the Lower Construction and the Ur-Nanshe Building. This would mean that the four corners of the relief also notionally indicated the cardinal points, beginning with north in the top left corner and followed by east, south and west (clockwise around the image), or west, south and east if the anticlockwise direction is preferred. It is, of course, theoretically possible that the left to right direction could have represented an opposite, SE–NW approach, but that would conceivably have seemed counter-intuitive because it would have contradicted the orientations of actual temples that are known to have existed on Tell K. The cardinal associations of the corners at the tops and bottoms of the image would then also have been reversed, with south being at the top and north at the bottom, and though the rightness or otherwise of this relationship is a cultural construct, the predominance of the north star in matters of navigation and surveying lends credence to the idea that it is one that would have been avoided.

For a long time, the figure in the Feathered Figure was commonly identified by commentators as a priestly king, an officiating high priest or a worshipping ruler (see Dolce 1997, pp. 2–3; and André-Salvini 2003, p. 68), but this was with reference to easily assimilated catch-all definitions of Sumerian officials that have often been too readily applied.

By contrast, Heuzey saw the figure as a divinity from the outset, and he even expressed confusion when his initial mistaken interpretation of the left hand as grasping one of the mace staffs seemed to undermine that (Sarzec and Heuzey 1912, p. 165). A close reading of the inscription and a consideration of the interplay between the text and the image confirms, as argued above, that the figure is indeed Ningirsu. This has been suggested by several scholars (Braun-Holzinger 2007, p. 18; Marchesi and Marchetti 2011, p. 195; and Lecompte 2020, p. 435), though often with extreme diffidence, largely due to the omnipresent (and actually rather absurd) authoritarian and hieratic theory of the priestly king that has cast a shadow over ancient Mesopotamian studies for generations. This takes the form of a long-standing, but misguided theory that the theocratic priest-king of ancient Sumer was a leader who held spiritual and temporal powers like the Pope or an Old Testament ruler, notably Melchisedech. In the case of the Feathered Figure in particular, none of the iconographic arguments that try to interpret the figure as a human actor in some temple ritual are tenable. The rounded beard, bare chest and long mesh or net skirt together display some similarities with the appearance of an Uruk theocrat, but the figure in the Tell K relief differs from the stereotype in some key respects: his hair is not gathered into a chignon, for example, and he is not wearing the theocrat's characteristic brimmed cap, while his ceremonial skirt is not transparent and frontally open. Similarly, he is not shown as a worshipper on his way to pray (as erroneously argued by Parrot 1948, p. 70) because his hands are not clasped in the conventional attitude of prayer. Pointing to the sacred enclosure with his left hand, while his right appears casual and relaxed, the figure's gesture is one of proprietorship, even of welcome. As the accompanying inscription makes clear, the god's portrayal shows him arriving at the temple's sacred threshold, which he formally institutes as a holy space by installing the requisite insignia of his divine office. The figure also resembles other depictions of Ningirsu, not least that on Fragment D of the Stele of the Vultures, but also (and still more strikingly) the remarkable portrait incised on a Presargonic shell plaque (Fig. 74) in which the iconography of the warrior god, who is seen fighting a supernatural, multi-headed hybrid beast, is closely comparable to that used on the plaque: he has the same long hair, a beard that begins at the jaw line, leaving the face free, and a headdress with two vertical feathers. Finally, the plausible but somewhat surprising comparison made in

FIGURE 74. Presargonic shell plaque, showing Ningirsu with a horned crown fighting a seven-headed monster.

the inscription between Ningirsu and a raven was perhaps a way of articulating Ningirsu's filial link with Enlil, who is also associated with a raven in ancient Sumerian mythology (cf. Veldhuis 2004, pp. 299–300).

Another remarkable fact is that the inventory of agricultural lands includes some toponyms or ceremonial names that are also found elsewhere in Presargonic texts from Girsu, as Wilcke has observed. For example, A-suḫur and SANGA$_x$ appear in later texts from Lagash–Girsu, while the BAD marsh (BE AMBAR in Sumerian) is also comparable, as noted by Lecompte, with various toponyms found in the archives and sets of texts that incorporate the sign AMBAR, such as Tir-ambar^{ki}. The case should not be overstated, however, because some of the other names that seem only to have been used on the Feathered Figure inscriptions have no known parallels elsewhere in the toponymy of the state of Lagash.

Metrological problems notwithstanding, it seems certain that the list of landed properties on the relief represented a very wide variety of surface areas, ranging from 6.48 ha to 1,166.4 ha to perhaps as much as 3,888 ha, depending on how the Sumerian numbers are converted (see Lecompte 2020). The lack of the names of any buyers and sellers of the plots of land excludes the idea that the inscriptions simply embody an archaic version of a later *kudurru* or boundary stone, and this is further confirmed by the sheer sizes of the surface areas in question. The inscribed doxology, which is punctuated by the repeated praise formula (zà-mì), translated as 'Ningirsu, you are the god of Girsu. Glory to Ningirsu!', introduces the idea of the (possibly progressive) acquisition and establishment of an agrarian estate belonging to the Ningirsu temple (see Lecompte 2020, p. 433). Such a domain could conceivably have been placed in the hands of the tutelary god of Girsu to celebrate the foundation of the temple institution when the Lower Construction was built and sanctified. In that case, the relief might have constituted a legal and divinely sanctioned contract of endowment that was drawn up at the behest of some unknown party. Conversely, however, the quasi-legal recitals were surely theoretical, acting as a way of justifying a post hoc land-grab of the territories that formed the emerging city-state of Girsu, the god's fiefdom. Accordingly, it is possible that the Feathered Figure provides evidence of the appropriation of an expanded area that might have been conceived of as the embryonic domain of the god and his temple establishment. It is also interesting to note that different general types of agricultural settings and local habitats are itemised, including fields, waterways, canals, orchards and marshes. The mixture might perhaps be considered to be a balanced portfolio of landed property (so to speak) that also represented a microcosm of the Sumerian world.

The difficulties of palaeography and metrology presented by the archaic inscription mean that it is impossible finally to calculate the sum total of the area of land owned by the temple, but it might have been as much as 4,166.64 ha or 5,119.2 ha (51.192 km^2) or even significantly more. Estates of this approximate size, which might have formed only the core of the overall amount of land owned by Ningirsu (the territory that the ancient Greeks would have referred to as the *khôra*), would have constituted a realistic agricultural complex for a religious institution that occupied a central place in the organisation of the city-state. Alternatively, the lands listed on the relief might document the acquisition or seizure of new plots in an attempt to consolidate Girsu's control over an ever-increasing expanse of countryside. In truth, it is impossible to know. Furthermore, while the risk of committing anachronisms makes it problematic to link the place names inscribed on the Feathered Figure with known Presargonic toponyms, it should be remembered that the A-suḫur and SANGA$_x$ waterways, recognised by Ur-Nanshe and his successors, were in the neighbourhood of Girsu, while the marshland listed as BAD (BE AMBAR) on the relief might tentatively be located further away in an area between Girsu and Lagash, if the epithet on the relief can indeed be correctly linked with the later place known as Tir-ambar^{ki}.

As has been proposed by Lecompte (2020, p. 423), the reference in the hymnlike composition on the obverse of the plaque to the 'long rope' that is laid down by the 'prince' surely refers to a surveyor's rope (èš.gìd.da). This is consistent with the demarcation of plots of land that seems to be a recurring feature of the text, and also with the key consecration and construction rituals that preceded the building of temples, namely the laying out of the sacred spaces with ropes and pegs. As argued in Chapter 14, this was carried out according to cardinal rules in the context of a world order that conceptually divided up the land into an unbroken or tessellated series of plots. Additionally, it is tempting to ask whether the rectangular boxes that are used to divide the text on the relief might also have related to this system. The idea becomes still more tantalising when the possibility that the carving itself might have acted like an orientation device that was calibrated (as it were) by the axis of approach to the temple depicted in the image is taken into account, as noted above.

Perhaps the thorniest question posed by the document—one that has been much debated and appears sadly incapable of satisfactory resolution—concerns the possible occurrence of the most revered epithet applied to Ningirsu's temple: Eninnu, or é.ninnu, literally meaning 'house fifty'. Since the first unequivocal use of the term probably dates from the reign of Enanatum I, it is extremely problematic to suggest that the only known precursor is found in the text inscribed several centuries earlier on the Feathered Figure. The likelihood that the word é.ninnu on the plaque is intended to signify the temple in the same way as it does in Under Enanatum I recedes still further when it is realised that the building in which the Feathered Figure was displayed—the Lower Construction, which was in all likelihood the foundational iteration of the Ningirsu temple on Tell K—would surely therefore also have been known as the Eninnu. This is highly improbable, however, because the successor temple built by Ur-Nanshe (known as the Ur-Nanshe Building) was not called é.ninnu, but rather é.^{d}nin.ğír.su or èš.ğír.sú, adopting the same official name as that which unequivocally designates the temple in the inscription on the reverse of the Feathered Figure: é.^{d}Nin.ğír.[su]. It might also be considered unlikely that the makers of the plaque applied two different epithets to the temple. All in all, it seems preferable to follow Lecompte (2020, pp. 431–2) in taking the occurrence of the term on the plaque to mean something other than 'house fifty'.

With respect to its iconographic and palaeographic content, the dating of the Feathered Figure has been the subject of much debate, but it seems certain that it was created in Early Dynastic I times. Whether it should be dated to the beginning of the Early Dynastic I period (2900–2800 BCE), making it the same age as the archaic tablets of Ur (Wilcke 1995, pp. 669–74), or to its later phase (2800–2600 BCE, previously known as the Early Dynastic II period, as suggested by Marchesi and Marchetti 2011, p. 43), is not easy to determine solely on palaeographic grounds. Lecompte (2000, p. 432) has proposed a middle way, suggesting a date between 2750 BCE and 2700 BCE, making the plaque slightly later than the archaic archive of Ur. The object's archaeological context, as already highlighted, is extremely obscure, not least because it was interred close to the Ur-Nanshe Building at a much later date in the Presargonic era. There is no doubt, however, that it was originally housed in the Lower Construction, and that it was probably fashioned to commemorate the temple's construction and inauguration. If the attempt, based on the meagre and problematic set of potsherds collected by Genouillac and Parrot, to reconstruct a chronological sequence for the early strata on Tell K is correct, then the idea that the relief dates to a time in the Early Dynastic I period (2900–2800 BCE) would appear to be the most likely conclusion. This would place it in the same time frame as the Lower Construction, with the Feathered Figure and the temple both therefore being later than the reliable chronological horizon that is provided by pavement V and its associated deposits that date back to Jemdet Nasr times (3200–2900 BCE).

The Girsu Land Stele

Dating from approximately the same time in the Early Dynastic I period as the Feathered Figure, and also originating from the Lower Construction, the fragmentary Girsu Land Stele (Fig. 75) is another outstanding artefact from archaic Girsu. Lacking the hymnic and mythological content of the Feathered Figure, the surviving portion does not have the same poetic resonance as the carved plaque, particularly for the modern viewer, but in other ways the two should be regarded as counterparts. Like the Feathered Figure, the Girsu Land Stele incorporates a title deed that lists some plots of land belonging to the god's estate. It was stored in the temple treasury, and should be understood in large measure as the archaic equivalent of the documents that would

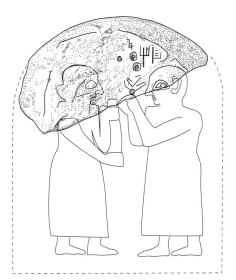 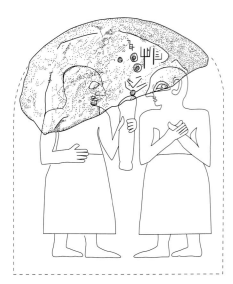 

FIGURE 75. Reconstruction of the Girsu Land Stele, with two possible versions of the obverse (left and centre) and the reverse (right).

today be found in a land registry—the vital difference being that the rights of ownership recorded on the Girsu Land Stele are, in principle, absolute because the itemised lands are considered to belong to Ningirsu. Historically, the stele sheds light on the territorial formation (or expansion) of the emerging city-state of Girsu, whose lands were administered as the property and acreage of Girsu's patron god.

The Girsu Land Stele is a fragment of grey limestone that is curved on top and broken diagonally below; measuring 0.21 m (w), it is inscribed on both sides and also around its thick outer rim. When it was made, it clearly had representational content on one side (which, by analogy with the Feathered Figure, might be referred to as the obverse), but the only section that survives is the upper segment of a man's bald head, including parts of the ear, eye and nose. The minimally preserved figure faces left, and though the area in front of his eye and nose is very badly eroded, faint traces of a right-facing counterpart can possibly be made out, notably the shape of the back of an eroded figure's head (with or without a chignon) and the arc of the right shoulder. The upper right edge of this side of the stone, above the man's bald head, is slightly damaged as well. The other side of the stele fragment (cautiously described as the reverse) is filled with two horizontal columns that are divided into rectangular boxes containing archaic signs. The segment above the uppermost horizontal divider is decorated with incised cross-hatching to create an irregular reticulated pattern, the central part of which is abraded. A similar pattern fills the stone's thick circumferential rim, where some triangles might also be visible. A vertical portion on the right of the stele's text-filled reverse is damaged, and a significant part of the inscription is lost.

The surviving remnant of the Girsu Land Stele recalls another rare object from the Early Dynastic I period that is one of a pair known as the Blau Monuments (BM86260), which are made of green schist (a rock formed by the metamorphosis of shale or mudstone). One of the two compares especially well with the Girsu Stele because it is a semi-oval with a maximum diameter of a little less than 0.18 m that has a similar curving shape to the Girsu stone and is also inscribed with figures and archaic signs. The style of the inscription on the reverse of the Girsu Land Stele is also reminiscent of the inscription on the Feathered Figure (see Parrot 1948, p. 56; and Marchesi and Marchetti 2011, p. 43).

The very limited extent of the surviving portion of the iconographic scene on the obverse of the stele means that it is, of course, impossible to make out what it showed with any degree of certainty, but the shaven-headed figure might well have been a ruler or perhaps rather a high-priestly administrator of the Ningirsu temple. Furthermore, if the worn-out marks to the left of the eye and the nose do indeed represent traces of a second, right-facing figure who was depicted with a bald head or a chignon, that would indicate either another tonsured priest or possibly an individual of higher status, perhaps a ruler, if the second figure's hair was shown tied back behind the head. The implication is that the lost scene depicted two individuals, maybe a ruler and a high priest, standing face to face, and conceivably in the act of performing a ritual of some kind. Among the many possible reconstructions, two seem especially likely: the first (Fig. 75 (left)) shows a ruler who is wearing his hair in a chignon and holding an object, while the facing high priest has both his hands raised; the second (Fig. 75 (centre)) shows two bald priests, with the figure on left holding what could have been a torch (the remains of which are perhaps just about perceptible on the fragment of stone), while the figure on the right has clasped hands. The maximum dimensions of the unbroken stele might originally have been around 0.281 m (h) × 0.23 m (w).

The inscribed text on the reverse of the stone records the respective surface areas of several obscure fields, while the grand total, which is thankfully preserved, is indicated on the obverse by the signs above the remains of the shaved head (Gelb et al. 1989–91, pp. 67–8). Despite the importance of the archaic inscription, and despite the fact that it has been subjected to thorough analysis by some renowned philologists, the generally accepted calculation and conversion of the total land area referred to is marred by a flagrant error that has never previously been highlighted. As published by Gelb et al. (1989–91, p. 67), the total is made up of 2 šar'u.gal 1 bùr, which they convert to 4,573 ha or 45.73 km², denoting a square of land measuring about 6.7 km × 6.7 km. If the linear length of 1 šar.gal equals 3,600 bùr, however (see Powell 1987–90, pp. 457–517), then 1 šar'u.gal (the surface area corresponding to 10 × 1 šar.gal) is actually equal to ten times that amount, or 36,000 bùr. Two šar'u.gal therefore make 72,000 bùr, and if 1 bùr is defined as a rectangle measuring 6 m × 10,800 m (= 64,800 m²), that means the initial calculation of 2 šar'u.gal 1 bùr works out at 72,000 × 64,800 m² = 4,665,600,000 m². If that figure is then divided by 1,000,000 to convert it to square kilometres, the actual sum total is 4,666 km².

Gelb et al. give an area of 45.73 km² for 72,001 bùr, which breaks down as 0.000635 km² or 635 m² per bùr. The figures are out by a factor of 100, which is a particularly tricky mistake to make with a predominantly sexagesimal system—one that suggests there is a modern calculation error somewhere.

It is true that the same figure has been published over a number of years by more than one author, and this makes it likely that errors have crept in and been compounded, perhaps through hypercorrection. There may have been some confusion about the difference between a square with sides of 2 šar.gal (a square with sides of 40 km being considered to be twice that of a 2 šar.gal square—with sides of 21.6 km) and the surface area of a block of land measuring 2 šar'u.gal. This might have resulted in a multiplication by 10, explaining why the calculation of the area is out by a factor of 100 instead of 1,000, but in any event the outcome to date has been incorrect and messy.

The conclusion is that the total surface area of the land mentioned on the obverse of the Girsu Stele ought therefore to be 4,666 km², equating to a square with sides of 68 km, which is a truly enormous figure (approximately a third of the total area of the modern Dhi Qar Governorate, which is 12,900 km²). It is significantly larger than, for example, the widely accepted estimate of the size of the Presargonic state of Lagash, calculated as about 3,000 km² of irrigated lands (see Diakonoff 1974, pp. 173–203; and Westenholz 2002, p. 26). To give a further sense of what this implies, the land expanse noted on the Girsu Land Stele is by far the largest of any of the blocks of land recorded on a single surviving object in Sumerian history.

Despite their incorrectly calculated total, Gelb et al. (1989–91, p. 68) nevertheless observe that, as with the estates recorded on the Feathered Figure, the size of the territory alluded to makes it extremely unlikely that the Girsu Land Stele was created as a contract or registry document to confirm the sale and purchase of the listed real estate. It was probably therefore drawn up either to register the legal transfer of landed property as a gift or grant (so to speak) in favour of the Ningirsu temple, or possibly as an inventory of the god's estates that had primarily symbolic rather than legal significance. As with the Feathered Figure, moreover, the Girsu Land Stele was doubtless produced in the context of a particularly significant ceremonial event, the exact nature of which cannot be known. One distinct, albeit speculative possibility is that the erection or perhaps the restoration of the Lower Construction on Tell K marked the initial acquisition or the symbolic renewal of Ningirsu's claim to his domain, depending on whether the god had previously been recognised as the chief deity of Girsu during the time horizon represented by and possibly preceding pavement V. In either of these cases, the records of the god's estates were immortalised on stone, and his earthly representative—the inferred ruler on the obverse of the stele—was confirmed as his administrator. Alternatively, the Girsu Land Stele might have been commissioned to commemorate the acquisition of new territories beyond Girsu's hinterlands in the wake of a successful campaign against a vanquished rival that was led by the supposed ruler portrayed on the stone. These theories cannot be confirmed, but in either case it seems that Girsu, whether by a process of organic growth or military conquest, achieved the status of a regional superpower in Sumer, becoming a veritable behemoth state.

Though the Girsu Land Stele derives from the same epoch as the Feathered Figure, it is impossible to know for sure which of the two artefacts is older. Nevertheless, it remains likely that the stele is later because there is little doubt that the Feathered Figure was an object of cardinal importance that was created in the context of the initial foundation of the Lower Construction.

The Stele of the Captives

Related in terms of chronology and pictorial style to the Feathered Figure and the Girsu Land Stele, the fragmentary Stele of the Captives, as it is referred to here (Fig. 76), is a third outstanding work of Sumerian art that originated from the Lower Construction. In view of its historical importance and aesthetic value, it is regrettable in the extreme that the carving was reprehensibly abandoned by Sarzec and left on the site to be engulfed in a spoil heap, destroyed or possibly disposed of illegally. It is a blessing that the object was photographed, but the fact that it subsequently disappeared and has never resurfaced makes it is one of the great lost objects

FIGURE 76. Reconstruction of the Stele of the Captives.

of Girsu, and its disappearance is rendered all the more painful because it was entirely avoidable.

The substantial fragment of a very large limestone stele made in Early Dynastic I times, measuring 0.8 m (h) × 2 m (w) × 0.2 m (t), and decorated with a shallow relief, was unearthed in its primary context on the pavement on the floor of the trophy room or treasury (room T) in the Lower Construction. It seems that Sarzec did not take the trouble to ship it back to France or deposit it somewhere for safe keeping on account of both its weight and his assessment of its poor condition (see Parrot 1948, p. 74). The colossal scale on which it was conceived makes it one of the largest Sumerian sculptures yet brought to light; to give just two points of comparison, it was much bigger than the Presargonic Stele of the Vultures (with overall measurements of 1.3 m (w) × 0.11 m (t)), and twice the size of Naram-Sin's Akkad Victory Stele (with a width of about 1 m).

The portion of it that was found preserved *in situ* was the section, including its uncarved base and part of the register immediately above, that contained the lower portion of an engraved scene showing the legs (below the knees) and feet of six men. Set against a plain background, two of the figures were portrayed wearing Sumerian kaunakes, two of them were apparently naked and two more were so badly damaged that it is not possible to be sure how they originally appeared. Nonetheless, it seems likely that the scene showed three pairs of figures, each pair being made up of a naked prisoner of war and a soldier wearing a ceremonial skirt with a fringed hem of lanceolate tassels. As indicated by the direction of the feet, the pairs of figures were depicted facing left, with each naked captive in front of the respective accompanying soldier. Though there is no way of knowing what was carved on the top two-thirds (approximately) of the monument, it is probable that there was an upper register that featured the ruler of Girsu in a warlike context. If the height of the plain base is added to the inferred heights of the two proposed registers (derived from the sizes and proportions of the preserved parts of the figures), it can be assumed that the stele might originally have been about 2.5 m high. The conjectured composition is a classic Mesopotamian victory scene, with parading warriors escorting naked captives after a battle. Already in use in the Late Uruk period, the subject would have drawn on figurative language that was typical of the third millennium BCE—the Standard of Ur providing a well-known example.

The Stele of the Captives is the earliest-attested Sumerian war monument on this scale that was carved in relief to commemorate or celebrate the conclusion of a triumphant military campaign, and as such it can be regarded as the Girsu precursor of the Stele of the Vultures. Kept in the trophy room of the Ningirsu temple, which also housed the Feathered Figure and the Girsu Land Stele, it was manifestly one of the city-state's most revered emblems. It is impossible to know which particular victory it was intended to honour, or indeed whether it related to an actual historical event. It might instead have showed a generic scene dedicated to the warrior god Ningirsu and his triumphant earthly army of human soldiers. What is abundantly clear, however, is that the stele's colossal size unequivocally expressed the military supremacy of archaic Girsu in a style that might be described as lofty, if not magniloquent or bombastic. It also seems reasonable to suppose that the inferred proximate positioning in room T of the Lower Construction of the Stele of the Captives and the Girsu Land Stele, with its inventory of lands, might have had a special significance. Conversely, though it is tempting to connect the victory scene with the hypothesised extension of the territory of Girsu that was conceivably represented by the areas listed on the Land Stele, it must be stressed that the two objects might not have been exact contemporaries, and might not have been commissioned by the same ruler. It cannot even be unconditionally supposed that they were displayed side by side in the temple. What can be affirmed is that, throughout the long life of the Ningirsu temple complex known as the Lower Construction, from its origins in the Early Dynastic I period through Early Dynastic IIIa times and down to its deconsecration and ritual interment in the reign of Ur-Nanshe, highly prized state monuments were stored, curated and displayed in one of the two rooms that made up the temple's inner sanctum. The artefacts seem all to have commemorated especially significant events relating to the foundation and grandeur of Girsu—its formation as a territory belonging to Ningirsu, and the expansion and consolidation that were achieved through and safeguarded by its martial strength.

The Circular Bas-Relief

Perhaps the most fascinating of the constellation of objects from the Early Dynastic I period that were found in, or closely

FIGURE 77. Reconstruction of the Circular Bas-Relief.

associated with, the Lower Construction was the Circular Bas-Relief: a small circular cylinder made of limestone, with a frieze-like relief of figures and cuneiform signs carved around its rim, and overall dimensions of 0.19 m (h) × 0.39 m (diameter) (Fig. 77). The fact that the sculpted cylinder survived the ravages of time to the extent that it did is particularly surprising, since the six shattered pieces (here labelled A to F) from which it was reconstructed were uncovered in several different places. As outlined above, Fragment A, measuring 0.08 m (h) and depicting two bald men and another man with long hair and a long beard, all left-facing, was found on the floor of room T inside the Lower Construction (Sarzec and Heuzey 1912, Pl. 1 ter (1b)). Three more pieces were found at the same level as Fragment A on the paving outside the Lower Construction, under the masonry that formed the encasing block that was added around the outer walls of the two-room temple: Fragment B, measuring 0.07 m (h) and portraying two high-ranking figures standing face to face; and Fragments C and D (with heights of 0.07 m and 0.1 m, respectively), representing two sections of the rounded base of the sculpture and showing the bottom parts of some of the figures, including their standing feet. The context of Fragment E, measuring 0.08 m (h) and showing four men with long hair and long beards, was not clearly recorded (Sarzec and Heuzey 1912, Pl. 1 bis (2)), though it was apparently found at a deeper level than the Feathered Figure. One more piece was excavated by Cros in his North Trench: Fragment F, which was part of the object's cylindrical interior, was not carved.

Sarzec and Heuzey (1912, p. 313) believed that the artefact was originally made up of two superimposed cylindrical blocks that were drilled with two almost circular perforations (with diameters of 0.06 m) running vertically and continuously all the way through them. Although this observation has never been questioned, it is in fact extremely unlikely that the sculpture was formed of two separate components in this way. First, because this completely unheard-of technique would have introduced a host of practical issues that would have unavoidably interfered with the sculpting of the circumferential scene; and secondly, because the photographic evidence leaves little doubt that the artefact was deliberately broken across its diameter (from top to bottom) and split horizontally through its circumference (from side to side) for reasons that are explored in detail in Chapter 15. The top surface of the object was probably drilled with two central holes, though it must be stressed that the trace of only one hole was preserved, and the existence of the second is entirely inferential.

From the outset, the Circular Bas-Relief was identified as perhaps a low base or pedestal that was used to display sacred objects, votive weapons or divine emblems (see Sarzec and Heuzey 1912, p. 313; and Heuzey 1900, p. 53), or a cult statue (as later proposed by Crawford 1987, p. 71), none of which survived. It is also possible that the object might itself have been a focus of worship, conceivably as a ritual appurtenance, in which case it could have been the crowning feature of a sacred installation (an altar, for example) rather than a pedestal. The two ideas are not mutually exclusive, however, so even in the latter setting the cylinder might still have been the support for a cult emblem.

The scene on the rounded surface of the artefact contains some of the most intriguing iconography that has been handed down from archaic Girsu. As already highlighted, the stone carving was in all likelihood commissioned to immortalise a pact that was made between two prominent leaders, who are shown holding weapons and totemic symbols of power that doubtless relate to their respective peoples or clans. Fortunately, their two facing heads were preserved on Fragment B, while their feet survived on Fragment C.

As reconstructed diagrammatically in Fig. 77, each leader was accompanied by a cohort of praying worshippers, all with characteristic clasped hands, which means that any treaty or agreement that the scene was intended to commemorate was ratified with the approval of the gods. The main, totem-holding figure on the left was accompanied by seven (theoretically) identical followers, all with long hair and long beards, while his counterpart on the right also almost certainly had seven followers, three with shaven heads and four with long hair and long beards (three of the hirsute heads being conjectural). The fact that the two principal figures had lines of followers behind them is confirmed by the opposed directions of some of the surviving heads and feet. This is especially interesting on Fragment B, where the two leaders are shown looking at each other, and on Fragment D, where the ends of the two processions can be seen, separated by a subgroup of three figures: a right-facing, supposedly bald musician (whose rank and function are confirmed below) and a left-facing man with surmised praying hands, long hair and a beard; between them is a half-size figure with raised arms. Placed diametrically opposite the two facing leaders, who must be regarded as the focal point of the tableau, the presence of this musical subgroup lends a superb symmetry to the circling band of carving. The entire scene, which is framed at the top and bottom by a narrow protruding border, is well modelled in shallow relief against a carefully sanded background, and the upper surface of the object is flat and similarly smooth.

The figures were each shown wearing a ceremonial skirt or kaunakes on which some of the participants' names were carved in cuneiform signs, and in one preserved instance a title was added. It is a matter of extreme regret that, because their lower bodies and skirts are mostly missing, the names of the two main protagonists are not known, but the inclusion of personal names surely provides incontrovertible evidence that, even if it includes symbolic or legendary elements, the scene was meant to record an actual historical event. In total, the skirts of nine individuals have partly survived: two worn by members of the procession on the left; four worn by followers of the leader on the right; and the three belonging to the subgroup that includes the confirmed musician. The names of the half-size figure and the man with the plain skirt to his right were apparently not shown on the relief, but otherwise five names have been transcribed. If it is reasonable to assume that the two leaders and all their followers were positively named (supported by the fact that vestiges of signs might be discernible on the two leftmost figures of the group on the left), as was the high-ranking musician, who was perhaps a harpist or a singer (see Parrot 1948, p. 73; and Marchesi and Marchetti 2011, p. 42), then it might tentatively be concluded that the half-size figure and the blank-skirted man to his right were subordinates of some kind, probably lower-status musicians or performers, whose personal identities were considered unimportant. Beginning with the chief musician, and looking at the reconstruction (Fig. 77) from right to left, the legible names are:

^{pa}pabilga$_x$(PAP.NE)^{ga} nar-gal: Pabilga, the chief or senior musician
lugal(LU$_2$.GAL)-^{a}asilal$_x$(EZEN): Lugal-asilal
KU.KUR$^?$.IR.IR: [reading order of signs unknown; name unknown]
ur-me-ku: Ur-Meku [name uncertain]
MUNUS.[AŠ$^?$].ŠE/[G]I: [name unknown]

The archaic scene is extraordinarily pregnant with historical and symbolic meanings that will for the most part probably never be finally elucidated. The identities of the two leaders of the respective groups involved in the depicted event have unsurprisingly been a source of much debate, as have the items that they are holding in their hands. The leader on the right, who is beardless and long haired, is carrying a slender, pointed stick or staff that rises almost vertically above the two facing heads and penetrates the slim horizontal border that frames the top of the relief. His other hand runs across the front of his chest in a gesture that seems analogous to the left hands of the figures standing behind him. The motif of an individual holding a rod is quite frequent in Early Dynastic images, where it is found associated with a wide range of actions, including persons walking in front of or behind a chariot, or holding the reins of horse that is pulling a chariot; herders leading livestock; and even figures (who could conceivably be judges or umpires) standing next to wrestlers. In the context of the Circular Bas-Relief, it should probably be assumed that the rod has symbolic connotations of leadership and authority that loosely relate to one or other of these actions, perhaps intimating that the principal figure is metaphorically herding or leading his flock of followers.

The iconography of the leader on the left is more difficult to assess. He is shown with long hair and perhaps also a beard, and (judging from the hem that can be seen in Fragment C) a plain skirt; he is holding a long-handled tool or weapon with a curving blade (perhaps a sickle sword) in his right hand, with the shaft resting on his right shoulder and the top of the blade roughly level with the top of his head. If the curved blade is compared with the object held in the right hand of Eanatum on the reverse of the admittedly later Stele of the Vultures, it might plausibly be concluded that both items are badges of office that signal the exalted or royal status of their bearers. In his raised left hand the same leader on the Circular Bas-Relief is holding up an enigmatic object that features a horseshoe-shaped bottom with a central groove running around its arc and horizontal stripes across its straight, narrow sides. Above that (below the thumb of the leader's left hand) is a series of four horizontal grooves bordered by a vertical stripe on the left, and above the thumb the object fans out towards a curving top edge. The upper segment is marked with perhaps two short vertical furrows just above the thumb, followed by an irregular set of four roughly transverse lines, and above that another set of vertical grooves or furrows with wider, flatter patches on both sides. It is not at all easy to make out the forms precisely, and the indented grooves might perhaps have been applied in order to suggest the ridges that appear on either side of them, particularly the ones just below the figure's thumb. Heuzey judged the object to be a fringed headband or some kind of bent article that was the reward for a victory, or perhaps a military emblem (Sarzec and Heuzey 1912, p. 356).

Another alternative suggested by its shape is that the enigmatic object might be a symbolic sandal. Though at first sight this idea might seem slightly curious, it should be remembered that ceremonial sandals made of silver and copper have been discovered in funerary contexts from the later Early Dynastic and Akkad periods (McMahon 2006, pp. 121–3). Furthermore, a sandal can be seen attached to the shaft of a standard featuring a ceremonial mace head on an Akkad cylinder seal from Nippur that shows a seated deity, possibly Enlil, being addressed by the gods of the storm and the moon, with a human worshipper in attendance (Fig. 78). Though the analogy should not be pressed too far, it is perhaps also worth observing that the foremost of the two gods on the seal (the one who is closest to the sandal-adorned standard) also carries a long-handled object in his right hand that rests on his right shoulder and is fitted on top with a curving appendage. But if the form in the Circular Bas-Relief is indeed a sandal

FIGURE 78. Akkad cylinder seal from Nippur that shows a sandal attached to the shaft of a standard featuring a ceremonial mace head.

(more precisely a left sandal, as suggested by its curving top edge), it must unquestionably have had a symbolic meaning. The foot or sandal as a symbol of domination, representing the placing of a foot on the neck of a defeated enemy, for instance, occurs in a range of contexts at different historical periods, most importantly for the present discussion in an important passage towards the end of Gudea's Cylinder Inscriptions (also referred to in Chapter 37 below), where, before welcoming Ningirsu into the New Eninnu, Gudea metes out justice to malefactors (B18): 'A day of justice dawned for him. He set his foot on the neck of evil ones and malcontents'. The logical extension from forceful subjection or the punishment of wrongdoers to the peaceful act of giving a ceremonial sandal to ratify the transfer of lands, is found in some cuneiform sources (particularly the Nuzi tablets), but the imagery on the Circular Bas-Relief does not seem to conform to either of these patterns. The use of the symbol was more explicit in ancient Egypt, where, for example, a high-ranking courtier who comes bearing a pair of sandals is represented twice on objects from the reign of Narmer: on the king's palette and on his mace head, both of which were made in about 3000 BCE and were therefore approximately contemporary with the Girsu relief (Fig. 79). In both cases the image of the sandal was presumably employed to denote sovereignty, and that is perhaps the best explanation for the introduction of the symbolic sandal on the Circular Bas-Relief, where the overall sense of equilibrium that the carving expresses is personified in the meeting of two equal and counter-balanced sovereign forces: the leader on the left with the sandal and sickle sword as emblems of his authority over the territory that he rules, and the leader on the right

FIGURE 79. A courtier at the court of Narmer of Egypt holding a pair of sandals belonging to the king. From the Palette of Narmer, c.3200 BCE.

with the long staff that signifies his equivalent supremacy. Accordingly, the two counterparts are depicted coming together as powerful equals.

Lined up behind the two leaders are their respective groups of seven followers, all of whom are depicted with their hands clasped in front of their chests in a gesture that is generally interpreted as one of prayer and attentiveness. All ten of the figures whose upper bodies are preserved have bare chests, including the two chief protagonists and the half-size figure, who is either a child or an unusually small adult. The lower bodies of six of the men belonging to the two principal parties are preserved, and they are all shown wearing skirts made up of flat panels at the top, with lanceolate strips affixed below. In addition, they are all also wearing open overskirts, or perhaps just two pieces of cloth that dangle down from the two sides of their waists, almost taking the form of cloth swords. The style of dress is typical of warriors (or charioteers), though it is noteworthy that the small member of the musical trio is similarly, though less elaborately attired. The four men with preserved heads and upper bodies, who can be seen standing behind the leader with the sickle sword on the left, uniformly have long hair and long beards, but the appearance of the men standing behind the leader with the stick on the right is more varied. Four heads and upper bodies have survived, three of which have fully shaven heads, while one has long hair and a long beard. Horizontal stripes are used to depict the hair and beards, and it is worth recalling that the same technique was used to represent the hair of the foundation figurines that were also found below the Lower Construction. It is typical of plaques unearthed at various sites that differently attired figures, with and without hair and beards, are shown together, and such details do not clearly correlate with specialised roles. For example, individuals carrying baskets are sometimes shown shaven and sometimes with long hair. One more definite point is that charioteers on preserved perforated plaques are always portrayed with long hair and beards. Conversely, however, shaven-headed warriors with chariots are represented in Early Dynastic glyptic work and inlays, for example on the Standard of Ur.

Diametrically opposite the two leaders, on the other side of the circular relief, is the group of three that includes the small figure with raised arms, who stands between two individuals who are facing each other (as can be confirmed by the positions of their feet), and seemingly looking at one another over the top of the smaller figure's head (as reconstructed in Fig. 77). The upper bodies of the two clearly adult members of the trio are missing, but it can be seen that they are both wearing plain, unpleated skirts, and as previously mentioned the skirt of the chief musician on the left has his name inscribed on it. The small individual has two or maybe three stylised locks of rather short hair that fall straight down over his forehead to about the level of his eyebrows, and he is wearing a pleated short skirt with an even hem that also features a thick belt at the waist.

Representations of diminutive individuals whose stature contrasts markedly with that of the figures around them are relatively frequent on Early Dynastic objects, and their smaller size can depend on a range of factors: sometimes it is used to suggest rank or age, and at other times it is more about the spatial arrangement and composition of the depicted scene. For instance, on artefacts associated with Ur-Nanshe it is common for the ruler to be shown as the huge central protagonist, with the other participants in the tableau depicted in a range of sizes, perhaps partly depending on their status, but also to fit into the available space around him. Similarly, attendants shown carrying various kinds of containers on surviving Early Dynastic plaques are often made smaller than the more important personages they serve. The diminutive figure who is shown standing in front of the onagers on the upper register of the presumed obverse of the Standard of Ur is an interesting example (Fig. 80). He is portrayed in the same manner as other subordinate members of the procession to the left of the enlarged central figure, but he occupies the space below the animals' heads: is that a realistic indication of his size, a way of filling what would otherwise have been an unwanted empty space or a way of representing his function, perhaps as a groom? The fact that the head of the smaller figure on the Girsu Circular Bas-Relief reaches the waists of the adjacent members of his subgroup means that he is not just slightly shorter than the people around him: he is actually half their size. That suggests either a child or an adult of particularly short stature, but the former is much more likely. One reason for that is the smaller figure's hair, which adds an extra element to the way he is differentiated from the other participants in the depicted ceremony. If he were a

FIGURE 80. The Standard of Ur (detail of the war panel). British Museum 121201.

small adult, might he not be expected to have either a shaved head or to be wearing his hair long? His idiosyncratic skirt also sets him apart, as does the position of his hands. These are speculative matters, but as was also inferred by Heuzey, he is presumably a child shown in the act of singing or dancing (Sarzec and Heuzey 1912, p. 354). A straightforward dance performance is surely less likely, however, because the putative dancer is not only out of sight behind the backs of all those who are taking part in the ceremony, he is further concealed between the skirts of his two companions. The idea that the three members of the subgroup form a musical trio is probably further confirmed by the fact that the adult on the right of the group seems perhaps to have been the only large figure whose name was not recorded—a lack that possibly means his subordinate status was equivalent to that of the anonymous child.

The significance of this rare masterpiece of archaic art was immediately obvious to Heuzey, who came up with a host of interpretations, including the coronation of a triumphant warlord, a crown prince being invested by a reigning ruler, a hegemonic king (lugal) receiving an emblem of power from a lesser ruler (ensí) as a sign of the minor leader's vassalage, or (conversely) a subordinate ally receiving the insignia of office from a greater ruler. A key model for Heuzey was the later Early Dynastic IIIa Mace of Mesilim, which bears witness to the dominance of the powerful king of Kish (the suzerain or lugal) over the vassal ruler of Lagash. In Heuzey's view, the enigmatic object held in the left hand of the bearded ruler who carries the sickle sword is a symbol of investiture: a turban-fringed band that is the insignia of governorship.

Heuzey is surely correct to say that the two lines of men, led by their respective chiefs, are shown converging, and that the scene enacted by the two leaders is the ceremonial subject of the piece. By contrast, Parrot believed that the groups of figures form a single procession composed of two parallel lines, led by two individuals—possibly a king and prince of Girsu—who are supposed to be walking side by side towards the Ningirsu temple. The thoroughly religious nature of the event is confirmed for Parrot by the clasped hands of the worshipping followers, while the musical subgroup adds sacred music, ritual incantations and hymns (Parrot 1948, p. 73). The unlikely idea of a dual procession, which is contrary to any known mode of ancient Sumerian visual representation, would render the circular form of the carving nonsensical, even though the makers clearly exploited its expressive capabilities. Nevertheless, Parrot goes on to interpret the scene as either the prelude to the departure of an army of soldiers in parallel formation or their return from a campaign.

The imagery is exceptional on many counts, and the difficulty of defining its meaning is compounded by the object's very uniqueness: it does not conform with any known genres (ritual banquets, victory parades, religious processions and so forth), and nothing else like it has been discovered. Only the two leaders are shown carrying weapons, emblems or symbols of office, while their followers are portrayed unarmed and at prayer. Similarly, there are no prisoners of war, but there are no religious offerings either. The only addition to the two main lines of figures is the musical subgroup, but whether the character of the music being performed is supposed to be festive or solemn is difficult to decide. Potentially significant by their absence are any symbols of divinity that might have introduced the idea of a presiding deity, but these might have been superfluous, partly because the relief was, in any case, kept in the temple, but also because the emblem of the god—unquestionably Ningirsu—would surely have been visible on the surmised object that was fitted into the holes on the upper surface of the Circular Bas-Relief, which acted in this respect as a supporting base. The object's original context is in fact crucial to any attempt to try to unlock the mystery of the carving, and to dissociate the Circular Bas-Relief from its inferred location in the treasury of the Lower Construction is to falsify its putative meaning. As already noted, this means that the ceremony depicted in the relief must have been celebrated under the auspices of Ningirsu, and this is confirmed by the praying followers. The mirroring of the two main lines of men, together with the secondary balance established by the placing of the two leaders and the musical trio on diametrically opposite sides of the circle, create the sense of a multifaceted occasion: a ceremony that is at the same time grave and joyful, festive and solemn, with the implied contrasts contained in a state of confident and harmonious symmetry that is lent further credence by the relief's circular or cylindrical shape.

The key question of whether or not the two leaders were considered to be of equal rank, or whether one is represented as a superior ruler and the other a vassal lord, or perhaps a high-standing official, cannot be answered solely on the basis of the particular items that the two figures are holding, or on account of their dress and facial appearances, even though these descriptive elements clearly show them as counterparts. The judgement has to be made by looking at the way the scene is put together as a whole, and also by considering the intrinsic character of the object. As indicated above, these features point decisively to an equilibrium of power. The symmetry that is built into the fabric of the scene suggests a pact between two counter-balanced forces that is ratified with the sanction of Ningirsu. Again, it is surely no coincidence that the object on which the meeting of sovereign equals is immortalised is a circular cylinder. The impression would have been quite different if the two sides had been shown on a flat surface—a stele, for example. In that case the meeting of the two leaders might have seemed more like a face-off between two competing rivals and their cohorts, but the fact that the scene is carved around a circular object invokes the metaphor of the concordant coming together of two mirroring groups, who are joined at the front by their respective leaders and at the back by the interposed musical subgroup that completes the two processions.

Can more be surmised? As with the Stele of the Captives and the Girsu Land Stele, it is important to remain cautious with such richly suggestive objects about which very little can be definitively known, but with respect to the Circular Bas-Relief it seems reasonable to postulate, drawing on what is known about the subsequent history of Girsu, that the exceptional scene shown on the relief might be a record of the original treaty that united Girsu and Lagash. As mentioned above, the fact that the personal names of the participants were documented clearly indicates an actual historical event. Similarly, if the symbolism of the sandal can be relied upon, that would add the notion of a mutual recognition and even a voluntary consolidation of sovereignty, with the two parties combining as powerful equals in a new political order. With respect to the broader iconography of the sandal, it is interesting to note another general point of correspondence with the Palette of Narmer, which depicts the unification of Upper and Lower Egypt, though Narmer's consolidation was achieved by military means. As also previously highlighted, there can be little doubt that the union of Girsu and Lagash was brought into being before the reign of Ur-Nanshe, but it also certainly predated the age of the Hexapolis that was presided over by the city of Kish. The coming together of the two states should probably therefore be sought in the heroic age of the Early Dynastic I period. Evidence of the historical connections between Girsu and Lagash—under the divine tutelage of Ningirsu—going back to the very earliest times is exceptionally strong, even to the extent that the two cities seem occasionally indistinguishable and interchangeable. The origins of their merger therefore conceivably reached all the way back to the time when the emerging state of Girsu was in the process of being formed—the era of the Lower Construction. The building of the temple might therefore be considered to have taken place when multiple influences coincided to crystallise the Girsu–Lagash union, and this, by the same token, might also be the historical moment that is recorded on the Circular Bas-Relief. As is detailed in a following chapter, the particular fate of this object, evidenced by the condition in which it was found, adds further force to this argument.

CHAPTER 14

The Tessellated Earth

THE FACT THAT THE FOUR CORNERS OF THE WALLS OF ancient Sumerian temples were carefully constructed so that they were aligned with the cardinal points has led to a generally received idea that the temple functioned as a kind of divine compass. The image that immediately springs to the modern mind is the familiar navigational instrument that takes the form of a graduated circle with a magnetised needle that turns around a central pivot. The analogy has perhaps been lent greater credence by the famous Babylonian world map, produced around 2,000 years after the time of the Lower Construction, on which the earth is outlined with two concentric circles that are surrounded with triangles (BM92687), but the idea that the Sumerians conceived of the cardinal points in terms of a circle with a centre should be categorically dismissed. The trivial reasons for the dismissal are that the magnetic navigational aid was only discovered around 200 BCE, and that the much later Babylonian world map, with perhaps seven triangular apexes regularly positioned around the concentric circles, was surely not designed to be a description of the earth that relates to the sort of map that could be drawn with the aid of, or used in conjunction with, a magnetic compass. The fundamentally important reason is that the cardinal orientation of Sumerian temples was established on the basis of astronomical observations, and this has some interesting consequences for the way in which the Sumerians conceived of the world in which they lived.

It is helpful to begin by considering how a Sumerian temple was probably laid out in practice, a subject that is touched upon above with respect to the anomalous positioning of the Lower Construction (Fig. 81). Suppose that a N–S axis was established by astronomical means, as it would also have been for navigational purposes, by taking readings from a generally recognised north star, which at that epoch was probably not Polaris but Thuban (Alpha Draconis). The astronomical data could then be translated into a line drawn on the earth, and a foundation peg hammered into the ground on the N–S axis to establish the position of the temple's N corner. A cord or rope fixed to the N peg could then be pulled taut exactly southwards, and fixed in place to mark the N–S line (but not, it should be stressed, the temple's S corner because Sumerian temples were not square but rectangular). The rest of the walls could then be pegged out with respect to that cardinal axis: first, by creating a N-pointing right angle at the N peg that was bisected by the N–S axis (Fig. 81.1). That would establish the lines of the NW and NE walls, which could then be pegged out in turn, allowing the W and E corners to be fixed at chosen distances along these NW and NE lines, with the exact placement of the W and E corners depending on the desired lengths of the respective NW and NE walls. More W-pointing and E-pointing right angles could then be created at the now defined W and E corners to establish the lines of the SW and SE walls, which could accordingly be pegged and marked out. The point at which they crossed would define the right angle at the temple's S corner.

If Sumerian temples had been square, the lines of the SW and SE walls would have met to form the S corner at a point on the original N–S axis, and the arrangement would have been like that implied by the circular geometry of a magnetic navigational compass, with the N–S and E–W diagonals of

194 | The Mound of the House of the Fruits

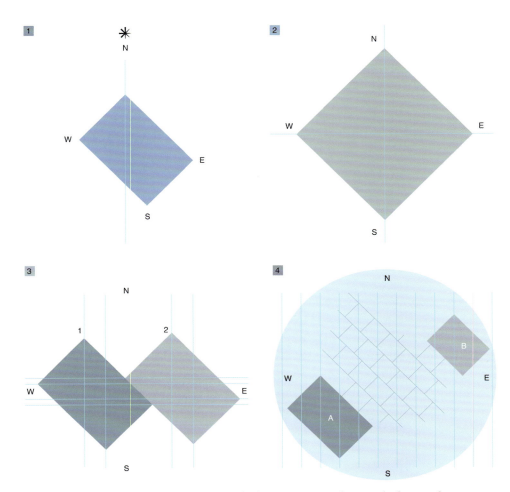

FIGURE 81. Diagrams showing the way in which Sumerian temples were laid out with respect to the cardinal points: 1. the usual layout with the N corner established on a primary N–S axis; 2. a theoretical square ground plan, comparable to a modern magnetic compass; 3. two adjacent temples with parallel N–S axes and E–W axes; 4. the tessellated earth, with numerous N–S axes notionally linking two distant temples (A and B).

the square crossing at the centre of the circle, and the cardinal points indicated by the four right angles (all bisected by the two diagonals) that formed the square's corners (Fig. 81.2). Since Sumerian temples were seemingly without exception rectangular, however, the S corner was not placed on the original N–S axis, and the E and W corners were similarly slightly displaced with respect to each other. Crucially, therefore, because the ground plan was rectangular, the initial N–S axis now manifestly acquired a counterpart because the S corner was placed on a second N–S line that extended through it. That second N–S line was, by definition, parallel to the first because the N and S corners were both correctly aligned with the cardinal points.

This might at first glance seem counter-intuitive. Surely, it might be objected, the two lines are not actually parallel because they will eventually converge at a single point of origin. But the ancient Sumerians did not know that the earth was spherical, such that all sufficiently extended N-pointing lines will eventually meet at the North Pole (facts that are exemplified in the symbolic import and operating principles of the magnetic compass). Even more importantly, they had no idea of the unimaginably large distance between the earth and the fixed north star (303.3 light years in the case of Thuban). That is why the two N–S lines, which are micro-millimetrically short by comparison with the stellar distance between the earth and the celestial reference point, are to all intents and purposes parallel, and why two travellers, one starting at Lagash, the other at Umma (for example), could both head north, strictly following the north star, and arrive a day later at two different places that were due north of Lagash and Umma, respectively. The way in which the astronomical data translated into lines on the surface of the earth not only meant that they were (for all practical purposes) incontrovertibly parallel, but also that they both unquestionably had equal status as cardinal axes. These understandings are reinforced when it is recalled that the full extent of the earth as conceived of by the Sumerians was approximately coterminous with the area now referred to as the Fertile Crescent, and that (for reasons it would have been very difficult to argue against at the time) it was considered to be flat. The situation is somewhat analogous to the continued use of the principles of Newton's theoretically outdated classical physics in an Einsteinian (or even a post-Einsteinian) universe: the reality is that they work. The difference is that, for the Sumerians, theirs was the only system they knew, and it must presumably have been painstakingly developed and refined over the lifetime of their culture.

Once the temple is pegged out in the way described above, the realisation of the existence of the second N–S axis potentially gives rise to a pattern (Fig. 81.3). Let the second axis be extended, and a second N corner be marked with a peg, in order to lay out a second rectangle with the same dimensions as the first, such that the SW side of the second rectangle touches the NE side of the first one (the temple). Having exactly the same orientation, the two shapes will be perfectly congruent, but offset, one with respect to the other, so that the NW and SE sides of the two are not aligned, but instead placed on parallel NE–SW axes. But the construction of the second rectangle implies the existence of a third, and the third a fourth, and the fourth a fifth, and so on. In addition, new rectangles can be constructed on all sides of the original one so that the series can be extended in any or all directions. Stated mathematically, the result is a tiling or tessellation: an arrangement of identical plane shapes that completely covers an area without overlapping. In practical terms, it would have been perfectly exemplified by the pavement that extended out from the NE side of the Lower Construction, for instance. The cardinal axis of the pavement was given by the cardinal axes of the temples (assuming that the Lower Construction's pavement V was laid as the foundation for an earlier, correctly aligned building that had exactly the same orientation as the surrounding block, P'Q'R'S'). The altered dimensions of the rectangular slabs or bricks used for different pavements at different epochs (the pavement on the NW side of the Ur-Nanshe Building, for example) would lead to superficial changes in surface appearance that would not affect the fundamental orientations of the tiling.

But there is no conceptual limit to the area that such a tiling or tessellation could cover. Imagine a secondary chapel dedicated to Ningirsu that was constructed in the countryside many kilometres away from Girsu. That sacred building would also have been pegged out so that its corners were aligned with the cardinal points. In theory, therefore, if the land were smooth and flat, and a sufficient number of well-cut slabs or bricks were available, it would have been possible to tile the space between the temple in Girsu and the outlying rural chapel with perfect mathematical precision because both temples and all the tiles would have been laid along axes that were established with respect to astronomical data (Fig. 81.4). What this thought experiment shows is not, of course, that actual tiles could in practice have been laid across an entire region, but that the astronomically determined alignments were real and ubiquitous because everything that existed or moved did so beneath the sky and therefore of necessity with respect to the cardinal points. Accordingly, positions in space were defined in relation to the framework of celestial lines that could be laid out on the terrestrial surface, and the clearest manifestation and indicator of the tessellated earth that was implied by that understanding was the temple. That is the sense in which it should be thought of as a divine compass.

The use of pegs and ropes to lay out plots of land and buildings is touched upon in the inscriptions on the Feathered Figure (discussed in detail above). On the obverse, after the two emblems of Ningirsu's temple—the 'mace head' and the 'fitting ornament'—are described, the 'prince' subsequently brings the 'long rope' to the banks of the river. As has been persuasively argued by Lecompte (2020, p. 423), the rope is doubtless a surveyor's rope, and the idea is confirmed on the plaque's reverse, where numerous contiguous lands belonging to the temple are said to be laid out. Much more comprehensive is the account of the construction of the New Eninnu on the Gudea Cylinders. From the outset, when Ningirsu approaches the sleeping Gudea and speaks to him in a dream, the god makes it clear that the temple must be constructed according to rules that he has inscribed in the night sky (A9): 'you who are going to build my house for me, Gudea, let me tell you the ominous sign for building my house, let me tell you the pure stars of heaven indicating my regulations'. Subsequently, when the ruler begins to mark out the lines of the temple's walls, he begins by laying out a rope on a N–S axis and fixing it with pegs, as explained above, and the laying out of the building instantiates a connection between the earth and the sky (A17):

Towards the house whose halo reaches to heaven, whose powers embrace heaven and earth, whose owner is a lord with a fierce stare, whose warrior Ningirsu is expert at battle, towards Eninnu-The-White-Thunderbird, Gudea went from the south and admired it northwards. From the north he went towards it and admired it southwards. He measured out with rope exactly one iku. He drove in pegs at its sides and personally verified them. This made him extremely happy.

With great ceremony, and after elaborate rituals have been performed, Gudea then lays the first brick, at which moment the temple is symbolically ready to enter. The preserved text does not explicitly state where the first brick is laid, but there can be no doubt that it must have been at the N corner: first, because it was laid at a point on one of the temple's outer walls, as is intuitively obvious, and further confirmed in the text by the notion that once the first brick has been laid Gudea can then metaphorically enter the sacred space, conceptually going from outside to inside; secondly and more importantly, because the S end of the N–S line that has been marked out with the rope does not determine the location of the temple's S corner, which means that only the N corner exists when the axis is laid down. The reason for this, as noted above and as a matter of historical fact with regard to the Ningirsu shrine at the heart of the New Eninnu, is that the temple was designed in the shape of a rectangle and not a square. This means that the rope stretched out by Gudea to establish the original N–S axis defined the precise position of the N corner, but not that of the S Corner because the latter had to be constructed geometrically when the walls of the building as a whole were demarcated. As this also implies, for incontrovertible reasons of geometry the only point in the temple's walls that can logically have been fixed by the N–S axis is the N corner, from which the other walls were subsequently derived. Consequently, after laying the first brick, Gudea calculates the ground plan of the edifice as though, like the goddess Nisaba, he is a consummate expert in mathematics (A19):

He put down the brick, entered the house and as if he himself were Nisaba knowing the inmost secrets (?) of numbers, he started setting down (?) the ground plan of the house. As if he were a young man building a house for the first time, sweet sleep never came into his eyes.

What is perhaps most fascinating and even touching about this passage is the way Gudea is compared with a 'young man' who is building his first house. The twofold implication is that he is sleepless with excitement like a bridegroom, but also that this is generally how people built their houses. Despite the reference to Gudea's 'secret' knowledge of numbers, the construction of buildings according to comparable rules was presumably a commonplace occurrence, though the familiar procedure should perhaps be understood with respect to the general method of marking out the lines of a building's walls, rather than ensuring that their corners faced the cardinal points, which might have been a special attribute of sacred edifices. It might also intimate that the geometrical skills needed to perform some of these operations were the preserve of trained surveyors, and it would follow that such people were probably priests, as corroborated by the special association between Nisaba and numbers.

It is also worth observing that, although the temple is expressly the house of Ningirsu, a pantheon of senior deities assist with its construction and sanctification, while others seem simply to stand back and admire the process. Consequently, after Gudea has stretched out the ropes 'in the most perfect way', Enki hammers in the foundation pegs, Nanshe interprets the oracles, and Gatumdug painfully gives birth to the bricks, which Bau anoints with oil and essence of cedar (A20). As they work, or perhaps when this phase of the work is completed: 'The Anuna gods stood there full of admiration'. Gudea then proceeds to mark out a series of seven 'squares', all furnished with emblematic motifs, that represent plots or spaces associated with the internal area of the rectangular temple or sacred complex (A20): 'He laid the foundation, set the walls on the ground. He marked out a square, aligned the bricks with a string. He marked out a second square on the site of the temple . . . He marked out a third square on the site of the temple, saying, "It is the Imdugud bird enveloping its fledgling with its wings..."' Later on, in a slightly enigmatic passage near the beginning of Cylinder B, shortly before Ningirsu enters his abode, the ruler appears to consecrate the corners and floor of the building, possibly in a kind of activation ritual (B3): 'Gudea made a paste with cornelian and lapis lazuli and applied it to the corners. He sprinkled the floor with precious oil'.

In general terms, a temple that was planned around the prime N–S axis was correctly situated with respect to the fixed point in the sky from which all directions could be calculated, and its spatial mode of being was realised. In addition, the way it was laid out also had a temporal meaning, and that is stressed in the inscriptions on the Gudea Cylinders by the temple's constantly reiterated connection with agricultural plenty. Ningirsu, who was, of course, the god of irrigation and agriculture as well as the warrior god, states the association between the properly laid out temple and the fruits of the earth at the outset when he speaks to Gudea in his dream (A11):

'I will call up to heaven for humid winds so that plenty comes down to you from heaven and the land will thrive under your reign in abundance. Laying the foundations of my temple will bring immediate abundance: the great fields will grow rich for you, the levees and ditches will be full to the brim for you, the water will rise for you to heights never reached by the water before. Under you more oil than ever will be poured and more wool than ever will weighed in Sumer.'

As alluded to in the discussion of the foundation figurines that were buried under the Lower Construction, the essential theme here is the passing of time, and especially the changing of the seasons: ideas that were expressed architecturally through the temple's E–W orientation. The positions of the building's E and W corners, which were not directly defined by celestial observations, were calculated after the N corner had been established. In practice, therefore, as described above, the two sides of a right angle placed at the N corner (with the angle pointing due north) could be extended along the resulting NE and NW lines. Two more E-pointing and W-pointing right angles could then be laid out at the E and W corners, respectively, and their SW and SE sides extended to form the S corner at their point of intersection. The four angles of the rectangle thus outlined would each measure ninety degrees, and the E and W corners would point due east and due west. These issues are considered in detail with respect to Gudea's New Eninnu in Chapter 40, but this does not mean that the sun would rise and set every morning and evening along the E–W axis because, in reality, it only passes precisely through the E–W axis twice a year, at the spring and autumn equinoxes, around 20 March and 20 September, respectively, when day and night are the same length, and (in astronomical terms) the sun crosses the celestial equator. Since these dates could be determined by plotting the sun's path with respect to the temple's E and W corners, the building itself could act as a seasonal clock. As discussed in detail in Chapter 40, it is highly probable that other significant dates in the solar and lunar calendars were expressed in the orientation of temples, though the precise extent to which this happened would presumably have changed and developed during Sumer's long history. By definition, however, the equinoxes were a chief frame of reference, as indeed was the appearance of the new moon (noted above with respect to the W corner of the Lower Construction). On account of the temple's rectangular outline, the E and W corners (like the N and S corners) also lay on parallel axes that would, in practice, have been a few metres apart. What impact, if any, this might have had on the resulting observations is not clear, but the fact that all known temples were laid out in this way means that any effects must have been systematically accommodated. In this respect, moreover, as argued exhaustively in Chapter 40, the slight offset between the parallel E–W axes worked together with the orientations of the temple's main façades (northeast, south-east, north-west and south-west, respectively) to give architectural form to seasonal meanings associated with the summer and winter solstices.

If, as seems self-evident, rectangles were the accepted primary shape in Sumerian sacred architecture that was seemingly because they dynamically generated the axes that gave form to the universal tessellation in a way that squares, with their single N–S and E–W axes crossing at a central point, did not. That does not, of course, mean that squares were not used, as indicated by the bricks used on the approach to the Ur-Nanshe Building (pavement F) or when Gudea is described laying out 'square' spaces inside the temple or sacred complex, for example (though the meaning of the word 'square' in this instance might not be as certain as the translation suggests). Similarly, as demonstrated above in Chapter 9 with respect to the Pillar of Gudea, Lagash II builders, for whom square bricks were the standard form, developed a relatively advanced understanding of the geometry of squares, though that probably does not imply that they were familiar with geometrical concepts that were used and taught in the Old Babylonian period (see Chapter 39 below). With regard to the laying out of the temple, however, it might conceivably imply that the square was regarded as a special instance of the rectangle—a rectangle with only one cardinal axis, perhaps analogous to the way in which, in much later geometry, the circle is regarded as a special instance of the ellipse (an ellipse with a single focus at its centre). Possibly for the same reason, the evidence from Girsu appears to suggest that Sumerians were not especially interested in the significance of the geometrical centres of the objects and buildings that they created. Where were the central points of the Lower Construction or the Ur-Nanshe Building, for example? It is possible to find them by drawing the diagonals of the rectangles on the plans, but nothing of any interest seemingly takes place there. Similarly, the square star-shaped section of tiling on the floor of the Lower Construction's trophy room—which was itself also square—was apparently not positioned in the middle of the room, but offset to one side. Its placement might have been significant relative to the other objects that were introduced into the space, but it was not laid to mark the centre of the square space that contained it. Conversely, as can be seen in the diagrams in Chapter 40 (Figs. 218 and 219), the location of the cult statue on its podium lay at the centre of a series of intersecting axes that were defined by the laying out and placement of the building.

An interesting question of politics is also built into the conception of the earth as a tessellation that was based on celestially determined cardinal points. Sumerian states (or city-states) developed as juxtaposed entities, each with their own chief god. Since the cardinal N–S axes that were derived from astronomical observations formed a potentially infinite series of parallel lines, all the temples in every polis could be oriented with respect to the cardinal points without priority being accorded to any of them. Built on a divine compass that was formed as a network of interlocking lines that did not allow for a central point, the divisions and orientations were not intrinsically hierarchical, so that the gods of each state—all members of the same pantheon, after all—could all be worshipped with equal confidence. This is quite unlike the situation in Christianity or Islam, for example, where the holiest place theoretically defines the spiritual centre of the whole world. For Christianity, that idea was given cartographic form in early medieval maps, and also symbolised by the orientation and layout of Christian churches, which were designed to indicate the eternal city of Jerusalem but also to rehearse the narrative of salvation in their architecture and decorations.

It is perhaps relevant in this respect to note that the Sumerian outlook contradicts the influential theory of Mircea Eliade (1959), who argues that, viewed from a sacred standpoint, the world is not homogeneous, but rather heterogeneously differentiated into sacred spaces, which are 'strong, significant', and non-sacred spaces that are 'without structure or consistency, amorphous'. For Eliade, therefore, when the domain of the divine breaks into the fabric of the world in the form of a 'hierophany' then a sacred centre is instantiated that reveals an 'absolute reality' that is categorically different from the 'nonreality of the vast surrounding expanse' (Eliade 1959, pp. 20–1). The occurrence of the hierophany would thus represent an 'absolute fixed point' or an *axis mundi*, as Eliade calls it: a 'centre' of the world that ruptures the illusory homogeneity of ordinary space, opening a passage to a transcendent, qualitatively dissimilar 'cosmic region' that discloses the cosmogonic principles that shape reality (Eliade 1959, pp. 36–7). Churches and other religious buildings are portals that lead from profane mundanity to the domain of the sacred, giving architectural and institutional form to the notion of a hierophany as an *axis mundi*. Though Eliade presents his ideas as the anthropological basis of religion in general, they are entirely alien to the Sumerian system of the world, in which, far from being invisible and transcendent, the sacred was everywhere manifest in the unbreakable connection between the earth and the sky. The hallowed precinct on the summit of Tell K, together with the sanctum sanctorum—the temple itself—were not qualitatively different places from the surrounding landscape, rivers and marshlands or distant rural chapels (or even the wilderness at the edge of the known world) because the cosmological principles that made the world 'function' as it should (to quote again the evocative phrase of Ur-Bau and Gudea that is discussed in Chapter 42) were always available and capable of being mapped onto the earth. Consequently, the distinction between the sacred precincts and the mundane world at large was merely one of degree. The sacred precinct on Tell K only brought greater clarity and a more immediately apparent sense of form to divine principles that were woven intrinsically into the fabric of reality in which everything was contained.

Accordingly, the Sumerians instantiated their cosmology in a radically different way to the religions described by Eliade because it was itself the reality of their world. When the people of Lagash sank a well such as the Well of Eanatum on Tell K, they dug down through the mound that had been raised over numerous generations and through the underlying raw earth until they reached the vast reservoir of sweet water that was believed to have been placed below the ground when the world was created. When they travelled north, south, east or west, they eventually encountered the encircling mass of salt water that also dated back to the very beginning of the cosmos. It is therefore not difficult to imagine why they might have thought of the earth as floating on potentially tempestuous masses of sweet and salt water like a ship at sea. Against this backdrop of uncertainty, the guarantor of spatial and temporal stability was the temple, which, as expressed in the inscriptions on the Gudea Cylinders, was not only secured by the foundation pegs that functioned like mooring posts, but was itself the mooring post that anchored the land amid the fluctuating cosmos (A22):

> The ruler built the house, he made it high, high as a great mountain. Its abzu foundation pegs, big mooring stakes, he drove into the ground so deep they could take counsel with Enki in the Eengura. He had heavenly foundation pegs surround the house like warriors, so that each one was drinking water at the libation place of the gods. He fixed the Eninnu, the mooring stake, he drove in its pegs shaped like praying wizards.

These matters are considered in detail in Chapters 43 and 44, but the idea expressed in the last sentence just quoted, that the Eninnu, the house of Ningirsu, is itself the universal fixing instrument is emphatically repeated in the paean of praise for the sacred complex that comes at the beginning of Cylinder B (B1): 'House, mooring post of the Land, grown so high as to fill the space between heaven and earth, Eninnu, the true brickwork, for which Enlil determined a good fate, green hill standing to be marvelled at, standing out above all the lands!'

The implication is that, when Sumerian high priests and architects pegged out their temples in accordance with the astronomical data, they laid out lines on the earth's surface that were determined by the real positions of the stars. These lines were not symbols in the way that word is now usually understood. They were rather the tangible manifestations of the substantial and unbreakable connection between the sky—the realm of the gods—and the earth, with a vast reservoir of sweet water beneath its surface and salt water all around.

Coda: The Temple Ideogram

The suggestion was tentatively made above with regard to the Feathered Figure (Chapter 13) that an informed viewer of the plaque might have connected the axis of approach to the temple that is emblematically portrayed on the relief with that of a real temple, perhaps the Lower Construction in particular. Furthermore, if the left to right direction in which the figure is shown moving is correlated with a NW–SE approach then the four corners of the relief can also be imaginatively linked with the cardinal points, with north in the top left corner, followed by west, south and east (anticlockwise around the plaque). The carving is also divided into boxes or fields: less so on the obverse, where the words are only separated horizontally by dividers, but completely on the reverse, where horizontal and vertical lines organise the text into a continuous series of adjoining rectangles that are demarcated like the plots of land listed in the inscriptions. As well as being literary and pictorial, that is, the plaque schematically signifies both the temple's mode of being and its function: images, words, lines, blocks of text and the stone's physical shape can be read as an integrated complex sign that expresses the many aspects that combine to make up the temple's meaning. With this in mind, it is noteworthy that the temple is not represented on the plaque as a sequence of rooms, but rather in terms of its orientation, its emblematic threshold, the fact that it is the house of Ningirsu, and its role in the landscape—which it occupies, overlooks and institutionally oversees—causing it to be marked out into fields, orchards and other plots with the surveyor's rope that is mentioned in the text, just as its own walls are (or have been) laid out.

The point being made is that the plaque functions as a readable schematic sign that stands for the temple as a constellation of processes, and that its key signified components relate not to its internal spaces, or even to its façades, but to its role in instantiating the principles of the tessellated earth, as expressed in the laying out and orientation of the building, the indicated axis of approach, the consequent analogies between the stone's corners and the cardinal points, and the use of the surveyor's rope to divide the land into plots—an action that is schematically repeated in the graphic dividers that are used to demarcate the boxes containing the inscription on the reverse. With this in mind, the further question arises as to whether these ideas might also have informed the way in which the temple was represented in the Sumerian ideogram é, meaning 'house' and by extension 'temple', or more broadly the 'household of the god'.

Sumerian é, which is one of the oldest and longest-lasting cuneiform signs, is attested from the dawn of writing (proto-cuneiform in the Uruk III period) all the way through to the Hellenistic era. Graphically stable over time, the early cuneiform examples of é take the form of an approximately rectangular grid-like composition that usually shows a regular arrangement of boxes or squares (sometimes including a line of rectangles) at one end, from where the containing and dividing lines that form the pattern of quadrilaterals are extended in one direction to make up the rectangle's length (Fig. 82). The number of adjoining boxes that form the orderly arrangement in the early pictographic examples could vary on average from about six or nine to as many as twenty-eight (as documented in the examples given in Labat and Malbran-Labat 1995, p. 148; and Fossey 1926, p. 605). From as early as the Ur III period, the sign was often rendered more schematically, and this tendency developed over time to make the representation increasingly abstract (but not by any means necessarily simpler), as its strokes became more distinctly cuneiform in character, even though it never lost touch with its original form. Superficial changes in appearance can be noted in specific examples that doubtless reflect the characteristic handwriting of individual scribes, but the way the sign evolved, especially during the first half of the third millennium BCE, is remarkable for its adherence to the basic pattern.

Scholars seldom discuss the sign é in studies of the origins and development of cuneiform writing because they prefer

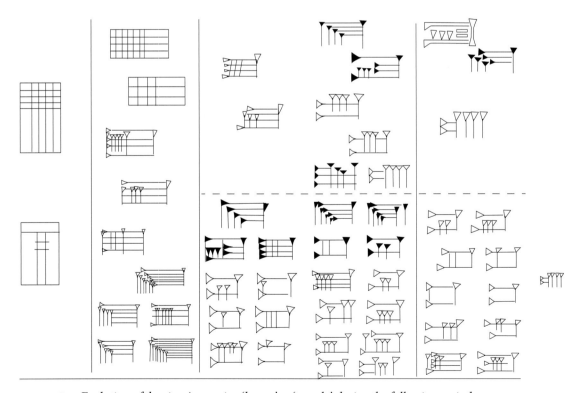

FIGURE 82. Evolution of the sign é, meaning 'house' or 'temple', during the following periods (left to right): Archaic, Ur III, Old Assyrian and Babylonian, Middle Assyrian and Babylonian, New Assyrian and Babylonian, standard Neo Assyrian (from Labat and Malbran-Labat 1995, p. 148).

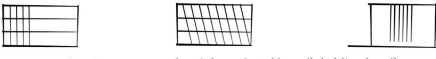

FIGURE 83. Three Sumerian signs, from left to right: é ('house'); kid ('reed mat'); gan₂ ('field').

ideograms, including ku₆, ka or šu, that exhibit more visually striking attributes as they gradually developed from pictograms to cuneiform marks. The é pictogram has traditionally been thought to represent a building, either in elevation or in plan, and the idea has been supported with reference to lexical series and the equivalence between é in Sumerian and the Akkadian word *bītum*, meaning house (see CAD, B, p. 282). The ascription is plausible, and it might be correct, though the very fact that it is a back-projection means it is inherently fraught with difficulties. An alternative has been suggested by Glassner (2000, pp. 200 and 214), who speculates that the origins of the sign é might relate to a loom or the weaving of a reed mat. Weaving, which, on account of its symbolic overtones, is regularly considered to be an activity of extreme importance by anthropologists, was undoubtedly a vital component of ancient Sumerian economic and cultural life. Glassner links the grid-like composition of the pictogram with the shapes of looms on the basis of glyptic representations (another back-formation that relies on the benefit of hindsight), while the idea of the reed mat draws on a rather unconvincing similarity between Sumerian é and the Sumerian sign meaning 'reed mat' (kid) (Fig. 83).

An apparently more promising association between é and the representation of a field is stymied at its source by the fact that the pictograms for 'house' and 'field' (gan₂) are so graphically distinct (Fig. 83). The sign for field, which looks like a series of uprights raised above an elongated horizontal line, with a slightly taller vertical at each end and a single crossbar running across the top, does not seem to bear any resemblance to a plan of adjoining fields laid out on the ground. Taken as an elevation, however, it would perhaps tend to describe a partially fenced-off strip, with the long horizontal at the bottom indicating the limited extent of the enclosure, and the uprights and crossbar signifying a paling—none of which should be taken too literally. Though it is a conjectural matter, the most obvious visual comparison would probably be with a sheep pen—an idea that would also make sense in terms of the sign's early cultural development and use. Again,

however, it is important not to confuse the subtle connotations evoked by Sumerian pictograms with the more straightforward semantics of infographics.

The discussion can be broadened if the house or building, and especially the temple, are considered not merely as material structures but as focal points of interaction that link human society with the earth and the gods. In this sense the temple (but also the household more generally) is more than a building. It is an institution or a locus of activities that encompasses multiple meanings and functions. That is the significance of the temple as it is represented on the Feathered Figure, for example, and this is perhaps also the best way to interpret the possible origins and schematic representation of é. There can be no doubt that the characteristic pattern of squares or boxes at one end of é looks like a kind of tiling, and if the context provided by the Feathered Figure and the principles of the tessellated earth can be relied upon then the tiling should be considered not as an arrangement of physical objects, but as a way of dividing up the land, which was an elemental part of Sumerian culture. When, in the Cylinder Inscriptions, Gudea plots the N–S line that will be used as the basis for the temple's ground plan, he does so by mapping a divinely given astral sign onto the earth with a rope and pegs. The same procedure is introduced, albeit more elliptically, in the inscriptions on the Feathered Figure when the 'prince' brings the surveyor's rope to the 'banks of the river' and the fields, orchards and temple are laid out.

Even more significantly, the bringing of the rope in the Feathered Figure inscriptions is associated with the act of creation itself: 'Amidst the meadows, the lord created the bison, and the gazelle is born. The long rope on the banks of the river is brought by the prince. The bison is born, and the gazelle is born'. Acts of surveying or demarcation and creation are closely linked, therefore, and both have divine connotations, but that is not their only or exclusive message. The text is also about husbandry: the laying out of the fields and orchards provides conditions in which the land can become abundantly productive. In this sense the link between the laying out of fields and the birth of grazing animals might also be termed a matter of good stewardship. When the text states that, 'Amidst the grasses, the master created them', it conceivably refers not only to the original creation of animal life, but also metaphorically to the birth and rearing of livestock. The necessary conditions for organised animal husbandry are created by marking out the fields or pastures. All of these meanings are contained in and expressed through the institution of the temple, and indeed the human household generally, which are both framed as manifestations of the relationship between humanity, the earth and the gods. As attested by the Feathered Figure, the Gudea Cylinder Inscriptions and the principles of tessellation described above, a key symbol of that nexus in ancient Sumer was the rope that was used to organise the land according to a pattern that originated with celestial observations. This could also be expressed in the marks that make up the é pictogram, where the tessellation is schematically described at one end, and the long ropes that are used to define it extend out from between the marked-out shapes to form the overall rectangle. That being the case, the pictogram stands graphically for the building not by portraying a simplified version of its physical appearance, but by invoking two interlinked and inseparable processes: the laying out of the temple and the division of the land into agricultural plots—activities that conceive of the building as a central link in what might be termed the Sumerian chain of being. With this in mind, the ropelike lines should not be treated too literally. Giving graphic form to the cardinal axis (or axes) that are plotted on the ground with reference to celestial observations when the temple is laid out, the pictogram evokes the building's capacity to instantiate the universal tessellation as a characteristic attribute of the place of humans in the world, with the earth under their feet and the heavens above.

CHAPTER 15

The Outer Block (P′Q′R′S′) and Associated Finds

ANY INTERPRETATION OF THE LAYOUT OF THE COMPLEX that was centred around the two-room Lower Construction must also explain the history and purpose of the enclosing block, P′Q′R′S′. The French excavators proposed several answers to this pivotal question, which has also been addressed in more recent studies. The first things to say are that the outer block was a later addition to the two-room core, and that some or all of the materials that were used to build it were salvaged: its walls were made of courses of fired bricks similar to those in the original building, combined with alternating courses of gypsum slabs taken from pavement V. The enveloping masonry, which was everywhere 2.15 m high, extended into the NW room (U on Plan C (2); Fig. 33), but not into room T on the SE side, where it blocked the doorway, leaving the room itself otherwise untouched. The old walls, which were 2.85 m high, stood 0.7 m higher than the top of the new block, including on either side of the doorway that led into room T, creating a void at the top of the opening that measured approximately 1.5 m (w) × 0.7 m (h). This led Heuzey to suggest that room T remained accessible (possibly via a ladder) and usable, perhaps as a storeroom, even after the outer block was built.

Contradicting Heuzey, however, Parrot (1948, p. 59) and Forest (1999, p. 13) both suppose that room T was deliberately filled with a mixture of rubble and mud-bricks, which Sarzec, for reasons previously discussed, did not record. Room U, on the NW side, was probably emptied of its contents before it was filled with courses of fired bricks and gypsum slabs. Room T, on the SE side, was not treated in the same way, and significant remains were found there, including the cruciform pillar (No. 1 inside room T on Plan C (2)) and the bottom part of the Stele of the Captives (No. 3 in room T on Plan C (2)), together with other movable objects, both in the inferred fill and on the paved gypsum floor, which featured the intact star-shaped arrangement of slabs in front of the cruciform pillar (No. 2 in room T on Plan C (2)).

Parrot (1948, pp. 54–63) and Crawford (1987, pp. 71–6) argue that the purpose of P′Q′R′S′ was to consolidate the two-room Lower Construction so that it could form a stable base for the new building that was eventually built on top of it. As discussed above, however, the precise placement of the block in relation to both the original walls of the Lower Construction and pavement V was noteworthy. Offset by about three degrees with respect to the core of the Lower Construction, the outer block was definitively aligned with pavement V. The differential between the old and new walls presented the builders with several problems of construction that are discussed below, but the very fact that they were willing to deal with them for the sake of the realignment indicates how important it was. The supposition (presented in Chapter 12) would appear to be that they took the opportunity to revise a given characteristic of the inner building that was considered unsatisfactory, inaccurate or no longer essential. The revision (if that is the right way to describe it) presumably related to the fact that the two-room core had earlier been misplaced with respect to the cardinal points, and it could well have signalled a change in the status of the inferred sacred obstacle that had necessitated the peculiar positioning of PQRS on the pavement. In any event, in terms of its placement, the orientation of pavement V was probably of fundamental importance because that is what dictated the ground plan of the outer block.

Whatever the criteria were, the builders went to great lengths to position P′Q′R′S′. This was particularly the case on the SW side, where (as noted earlier) the gap between the old and new walls gradually decreased from a maximum of 0.4 m in the S corner (R on the old walls) down to zero where the E corner of the old building (Q) coincided with the new wall (Q′R′). The regular angle (or bevel) of the new SW wall, which was made of fired bricks and fragments of gypsum (presumably chips or pebble-like pieces taken from pavement V), could well have required the use of a formwork into which the building materials could be poured or strewn. The scrupulousness of the approach seems all the more noteworthy in view of the positioning of the subsequently superimposed Ur-Nanshe Building, which was not placed above the centre of the block (P′Q′R′S′), but almost exactly over the walls of the original, two-room Lower Construction (PQRS), with the noteworthy difference that, unlike its predecessor, the Ur-Nanshe Building was properly oriented with respect to the cardinal points.

Forest (1999, pp. 14–15) explains the arrangement as a compromise between the need to fortify the old remains (PQRS), which the surrounding block successfully did, and a desire to keep parts of the lower level in use. This leads him to speculate that the new block was part of a refurbishment programme that turned the original core of the Lower Construction into a transitional variant of the temple that was later superseded by the Ur-Nanshe Building. Assuming that there were one or two mud-brick corridors around the two original rooms, he therefore suggests that the old core of the building was largely relinquished, and that the closest adjacent hallways, especially on the NE and SE sides, were filled with masonry belonging to the new block. The builders encroached less upon the innermost hallway on the other two sides, where the new block was narrower, but any problems that might have eventuated would in any case have been minimised by the presumed existence of a second peripheral corridor that was further away from the core walls (PQRS). The proposed new structure, supposed to have been an intermediate development that was carried out after the closing of the original Lower Construction, but before the later erection of the Ur-Nanshe Building, thus reused as much as possible of the old base, though some of it inevitably had to be given up for technical reasons.

It is extremely unlikely that the upper surface of the new block was intended to be a floor—a proposal first advanced by Heuzey for the filling in room U on the NW side, and later taken up by Parrot (1948, p. 59) and Crawford (1987, p. 73). The simple reason for this is that additional bituminated cavities were incorporated into the top of the new block, inside and outside room U. As in the original building, these vase-shaped openings were presumably anchoring points for projecting poles that formed the stays for reed screens (or adobe walls, in Forest's view, though for the reasons discussed in Chapter 12 it is unlikely that the rather light framework would have been used to brace a rigid, but relatively brittle structure). They would thus have created the outlines of a slightly larger building in which (Forest argues) the size of room T on the SE side was increased towards the north-west because the reed screen on top of the original partition wall was replaced by a new one on the filling inside room U (with the top of the new block being raised to house the protruding tops of the old walls). The dimensions of room U on the NW side did not change, but it was displaced slightly, also towards the north-west, where it was bounded by the new reed screens (or adobe walls) that were anchored by the new bituminated capsules.

The importance attached to the orientation of Forest's proposed transitional building was shown by the care with which the new SW wall (Q′R′) was constructed, and also confirmed by the placement of the later generation of bitumen-coated cavities that adjusted the space formerly occupied by room U to make it follow the lines of the new block. The dimensions of the inferred structure, in so far as Forest can estimate them, were the same as those of the later Ur-Nanshe Building. The disposition of the new NW walls and the conjectured niche that was fashioned inside the old walls of room U became features of the new building by virtue of the structures that the bituminated cavities were installed to support. Since no new cavities were found in the new block on the SE side of the building, any reed screen or adobe walls in that area must have followed the lines of the cavities in the original walls, perhaps even reusing some of the original stays. The upshot is that the inferred transitional temple must have measured approximately 6.25 m × 9.35 m, the same as the Ur-Nanshe Building, and that, except for the positioning of the niche created by the repositioned reed screen or adobe walls in the vicinity of room U, the ground plans of the two structures were identical.

Difficulties are presented for the theory due to the height of the walls of the two-room Lower Construction, which rose about 0.7 m above the top of the new block. This was a major obstacle on the NW side of the building, where the protrusions would have dramatically reduced the available space in the new NW room, possibly rendering it unserviceable. It was less problematic on the SE side, where any new reed screens or adobe walls could have reused the first generation of bituminated capsules, but even there the coincidence was only partial because of the changed orientation of the new structure, which was more marked on that side. For this reason, Forest considers that the height of the entire new block must have been raised by the addition of several layers of mud-bricks, creating a new floor that was not identified as such by Sarzec, partly for the familiar reason that he took no notice of mud-bricks, but also because this was the level at which the mud-brick platform of the Ur-Nanshe Building was later constructed above the original walls. Laid at the same level as the top of the filling of mud-bricks that formed the raised floor of the new block, but situated only above the original walls, the Ur-Nanshe foundation that Sarzec did record was made up of a layer of gypsum slabs (taken from pavement V, which, it should be noted in passing, must have been readily accessible when Ur-Nanshe's builders sealed the old temple) that were laid on a bed of bitumen, followed by three layers of fired bricks that were covered with another coating of bitumen (as shown on the section on Plan C (2)).

This elaborate proposal seems far-fetched, not least because it interpolates a construction phase for which there is no evidence, while placing far too much reliance on features that Sarzec is supposed to have overlooked rather than on his expressly recorded finds. Nor does it reconcile the apparent continued existence of some of the Lower Construction's original underground corridors with the now raised cella and trophy room. Furthermore, the transitional structure is framed in large part to account for the installation of seven bituminated cavities in the NW side of the outlying block, but the assumed need to raise the top of the block with mud-bricks to create a floor to accommodate the protruding remains of the old walls places the new cavities (but not the original ones that were in the older, higher walls) under a layer of mud-bricks that was 0.7 m thick. This, it should be stressed, is not the layer that was found by Sarzec between the top of the Lower Construction and the base of the Ur-Nanshe Building. It is the filling that Forest supposes must have been added on top of the part of the block that extended inside room U to establish a new floor level.

The simpler, more logical conclusion, which is also more consistent with the recorded data and does not require the introduction of an undated transitional event for which there is no evidence, is that the erection of the new block was associated with the decommissioning of the older temple in preparation for the construction of the superimposed Ur-Nanshe Building. This would mean that the new block (P′Q′R′S′) was a coffer designed to enclose the original temple (a potent holy space) as part of a closing phase or ritual interment. In the process, the mud-brick walls that made up the encircling platform, with its corridors and other spaces, would have been taken out of service so that the materials could be reused in the ritual burying of the shrine. This would also explain why the older foundation platform, pavement V, was so badly preserved: the pavement itself had finally reached the end of its useful life because the uppermost ground surface of the central part of the mound was about to be elevated by about 4 m to the new Ur-Nanshe base level (12.83 m on Sarzec's Plan C (2)), so its gypsum slabs were partly salvaged by Ur-Nanshe's workers to be recycled in the coffer.

Room U, on the NW side of the temple, was infilled during this phase (as discussed above and recorded on Plan C (2)), which is typical of the ritual closure of a sanctum sanctorum. Room T, on the SE side, was also infilled, but in a different manner, with certain select objects being retained, ceremonially broken and deliberately replaced in the decommissioned sacred space. The elaborate layers that were added on top of the old temple walls, but not on the surrounding block, as can be seen on the section on Plan C (2), clearly demonstrate that it was the old building in particular that was being sealed. This again confirms an act of ritual deconsecration, as does the intricate texture of the sealing layers: a layer of bitumen (0.05 m), a tiling of gypsum slabs (0.2 m), three beds of baked bricks bonded with bitumen (0.24 m) and another, uppermost layer of bitumen (0.06 m). In addition, as is detailed below, some significant objects were found associated with these layers. Deposited on top of them was part of the mud-brick platform (here 0.7 m thick) that was the foundation for the Ur-Nanshe Building.

The fact that the enclosing block reverted to the outlines provided by pavement V shows that the problem that had led to the apparently unorthodox placement of the two-room core had now presumably been resolved. The nature of the difficulty and the eventual solution cannot be known with certainty, but if the ground plan of PQRS had been adapted to accommodate an immovable sacred obstacle (as discussed above) then that sacred entity could have been deconsecrated when the rest of the old temple was decommissioned. This would have allowed the builders, without any hint of sacrilege, to fit the block to the lines of the pavement, as they very carefully did.

One other difficulty that cannot currently be resolved with finality is the fact that the builders fitted seven new bituminated cavities in the coffer: four along its NW face, and three in the area of room U. If these were indeed the anchors for vertical poles, there are perhaps three possibilities. First, the block and the two-room core could temporarily have performed a single function, with the new poles at the NW end of the block being used in conjunction with some of the older ones at the SE end to form the outlines of a provisional temple. To all intents and purposes, this is Forest's transitional building hypothesis, and for the reasons previously outlined it is unconvincing, perhaps most importantly because it would imply the existence of an unattested ruler who commissioned the structure but left behind no deposits or other memorials to commemorate the event. Secondly, again on the assumption that the new poles at the NW end of the block were used in tandem with some of the original poles at the SE end, they could have been markers that were meant to protrude above the mud-bricks that were deposited on top of the Lower Construction after it had been deconsecrated. This would have helped the builders to establish the layout of the new walls of the Ur-Nanshe Building above the cella and trophy room of the Lower Construction, though the whole arrangement of the new building would thereby have been pushed over a little towards the north-west, with the lines demarcated by the new poles in and around the old room U providing the plan for the new cella, while several of the older poles (presumably omitting the ones around the doorway in the SE wall) marked the outlines of the trophy room. This is not inherently implausible, particularly as pavement F (on Plan C (1); Fig. 33), which was the main approach to the Ur-Nanshe Building, extended out from its NW façade, in front of the cella, whose changed location might have been carefully defined by the poles fitted in the NW end of the enclosing block. The positioning of a new temple with respect to an older one was, of course, a matter of the highest religious importance, but why would the builders go to the elaborate lengths of fitting new cavities into the enclosing block that were intended to be nothing more than disposable markers? Simple sticks stuck into the ground would have done the same job without the need for such laboriously installed infrastructure. In addition, the axis on which the new building was to be constructed, and the exact lines of its walls, would unquestionably have been freshly pegged out on the basis of astronomical observations (as described above) after the raised ground had been prepared, and that means that the desired degree of congruity could have been achieved with a single pole in the N corner.

The third possibility draws on the probability that the permanent removal of the cult statue from the current cella and its eventual reinstallation in a new home were momentous events that must have been planned in minute detail and accompanied by a lengthy succession of liturgical rites. It was surely not just a case of taking the statue out, transporting it to a secondary chapel (or a sequence of chapels in different locations) and then placing it in the new cella in the Ur-Nanshe Building on Tell K when the later temple was finally ready. The significant raising of the sacred floor level from 8.48 m to 12.83 m (Sarzec heights), for example, might have had particular symbolic importance precisely because the elevated ground on which the new temple was going to stand was essentially a new fabrication that was the work of human hands that had to be transformed to make it suitable as the domain of the deity. It could, for instance, have required that the statue be elevated in stages, defined by the progress of the building works, from its old pedestal in the Lower Construction to a provisional platform that was created by the new reed screens installed over the new cavities in and in front of room U, and from there to the permanent new ground level above. That way, the sacred character of the raised level, which was in some vital respects a freshly created patch of unsanctified earth that had been brought into being not by the gods but by human endeavour, could have been duly established before the god was temporarily removed from Tell K, such that the new building could be constructed on already hallowed ground with divine sanction. Nor should it be forgotten that the bituminated cavities in the masonry that made up the Lower Construction's surrounding block were placed at a Sarzec height of 10.88 m, just 0.7 m below the tops of the temple's walls (at 11.58 m), which must have been situated at about the same level as the summit of the mound when the underground rooms of the Lower Construction were in service. This might well confirm that the top of the block, with its presumed reed screens supported by the bitumen cavities, represented an intermediate and temporary stage in the overall raising of the sacred floor.

An operation of the sort just described was perhaps the historical obverse of the negative story told in Genesis 11:1–9, where the raising of the ground through the cooperative effort of humanity leads to the construction of the Tower of Babel. God considers this to be such a dangerous challenge to his power that he scatters the people and 'confounds' their speech, causing them to speak a host of mutually unintelligible languages. The parable, which treats the construction of the tower as a symbol of consolidated human action against the God of the Old Testament is a piece of anti-Babylonian propaganda, but the very fact that the building could be conceived in this way might suggest that the elevation of the ground did indeed have potent religious connotations. In that case, the events hypothesised above might have been procedural elements of the interconnected ritual deconsecration of the old building and the sanctification of the new one, including, perhaps most significantly, the lately raised surface on which it was built: the sacred locus being transferred from the lower place to the higher one (and shifted a little to the north-west) in defined stages in order to sanctify the new ground and gain divine protection for the fundamental changes wrought on the earth by human actions. This is perhaps the most likely explanation, but in the absence of further epigraphic or archaeological evidence it must remain a matter of conjecture.

The Small Square Pit

One other installation, which is not shown on Sarzec's plans, was excavated outside the Lower Construction on pavement V. To the north-east of the inner E corner (S), at a distance of 4 m, Sarzec discovered a small square pit with sides measuring 0.8 m. Heuzey (1900, p. 48) calls it a well, but this is undoubtedly inaccurate, as he himself acknowledges, because its walls were plastered with a mixture of clay (adobe) and chopped straw, making it unsuitable for water. Excavated down to a depth of 4 m (beyond which the local workmen refused to dig, so it is impossible to know whether it was considerably deeper), it was found to be full of ashes. As indicated by its depth of at least 4 m, however, it could not have been a hearth. Heuzey hesitantly wonders whether it might have been dug to contain the remains of burnt offerings from an inferred sacrificial altar that might have been installed nearby, but nothing of the kind was noted in the vicinity. If it dated back to the time when the Lower Construction was surrounded with underground walkways, it could indeed conceivably have been a repository for sacrificially burnt remains, but that would also suggest that an associated altar must either have been in one of the two holiest rooms, which were open roofed, thus allowing smoke to escape, or that a chimney was built that passed through the mud-brick mass that formed the ground level above the inferred underground space. The described location of the pit suggests that it must have been placed comfortably within the confines of pavement V, fairly close to its SE edge, but Heuzey does not explicitly say this and he gives no information as to whether its top rose up above the paved floor. It could conceivably have been a later feature that was ritually linked with the ceremonies that were carried out to accompany the eventual closure of the temple, but again this is pure surmise.

The Ritually Buried Objects

The recorded objects that were associated with the two-room temple—some fragmentary, and some significantly intact—can all be shown to confirm the hypothesis of a ritual interment. The NW room of the Lower Construction (room U), which was the cella that housed the cult image and its podium, was emptied and infilled, as previously described. The SW room (T) was the associated trophy room that contained objects of particular divine significance. These included the bottom part of the Stele of the Captives, the fragmentary Circular Bas-Relief and the Girsu Land Stele, all of which were found in or around the room when Sarzec uncovered it, and the precise way in which these objects were deposited, as well as the states in which they were discovered, reflect procedures that must have been expressly carried out as part of the rites that were solemnised before the building was formally deconsecrated. Uncovered in a layer of infilling in the sacred space where they originated, the objects found in room T had undergone special treatment before being buried in the deposited filling when the core Lower Construction was encased in the surrounding block, and when the NE room was also closed off. The bottom part of the stele, the damaged bas-relief and the Girsu Land Stele were all found fractured but not randomly discarded or abandoned. Over a period of many centuries they were subsequently subject to accidental deterioration (natural breaks and erosion, for example), but when the temple was decommissioned they were almost certainly carefully and purposefully broken prior to their ritualised interment.

The limestone Stele of the Captives was found still standing on the pavement in front of the doorway inside room T, where it had in all likelihood acted as a kind of monumental screen. Inexcusably discarded by Sarzec, the photo taken on site (Fig. 44) and the drawing made of its obverse (Fig. 76) show that the preserved part was roughly rectangular. This points to the fact that it was broken intentionally and in a controlled manner (perhaps sawn in two at the height of the waists of the figures), but it was not otherwise reworked or smoothed because the upper edge in particular, as well as the lower edge, were irregular. Almost exactly the same procedure was carried out on the Circular Bas-Relief (Fig. 77): this too had been sawn through laterally along the line of the waists of the figures. In addition, it had been broken into small pieces of which only six were found: one was buried in room T, presumably as a *pars pro toto*, a fragment chosen to represent the whole; four more pieces were apparently found close to the building on pavement V, while a sixth was found 20 m away in Cros's Trench 5, incorporated into the NE corner of the terrace platform built by Ur-Nanshe. The fact that neither the Stele of the Captives nor any of the pieces of the Circular Bas-Relief exhibited signs of having been defaced, erased, reincised or otherwise malignly damaged leads to the conclusion that they were ceremonially fractured, probably as a way of deactivating their sacred aura and symbolic significance, before being carefully positioned and solemnly interred. Incidentally, it has occasionally been pointed out that there is perhaps an oblique shallow indent below the corner of the eye and towards the nose of the leader on the left of the scene on the Circular Bas-Relief that might be interpreted as a sign of intentional defacement or *damnatio memoriae*. Any mark is so slight as to be barely perceptible, however, and it is therefore an extremely small and isolated instance that does not reflect a pattern of defilement that affects the key sensory centres generally, such as is more clearly found, for example, on the Stele of the Vultures (discussed in Chapter 20 below). The face of the leader on the right of the same scene is pristine, and the surviving faces of the other participants in the depicted ceremony show no marks of targeted mutilation. Heuzey (Sarzec and Heuzey 1912, p. 357) noted from the outset that the way the cylindrical object had been broken was probably not accidental, and this is accounted for by the fact that it was ritually buried, but the observable trace of a single crack that could have been produced inadvertently provides no evidence of systematic desecration.

The discovery of a fragment of the Circular Bas-Relief, together with two slabs of gypsum that were probably taken from pavement V, in Cros's Trench 5, in the NE corner of the raised mud-brick platform established by Ur-Nanshe, would again indicate that the ritual interment of the core Lower Construction took place under Ur-Nanshe's authority, as part of the programme of building works carried out during his reign. The stratigraphy is also consistent with the sequence of deposits that were carefully used to seal off the top of the old temple. With reference to Forest's thesis, the idea that the surviving objects, together with the block and its appurtenances, were the battered and levelled remains of a lost transitional temple that otherwise left no trace adds unwarranted complications for which there is no evidence. The capping layers added to the top of the old building, which were scrupulously placed only over its original walls, are far more convincingly explained as the ritual sealing of the holy spaces than as the partial floor of an intermediate building—a solution that creates a host of new problems. On the contrary (as Heuzey correctly argued), the composite cover built on top of the old temple represents a cleansing and sealing layer that formed a ritually cohesive substructural base for the platform of mud-bricks, complete with recorded foundation deposits, that was installed to support the Ur-Nanshe Building.

Some votive objects were found at different depths within the mud-brick infrastructure that was associated with the elaborate capping layers that secured the Lower Construction. These, it should be said, were dedicatory not commemorative, which is a vital distinction. Commemorative objects, meaning artefacts that were intended to be foundation offerings, were ritually buried to accompany a new building phase that was carried out under the auspices of a new ruler, and they were accordingly inscribed in that ruler's name to memorialise his work. By contrast, dedicatory objects, such as votive artefacts, were placed first and foremost in honour of the god, in this case Ningirsu, whose protection was sought. The rare objects found buried in the mud-brick foundation that surrounded and lay between the closed Lower Construction and the Ur-Nanshe Building, notably the Mace of Mesilim and the inscribed Copper Blade that was figuratively decorated with ornate lions, both fall into the latter category because they were found in the lowest layers of the mud-brick mass that formed the substructure of the raised Ur-Nanshe platform. As is clarified below, the Colossal Spear Head inscribed in the name of another king of Kish, which has caused numerous interpretative problems for generations of scholars, should also be included in this group.

The Mace of Mesilim (AO2349; Fig. 28) is an oversized, and therefore symbolic limestone votive mace head, measuring 0.19 m (h) × 0.16 m (diameter), that is decorated with reliefs on its top and around its circumference. The relief on the upper, unpierced face of the ceremonial weapon shows a lion-headed eagle with outstretched wings. Around the edge are six half-erect leaping lions that appear to be chasing and grasping each other. Their bodies and raised tails are shown in profile, while their heads are all presented frontally. The creatures' eyes were originally encrusted, probably with lapis lazuli or shells, which were missing when the object was found, but traces of blue pigments have been detected. A short inscription is carved on the body of two of the lions (RIME 1.8.1.1): 'Mesilim, king (lugal) of Kish, temple builder for the god Ningirsu, deposited(?) this mace for the god Ningirsu. Lugalshaengur (is) the ruler (ensí) of La[gash].'

The Copper Blade with Lions (Fig. 28), which was one of the most beautiful pieces of metalwork to have originated from Tell K, measured 0.41 m in length, and it had two lions engraved on its hilt. The animals were depicted belly to belly, with elongated and entwined tails, while their front paws were shown holding the thick lanceolate blade that had a double slope. At the bottom of the weapon was an inscription that mentioned an administrator (sanga) of the Ningirsu temple. Unfortunately, this remarkable object disappeared when it was being transported from Tello to Istanbul (or Constantinople as it was then), and nothing is known of its subsequent fate. Based on the photo published in Sarzec and Heuzey 1912 (Pl. 6 ter (2)), the deciphered inscription shows a free arrangement of signs that is a stylistic trait typical of the Fara or Early Dynastic IIIa period (see Braun-Holzinger 1991, p. 88; and Marchesi and Marchetti 2011, p. 43). The translation reads: 'Copper (?) dagger dedicated to Ningirsu by a temple administrator (sanga)'.

The reason why the Colossal Spear Head (AO2675; Fig. 28) has not hitherto been included among this group of dedicatory objects is that its find location was confusedly misrepresented by Heuzey. This is a clear example of an artefact that was mistakenly attributed to the wrong archaeological context either because of poorly recorded data or (more probably) because the data was inattentively handled. This has misled scholars into thinking that the Colossal Spear Head, which was inscribed in the name of Lugalnamnirshumma, who styled himself king of Kish, was dedicated in (or even slightly after) the reign of Ur-Nanshe, when in fact it dates back to the Early Dynastic IIIa period. The error has created a host of historical problems, not least the need to explain how, after the rise of the powerful dynasty founded by Ur-Nanshe, Girsu–Lagash might once again have been subject to the overlordship of Kish. The difficulty has been further compounded by the theory that kings of Uruk might perhaps have assumed the catch-all title of king of Kish, such that, in spite of the inscription, Lugalnamnirshumma might actually have been a king of Uruk (Marchesi 2015, pp. 144–5). With regard to the spear head's previously accepted archaeological context, none of this makes sense. The problem derives from Heuzey's earlier account of the object (1900, p. 25), where he states that it was found some 7.5 m from the E corner of Ur-Nanshe Building (9.4 m on Plan C (1), where it is marked as No. 16) and 0.15 m above the Ur-Nanshe base level (12.83 m), which would place it within the same stratigraphic horizon as the remains associated with the time frame of the Ur-Nanshe Building itself. In the more precise and thorough description of the artefact (Sarzec and Heuzey 1912, p. 261), Heuzey writes that it was found 7 m away from the Ur-Nanshe Building, a little above its 'lower level' (*niveau inférieur*), by which he presumably means the temple's substructure, or *sous-sol*, which is the word used on Plan C (2) to describe the capping layer at the top of the Lower Construction, rather than the *sol* (or ground), which refers to the Ur-Nanshe base level. This would confirm that the Colossal Spear Head was almost certainly found in the mass of mud-bricks below the Ur-Nanshe Building at a Sarzec height of about 12.28 m (or 0.15 m above the height of the capped top of the Lower Construction, which lay at 12.13 m), in the same horizon as the Mace of Mesilim and the Copper Blade with Lions.

The placement of the Colossal Spear Head in this stratigraphic layer is in accord with its presumed date of manufacture in the Early Dynastic IIIa era, and it replaces the previously confused historical context with an intelligible chronology. Lugalnamnirshumma, whose name means 'the lord is endowed with authority' (Marchesi and Marchetti 2011, p. 124), was doubtless one of Mesilim of Kish's successors, and therefore in all likelihood another foreign overlord of Girsu in the period before Ur-Nanshe ascended to power. The time frame also helps to explain some generic similarities between the spear head and the Mesilim mace, both of which are oversized, while both votive weapons are expressly dedicated to Ningirsu. Measuring 0.85 m (l) × 0.135 m (w), the spear head takes the form of a lanceolate leaf with a double slope. The stem of the blade, which tapers towards the base, is shaped into a long tang with four holes, indicating that the ceremonial weapon must have been fitted with an imposing shaft that was secured with rivets. The elongated blade is decorated with an engraving of an upright lion with an erect tail, and the positioning of the lion and the inscription would further suggest that the piece was displayed upside down, with the blade pointing towards the ground and the shaft in the air.

Bearing the name of Lugalnamnirshumma of Kish, the Colossal Spear Head therefore has a comparable pedigree to the mace connected with Mesilim of Kish—a foreign overlord from a previous epoch who was subsequently venerated almost as a legendary figure. Comparably, the inscription on the Copper Blade with Lions records that the fine dagger was also dedicated to Ningirsu, but by a temple administrator or high priest (sanga). Since nothing further is known about this person's name and origins, it is impossible to say whether he also might have been from Kish, but the three objects, which were found in pristine condition, relate to the fragmentary pieces that were found ritually buried in room T: the bottom part of the Stele of the Captives, the Circular Bas-Relief and the Girsu Land Stele. Considered as an ensemble, they comprise a group of similarly ancient relics that were probably safeguarded and displayed as ex-votos inside the shrine of the Lower Construction before later being carefully disposed of when the temple was deconsecrated and sealed. It should also be noted that the artefacts were treated differently according to their intrinsic characters and the messages they conveyed: the ceremonial weapons, which were all (perhaps including the dagger) conceivably donated as precious ornaments by high-ranking figures from outside Girsu–Lagash, were buried intact, but the Stele of the Captives, the Circular Bas-Relief and the Girsu Land Stele, which can broadly be interpreted as foundational artefacts that record the earliest history of the state (as argued in Chapter 13), and therefore of supreme religious significance, were broken and desacralised.

The fragment of an onyx bowl inscribed in the name of Ur-Nanshe and dedicated to the goddess Bau that was found elsewhere in the mud-brick foundation, at an overall depth of 0.05 m below the Mace of Mesilim, has caused major problems for the transitional temple theory proposed by Forest and others (outlined above) precisely because it dates to the time of Ur-Nanshe. Presuming that Ur-Nanshe was only active when the supposed transitional period was drawing to a close, the proponents of the theory are forced to argue that this fragment must have come from a trench that is not named in the published accounts—one that was not explicitly described by Sarzec (see Marchesi and Marchetti 2011, p. 43). The fact that it is a stray object—more precisely, a displaced object that belongs in the tertiary category of contextualisation laid out in Chapter 10 above—is beyond doubt. As with other fragments of Bau vessels found in tertiary contexts at a variety of locations across the whole site, therefore, it might well have originated on Tell A, but there is no reason to attribute the decontextualisation to the excavator, thereby creating an unrecorded trench for which no evidence exists. On the contrary, its find location is precisely described in the literature: it was discovered towards the bottom of the extensive mud-brick infrastructure that entombed the capped Lower Construction, where it was no doubt randomly mixed in with the clay and any other discarded materials that were used to form the mud-brick mass in which it was found. As such, it constitutes a perfect piece of dating evidence for the proposed construction sequence that has been outlined in detail above, confirming that the sealing of the Lower Construction and the addition of the related mud-brick layers were part of the ritual interment of the older temple, followed by the preparatory work for the new temple that was built during the reign of Ur-Nanshe.

The Cache of Eight Archaic Tablets

As is further discussed below, the intermediate layers around and between the old and new temples yielded other objects that Heuzey, apparently for simplicity's sake, preferred to deal with in his account of the Ur-Nanshe Building. Including the enigmatic cache of eight 'very archaic' tablets, he connects them mostly with pavement F, which extended out to the north-west from the NW face of the later temple, probably because Sarzec recorded them as having been found at about this topographical height. When Heuzey describes the eight archaic tablets more precisely, however, he himself indicates that they were actually found beneath pavement F, in the upper section of the intervening layers between the old and new temples. This important nuance, which has consistently been overlooked, has led to some major misunderstandings, the resolution of which allows for a major reassessment of the stratigraphy of the upper parts of the mound.

Sarzec's discovery of the cache of tablets—a set of administrative clay documents dating to the Early Dynastic IIIa period—is nothing short of a conundrum. They were found hoarded together about 0.1 m below the Ur-Nanshe horizon at a Sarzec height of 12.73 m, 6.8 m south-west of the SW wall of the Ur-Nanshe Building, and therefore interred in the Ur-Nanshe layer of mud-bricks that was deposited immediately below the new temple. This particularly enigmatic deposit is a one-off recovery that stands out distinctly from the entire corpus of finds deriving from Tell K. Apart from the odd stray example, no clay tablets that were inscribed by book-keepers (accountants or clerks, as they might also be called) were recovered on Tell K in any of the French excavations. Contemporary with the latest phase of the Lower Construction, they came from an Early Dynastic IIIa temple archive that was presumably housed outside the sacred precinct of Girsu, probably on Tablet Hill (Tell V), a complex that included administrative (and other) buildings in a time span ranging from the Early Dynastic III period down to Lagash II and Ur III times. But why was this particular collection of documents placed in the foundation layers associated with the Ur-Nanshe Building? Were they deliberately buried to fulfil some religious or ritual purpose relating to the administration of the estates belonging to the decommissioned Lower Construction, or left there for some other reason that is perhaps destined to remain elusive?

Published by Thureau-Dangin in 1903, the eight tablets contain administrative data relating to the distribution of livestock, land and produce (cattle, fields, wool, bread, flour and grain), together with lists of named persons about whom nothing is known. Apart from the listings themselves, no further information is recorded that might provide any kind of historical context. In the *Recueil de tablettes chaldéennes* ('Collection of Chaldean Tablets') they are indexed as follows: RTC1 (AO410), RTC2 (AO407), RTC3 (AO412), RTC4 (AO406), RTC5 (AO411), RTC6 (AO282), RTC7 (AO408) and RTC8 (AO405). If the group of tablets is thought to have been ritually buried in a favissa then they could perhaps have been deliberately selected from a much larger archival corpus as representatives of the whole. That might, for example, help to explain the wide range of items and subjects that are recorded on them, but it is impossible to be sure. The difficulty is exacerbated by the fact that no archival material from this early period survives that could shed light on whether the collection of deposited tablets was considered to be a self-contained dossier of mutually related items or a curated selection of generic types. The idea that they could be a specially assembled selection is probably contradicted by their diversity, however: six contain straightforward inventories, while two specifically record lists of offerings. The breakdown of their contents is similarly varied and inconclusive: single tablets are respectively devoted to flour, bread, grain and small cattle, but two tablets contain lists of persons and two more contain lists of fields. Accordingly, the range of text types and subjects tends to discredit the curated selection hypothesis, but there is no evidence to support the dossier theory either. They might have been randomly discarded, but their archaeological context and the fact that the eight tablets were found together as a cache would tend to refute that argument. As with any human situation, there could have been a host of reasons why some individual or group of individuals might have wanted to bury or dispose of items of personal or administrative significance, perhaps as a private or semi-official memorial that would have required the express approval of Ur-Nanshe or his officials, or even for some less honourable, even clandestine reason. Maybe, on the one hand, a clerk or a body of clerks (or their descendants) wished to commend themselves to the deity or to posterity. On the other hand, if there was something amiss in the records that one or more individuals wished to erase (even without formal sanction), it would conceivably have been simpler to pulverise the clay tablets and scatter the remains, but the sacred character of the archive might have made this impossible for a host of readily comprehensible reasons, in which case the eight tablets could have been buried as a private or official act of atonement. There is simply no way of knowing, but the uncertainty surrounding the anomalous cache evocatively recalls the fact that the intelligible archaeological remains reflect only a tiny part of the full range of human experience, much of which has been lost.

CHAPTER 16

The New Sanctuary: The Ur-Nanshe Building

UR-NANSHE (C.2460–2425 BCE), WHO FOUNDED THE First Dynasty, was evidently a ruler of epoch-defining vision and charisma. The son of a certain Gunidu, whose origins are unknown, he usually styles himself 'king' (lugal) of Lagash in his royal inscriptions, contrasting with his immediate successors, who generally prefer the title ensi, which has the broader connotation of 'ruler'. His enduring prestige is probably affirmed by the fact that his personal god, Šul.MUŠ×PA (Šul.utul$_{12}$), was passed on from ruler to ruler for the next four generations at least. Issues of warfare and foreign policy are almost entirely absent from Ur-Nanshe's preserved inscriptions, which contain just one mention of a victorious military campaign against Umma and Ur, during which Pabilgatuku, the ruler of Umma, was taken prisoner (RIME 1.9.1.6b). Conversely, as witnessed by the references in numerous dedicatory inscriptions to temples and divine statues in the cities of Lagash and Girsu, Ur-Nanshe's focus seems to have been very much on religious matters. This was not necessarily an indication of his unusual piety, however, because (as discussed in Chapter 11) Ur-Nanshe shrewdly grasped the importance of religious worship as a binding agent in the formation of Lagash, Girsu and Nigin as a composite political entity. The three main deities named in his inscriptions are his namesake, Nanshe, who appears about twenty-five times, and Ningirsu and Gatumdug, who are both mentioned about ten times. No administrative texts can be dated to Ur-Nanshe's time, but some forty royal inscriptions bear witness to his many building activities in the extended state of Lagash, and this seems to confirm the commonly held assumption that he enjoyed a long reign.

Although the preparatory work overseen by Ur-Nanshe for the construction of his new sanctuary was carried out on a massive, perhaps unprecedented scale, it also paid due regard to long-established traditions. The old building was ritually decommissioned, as befitted the holiest site dedicated to the city's chief god, Ningirsu, and tributes were offered to Ur-Nanshe's predecessors, the architect rulers who had built earlier temples on Tell K, as well as to the ancestral overlords of Kish—in particular Mesilim—who had achieved legendary status and were invoked throughout the Early Dynastic period not only as heroic figures but also as the mediators of venerable, divinely sanctioned treaties. Notable among these was the highly significant settlement negotiated by Mesilim in the Early Dynastic IIIa period, about a century before the reign of Ur-Nanshe, that secured Girsu within recognised boundaries by resolving (provisionally, as it turned out) the Umma–Lagash border conflict, one of the earliest recorded boundary disputes between states in human history, and one that was a constantly recurring issue in the story of the neighbouring territories. Paying due regard to interrelated spiritual and civic practices, therefore, Ur-Nanshe initiated a comprehensive construction programme in Girsu that was focused on religious buildings. He restored and refurbished shrines and cult locations, commissioned divine statues and ordered new liturgical hymns. The totality of his vision meant that he was responsible for thoroughly reshaping the landscape of the holy city, which was, it should be stressed, a space in which the sacred and the secular were inseparably fused, and his reforms extended to the state of Lagash at large. The centrepiece and starting point for the entire scheme was the

FIGURE 84. Reconstruction of the Ur-Nanshe Building on the summit of Tell K, viewed from the north-east, with the stairway ascending the stepped mound and the chambered gateway in the temenos wall.

splendid new Temple of Ningirsu on Tell K that is referred to, following the original French nomenclature, as the Ur-Nanshe Building (Fig. 84).

A Three-Step Platform

To accommodate the new sanctuary a colossal platform was constructed that raised the mound to the Sarzec reference height of 12.83 m, sealing and enveloping the old temple with a huge mass of substructural deposits that was made principally of a solid core of planoconvex mud-bricks (Fig. 85). What this means, which is detailed in Chapter 12 above, should be re-emphasised. The base level of the Lower Construction was 8.48 m, but as the main temple rooms lay underground, where they were surrounded by subterranean corridors and presumably service rooms, the surface of the mound in the vicinity of the temple, was already at a Sarzec height of around 11.58 m (calculated by adding the combined height of pavement V (0.25 m) and the Lower Construction's walls (2.85 m) to the Lower Construction's base height). How much of the mound rose to 11.58 m in the era of the ancient shrine, and indeed whether the central area of the mound's summit was higher than that indicative value, is difficult to say, but if, as seems to be the case, Ur-Nanshe added about 0.7 m of mud-bricks on top of the sealed older temple and its underground annexe walls, it would suggest that a considerable area of the summit already lay at a Sarzec height of between 11.58 m and 12.13 m (subtracting 0.7 m from the Ur-Nanshe base height of 12.83 m). Amidst the array of details, it is vital to stress at the outset the profound significance of Ur-Nanshe's action, because he did not simply elevate the mound as one might add a storey to an existing building. On the contrary, by constructing a temple on the newly established surface he raised the sacred level—the divinely charged abode of the god—from 8.48 m to 12.83 m, and in so doing he dramatically changed the character of the entire upper surface of the tell.

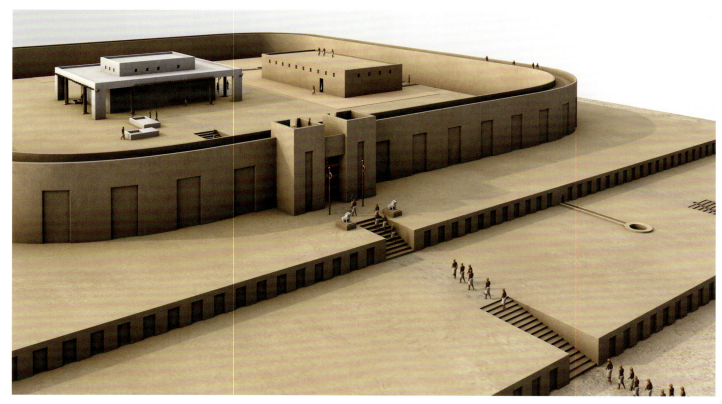

FIGURE 85. Close-up of the massive platforms of Tell K, including the ceremonial stairway, the chambered gateway and the temenos wall, looking towards the E corner and SE façade of the Ur-Nanshe Building, with the brewhouse to the right of the temple.

Ur-Nanshe's enormous platform stretched out expansively across the mound, such that Sarzec and especially Cros found its remains in the central sector (the area of the upper sacred precinct), and in Cros's West Trench, North Trench and South Trenches (the area marked as *Maison des Fruits* and Trenches 5, 8, 9 and 10 on Cros's Plan B; Fig. 36), and also lower down on the E or SE slope of the tell in one of the rectangular blocks of earth left behind by Sarzec, where Cros found a substantial section of the thick mud-brick platform. In the central sector, where it rose above the capping layer of gypsum, fired-bricks and bitumen that had been used to seal the Lower Construction (at a Sarzec height of 12.13 m), the mud-brick mass was about 0.7 m thick. At the bottom of Trench 8, a little to the west of the Ur-Nanshe Building, where the new layer was also 0.7 m thick, a drain was installed, probably at the interface with the decommissioned Lower Construction; sloping away to the south-west, it was built of planoconvex fired bricks that were signed with the single thumbprint that was Ur-Nanshe's regnal marking.

In Trench 5, to the north-east of the new temple, significant remains of the mud-brick platform were exposed to a depth of 1.7 m, overlaying part of the earlier elevation. In the South Trenches (9 and 10), probably demarcating the SE edge of the enlarged mound, a mass of mud-bricks was found covering an area that measured 6 m × 30 m and descending to a depth of 6 m. As these discoveries clearly show, the new platform enveloped and significantly extended its precursor.

Remains of the mud-brick substratum were excavated in all directions in the more immediate vicinity of the Ur-Nanshe Building, radiating out to distances of between 12 m and 25 m, and reaching depths of between 0.3 m and 1.7 m below the level of the Ur-Nanshe base, while traces of a lower platform were also exposed by Cros in one of Sarzec's rectangular blocks near the Pillar of Gudea. When he was writing up the data recorded by Sarzec, Heuzey soon realised the range and depth of this immense new terrace platform, which can now be estimated to have occupied a total area of about 125 m × 110 m = 13,750 m². Numerous votive objects were buried in the mud-brick mass, including foundation figurines, plaques and tablets. It should be reiterated here that the mud-brick deposits that were laid down around the Lower Construction to encase the building and also to consolidate the overall raising of the mound merged homogeneously with the uppermost layers that were placed above the capped older temple, including the 0.7 m-thick deposit of mud-bricks to which Sarzec exceptionally paid attention (as previously noted). With reference to the locations of the objects that were found buried in the compacted beds of mud-bricks below the Ur-Nanshe base level, where they lay around and above the Lower Construction, therefore, the key differentiator is the height at which they were found because, largely due to the inadequacies in the recorded data, it is not possible to discriminate between the qualities of mud-brick deposits that entombed and covered the Lower Construction, on the one hand, and those that were used to raise and prepare the mound for the erection of the Ur-Nanshe Building on the other.

One of the seismic innovations introduced by Ur-Nanshe was a change in the conventions surrounding the ancient ritual of burying of foundation pegs at highly charged spots under sacred structures (Fig. 86). Whereas the pegs found under the Lower Construction were free of cuneiform texts, Ur-Nanshe's copper figurines were inscribed with a dedicatory text that named him as the ruler who had deposited them, and they were additionally accompanied by an inscribed stone tablet in the shape of a planoconvex brick. Furthermore, the pegs associated with the Lower Construction were each made from a unique mould, and the way in which they were cast and finished meant that they were all crafted as one-off objects, each slightly different from all the others. By contrast, the Ur-Nanshe inscribed pegs were all cast from the same mould—mass-produced, so to speak—as positively identical objects. In practice, the large numbers of pegs required could not have been produced from just one master mould, so they were presumably made in batches from substantially similar moulds, but the intention was to manufacture multiple copies of the same figure rather than to create individualised sculptures. Five deposits are listed by Parrot (1948, p. 63), four of which are marked as a, b, c and d on Sarzec's Plan C (1) (Fig. 33). They take the same identical form of an anthropomorphic figure with a carefully modelled head, prominent nose, large eyes and a small mouth that is shaped into a serene smile. The hair of each is styled into ringlets or locks that fall down behind the head onto the back between the shoulders. The arms, which are carefully modelled, are attached to the torso, while the hands are clasped together at the chest, with the left hand wrapped around the right from below in the conventional Sumerian gesture of prayer. The torso tapers down to a point that forms the peg or stake that was driven into the ground, and the same cuneiform inscription, which reads 'Ur-Nanshe built the sanctuary of Girsu', runs down the length of the back of each figure. Ranging in height between 0.14 m and 0.16 m (depending on the preserved lengths of the spikes), the Ur-Nanshe figurines were found inserted vertically as far as their joined hands into holes in inscribed copper discs or collars that terminate behind the heads in splayed out swallowtail (or perhaps dovetail) appendices (Fig. 86), and the points of the pegs below the copper collars were implanted in the sacred mound. The inscription on the copper surfaces is a slightly extended version of the one on the figurines (RIME 1.9.1.7): 'Ur-Nanshe, king of Lagash, son of Gunidu, built the sanctuary of Girsu'. As noted in Chapter 1, it is important to recall that the key term, the 'sanctuary of Girsu', was used as a cognomen for the Temple of Ningirsu.

The function of the copper discs with their flaring, upward-angled tails, was to provide additional support for the third element of the deposit: an inscribed stone tablet, carved in the shape of a planoconvex brick, that was carefully positioned on the head of the figure at the front and on the tail of the copper disc behind. By contrast with the short inscriptions added to the figurines and the copper supports, the stone tablets feature a longer text that details some of Ur-Nanshe's building projects and pious deeds. At first glance, the tailed copper discs or collars might seem like a slightly cumbersome way of supporting the stone tablets, but the distinctive shape of the discs and the way they were manufactured to fit precisely over the top of the figurines makes it likely that they were intended to represent the loop and knot of a surveyor's rope fastened around a surveying peg. As detailed above with respect to the Lower Construction and the principles of the tessellated earth, these were fundamentally important objects in the laying out of buildings that also had wide-ranging significance in the context of Sumerian culture generally. The pegging out procedure is described in detail in the Gudea Cylinder Inscriptions, where (again as discussed in Chapters 14 and 44) the ruler himself pegs out the cardinal N–S axis, just as he moulds and lays

FIGURE 86. A two-part copper foundation deposit from the reign of Ur-Nanshe, comprising an inscribed figurative peg and an inscribed collar. British Museum 96565.

the first brick with his own hands. The royal associations of the pegging out process were later given emblematic form in the symbol of the rod and ring, probably representing a foundation peg and a coil of surveying rope, that became the acknowledged sign of divinely approved kingship.

The inscriptions on Ur-Nanshe's foundation tablets each present nuanced, slightly different accounts of his colossal project. Two examples illustrate some minor variations and give a flavour of the rich legacy Ur-Nanshe was in the process of creating (RIME 1.9.1.9 and RIME 1.9.1.11):

Ur-Nanshe, king of Lagash, son of Gunidu, (Gu.NI.DU was) 'son' (citizen) of Gursar, built the 'Shrine-Girsu', formed the statue of Shulshaga, formed the statue of Gushudu, formed the statue of Kindazi, built the temple of Nin.MAR.KI, formed a statue of Lamma. shita.e, dug the Asuhur canal, dug the 'Ditch of the Southern Wood', dug the 'Great Reservoir' at the Enlilpada canal, dug the 'Canal Moving like a Falcon', dug the Nin.sanga.ba.DU canal. He is the one commissioned by the goddess Nanshe.

Ur-Nanshe, king of Lagash, son of Gunidu, (Gu.ni.du was 'son' of) Gursar, built the temple of the goddess Nanshe. He formed the statue 'the goddess Nanshe is a mighty lady'. He built the 'Shrine-Girsu'. He formed a statue of Shulshaga. He built the Ibgal ('Great Oval'). He formed a statue of Lugal.urtur. He formed a statue of the god Lugal.uru×kár. He built ki.nir. He formed a statue of Nin.réc$_{107}$-èš. He formed a statue of Nin-gidru. He built the temple of the goddess Gatumdug. He formed a statue of the goddess Gatumdug. He built the Bagara, built the E.dam, built Abzu.e, and built Tirash.

The inscriptions further corroborate the point made in detail above (Chapter 11) that Ur-Nanshe used the unifying force of religion to help consolidate and reshape the already established Girsu–Lagash alliance. This is reflected in the stress placed not just on the worship of Ningirsu but on the construction of temples and the creation of statues for a pantheon of Lagash deities. The promotion of the goddess Nanshe, for example, recalls the fact that Ur-Nanshe was a native of the district of Nigin, and he therefore wished to introduce Nanshe, as both the patron goddess of Nigin and his namesake, into the enlarged divine household of Ningirsu that was being established in Girsu. Incidentally, there is no archaeological or epigraphic evidence to support the idea that the sweeping programme of religious renewal was inaugurated in response to an unproven campaign of destruction in Girsu–Lagash that was carried out prior to Ur-Nanshe's rise to power, as is sometimes suggested (Schaudig 2012, pp. 123–49).

The re-establishment of the state's most sacred precinct on Tell K, including the ritual interment of the Lower Construction and the concomitant desacralisation and ceremonial burying of its holiest artefacts, can also be understood in the context of Ur-Nanshe's comprehensive politico-religious transformation. When Ur-Nanshe took control of the Girsu–Lagash union, at a time when the power and prestige of Kish was diminishing and the Hexapolis had fallen apart, for strategic as well as personal reasons he brought the coastal region of Nigin into the alliance. That is presumably why he was happy to trumpet his Nigin birthplace, Gursar, on his royal inscriptions, and partly why his regnal name, Ur-Nanshe, is repeated so frequently. In modern parlance, he was seemingly engaged in an information or propaganda campaign that was designed to bolster his position as the ruler of an enlarged, but also fundamentally redefined kingdom that could be sustained as a political entity into the future. The reformation of the Lagash pantheon, accompanied by the rebuilding of city temples and other places of worship, as well as the inauguration of new divine statues and the commissioning of fresh liturgical hymns were all part of the same effort. As an evolutionary development rather than a revolutionary upheaval, it involved respectfully drawing a line under the past while announcing and cementing the new order. It required Ur-Nanshe to supersede former traditions without obliterating them from the record, and this is reflected in the way he dealt with the Lower Construction and its appurtenances. He painstakingly entombed the deconsecrated temple, whose walls were preserved and left standing, and he buried the deactivated sacred objects, particularly those that represented antiquated political treaties or contractual agreements: the Circular Bas-Relief that documented the original pact of union between Girsu and Lagash; the Stele of the Captives that commemorated a defining historical victory; and the Girsu Land Stele that contained a now outdated record of the territories controlled by the state. The binding significance of these objects was rendered null and void by meticulously administered defacements that severed the legal obligations that they enshrined. The Feathered Figure, which was not subjected to the same treatment, apparently retained its foundational importance, possibly until the reign of Enmetena, and this is hardly surprising because of its paramount status. With its hymn to Ningirsu and the image of the god entering what must be considered to be the first Temple of Ningirsu on Tell K, and the concomitant organisation of the god's primordial domain, centred around Girsu, the Feathered Figure was surely held to be much more than a memorial to the relatively recent past, namely the era of the building of the Lower Construction in Early Dynastic I times. By its very nature, it evoked the mythical beginnings of the state for all time, and its import could therefore be seen as elemental.

With this in mind, it should also be recalled that the state was a model of the cosmos, so the retention of the Feathered Figure in the context of an inclusive programme of renewal might also have been considered to be a tangible sign of the continuing vitality of the cosmic order. In general terms, that could not be restored as such, but it could perhaps have been reflected more clearly in the patterns of life that were expressed in and governed by the actions associated with the newly constructed and refurbished sacred places and objects.

This could further help to explain the sheer number of different subjects that are recorded on the Ur-Nanshe foundation tablets, which celebrate the creation of a cohesive network of cult places, all linked by their shared connection with and reliance on the temple of the city's chief god, Ningirsu, rebuilt on the site of his original dwelling on Tell K. As noted above, the use of diverse texts was an innovation on the part of Ur-Nanshe that differentiates his foundation deposits from those found at other sites, where the same text was often repeated over and over again like a mantra. It is surely also significant that the all-embracing outlook that characterises the inscriptions on the Ur-Nanshe foundation tablets that were buried in the extended platform was not replicated on bricks that were specifically and directly placed in the walls of the temple itself, which was, as it were, the self-sustaining core on which the rest depended. The inscriptions on bricks built into the temple walls, which are variants of the short dedications found on the foundation pegs and their copper collars, expressly introduce the name of the god (RIME 1.9.1.19): 'Ur-Nanshe, king of Lagash, son of Gunidu built the temple of Ningirsu (é.Ningirsu)'. By contrast, the inscriptions on the door sockets that were placed at the temple's thresholds were more outward-looking and expansive in their intent (Fig. 87). The one marked as No. 2 on Sarzec's Plan C (1), for example, which begins by mentioning the Ningirsu temple, goes on to record the fact that Ur-Nanshe's reach extended as far as the 'foreign lands' from which he exacted tribute (RIME 1.9.1.22):

Ur-Nanshe, king of Lagash, son of Gunidu, (Gu.NI.DU was) 'son' of Gursar, built the temple of the god Ningirsu, built the temple of the goddess Nanshe, built the temple of the goddess Gatumdug, built the E.dam, (and) built the temple of the god Nin.MAR.KI. He had ships of Dilmun submit timber as tribute from the foreign lands (to Lagash). He built the Ibgal ('Great Oval'), built the KI.NIR, (and) built the E.PA.

Heuzey, later followed by Cros, postulated that the main mud-brick terrace that formed the freshly raised mound on which the temple was built probably also featured staged

FIGURE 87. An inscribed door socket of Ur-Nanshe. Musée du Louvre AO252.

lower platforms. The reason for this was the significant height differences between contemporaneous constructions dating to the Early Dynastic period that were found in the central area and on the periphery, including stairways, cisterns and associated installations, particularly on the NE and SW edges of Tell K, and also along and within its sloping sides. For example, some 40 m to the north-east of the Ur-Nanshe Building, in an area referred to by Heuzey as Tell J (marked simply as J on Sarzec's Plan D; Fig. 34), Sarzec unearthed a large, bitumen-coated reservoir (described as a *piscine* or pool) and a neighbouring enigmatic structure: a small block of planoconvex fired bricks that were impressed with a single thumbprint (see Pl. 57 bis (2); Fig. 47) that securely dated them to the reign of Ur-Nanshe. The Tell J reservoir and the small block both stood at around the same Sarzec height of 10.8 m, about 2 m below the base level of Ur-Nanshe's pavement F. A second instance is provided by the landing on the Large Stairway by the Pillar of Gudea (noted on Sarzec's Plan D and Cros's Plan B), which was recorded at a Sarzec height of about 6.8 m, with the upper flight of steps rising a further 2 m to about the same level as the base of the Lower Construction. Finally, along the NE slope of Tell K, Cros's Double Stairway (in fact a series of superimposed Early Dynastic flights of steps) and the adjacent water supply network (all marked on Cros's Plan B), which almost certainly range in date from the reign of Ur-Nanshe through to the time of Urukagina, were exposed at comparable Sarzec heights of between 6.8 m and 8.8 m.

As these examples indicate, when Ur-Nanshe's new sanctuary is viewed as a composite whole, it becomes clear that it was built on a series of three stepped mud-brick platforms, each about 2 m high, that incorporated ceremonial stairways and embedded water supply and drainage installations, all made of fired bricks. The stairs and conduits were generally excavated near the edges of the massive stepped platforms, with the stairways on the outer surfaces of the slopes and the water channels and drains buried inside them, and they were found in a variety of areas and at a range of heights, with the lowest placed at a Sarzec height of around 6.8 m.

The Oval Enclosing Wall

Forest (1999, p. 25) persuasively argues that the higher parts of the entire tell were enclosed inside a huge curving wall, with a thickness of perhaps 3 m, that was a principal feature of the Tell K complex from the time of its construction under Ur-Nanshe to the end of the Early Dynastic period (*c*.2300 BCE), when the whole site, including all its buildings and installations and Ur-Nanshe's enclosing wall, were finally razed to the ground by Lugalzagesi (see Fig. 59). Constructed on the middle of the three mud-brick platforms, at a Sarzec height of around 10.8 m, the wall's SE corner is presumed to have run along the outside of the structure marked *Mur de construction plus récente* on Sarzec's Plan D, which in fact records the location of a fired-brick drain or water channel that was built into the mud-brick mass, probably in the reign of Enmetena. The inaccuracies relating to the description of the 'more recent' wall and its placement on Plan D are discussed above in detail with respect to Sarzec's photo (Pl. 58 bis (2); Fig. 50), but it should be stressed again here that the curving structure was in reality undoubtedly found further towards the south-east than it appears on the plan, closer to the marked position of the top of the Small Stairway. Along the enclosing wall's NE face, there was (Forest argues) an imposing chambered gate, marked *vestiges* on Plan D, that was approached via the Large Stairway that ascended from the bottom of the outermost platform. The combination of the stairs and the imposing gate created a monumental entranceway that ascended up the three platforms, giving access to the higher parts of the sacred site. The gatehouse and the stairway were both subsequently refurbished by Eanatum and Enmetena, respectively.

Based on the probable curve of the E corner, the enclosing wall's overall shape must have taken the form of an oval (or perhaps more accurately a rounded rectangle). Forest (1999, p. 23) also notes that the angle of the Tell J reservoir and its adjacent rectangular block near the N corner of the tell's middle platform (outside the unshaded area on Plan D) was turned a little towards the south or south-west, as can be seen on the plan, which indicates the curving path taken by the wall at this point. The Tell J reservoir and rectangular block are assumed to have been placed inside the wall (at a Sarzec height of about 10.8 m), and this makes it likely that the wall also framed a series of demarcated spaces, rooms and installations that abutted onto its inner face.

Why, though, did the excavators find no trace whatsoever of this massive structure that is supposed to have been maintained for about a century and a half until the very end of the Early Dynastic era? To be sure, it was made of mud-bricks, which Sarzec generally ignored, but Cros, who took more careful note of such remains, did not record further traces of it around the mound, other than those noted in the rectangular blocks by the Pillar of Gudea. In addition, close examination of Pl. 58 bis (2) suggests that the right-hand side of the photo shows the outer SE face of the mud-brick mass that formed the upper terrace, while the rise in the foreground represents what appear to be the levelled mud-brick remains of a large structure fronting the water channel. The most likely reason for the absence of more substantial remnants of the oval wall is that (as mentioned above and as is considered further below) it met the same fate as the rest of the structures on Tell K at the end of the Early Dynastic period, when it was deliberately destroyed by the invaders from Umma. This was a frequent occurrence in ancient Mesopotamia in the wake of a successful conquest, as is attested in many sources and described in a poetic lament that was written even as the invading army led by Lugalzagesi of Umma (and Uruk) was approaching Girsu (discussed in Chapter 20). One further factor is that, about two centuries after the wall had been levelled, Gudea built a fired-brick block (again recorded on Pl. 58 bis (2)) near the enclosing wall's original SE corner that seems to have been intended to support the side of the mound's upper terrace, which was then probably transformed into the commemorative monument that is considered in Chapter 21.

Ur-Nanshe's New Ningirsu Temple: Stratigraphic Problems

At the heart not only of the sacred complex itself but also of Girsu's general spiritual and civic renewal was Ur-Nanshe's new Temple of Ningirsu. Rising above and dominating the peripheral structures, it superseded its illustrious predecessor, while markedly proclaiming the importance of its heritage by incorporating a number of striking similarities into its design. The Lower Construction was accordingly echoed in the orientation and alignment of the Ur-Nanshe Building's walls, and reflected in the juxtaposition of the two unequally sized inner rooms. As in the Lower Construction, the smaller NW room (B on Sarzec's Plan C (1); Fig. 33) was the cella, while the larger space to the south-east (room A) was the trophy room or treasury. The core footprint of the structure being a little smaller than that of the older building, it occupied an area that measured about 8 m² less, with the difference mainly affecting the cella on the NW side. It can also be reasonably assumed that the general orientation of the Lower Construction was retained in the positioning of the principal access route (pavement F on Plan C (1)), in front of the cella.

Despite these apparent similarities, which express religious continuity and the permanence of the sacred, Ur-Nanshe's sanctum sanctorum adopted a dramatically changed architectural principle. Most obviously, unlike the Lower Construction, it was not semi-subterranean. Instead, it stood on top of the newly raised mound, which must almost certainly at that time have been the highest elevation in the vicinity, and it was whitewashed with gypsum or limestone, all of which made it into a landmark that must have been visible from a considerable distance. The sense of openness was further enhanced by the peristyle of wooden columns (marked H on Sarzec's Plan C (1)) that extended out on all sides, complemented on the NW side by the paved ceremonial approach (pavement F) that was the same width as the NW façade.

At this level, as was also the case lower down in the mound, any annexes or adjacent installations made of unbaked mud-bricks were reduced to dust with a few rapid blows of Sarzec's pickaxes, but much less survived of the Ur-Nanshe Building than of the Lower Construction, which had been carefully encased in its enclosing block, so that its walls were preserved to a recorded height of 2.85 m (as discussed at length above). In stark contrast, the Ur-Nanshe Building was eventually deconsecrated before being mostly demolished and reconstructed to create a replacement temple that was itself, in due course, also superseded. It is a blessing that the state in which the retained heights of the Ur-Nanshe walls were found incorporates a wealth of information about their prior history, but it is also a matter of regret that the same cannot be said for the later sequence of events that occurred between the time of Enmetena and the final razing of Tell K at the end of the Early Dynastic period.

This is because a critical problem affects any attempt at a precise reconstruction of events that took place between the time of the sealing of the Ur-Nanshe Building and the construction of the much later, Akkad wall that is marked *Mur* on Sarzec's Plan C (2) (Fig. 33). When Sarzec dug down from the base of *Mur* at the Sarzec height of about 14.5 m to the uppermost layer of bitumen on top of the Ur-Nanshe walls at a height of approximately 14.05 m (referring to the line marked DAE on Plan C (2)), he noted the discovery of some important artefacts, but gave no details whatsoever of any structural remains that had been deposited in this significant stratum. Yet, as is described below, three momentous occurrences took place in the time span represented by this hiatus in the stratigraphic record: first, Enmetena raised the mound and reconstructed the Ur-Nanshe Building; Urukagina then almost certainly renovated Enmetena's temple and also added to the top of the mound; and finally, at the end of the Early Dynastic period, the complex was razed to the ground by Lugalzagesi (Fig. 60). Sarzec, as has been stated many times, took little or no notice of mud-brick remains, so that any undestroyed traces of mud-brick walls built by Enmetena and Urukagina between the Sarzec heights of approximately 14.05 m and 14.5 m were presumably treated as though they were part of the general mass that made up the bulk of the mound, which was considered by Sarzec to be amorphous and unworthy of notice. To exacerbate the problem, any fired-brick or other structures that were built between these heights that Sarzec might potentially have considered to be significant were also torn down in antiquity by the hostile invaders from Umma. Consequently, there is a gap in the stratigraphic record that makes it extremely difficult to determine the sequence of events between the closing of the Ur-Nanshe Building and the construction of the Akkad wall *Mur* with any finality.

To clarify this a little further, when Sarzec started digging, the truncated walls of the Ur-Nanshe Building were no higher than 1.12 m, to which the sealing layers of bitumen and fired bricks added a further 0.1 m, altogether placing the levelling horizon at a Sarzec height of about 14.05 m, almost 3 m below the summit of the tell as it was when Sarzec began work in 1888. It is important to stress that the levelled walls did not result from the final razing of the reincarnated temple, as is detailed below. What is called, for convenience's sake, the Sarzec gap of about 0.45 m in the section on Plan C (2), between the sealing layer on top of the Ur-Nanshe building and the base of wall *Mur* at the Sarzec height of 14.5 m, includes a destruction horizon in which the only recorded finds were fragments of the Stele of the Vultures and other objects (some of which no doubt came from the temple) that were found purposely smashed and scattered. No trace was logged of the Urukagina walls that preceded the construction of wall *Mur*, but it is safe to say that they must have been placed around the height of the destruction horizon, as evidenced by the recorded heights of the stele fragments and other broken objects, while the only data relating to Enmetena's probable construction phase are the capped Ur-Nanshe walls. The key to understanding how events unfolded in the time frame represented by the Sarzec gap is therefore to collate the likely sequence in the central area of Tell K with stratigraphic evidence from other areas of the mound. Briefly stated, this suggests that Enmetena sealed and rebuilt the Ur-Nanshe temple as part of his extensive raising of the entire complex. Urukagina also elevated the sanctuary, though it seems likely that Enmetena's temple walls were not demolished at this stage, but the floors and thresholds could have been lifted to complement the new height of the top of the mound. Any inferred, probably mostly mud-brick remains that might have survived the final razing of the mound by Lugalzagesi, perhaps to heights of just a few centimetres, were sadly missed by Sarzec. Despite that, the ways in which events concealed by the Sarzec gap relate to finds made in other areas of the tell has often been overlooked or misunderstood by previous scholars, but those correlations provide clues to the stratigraphic puzzle that has impeded a fuller understanding of the Ur-Nanshe Building. Consequently, a thorough re-examination of the stratigraphy across the whole of Tell K facilitates the reconstruction of a general matrix for the entire temple complex.

Understanding the Ur-Nanshe Walls

From the outset, the lack of any mud-brick structures that could be associated with the Ur-Nanshe Building presented researchers with a problem because that absence was puzzlingly at odds with the composite character of the core walls, which were made of a planoconvex mud-brick core that was laid in a herringbone pattern and faced with fired bricks. A second anomaly was that no openings were found in any of the walls, but the discovery of door sockets and other door furnishings indicated that the walls must have been fitted with doorways. Regarding the problem of access, Heuzey (1900, pp. 8–9) presumes that the building was entered from above via mud-brick or wooden stairs. This was the solution he arrived at after relinquishing his earlier idea that the two protrusions (D and E on Plan C (1 and 2)), located at the levelling height on the SE and NW faces, somehow provided entry and exit points. As a result, however, he argues that the building must have been a granary or a storeroom for provisions (hence the familiar name, the House of the Fruits, or *Maison des Fruits*). This interpretation was also based on a misreading of some much later inscriptions in the name of Enmetena that were translated in 1887 by Amiaud, where the epithet used to designate the temple (actually not the Ur-Nanshe Building but a later iteration, as is explained below) was the 'sanctuary of the reeds of Ningirsu'. This led Heuzey to make the incorrect and anachronistic leap from 'reeds' to agricultural 'fruits' (see Heuzey 1900, pp. 2, 7 and 10).

In Forest's view (1999, p. 9), the plans that were drawn up using Sarzec's notes (Plan C (1and 2)) confuse two radically distinct construction phases, both carried out during Ur-Nanshe's reign, that were associated, respectively, with two structures (the original building and a comprehensive renovation) that were separated by nearly 1.2 m of infill. For Forest, the fired-brick walls that Sarzec took to represent the building's original ground plan were only added supports that were applied to bolster the mud-brick walls in order to allow them to serve as the foundation for a renovated temple. Conversely, Heuzey considered the fired bricks to be primary and the mud-bricks found inside the fired-brick facings to be later infillings of spaces he believed were originally internal corridors that ran around the two rooms. This is how the building is laid out on Sarzec's Plan C (1), where the unshaded areas represent interior voids. Reversing Heuzey's argument, Forest maintains that the mud-brick walls, which came first, were the walls of the original Ur-Nanshe Building, and that they filled the temple's interior with the exception of the spaces needed for the two rooms (A and B) that were separated by a thick partition (including the supposed niche marked C on Sarzec's plan, which was not a niche at all). The original mud-brick walls (Forest argues) were subsequently fitted with supportive fired-brick linings when the building was renovated, also by Ur-Nanshe.

In Forest's opinion, therefore, the mud-brick walls of the original Ur-Nanshe Building, which were found preserved to a height of about 1.12 m, and were nearly 0.8 m thick, delimited a rectangle of approximately 9.5 m × 6.25 m (making a total area of nearly 60 m²). An interior partition of the same mud-bricks subdivided the space to make two unequally sized rooms measuring 4.6 m × 4.6 m and 4.6 m × 2.3 m (covering areas of 21 m² and 10 m², respectively). The herringbone pattern exhibited by the mud-brick brickwork was common at the time in Sumer and very occasionally found elsewhere on Tell K, notably in the Well of Eanatum (though Heuzey does not record whether the mud-bricks in the Ur-Nanshe temple walls were laid vertically or horizontally). The brickwork projection that protruded from the NW side of the thick partition wall between the two rooms into the NW room (room B on Sarzec's plan) was the mud-brick podium that held the cult statue.

The renovators of this mud-brick building, Forest supposes, respected its outlines, but not its elevation. They installed fired-brick cladding around the original walls to the general levelling height of about 13.95 m on the Sarzec scale (12.83 m + 1.12 m). At the same time, they bricked in the bottoms of the doorways, which were now redundant, since the floor of the surmised new building had been raised, and that is why Sarzec did not find any openings in the building's levelled remains. The locations and dimensions of the first building's doorways can easily be reconstructed (Forest suggests) by following the outlines of the Lower Construction. They were on the long axis of the building, on the narrower NW and SE faces, and each was formed as a kind of vestibule that projected out from the building's core walls to serve as independent chambered rooms. Probably about 1.5 m wide, the openings must have had double-leaf doors. The two identical limestone door sockets—one collected in the SE room, and the other outside the building—must originally have belonged to one of these supposed doors, while the third socket, also found in the SE room, which was different from the other two, must have belonged to the other door.

As is considered in much greater detail below and in later chapters, Forest's and Heuzey's assumptions are both mistaken. The reason Heuzey cannot account for the mud-bricks found inside the fired-brick casings is because the original walls were almost certainly a thick composite that was made of both kinds of bricks. Accordingly, the supposed corridors illustrated on Plan C (1) did not exist because, except for the two rooms, the purported inner spaces were actually occupied by thick internal walls. Forest is right on this point, but wrong to suggest that the two kinds of bricks represented two construction phases. On the contrary, the fired bricks and the mud-bricks together formed the consolidated structural walls of Ur-Nanshe's original temple, which was subsequently renovated, but not under Ur-Nanshe as Forest supposes. As the stratigraphic analysis demonstrates, the renovation took place about a hundred years later, during the general refurbishment of the upper sacred complex that was carried out by Enmetena.

The Covered Gallery and Peripheral Corridor

The gallery or peristyle, which the surviving evidence suggests was an extremely rare, if not unique feature of Sumerian architecture, has been the subject of much debate, though it should be stressed in this regard that the Ur-Nanshe Building was by its very nature a pioneering construction (Fig. 88). In any event, there can be little doubt that the line of wooden pillars (H on Plan C (1)) demarcated a peripheral covered gallery that measured some 16 m × 19 m, making an area of approximately 310 m², including the footprint of the building itself. The fact that the pillar bases were regularly and symmetrically placed when Sarzec found them suggests that none were missing, but their spacing requires a further inference, which is that the covered gallery must have had walled corners made of mud-bricks, and almost certainly also some additional mud-brick walling in the middle of the two longer sides to the north-east and south-west.

The reason for this is that, as Heuzey (1900, p. 14) points out, the posts were arranged such that they could not by themselves have supported the colonnade's assumed roof. This is not only because the spans between them were considerable (7.4 m on the NW and SE sides; 10.5 m on the NE and SW sides), but most significantly because no pillar bases were found at the corners. The possibility that several lengthy cantilevers were somehow fitted to the sides and corners of the building must be categorically ruled out, which means (as Heuzey argues) that there must have been ground-based supports, certainly in the corners and probably also in the middle of the long walls. Since no supports were recorded, they must in all likelihood have been made of mud-bricks, unlike the pillar bases, which were built of square fired bricks. The supposition is therefore that mud-brick supporting walls were built in each of the four corners, and that there were probably also median supports in each of the two long sides. This presumes spans of the order of about 5 m between pillared and walled supports on the long walls, increasing to about 7 m on the NW side, where pavement F was the same width as the façade, and perhaps also (retaining the symmetry) on the SE side.

In addition, it should be noted that, as illustrated on Plan C (1), the pillar bases were systematically offset from the extension lines of the walls. Thus, the outer edges of the bases on the NE and SW sides of the building were not aligned with the axes determined by the walls, but seem rather to have been placed in the middle of, or possibly (for the N and S bases, in particular) outside those axes, while the bases on the NW and SE sides were located so that the notional extension lines of the walls met the middle of their inner edges. This indicates that the covered gallery was probably stabilised by a series of beams that projected out from the walls of the building and rested on the girder (or architrave) that was supported by the pillars, mud-brick corners and median mud-brick uprights.

If the space between the temple façades and the gallery walls is supposed to have been empty then the projecting beams (perhaps made of wood, like the columns, though they could just as well have been thickly bundled reeds) would each have had to be about 6 m long, which seems excessive. But this is unlikely because between the outer walls of the building and the lines marked out by the pillars (H) that define the outer edges of the covered gallery there was almost certainly an additional rectangle of mud-brick walls that surrounded the building to create an enclosed circumambulatory corridor, together with a series of secondary spaces between the corridor and the line of pillars that formed the outside of the gallery. Crucially, this mud-brick wall would also have provided an intermediary load-bearing structure between the temple walls and the architrave of the gallery, thereby reducing the required length of the projecting beams very considerably. The proposed intervening mud-brick structure was not detected by Sarzec, but it must have spanned about 11.5 m on the NW and SE sides and about 13.5 m on the longer NE and SW sides. The double cistern (G), which is marked on Plan C (1), close to the pillar (H) on the SE side of the building that is line with the building's SW façade, stood in the secondary void between the inside of the covered gallery and the exterior face of the assumed intermediary mud-brick wall. Indeed, the NW side of double cistern G (which was also eventually levelled) in all likelihood abutted directly onto the interposed mud-brick wall.

The Destruction of the Temple: The Catastrophic Fire Hypothesis

When Sarzec excavated the Ur-Nanshe Building he found that the two inner rooms were filled with ash, pieces of bitumen and charred bricks, and he also found some charred remains of wooden posts in the pillar bases (H) outside the

224 The Mound of the House of the Fruits

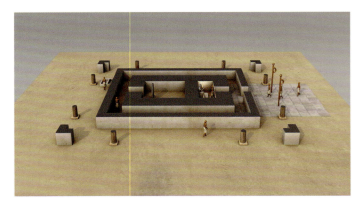

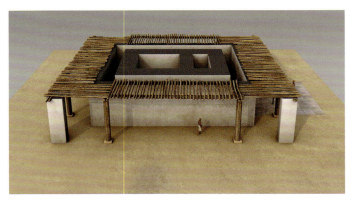

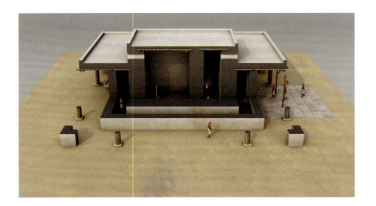

FIGURE 88. Four reconstructed views of the Ur-Nanshe Building, looking from the north-east and showing (from top to bottom): 1. the layout of the temple, with the cella and pavement F (right), the antecella (left) and the bases of the wooden pillars and mudbrick corners that supported the roof of the colonnade on all four sides; 2. the reed or wooden structure of the colonnade's roof; 3. the colonnade and lower level of the temple roof, presumably coated with bitumen and whitewashed; 4. a cutaway view of the finished temple.

building. As noted previously, Heuzey explicitly says that the posts, which were made of cedar, were square in shape like the bases, but this seems unlikely, not least because they must have been made of imported timber that was presumably delivered in the form of roughly cylindrical tree trunks, and also because it is not how their remains are drawn on Plan C (2), where they are shown as round. It should probably therefore be assumed that they were cylindrical columns with diameters of about 0.45 m. It must be stressed that it is not at all clear how much burnt wood was found (with one exception, it might have been hardly more than a few scraps), and it is impossible to be sure whether burnt residues were found in all the bases or just some of them. Nevertheless, these finds led Sarzec and Heuzey to suppose that the building must have been catastrophically destroyed by fire at the end of the Early Dynastic period, when the tell was eventually levelled. This mistaken point of view is addressed below, but it is worth noting immediately that there is a contradiction in Sarzec and Heuzey's account. They assume that the temple was destroyed by fire, and that its walls were reduced to a height of about 1.12 m (approximately 13.95 m on the Sarzec scale), but any actual evidence of a destruction horizon was found above this level in the Sarzec gap, as evidenced by the excavated fragments of the Stele of the Vultures and other objects, some of which came from inside the temple. Furthermore, traces of the inferred fire that they associate with the destruction horizon were also supposedly identified in the form of the ash and other burnt remains found inside the two rooms, but that ashy infilling was separated from the other objects that they think were damaged at the same time by a levelling layer made up of a bed of fired bricks and a coating of bitumen. Overall, the account is extremely confused and inconsistent, but that is hardly surprising since all the events that took place between the levelling of the remains of the Ur-Nanshe walls and the much later construction of wall *Mur* on Plan C (2) were swallowed up, from Heuzey and Sarzec's point of view, in the Sarzec gap and thus rendered indistinguishable.

Forest, who wholeheartedly embraces the fire narrative, takes it as the basis for an imaginative theory of construction phases, according to which the building burned down during Ur-Nanshe's reign and was immediately renovated, also by Ur-Nanshe, who rebuilt the temple—levelling, repairing and reinforcing the less-damaged bottom sections of the walls so that they could form a secure base for the replacement construction. The second Ur-Nanshe temple was conceived of by its architects not as an entirely new temple but as a comprehensive renovation, which is why (in Forest's view) Ur-Nanshe's immediate successors (his son, Akurgal, and grandsons, Eanatum and Enanatum I) seemingly left no commemorative inscriptions on bricks, door sockets, foundation deposits or elsewhere to record any construction work of their own on the site. It also explains the presence of seven slightly different bricks that were found in the W corner of the levelled base, alongside the bricks that were used to build the rest of the lower parts of the walls: some mud-bricks were doubtless reused, while the bricks for the fired-brick cladding were newly made, but in any case the seven bricks in the W corner that were inscribed in Ur-Nanshe's name were assuredly laid by his own bricklayers in the reconstruction phase. As is explained below, the placing of the excavated ritual objects and fixtures and fittings is far more convincingly accounted for when the detailed stratigraphy of Tell K more generally is taken into consideration, and there is similarly no reason to suppose that the seven bricks indicate a second construction phase. Despite these objections, the question of the fire is an important one that deserves serious reappraisal.

The first thing to say is that, although the two inner rooms were filled with burnt materials, the inner and outer walls showed no signs of having been burnt, scorched or blackened by soot. This is evident in Pl. 54 (1) (Fig. 39), where the entire SW façade can be clearly seen, as can parts of the building's interior. Little or no sign of fire would be expected on the inner face of the NW façade (on the left of the photo, where the long guy rope from Sarzec's tent seems almost to touch the NW wall) because the space seen in the photo (as Forest correctly thinks) would have been filled with the original mud-brick walls. Since Forest assumes that the mud-brick walls were later cladded, his theory is not impeded by the fact that no evidence of damage can be seen on the inside of the NW wall of the NW room (room B). But this clarification does not apply to Sarzec and Heuzey, who consider the fired bricks to be primary and could therefore have been expected to have paid attention to any fire damage to the walls inside room B, but none is recorded in the literature and none is visible in the photo.

The absence of relevant damage on the surviving walls could be explained by the surmise that the upper part of the building and the covered gallery caught fire, but that the flames did not envelop the whole structure, leaving the lower parts of the walls relatively unscathed. Although this changes the narrative from an absolutely calamitous fire to a very bad (or even just a fairly bad) one, there are reasons why it might have been the case. First, the most flammable parts of the structure would no doubt have been the roof of the main building, which was probably made of bituminated reed screens, and especially the higher parts of the covered gallery, including its roof (no doubt also made principally of reeds), with its projecting beams (made of reeds or wood), and the architrave (also made of reeds or wood) that ran across the tops of both the pillars and the proposed mud-brick portions of the gallery walls. Similarly, the cedar pillars would have been vulnerable, as would any reed screens (analogous with those presumably installed on the tops of the walls of the Lower Construction) that might perhaps have been incorporated into the vertical sides of the colonnade. In addition, the Ur-Nanshe Building's original walls were presumably at least as tall as the surviving sections of the equivalent walls of the Lower Construction, and they might therefore have been considerably taller than the top of the colonnade. That being the case, a fire that mainly affected the surrounding gallery and perhaps also the upper parts of the building would not necessarily have spread down to the lower sections of the walls.

Paying no attention to such details, Forest assumes the building was consumed by a disastrous conflagration and goes on to argue that, when the blaze subsided, the remains of the structure were shrouded in a heap of debris from the collapsed roof, upper walls and covered gallery. Trenches were then dug down to the level of the old floor (the top of pavement F) in order to access and repair the lower walls, fill the original doorways and install a fired-brick reinforcement layer to strengthen the old mud-brick walls so that they could serve as the foundation for the renovated temple. These supposed trenches, inside and outside all the original walls, gave access to the inner rooms, with whatever remained of their precious contents, and provided an opportunity for the two mismatched door sockets, which were doubtless (Forest thinks) rescued from the wrecked building, to be left in their unserviceable positions in the corners of the SE room. The copper blades that were found inside the building might have been deliberately placed as foundation deposits, though it is more likely, in Forest's view, that they were discarded in the excavated spaces inside the collapsed building and then inattentively covered when the trenches were refilled. The two rooms were filled with a mix of burnt remains, all of which could have come from the collapsed roof, including organic materials and bitumen, which would have been applied as a waterproofing agent.

Finally, the foundations were established and sealed with a coating of bitumen (0.05 m thick) and a bed of fired bricks (not marked on Sarzec's section on Plan C (2)), and the surrounding terrain was raised and levelled with the addition of several layers of mud-bricks. Exactly following the same ground plan as its burnt-down predecessor, a second Ur-Nanshe temple was then built, with a base (including the sealing layer) that was about 1.22 m higher than the base level of the older fire-damaged Ur-Nanshe Building, at a Sarzec height of about 14.05 m. Forest argues that the sealed leftover of the old building, newly lined with fired bricks, marked the level at which the new mud-brick walls began. The mound in the vicinity of the building having been now generally raised to the Sarzec height of about 14 m, he also assumes that the remnants of any nearby annexes or installations were cut down to the same height. The small fired-brick protrusions, D and E, were probably now installed at the new ground level on the SW and NE sides of the updated temple, and a new peripheral gallery was probably built. Nothing survived from the renovated temple; nor was any trace of the revised gallery found. The pillar bases (H) of the original gallery were buried in the mound when it was raised to the new levelling height of the supposedly restored Ur-Nanshe temple.

The Fire Reconsidered

The first problem with Forest's theory is that there is actually very little positive evidence for a devastatingly massive fire, though certainly some fire damage was found. As is argued in detail below, the ashy infills in the two rooms are far more readily explained as ritual deposits, comparable examples of which were found nearby on Tell A. Furthermore, the fact that Sarzec did not record any evidence whatsoever of flames having touched the walls, particularly the inner walls of the two rooms, together with the absence of evidence of any such damage on Pl. 54 (1), convincingly suggests that the fire that affected the original temple was probably not on anything like the scale presumed by Forest. It should also be re-emphasised that, unlike Forest, Sarzec did believe that the fired-brick layers found on the walls were part of the original construction and could therefore reasonably be expected to display signs of damage.

Doubts about the actual extent of the fire also have a bearing upon the two dissimilar limestone door sockets that were found in the SE room (Nos. 1 and 2 in room A on Sarzec's Plan C (1)), where they were stuck to the floor with bitumen, which was regularly used as an adhesive, not only for working accessories, but also for foundation tablets and other commemorative and dedicatory artefacts. These limestone fittings, which surely came from the original building, were not recorded as showing signs of fire damage, even though limestone is particularly susceptible to it. Nor were they found in functional locations because they were completely different in size and shape (one being hemispherical, the other conic), and also because their positions in the corners of the room would have meant that the entire SE wall (measuring 4.6 m) would have been taken up by a double door. This would definitely contradict the ground plan of the Lower Construction, which is reasonably supposed to have provided Ur-Nanshe with a template, and would make a nonsense of the placement of a stele inside the SE opening. On the contrary, therefore, the door sockets, which had almost certainly not been damaged by flames, were glued to the floor as foundation deposits, not during the reign of Ur-Nanshe but many decades later, as is argued below.

It is also unwarranted to argue that the fired bricks and mud-bricks found in the original walls were laid at two different times, and indeed there is every reason to suppose that the fired-brick layers and mud-brick cores were erected as part of the initial construction to create composite walls. The putative niche (marked C on Plan C (1)) that Heuzey takes to be set into the wall of the supposed passageway between the two rooms was actually the original podium that was built into the SE wall of the cella (room B), where the statue of Ningirsu was placed. Forest is right to say that the dentil-like interruption in the line of the SE wall of room B was a protrusion into the room rather than an outer recess because the imagined space between the rooms that is illustrated on Plan C (1) was not a walkway but a thick wall. He is again wrong to assume, however, that the ensemble of mud-bricks sandwiched by fired bricks was the result of two construction phases. In this regard, it is important to note that the composite formation of the walls that surrounded the innermost sanctum (the cella and the treasury) had a symbolic meaning as well as an architectural purpose: like a double skin or protective screen, the dual walls were intended to contain the power that emanated from the cult statue within. Comparable arrangements were not uncommon in Mesopotamian sacred architecture, and variants of the principle are commonly found in sacred buildings more generally, where the holiest spaces are very often physically and (or) symbolically set apart from the rest of the building in which they are housed.

Another source of fierce debate are the seven inscribed Ur-Nanshe fired bricks that were found, allegedly in a reused context, in an uppermost section of wall in the levelled Ur-Nanshe Building's W corner. The question of their archaeological provenance, and in particular whether or not they were found *in situ*, doubtless originates with Heuzey (1900, pp. 4–7), who is clearly confused about the association between the seven inscribed bricks and the overlying layer of smaller fired bricks (neither kind being explicitly illustrated in the section on Plan C (2)), all sealed with a coating of bitumen. Despite Heuzey's confusion, the seven Ur-Nanshe inscribed bricks were undoubtedly found in their primary context because they were intact, bonded with bitumen (like the rest of the wall) and well aligned with the facings of the surviving sections of the building's walls. Incidentally, the assumption that they were in a primary context would not be contradicted even by Forest's now rejected hypothesis, according to which all the fired bricks were part of the same phase. That their format was slightly different from that of most of the other contemporaneous fired bricks found nearby (though they were also planoconvex and marked with a single thumbprint) does not support the idea that they were strays from elsewhere that were reused in a tertiary context. Nor is it significant that six of the seven celebrated the construction of the 'shrine of Girsu' (èš.ĝír.sú), while the other one changed the ending of the dedication to the 'temple of Ningirsu' (é.^{d}nin.ĝír.su). These are some of the earliest-known inscribed commemorative bricks that have survived, and as previously noted, the Sumerian terms èš.ĝír.sú and é.^{d}nin.ĝír.su were interchangeable. Furthermore, their placement in the upper part of the walls that formed the W corner of the building is in accord with the find locations of inscribed bricks in the corners of many other buildings. It perhaps also reflects the special import of this part of the Lower Construction, where an elaborate foundation deposit was buried under the W corner in particular, as discussed in detail above.

Excursus: The Enmetena Renovation

A large part of the explanation for the condition in which Sarzec found the Ur-Nanshe Building, as illustrated (though not, of course, with perfect precision) on his Plan C (1 and 2), is that the original building was subsequently renovated. Working on the assumption that it was calamitously damaged by fire fairly soon after it was completed, Forest argues that it must also have been restored during Ur-Nanshe's reign, but the date can be more accurately estimated by comparing the stratigraphy of the central part of Tell K with that of other areas in the vicinity. This strongly indicates that the original Ur-Nanshe Building was kept in service for a period of about a hundred years until it was eventually renovated during the reign of Enmetena (*c*.2370–2335 BCE), who triumphantly once again re-established the state's territorial boundaries after his military exploits, thereby ushering in an era of peace and prosperity that was commemorated in a sweeping programme of construction and restoration at several locations in Girsu. The detailed stratigraphic evidence for this is considered in Chapter 19, but it is important to outline the signs of the deconsecration process and the preconstruction phase that can be attributed to Enmetena in the levelled structure.

Before the Enmetena renovation, the Ur-Nanshe Building, like the Lower Construction, undoubtedly had doors in its NW and SE façades. The bottom sections of these openings (below the levelling height) were blocked during the renovation phase (as also assumed by Forest). The procedure was not noticed by Sarzec, but that is perhaps unsurprising in view of the poor and untidy state of the walls—evident in the photos (Pl. 54 (1 and 2); Figs. 39 and 40). All the walls above the height of the blocked bottom sections of the doors were demolished, while the floors inside the two inner rooms (A and B), which had been cleared of their cultic artefacts, were filled to the levelling height. Prior to this, the two door sockets in the S and E corners of room A, which had been removed from their locations at the sides of one or both of the NW and SE entranceways, were glued to the original floor and ritually buried under the backfill.

The closing layers and subfloor packings inside the two rooms were fills made up of ash, bitumen and charred bricks, the compacted remains of which can be seen in the photos (particularly Pl. 54 (1)). Heuzey and Forest both interpret the mix as direct traces of a fire that had dramatically destroyed the entire temple, but this is unlikely, not only because the evidence of a fire on the scale suggested is scant, but also because the fill was not random. It was composed of bitumen sherds and pieces of burnt brick that were mixed with ashes that contained no recorded traces whatsoever of carbonised wood, reeds, larger fragments of other building materials or the remnants of any scorched or broken objects. This almost certainly demonstrates that the ash had been ritually sifted. In a procedure that was replicated in other excavated locations in Girsu, the rooms were filled with sanctified materials as part of the deconsecration of the original Ur-Nanshe Building prior to the construction of a newer instantiation of the temple above it. Having taken down the upper parts of the structure and blocked the openings at the bottom of the NW and SE walls, Enmetena laid foundation deposits in the decommissioned rooms and filled them with a ritually purified mixture. He then sealed the top of the truncated building in a manner comparable to that in which the Lower Construction had previously been capped by Ur-Nanshe. What was left of this when Sarzec uncovered the remains was a course of reused Ur-Nanshe bricks (of apparently slightly varying sizes) that were laid on a layer of bitumen that was 0.05 m thick. It should be noted again that the top of this capping layer stood at an overall Sarzec height of about 14.05 m, calculated by adding the heights of the truncated walls (1.12 m) and the capping layer (approximately 0.1 m in total) to the Ur-Nanshe base height of 12.83 m. As is discussed in Chapter 19, this was a little higher than the general elevation of Enmetena's raised mound (Fig. 60).

Other than the sealing layer, no traces of Enmetena's renewed temple were recorded because any walls he built were situated in the Sarzec gap in the section on Plan C (2) between the top of the old Ur-Nanshe walls and the base of *Mur*. The features that positively did survive—as noted in the reports—were a number of items inside and outside the building that were buried in the mound when Enmetena raised its level. They include the ritually buried artefacts that are detailed in Chapter 19, but also the brick pillar bases with their charred wood remains. That is undoubtedly why the pillar bases were all found *in situ*—untouched and well preserved, apart from the fire damage that was found on the wooden pillars themselves. The eight brick bases survived intact because they were interred in the mound by Enmetena when he reconstructed the temple. Whether the fire was the catalyst for the architectural project cannot, of course, be stated with certainty, but it might be a fair assumption.

As previously indicated, the Enmetena reconstruction was itself later refurbished by Urukagina towards the very end of the Early Dynastic period, though it is probable that Urukagina mostly retained Enmetena's walls, while raising the levels of the temple's thresholds and doors to bring them into harmony with the newly elevated summit of the mound more generally. The base of that final Early Dynastic temple, which was probably a fusion of the buildings constructed by Enmetena and Urukagina, must have stood at a Sarzec height of around 14.33 m (or possibly a little higher, as considered in Chapter 20), in the Sarzec gap between the sealed top of the Ur-Nanshe Building and the fragment of Akkad wall marked *Mur* on Plan C (2). In common with all the other structures and installations on the site, including the massive enclosing wall built by Ur-Nanshe, the Urukagina temple was razed to the ground by Lugalzagesi towards the end of the Early Dynastic period, during Urukagina's reign (*c*.2316–2307 BCE). One tangible sign of that final destructive levelling, which is discussed further below, is the pitiful state in which the Stele of the Vultures was found. Commissioned by Eanatum (*c*.2420–2390 BCE) to commemorate his resounding victory over Umma, it postdates Ur-Nanshe, but was almost certainly installed in the trophy rooms (later equivalents of room A on Plan C (1)) of successive temples to Ningirsu from the reign of Eanatum through to the Urukagina temple. Unlike its counterpart in the Lower Construction, which was ritually processed by Ur-Nanshe when the building was decommissioned, the Stele of the Vultures was purposely desecrated by Lugalzagesi, the conqueror of Lagash, who smashed it into pieces that were then scattered around the tell.

The Ur-Nanshe Objects and Temple Installations

The base of the floor on which the truncated walls of the Ur-Nanshe Building stood was 12.83 m, as calculated by Sarzec and marked on the section on Plan C (2). According to the plan, the Ur-Nanshe base height was the same for the bottom of the levelled temple, the underside of pavement F, which extended out from the temple's NW façade, and the bottoms of the brick bases of the wooden pillars (H) that were part of the surrounding peristyle or covered walkway. An exceptional hoard of artefacts was uncovered at or around this level, including the genealogical plaques and other dedicatory and commemorative objects associated with Ur-Nanshe, together with a number of more ancient sculptures and cult accessories: the Feathered Figure, the copper remains of a substantial ring post, two copper bulls' heads and a number of lions' heads made of stone. Since the time of Heuzey, the general consensus has been that this diverse inventory of artefacts was probably housed in the Ur-Nanshe Building's two rooms or displayed elsewhere inside the temple complex, before later being removed and dispersed when the site was ransacked. There can be no doubt that most of the artefacts found at this level were indeed featured in Ur-Nanshe's original construction, but their subsequent history was quite different from the one that has been widely retold, as is argued in Chapter 19. One reason why this has not been noticed is that, as previously mentioned, the precise archaeological contexts of many of the items found near the level of the Ur-Nanshe base were oversimplified by Heuzey when he compiled the concluding instalment of *Discoveries in Chaldea* (1912). In general terms, he seems to place them indiscriminately at the Ur-Nanshe base level, but his detailed descriptions paint a much more nuanced picture, according to which some were found slightly above or below the level of pavement F, as has been highlighted with respect to the enigmatic cache of eight archaic tablets discussed in Chapter 15, or the Colossal Spear Head that was mistakenly said to have been found above the height of the Ur-Nanshe horizon. Other artefacts were uncovered in a range of very different settings: in a compact mass of mud-bricks, on pavement F, and in a deposit of black soil, to name three examples.

Furthermore, it is important to note that none of the objects that were recorded as having been found at the Ur-Nanshe base level were actually found inside the Ur-Nanshe Building's main walls. On the contrary, all of them were uncovered inside the confines of the adjacent space that was delimited by the square bases of the wooden pillars (H) that formed the peristyle. As argued above, this space doubtless included an intermediate mud-brick wall that ran between the outer walls of the building and the sides of the covered gallery, where it created an enclosed circumambulatory corridor and a series of secondary spaces, and also acted as a support for the gallery's roof beams.

Three additional installations were uncovered within the Ur-Nanshe horizon in the vicinity of the temple: the two cisterns and attached blocks (IJ and KL), and an associated channel (M) that were all found about 8 m east of the building's NE wall (therefore outside the covered gallery), but on the extended Ur-Nanshe terrace platform at a Sarzec height of about 12.83 m. Made of planoconvex fired bricks that were impressed with the thumbprint that was Ur-Nanshe's regnal mark, the cisterns and blocks had been levelled and sealed with a layer of bitumen. Channel M, which sloped down towards the north-east and was embedded in the fabric of the upper mud-brick platform, probably near its outer edge, was more or less aligned with the inferred chambered gateway that was a feature of the substantial oval wall that surrounded the complex and the Large Stairway by the Pillar of Gudea, which were placed, respectively, on the two lower platforms that made up Ur-Nanshe's three-stepped mound. It therefore seems reasonable to suppose that the monumental ascent from the Large Stairway through the chambered gateway in the oval temenos wall was completed by a further stairway, probably adjacent to (and following the line of) channel M, that gave access to the topmost central area of the tell. This would have referenced and emphasised the principal NE–SW approach axis to the commanding upper level, and would also have meant that the water supply and drainage facilities could be installed in the same stepped incline as the stairways. A comparable arrangement of stairways and adjacent, ancillary cisterns and water channels was found by Cros in Trenches 6 and 7.

The Genealogical Plaques of Ur-Nanshe

The primal significance of the Feathered Figure is discussed above, and the circumstances of its interment in the sacred ground of Tell K are addressed in Chapter 19, where the ring post and animal sculptures found in the Ur-Nanshe horizon are similarly scrutinised, because these artefacts were in all likelihood processed and deposited by Enmetena when the Ur-Nanshe Building was deconsecrated. Of immediate importance for an understanding of the momentous changes brought about in Lagash by Ur-Nanshe are the Ur-Nanshe Plaques, which were presumably installed in the temple itself (in the main rooms or in the temple complex) as a way of cementing Ur-Nanshe's claims to power, boosting his personal and regal prestige, and elevating the status of his sons, including his nominated successor.

The Ur-Nanshe Plaques (Fig. 89), also known as the genealogical reliefs, are part of the rich ideological apparatus that was utilised by the founder of the First Dynasty to legitimise his wide-ranging programme of political and religious reforms. Ur-Nanshe fundamentally reshaped the politico-religious fabric that was an inalienable part of every aspect of life in Lagash, but he also wished to validate his sovereignty and his rightful claim to the throne, and to establish a long-lasting legacy by ensuring that the kingship would henceforth be passed by hereditary right through the male line—the agnatic principle being confirmed by the dramatis personae on the reliefs. The constellation of intentions was supported on the carvings through the mention of Ur-Nanshe's father and his place of birth (Gursar), together with portrayals of his sons and select courtiers (and possibly his wife or daughter in one instance, though this suggestion is refuted below). With the presumed backing of the gods, the aim was to create a personal and historical narrative framework that would underpin the foundation of an Ur-Nanshe dynasty. As far as is currently known, the idea that the succession of power could become the birthright of the sons of reigning rulers was, at the very least, uncommon in ancient Sumer, but little or no evidence survives.

Four plaques were unearthed. As discussed above, Plaques A, B and C (AO2344, AO2345 and EŞEM401) were discovered by Sarzec to the west of the Ur-Nanshe Building in 1888 (A and B) and 1889 (C); the fourth, Plaque D (EŞEM1633), which was also excavated by Sarzec, was not published in either of the early studies (Heuzey 1900; and Sarzec and Heuzey 1912), and its archaeological context is unknown. Made of white limestone, the carved plaques are all perforated in their centres with a circular hole (with diameters ranging between 0.04 m and 0.05 m) that probably allowed them to be fixed to one of the inner walls of the Ur-Nanshe Building, conceivably with some kind of peg. Carved in bas-relief, their representational contents depict Ur-Nanshe with his sons and some court dignitaries, including his cup-bearer, chief snake charmer and chief scribe. The names and titles of the figures are mostly included in the accompanying inscriptions (though some names have been lost), together with a commemorative text that records Ur-Nanshe's construction of several temples: first and foremost, the sanctuary of Ningirsu on Tell K, or the House of Ningirsu, as it is referred to.

Although at first glance the four votive plaques seem rather similar to each other in appearance (especially Plaques A and D), they differ in detailed ways that make them all unique.

The New Sanctuary: The Ur-Nanshe Building 231

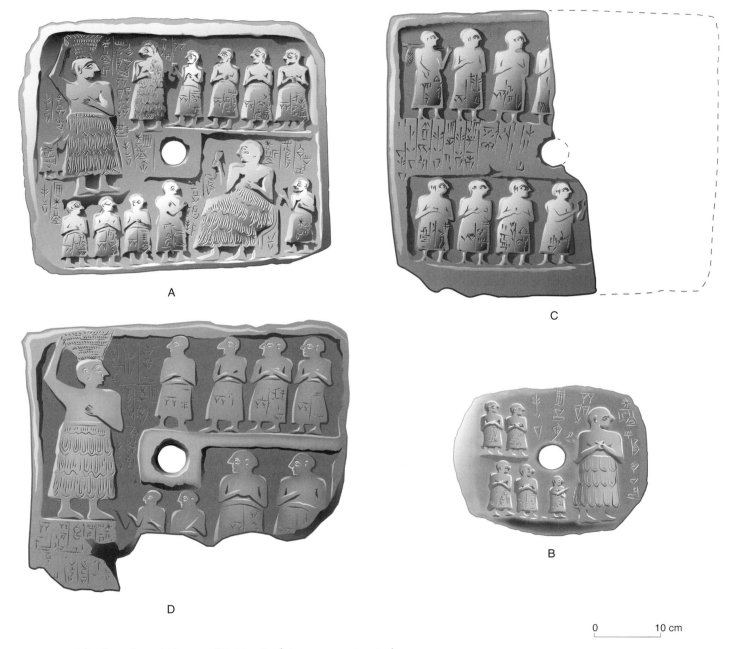

FIGURE 89. The Genealogical Plaques of Ur-Nanshe (Plaques A, B, C and D).

The variety, which was undoubtedly intentional, cannot be ascribed to technical shortcomings on the part of their makers. Three plaques (A, C and D) are rectangular, while one (B) can be described as roughly oval. Since this is the only known example of an oval (or nearly oval) Early Dynastic votive plaque, it is evident that Plaque B must have been reworked before its final decommissioning, and this is further confirmed when its shape and condition are compared with its more conventional counterparts. Indeed, as detailed in the discussion of Plaque B's condition in Chapter 19, the scene as it is known today almost certainly represents only about a quarter of the original carving because significant portions to the right and above the existing oval were deliberately (or perhaps accidentally) removed. The rectangular plaques all measure approximately 0.4 m (h) × 0.5 m (w), though the half-preserved one is proportionally smaller because it has been irregularly broken or cut down along a more or less vertical line that runs through the central perforation. The oval one is notably smaller, measuring 0.23 m (h) × 0.29 m (w). Their thicknesses differ: Plaque A is 0.065 m thick; B and C are 0.07 m and 0.08 m thick, respectively; Plaque D, which is the thinnest, is just 0.04 m thick. The edges of all the plaques are unevenly worked (though some of the irregularities are perhaps partly due to erosion or accidental breakage), and it seems that each of the carved scenes was originally framed with a narrow raised border that ran all the way around its edge. The thickness of the relatively well-preserved frame on Plaque A is variable: markedly thinner at the bottom, it is thickest on top and around the top left corner. Only the bottom band of the frame of Plaque B (the oval) remains, along with vestiges of the left vertical, where the approximately rectilinear protrusion seems generally to have been cut back so that the carved scene sits proud of it. The thin fringe of unworked stone that is visible in this area was conceivably covered with plaster when the plaque was reattached to a wall after it had been cut down and remodelled. The bottom edge of the surviving half of Plaque C is apparently unfinished below the frame, which is seemingly thicker along this side than on the left and above. Interestingly, the wide central band of inscriptions that runs horizontally across the plaque, separating the upper and lower registers, merges with the frame on the left edge, where the writing extends into the border. This differs from Plaque A, where the floor of the upper scene on the right, which acts as a dividing line between two interlocking registers, is clearly separated from the adjacent vertical frame. The border of Plaque D, which is very badly damaged, survives only as a thin line above the relief on the upper edge, especially towards the top left corner, though even here the traces are extremely faint. The central perforation in Plaques A and D, both of which show Ur-Nanshe carrying a basket on his head, is bordered with a frame that is carved in relief, while the hole in Plaque C might not have been framed, but the area is so damaged that it is impossible to be sure—in any event, the perforation is placed in the middle of the raised wide band of inscriptions that separates the upper and lower registers. The perforation in Plaque B, the reworked oval, is unframed and placed on the flat background so that the carved tableau projects out above it. The placement of Plaque B's perforation is deceptive, however, because of the extent to which the original was cut down. As argued in the discussion of its condition in Chapter 19, the existing hole is probably a later addition.

On all the plaques the figures emerge in relief from a background that is plain except for the incised inscriptions, and they are arranged in two registers that are separated by raised bands of varying breadths: narrow on Plaques A and B; wide on Plaque D; and extremely wide on Plaque C. In all the scenes (probably including Plaque C, where he was presumably placed in the missing half) Ur-Nanshe is oversized, and in all cases he interrupts the registers, which are, so to speak, too small to contain him. This creates a noticeable pattern on Plaque A, where the upper divider (the floor under the feet of the smaller figures at the top on the right-hand side) and the lower divider on the left (the floor on which the oversized figure of Ur-Nanshe is placed) are visually connected by the frame of the central hole to create a stepped or interlocking effect. In all cases, the ruler, who is clean shaven, bald and bare chested, wears a long kaunakes or ceremonial skirt that is formed of lanceolate tufts, while the caption that identifies him is always carved by his side and never on his person or clothing (though the patterned skirt would have made this unlikely in any event). The other figures are also mostly bald and clean shaven, and their hands are generally clasped in front of their bare chests in attitudes of attentiveness or prayer. The subsidiary figures' baldness and lack of beards stresses their priestlike piety and reverence, though whether that is also the implication of the king's appearance is less clear, except on Plaque B, where he is portrayed with the same joined hands as the worshippers behind him. With one preserved exception, the lesser characters all wear plain skirts fastened with belts that are seemingly tied behind their backs, and they all have their names and titles inscribed on the skirts' plain fronts.

Plaque A, which measures 0.4 m (h) × 0.47 m (w) × 0.065 m (t), depicts Ur-Nanshe carrying a basket on his head that is presumably filled with bricks: about ten parallelogram-like blocks can be seen emerging from it at the top, where they radiate outwards, extending the angled lines of the two sides of the receptacle. The fact that the forms sticking out of the basket represent finished bricks excludes the possibility that the sculptors intended to show Ur-Nanshe carrying the wet clay that was used to mould the first brick that was laid in the temple walls: a ceremonial component of the preparatory rituals that were carried out before the construction work got under way, as described on Gudea's Cylinder A. In the Gudea Cylinder Inscriptions the ruler also carries a basket of bricks on his head, and it is expressly compared to a crown (A20): 'Gudea, in charge of building the house, placed on his head the carrying-basket for the house, as if it were a holy crown'. The same association is undoubtedly present in the portrait of Ur-Nanshe on Plaques A and D, where the symbolic 'holy crown' adds to the ruler's physical stature, but most importantly, as in the later Gudea text, confirms his status as the chosen instrument of the god's will.

The small figure behind the ruler is one of his sons, Anita, who raises a spouted vessel in order to pour a libation. Anita's feet are placed at the level of the hem of Ur-Nanshe's skirt, while the ruler's feet are on a narrow floor or ledge that separates him from the register below. Facing him on the upper register, which is subdivided into two levels, are the other individuals who are taking part in the ceremony. The first figure in the line, who looks towards Ur-Nanshe with his or her hands clasped in the conventional attitude of prayer or reverence, is quite a lot taller than the ones behind, but the extra height is generally incorporated into the upper register by the lower placement of the floor on which he or she is standing. This person, whose name (ÁB.d[a]?) is unclear, wears a robe that is similar to the king's skirt except that it has five lines of lanceolate flounces (compared to three on Ur-Nanshe's kaunakes) and it includes an upper piece that covers the left shoulder and falls to just below the left forearm. Above the figure's head is a sort of crestlike form (similar to a cockerel's comb) that is formed of carved oblique hatching. Shrouding the back of the head, it does not cover the person's ear, and it seems to get wider as it descends past the back of the neck onto the shoulder. The relief is so badly damaged at this point that it is very difficult to know whether the shape is supposed to represent long hair or a kind of hood, though in any event it seems distinctly different from the upper part of the garment, so the two are presumably not supposed to be joined. This enigmatic individual has been variously identified as the ruler's daughter or wife, a diviner or even as a military officer, since shawl-like garments are worn by soldiers in other carvings, for example by Eanatum when he leads the army into battle on the Stele of the Vultures. The idea that the person portrayed might have been a woman can be ruled out with a high degree of confidence on two grounds: first, it is hard to see why the king's wife or daughter would be shown on a carving of this nature—above all in this sacred context—with her breast bared, unless she were depicted nursing a child (perhaps in a semi-legendary setting, as Nanshe is said to have suckled Eanatum in the text inscribed on the Stele of the Vultures, for example); and secondly, because the purpose of the genealogical theme that runs through the plaques (most notably on A and D) is almost certainly to establish the transmission of the kingship through the male line. In consequence, for reasons of policy, the figures on the plaques are shown as—and in most cases explicitly identified as—men or boys, making the presence of a woman extremely difficult to account for. The other possibility, which is probably the correct one (as discussed further below), is that the enigmatic figure was Ur-Nanshe's first-designated successor, who might have been subsequently killed in battle and replaced as crown prince by Akurgal, another of his sons (see Tunca 2004, pp. 22–3). It should be stressed that the identification of the enigmatic figure must depend on an overall interpretation of the meaning of the scene because the significations of the Sumerian characters that name him are ambiguous.

The four individuals behind the enigmatic figure, all facing Ur-Nanshe, are also sons of the king. Named Akurgal, Lugalezem, Anikura and Mukurshubata, they are depicted from left to right in order of increasing size, perhaps according to their ages, though it is not immediately clear how that would tally with the fact that the smallest of them, Akurgal, eventually became Ur-Nanshe's successor, unless the others perhaps all died prematurely, or unless the hereditary principle was not based on seniority, which is practically unimaginable. In this regard, it should be recalled that the carvings were presumably made towards the beginning of Ur-Nanshe's long reign, probably around the time of the construction of the Ur-Nanshe Building. Many decades therefore elapsed before Ur-Nanshe eventually died, leaving Akurgal to be installed as ruler, and that intervening history, comprising most of Ur-Nanshe's kingship, could not by definition have been taken into account when the reliefs were sculpted. The size order of the figures is inverted in the line of figures who face the seated king on the lower register, where the taller ones are at the front. Though some of them are also Ur-Nanshe's sons, they are all different people from the persons shown in the upper register, and it might be that the two at the back of this group were represented without any concern for realism or even symbolism, but purely in order to fit them into the space below the feet of the outsized form of Ur-Nanshe on the register above (on the left). Akurgal, who leads the line on the upper register, has long hair that is gathered at the back of his head in a flattened double chignon tied with a band. He is holding a spouted vessel, and is perhaps intended to be shown flanking the enigmatic figure in front of him—the further inference being that the two might both be involved in the depicted ceremony, together with Ur-Nanshe and Anita (all of which is considered at greater length below).

In the lower register the ruler is seated on the right, facing leftwards, and he raises a beaker in his right hand, possibly indicating that the scene shows a banquet celebrating the temple's inauguration. The smaller figure behind him, who is holding another spouted vessel (making three altogether), is an individual named Sangdingirtuku, who is not described as a son of the king. In front of the ruler stands Balul, the chief snake charmer, who is taller than the figures behind him. He has his right arm bent, with his open hand raised almost to the height of his shoulder, while his left arm is placed across his chest. He might perhaps be shown in the act of singing a hymn or reciting some words (conceivably a eulogy, though that is purely speculative) because his posture echoes that of figures in Early Dynastic banquet scenes that include depictions of musicians. It is, of course, highly likely that a celebratory feast would have been accompanied by music, and this might confirm the meaning of Balul's gesture as one of performance rather than some other kind of service. Behind him are three more of Ur-Nanshe's sons, named (from right to left) Anunpa, Menusu and Addatur.

The scene on Plaque B (the oval), which measures 0.23 m (h) × 0.29 m (w) × 0.07 m (t), shows all the figures facing to the right with their hands clasped at their chests, except for the smallest one, Anita, who is raising a spouted vessel, as on Plaque A, though in this case he is not specifically referred to as Ur-Nanshe's son (dumu in Sumerian). Anita stands behind the oversized figure of Ur-Nanshe, who is almost as tall as the plaque's two registers combined, and about twice the height of the individuals behind him. The person immediately behind Anita on the lower register is Akurgal, who is named as the king's son, while another son, Lugalezem, appears on the upper register, though without the designation dumu. Lugalezem is followed by Gula (yet another son, though again not titled as such in this instance) and Barasagnudi, who is possibly a member of the king's court. As is considered in detail in Chapter 19, the scene on Plaque B, which is clearly incomplete, lacks about three-quarters of its original content, but it probably depicted one or more ceremonies relating to the inauguration of the temple as the abode of the god.

Eight figures are preserved on the surviving half of Plaque C, which measures 0.45 m (h) × 0.3 m (w) × 0.08 m (t), and they are all facing to the right, possibly looking at the lost figure of Ur-Nanshe, who was probably much larger than the rest, such that his image must have broken through the broad central dividing band between the two registers. A small corner of his skirt can perhaps be made out on the lower register. The figures all hold their hands in the conventional Sumerian attitude of worship, apart from Hursagshemah, on the far left of the upper register, who is shown holding a long stick in his left hand (resting on his left shoulder) that has a reticulated object shaped like a teardrop dangling from it, and Anita, on the right of the bottom register, who is again holding a spouted vessel that can be associated with a libation ritual. The half-figure on the right of the upper register is Awilkinatim, who is not recorded as being a son of Ur-Nanshe, unlike the two immediately behind him, Lugalezem and Mukurshubata (from right to left), who are both named as sons. Figures carrying sticks to which hanging objects are fixed are relatively common in Early Dynastic art, and they are regularly found in scenes of banquets and ceremonies, often in conjunction with men carrying vessels and boxes. The stick might be an emblem of trade or the spoils of war, in which regard it is worth noting that the plaque's inscription mentions the transportation of wood from the distant land of Dilmun (discussed further below). On the lower register, behind Anita, who is acting as cup-bearer, is Balul, the chief snake charmer, who is not referred to as a son. Behind him comes Ur-Nanshe's son Akurgal, and bringing up the rear is Namazu, the chief scribe.

Plaque D, which measures 0.43 m (h) × 0.495 m (w) × 0.04 m (t), again shows Ur-Nanshe carrying a basket on his head, doubtless as part of the preconstruction rites for the shrine. In this instance no bricks are visible, though it is difficult to say whether that is simply because the top of the stone above the basket is damaged. Facing the king are eight males on two registers, all displaying the same attitude of devoutness, except for the first of the two very small figures below the frame of the central hole. He carries a spouted jug and can again tentatively be identified as Anita, despite the fact that his inscribed skirt is missing. Unlike on Plaque A, he is facing Ur-Nanshe. The four men shown on the upper register, who are all explicitly referred to as sons, are divided into two groups: a single figure, Lugalezem, and a trio behind him and slightly separated from him, named as Anikura, Mukurshubata and Akurgal. The arrangement of the single figure with respect to the group behind him compares reasonably closely with Plaque A (with the notable absence of a cup-bearer on Plaque D), although the separated individual in this case is not noticeably bigger than the others, and he is not differently attired. Since the skirts of the figures on the bottom register are missing, their names have been lost apart from the third one from the left (after the two diminutive individuals below the frame of the central perforation), and he is named as Ur-Nanshe's son Gula.

As noted above, the subsidiary figures have their names and titles inscribed on their skirts, but Ur-Nanshe's name is consistently placed on the background with the rest of the commemorative text. All the plaques refer to Ur-Nanshe as the king (lugal) of Lagash and the son of Gunidu, while on Plaques A and D, where he is shown carrying the basket on his head, he is also called the 'son of Gursar', which is the name of his birthplace. Plaques A and D record that wood has been brought from Dilmun at the behest of Ur-Nanshe, who 'had ships of Dilmun submit timber as tribute from the foreign lands (to Lagash)'. All the plaques name Ur-Nanshe as the builder of the Temple of Ningirsu, and he is additionally credited with the construction of the Abzubanda (the Little Fountainhead) and the Nanshe temple on all of them except for Plaque B (the oval). Plaques C and D specifically record that he built the Sheshgar, the Temple of Nanshe in Girsu.

Of the other characters, Akurgal and Lugalezem are mentioned on all the plaques, while the name of Anita (the cup-bearer) is only missing from Plaque D, but it was almost certainly recorded on his lost skirt. The name of Mukurshubata is shown on all the plaques except for Plaque B; Balul, the chief snake charmer, is named on Plaques B and C (the half-plaque); Anunpa and Anikura are named only on Plaques A and D, which show Ur-Nanshe carrying his basket; Sangdingirtuku, Menusu, Addatur and the enigmatic figure (ÁB.d[a(?)]) are named only on Plaque A. Gula is mentioned on Plaques D and B, while Barasagnudi's name only appears on Plaque B. Lastly, Namazu (the chief scribe), Awilkinatim and Hursagshemah are attested only on the preserved half of Plaque C.

Some suggestions can tentatively be made about three of the most frequently named individuals on the Ur-Nanshe Plaques: Akurgal, Lugalezem and Anita (see Romano 2014 for a recent discussion that reaches different conclusions). The first two are named on all the plaques, and it is generally accepted that Akurgal, whose reign was short, ascended to the throne after Ur-Nanshe's death. On Plaque A the enigmatic figure (ÁB.d[a(?)]) who stands in front of Ur-Nanshe on the upper register can most plausibly be identified as his chosen successor, the crown prince. That is presumably why he is set apart from the figures behind him by his clothes, which compare to the kaunakes worn by the king, and his size: he is placed on his own individual floor (as it were) and he is quite a lot bigger than all the other secondary figures. On Plaque D this key position is taken by Lugalezem, who stands slightly apart from his three brothers behind him, including Akurgal, who is at the back of the group. This might well indicate that the enigmatic figure, possibly Ur-Nanshe's firstborn son, was nominated as the king's successor, but subsequently died, perhaps killed in battle, as argued by Tunca (2004, pp. 22–3; see Romano 2014 for some alternative views). That being the case, he was in all likelihood replaced by Lugalezem, who was doubtless alive when all four carvings were made, as evidenced by the fact that he is portrayed on all of them. This would imply that, chronologically, Plaque A was made before Plaque D, and that D was commissioned as a replacement following the death of the crown prince, the enigmatic figure shown on A.

This inferred chronology would also account for some of the similarities and perhaps also the differences between the two plaques. The upper registers, which show Ur-Nanshe with his crownlike basket of bricks facing a group of his sons, including a surmised designated successor, are very nearly the same. The lower register of Plaque A includes a scene that has been interpreted as a ceremonial banquet, but this has been replaced on Plaque D by another line of praying figures (whose names have been lost apart from the king's son Gula on the far right), and the change might conceivably have been made in response to the death of Ur-Nanshe's presumed eldest son. That would help to account for the change on the lower registers from a scene of celebration on Plaque A, including the inferred performance given by Balul, to an atmosphere of greater solemnity on Plaque D. It might also be hypothesised that the reason why Lugalezem is more plainly dressed on Plaque D than the enigmatic figure on Plaque A is that the less elaborate clothing was an implicit acknowledgement of the fact that being named as crown prince did not guarantee a future accession to the throne.

In other words, the dress (and the size) of the enigmatic figure seem definitively to place him in the same category as Ur-Nanshe, whereas the clothes of Lugalezem, together with his size, which is closely comparable to that of his brothers behind him, indicate that his status is still necessarily provisional.

In the event, for reasons that cannot be known, Lugalezem did not actually succeed his father, and that honour fell to Akurgal, who is named on all the plaques. Romano (2014, pp. 188–91) envisages a power struggle between the two sons, though there is nothing specific in the iconographic evidence to support the idea. As previously noted, however, the order of the sizes of the figures on the upper register of Plaque A might suggest that Akurgal is a younger brother (and not an anointed crown prince), and this might be confirmed by the fact that, like Anita, he is also shown holding a spouted vessel. One highly plausible inference is that he is acting as cup-bearer to his surmised elder brother, the enigmatic figure (ÁBd[a(?)]), just as Anita is cup-bearer to the king. This would endorse the idea that all four are taking part in a ceremony (perhaps of investiture) and corroborate the correspondence between the king and the crown prince, and it would also identify Akurgal and Anita as younger brothers. The relative youth of Akurgal might be further confirmed by the fact that, on Plaque D, he is placed at the back of the line of brothers who are shown standing behind Lugalezem, while only one cup-bearer is shown on the same carving: the small figure facing the king on the lower register, who might again cautiously be identified as Anita, even though his skirt containing his inscribed name is missing. Many of these matters are unavoidably speculative, but the clear correspondences and divergences between Plaques A and D provide some convincing circumstantial evidence of a provisional chronology and order of succession.

Finally, a closer examination of the figure of Anita might contribute a little more to an understanding of the order in which the Ur-Nanshe Plaques were made. On Plaques A and B (the cut-down oval), he is shown in exactly the same position relative to his father (standing directly behind him), and he is about the same size on both plaques. His diminutive stature is a little deceptive on Plaque A, where he stands on his own raised platform, but if his feet were placed at the same level as those of Ur-Nanshe then the top of his head would be roughly in line with the bottom of the uppermost row of flounces on the king's kaunakes. He is a little shorter on Plaque B (where his feet are again positioned somewhat higher than those of Ur-Nanshe), but if they were on level ground, his head would reach at least as far as the bottom of the middle row of lanceolate flounces. These similar portrayals contrast markedly with the way he is depicted on the broken Plaque C, where he is shown standing in line with two members of the king's court (Balul the snake charmer, who is immediately behind him, and Namazu the scribe at the back of the group) and his brother Akurgal, who is placed between the two functionaries. Standing at the front of the line, Anita is distinguished from the rest only by the fact that he is again acting as the cup-bearer in whatever ceremony was recorded on the lost half of the relief, while the figures behind him are all shown with their hands clasped in front of their chests. Otherwise, he is physically identical to the people who complete the group: he is depicted in precisely the same manner, and no longer distinguished by his reduced stature. The imagery on the carvings is not, of course, intended to be realistic as that word is now understood, but the changed iconography of Anita's portrayal makes it plausible to suppose that he is bigger and therefore older on Plaque C than he is on Plaques A and B. That being the case, it can tentatively be proposed that there was a time lag between the carving of Plaques A and B, which were (it might be further surmised) produced as a pair when the temple was inaugurated, and the making of Plaque C, which came later. Apart from the fact that it is later than Plaque A (and therefore almost certainly later than B), it is difficult to estimate precisely where Plaque D would fit into the order of making, especially as the cup-bearer on the lower register cannot categorically be named as Anita. If that diminutive figure is indeed Anita, however, it would imply that Plaque D was made relatively soon after Plaques A and B.

CHAPTER 17

The Eanatum Extension Phase

DURING HIS LONG REIGN, WHICH LASTED ABOUT thirty-five years, Ur-Nanshe remodelled Tell K as part of his comprehensive reshaping of the entire city-state. The breadth and depth of his activities were recorded and celebrated in numerous surviving inscriptions, some of which, particularly those found near the Temple of Ningirsu on Tell K, adopt the expected mantra-like formula; those found further afield, which connect other buildings, installations and ritual practices with the core beliefs that found an architectural focus in the spiritual and civic hub that was the Ningirsu temple—the èš-ĝír-sú or é-^{d}nin-ĝír-su—take a much wider variety of forms. Considered as a whole, they paint a picture of Ur-Nanshe as a ruler of immense vision, drive and powers of organisation. It is probably fair to assume that Sumerian rulers were not generally lacking in confidence, but, to use a modern phrase, Ur-Nanshe must have been an extremely hard act to follow, and it appears that his immediate successor, his son Akurgal (c.2425–2420 BCE), whose reign was extremely short and seemingly lacking in incident, was content to keep things largely as his father left them. Perhaps there might even have been a sense that, after what must have been the ceaseless activity of Ur-Nanshe's more than three decades in power, the state needed to catch its breath. Akurgal is a prominent figure on the Ur-Nanshe Plaques (discussed in Chapter 16), where he appears to be one of the youngest of Ur-Nanshe's numerous sons, but nothing definite is known about how he eventually rose to power and what became of his many elder brothers. Otherwise, very little further information about him has been preserved. Among the very few inscriptions in his name, one mentions the building of the non-urban Antasura temple of Ningirsu in the Gu'edena borderlands (RIME 1.9.2.1).

Akurgal was succeeded by his son Eanatum (c.2420–2390 BCE), who, like his grandfather, enjoyed a long reign and was extraordinarily active in more ways than one. He was an energetic warrior, who fought mainly defensive wars against a coalition of other cities and foreign powers—notably Elam—and he was able to defend and maintain the threatened integrity of the state of Lagash. This, in turn, meant that the balance of power in Sumer generally was stabilised. Recalling venerated sovereigns of the past, notably including Mesilim, he occasionally styled himself king of Kish—a cognomen meaning 'world king' (as noted in Chapter 15)—but in Eanatum's case that was a bombastic claim, and the adoption of the title was probably little more than political hyperbole. With reference to his military exploits, he is also known by his battle name, LUM-ma (RIME 1.9.3.5). His royal inscriptions, which frequently refer to him as the ruler (ensí) of Lagash, record victories over rival city-states in Sumer (Umma, Uruk and Ur), as well as in the northern region of Upper Mesopotamia (Subartu and Mari), and further afield, particularly in the east, in Elam (Arawa and Mishime). Central to Eanatum's military undertakings was the renewed border conflict with the neighbouring city-state of Umma. His decisive victory was commemorated on the Stele of the Vultures, one of the most outstanding artworks of the entire Early Dynastic period, whose surviving fragments are discussed in detail below. Eanatum's triumph might have brought some years of peace to the region, at least for the duration of his reign, but the conflict between the two city-states was a recurring feature in the history of Lagash from the previous Early Dynastic IIIa era, when Mesilim of Kish negotiated a resolution, through to the Presargonic period, when Lugalzagesi of Umma defeated Urukagina, overran the state of Lagash and razed the sacred precinct on Tell K to the ground (as noted previously). Generally, the events recorded in Eanatum's inscriptions, and in relief on the Stele of the Vultures, suggest that he enjoyed a long reign that was focused on warfare and foreign policy, but he seems also to have inherited some of the architectural interests and ambitions of Ur-Nanshe. His preserved inscriptions provide a wealth of information relating to his building activities, especially the enlargement of Ur-Nanshe's religious complex on Tell K.

An Overview of the Eanatum Phase

About 25 m north-west of the Ur-Nanshe Building, in the extended area that surrounded it, Eanatum built a large well that became a tremendously significant and extremely long-lasting feature of the sacred complex on Tell K (Fig. 59). Despite the fact that it was covered only by a very shallow layer of earth, it survived largely intact until it was excavated by Sarzec in the late nineteenth century, and when Cros arrived at the site more than two decades later in 1903, he noted that it was still a very prominent landmark. The well was made of one or more types of inscribed planoconvex fired bricks, some of which formulaically record the details of its construction in the following words (RIME 1.9.3.9):

> Eanatum, ruler of Lagash, granted strength by the god Enlil, nourished with wholesome milk by the goddess Ninhursag, nominated by the god Ningirsu, chosen in the heart by the goddess Nanshe, son of Akurgal, ruler of Lagash, defeated the mountain land of Elam, defeated Arawa, defeated Gisha (Umma), and defeated Ur. At that time, he built a well of fired bricks for the god Ningirsu in his broad courtyard (kisal.dağal). His personal god is Šul.MUŠ×PA. Then, the god Ningirsu loved Eanatum.

The term kisal.dağal, in which kisal means 'courtyard' and dağal is translated as 'broad', is especially revealing because it does not seem to have connoted a standard part of either a temple or another kind of building, and it is not known as a formulaic epithet. Since a 'narrow courtyard' in this ceremonial sense is almost a contradiction in terms, the word dağal is taken to mean 'big', and when it is applied to a space or an expanse of ground rather than an edifice, it seems to signify something along the lines of 'spacious' or 'broad'. The act of enclosing an extensive area as a courtyard—and proclaiming the fact in an inscription for all the world to see—was presumably a demonstration of Eanatum's power, though the well that he built in the kisal.dağal of Ningirsu, whose brick-lined shaft descended from the top of the mound towards the water table many metres below, was unquestionably an exceptional feat of engineering that was commensurate with the grandiose terminology. The phrase kisal.dağal does not appear in any of the surviving Ur-Nanshe inscriptions, but one illustrious precedent for it is found in the Sumerian version of the Gilgamesh epic, where the hero does something (perhaps builds or installs something—unfortunately the remainder of the passage is lost) in the kisal.dağal of Inanna in Uruk. Against this background, Eanatum's use of the term kisal.dağal is therefore taken to indicate that, in addition to the well, he made some improvements to the area around the temple on the sacred summit of Tell K. The idea gains further support by his declaration that he constructed (or refashioned) the 'enceinte of the holy precinct', and a fragmentary inscription on a limestone plaque that was found in a Tell K spoil heap as recently as April 2015 further emphasises his activities as an indefatigable sovereign builder.

The principal features of the remodelled annexe to the north-west of the temple included the Well of Eanatum and an earlier version of the impressive Oval Reservoir that was excavated and photographed by Sarzec (Pl. 55 (2); Fig. 42). The underlying Eanatum reservoir (which was logged by Sarzec as a layer of fired bricks that he interpreted as part of the foundation mass for the uppermost structure), together with an associated set of installations, were housed in an area measuring about 25 m × 10 m that was built on a NE–SW axis and almost certainly closed off by mud-brick walls. It was accessed by a gate on its SW side, part of which was found by Sarzec. This walled area (anachronistically referred to as the Enmetena Esplanade, even though the features attributed to Eanatum were built before Enmetena's time), together with the Well of Eanatum, were all placed at the same Sarzec height of 12.83 m as the base of the Ur-Nanshe Building and pavement F on the temple's NW side. The floor of the whole remodelled space, including the ground in the vicinity of the well and the walled space around the Eanatum reservoir and its nearby cisterns, was probably paved with fired bricks that were similar in size to those used to build the well shaft. The extended sector, which measured perhaps 20 m × 50 m (overall) and was situated along the NW edge of the tell's upper terrace, formed the most significant recorded part of Eanatum's 'broad courtyard' (kisal.dağal).

Although the well was the crowning architectural achievement of Eanatum's reign, traces of his work were detected at other places on the tell, notably around the Double Stairway and water supply network in Trenches 6 and 7 (on Cros's Plan B; Fig. 36), and in the area of the Pillar of Gudea, where the Large Stairway was possibly built or restored by Eanatum.

The Well of Eanatum

The relationships between the different elements constructed by Eanatum are extremely hard to disentangle because the data in the French reports is often contradictory, and some of the recorded information is little more than approximate. The well itself has the merit of being dated, however, and the Eanatum text that is associated with it is particularly interesting not only on account of its terminology, as just described, but also because it shows that there can be a perfect concordance between architectural remains and their commemorative inscriptions. It is clear that the uppermost section of the well was built in two phases: in the first phase, which was carried out by Eanatum, the wall that formed the mouth of the well shaft was approximately level with the surface of the tell at the key Sarzec height of 12.83 m (the Ur-Nanshe base level). Enmetena subsequently raised the well's opening by adding a coping and a dome that increased its total height by a further 0.9 m. The walled well shaft was sunk by Eanatum to a depth of around 14 m or 15 m, cutting through the mudbrick mass of superimposed Early Dynastic platforms and underlying Uruk and Ubaid layers to access the groundwater below the water table, which was, it is again worth noting, point zero on the Sarzec scale of heights. The bell-shaped cuts and compact infillings of Early Dynastic IIIb potsherds are well recorded in the photos taken by Sarzec and Genouillac (Figs. 46 and 58), while the relationship between the original walls and the well's later domed top can be seen in Pl. 57 (2) (Fig. 46).

Below the Enmetena Esplanade

The connections between the Well of Eanatum and the structures that were exposed beneath the Enmetena Esplanade present some thorny problems that can be solved by comparing the archaeological contexts, relative heights, types of brickwork and stratigraphic sequencing in the two areas. The complex stratigraphy of the Oval Reservoir and its underlying predecessors includes three distinct phases. The well-preserved Oval Reservoir at the top of the sequence that was excavated and photographed by Sarzec was a composite installation, with a sloping bitumen-bonded surface, surrounded by a coping, that also featured a T-shaped junction on its NE side. Its unusual shape and the carefully designed surface curvature of its internal floor indicate a specialised function that was related to the production of beer, and it is reasonable to assume that the three smaller bituminated cisterns found close by at the same level (the two rectangular structures with double cavities and a third with three cavities that are illustrated on Sarzec's Plan D (Fig. 34)) were also built to aid to the brewing process, as is discussed in detail in Chapter 19.

Two more superimposed reservoirs were found below the Oval Reservoir. They had the same elliptical shape as their successor structure, but they survived only as single courses of fired bricks that Sarzec took to be part of an intricate underpinning. The fact that all three presumably served similar purposes at different times confirms that, for a long period, this part of the tell was the site of a brewery. Sarzec did not record any bituminated channels that were associated with the lower two structures, and their excavated remains seem to have been flat, but the fact that they both had had later constructions built on top of them means that their original profiles could well have been disregarded or refashioned in later phases. The topmost Oval Reservoir was probably built during the reign of Urukagina. Below that, the middle one was built by Enmetena, and the bottom one—the Eanatum reservoir—was installed as part of Eanatum's courtyard project at about the same time as the Well of

Eanatum. The Eanatum reservoir was made of fired bricks measuring 0.31 m × 0.23 m × 0.07 m. Inserted underneath its brickwork was a curious single brick with dimensions of 0.32 m × 0.22 m × 0.06 m that was marked with an unusual, deeply incised marking in the form of a double-barred cross, with the bars angled upwards on either side of the vertical. The base of the Eanatum reservoir was associated with a fired-brick paving made with uninscribed flat bricks measuring 0.32 m × 0.22 m × 0.05 m that had been very carefully manufactured and particularised. They were marked on one side with a longitudinal stroke (like the later bricks of Enmetena), and further distinguished with a rectangular groove running all the way around the same face like a frame (Heuzey 1900, p. 84). The paving was laid at the same height as the bottom of the threshold in the gate to the south-west of the reservoir, a correlation that would place the base of the Eanatum reservoir and the associated pavement made of fired bricks marked with framed finger strokes at the key Sarzec height of 12.83 m—the same as the general Ur-Nanshe base height, which was left unaltered by Eanatum. Remains of the Eanatum pavement were recorded at unspecified distances around the reservoir, the implication being that it was a prevailing feature of the Eanatum extension phase in this area of the tell.

The gateway raises some difficulties that can be relatively easily resolved. As excavated by Sarzec, it featured two fired-brick piers or door jambs that were placed on either side of a threshold that was eight courses of bricks high and 1.7 m wide. The fact that the base of the threshold and the masonry piers were found flush with the Eanatum pavement at the Sarzec height of about 12.83 m strongly suggests that the eight courses of bricks that formed the threshold were a later addition to Eanatum's original gate (built at the same time as his well, pavement and reservoir). As discussed below, the extra courses were almost certainly installed in the threshold when the overall height of the mound was elevated by Enmetena as part of his comprehensive renovation and refurbishment programme. A question that is less easily answered is whether the gateway and associated mud-brick walls that housed Eanatum's reservoir (presumably the centrepiece of his brewery) was a building with a roof or whether it was open to the elements. As is argued below, however, the production processes that were carried out in the area would probably have been closed off and protected from airborne dust, dirt and flies, for example, and this suggests that Eanatum's brewing facility was probably covered with a roof.

Eanatum's well was pointedly referred to in the important inscription quoted at the beginning of this chapter as having been built in Ningirsu's 'broad courtyard', which is taken to mean the temple's sacred precinct at large. The further inference, that he carried out works in the vicinity of the temple but left the Ur-Nanshe Building intact, is strongly supported by the evidence. His new structures were founded at the same level as the Ur-Nanshe base, while the focus of his main construction project seems to have been the well, which was undoubtedly a major undertaking, and also the brewing enclosure on the NW edge of the tell. Nevertheless, he did make one highly significant change within the confines of the temple walls: in all likelihood, as is argued in Chapters 18 and 19 below, he enshrined the Stele of the Vultures in the Ningirsu temple, probably inside the opening of the door that led into the SW room (Sarzec's room A on Plan C (1); Fig. 90). The fact that there was a stele in the corresponding place in the Lower Construction would indicate that the tradition of placing a commemorative sculpture of this type in the same position in the temple's trophy room was a time-honoured one. Whether or not Eanatum replaced an older stele with the Stele of the Vultures cannot finally be known, but the historic significance of Eanatum's victories on the battlefield, which secured the borders of Lagash and maintained the state's standing as pivotal regional power, might well have justified such a substitution. As is discussed in detail below, the Stele of the Vultures was later desecrated and broken into pieces that were randomly scattered when the entire temple complex was razed to the ground at the end of the Early Dynastic period.

Coda: Enanatum I

Eanatum's successor was his brother Enanatum I (c.2390–2370 BCE). Since Eanatum probably ruled for about thirty years, it might perhaps be assumed that Enanatum I was relatively advanced in age when he succeeded to the throne, but he nonetheless reigned for about twenty years. Despite his illustrious older brother's military success, the ongoing conflict between Lagash and Umma flared up again during Enanatum I's reign, and it is recorded that he successfully

FIGURE 90. The Ur-Nanshe Building in the reign of Eanatum, seen from the south-east, with the door to the antecella in the foreground. Inside the antecella are the Stele of the Vultures (screening the entrance), together with a number of sacred artefacts, including three of the Ur-Nanshe Plaques on the NW wall.

countered cross-border incursions undertaken by troops from Umma (RIME 1.9.4.2). His temple building activities were focused on the goddess Inanna, in particular the construction of the Eanna (Inanna's inner sanctum) in the Ibgal temple in Lagash, which is mentioned around ten times in a number of surviving inscriptions (RIME 1.9.4.2 and RIME 1.9.4.6). The Eninnu of Ningirsu in Girsu, meaning the Tell K temple, is also mentioned in his royal inscriptions, and one text, which was inscribed on a brick found in the vicinity of the sacred precinct's temenos wall, indicates that Enanatum I carried out some refurbishment work on the building (RIME 1.9.4.3):

> Enanatum, ruler of Lagash, son of Akurgal, ruler of Lagash, when the god Ningirsu chose him in his heart, he brought white cedars down to him from the mountains. When he had filled in the temple with them he laid its roof thatch(?) of white cedar. The poplar lions that he installed for him there as gatekeepers, he set for the god Ningirsu, his master who loves him.

This seems strongly to suggest that Enanatum imported cedar that was used to repair (or 'fill') some parts of the Ur-Nanshe Building and that he oversaw the resurfacing or renovation of its roof, which was also made partly of cedar. The idea that it was 'thatched' with cedar is surely highly unlikely, unless some smaller branches were used in process, but a bitumen-coated reed screen would surely have been the most convenient and suitable roofing material. That being the case, it might be surmised that some cedar roof beams were replaced. The inscription provides no clue as to why these repairs were carried out, but it should be recalled that the temple was probably in excess of fifty or sixty years old by this date (Ur-Nanshe having reigned for thirty-five years, followed by Eanatum, who reigned for a further thirty) so the passage of time might have begun to take its toll on the more perishable structural features. In addition, Enanatum commissioned some poplar carvings of lions that were displayed as 'gatekeepers', but whether this means they were installed directly outside the temple (on pavement F, for example) or at the ceremonial access point to the sacred precinct that was associated with the Large Stairway by the Pillar of Gudea (near Tells I and I') cannot be determined. It might be further assumed, however, that he built a commemorative structure (perhaps a pedestal) near the Large Stairway to celebrate the repairs carried out on the temple.

Two inscribed votive artefacts of special interest that derive from the reign of Enanatum I are a stone mortar (Fig. 27) that was used for crushing garlic for the god Ningirsu in his Eninnu (RIME 1.9.4.4) and a mace head (Fig. 91). The mortar was unearthed along with three fragments of the Stele of the Vultures and the border stone (described in Chapter 20) that commemorates Eanatum's reconquest of the frontier territory of Gu'edena. The superb mace head found its way onto the antiquities market, but was later acquired by the British Museum (BM23287). It is dedicated to 'Ningirsu of the Eninnu' by the 'minister' (sukkal) Barakisumun (Baraki.TIL) to safeguard the life of Enanatum I (RIME 1.9.4.19).

FIGURE 91. The Thunderbird Mace Head. British Museum 23287.

CHAPTER 18

The Stele of the Vultures

THE STELE OF THE VULTURES (FIG. 92), WHICH WAS made during the reign of Eanatum, is a supreme monument of Sumerian art and literacy, and like other treasures of Mesopotamia, including the ceremonial Vase of Uruk and the Standard of Ur, its epoch-defining pictorial programme and accompanying cuneiform signs encompass the whole theological metastructure of Sumerian thought and ritual. Carved in relief, the stele's iconographic and epigraphic contents revolve around the cult of the triumphant hero god, Ningirsu, and his chief symbol, the Thunderbird, celebrating the god's power and his divinely sanctioned claim to the state of Lagash, including all its territories. This is a legal claim that is upheld in the human world by force and military might, in this case under the leadership of Ningirsu's earthly nominee, the ruler Eanatum. Accordingly, the monument commemorates and celebrates Eanatum's triumph over the city of Umma, the arch-enemy of Lagash, in the latest episode of the long-running dispute over territory and natural resources. The stele also has clear legal ramifications for the ongoing behaviour of the two states: it records the oaths sworn by the defeated ruler of Umma and affirms the re-established border between the two city-states, documenting arrangements regulating the use of the land and water resources in the frontier regions. Rectangular in shape, with a rounded top, the fragmentary remains of the stele represent a white limestone monument that is thought to have measured 1.8 m (h) × 1.3 m (w) × 0.11 m (t). It bears an inscription and a pictorial representation in shallow relief on its front and back faces, and on its narrow sides. Commissioned by Eanatum, it was almost certainly kept in the trophy room of the Ningirsu temple on Tell K.

As previously noted, six fragments were found on the site by Sarzec (here labelled A to F), one of which (B), containing the head of the god's mother, Ninhursag, on one side and showing corpses on the other, was unearthed on Tell A, while the other five fragments came from Tell K (Sarzec and Heuzey 1912, pp. 36 and 67–8). Sarzec's workmen discovered Fragment C, again depicting Ninhursag and a heap of corpses on its respective sides, at the base of Tell K, in the depression between Tells I, I' and J, where it lay 1 m below the ground, close to the Tell J reservoir. Fragment A, with birds of prey carrying human body parts, was found 1 m away from Fragment C at the same depth. Fragment D, which shows Ningirsu, was uncovered to the south-west of the Ur-Nanshe Building, while Fragments E and F were found to the east of the temple, and all three pieces were found lying above the level of the structure's sealed walls, in the Sarzec gap that includes the destruction horizon associated with the temple. Finally, Fragment G, which was probably stolen and illegally sold, was eventually bought in 1898 by the British Museum and subsequently donated to the Louvre in 1932 to be restored and reunited with the other surviving pieces (see Sarzec and Heuzey 1912, p. 357; and Barrelet 1970, p. 234).

The front and the back of the stele are commonly referred to as the 'mythological' and 'historical' sides, respectively, with the mythological obverse devoted to divine subject matter—Ningirsu in particular—and the reverse showing battle scenes in which Eanatum and his troops defeat the enemy forces of Umma. As was the case with the earlier Uruk Vase and other artefacts from the third millennium BCE, notably the Standard of Ur, the pictorial representations on the Stele of the

244   The Mound of the House of the Fruits

FIGURE 92. Reconstruction of the Stele of the Vultures, showing the mythological obverse (left) and the historical reverse (right).

The Stele of the Vultures 245

Vultures were probably intended to be read from bottom to top, and since the figures mainly face to the right, the direction of the lateral movement and action in the scenes is also taken to be from left to right. As it emerges from the background, which is almost entirely covered with the incised inscription, the bas-relief is relatively high and flat, though with rounded edges. The figures are well modelled and the details are carefully incised. Unfortunately, so little of the stele has survived that it is only possible to reconstruct its original contents very tentatively and with a high degree of uncertainty.

The Mythological Obverse

The inscription that begins at the top of the mythological side of the stele would confirm that this was indeed intended to be the front of the monument. It is assumed to have been divided into two registers by a thin band of transverse relief, above which the upper register took up more than half of the stele's total height. Ningirsu, who was the principal subject of both registers, was shown standing in the upper tableau, and driving his chariot below, and in both scenes he was watched by his seated mother, Ninhursag. The main figure can be confidently identified as Ningirsu (and not Eanatum) on account of the skirt or kaunakes that he wears, the mace that he holds in his right hand, and also because of the presence of Imdugud, the Thunderbird (in his left hand)—all in the upper register and all visible on Fragments D and E. Ninhursag, the Lady of the Mountain, is closely associated with her son in all the myths relating to the warrior god, and she appears on the obverse in Fragments B and C, both times wearing a Thunderbird crown, while in Fragment C (the upper register) the association is further strengthened by the addition of a standard that is topped with another Thunderbird or possibly an eagle (as argued by Heuzey in Sarzec and Heuzey 1912, p. 101; and Parrot 1948, p. 97). For all of these reasons, Parrot's suggestion (1948, p. 97) that the seated deity might instead have been Ningirsu's wife, Bau, can be safely rejected.

Beginning with the lower register, of which almost nothing remains, and referring freely to the reconstruction, Ningirsu was shown seated in his chariot, which was placed towards the left side of the carving. The point of his spear (the shaft of which is partly preserved in Fragment F) was lowered towards the ground as he approached his mother, probably to receive her blessing. The god's crown is not preserved in any of the fragments, but it seems reasonable to assume that it was also decorated with a Thunderbird motif, like his mother's. As can be seen on Fragment F, the reins of the divine chariot were threaded through two conjoined rings decorated with a single heraldic lion passant, while a double-arched shaft or draught pole was also seemingly reinforced with metal loops or struts. The double arch might well have been intended to show that the chariot was pulled by two animals and not just one (as in the reconstruction).

Above the lion passant can be seen the remains of a bird's wing (identified by comparison with the well-preserved wings of the Thunderbird on the upper register (Fragment D)), and this was probably part of an Imdugud figurine that adorned the top of the compartment at the front of the chariot where the god's whip and other weapons were stored. The whip is represented in Fragment F by the two wavy lines (indicating lashes) that fall down from the Thunderbird's wing onto the back of the heraldic lion, and the same arrangement, minus the Thunderbird figurine, can be seen clearly on Eanatum's chariot on the reverse of the stele (Fragment E). Chariots with curved shafts could be either two- or four-wheeled, but Ningirsu's chariot might perhaps have had two wheels because of the pronounced downward curve of the shaft's arch; conversely, four-wheeled chariots generally had straight draught poles that extended out over the animals' backs (see Barrelet 1970, p. 242). In parallel depictions from a similar period, charioteers are shown both standing and seated. This is the case on the bottom register of the Standard of Ur, for example, where both positions are recorded. If Ningirsu had been shown standing, however, he would have had to be compressed in order to fit into the shorter lower register, thus making him the same size as, or probably considerably smaller than, his mother. For this reason, it seems more likely that he was shown seated, as in the reconstruction, since this allows the proportionate statures of the god and Ninhursag to appear at least equal, though the god was of course deliberately made much larger than her on the upper register.

Ningirsu's two-wheeled chariot might have been pulled by two onagers (wild asses), as on some later Gudea steles, where the god's conveyance features a similar double-arched shaft and its front is also decorated with a Thunderbird figurine (Fig. 93 (left)). Alternatively, the divine chariot might have been drawn by winged lions (Fig. 93 (right)). The creature is found in association with a bird that can feasibly be seen as Imdugud on an Early Dynastic engraved shell plaque from

FIGURE 93. Two possible views of Ningirsu's divine chariot, showing it being pulled by onagers (left) and winged lions (right).

Girsu (see Sarzec and Heuzey 1912, p. 271). Furthermore, as has been noted by various scholars, a later Akkad carving shows the god's chariot being drawn by a winged lion whose paws are replaced by the talons of a bird of prey (see, for example, Barrelet 1970, pp. 253–4; and Winter 1985, pp. 15–16). With respect to the dimensions and arrangement of the figures, winged lions would surely have been visually more suitable than onagers for the lateral space between the chariot and Ninhursag; similarly, as on the reconstruction, the lions would not have interrupted the notional line linking the faces of the god and his mother in a way that the larger and more upright onagers might have done. The pronounced curve of the draught pole might also be explained by the winged lions' smaller stature. Trying to decide what kind of animal was shown pulling the god's chariot, Heuzey draws attention to a possible relief fragment that was found and photographed by Sarzec towards the end of his time in Tello, but which later went missing (Sarzec and Heuzey 1912, p. 375). Heuzey mentions that he himself searched for it in Paris and Constantinople, but with no success. According to Heuzey, who of course had nothing but the photo to guide him, the supposed carving on the fragment bore a definite similarity to the relief on the Stele of the Vultures. As can be seen on the photo, however, any carved forms and stylistic features are extremely difficult to decipher, making the comparison inconclusive at best. Finally, therefore, the present reconstruction includes a winged lion, but the drawn shapes are entirely provisional as no reliable information survives, though it is likely that the chariot was pulled by two animals.

Sitting in front of the chariot and facing her son, Ninhursag wears a Thunderbird crown decked with a lion-headed eagle that is also seemingly horned (see Romano 2008). Her crowned head is visible on Fragment B, as are the tips of some mace heads behind her shoulders—a set of motifs that can also be made out on the upper register on Fragment C. With the obvious exception of the gigantic figure of Ningirsu in the stele's main scene, representations of standing deities are not common in the Early Dynastic period, and this is one reason why it should probably be assumed that Ninhursag was shown seated (see Barrelet 1970, pp. 240 and 244–5), possibly on a throne decorated with pebble-like rock forms to represent the mountain with which she is associated. Also important is the fact that, as with Ningirsu, the size constraints imposed by the lower register would seem to make a seated position more likely. The goddess's hands might have been clasped at her waist (in a manner comparable with the Sumerian gesture of prayer) or she might have had her right hand raised in an act of benediction, while the other lay in her lap, as in the reconstruction. Her dress in the reconstruction is interpreted as having been plain, like Ningirsu's skirt (parts of which survive on the top and bottom registers on Fragments E and F). Behind her crown is a small, left-facing lion passant that might suggest part of a temple façade, or (though perhaps less likely) a canopy, as Heuzey suggests (Sarzec and Heuzey 1912, p. 101). Resembling the top of the net on the upper register, the lion might have been coupled with a counterpart that faced the opposite direction, with the two surmounted by (or possibly grasped by) a Thunderbird—an emblematic combination that is well attested in several contemporary sources (see Van Dijk and Coombes 2017). These probabilities are all reflected in the reconstruction of the bottom right corner of the obverse.

On the upper register, the huge form of Ningirsu, who is by far the largest figure on the monument, holds in his left hand a casting-net that is loaded with vanquished enemies. It is worth recording that Heuzey believed that the oversized god was Enlil because Enlil's net is mentioned in the cuneiform inscription (Sarzec and Heuzey 1912, p. 362), but the casting-nets of numerous deities are introduced in the text, always in support of Eanatum's intention of confirming Ningirsu's ownership of the lands recovered from Umma, and there is little reason to doubt the identity of the principal figure, which is confirmed by the presence of the divine mace and Imdugud—both integral parts of Ningirsu's iconography. Accordingly, in his right hand Ningirsu holds a mace that he uses to strike a skull that emerges from his net. Since the protruding head is larger than those of the other captives, it is perhaps intended to be that of their leader. All of these details are visible on Fragments D and E, where the god's long, wavy hair can be seen tied back in a chignon (an attribute of royalty, or in this case divinity), while a long beard falls down in five thick, undulating bands onto his broad, bare chest. As also preserved on Fragment E, Ningirsu wears an extended skirt that is plain except for two central narrow borders that run from the waist down towards the hemline, and the garment is secured above his waist by a wide belt. The net of prisoners is closed with a Thunderbird figurine (with outspread wings) that is shown standing above (or on the backs of) the two protomes of lions discussed above, while the god is seen firmly grasping the legs of the Thunderbird with his left hand. The enemies trapped in the net are small and naked, with shaved heads and faces, while their bodies are twisted and contorted in unnatural positions that emphasise the extreme degradation to which they have been subjected (see Fragment E).

Towards the left side of the stele, behind the god's enormous frame, Ninhursag observes her son's triumph. Only the top of her head (her eye and nose), and her Thunderbird crown and standard (seen behind her) are preserved on Fragment C, but it can be surmised that she was probably raising a celebratory beaker and holding a bunch of dates. The bird-topped pole was held by a standard bearer, whose fingers can be seen behind Ninhursag's head on Fragment C. Whether the goddess was standing or seated (in the reconstruction she is shown on her throne), the flat surface of the stone between the ground beneath her feet (and those of her attendant) and the bottom of the upper register was probably free of representational content and therefore presumably filled with parts of the cuneiform inscription. Of great interest is the correspondence between the front and back faces of Fragments B and C on the lower and upper registers. In both cases, the spaces on the other side of the monument that are diametrically connected with the areas occupied by the two portrayals of the goddess on the obverse are filled with mounds of dead bodies. This is certainly much more than mere coincidence because in Sumerian mythology Ninhursag was closely associated with the cosmic mountain known as kur, which was traditionally linked with the hostile foreign land that bordered Sumer. According to the myths (Bottéro and Kramer 1989), in his guise as the heroic god, Ningirsu conquered kur, making the territory an important source of valuable raw materials, including metal ores, stone and wood. A meaningful relationship between the two faces of the monument seems also to have been created on Fragment D, where the front and back depict Ningirsu and Eanatum, respectively. The mirroring effect was doubtless intended to reflect the bond between the divine triumph of Ningirsu and the human victory of his earthly representative, Eanatum, who leads the army of Lagash into battle.

The Historical Reverse

The reverse of the stele, which was devoted to Eanatum's verifiable historical defeat of Umma, was divided into four registers by three thin bands of horizontal relief, and it might possibly have focused on two distinct moments in Eanatum's long struggle against the neighbouring enemy state (see Cooper 1983, p. 26). Looked at from the bottom to the top, an earlier episode in the ongoing conflict was conceivably the subject of the two lower registers, while later events, including the conclusive victory, were shown on the two upper registers. Alternatively, the entire reverse might have pictured a single battle, punctuated with a sacrifice that was carved on the second register from the bottom (Alster 2003–4, p. 4). Unlike the front of the stele, which was unevenly divided along its height into a taller upper register and a shorter lower one, the four registers on the reverse probably divided that side of the stone into two roughly equal halves.

Only a very small part of the scene carved in the bottom register has survived, and it seems perhaps to show Eanatum using a long spear to pierce the fully shaven, left-facing head of the ruler or ensi of Umma (Fragments B, F and G). The victim is shown bringing his right hand up to the side of his face, either in a futile gesture of self-protection or as a sign that he is pleading for his life. In front of him can be seen the remains of the tops of the right-facing bald heads of three shorter men—probably warriors from the army of Umma who were conceivably being pressed forward by a Lagash soldier in the direction of their vanquished leader, and it is likely that they were naked and had their hands tied behind their backs (as on the reconstruction). Otherwise, they could have been enemies fleeing from the victorious ruler of Lagash, though this might be less likely. To the right of the preserved text that runs around the defeated soldiers' heads, the right side and bottom right-hand corner of the lower register are missing, but the imagery might have included more captured troops who were associated with their leader, but perhaps marching rightwards, as can be seen on other Early Dynastic war monuments, notably Standard of Ur and the inlay panels from Kish and Mari (see Aruz and Wallenfels 2003, pp. 90–1 and 157). In any event, all the enemies of Lagash were surely shown humiliated in defeat—wounded, weaponless and naked. As in the reconstruction, the lost part of the left side of the bottom register was probably filled with a portrait of Eanatum, shown holding his long spear as he kills his principal foe.

The carving on the second register up from the bottom was devoted to a ceremony performed before the seated ruler of Lagash, who is recognisable by the bottom of his skirt that is made up of lanceolate strips, with his bare feet resting on a simple slanting footrest (as can be seen on Fragment F). Though Heuzey (Sarzec and Heuzey 1912, p. 175) states that the figure could have been a god, this suggestion can be discounted because the skirt worn by the seated figure is identical with that of Eanatum on Fragment D (above). Seated in this predominantly martial context, just to the right of the centre of the stele and facing left, Eanatum was probably shown wearing his helmet and perhaps holding up his mace, as on the later cylinder seals of Ishqi-Mari (see Margueron 2004, p. 311). Figures taking part in rituals were usually shown fully shaven, in the act of raising a beaker and holding a palm frond or a bunch of dates, but the soldierly portrayal is more consistent with the imagery on the stele as a whole, and if a semi-realistic note is admissible, the ceremony might represent a pause in the action to allow for the proper burial of the dead (as intimated in the inscriptions and discussed further below). That said, if Eanatum was instead shown raising a sacramental drinking vessel, that might well have corresponded with the inferred depiction of Ninhursag on Fragment C on the obverse of the carving (in the upper register).

Behind the ruler, in the space towards the right side of the stele, were probably one or more attendants or soldiers, as on Early Dynastic banquet scenes and votive plaques, including Ur-Nanshe Plaque A (see Chapter 16). This would also be consistent with the iconography of the Ishqi-Mari seals.

In front of the ruler, on the far side of the vignette that contains the ritual, can be seen two men wearing kilts or skirts with fringed hems and belts (possibly with attached daggers). Carrying baskets full of earth on their heads, they are climbing a heap of naked corpses, presumably to bury the bodies in a sepulchral mound (Fragment B). The corpses are neatly arranged in layers, with their heads and feet alternately pointing to the right and left, while the extremely short mound-builders face leftwards, with their backs to Eanatum. The overall shape of the piled-up corpses reflects the form of the large quantity of sacrificed animals (possibly intended to be sheep or lambs) seen immediately to the right on Fragment G. In the ritual scene, a naked, fully shaven cult celebrant, whose oversized legs are partly preserved, is shown pouring a libation, conceivably using a spouted vessel. The vessel depicted on the frieze has not survived, but a stream of what must be water can be seen flowing down into two big pots that apparently have date palms growing in them: one pot is on Fragment G, while the other is on Fragment F (in front of Eanatum's knees and shins). The dates protrude in thick bunches, while broad palm leaves can be seen flopping down between the pot and the heap of sacrificed animals on Fragment G, and close to Eanatum's skirt on Fragment F. Also on Fragment F, on the ground in front of Eanatum's feet, can be seen a bull that is lying belly up on the ground, with its legs extending over its upward-facing neck. Its front hooves are tied to a short post next to Eanatum's footrest on Fragment F, while its hind legs are fastened with a rope to a similar post on Fragment B, where the rope's twisted strands and the serpentine form of the knot are sharp and well preserved.

It has been argued that the supposed ritual scene actually represents the dream that is mentioned in the inscription that Eanatum reportedly had before the battle (Winter 1985, pp. 19–20), but that seems unlikely, and very hard to correlate with the narrative of slaughter in the register below. Scholars generally agree that the tableau is intended to record an actual event, but they disagree on the identity of the dead. In Heuzey's opinion (Sarzec and Heuzey 1912, p. 99, followed by Romano 2007, p. 14) the corpses in the burial mound must be those of the defeated enemies of Lagash because the propagandistic function of the monument would have been undermined by the recollection of Lagash soldiers who lost their lives. By contrast, Selz (2015, pp. 393, 396 and 401–2) argues that the bodies are indeed those of killed Lagash troops, who are being ceremonially buried with accompanying rites, as confirmed by the rich offerings shown on Fragments G and F, but also because of the strong differentiation between the orderly arrangement of their bodies and the messy heap of dead Umma enemies that can be seen below and to the right of the vultures on the top register (on Fragment C). With the possible exception of the corpses shown on the reverse of Fragment B, the mistreatment of enemy bodies and prisoners of war seems to have been a ubiquitous feature of the stele's imagery, the model instance being provided on the obverse by Ningirsu with his netload of captives and corpses. One other alternative is that two ways of dealing with the remains of killed enemy soldiers might have been intended to convey a narrative in which Eanatum begins by showing pious compassion and burying the enemy dead with military honours, before becoming more hard-hearted and deciding to mishandle the corpses when the army of Umma persists in opposing him (see Selz 2015, p. 398). Surely a far more convincing reading is that the Stele of the Vultures was intended to be a war memorial in the most comprehensive sense of the term, and that its makers therefore did not shrink from acknowledging and honouring the Lagash soldiers who inevitably did make the ultimate sacrifice, giving up their lives for the sake of their leader, their country and their god. This might also accord with the inscription, where the building of numerous tumuli is specifically mentioned (as discussed below).

The third register up from the bottom of the reverse shows a battle scene in which Eanatum, the largest figure in this register, can be seen standing in his chariot, holding a long lance high in his left hand in an attack position (see Fragment E). As on the bottom register, the blade of the weapon was possibly piercing the head of an enemy, who might have been just to the right of centre, as in the reconstruction. Unlike Ningirsu, the human ruler of Lagash is beardless, while strands of his thick, long wavy hair can be seen protruding out from under the bottom of his pointed helmet and falling down onto his shoulders. Above that, the bulk of his hair is formed into a chignon that is held in a bipartite band, with the whole arrangement recalling the helmet of Eanatum's contemporary, Meskalamdug, king of Ur (see Aruz and Wallenfels 2003, p. 35). Eanatum is wearing a skirt that is formed of horizontal flounces of lanceolate clusters, with a stole or tunic made of wavy tufts of material covering his torso and his left shoulder, but leaving his right shoulder bare. In his right hand he is holding the handle of an S-shaped weapon that appears to be made of three thin bands or rods that are fixed together with two loops or straps. Though it is a similar shape to the sickle sword that can be seen, for example on the Circular Bas-Relief from the Lower Construction (Fig. 77), Heuzey interpreted it as a projectile, perhaps a sort of boomerang (Sarzec and Heuzey 1912, p. 177). Javelins and various pointed weapons, doubtless including arrows, some of which are horizontal and some crescent-shaped according to Heuzey (Sarzec and Heuzey 1912, p. 176), together with an axe and a whip, can be seen in the quiver-like compartment that is fitted to the front of the chariot. The conveyance's two reins and part of the curving draught pole can be seen below the weapons, and it seems reasonable to assume that the vehicle was pulled by onagers, as shown in the reconstruction. It is probable that a second warrior was also standing in the royal chariot, behind Eanatum, as evidenced by the shaft of a second spear that can be seen below the ruler's right forearm. The soldier carrying it was expunged by a circular hole that was drilled in the carving at a later date, as is considered in more detail below.

Behind the chariot are two ranks of marching soldiers, all wearing pointed helmets, plain stoles that cover their left shoulders (as Eanatum's covers his) and the same type of skirt as the ruler. They all hold spears in their right hands and axes in their left hands, with all the shafts pointing slightly backwards over their shoulders and up towards an inferred sky. The image of the marching men extends around the side of the stele (on the narrow outside edge of Fragment E), where the partial remains of the leg of a slaughtered foe can be seen beneath their feet. This presumably implies that the whole unit of Lagash soldiers, including those seen on the reverse of the stele on Fragment E, were originally depicted marching on their enemies' dead bodies, as they are on the upper register (Fragment D)—a view advanced by Heuzey (Sarzec and Heuzey 1912, p. 180).

Near the right edge of the same register, just below the horizontal band of relief that separates it from the top register above, can be seen possible traces of a head and a spear point (at the bottom edge of Fragment C). There has been some disagreement about what the surviving forms represent. Parrot (1948, p. 99) argues that the carving is only of a very damaged head, while Heuzey (Sarzec and Heuzey 1912,

p. 97) interprets the faint vestiges as a bald head and a spear, an idea that might suggest the image of an enemy soldier fleeing the approaching ruler on his chariot, except for the fact that the figure is seemingly armed and the tip of his spear is probably facing upwards in a neutral position. Alster (2003–4, p. 3) believes the head is facing to the left, and that the soldier is therefore the intended victim of the ruler's brandished spear. As seen on the reconstruction, it is perhaps most likely that the soldier was not bald, but rather protected by a plain helmet like the ones worn by the ranks of soldiers behind the ruler's chariot on Fragment E, and that he is facing right, all of which suggests that he was probably a Lagash soldier who was positioned in advance of the chariot, as can be seen on other Early Dynastic plaques (see, for example, Boese 1971, Pls. I.2 and V.2) and on the Standard of Ur. The scenes shown in those comparison cases depict either the end or the aftermath of a battle, but on this register of the Stele of the Vultures the events of the battle and its conclusion might both have been condensed into a single tableau. The fact that the top of the soldier's helmet was at about the same level as the head of Eanatum, who towers above his men, partly because he is slightly oversized and partly because he is portrayed standing in his chariot, means that the soldier in the advanced position could not realistically have been shown with his feet directly on the field of battle. The corollary is that he might have been positioned above—on top of, or notionally behind—some dead enemies who were lying scattered on the ground. An analogy might be found in the figure pouring the libation in the ritual scene on the register below, where the celebrant is also shown above, or possibly behind, the pile of sacrificed animals on the ground below him.

Eanatum, who occupies the centre of the top register, holds the curved weapon that is seen in Fragment E (below) close to his chest in his right hand. It is important once more to note the correspondence between Eanatum on the reverse of Fragment D and Ningirsu on the obverse: the two sides of the relief are constructed in a way that depicts the god and his human representative as symbolic counterparts. Below the curving top of Fragment A can be seen the vultures that give the stele its familiar name. It is not surprising that this vignette caught the attention of Sarzec and Heuzey since it is a particularly dynamic passage of carving that shows the birds of prey clutching human carrion, including several heads, as well as human hands and forearms, and it seems likely that more birds were seen to the left of the preserved flock, as on the reconstruction. Part of an oblique stick is visible below the vultures at the bottom left corner of Fragment A, and this was probably the shaft of Eanatum's downward-pointing spear (the handle is too long to have belonged to a mace or a battle axe). Heuzey (Sarzec and Heuzey 1912, pp. 96 and 179) suggests it might have been the weapon of a defeated enemy, but the presumed position of the shaft with respect to Eanatum's torso in Fragment D makes that less likely.

Behind the ruler on Fragment D is a well-preserved phalanx of soldiers in battle order, carrying their spears horizontally and protecting themselves with an orderly arrangement of shields; some of the men are also armed with axes. Wearing pointed helmets from which their long, wavy hair emerges over the backs of their necks, they are seen marching over the naked and debased bodies of their enemies. It is noteworthy that the surviving figures on the top two registers seem compositionally to have been arranged chiastically. Accordingly, the oblique angle of the ruler's inferred spear on the upper register is echoed in the weapons of the advancing troops on the register below, while the horizontal position of the soldiers' weapons on the top register is repeated in the angle of Eanatum's spear below. To the right of the ruler on Fragment C, on the extreme right edge of the stele, is a mass of shaven and naked enemy bodies that are being heaped up by two or three (or perhaps more) standing figures. Traces of a left-facing standing man can perhaps be made out at the bottom of Fragment A (above), so that might have been the top of the mound.

It is feasible that Eanatum was portrayed in the act of killing a high-status enemy with his spear. Though no direct evidence of that has survived, a similar image is found on the Standard of Ur, in the centre of the middle register, where a warrior, who is significantly positioned directly below the king of Ur (on the register above), can be seen stabbing an enemy soldier lying on the ground. Restrictions of space might have made that unlikely on the Stele of the Vultures, however, in which case Eanatum might simply have been directing the point of his spear towards the mound of defeated dead, thereby drawing attention to the miserable fate of Ningirsu's enemies.

The Inscription: Words and Images

The stele bears an inscription that was carved on the stone's flat background after the pictorial representations had been applied (Fig. 94). Beginning at the top right corner (or more

252 The Mound of the House of the Fruits

FIGURE 94. Reconstruction of the obverse (left) and reverse (right) of the Stele of the Vultures, highlighting the positions of the names of gods, people and places.

The Stele of the Vultures 253

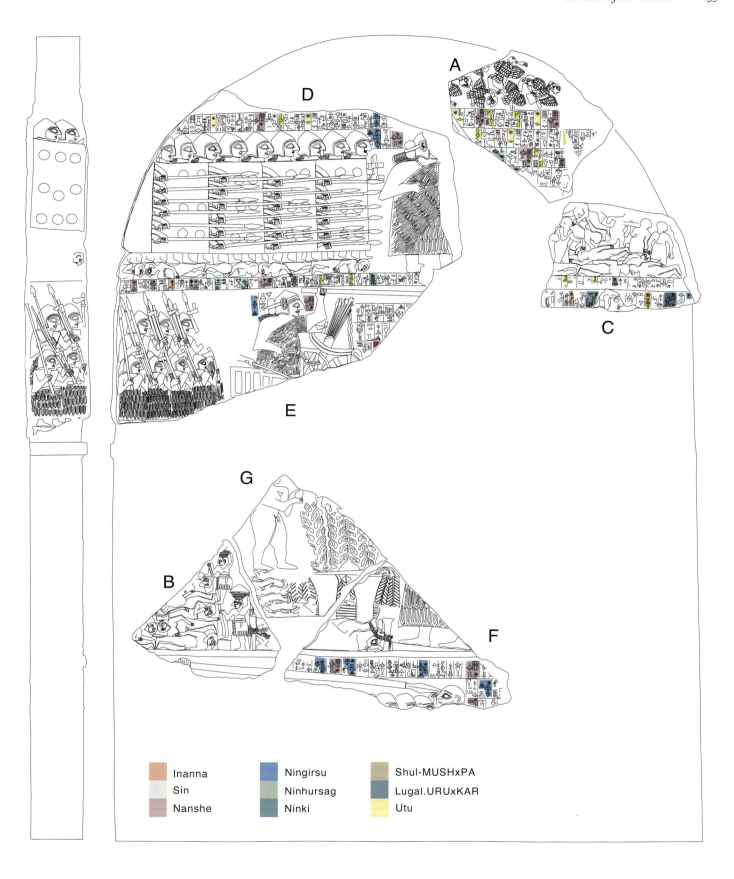

accurately the curve) of the mythological obverse, the preserved text (RIME 1.9.3.1) is made up of twenty-two columns on the front and twelve on the back, making a total of more than 830 surviving lines, of which 130 are incomplete. The text reads horizontally across the stone from right to left. In addition, two cartouches or labels are included that identify Eanatum individually.

On the upper register on the mythological side, the inscription narrates the long-standing conflict between Lagash and Umma over the ownership of land and control of water supplies in the border area, known as the Gu'edena (Fragments A, D and C). The problem is traced back to the reign of Akurgal, Eanatum's father, and Umma is accused of failing to respect a kind of loan or tenancy agreement that allowed the citizens of Umma to exploit some border areas that were considered to belong to Lagash, or more specifically to Ningirsu. The people of Umma have persistently failed to pay the rent on the land: a charge that was paid as a share of the grain harvest, and at the same time they have aggressively changed the agreed boundary line between the two states in order to expand their territory. After this preamble, the focus shifts to the coordinated resolve of Ningirsu and Eanatum to punish Umma and restore justice (Fragments D and C). Eanatum's glorious heritage and his divine right to rule are described. The god is said to have been miraculously instrumental in his conception, and it is even intimated that Ningirsu might in some sense be Eanatum's father. After his birth, the ruler is named by Inanna and suckled by Ninhursag, then Ningirsu lays his giant hand (five cubits wide) upon the infant and bestows the kingship of Lagash upon him. Umma is then declared to be the sworn enemy of Lagash because the ruler of Umma has taken possession of the Gu'edena, Ningirsu's 'beloved field', and Eanatum is sent a dream in which Ningirsu stands by his head and instructs him to take up arms against the foe. Utu, the god of the sun and of justice, appears, confirming the legitimacy of the cause by his presence, then Eanatum dreams of destroying countless Umma enemies of Lagash until the citizens of Umma finally rise up against their leader and kill him in his own city.

Next comes the account of the battle (Fragment D). Eanatum, who personally heads the vanguard, is immediately wounded by an arrow, which he removes from his body. He then assails the enemy like a destructive 'rainstorm' that overwhelms them in an all-consuming 'deluge'. The imagery is extraordinarily potent, and so culturally evocative that it was employed repeatedly in similar martial contexts until at least the first millennium BCE, during the Neo-Babylonian period. It should not be overlooked that Ningirsu was, of course, the god of thunder, as witnessed by his taming of Imdugud, and the imagery of storms and flooding accordingly symbolises his participation in the events, further confirming the fact that Eanatum is his representative and earthly counterpart. Once the battle is won, Eanatum re-establishes the border with Umma, erecting a stele (a border stone) to mark its location (Fragments D and C). He then buries the numerous dead in twenty tumuli. Doubts have been expressed about the identity of the dead, but—with all due caution—two small clues suggest that this burial might be carried out to honour Eanatum's men who have been killed in the battle. First, the soldiers of Umma are previously said to have been swept away in a destructive deluge, a metaphor that surely indicates a categorical disregard for the Umma dead, who are simply obliterated—a fact that is graphically confirmed on the monument in the climactic image of the vultures carrying away their body parts. Secondly, despite the rather poor condition of the text, the narrative seems to mention that Eanatum buries the Lagash dead with honour: 'He defeated Gisha (Umma) and made twenty b[urial tumuli (honouring his dead)] for it'. Immediately thereafter, Eanatum's personal god (Šul.muš×pa) cries 'sweet tears (of joy)' over the victorious and dutiful ruler. The words and images seem at this point to express a complex mixture of sadness at the loss of Lagash lives, tempered with happiness at the recovery of the stolen lands. Finally in this section, Eanatum is said to have 'obliterated many foreign lands' on behalf of Ningirsu—a boast that is repeated elsewhere. The lower register of the obverse (Fragments G, B and F) contains a long inventory of the recovered lands.

There follows a quasi-judicial ceremony in which Eanatum forces the ruler of Umma (who evidently survived the battle) to swear an oath on the respective casting-nets of a pantheon of divine witnesses (on the obverse of Fragments G, B and F, and the reverse of Fragments A, D and C). In the presence of one deity after another, the defeated ruler of Umma is compelled to avow a series of commitments, including that he will henceforth respect Ningirsu's ownership of the disputed lands, that rent will be duly paid on the fields that the citizens of Umma are permitted to cultivate (the lands will henceforth be exploited as 'an interest-bearing loan'), that he will maintain the levees 'up to the spring', that he will not interfere with the Lagash levees and irrigation ditches, and that he will not smash the border steles. Finally, the agreement shall be valid in perpetuity, and if the ruler of Umma breaks it then the casting-net (or nets) of the god (or gods) shall fall from the sky and destroy him. After each repetition of the agreement, Eanatum very 'cleverly' (as the text says) further affirms its validity by sending a token (typically two doves that have had their eyes anointed with kohl and their heads with cedar resin) to the god whose net is invoked. It is surely highly significant that the swearing section of the inscription begins on the mythological obverse and continues over onto the historical reverse because the agreement that is sworn multiple times is approved by the pantheon of deities, while its effects will be felt by the rulers and citizens of Lagash and Umma on a day-to-day basis forevermore: the connecting of the obverse and the reverse thus manifests the concordance of divine and human intentions.

Since the time of Heuzey, the introduction of the nets has caused considerable scholarly confusion, mainly because the first one belongs to Enlil, and it has therefore been thought that the net used by Ningirsu on the obverse must be that of his father and not his own. In fact, the ruler of Umma is made to swear on the casting-nets of Enlil, Ninhursag, Enki, Sin (the 'impetuous calf' of Enlil) and Utu, so the net motif is a literal and metaphorical catch-all for the divine wrath that will befall Umma if the oath is broken. Ningirsu discharges the will of the gods, but he does so as the appointed executive of the entire pantheon, including himself, all of which further reinforces his claim (and therefore that of Lagash) to the disputed territory. Nor can there be much doubt that the net he holds on the obverse is his own personal one because it is strikingly closed with a clasp or fastener in the shape of the Thunderbird that the god holds in his left hand. The preserved text breaks off on the mythological front after the invocation of Sin. When it continues on the historical reverse, the first god to be mentioned is Utu, after whom comes Ninki, the earth goddess, who will not strike with a net from above if the people of Umma break the sworn oath, but will instead cause snakes on the ground to fasten their fangs into the feet of the miscreants, so retribution for any perfidious behaviour will come from both the sky and from the earth. It should be further remarked that the principal image of Ningirsu with his net, as he is shown on the front of the stele, almost certainly performs a dual function: most obviously, it affirms the god's role in Eanatum's devastating defeat of Umma, but it is also proleptic, indicating that this is the punishment that will be meted out by the divine owner of the lands—who is also the enforcer of the resolution adopted by all the gods, as recorded in the accompanying text—if the ruler and citizens of Umma treacherously fail to live up to their sworn obligations in the future. Standing for the roll-call of deities with their respective casting-nets, the oversized figure of Ningirsu grasping the Thunderbird-handled net on the obverse sums up the judicial force of the contract that the ruler of Umma has effectively signed by swearing the oath demanded of him by Eanatum.

On the historical reverse (Fragments C and E) the narrow dividing line between the top register and the one below it again enunciates Eanatum's pedigree and the excellent characteristics that have been bestowed upon him by numerous gods: Enlil gave him strength, Ninhursag fed him with her own breast, Inanna named him (with the connotation that his reputation is surpassing), Enki made him wise, Nanshe chose him as her favourite, and so forth. And he is again commended as the 'subjugator of many foreign lands' on behalf of Ningirsu. In particular, he is said to have conquered Elam and Subartu, giving Lagash control of their timber and other goods, and he has subdued the cities of Susa and Ur. Lastly, at the bottom of the historical side, above the spear and the shaven heads (Fragment F), is a passage of text, separated from the rest of the inscriptions, that seems to provide a record of the words inscribed on the border stele that Eanatum erected in Ningirsu's honour on the Gu'edena frontier. After introducing the king of Kish, either as the broker of the original treaty that established the border some centuries earlier, or in a general sense as a way of referring to Eanatum as the king of the world, it reads (in a translation adapted from RIME 1.9.3.1):

The name of the monument is not the name of a man. He proclaimed its name: 'Ningirsu, the lord, crown of LUM.ma is the life of the Pirig̃-Edena-Canal!' He erected for Ningirsu the monument of the Gu'edena, the beloved field of the god Ningirsu, which Eanatum restored to the god Ningirsu's control.

In a general sense, the Stele of the Vulture's words and images do not correspond exactly because each stresses different aspects of the narrative and theme, and each mode of expression records distinct details. This depends partly on the particular strengths of the visual and written languages, which derive from distinct traditions (Winter 1985, p. 23). The first contrast, which is formal, concerns the respective orientations of the pictures and words. The inscription starts on the top right of the mythological obverse, from where it reads downwards and across, continuing at the top right of the historical reverse. By contrast, the pictorial narrative proceeds in the opposite direction, being read from bottom to top and generally from left to right. Nonetheless, in terms of content, text and imagery are well coordinated. In the inscription, the war against Umma is waged first and foremost at the behest of Ningirsu because he is the owner of the land that has been illegally exploited and occupied. Consequently, it is Eanatum's duty, as the ruler of Lagash, to prosecute the war in order to fulfil Ningirsu's wishes and restore justice, with reference to the legal agreement that was previously entered into by both parties to regulate the ownership and use of the land. Similarly, in the relief, Ningirsu's crushing of the enemy on the obverse and Eanatum's victory on the reverse communicate the same message as the text, using pictures to contribute to the narrative and to legitimise and validate the recorded events.

The written and visual accounts both set the proceedings in temporal and spatial frameworks that have narrative coherence. Despite that, although both expressive modes draw on a before-and-after structure, they only partially overlap, at least in terms of the surviving contents. For example, as far as can be known, the inscribed narrative preamble that briefly details the background to the conflict is missing from the relief. The untrustworthy and aggressive enemies are not shown carrying out the misdeeds that they are accused of in the text, which details a set of complicated legal and moral issues, including the idea of unfulfilled contractual obligations that are understandably difficult to portray through the scenic medium of pictorial carvings. Instead, only the battle and its aftermath are shown, resolving the complex historical background into a chronicle of just punishment through military defeat.

The lower registers of the relief on the obverse depict happenings that chronologically precede those represented above: Ningirsu is shown receiving his mother's blessing before the battle in the register below, but with his net filled with corpses, after the war has been won by Eanatum, in the imagery above. The fact that the situation on the reverse is more complicated is perhaps a consequence of its historical content as opposed to the mythological or even theological content of the obverse. Three of the four registers on the historical side show scenes of fighting. Only the second register from the bottom contains contrasting content, in the form of the ritual burial of the dead, but here, as in the other three registers, heaped corpses also proliferate, though in a context that might tentatively be interpreted as more compassionate.

Overall, the relief is not mainly concerned with a chronological account of successive incidents, but with the celebration and thematic linking of the two protagonists, Ningirsu and Eanatum. This provides the religious justification for the war, and one way that it is stressed visually is in the similar but varied appearances of the god and the ruler. Both wear their hair in chignons, for example, but while the god has a long beard, the king is clean shaven. Also, they are both shown driving chariots, but the god's (presumably) two-wheeled conveyance was probably swifter, lighter and drawn by winged lions, whereas that of Eanatum conceivably had four wheels and was pulled by onagers. Similarly, while the god was alone in his vehicle, the king was accompanied by an attendant—an assistant charioteer or a guard. The correspondences between Eanatum and Ningirsu are clearly accounted for in the text, where it is hinted that Ningirsu was instrumental in bringing the ruler into being as his divine begetter, and the ruler is said to have received numerous personal and formal benefits from a host of gods and goddesses. The pantheon of supreme deities that bestow favours upon Eanatum and unconditionally support Ningirsu's claim to the misappropriated and misused lands is not directly represented on the relief, however. In the preserved parts of the stele's pictorial programme Eanatum is seen only in association with Ningirsu and Ninhursag, and his relationship with both deities is made richer by the fact that the goddess, who is the mother of Ningirsu, is also said to have suckled Eanatum. Ningirsu has already been identified as the ruler's divine father, but the two are also, in a sense, brothers because they were both nursed by the same mother. The dizzying complexity of the theology is fraught with spiritual mystery that is not entirely unfamiliar from later conceptions of the relationships between humans and gods, including that found in the Christian trinity, with Mary as the maternal fourth presence. The absence of portraits of any deities other than Ninhursag and Ningirsu, coupled with the fact that Ningirsu's colossal form dominates the memorial, is probably explained by the fact that the stele was expressly dedicated to Ningirsu and displayed in his temple on Tell K.

In the surviving text, the battle is condensed into the images of the rainstorm and the deluge, which are placed in a mythical framework on the obverse by the introduction of the Thunderbird as the emblem of Ningirsu in his role as the god of the storm. It may well be that descriptions of battle scenes were multiplied in the inscriptions as a whole, as is generally the case in later epics of warfare from all periods, but any presumed additional action narratives on the Stele of the Vultures would have been couched in particularly formulaic terms because the outcome of the war is never in doubt. The story begins somewhat surprisingly, when Eanatum is shot with an arrow, but the occurrence is devoid of tension because he simply removes the projectile from his body and carries on with characteristic (and symbolic) energy as a 'man of the wind' (according to the text he 'breaks' the arrow that has wounded him, snapping the shaft without removing the arrowhead). In stark contrast, the amount of information conveyed about the battle increases exponentially in the pictorial representations, where the ruler and his soldiers are seen in several fighting modes. There are also burials, a solemn ritual, heaps of mutilated and degraded corpses, vultures that feed on the bodies of dead soldiers that have been abandoned on the field of battle when the fight is over, and the taking of prisoners of war. The illustrated incidents on the historical side of the relief take place in a temporal framework: the battle is made up of episodes (shown in the different battle formations on the bottom and the top two registers), with the ritual interlude coming somewhere in the middle, and the aftermath that is invoked when the carrion birds take possession of the field. Conversely, the scenes on the mythical side take place almost in an extra-temporal dimension. This is clearest in the image of Ningirsu with his casting-net, the stele's 'culminating scene', as it is called by Winter (1985, p. 14), which represents not only the conclusion of this particular battle, but also the consequences for any future violations of the oaths sworn on the nets of the gods, as described in the text. Accordingly, whereas the imagery on the historical reverse is, to all intents and purposes, a pictorial chronicle of things that might have actually happened, the images on the obverse invoke a divine dimension through a mode of representation that might be described as iconic.

Imdugud, the hybrid Thunderbird, who is half-lion and half-bird, is conspicuous by his absence from the preserved text, but he is represented several times on the relief, not only in the various images that portray him specifically (the net fastener and the Thunderbird crowns on the mythological side, for example), but also in the correlations and contrasts between Imdugud and the birds of prey. A key feature of his iconography is that, on the mythological side of the stele, the Thunderbird appears immobile and hieratic: he is active only in the abstract as the invisible driving force that manifests itself in the destructive power of the god and the ruler. The vultures, his counterparts on the historical side of the memorial, by contrast, are vigorously and evidently engaged in the action as rowdy, turbulent and voracious predators that seem almost more frightful than the mythological bird himself. They appear as exact, but living counterparts of the static creature on the divine emblems, connoting the destructive actions on the part of the ruler that are as tremendous and merciless in their earthly way as those of the storm god.

As seems natural, Ningirsu is the deity who receives most mentions in the surviving parts of the inscription (about thirty-seven), which is almost exactly the same number as his human counterpart, Eanatum, whose name is mentioned about thirty-nine times. Whether this is reflective of the lengthy original inscription as a whole cannot be known, but it would seem to stress the propagandistic intention of the monument, which is all too easily overlooked when the exegesis focuses on reconstructing the rich and intricate historical and mythological meanings that the makers expressed so vividly. It must always be recalled that the political purpose of the stele was to reinforce the connection between Eanatum and Ningirsu as a way of consolidating Eanatum's power and legitimising Lagash's claims to the occupied lands that the ruler of Umma might doubtless have argued were disputed territories. The inscription on the stele's mythological face details the innate and divinely bestowed characteristics possessed by Eanatum that will be instrumental in his efforts to defeat Umma, while the relief on this side of the stone is focused almost exclusively on Ningirsu. As far as can be known from the surviving fragments, there was no depiction of Eanatum among the mythological scenes. This absence—if such it was—is interesting in itself because the fascinating subject matter of the ruler's birth and upbringing might have provided a fruitful source of inspiration. On the historical face of the stele, in the text as well as in the relief, the focus is on the mature Eanatum as the strong ruler who recovers the god's stolen lands and (by extension only in the relief) conquers new territories on Ningirsu's behalf. In this regard, it is noteworthy that city-states other than Lagash and Umma are named only on Fragment E (in front of Eanatum's chariot), and in the quotation from the text that was inscribed on the Gu'edena stele (on Fragment F, above and around the spear shaft), where Kish is mentioned.

In the surviving texts the (unclear) name of the ruler of Umma is stated only once, while the word Umma appears forty-four times (including numerous mentions of the 'ruler of Umma'). By contrast, Lagash is named only eight times, including when Eanatum is called the ruler of Lagash. The army of Lagash is not mentioned in the inscription, a fact that makes the ruler appear almost as though he is a lone protagonist. This contrasts with the relief, where Eanatum's soldiers are well represented. As far as the gods are concerned, the name of Ningirsu's mother, Ninhursag, is inscribed around nine times, mainly on the mythological side (on Fragments A, B, F and G), and just once on the reverse (on Fragment E). Inanna and Utu are named six and seven times, respectively. Utu, the god of justice, is mentioned just once on the mythological side, near Imdugud's wing at the top of the casting-net on Fragment D, and many more times on the reverse on Fragment A in the top register, where the final victory of Eanatum is represented, together with the symbolic punishment of the enemy dead, who are reduced to carrion for the vultures to feast on. On both sides the inscribing of Utu's name occurs in significant pictorial contexts, where the subject is the restitution of justice and the retribution that is exacted on the wrongdoers. Inanna's name appears mainly on the mythological side on Fragment A, and twice on the reverse. Similarly, Enlil's name appears five times (including when Sin is called his 'calf'), Enki's appears seven times, and Sin's six times, mostly on the lower register of the mythological side (Fragments B, F and G). Seven mentions of the earth goddess, Ninki, who is also associated with snakes and the underworld, are found in a significant position at the top of the historical side (Fragments A, C and D). Finally, a number of other gods (Lugal.URU×KAR, Hendursag, Dumuziabzu and Nanshe) are each mentioned just once on the historical face, with the exception of Šul-MUŠ×PA, Eanatum's personal god, whose name is inscribed below the wing of the Ninhursag's bird-topped standard (an eagle or a Thunderbird) on the mythological side of the stele on Fragment C.

CHAPTER 19

The Enmetena Restoration

ENMETENA (C.2370–2335 BCE), WHO WAS THE SON and successor of Enanatum I, undertook the first major restoration of Tell K since the comprehensive remodelling of the whole city-state by his great-grandfather, Ur-Nanshe. Represented on more than thirty royal inscriptions, including some that were found outside the borders of Lagash, Enmetena is one of the best documented rulers of the Lagash I period. The evidence derived from administrative tablets suggests that he was the ruler (ensí) of Lagash for at least nineteen years, but the events recorded in his royal inscriptions suggest that his term of office was considerably longer. Yet again, the border dispute with Umma broke out during his reign, even though it seemed to have been resolved by his father. An inscribed clay cone, known as the Cone of Enmetena, recounts the defeat of Urlumma, the ruler of Umma, followed by the accession to power of the new ruler, named Il, and a fresh settlement that involved the construction of an embankment or levee stretching from the Tigris to the Nun canal (RIME 1.9.5.1). The text includes a historical narrative that traces the dispute all the way back to the pivotal treaty negotiated by Mesilim of Kish in the Early Dynastic IIIa period. A fragmentary inscribed clay cone (AO4399) also mentions incursions into Lagash that were carried out during Enmetena's reign by the 'man of Umma'.

Away from the conflict with Umma, Enmetena seems to have extended his rule outside the city-state of Lagash, possibly even enlarging the territories under its control. This is intimated by inscriptions found in Uruk, Ur and Badtibira as well as by claims to overlordship that are made or implied in other inscriptions, notably a vessel fragment from Uruk that carries lines of text from the Cone of Enmetena (RIME 1.9.5.1), and an inscribed statue from Ur that celebrates Enmetena's achievements, including the building of temples and shrines (RIME 1.9.5.17). His construction of the Emush temple in Badtibira, dedicated jointly to Inanna and Lugalemush, is attested by numerous sources, including about forty inscribed clay nails that were fixed into the walls of the Badtibira shrine at Enmetena's behest. Since the building of temples was the sole prerogative of the ruler of a city or state, it must be presumed that Badtibira had previously been annexed by Enmetena. His direct control over the city is further confirmed by accounts of the construction of the Inanna and Lugalemush temple that mention the cancelling of debts for citizens (RIME 1.9.5.4)—another privilege that could only be exercised by a head of state. The texts on the clay nails that were inserted into the walls of the Badtibira temple (RIME 1.9.5.3) also record a pact of 'brotherhood' (nam.šeš) that was established between Enmetena and the ruler of Uruk, Lugalkiginedudu. The nature of the arrangement is unclear, and it is not known whether it meant that Uruk owed allegiance to Lagash, but the fact that it is repeated on every one of the forty clay nails that carry Enmetena inscriptions is noteworthy, especially when the votive import of such objects is taken into account.

Enmetena's inscriptions also record his architectural activities in the city-state of Lagash at large, where he focused on the state's principal deities, including Ningirsu and Nanshe, though he also dedicated a temple to Enlil, the chief god of the Sumerian pantheon (RIME 1.9.5.17). This is a significant text because, although Enlil is frequently mentioned in

260 The Mound of the House of the Fruits

Lagash I royal inscriptions, it is the first recorded mention of a temple that was exclusively devoted to him. Nevertheless, Ningirsu is the deity whose name occurs most frequently in the entire corpus of more than thirty Enmetena royal inscriptions. He is named about twenty-five times with reference to various constructions that were erected in his honour.

Enmetena's work on Tell K was carried out on a huge scale (Fig. 95). He oversaw a major renovation of the Ur-Nanshe temple to Ningirsu, in which context the whole upper terrace was raised by about 0.8 m. In addition, he laid a new pavement that extended out from the Well of Eanatum, and he added a domed cover to the top of the well shaft. On the W edge of the tell, he built the very large brickwork mass that is referred to as the Enmetena Block, and he constructed the impressive curving channel that stretched around the mound's E corner.

He also raised the floor level of the brewery area, known as the Enmetena Esplanade, constructing the second variant of the three attested shallow reservoirs that were found on the same spot, and he built up the existing threshold at the gateway to the brewery complex (previously established by Eanatum) so that it could accommodate the elevated ground level and new pavement. Finally, the raising of the top of the tell must have required modifications to the stairways that led up to it, and it is likely that Enmetena rebuilt the Large Stairway to the north-east and made additions to the Double Stairway that was found near the N corner of the mound in Cros's Trenches 6 and 7 (marked on Cros's Plan B; Fig. 36).

With regard to Tell K, several interesting Enmetena inscriptions were found on a variety of ex-votos, including foundation tablets, door sockets and bricks. As well as affirming the

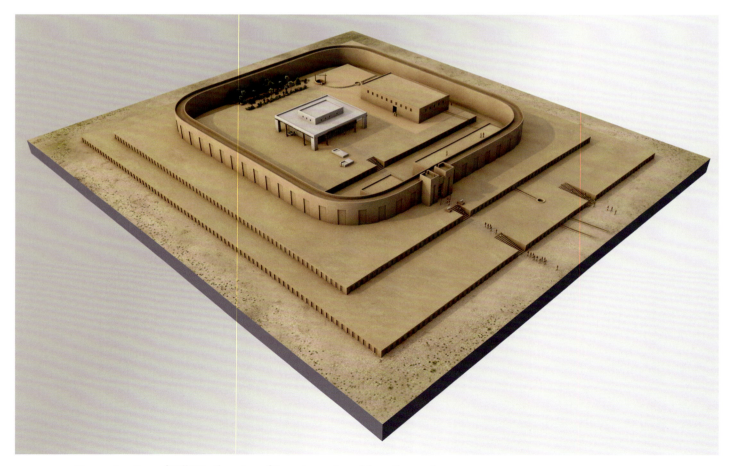

FIGURE 95. Reconstruction of Tell K in the reign of Enmetena, viewed from the south-east, showing the raised mound with its ascending platforms, the restored temple (centre) and the brewhouse (right). Additional structures are visible on the SE side, inside the SE temenos wall; the gardens and the Well of Eanatum are to the north-west.

scope of his architectural vision, they commemorate the construction of what is called the 'reed shrine' of Ningirsu's giguna (referred to either as èš.gi gi.gù.na ^{d}Nin-ĝír-su or èš.gi ^{d}Nin-ĝír-su). As is usual for cardinal proclamations of this kind, both variants were found repeated: the latter on five bricks, of which one was laid in the Enmetena Block; and the former on three bricks, one of which was excavated in the Enmetena Esplanade or brewery area. The particular 'reed shrine' formula, which is examined in detail in the general introduction to this book (Chapter 1) also appears on one or more door sockets. As far as can be ascertained, this was the first time that the epithet 'reed shrine' had been used to describe the Ningirsu temple, and it might well be an acknowledgement of the fact that Enmetena renewed the Tell K temple as part of his work on the whole site. As Forest (1999, p. 19) argues, the phrase was probably introduced to connote the core temple building in the context of the complex as a whole. Despite that, it might seem curious to find reeds mentioned so prominently on fired bricks, but the word was probably used in a figurative sense. A 'poliad' deity, or god of the polis, as the Greeks would have called him, Ningirsu was also endowed with elemental creative attributes that are notably stressed in the surviving lines of Lugale, the poem written in his honour (described in Chapters 1 and 47). Accordingly, like Enki, Ningirsu could be linked to the southern Mesopotamian marshlands, which was among the most potently generative environments that could be conceived of, and a similar association is found in the Hymn to the Reeds, written during the reign of Ur-Nanshe. Invoking Ningirsu in his generative guise to aid and inspire Enmetena's programme of construction, the term 'reed shrine' should therefore probably be understood metaphorically. The word giguna, which denoted a sacred edifice that was raised up on a high platform, might also have been a particularly expressive choice, as it seems previously to have been used only by Eanatum in one surviving instance. As argued above, it seems that a new epithet was applied to the shrine in its entirety to memorialise the work of renewal and reshaping that was carried out by Enmetena.

The Well of Eanatum

The closeness and relative heights of the Well of Eanatum and the Enmetena Block, which were both found by Sarzec shortly after he began work on Tell K, make it expedient to deal with them first before moving onto the changes Enmetena made to the rest of the sacred complex. The well, which rose to the Sarzec height of 12.83 m when it was completed by Eanatum, was extended by Enmetena, who added a coping and an associated domed extension or cover. Built directly on top of Eanatum's circular well shaft, the new coping was 0.3 m high, while the domed section added a further 0.6 m, meaning a total of 0.9 m of new brickwork was installed on the existing well. The internal and external dimensions of the coping (2.8 m and 4.25 m, respectively) were much greater than the size of the walled shaft, which measured 1.6 m internally and 2.8 externally. The coping and dome increased the overall height of the well's opening from the Sarzec height of 12.83 m to the new height of about 13.73 m. Since Enmetena raised the whole upper terrace by 0.8 m (from the Sarzec height of 12.83 m to 13.63 m), the figure calculated for the refurbished opening correlates closely with the level of the newly elevated summit, and it should also be recalled that the mound sloped away in this SW area, meaning that the Ur-Nanshe horizon of 12.83 m, which was left unaltered by Eanatum, should be considered as indicative around these installations, such that the actual altitude might in practice have been a little lower.

An unresolved question concerns the level of the adjoining bituminated water channel on the E side of the well that ran eastwards before curving towards the north-west, where it flowed into a small circular cistern (all shown on Sarzec's Plan D). Was this pipework (so to speak) also added, or raised and renewed, as part of Enmetena's restoration project? Unfortunately, Heuzey and Sarzec are silent on this point, giving no information about the height at which it was found or any details about its brickwork. Nevertheless, it seems highly likely that the channel recorded by Sarzec was also built by Enmetena (whether earlier versions of it were installed below is not known). A crucial reference point is provided by the stone door socket that was found 4.7 m away (4 m north-east of the well in Sarzec and Heuzey 1912, p. 420), which was inscribed in Enmetena's name and seemingly found in its primary context, as it was fixed to a fragment of tiling from the Enmetena pavement, part of the Enmetena Esplanade (discussed below). Reflecting the overall level of the Enmetena horizon, and in accordance with the indicative altitude of the refurbished top of the well, the paving and door socket were in all likelihood placed at a Sarzec height of approximately 13.63 m.

The Enmetena Block and the Raising of the Mound

An understanding of the function of the Enmetena Block, which was an extremely significant structural feature of Enmetena's overall programme, helps greatly to clarify the effects of his work on the three-step mound as it had been left by Ur-Nanshe. The block stood about 15 m west of the temple (still referred to for convenience's sake as the Ur-Nanshe Building) and a few metres south of the Well of Eanatum, where it marked the south-westernmost edge of the sacred precinct's upper platform. The sweeping nature of Enmetena's plans was commemorated in the inscriptions discussed above that were found on some of the bricks used to build the block, where the entire sacred mound (the giguna), with the temple (the 'reed shrine') at its heart, is used as a synonym for the Eninnu, or the establishment of the god (RIME 1.9.5.11):

> For the god Ningirsu, warrior of the god Enlil, Enmetena, ruler of Lagash, chosen in the heart by the goddess Nanshe, chief executive (ensí.gal or great ruler) for the god Ningirsu, son of Enanatum, ruler of Lagash, who built the 'reed shrine' of the god Ningirsu, may his personal god, the god Šul-MUŠ×PA, forever stand (interceding) before the god Ningirsu in the Eninnu for his life!

The inclusive connotation is confirmed by the inscribed silver Vase of Enmetena, which depicts Ningirsu's most potent emblem, the lion-headed eagle (the Imdugud or Thunderbird), and also by an inscribed bitumen (or possibly slate) plaque, with a text that commemorates the fact that it was commissioned by Dudu, the hieratic administrator of the temple under Enmetena. Both were discovered in the vicinity of the Enmetena Block, and both were devoted to Ningirsu as the patron god of the Eninnu in its entirety.

Thanks to the dedicatory bricks that were found in it, the block can be dated with some certainty, even though the inscriptions themselves use epithets to refer to the temple and the sacred precinct that complicate the picture. Abundantly described in the literature, the block seems at first glance to present no difficulties, except for an important discrepancy about its length, with the written accounts suggesting it was actually much longer than it appears to be on Sarzec's Plan D (Fig. 34), though, as discussed in Chapter 9 above, since the plan is inaccurate in other respects, it could also be defective in this instance. The idea that the structure was built (perhaps with some partial restoration of existing elements) as part of a major refurbishment of the SW containing wall of the upper terrace, which in turn was linked to the general raising of the top area of the mound by Enmetena, is extremely attractive. It would explain why the block was placed on, and protruded above, the mud-brick core of Ur-Nanshe's middle platform. The higher sections of the block formed the newly raised outer edge of the uppermost terrace, while its base formed the corresponding edge of the middle platform that had been established by Ur-Nanshe some decades previously, and now proportionately raised by Enmetena.

The situation begins to look far more problematic when the cross-section of this part of the tell is taken into consideration, however. According to Cros's SW Section (Fig. 37), the top of the block was seemingly found about 3 m below the original surface of the mound, while the top of the more or less adjacent Well of Eanatum was found at ground level. How is that differential to be accounted for? As Forest argues, it is conceivable that the top of the block might have been built up with mud-bricks to the same height as the mouth of the well (recalling the acknowledged point that such materials were disregarded by Sarzec). And yet, even as it is represented on Cros's section, the block was in a poor, misshapen condition, which surely would not have been the case had it been protected by a mass of mud-bricks that was 3 m thick. On the contrary, the state in which it was preserved strongly suggests that it had suffered from erosion, but this, in turn, seems incompatible with the fact that, at a distance of just 3 m, and supposedly rising 3 m higher than the top of the block, was the perfectly preserved well, which was also mostly older than the block.

A far more convincing explanation derives from a careful consideration of Cros's SW Section, especially when it is compared with the evidence recorded by Sarzec. The relative heights of the two features as shown on Cros's section are difficult to correlate with Sarzec and Heuzey's account, where it is stated that the block was found close to ground level, like the neighbouring well (which even rose above the surface of the ground). The existence of the well was common knowledge among the local Arab population (Sarzec and Heuzey 1912, p. 406), who believed it was haunted by jinns or spirits, and Sarzec noted signs of the block's presence from the time of his 'first excavations' on Tell K (Heuzey 1900, pp. 69 and 77–80). This might at first glance suggest that the top of the well and the top of the block ought to appear at about the same level on Cros's section, with the top of the block a little lower, partly because the well stood proud of the surface and partly because the block was found further down the tell's gently sloping side—a point that is well made by Forest, and one that can also be confirmed by comparing Sarzec's photo (Pl. 55 (1); Fig. 41). But the straightforward conclusion is affected by an understanding of what Cros's section was intended to show, and this is where difficulties arise. Cros's aims in the SW Section were seemingly contradictory because the drawing combines an indication of the state of the mound as it was before the excavations started with a depiction of how it looked when the diagram was made, probably in 1903, when Cros carried out initial surveys across the site. These two issues lead to considerable confusion, particularly with respect to the height of the top of the well.

A main indicator of the site's original condition on the section is the overarching profile of the mound's summit. By 1903 it had been dramatically truncated down to the levels of the Sarzec Esplanade, which is shown running horizontally (with several ups and downs) through the middle of the tell. The issue with the well is that it is shown stratigraphically not as it was in 1903, but as though its highest point still lay at about the same level as the summit of the mound, as it did when Sarzec found it. This is simply incorrect, as even the manner of the well's portrayal suggests, because although it was still a prominent landmark when Cros first saw the site, by the time of his arrival the upper parts of the structure had been dismantled some years previously by Sarzec. This is already apparent in Sarzec's photo (Pl. 57 (2); Fig. 46), which was taken after he had removed the domed extension with which it was capped and had begun work on the associated coping. Cros's section shows only the preserved part of the cylindrical well shaft, after the dome and coping had been taken away, and perhaps also after further courses of bricks had been removed from the top of the shaft, whether systematically or by looters. But the preserved extent of the shaft is shown as though it rose to the level of the original summit of the mound, which was not the case, since the coping and the domed addition increased the overall elevation of the top of the shaft by at least another 0.9 m. Therefore, as regards the SW edge of Tell K, particularly in the vicinity of the Enmetena Block and the Well of Eanatum, Cros's SW section is unreliable. If it was intended to depict the position of the tops of both the block and the well with respect to the upper surface of the mound, where they were found by Sarzec, it should show them both close to, or touching (or in the well's case a little above), the sloping line that describes the tell's original summit. If it aimed to show the excavated state of the structures as Sarzec had left them after his final excavations, the top of the well should be placed at least 0.9 m below the original summit of the tell to take account of the fact that the coping and domed addition had been removed. In reality, additional courses of bricks would also almost certainly have been removed by the time Cros first visited Tell K, so that the top of the well had probably been reduced by considerably more than 0.9 m when the plan was sketched, and this would have placed the surviving part of its shaft closer to the level of the preserved upper part of the block. All of this can be further verified by comparing Cros's published account (1910, p. 72), where he states that, when he first saw Tell K, the top of the well stood 1.5 m above the Sarzec Esplanade. If that figure of 1.5 m is plotted on the section (using the scale provided), it does indeed place the surviving top of the well just a fraction higher than the top of the adjacent block, both of which were preserved when Cros first visited Tell K in 1903 to a Sarzec height of roughly 10.5 m.

In a sense, however, the problems with Cros's section are largely irrelevant because what is of primary concern is the stratigraphic relationship between the top of the block and the top of the well as those features were left by Enmetena, and this correlation was observed by Sarzec when he came across both the well and the block close to the upper surface of the tell. As noted above and discussed in more detail below, Enmetena raised the top of the mound from the Ur-Nanshe horizon of 12.83 m by 0.8 m, which is in accord with the elevated opening of the top of the well (at about 13.73 m or a little lower, as stated above). The top of the Enmetena Block was therefore also at about the same approximate Sarzec height of 13.63 m or 13.73 m, which places it within the Enmetena horizon. This would situate the top surface of the block at about the height of the raised mound's upper terrace, notably represented by the pavement that was laid in the area of the Enmetena Esplanade (discussed below), which was at the same Sarzec height of 13.63 m.

Also, and again as mentioned above, the vertical profile of the block was generally L-shaped, with the bottom bar of the L jutting out towards the south-west, away from the principal areas of the tell, out towards the surrounding plain, while the height difference between the top of the block and the surface of the bottom bar of the L was 1.7 m, as mentioned by Heuzey (1900, p. 77). As can be seen on Sarzec's photo (Pl. 55 (1); Fig. 41), the well-preserved lower section of the block (the base of the L) was formed of a significant but unknown number of courses of bricks, four of which can be seen in the photo. The thickness of the bricks being 0.06 m (plus mortar), this would place the base of the bottom bar of the L at least 2 m lower than the top of the block, at a minimum Sarzec height of 11.63 m. Heuzey (1900, p. 78) goes much further than this, suggesting that Enmetena wished to site the block's foundations at the same level as the 'ancient ground' of the Lower Construction. While it is surely an exaggeration to say that the foundations of the Enmetena Block might have descended to a Sarzec height of 8.48 m, more than 3 m lower than they appear on the photo, this nevertheless points to the crux of the matter. The purpose of the L-shaped block was to bolster and partly to extend the newly raised upper surface of the mound at the Sarzec height of 13.63 m, and at the same time proportionately to elevate the height of the middle terrace that had been established by Ur-Nanshe when he remodelled the entire tell. Accordingly, the Enmetena Block formed part of the new retaining structure that was built when Enmetena elevated the mound's upper terrace by 0.8 m and correspondingly raised the lower two terraces that dated back to the time of Ur-Nanshe.

Though not identified as such by Sarzec, further evidence of Enmetena's reconstruction of the mound's massive supporting platforms was provided by the discovery of the extensive, extremely well-preserved section of curved channelling that ran around the E corner of the middle one of the three colossal terraces. As argued in Chapter 9, the channel is mislabelled on Sarzec and Heuzey's Plan D, where it is called a 'more recent wall'—an epithet that should have been applied to the Gudea block of fired bricks that can be seen in the photo (Pl. 58 bis (2); Fig. 50), but which is not marked on the plan. Similarly, the curving channel is also inaccurately placed on the plan, because the wider section that is seen on the photo and clearly drawn on the diagram was in reality further to the south-east than it appears, and therefore much more in line with the tell's E corner than the plan suggests. Almost certainly built with the same fired bricks as were used in the Enmetena Block (again as argued above), the channel was situated on the middle one of the three principal platforms that made up the tell at an estimated Sarzec height of between 10.8 m and 11.6 m (calculated by adding 0.8 m to the height of the Tell J reservoir (J on Plan D)). This was presumably not the only alteration that Enmetena made to the tell's water-carrying systems. In addition, though Cros's account again presents difficulties, it is possible that Enmetena did some refurbishment work on the installations referred to as the water supply network, and particularly the reservoir referred to as the Rectangular Construction, since at least some of the rectangular bricks referred to by Cros (1910, pp. 90–4) as post-Enmetena surely originated in his reign.

Enmetena's general elevation of the three-step mound must, of course, have required additions to the stairways that provided access to the site, and this would presumably have been most noticeable on the monumental entranceways. Evidence of significant work was found on the Large Stairway that lay about 35 m to the north-east of the Ur-Nanshe Building, where a flight of steps ascended towards the middle of the NE side of the tell. Built of bricks that displayed Enmetena's regnal marking (a single longitudinal fingerstroke), the surviving flight formed a gentle ascent that rose to meet a landing at the Sarzec height of about 8.48 m. This transitional platform was laid on two substantial brickwork blocks in which were found the two wide-bellied bituminated cavities, referred to previously, that might have been the bases for significant flagpoles or ring posts. It has been argued that this monumental ascent was formerly established by Ur-Nanshe, and that it led to a chambered gateway (restored by Enanatum I) in the massive temenos wall that enclosed the upper mound, from where it gave access to the tell's sacred summit (see Chapter 16). That being the case, and since no identified traces of Ur-Nanshe bricks were recorded by Sarzec on the Large Stairway, it must be assumed that Enmetena painstakingly renewed it, and that, some considerable time later, it was again refitted by Gudea. More signs of Enmetena's work on the stairways of Tell K were found by Cros in Trenches 6 and 7, where the two flights of stairs on the Double Stairway (below which lay two previous iterations of the ascent) were built with bricks from the reign of Eanatum, together with bricks bearing Enmetena's regnal marking. The fact that the two types were in some cases found side by side on the same treads clearly shows that Enmetena refashioned or repaired the ascent. The extent of the refurbishment is impossible to determine, but it was evidently not as comprehensive as the work carried out on the Large Stairway. What seems certain in both cases is that Enmetena increased the heights of the Large Stairway and the Double Stairway in the context of his overall raising of the three-step mound.

The Hanging Gardens of Girsu

The understanding that the Enmetena Block, which was built as a massive support for the freshly raised mound, had an L-shaped profile that followed the tell's stepped outlines might shed further light on the meaning of the epithets that were introduced by Enmetena to refer to the sanctuary: the 'reed shrine' and 'giguna' of Ningirsu. Perhaps the best way to broach that issue is by raising a further question: why did Enmetena reinforce just this relatively limited part of the SW side of the sacred complex with fired bricks, and not the whole perimeter? The fact that the bolstering structure was made only of fired bricks in this rather confined area is demonstrated by the apparent cohesion of the block as a unit, and also by the fact that no trace of a related fired-brick support was found anywhere else around the site, not even by the stairways that Enmetena is known to have raised. Since the possibility that the decision was forced upon the builders due to a lack of materials is unimaginable, it must have been a positive choice. But what possible reason could there have been to use fired bricks only on this side of the sanctuary, and especially bricks that bore the dedicatory text quoted above that includes the novel appellations?

The general consensus with regard to the Sumerian word giguna is that its core definition relates to a 'sacred edifice built on a high platform or terrace' (as it is defined in CAD, G, pp. 67–70), which seems to correspond exactly with the physical reality of Early Dynastic Tell K. But the word giguna, which embraces a constellation of meanings, is a more complex term than this implies. The etymology of the word suggests a structure made of reeds, and in Early Dynastic texts the word giguna is closely connected with small plantations or thickets (Cavigneaux 2016). That is why, although the usual modern translation is 'raised terrace' or 'temple', it is also sometimes translated as 'grove'. Consequently, inscriptions from the last part of the third millennium and the early part of the second millennium describe a giguna as growing on pure ground, as something that is holy and sometimes also green; it is said to connote a secret place and something that smells of cedar, but it is also associated with something that is lofty like a mountain. Finally, it is described as a kind of residence (see Szarzyńska 1992, pp. 278–80).

As the diverse usages demonstrate, the word giguna could be applied to artificially created pleasure gardens: groves planted with cedars or other aromatic trees and plants. That meaning links to the elevated temple because the term seems also to have meant 'a reed structure erected on an artificial mound', while giguna (or gi-guna to clarify its composite form) might literally denote 'multi-coloured reeds' (see Cavigneaux 2016). Since reeds are not intrinsically colourful, either when they are growing or after they have been cut and dried, the essential idea must presumably have had metaphorical overtones that connected the word giguna with attractive or flourishing vegetation. The connotation of a temple on a high platform, or a divine house with a stairway as it became in later Akkadian (drawing on the Akkadian word *bītum*, meaning house, and also *simmiltum*, meaning stairway), was therefore related to a shrine built at least partly of reeds that was also green and redolent of sweet-scented trees and flowers. As it evolved in one direction, the word came to designate the platform terraces on which temples were built, but if that meaning is reconnected with the core sense of colourful or fragrant plants, and also with greenery, then it is inherently feasible that to refer to a stepped temple platform as a giguna would also imply that the sanctuary was planted (Cavigneaux 2016). The giguna, which was an assemblage enjoyed by a number of gods and goddesses, was therefore an elevated divine house with an associated pleasure garden.

If that is taken to be the meaning of the word as it was used by Enmetena then it might further be assumed that the stages of the L-shaped Enmetena Block were planted with horticultural trees, shrubs and flowers, perhaps climbing (or trailing) plants that covered the walls, or possibly vines, wisteria or even willows (Cavigneaux 2016). In other words, the stepped structure can plausibly be interpreted as the base for what should be called the hanging gardens of Girsu (Fig. 96), but how might such a garden have been established? It is unlikely that any standing or hanging plants would have been grown directly in the mud-brick substructure on the topmost level (to the north-east of the fired-brick walls of the Enmetena Block). For one thing, the roots of any larger trees, shrubs or vines would have soon interfered with the masonry. More importantly, the tell's usual ground, which was made of mud-bricks

266 | The Mound of the House of the Fruits

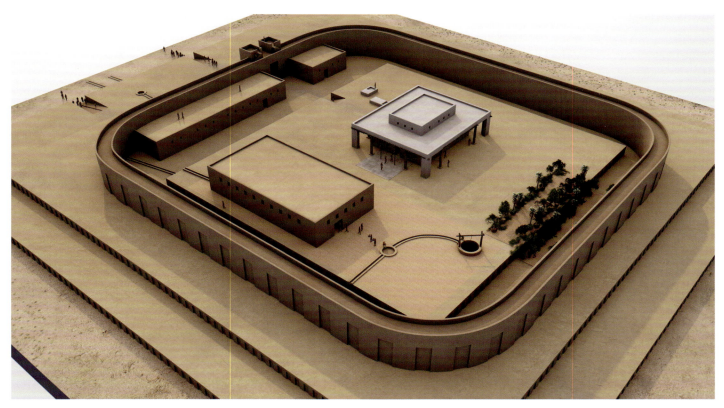

FIGURE 96. A view of the hanging gardens planted on Tell K by Enmetena, looking towards the W corner of the Enmetena temple, with the grove and the Well of Eanatum (right).

or compacted clay, would have absorbed a great deal of water, and the ground would presumably have needed a great deal of added organic matter to make the raw clay into more fertile soil. It would possibly have been difficult to contain the water in relatively open ground, while the clay base material would have become rock-hard during the baking hot summers—which is precisely why clay could be used as a building material. Similarly, the surface of the block's L-shaped protrusion on the mound's middle terrace was made of fired bricks, so unless that whole fired-brick shelf (so to speak) had been fenced in (or walled in) and filled, thereby effectively raising the level of this short stretch of the middle terrace, then nothing could be planted directly in the fired-brick ground.

Accordingly, it is far more likely that, on both the uppermost and the middle terraces, the necessary volumes of prepared soil—presumably a mixture of clay and organic materials—would have been decanted into specially made (fired or unfired) clay pots in which growing conditions, especially with regard to irrigation and water conservation, could be more precisely controlled. The fact that the sacred garden was planted exclusively on the SW side, which is the only place where traces of a fired-brick block were found, would have made it a particular feature of that part of the mound, distinguishing it from the rest as it presented a green and colourful appearance against the muted palette of earthen colours that characterised the sides of the mound generally. In terms of the exact positioning of the planted area, a key issue of logistics was probably of even greater significance than the festive aspect of the mound's SW face, however, because the Enmetena Block was built right next to the Well of Eanatum, from where sufficient water could relatively easily have been obtained and conveyed by bucket or bituminated conduit to supply the garden's thirsty soil.

The Enmetena Esplanade

As already mentioned, in the area known as the Enmetena Esplanade, Sarzec unearthed a number of inscribed objects on which the expression èš.gi.gi.gù.na, meaning the 'reed sanctuary of the giguna', or the 'multi-coloured reeds', was again used to refer to the sacred complex (RIME 1.5.9.10). Other inscriptions commemorate the construction of a brewery, or é.bappir (RIME 1.9.5.13) and a coach house, é.ǧešgigír.ra (RIME 1.9.5.14), both dedicated to Ningirsu—all found *in situ* to the north of the Ur-Nanshe Building, in or around the Enmetena Esplanade, suggesting that the planners intentionally placed the buildings close to one another in that area. It is interesting to note that the Enmetena proclamations correlate with information recorded on Gudea Cylinder A, which speaks of the 'brewery' and the 'coach house' as neighbouring installations (A28), indicating that there was continuity between the sacred complex on Tell K and Gudea's New Eninnu on Tell A, and that these buildings were regarded as somehow belonging together.

With respect to the work done by Enmetena, the stratigraphy in the vicinity of the Enmetena Esplanade is clear because there is unequivocal evidence that the level of the tell in this area was raised with a mud-brick mass to establish a new upper terrace surface. Indeed, Sarzec exceptionally described the courses of mud-bricks that were placed under the Enmetena reservoir (the middle one of the three that were superimposed) and it is worth recapping what was recorded. In total there were six courses of mud-bricks with dimensions of 0.21 m × 0.14 m × 0.05 m or 0.06 m (t). The top two courses were laid vertically on their long sides in a herringbone pattern, with a course of bricks laid flat under each course, and below them were two further courses that were laid vertically, again in a herringbone pattern. This gives a thickness of 4 × 0.14 m for the vertically laid courses plus 2 × 0.05 m or 0.06 m for the flat courses, making approximately 0.68 m plus (approximately) 6 × 0.02 m for the clay bonding. That gives a total of about 0.8 m for the mud-brick deposit under the reservoir, which is exactly in line with the benchmark figure for Enmetena's general raising of the mound from 12.83 m (the Ur-Nanshe base level, which was left unchanged by Eanatum) to 13.63 m (12.83 m + 0.8 m). Buried in the mud-bricks was a set of five foundation deposits in the form of large copper figurines (about 0.25 m tall) that were accompanied by stone tablets inscribed in the name of Enmetena to commemorate the construction of the 'reed shrine' of Ningirsu's giguna (Fig. 97). Incidentally, in view of the interesting details that were recorded about the layer of mud-bricks that was found under the superimposed reservoirs, it is all the more regrettable that this is the only place on Tell K where Sarzec applied his considerable powers of observation to this vital material.

Although the design of Enmetena's preserved foundation deposits is markedly different from that adopted by Ur-Nanshe, there is nevertheless some continuity between the two types: both include anthropomorphic copper surveyors' pegs with dedicatory inscriptions, together with stone tablets shaped in the form of planoconvex bricks and inscribed with an elaborate dedication. Two significant departures from the earlier practice are that the Enmetena figurines (with heights ranging between 0.24 m and 0.28 m) are larger than their Ur-Nanshe predecessors, and they are not fitted with the copper collars that were used by Ur-Nanshe to support the accompanying stone tablets. Most importantly, the heads of the Enmetena figurines are each adorned with a single pair of horns—a clear attribute of divinity. This innovation was not introduced by Enmetena, however. The foundation deposits of his father, Enanatum I, that were retrieved from the Ibgal temple of Inanna in Lagash already displayed this distinctive feature, and those deposits were also found placed below the sanctuary's mud-brick platform and within the outlines of its walls. Enanatum I's figurines were placed vertically between the bricks in an initial course of mud-bricks, with their pointed tips touching the ground surface below, and they were then encased up to their necklines by two further courses of mud-bricks. The inscribed stone tablets were positioned horizontally on top of the third course, behind the heads of the figurines, so that the tops of the heads and the upper surfaces of the stones were flush. The carefully arranged ensembles were then covered with more courses of mud-bricks (Hansen 1992, p. 208).

The inscribed stone tablets that are components of the five Enmetena foundation deposits found *in situ* in the Enmetena Esplanade were all made with holes running all the way through their centres so that they could be fitted over the heads of the figurines before the deposits were buried in the mud-bricks. The figurines themselves display carefully modelled heads, prominent noses, serene smiles and large eyes that are wide open, as though to express a state of exaltation. The hair on each is styled into a series of ringlets or locks that fall down the figures' backs almost to their waists. Their arms are carefully modelled, with the hands clasped to the chests (the left in front of the right), and their torsos taper down to narrow points that again resemble the form of surveying pegs.

268 The Mound of the House of the Fruits

FIGURE 97. An Enmetena foundation deposit, including a copper peg and an inscribed planoconvex tablet made of sandstone. Musée du Louvre AO2353.

The dedicatory inscriptions on the figurines record Enmetena's construction of the brewery for Ningirsu (RIME 1.9.5.13): 'For the god Ningirsu, warrior of the god Enlil, Enmetena, ruler of Lagash, son of Enanatum of Lagash, who built the brewery of the god Ningirsu. His personal god is the god Šul-MUŠ×PA'. As on the foundation deposits of Ur-Nanshe, the texts on the tablets describe Enmetena's overarching project, the scope of which reached well beyond the confines of the Ningirsu complex on Tell K. Following in Ur-Nanshe's pioneering footsteps, Enmetena seems purposefully to have emulated his distinguished forefather (RIME 1.9.5.12):

For the god Ningirsu, warrior of the god Enlil, Enmetena, ruler of Lagash, son of Enanatum, ruler of Lagash, descendant of Ur-Nanshe, king of Lagash, built the Eshdugru ('Shrine [in which] Pots Are Arranged') for the god Ningirsu, built for him the Ahush 'Terrifying Water' the temple where (the god Ningirsu) looks approvingly upon (Enmetena). For Lugal.URU×KAR he built his 'palace' of (the town of) URU×KAR, built the Eengur 'Temple of the Fountain-head' of (the town) Zulum for the goddess Nanshe built the Abzu.pasira 'Fountainhead with Narrow Channels' for the god Enki, king of Eridu, built the giguna ('Multi-coloured Reeds') of the shining grove for the goddess Ninhursag, built for the god Ningirsu the (town) Antasura ('[Northern(?)] Boundary') (whose) temple's awesome splendour covers all the lands, built the Eada ('House of the Father') of Imsag for the god Enlil, built the temple of the goddess Gatumdug, built (the town) Shapada ('Chosen (in) the Heart') for the goddess

Nanshe. At that time, Enmetena built for the god Ningirsu, the master who loves him, his (Ningirsu's) brewery. Enmetena, who built the brewery of the god Ningirsu—his personal god is the god Šul-MUŠ×PA.

On top of the mud-brick layer in which the elaborate foundation deposits were buried, the Enmetena pavement was tiled with square fired bricks (Heuzey 1900, p. 86). Sarzec and Heuzey give no further details about their size or manufacture, but the tiling seems to have covered a wide area that stretched out to the Well of Eanatum, taking in the gateway with the raised threshold that stood at the entrance to the esplanade (north-east of the well and south-west of the topmost Oval Reservoir on Sarzec's Plan D), and probably radiating outwards towards the north-east. A number of fragments of square-brick paving were recorded in the extended area, some with door sockets fixed to them, notably the one mentioned above that was found about 4 m north-east of the well.

Since the Enmetena pavement was placed at a Sarzec height of 13.63 m, that puts it within the same horizon as the raised level of the corresponding Enmetena paving associated with the coping and domed extension that was added to the top of the Well of Eanatum. As noted above, the upper surface of the added dome lay at an approximate Sarzec height of about 13.73 m, but was almost certainly a little lower than this in reality due to the profile of the ground. The height of the elevated threshold in the gateway that fronted the esplanade also correlates neatly with these figures because the eight courses laid in the opening lifted the threshold by about 0.8 m, which is again consistent with the overall height of the newly installed Enmetena pavement (also 0.8 m above the old base). By the gate was found another inscribed stone door socket, identical to the one found approximately 4 m north-east of the well, on which mention is made of the 'sanctuary of the reeds' of Ningirsu, using the same phraseology as the bricks found in the Enmetena block. The middle of the three superimposed reservoirs, built with Enmetena bricks, was constructed on a platform that had been raised by the same amount (0.8 m), while the three smaller rectangular blocks that were fitted with bituminated compartments were also brewery installations that were most probably built during the same Enmetena construction phase. No information was recorded by Sarzec about the Enmetena paving that was laid in the vicinity of his reservoir, but the stone door socket that was identical to the one attached to a square Enmetena brick would presumably indicate that the floor of the Enmetena brewing facility was also paved with the same square tiles.

The Brewhouse

The outstandingly well-preserved installation that was the main feature uncovered by Sarzec on the Enmetena Esplanade was the Oval Reservoir (*Bassin Ovale*), which was almost certainly built by Urukagina, though no certain evidence of that fact was recorded. The French word *bassin* is a catch-all that Heuzey and Sarzec apply, sometimes misleadingly, especially when the word is literally translated into English, to a range of concave or cavitied fixtures, including this one, whose uses were not always immediately obvious. In fact, the Oval Reservoir was a large, open fermentation vat or tank, with an approximate capacity of a little less than 3,000 litres, and in conjunction with the Well of Eanatum, it was at the heart of Tell K's beer-making industry. The installation that Sarzec first found (the topmost of three that were superimposed), which postdates Enmetena, was clearly not associated with a comprehensive refurbishment of the whole brewing complex, but was rather an updated replacement vat or tank for the one constructed by Enmetena. Apart from the addition of the new fermenter, therefore, the layout and operation of the brewhouse in all likelihood remained as they were in the time of Enmetena, after he had expanded the first iteration constructed by Eanatum, whose well supplied the necessary water. For these reasons, and also because the archaeological ramifications of making beer on this scale and at this location on Tell K would have been comparable in all three instances, it makes sense to discuss the brewing operation here, using the Oval Reservoir as the paradigm case.

To simplify matters, the capacity of the fermenter (the Oval Reservoir) can be calculated by treating it as a regular ellipse, with axes measuring 5.1 m and 4.6 m (the dimensions recorded by Sarzec), subtracting 0.5 m to account for the width of the low coping (made of bricks measuring 0.32 m × 0.25 m × 0.05 m), and estimating its overall depth as 0.2 m (the three courses of bricks in the coping plus mortar), which gives: 2.3 m × 2.1 m × π = 2.96 m^3, or 2,960 litres. In order to lay down a benchmark, it is estimated that beer containing about 4% alcohol requires roughly three parts water to one part grain (taste and strength being determined by the chosen proportions), which works out for this reference example as 2.22 m³ (or 2,200 litres) of water for 0.74 m³ (or 444 kg) of grain, calculated (again for simplicity's sake) as though it were straightforward grain barley.

These are spectacular numbers, and even if there is a margin of error of 10% or 20%, the unequivocal conclusion is that beer production in these quantities could not have been conducted without sophisticated, well-planned infrastructure. First, 2,200 litres of water, which could not easily or hygienically be carried in buckets or large jars in the volumes required, had to be piped from the Well of Eanatum to the T-shaped junction on the fermenter's NE side. The hydrodynamics of this means that the water, once extracted from the well, had to flow downhill for a considerable distance, first north-westwards towards the edge of the tell, and then from the south-west to the north-east until it reached the brewery. This could have been effected: a) by utilising the existing slope of the mud-brick mound; b) by remodelling the mound to accommodate the flow; or c) by using a purpose-built aqueduct (Figs. 98 and 99). Since there were installations on the SE side of the fermenter, the inlet must have been on the NW side of the T-shaped junction, which would have needed to be higher than the outlet on the SE side. Happily, Sarzec's photo (Pl. 55 (2); Fig. 42) shows exactly this view, and (possible perspective distortions notwithstanding) there does indeed appear to be a gentle slope from the north-west down to the south-east (from right to left as we look).

The large amounts of processed grain needed, which were presumably supplied from the temple's estates, which included fields and granaries, had to be delivered to the upper part of the tell. The grain could have been carried up the stairs in baskets by labourers, brought up using pack animals or possibly driven up in wheeled transport that might have ascended via a smooth, or perhaps very gently stepped slope. Though no candidate for such a slope has been identified, the fact that a coach house dedicated to Ningirsu was situated right next to the brewhouse would surely imply that coaches and chariots could ascend to the upper level. The processed grain came principally in the form of barley cakes, or bappir (a word that occurs in the Enmetena inscription (RIME 1.9.5.13)

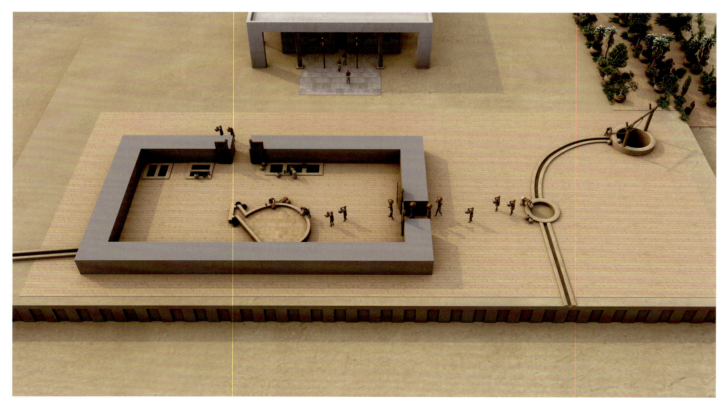

FIGURE 98. Reconstruction of the brewhouse, seen from the north-west, with the Well of Eanatum (right).

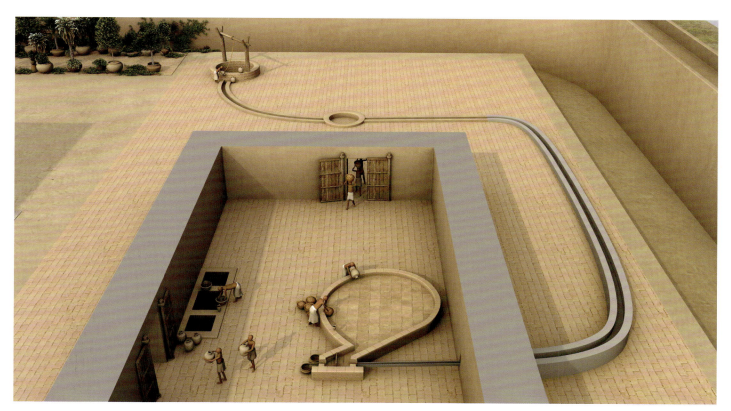

FIGURE 99. A cutaway view of the reconstructed brewhouse, seen from the north-east, showing a possible aqueduct supplying water from the well to the Oval Reservoir's T-shaped junction.

quoted above), which were made of malted (meaning partly germinated) barley that was dried, milled and formed into cakes that were very lightly baked at low temperatures (see Paulette 2020, pp. 74–9, for bappir and other beer-making ingredients). These processes turned the starch into carefully conditioned sugars and broke down the grain's chemical contents to make them more readily fermentable. The dry ingredients (with groats, roasted grains and aromatics as optional substitutions and additions) were presumably shovelled into the deeper belly of the fermenter, behind and below the T-shaped junction in the photo, where they were beaten and mixed with water to make the infusion (mash or wort) that dispersed throughout the fermenter as more water was steadily added until the tank was full.

Sarzec noted that the base of the installation sloped down towards the north-east, as can clearly be seen in the photo. Accordingly, when the fermented liquid was ready, the lower outlet on the SE side could be opened, and the liquid would flow down and out into nearby receptacles. The rate of flow would have been regulated naturally by the shallowness of the slope, and manually promoted by human operatives where necessary, while the belly under the T-shaped junction would conceivably have acted as a sump to catch some of the plentiful solid deposits that were left over from the fermentation. This valuable by-product could have been used for animal feed or fertiliser, as it still is today. There is a generally received idea that Sumerian beer was thick and porridgy (see Paulette 2020, p. 68), but the fermented liquid from this production line could have been filtered through a fine mesh as it passed through the outlet, and the possibility of further clarifying and conditioning at this stage is discussed below. In consequence, it is perhaps conceivable that the beer made on Tell K was not necessarily as thick as is often supposed. Optimal temperatures for the fermentation of ales such as this range between sixteen and twenty-two degrees centigrade (see 'fermentation' in Oliver 2012), which means brewing must have been seasonal (taking place during the cooler months). The fermentation time was a few days, implying probably one production cycle a week, and the finished product that resulted from each batch of raw ingredients would presumably have amounted to some 400 litres of beer (tentatively assuming a ratio of about five to one), some or all of which had no doubt eventually to be stored in suitable receptacles in the coolest available place, perhaps elsewhere on the site and possibly underground.

The entire process had considerable consequences for the building's architectural features (Fig. 100). To prevent unwholesome bacterial infections, the inside of the brewhouse, including the fermenter and all the other installations had to be kept scrupulously clean, which would have required lots more water. In addition, the necessary high degree of environmental control meant that the building must have been roofed to keep out dirt, dust, birds and flies, for example. And yet, the fermentation process also required excellent ventilation (as it does today, especially when such open shallow tanks are employed). This is for four main reasons: the fermentation of cold-water mashes is assisted up to a certain point by aeration that supplies oxygen (see 'oxidation', in Oliver 2012); wild yeasts, which presumably played an important role, are carried on currents of air; the gaseous by-product of fermentation is carbon dioxide, which is toxic in high concentrations and would have had to be expelled; and finally, fermentation is exothermic (it generates heat) so a good air flow would have helped to control the temperature inside the building. To create a through-draught, therefore, the brewhouse must have had several large window openings that would surely have been protected with screens (possibly removable ones), perhaps made of tightly woven reeds or cloth. Finally, although it is possible to brew beer in an open shallow tank of this kind using only airborne wild yeasts, the relatively warm ambient temperatures, in combination with the general set-up, leads to top fermentation, which means that the yeasts produced while the sugar was being consumed and turned into alcohol would rise to the top of the tank as foamy flocculations that could be skimmed and set aside to be used in the next fermentation (thus making the

FIGURE 100. A view of the interior of the brewhouse, seen from the north-east, showing the Oval Reservoir, the respective doors in the SW wall (behind the reservoir) and the SE wall (left), the partly subterranean conditioning vats (left) and the screened windows.

procedure still more controllable) or mixed in with the other by-products and used as animal feed or fertiliser. Incidentally, Sarzec noted that the inner floor of the fermenter sloped down towards the T-shaped junction at the NE end, but also across the width of the installation from the north-west to the south-east (towards the centre of the tell). In addition to promoting the flow of beer out of the vessel, the two gradients would presumably also have aided thermal circulation in the fermenting liquid, and further facilitated the collection of spent solids.

Also found in the brewhouse, next to the Oval Reservoir, were three rectangular containers (*bassins* in French) that were built of fired bricks and situated on the SE side of the fermenter (see Plan D): one had three compartments (clearly visible in Sarzec's photo (Pl. 55 (2)), and the others each had two. Heuzey (1900, pp. 82–3) records that the cavities of all three were coated with bitumen, which indicates that they were intended to hold liquids, while their position on the SE side of the fermenter, close to the outlet on the T-shaped junction, suggests that they might have been vats used to clarify and condition the fermented beer after it had been evacuated from the fermenter but before it was decanted into manageable containers and removed from the brewhouse. The clarification stage, where the liquid rests to allow any residual solid particles to sink to the bottom of the container, is a documented process in ancient Mesopotamian brewing (Hartman and Oppenheim 1950, p. 16), while conditioning is a universal feature of beer making everywhere. As can be seen in the photo, the top of the three-part container stood at about the same level as the base of the fermenter, meaning that the bituminated cavities could have been below ground, which would have made sense in terms of temperature management and access, and would also have assisted the flow of the fermented liquid from the more elevated outlet on the fermenter to the underlying openings of the containers.

Heuzey gives no dimensions for the three installations, but he does record that the bricks measured 0.3 m × 0.25 m × 0.06 m, and more information can be gleaned from the photo, where ten vertical courses can be counted on the three-part container, meaning it must have been about 0.8 m tall (again factoring in 0.02 m for each of the courses of mortar). The outer and inner lengths and widths of all three containers can be derived from the scale drawing on Plan D, according to which the three-part container was 6 m × 1.5 m (overall), with inner compartments measuring 1 m × 1 m; the adjacent two-part container (the middle one of the group) was 1.83 m × 1.83 m (overall), with inner compartments measuring 1.5 m × 0.67 m; and the two-part container to the north-east was 3.16 m × 2 m (overall), with inner compartments measuring 0.67 m × 1.33 m. If, for the sake of argument, it is assumed that the bases of the containers were made of three courses of bricks (the same as the coping around the sides of the fermenter) then the internal height of the individual compartments must have been approximately 0.8 m − 0.24 m = 0.56 m, which produces the following capacities. The three-part container held: 1 m × 1 m × 0.56 m = 0.56 m^3, or 560 litres; the adjacent two-part container: 1.5 m × 0.67 m × 0.56 m = 0.5628 m^3, or 560 litres; and the NE two-part container: 0.67 m × 1.33 m × 0.56 m = 0.499 m^3, or 500 litres.

The figures collate remarkably well with each other and with the roughly estimated benchmark yield of the fermenter (400 litres), and it should also be borne in mind that, for weaker beers, which were very commonly drunk instead of plain water in the ancient world due to the purifying effect of even very small amounts of alcohol, the yield would have been greater because they were made with more water and less grain. In any event, it does not seem unreasonable to suppose that each of the seven bituminated cavities was a conditioning and clarifying vat that was designed to hold a single batch of beer.

Finally, there is a significant space of about 4 m between the single, three-part container (on the left on Plan D) and the pair of two-part containers on the right, and it is conceivable that this was the setting for a service door through which jars of clarified and conditioned beer could be carried out of the brewhouse and taken away for distribution or storage. There are at least three good reasons why it would have made excellent sense to position an exit point in the wall close to the outlet on the fermenter's T-shaped junction: first, the filled vessels, doubtless made of terracotta, would surely have been heavy; secondly, it was also necessary to remove around 400 kg to 500 kg of water-saturated spent grain from the fermenter, together with any unwanted yeast; and thirdly, cleanliness being of the highest importance, it would have obviated the need for gangs of labourers to carry the products and discards through the interior of the building to the main door in the SW wall. It is impossible to say this with certainty, but a service exit on a manufacturing facility of this kind might have been a double door with two leaves, making it cheaper to build and more convenient to use. Supplies of raw materials could also have been brought into the building at this end, but the idea that entry and exit points were on different sides of the building seems logistically more attractive.

It is noted above that beer production, which was of course a major activity in ancient Sumer, must have been seasonal, and that beer was consumed at religious festivals and other cult occasions, and also when divine offerings were made. It is therefore not surprising to find a sacred brewhouse in such a prominent location in the Ningirsu complex on Tell K. What has not perhaps previously been understood is the sheer scale of beer production, which has sometimes been treated as though it were exclusively a cottage industry that was carried out in individual households. There is no doubt that beer-making was widespread, if not ubiquitous, but it is also to be expected that a populous institution such as that represented by the Ningirsu temple would have needed to brew beer to satisfy the needs of the priests, administrators, officials and functionaries employed there, as well as those who attended the many religious events that took place in the sacred precinct. The preserved inscriptions state that the necessary barley and grain came from the institution's fields and storehouses that were managed by the ruler and the high priests of Ningirsu. Otherwise, the surviving ancient texts from Girsu provide lots of information about brewing generally, but little if any about the brewery installations in which beer was made.

The Presargonic archives of the last queens of Lagash (the é.mí, or 'house of the women', that was later renamed by Urukagina as the institution of the goddess Bau, the é.Bau (é.^{d}ba-ba$_6$), or 'house of Bau') does, however, offer some extraordinary insights into the state's cultic celebrations and festivals, together with its religious calendar, and they confirm that emmer (a kind of wheat) and black (or perhaps rather 'dark') beer were of high importance in the lists of offerings and ritual processions. Among the most important Ningirsu festivals that marked the cultic calendar year were the 'Barley-Consumption Festival of Ningirsu' (ezem.še.gu$_7$.^{d}Nin.ğír.su) and the 'Malt-Consumption Festival of Ningirsu' (ezem.munu$_4$.gu$_7$.^{d}Nin.ğír.su). As described above, the harvested barley was malted, or partly germinated, before being processed to make barley cakes, or bappir, and the names of these festivals suggest that they were closely associated with the necessary procedures. Evidence from the offering lists records that the principal religious feasts in honour of Ningirsu were probably staged twice a year in spring and autumn (in the months of iti ezem še gu$_7$ ^{d}Nin.ğír.su and iti ezem munu$_4$ gu$_7$ ^{d}Nin.ğír.su, which correspond to months 1 (or 4) and 9 or 10 of the Lagash religious calendar). Finally, preserved texts relating to expenses incurred for sacrifices show that the celebrations lasted for three or four days.

The Stratigraphy of the Central Area

The overall raising of the top of the tell by 0.8 m must also have applied to the central area of the mound, namely the area occupied by the Ur-Nanshe Building, or the Temple of Ningirsu. This can be confirmed by the reinterpretation of the French results from Tell K that is presented in this book, which reveals that the stratigraphic sequence that was recorded by Cros included archaeological remains that had not been disturbed by Sarzec. They show that the platform associated with the base of the Ur-Nanshe Building had almost certainly been systematically sealed with a layer of sand, on top of which was a mass of mud-bricks with a thickness of 0.7 m. This layer was found by Cros in Trench 8 (marked on Cros's Plan B; Fig. 36), slightly to the southwest of the Ur-Nanshe Building, approximately in the space between the temple and the Enmetena Block. Furthermore, the strata of sand and mud-bricks that Cros uncovered, which can almost certainly be attributed to Enmetena, were found beneath a deposit of black soil and miscellaneous debris that was 0.3 m thick, and this leads to a clear conclusion: if the substratum of sand and mud-bricks in Trench 8 provides evidence that the raised Enmetena platform extended comprehensively across the entire sacred precinct then the ground around the base of the Ur-Nanshe Building must also have been raised by Enmetena. In point of fact, since the zone between the well and the Enmetena Esplanade was comprehensively elevated it could not have been otherwise, but the recognition of the sealing layer covered by an occupation layer provides confirmation. This means that pavement F (based at the key Sarzec height of 12.83 m) and all its associated features, including the bases of the wooden columns and the numerous objects that were found at this topographical level, were all purposely covered by the later Enmetena foundation platform that was not recognised by Sarzec, but which, as has been repeatedly mentioned, was recorded a posteriori on the section on Plan C (2), where it is embedded in the deposits marked *Brique crue*.

If the layer of mud-bricks found by Cros in Trench 8 extended into the area around the innermost sanctum then the fact that it appears to have been slightly shallower than the 0.8 m of mud-bricks that was added in the vicinity of the Enmetena Esplanade requires a word of explanation. It was built up with the addition of an unmeasured amount of sand (as noted), but this does not mean that the base of the Enmetena temple that succeeded the Ur-Nanshe Building was either relatively low compared to the surrounding areas, or even at the same height. On the contrary, it was quite considerably more elevated because, although the Ur-Nanshe Building was founded on the Ur-Nanshe base (at a Sarzec height of 12.83 m), 1.12 m of its truncated walls were preserved above that (as noted by Sarzec), and on top of them was a bitumen and brick sealing layer that had an estimated thickness of at least 0.1 m. This means that the tops of the old Ur-Nanshe walls were capped at a Sarzec height of approximately 14.05 m (12.83 m + 1.12 m + 0.1 m), and this, in turn, shows that the capping layer was placed at least 0.42 m above the general Enmetena altitude of the sacred precinct, which lay at a Sarzec height 13.63 m. The minimum elevation of the base of the new Enmetena walls was therefore 14.05 m, but the exact height at which they were founded would have depended on whether the reconstructed building stood directly on top of the sealed Ur-Nanshe walls or whether further layers of mud-bricks were added (as seems inherently likely), and therefore whether the Enmetena sacred edifice was raised above the rest of the mound on a podium of some kind, which again seems plausible. This fundamental point has to be borne in mind in the course of the discussion that follows: the general raising of the mound by Enmetena (and subsequently by Urukagina, as is detailed below) should be carefully and cautiously distinguished from the height at which the temple walls were successively founded. During the reign of Enmetena the base of the temple was raised above the rest of the mound. This might also have been the situation under Urukagina, but the evidence is less conclusive for that later period, and it is not inconceivable that the summit of the mound was at that point uniformly elevated to the same level.

The realisation that the area around the temple was raised to at least 13.63 m by Enmetena has a seismic implication: the artefacts that were found on and around pavement F were almost certainly not, as has previously been the unquestioned orthodoxy, haphazardly scattered when the temple was violently desecrated, thereby forming part of the destruction horizon created at the end of the Early Dynastic period. Rather, the objects associated with the levelled Ur-Nanshe Building were deposited by design in or beneath the structural mass of mud-bricks that was added to the mound in the course of Enmetena's restoration project. Sarzec's own findings confirm this (though again it is a point that has previously gone unnoticed) because his discovery of fragments of important artefacts, including three broken pieces of the Stele of the Vultures, at the Sarzec height of more than 14 m (the figure is unfortunately not given precisely) demonstrates that the destruction horizon was actually situated at least 1.17 m higher than the base of pavement F, though that figure is undoubtedly an underestimate.

It is also noted several times above that Heuzey contradicts himself about the find heights of objects connected with the Ur-Nanshe Building. In his sweeping introductory account he places all the objects at or around the base level of the temple and pavement F (12.83 m), but in his more detailed discussions he reveals that the objects were actually unearthed in a wide range of archaeological contexts. The reason for this is presumably that, although the master narratives of the fire and the later wholesale destruction that Heuzey drew on in order to make sense of the archaeology were contradicted by the details, he nevertheless scrupulously recorded the measurements as exactly as he could because he was, above all, a first-class scholar. The only way to evaluate the situation now is therefore to reappraise the objects associated with the Ur-Nanshe Building, reconsidering them both individually and as a group, and also to look again at the state in which they were found and their precise archaeological contexts: whether they were found singly or alongside others, and whether conclusions can be drawn about the stratigraphic relationships between them.

First, as far as can be ascertained from the published reports, the heights that Sarzec recorded for these objects were relative, mostly taking the base level of the Ur-Nanshe Building as the point of reference, but in many cases this benchmark is not explicitly mentioned by Heuzey, who also usually gives no indication as to whether or not the deposits being discussed were, or might have been, associated with each other. One thing that is unambiguous, however, is that the items that were found above the height of the levelled Ur-Nanshe Building (demarcated by the line marked DAE on Plan C (2); Fig. 33) were differentiated from those found lower down, around the height of pavement F. As just mentioned, those actually found in the black soil notably include three fragments of the Stele of the Vultures, together with the Stone Monument of Eanatum and the broken Mortar of Enanatum, which were all found above the height of the levelled building (DAE on Plan C (2)). Accordingly, if any of the other recorded finds had been excavated in the upper deposit of black soil, there is little doubt that Sarzec would have noted them as such. What he positively did record was the mass of mud-bricks encasing the levelled Ur-Nanshe Building that Heuzey later reconstructed when he helped to draw up the published section on Plan C (2). Consequently, the majority of the finds listed by Heuzey in the relevant parts of the reports were clearly made at heights slightly above, below, or at the level of pavement F.

A comparison of the artefacts found above the height of the levelled building (DAE, generalised as the Enmetena levelling horizon) with the group found lower down near the Ur-Nanshe base (generalised as the Ur-Nanshe horizon) shows that they were handled very differently and met very different fates. The Stele of the Vultures, which Heuzey significantly says was found above the sealed building, had been desecrated and unmethodically smashed into pieces, but the objects associated with pavement F displayed no traces of having been burnt, malignly broken or defaced. On the contrary, notwithstanding the inescapable effects of having been buried in the ground for many centuries, they were in extremely good condition and certainly not shattered into fragments as the Stele of the Vultures was. Despite that, on closer inspection, some signs of minor, but deliberate damage can perhaps be discerned, as can be detailed most effectively with respect to the Ur-Nanshe Plaques (Nos. 4–6 on Plan C (1); Fig. 33), which are discussed immediately below.

The Condition of the Ur-Nanshe Plaques

The Ur-Nanshe Genealogical Plaques exhibit areas of small, almost unnoticeable traces of calculated damage that were inflicted on some of the carvings' particularly meaningful motifs. To name one evident instance, these include the eyes, ears and hands of some of the depicted figures, as though the protagonists in question have had their senses of sight, hearing and touch annulled. Unlike the signs of violent defacement that can clearly be seen on some of the other significant monuments from Tell K, the slight disfigurations found on the Ur-Nanshe Plaques suggest that the objects were probably ritually desacralised. The key cult artefacts that were placed in Sumerian temples were held to be receptacles of the sacred energy that was infused into them when they were solemnly consecrated on being introduced into the holy spaces. It is clear that sacred statues, above all the representation of the god or goddess, were deemed to inhabit a liminal dimension between the earthly and the celestial, and that the principal divine effigy, for example, was thought in a very real sense to be an emanation of the deity. Important objects in the sanctum sanctorum of a Sumerian temple were considered to be comparably animated with divine potency as a consequence of transformative rites performed by high priests. Accordingly, when they were taken out of service and decommissioned before being ritually buried, for example, they were desacralised—made less sacred in ceremonies that were intended wholly or in large part to undo the transformation they had previously undergone. The Ur-Nanshe plaques, which were displayed in the Ningirsu temple on Tell K, were among the holiest artefacts in Girsu. When the Ur-Nanshe Building was eventually refitted or rebuilt, and (for whatever political or religious reason) the plaques were considered surplus to requirements, they could not therefore simply be discarded. On the contrary, they were scrupulously processed and buried in the fabric of the sacred mound, which, it should be recalled, was not raw earth, but a hallowed artificial creation that was considered to be blessed in its entirety.

Plaque A (AO2344), which contains the double image of the ruler, is the best preserved of the four. Its corners are broken, in particular the two on the right, and the relief frame is chipped in several places, especially the top horizontal. Plaque B (the oval) is also well preserved, but it was undoubtedly cut down and reworked (as discussed in detail below), perhaps in part so that it could be plastered into one of the temple's inner walls. Plaques C and D both present central vertical fractures that split the objects in two, and in the case of Plaque C the right half has completely broken off and been lost. Plaque C also displays an oblique fracture that runs in an almost straight line from the bottom left part of the perforation down through the broad dividing band that is filled with inscribed text and into the lower register, where it cuts through the chin of the leftmost figure and continues down through the left border. As previously noted, the archaeological context of Plaque D (EŞEM1633), which is the worst preserved of the set, was not recorded, and since the object's precise find location and condition are evidently crucial to any understanding of its fate, the absence of this information must always be taken into consideration. With that caveat in mind, in addition to the central vertical break that splits the stone into two halves, a large chunk on the bottom, especially the bottom right, including the lower parts of the bodies of the figures on that side, has not survived. The broken lower edge is very irregular, with a profile of several curves that create a nearly serpentine profile. The bottom left corner has broken away completely, but the left vertical is reasonably intact, as is the top left corner, even though it is fractured. As regards the inscriptions, the texts on Plaques A and B are well preserved; the inscriptions on the surviving half of Plaque C are mostly sharp and distinct, though some text has seemingly been lost around the perforation. The inscriptions on Plaque D are extremely flat and worn, and much of the text is, of course, missing, as is to be expected.

Some of the figures on Plaque A, which are largely in good condition, seem to have been selectively treated. The basket that is carried by the standing figure of Ur-Nanshe is slightly chipped, as are his forehead above the front of the eye and the bridge of the nose, along with his left and right forearms (including the inside of his right wrist towards the hand), and his upper right arm, below the bicep. On the lower register the area around the ear of the seated portrait of the king has been noticeably chipped away, and there is a marked abrasion in the second row of his skirt strips, directly in line with his head, in the vicinity of his crotch. The image of the ruler was clearly not brutally defiled, however. On the contrary, if the damage is cautiously considered to have been carried out deliberately then it seems to be associated with particular activities and physiological functions: the ritual bringing of the basket, for example, as indicated by marks applied to the receptacle and to the ruler's arms; the area above the eyes, perhaps connoting the perspicacious intellect; the wrist, with its beating pulse; the ear of the king on the lower register, where he sits listening to the chief snake charmer, Balul, who is shown singing hymns or reciting texts; and the groin area of the seated monarch, representing the source of Ur-Nanshe's evident virility, as witnessed by the relief portraits of his numerous sons. The impacts might be regarded as quasi-surgical in their intent: not insolently smashing the image of Ur-Nanshe, but rather deactivating its vital forces in a controlled and respectful way.

Behind the ruler's back is the diminutive figure of his son Anita, whose head, right shoulder and left upper arm have been deliberately chiselled off. The damage has not affected the rest of the body, and the relief portrait appears to be about the same overall thickness as (or possibly slightly shallower than) the upper surface of the plaque's largely intact margin to the left of his head, all of which would tend to rule out accidental breakage. The elaborately dressed figure wearing a flounced kaunakes and a shawl who stands facing Ur-Nanshe has also suffered damage: the lower part of the head, including the mouth and chin, have been removed, while the cloth at the back of the skirt is slightly abraded, perhaps through natural erosion. Behind the skirted figure (identified as a man in the detailed description in Chapter 16) stands Akurgal, Ur-Nanshe's eventual successor and another of his several sons, who holds a spouted vessel in his right hand. His depiction is unusual in that, apart from the elaborately attired man in front of him, Akurgal is the only one of all the characters on all four plaques whose hair is not shaved off. Instead, he wears it in a double chignon that is secured with a band. The hair around the form of his skull has survived, but the protruding chignon behind his head has been chiselled off, and there is also some notable damage to the left side of his skirt that particularly affects the Sumerian sign for 'son' (dumu). The skirts of Anikura and Mukurshubata, the last two sons on the right of the group of four that includes Akurgal, have also been slightly damaged. On the lower register the right shoulder and arm of the chief snake charmer (in front of the seated ruler) has been broken, while his upper back above the waist seems to have been chiselled off, and a particularly straight vertical cut can be seen at this point (perhaps following the upright of a lost cuneiform sign).

A twofold intentional pattern can tentatively be identified in the areas of damage. The excisions seem to have been applied to individuals who play chief roles in the depicted ceremony, including Balul, the performer, but more especially to those who are closely related to the king. This would explain why Sangdingirtuku, the subordinate participant behind Ur-Nanshe, was left untouched because he is not identified as one of the king's sons. When considering why some figures are more damaged than others, it has to be remembered that many decades elapsed between the time when the plaques were sanctified and the date of their decommissioning. When the reliefs were carved, the lives of the participants still lay ahead of them, but when they were taken out of service, the characters were all dead and their life stories were part of the history of Lagash. This applies particularly to Akurgal, who became Ur-Nanshe's successor, but no information has survived about the ruler's other sons, especially the important personage who stands in front of Ur-Nanshe on the upper register. It is quite possible (indeed likely) that some or all of them also played memorable roles in the governing of the state, and that this knowledge, which can probably now never be recovered, influenced the priests, diviners or other high-status functionaries who determined the exact form that the desacralising treatments should take.

On Plaque B (the oval) a single trace of intentional damage is discernible, again on the forehead of Ur-Nanshe, and also above the eye. The left leg of Lugalezem, the first individual behind Ur-Nanshe on the upper register (who is not named as a son in this instance, though he is elsewhere), is chipped just below the skirt, but this does not appear to have been done deliberately. Ur-Nanshe's son Anita, who is shown standing behind the ruler, again performs the role of cup-bearer (as on Plaque A), but in this case he is not explicitly named as the king's son. Behind him is Akurgal, who is named and further identified as a son with the Sumerian sign dumu. Neither figure has been damaged, but the way in which the subject of the relief has been generally modified might help to account for this. Vestiges of the plaque's left-hand frame have survived, but no sign whatsoever of a border is evident on the right. In addition, the figures are all looking towards the right, and the plaque, which was presumably originally rectangular, was probably similar in size to the other plaques, with a possible width that might have been a little under 0.5 m (Plaques A and D being the representative examples). This makes it likely that a third or more of the scene is missing from the plaque's right-hand side (taking into account that the surviving width is 0.29 m and provisionally assuming an original overall width of between 0.45 m and 0.5 m). Whatever was in that lost portion must have completed the depicted ceremony, which is clearly partial in its surviving form, and it may be that the removal of that tableau meant that no further treatment was required. Similarly (though again with a high degree of caution), it is significant that the height of the surviving part of Plaque B is 0.23 m, while the heights of A, C and D are almost double that (0.4 m, 0.45 m and 0.43 m, respectively). The implication is that Plaque B in its current state represents about a quarter of the original carving, which presumably had overall measurements of about 0.45–0.5 m (h) × 0.4–0.45 m (w). In this regard, it is also relevant to consider the perforation on Plaque B. Unlike the ones on Plaques A and D, it is not framed, but drilled directly into the background, and it is also markedly irregular, particularly on the right-hand side, though this could of course be due to erosion. It is impossible to say whether the perforation in Plaque C was framed or not, which means that, in and of itself, the absence of a frame around the hole on Plaque B may not be conclusive, but what does seem clear is that all the holes were drilled in the centre of the stones. This means that, if three-quarters of the carving above and to the right of the preserved scene on Plaque B are missing, the existing hole was probably added when the carving was cut down and reshaped, and this in turn would mean that the original perforation was somewhere in the missing portion, to the right of Ur-Nanshe and probably a little higher than the top of his head, though its exact location would depend on the precise size of the original plaque, which is unknown.

What did the missing scene contain? One important clue is provided by Ur-Nanshe's stance, which differs conspicuously from the way he is standing on Plaques A and D, where he is shown carrying his basket of bricks. By contrast, on Plaque B he has his hands clasped in an attitude of prayer or extreme deference. In the other scenes (probably also on Plaque C, where his image was almost certainly in the lost half), Ur-Nanshe is the recipient of this reverential gesture, such that the other figures, who are mostly placed in lines in front of him, almost invariably have their hands deferentially joined as they face him—the exceptions being individuals who are actively playing their parts in the depicted ceremonies that revolve around him. On Plaque B, however, Ur-Nanshe himself is shown in an attitude of dutiful devotion, as emphasised by the presence of four similarly reverential figures behind him, thereby indicating that he is taking part in a ceremony in honour of someone or something other than himself. To whom might Ur-Nanshe offer that gesture in this sacred setting, and in the context of the narrative strand running through the plaques that relates to the construction of the temple? The only answer is surely Ningirsu, whether in person or as represented by his attributes or his holy dwelling. Whereas the subject of Plaques A and D is the building of the temple, therefore, the presumed subject of Plaque B, including the missing part, was probably its dedication or opening, and Ur-Nanshe is accordingly shown in an act of worship as the god takes up residence in his new abode, the Ur-Nanshe Building. That does not mean that Ningirsu was necessarily represented on the missing part of the plaque, but it might plausibly suggest that the scene as a whole was in all likelihood designed to commemorate the completion and inauguration of the new temple, including any associated rites.

As noted previously, Ur-Nanshe is not shown on the surviving half of Plaque C, presumably because he was in the missing portion to the right. Similarly, the first figure on the right of the line in the upper register has been lost almost completely. Behind that half-figure is Lugalezem, one of Ur-Nanshe's sons, whose portrayal exhibits some slight damage, similar to that on Plaques B and D. In particular, the damage here is also around the skirt, as on Plaque B. The oblique fracture that runs from the central perforation downwards and out to the left, which is clearly unintentional, touches the top of Akurgal's head and cuts through the jaw and right shoulder of the leftmost figure on the bottom register, who is identified as the chief scribe.

On Plaque D the king's head and right upper arm are damaged, but this seems to have been caused by an irregular fracture running generally across the top left corner that was surely accidental or the result of natural processes. The breadth of the break makes it difficult to say whether it masked any deliberate erasures. The forehead area above the eye that was targeted on Plaques A and B seems mostly untouched in this instance, apart from a small fissure at the bridge of the nose, but this is by no means conclusive. Below the right upper arm, the right side of the ruler's chest is severely abraded. It is again hard to say whether this might have been done deliberately, but in any event it would imply a different pattern of intent from the damage applied to Ur-Nanshe on the other plaques. An oblique fracture, which is probably the result of accidental breakage, can be seen running from the centre of the left edge of the stone, angled downwards and towards the right, and cutting through the lower left corner of the king's skirt, affecting his right foot and the inscription. The vertical break that runs through the centre of the carving and around the right side of the perforation cuts through the figure of the king's son Lugalezem, who occupies a highly significant position with respect to Ur-Nanshe in this scene. The fracture slices through the back of his head, his chest, hands, skirt and left foot. The right side of the skirt of Anikura, the second son on the upper register, is pitted, and his name has been destroyed; behind him, the skirt of the third son, Mukurshubata, is slightly damaged on the left, while that of Akurgal, the son on the extreme right, is also partly erased below his left forearm. The lower bodies of the four men on the register beneath are all missing, while the head of the cup-bearer (the small figure at the front of the line on the left), who is again most probably Anita, has been broken around his ear, though less seriously than on Plaque A. The clasped hands of the man behind Anita and also of the man at the end of the line on the right are missing, as are the lower parts of the skirts of the two men on the extreme right, and their names are consequently only partially preserved. A tiny fracture can be seen passing through the head of the king's son Gula (the third figure from the left on the lower register), but this does not seem to be intentional. The extremely poor condition of Plaque D makes it impossible to identify deliberate breakage, and it is of course vital to compare any patterns of erasure with those found on the other plaques. Overall, however, the forensic assessment is inconclusive, and the total absence of any archaeological context makes it impossible to judge whether Plaque D was ritually buried along with the other three.

The Copper Heads of Bulls and the Stone Heads of Lions

As is exemplified by the close examination of the condition of the Ur-Nanshe Plaques, the objects that were found outside the walls and within the range of the Ur-Nanshe horizon were in a similar state of preservation to those found inside the temple's ritually sealed rooms, including the door sockets inscribed in the name of Ur-Nanshe. Considered together, therefore, these artefacts appear to form a coherent ensemble that all came originally from the temple, where they were presumably installed as ornamental sacred fittings, or in one or two rare instances as votive objects. The items that were an inherent part of the temple's sacred fabric as defined by Ur-Nanshe include the ritually decommissioned Ur-Nanshe Plaques that presumably adorned the temple's inner walls, the ring post found on pavement F (No. 17 on Plan C (1)), the Stone Heads of Lions (No. 7 on Plan C (1)) and the two Copper Heads of Bulls, one of which was inscribed. The Feathered Figure, which was a cardinal votive object, was a carving of the highest cultural and religious significance because (as detailed above) it represents the moment when the god took possession of Tell K.

A further compelling point emerges when the exact find locations of these buried items are taken into account because subgroups of similar artefacts were found together. The two Copper Heads of Bulls were found on the SE side of the temple, together with a copper libation vase (recorded in Heuzey's text but not specifically marked on the plan), while the five stone lions' heads (including a grouped identical pair) were clustered on the NW side of the building. These are relatively clear examples of artefacts that were interred in ritual pits or favissas, with regard to which it should also be stressed that Heuzey plainly states that the copper bulls' heads and the libation vase were found inserted into the compact mass of mud-bricks, not on a floor or pavement. This, it can be added, was a continuation of the mud-brick substratum that was uncovered in Cros's Trench 5, situated on the NE side of the central area.

The two Copper Heads of Bulls (AO2676 and EŞEM1576) were discovered together with a long-spouted copper vessel (the length of the spout being 0.25 m). The appearance of the bulls' heads, which were expressively modelled using the lost-wax technique, is vividly arresting (Fig. 27). According to Heuzey (Sarzec and Heuzey 1912, p. 238), their hollow interiors were filled with bitumen, but no remains of that have survived. The heads are fitted with extended slender horns that project outwards before curving upwards and slightly inwards in delicate arcs, while the spoon-shaped or even flower-shaped ears, which are slightly stylised, protrude out on slim stems on either side. The animals' large eyes are inlaid with lapis lazuli and shell (though one eye has been lost) and framed with thickish eyelids. The marked outlines of their snouts are formed with large volute nostrils, and the mouths are closed. Perforations or mortises that were designed to receive tenons can be seen on their two sides, and it is probable that the bulls were created to decorate the soundboxes of lyres such as those discovered in the Royal Cemetery of Ur and frequently depicted in Early Dynastic art, including on the Standard of Ur. It is also possible (but much less likely) that they were decorative elements made to adorn ceremonial seats, either self-standing or in chariots (see Parrot 1948, p. 106), and they could conceivably have been architectural fittings that were attached to panels, though that is again doubtful.

Heuzey (Sarzec and Heuzey 1912, p. 238) records that the heads measure 0.1 m and 0.12 m in length, respectively, but the actual measurements of head AO2676 are 0.19 m (h) × 0.167 m (w). The bull is inscribed on its forehead with a dedication to Ningirsu in the name of Lugalsi, a high priest of lamentations from Uruk (Marchesi and Marchetti 2011, pp. 44 and 124, and n. 244), and this would tend to confirm that the heads were ornaments for musical instruments because Lugalsi's main duties presumably included singing and playing on liturgical occasions (Fig. 101). The heads are both well preserved (particularly in their restored states), but both have one broken horn (the right horn of AO2676, and the left one in the case of EŞEM1576). Though the projecting ends of the horns were understandably rather fragile

FIGURE 101. Reconstruction of a bull lyre from Girsu.

and vulnerable to breakage compared to the sturdy skulls, that fact that only one of each is broken makes it tempting to suppose that the horns were snapped off deliberately and in a complementary fashion (one on the right and one on the left). In addition, EŞEM1576 lacks its right eye and left ear. Despite the other suggestions mentioned above, all the evidence indicates that Copper Heads of Bulls were probably fitted to the soundboxes of lyres and that they were donated by Lugalsi to form part of the temple's cultic apparatus.

Incidentally, the oversimplified explanation that bulls' heads were used to decorate lyres because the sound of the lyre recalled the bellow of a bull (see, for example, Van Dijk 2013, p. 13) should be reappraised. One reason why the comparison has retained currency is because of the image of the roaring bull that is used in the Gudea Cylinder Inscriptions (A28). This was translated by Edzard (1997, p. 87) as 'its harp chamber is (like) a roaring bull', where the Sumerian text is taken to refer to the sound box of the lyre, while Sjöberg (1984, p. 76) simply assumes a likeness between the lyre and a 'softly lowing bull' (quoted in Van Dijk 2013, p. 13). By contrast, the more recent translation for the ETCSL project (Electronic Text Corpus of Sumerian Literature) renders the key line (773) as 'Its drum hall is a roaring bull' (a.ga balaǧ.a.bi gud gu$_3$ nun di), and the important word balaǧ does indeed appear to have had associations (particularly strong in the Early Dynastic period) with both stringed instruments and also with drums (Gabbay 2014)—possibly, in part, because the sound box could be used to create percussive sounds. These more complex meanings pave the way for increasingly subtle associations between lyres and bulls. The first and most significant reason to doubt the straightforward sound comparison is that a bellowing bull, which produces a prolonged roar, sounds nothing like a lyre (or any equivalent modern string instrument) and much more like a member of the woodwind family. The more persuasive alternative connection between bulls and drums that is made explicit in the ETCSL text was presumably based principally on the thundering sound of a bull's hooves, and this was perhaps boosted for ancient Sumerians by the fact that actual drumheads were made of the dried skins of animals, possibly including the hides of cattle.

More specifically, however, the absence of a comparison between the bellow of a bull and the music of the lyre is implicit in the way the Copper Heads of Bulls from Tell K (like most if not all other busts of bulls from lyres) are sculpted with their mouths closed. A partial exception to this is the image of the lyre on the Standard of Ur (Fig. 102), where the mouth might be slightly open, though the inlaid mosaic makes it difficult to be sure. Nonetheless, if the sound of the lyre had been generally likened to that of a roaring bull then it would surely have made more sense for the bulls' mouths to have been depicted as if they were open—perhaps even wide open. And yet, as Van Dijk notes, many (if not most) bull lyres were manufactured as representations of the whole animal, in some cases with legs, as though the bull was standing, and in others with the animal's legs discreetly folded beneath its body. The bull lyre shown on the Standard of Ur does not seem to be fitted with legs (though they could just about conceivably be under the body), but it clearly shows the way a connection was made between the whole forms of the instrument and the animal. Accordingly, the body of the bull is the soundbox, with the long, rather thick strings emerging from a lateral split in its side. Those strings were unquestionably made from natural gut (often misleadingly known as catgut), by which is meant dried and twisted strands from the intestines of animals, including cattle. In other words, the lyre in its entirety was conceived of as being like a transfigured bull, with a head and a body (the sound box) from which its adapted intestines emanated as the strings that were plucked or strummed to produce music. The intended effect might be described as a strange metempsychosis or transubstantiation in which the bull is reborn as an instrument and given a voice (or caused to speak) after its death. That opens the way to a much more subtle comparison between the rather gentle sound of the lyre and the muted voice of a bull that is mastered and subdued in death, while its formidable raw power is harnessed and transformed to create musical harmony.

The small Stone Heads of Lions (Fig. 27) that were found together on the SE side of the temple are made up of two groups: three heads, of which two were sculpted in limestone and one in alabaster (AO231, AO232 and AO233) and an identical pair made of gypsum (EŞEM456 and EŞEM458). Head AO231, which measures 0.101 m (h) × 0.07 m (w), has a mane formed of elongated shallow tufts with rounded ends, and they are all incised with an inner line that reproduces their outlines. The large, round ears have very distinctly flattened tops, while the slightly bulging, upward-pointing eyes are articulated above with thick lids that are carved as two almond-shaped arches. The lion's stylised nose is interesting because it projects unnaturally beyond the rest of the animal's

FIGURE 102. Detail of a lyre player and a singer on the peace panel of the Standard of Ur. British Museum 121201.

muzzle. Indeed, when looked at in profile, the nose, which is clearly not based on sketches of a real lion, looks rather like the characteristic human noses that are seen on Sumerian reliefs—on the Ur-Nanshe Plaques, for example. This adds an almost grotesque quality to the representation, particularly when the more complete profile (with the lion looking from right to left) is considered. Below the nose, the short snout is noticeably cylindrical when viewed face on, and it is articulated above with incised oblique whiskers that radiate out from a central point. At the centre of the mouth is the protruding tongue, which sticks out about as far as the nose (or a little less) when seen in profile (adding to the gargoyle-like effect). It is not at all clear what the sculptors had in mind when they decided to make the tongue stick out in this way: is it to be associated with eating, licking or ferocity, for example? The bared teeth that are conspicuous on both sides of the tongue certainly seem to connote aggression. The middle teeth, closest to the tongue, are squarish and arranged in two rows; those nearer to the sides of the mouth, which are single and pointed, are presumably meant to represent the sharp canines (cuspids or eye teeth) that are a memorable feature of real lions' mouths. When looked at in profile (with the muzzle on the right), the back part of the lion's head is so badly broken that the ear and part of the mane are missing. On the other side, the curve of the flattened right ear is slightly chipped at the top, while the upper section of the nose (the part between the eyes) and the tongue are abraded.

The appearance of the surviving fragment of AO232 suggests that it was very similar to AO231, but carved in alabaster instead of limestone. The preserved piece, which measures 0.059 m (h) × 0.067 m (w) × 0.025 m (t), shows part of the right side of the lion's head, including its right eye and ear (which is flattened like the ear of AO231), and its mane, which is similar to that of AO231, though without the repeated inner outline. Head AO233, which has a plain mane that is formed into a gentle point in the middle, above the eyes, measures 0.09 m (h) × 0.078 m (w). The shape of the head is like the front-facing heads of the lions carved on the Mesilim Mace Head, except that the Mesilim lions, which are adorned with extravagant manes shown in shallow relief, are clearly identified as male. Head AO233 does not feature the elongated rectangles with rounded ends that are used on AO231 and AO232 to describe the lions' bushy head hair, and their absence might intimate that AO233 represents a lioness. If that was indeed the intention then the fact that AO233 is otherwise so similar to AO231 (they are almost exactly the same size and both are made of limestone) might mean that they were made as a pair: one male and one female. It is, of course, impossible to be categorical about this, but the visual evidence seems plausible. The short, wide ears of AO231 are placed on the top of the head, where they stand up in irregular circular segments that are somewhat broken. The ears are not flattened out on top like those of AO231 and AO232, while the outsides of the eyes, which are framed by thick downturned lids also point downwards to create an expression that would now be regarded as one of melancholy, though whether a similar emotion can be attributed to AO233 is doubtful. In any case, the impression created is quite different from the eyes of AO231, which point upwards and seem to glare. Similarly, although the outline of the nose of AO233 is pronounced, it does not protrude in the same stylised way as that of AO231, and it is perhaps more in harmony with the shape of the cylindrical mouth. As with AO231, the tongue of AO233 originally stuck out from the middle of the mouth, but only its stub has survived. Pointed teeth are visible below the radiating whiskers, but the way the teeth are carved is less realistic than the teeth of AO231 because they are all sharp, with no attempt being made to differentiate between the canines and the rest. At the back of the head, behind and below the ears, a circular hole designed to hold a tenon has been drilled all the way through the stone from one side to the other, and there is an inscription carved on the back of the head between the ears that reads: 'Ur-Nanshe, king of Lagash, son of Gunidu' (RIME 1.9.1.24b). The ears and nose of AO233 are chipped, but not badly, and the tongue has been broken off. In addition, the bottom part of the inscription is damaged, and this might have happened when the head was detached from its support. There is also a notable fracture behind the hole beneath the right ear.

Heads EŞEM458 and EŞEM456, which were part of the cache discovered by Sarzec and are now in the Museum of the Ancient Orient in Istanbul, form a matching pair. Made of gypsum, both are 0.09 m high. They are similar to AO233, except that their eyes are rounder, while the tops of their heads are not pointed and their manes are longer. Head EŞ458 is inscribed, but the only word that is preserved is the single verb form mu.dù, meaning 'built the' (RIME 1.9.2.2a). Like all the other heads of lions (presumably including the fragmentary AO232, although that cannot be confirmed), EŞEM458 and EŞEM456 also have protruding tongues.

Generally, the carved heads of lions were associated with kingship and temple building in ancient Sumer, and in the case of the lions found on Tell K the more particular connection is with Ningirsu and the Ningirsu temple. In view of the intended frightening appearance of at least some of them (notably AO231), they might have served an apotropaic or protective function, perhaps being placed at the entrances of passageways to ward off miscreants, evil spirits or other malign supernatural beings. The drilled mortise holes (which were presumably originally features of all the heads) indicate that they were fastened onto lost supports by means of tenons, and they might possibly have been the crowning features of decorated door posts, or they might have been fitted to gate panels. Alternatively, and especially on account of their smallness (all are about 0.1 m high) and the presence of inscriptions on some of them, they might more probably have been ornamental elements that were fixed to pieces of temple furniture: thrones or an altar. Indeed, they could have been designed to adorn a range of sacred appurtenances inside the sanctum sanctorum

The Placement of the Buried Artefacts

The Ur-Nanshe Plaques and the other important artefacts unearthed at different spots around the temple were almost certainly not randomly placed, but specifically positioned with respect to both the temple and each other. It is also possible that their interment locations represented notional geometrical points that could theoretically be joined to form concentric rectangular lines that enclosed corresponding spaces. The three Ur-Nanshe Plaques (A, B and C), for example, were excavated on a NW–SE alignment that ran more or less along the same axis as the temple's SW colonnade (H–H on the SW side of the building on Plan C (1)), while two of the three were placed extremely close to two of the SW column bases. Notwithstanding its inherent fragility, the extremely large ring post was found in an exceptionally well-preserved state on pavement F, where it was carefully placed along and adjacent to the NW façade wall of the temple, where the door that led into the cella would originally have been. On Plan C (1) the ring post is shown with its full length intact on the pavement outside the NW façade, but on the photo (Pl. 57 (1); Fig. 45), where it is pictured on a surface of mud-bricks, it is in two parts that lie side by side. Whether it was found in one piece, as on the plan, or broken, as in the photo, is not certain. As suggested previously, however, the inferred inner core of bundled reeds must have decayed over time, leaving behind only the thin cylindrical coverings of beaten copper in which they were encased. Separated from their internal support, these sections of copper casing must no doubt have very easily come apart when the object was moved from its find location, prior to being photographed. Presumably while it was still in one piece, therefore, the post was symbolically placed across the line of the doorway that had formerly led into the space from which the statue of the god had been removed. The ring post would probably have been one of a pair that stood on either side of the entrance to the cella, conceivably outside the H–H line of the colonnade on pavement F, and its placement in front of the door of the cella again points to the ritual interment of a sacred object: the part representing the whole, and the post itself demonstrating that the inner sanctum, which was still in some vital respects a holy place, had nonetheless been deconsecrated.

For the individually deposited objects, any intended pattern is more difficult to define, though a general trend does seem to emerge: they were placed around the temple, all at about the same distance from it, to form an outlying concentric rectangle that conceptually cordoned off the building, as it were. Included in this possible arrangement were the third Ur-Nanshe door socket (No. 3 on Plan C (1)) that was found to the north-east of the temple, as well as the archaic Feathered Figure that was found to the north-west of it. Additionally, the favissa that held the Stone Heads of Lions was placed by the NW pillar base, while the other favissa containing the Copper Bulls' Heads (No. 18 on Plan C (1)) and the spouted libation vase (not marked on Plan C (1)) was found on the SE side of the temple, almost in line with the building's NE wall. The overall pattern might conjecturally be defined as a progression of rectangular spaces, centred around the Ur-Nanshe Building and similarly oriented north-west–south-east, that embrace, or perhaps fence off, the desanctified temple, creating a defensive barrier around it, so to speak, just as the ring post created a symbolic line of defence in front of the door of the decommissioned cella. It may also be that there was a progressive hierarchy of sanctity that dictated how close or far the artefacts were from the temple walls.

Overall, what emerges is the probable systematic deposition, in and around the Ur-Nanshe Building, of a set of symbolically charged objects, mostly dating from the time when the temple was built, but with one significant exception: the Feathered Figure, which was moved by Ur-Nanshe from the Lower Construction to his new temple, and finally deconsecrated by Enmetena along with the rest of the Ur-Nanshe objects, perhaps (though this is speculative) because it was felt that there was no longer any special need to affirm its foundational message, since the changed regime ushered in by Ur-Nanshe was now long established. The interments, which clearly had potent symbolic and ritual connotations, were intended to close off, desanctify and safeguard the building's most holy spaces in preparation for the erection of a renewed temple on the freshly raised ground above, as part of a general raising of the mound and a major overhaul of the entire sacred precinct. What is perhaps most remarkable about the depositions as thus interpreted is that the pattern they exhibit is comparable to that observed in connection with the ritual deposits laid down by Ur-Nanshe when he closed the Lower Construction.

There is also a crucial difference between the way the two buildings were handled, however, because, whereas the Lower Construction was taken out of service and painstakingly buried in its entirety in preparation for the erection of Ur-Nanshe's radically new temple, by which it was categorically superseded, Enmetena's building is perhaps best regarded as an extension or continuation of its predecessor. Indeed, the lower parts of the walls of the Ur-Nanshe Building, preserved to a height of about 1.12 m, provided the sealed support (and the ground plan) for the Enmetena extension, while the bottom section of the old sacred spaces, filled with ritually purified deposits, still existed as a kind of underfloor below Enmetena's new base. The doors of the Ur-Nanshe Building had, of course, been bricked in, but users of the later Enmetena temple must have been acutely aware of the fact that the former sanctum sanctorum lay just below their feet.

Furthermore, it is vital to recall that the relationship between two generations of working temples that seems to be exemplified in the two buildings under discussion must have been a relatively familiar one throughout the region. The inauguration of the Lower Construction and the dramatic reforms undertaken by Ur-Nanshe represented step changes on Tell K that were undertaken in the context of revolutionary moments in the history of Girsu. Much more frequent would have been the alterations, repairs or improvements that were made to existing buildings by new rulers, all of which, like everything else in ancient Sumer, must have been subject to complex sets of constantly evolving ritual procedures that had been brought into being over the lifetime of the religious culture. Such construction works must quite frequently have involved raising a sacred mound by relatively small amounts—0.8 m in this case, and subsequently by a further 0.7 m in the reign of Urukagina, as is discussed in Chapter 20—so the protocols for these comparatively frequent occurrences were presumably well established, notwithstanding the inevitable variations that would have depended on time, place and observed portents, interpreted within the accepted framework of beliefs.

There can be no doubt that in this case the ruler who reworked the top of the tell, including the Ur-Nanshe Building, was Enmetena, and that the temple he created was a successor building rather than an epoch-defining recreation of the sanctum sanctorum at the heart of the sacred precinct. Enmetena's name was broadcast on inscriptions that were found on a wide range of artefacts (bricks, foundation figurines and tablets, and door sockets), all memorialising the overhaul and reconstruction of the complex, with the renewed temple at its heart. The redevelopments were implemented on a wide-reaching scale, and so, to mark the transformation, the site was seemingly endowed with a novel epithet, giguna, or 'reed sanctuary'—a term whose wide-ranging significance is outlined above. Nor is it a coincidence that most of the objects excavated around the base of the temple's walls were fittings that had previously adorned the old Ur-Nanshe Building. These sacred emblems of the architecture of the past were ritually buried in order to ensure that the refurbishment was properly ratified and undertaken in accordance with established customs.

The reason why none of the buried objects that were found were inscribed in the names of rulers of Girsu that reigned in the generations between Ur-Nanshe and Enmetena is surely because the lineage of the previous temple was not broken and re-established to usher in a new era, but rather perpetuated in the renewed structure to the extent that portions of its most hallowed spaces still existed beneath the capping layer and inside the former doorways that Enmetena had blocked. This was, as it were, a translation—the raising of the holy essence to a new height, and not a rupture. Ur-Nanshe's legacy was therefore honoured and kept alive by the entombment of its most important symbolic artefacts, while the esteem that Enmetena felt for Ur-Nanshe was expressed in his inscriptions, where he dubbed himself the 'descendant' or 'inheritor' of Ur-Nanshe—a declaration that was made by no other ruler. The one important variation on this theme was the preservation of the Stele of the Vultures, which was created to celebrate the achievements of Eanatum and to commemorate his role in safeguarding the boundaries of Lagash. Though the dispute flared up again repeatedly, and Eanatum's success was therefore provisional, the importance of the victory that he won seemingly bestowed upon him a status comparable with that of the almost legendary Mesillim of Kish. The Stele of the Vultures was almost certainly placed inside the trophy room of the Ur-Nanshe Building by Eanatum, screening the entrance in accordance with the convention that can be traced back as far as the Lower Construction, in which the Stele of the Captives performed the same function. The Stele of the Vultures must surely have been preserved by Enmetena: removed to safety while his architectural plans were executed and then returned to its place of honour in the victory room, where it remained until it was later transferred into the same position in the last Early Dynastic temple on the mound that was renovated by Urukagina. It was displayed there until it was finally destroyed by Lugalzagesi after his devastating conquest of Lagash.

Lastly, the surmised solemn burial of the archaic Feathered Figure at the same time as the other objects deposited around the level of the preserved section of the old Ur-Nanshe walls must be considered an event of the highest significance. There can be no doubt that, in the Early Dynastic era, from the time of Ur-Nanshe to that of Enmetena, it was regarded as an exceptional sculpture. Found in almost mint condition, and dating back to the Early Dynastic I period, it must have been fastidiously looked after as a precious relic from the revered past for some four centuries. The significance of the stone relief is described in great detail in Chapter 13, but it is worth reiterating that it depicts the moment when Ningirsu, complete with the Thunderbird attributes that are shown on his feathered headdress, takes possession of the temple, which is symbolised by the paired mace heads that are fixed to emblematic doorposts. The prominent feathers and the warlike connotations of the mace heads recall the fact that Ningirsu subdued Imdugud, the Thunderbird, but did not kill it. Instead, he tamed its tremendous power, which can be interpreted as a sign of the potency of the two rivers, the Tigris and the Euphrates, thus confirming Ningirsu's dual identity as the warrior god, but also the god of irrigation and agriculture. Lists of lands and a hymn of praise, including a creation myth that evokes the demarcation of the land with surveyors' pegs and ropes, are also inscribed on the stone, so that its words and images work together to express the unbreakable chain that was believed to exist between the divine and the earthly: the expression of the god's identity being inextricably linked with the lands associated with his temple on Tell K and the laying out of plots of earth more generally. All of these meanings are decisively summed up in the temple's cardinal epithet, whose first recorded instance is found on the Feathered Figure: the House of Ningirsu (é.^{d}Nin.ĝír-su).

The prime importance of this object, with its foundational imagery and texts, is clear, and it might well have been considered to be the primordial token of the covenant between the people and the god that sanctioned the inauguration of the temple on the mound. It can therefore be assumed that the Feathered Figure was created when Tell K became the sacred centre of the cult of Ningirsu—the moment when Ningirsu was first institutionally worshipped as the god of Girsu. Accordingly, the pious deposition and interment of this plaque, which was supercharged with sacred meanings, must have been an event of the utmost importance. It was found to the north-west of the temple walls, alongside and aligned with the Ur-Nanshe Plaques and other temple appurtenances of high cultic significance. The most ancient deposit was thus interred in order to signal a new beginning for the age-old tradition—Enmetena's renovation of the temple, which was in every sense a continuation of the past.

Excursus: The Divine Nature of Objects and Phenomena

As is confirmed by textual evidence, cult objects such as those unearthed around the capped Ur-Nanshe Building were the focus of complex rituals that related to their consecration, installation, ongoing maintenance and eventual deconsecration. Like cult statues, they might also have undergone transformation rites that were believed to invest them with divine properties (see Selz 1997, pp. 167–209). The kind of divinity enjoyed by particular appurtenances, and whether or not artefacts that were intrinsic to the god or goddess's identity partook of his or her godhead, is a fascinating topic, but of more immediate interest is the fact that symbolic temple artefacts were unquestionably regarded as essentially sacred or holy, and that they were accordingly the focus of specific rituals. Indeed, the question of the relative divinity or holiness of individual objects might have been merely a matter of degrees of sanctity, with objects being placed on a continuous or sliding scale, as it were. A comparable idea can be applied to sacred spaces, which are judged to have been more or less holy or divine, according to their proximity to the deity. As this suggests, Sumerian religion was not framed in terms of a binary dichotomy between the profane and the sacred. On the contrary, everything was thought of as sacred, and the differences were formulated as degrees of sanctity.

In a related manner, from archaic times in Mesopotamia, cult images and some associated objects were understood to be material representations of 'divine powers' (Selz 1997). References to such holy entities are found throughout Sumerian textual sources, where they are distinguished by the addition to their nomenclature of the sign DINGIR, which classified them as belonging to the divine sphere (Selz 1997). It should be noted that the situation is not as straightforward as it sounds because of the difficulty of discriminating between objects or artefacts (including natural phenomena and events) that were believed to be endowed with a measure of actual divinity and those that had purely symbolic value. Included in the list of things that are known to have partaken in the divine nature of the godhead are emblems and appurtenances (including royal insignia), sacred offices, accomplishments of high cultural significance, musical instruments and glorified animals. The Early Dynastic period is the first time that such objects and phenomena are known to have been endowed with divine qualities, but the nature of their divinity is an unresolved question: were artefacts, living beings, sacred offices or functions and other phenomena conceived of as being deities in some sense? Were they invested with spiritual essences, for example—given souls, so to speak? Or were they exalted and made fit to be divine attributes or to form part of the divine household, either in perpetuity or until the time when they were desacralised? Administrative documents from the archives of the queens of Lagash (the é.mí, or 'house of the women'), who were the administrators of the estates of the goddess Bau, contain several texts that list offerings made to a great number of gods on various occasions, together with inscriptions that record votive donations to a select group of deities, and also donations to cult objects. As these documents demonstrate, all the recipients of either offerings or votive donations were invariably defined as 'divine' by the addition of the sign DINGIR. The cult objects included in the divinified categories have been tentatively grouped by Selz (1997, pp. 173–4):

1. Images: statue(s) (alan) or bas-reliefs (na.rú 'stele(s)').

2. Divine emblems: the Great Pole (of) the Abzu (ᵈdim-gal.absu), the bronze date-palm (gišimmar.urudu), the Lord who smashes the Mountains (lugal.kur.dúb).

3. Paraphernalia and cultural achievements (especially associated with kingship): the staff of the leader (ᵈhendur.saĝ), the sceptre (ᵈPA), the sheep shearing (zú.si).

4. Musical instruments: harp(s) (balag) and holy drum(s) (ub₅.kù).

5. Professions: the expert (ᵈgašam), the righteous barber (ᵈkindá.zi), the tax collector (ᵈsag.kud).

6. Divine animals: the young ewe (MÍ.U₈.sig), the lady falcon (ᵈnin.šará), the wild-cow (sún).

7. Other objects: the chariot (ᵍᶦˢgigír).

With regard to the kinds of offerings recorded in the archive as having been made to deified objects, it is noteworthy that the sizes of the gifts and the specified amounts of various commodities are usually fairly insignificant (Selz 1997). This might tentatively be interpreted as a sign that the phenomena elevated through the addition of the DINGIR sign were regarded as being of minor importance by comparison with the acknowledged major gods. Matters might not be so simple, however, because some documents show that sacred objects themselves were occasionally the recipients of votive gifts, even though, as a rule, such offerings were only supposed to be made to the professed major gods (Selz 1997, p. 175). For example, texts DP69 and DP71 record the following:

1 bronze-vessel (in the shape of) a Dilmun boat, 1 crown, covering the head, 1 necklace (for) the god Nin.MAR.KI; 1 crown (for) Etur; 1 crown (for) Igi'amashe; 1 crown (for) the stele: (these gifts come) from queen Shasha. 1 bronze-vessel (in the shape of) a Dilmun boat, 1 crown, 1 necklace (for) the god Nin.MAR.KI: (these gifts come) from Engisa. At the 'festival, when the young animals are "filled" into the grown-ups' did Shasha, the wife of Urukagina, the king of Lagash, dedicate (these gifts) ex-voto. 2nd year.

1 large spouted(?) vessel, 1 crown, covering the head, 1 necklace (for) the goddess Nanshe; 1 crown, 1 necklace (for) Gan.tur; 1 crown, 1 necklace (for) AB-irnun; 1 crown, 1 necklace (for) the Holy Drum; 1 crown, 1 necklace (for) Nintu.zaga. At the barley-eating festival of Nanshe did Shasha, the wife of Urukagina, the king of Lagash, dedicate (these gifts) ex-voto. 2nd year.

As these texts show, the listed gifts were delivered during religious festivals. In the first instance quoted, the ceremony of donation was performed at Gu'abba (é.Nin.MAR.KI), while in DP71 it was carried out in the region of Nigin. The written records are further supported by the names of the divine recipients, who are known to have had their main cult places in these locations. Each text mentions important offerings that were made to a stele and a holy drum, and the evidence overall therefore suggests that not only statues, but also cult objects underwent rituals that confirmed or endowed them with divinity. In some cases this was accompanied by the giving of a new name that connoted the creation of the object's glorified identity; also important are the process of induction, including the provision of an appropriate cult locus, together with the making of offerings and finally the procedures for deconsecrating the glorified object prior to its ritual interment (see Selz 1997).

The Renewed Temple

It is impossible to know exactly what the Enmetena temple looked like because none of its upper walls survived. The temple was firstly renovated and perhaps raised to a slightly higher level, along with the rest of the uppermost part of Tell K, by Urukagina, before being subsequently razed to the ground when the site was finally ransacked by Lugalzagesi at the end of the Early Dynastic period. The only vestiges that remained were the course of bricks and bitumen coating that sealed off the truncated lower sections of the Ur-Nanshe Building, at an overall Sarzec height of 14.05 m, with its purified infills, blocked entrances and foundation deposits. As noted above, these architectural remains were safely buried in the mound when the temple was decommissioned, and it is also conceivable that the capping layer on top of the Ur-Nanshe walls was supplemented with layers of mud-bricks that went undetected by Sarzec. Nonetheless, despite the inadequate recording of the data, it is possible to form an idea of the Enmetena temple's overall shape. Standing directly on top of the Ur-Nanshe walls, it must almost certainly have adopted the same ground plan, thereby referencing its precursor and emphasising the permanence of the sacred in its layout and arrangement, including the principal NW–SE axis and the doorways in the NW and SE façades. It is therefore readily conceivable that the new building was in most respects very much like a version of the Ur-Nanshe Building that had been elevated above its predecessor, and it should be further recalled that the Ur-Nanshe ground plan was modelled on that of the interred Lower Construction, so that the traditional layout might have been considered to be part of the intrinsic character of the Tell K Temple of Ningirsu.

Two certain additions were the protrusions on the NE and SW sides (D and E), though what their functions might have been cannot be known, and the way they are illustrated on the section on Plan C (2) (Fig. 33) is slightly misleading. Their upper surfaces are shown at the same level as the top of the Ur-Nanshe walls, and they themselves are drawn as though they were also covered with the same bitumen layer as the rest of the old temple. The installation level perhaps makes sense, as this would suggest that the courses of bricks that were excavated by Sarzec provided shallow foundations that were embedded in the newly raised ground that was established around the Ur-Nanshe remains. But they were not in fact coated with bitumen, as can be confirmed by comparing the photos (Pl. 54 (1 and 2); Figs. 39 and 40), where the narrow protrusion D is visible in the immediate foreground of both images. Bitumen was therefore applied only to the top of the old building, which would again make sense since this was the remnant of the former sacred structure that needed to be solemnly sealed.

Two interesting questions are whether Enmetena recreated the porticoed colonnade that seems to have been an especially innovative feature of the older temple, and what happened to the original covered walkway that was built by Ur-Nanshe. One thing that can be said for certain is that Ur-Nanshe's fired-brick pedestals were in extremely good condition and in their original positions when Sarzec excavated them, though the charred wood remains of the cedar pillars suggests that they had been damaged by fire. As detailed in Chapter 16, the catastrophic fire hypothesis should be abandoned because there is no evidence that the Ur-Nanshe Building in its entirety, including its inner walls and outer façades, had been affected by a conflagration. The colonnade, however, which must in any case have been the most combustible feature of the structure (as noted above), does seem to have been burnt, and since there is no epigraphic or archaeological evidence that Tell K was the target of a successful hostile conquest or invasion between the reigns of Ur-Nanshe and Enmetena, it should probably be assumed that it caught fire by accident. This is in no way unlikely, considering that fires were needed for numerous ceremonial and practical purposes in the sacred precinct, not least the numerous burnt sacrifices that must have been carried out every year. The area is also subject to wild thunderstorms, as can be illustrated with a little anecdote from the British Museum team's work on the site. During a very violent storm that raged one night in 2018 the team took cover, partly to shelter from the rain, but also because of the risk of being struck by lightning. It turned out to be a wise precaution because a bolt of lightning did indeed strike a post belonging to a nearby security checkpoint, setting it alight. In their prominent position, rising to a height of perhaps 13 m above the surrounding plain, the wooden pillars that supported the Ur-Nanshe colonnade would no doubt have made extraordinarily good lightning rods, and over a period of about a hundred years (between the reigns of Ur-Nanshe and Enmetena) there must be a reasonable statistical possibility that one of them might have been struck. If that is indeed what happened then Ningirsu's Thunderbird might conceivably have made its presence felt in the most portentous way imaginable.

Whether the fire in the peristyle (however it was caused) was the catalyst for the renovation, or whether Enmetena was addressing the consequences of a fire that had happened sometime previously, cannot now be known. What is clear is that the brick pillar bases and the burnt remains of the wooden pillars were buried by Enmetena when he raised the ground level at the top of the mound around the truncated and sealed walls of the old temple. This is proven by the fact that the bases (H on Plan C (1); Fig. 33) were found *in situ*, where they had been installed by Ur-Nanshe, and that none were missing—an extremely unlikely outcome for such relatively movable features if they had been left exposed, even for a short time. Accordingly, they must have been preserved intact and in place in the mud-brick mass that was deposited by Enmetena. Whether Enmetena rebuilt the colonnade remains a matter of conjecture, however. More certain is the fact that the new temple was probably raised on a podium, as the stratigraphy seemingly demands. This is because of the differential between the generally raised Sarzec height of the mound (13.63 m) and the Sarzec height of the capped temple walls (14.05 m). The Enmetena temple was therefore based at a higher level than the surrounding ground, and additional mud-brick layers might have further increased the differential. All of this would indicate that the Enmetena temple was built on a raised platform, and that might in turn suggest that there was no need to distinguish the building from the surrounding area with the addition of a colonnade, though none of this can be stated conclusively. In any event, Enmetena presumably created a new iteration of Ur-Nanshe's ceremonial approach (pavement F) on the NW side of the building, above the Ur-Nanshe paving, which was also buried in the newly raised mound.

CHAPTER 20

From Enmetena to the Destruction of the Early Dynastic Complex

From Enmetena to Urukagina

There is scarcely any evidence to suggest that the rulers who held power between the reigns of Enmetena and Urukagina (*c*.2316–2307 BCE) undertook any widespread construction work on Tell K or in the cultic district of Girsu more generally. Enmetena, who enjoyed a long and well-documented reign, was succeeded by his son, Enanatum II (*c*.2335–2327 BCE), who was also directly descended from Ur-Nanshe and probably represented the end of the genealogical sequence that had seen the kingship passed down through the male line for a period of five generations. The lack of administrative texts and royal inscriptions in Enanatum II's name suggests that his period in office was short. Indeed, the only preserved inscription dating to his reign refers to restoration works that were undertaken on the edge of Tell K, and they were probably carried out on constructions previously built by his father. Enanatum II's single text was found repeated on at least one of four stone door sockets that were excavated in the vicinity of the Tell J reservoir (J on Sarzec's Plan D; Fig. 34), situated to the north-east of the temple on the middle one of the mound's three massive terraces. It records that he restored a brewery (é.bappir) on behalf of the god Ningirsu (RIME 1.9.6.1), but the archaeological status of the door sockets is unclear, and it is impossible to know whether they were found in a primary context. All that can be said with any certainty is that they were apparently excavated close to each other and might therefore have originally been installed in a brewing facility in the vicinity of the Tell J reservoir. This might further indicate that the reservoir itself was a fermentation vat for the production of beer, but the evidence is far from conclusive.

The implication is surely not, however, that Enmetena's brewhouse was transferred down to the middle terrace by Enanatum II because the production centre in the sacred precinct on top of the tell was clearly still in use after his reign (unless there was a hiatus, but the deposits found under the Oval Reservoir make that highly unlikely), as confirmed by the later work carried out there by Urukagina (detailed below). Enanatum II might conceivably have done some repairs to the brewhouse, but the idea that these were extensive enough to necessitate replacing the doors (as might be suggested by the door sockets) seems improbable. Alternatively, did Enanatum II construct or enlarge a supplementary brewing facility in the area of the Tell J reservoir in order to meet the high demand for beer, for divine offerings as well as for consumption at the numerous annual festivals that took place not only on Tell K itself but also in the ceremonial square of the Urukug (the temple district of Girsu more broadly)? The latter are well attested in ancient inscriptions and further confirmed by the excavations undertaken by the British Museum team in the sacred precinct, as detailed in Part 3 below. It could also be, for example, that a second facility was established or refitted to brew other kinds of beer than the sorts produced in the upper brewhouse. Any attempt to suggest an answer to this question is impeded by the problem of calculating the capacity of the Tell J reservoir with any real accuracy because Sarzec recorded its overall size (6.5 m × 3 m) and the fact that it was found at ground level (at a Sarzec height of about 10.8 m), but the text gives no information about its depth or the size of the unmarked square bricks that were used to build it. A suggestive fact might be that the impressive Enanatum II door socket was found adjacent to the reservoir at a depth of about 1 m (a little lower than both of the fragments of the Stele of the Vultures), and this might have been the associated floor level (see Sarzec and Heuzey 1912, p. 115). Very tentatively, therefore, if the reservoir was positioned above ground, and built (for the sake of argument) of bricks that were 0.05 cm thick, that would mean it had a capacity of approximately 6 m × 2.5 m × 0.8 = 12 m³, or 12,000 litres (allowing three courses of bricks for the base of the bituminated cavity and subtracting 0.5 m from the overall lengths to account for the thickness of the walls).

If it had held even a half or a third of that (6,000 litres or 4,000 litres), that would still have been a considerable amount of water to deliver to that intermediate location halfway up the NE side of the tell on the middle one of its three terraces. It should also be borne in mind that lots more water would have been needed for the various cleansing operations carried out in a brewery. But no well was detected in the vicinity, while the Well of Eanatum was very far away on the SW side of the top of the mound, and the nearby water supply and drainage network to the north-east (shown on Cros's Plan C; Fig. 38) was considerably lower than the Tell J reservoir, at an approximate Sarzec height of 9 m (see Chapter 6), so the natural direction of flow from there would have been unworkable. It should also be recalled that the only surviving evidence of a possible brewing installation on Tell J was a door socket, which would confirm that the fermentation tank (if that is indeed what it was) was sited inside a building, as would in any case have been dictated by the nature of the manufacturing process (detailed in Chapter 19), so the necessary infrastructure must have been reasonably sophisticated. No traces of this were preserved, however, so it is finally impossible to say whether further water storage reservoirs were built nearby or whether water might have been supplied via pipework that was subsequently destroyed or overlooked by the excavators, or whether it was simply carried in buckets. Since there is no clear archaeological context for the door sockets, it is also possible that they were stray objects that had been displaced from elsewhere, but this again is little more than guesswork.

With respect to the rulers who came after Enanatum II, a large number of administrative documents have survived from the time of Enentarzi (c.2327–2322 BCE), styled ruler (ensí) of Lagash, who was formerly an administrator (sanga) at the Ningirsu temple during the reign of Enmetena, but nothing is known about his filiation. No royal inscriptions from his reign were preserved, and the only monumental inscription, which concerns his daughter Geme-Bau, pre-dates his accession to the throne (RIME 1.9.7.1). The date formulae on Enentarzi's administrative texts indicate that he ruled for five years, and he was succeeded by Lugalanda (c.2322–2316 BCE), who is identified as Enentarzi's son on a clay cone from the reign of Enmetena that was inscribed when Enentarzi still held the office of temple administrator (sanga). Inscriptions from the reign of Lugalanda are mostly administrative texts, but a rare royal inscription that mentions his name and title is preserved on some seal impressions (RIME 1.9.8.1), while a further inscription that was previously attributed to Urukagina mentions the raising of a stele (RIME 1.9.8.2): 'He erected a monument and named it Ningirsu is the Lord Eternally Exalted in Nippur'. It was found on a stray fired brick that doubtless came from a pedestal that formed the base of a stele that must have been installed somewhere inside the religious complex, perhaps near a stairway or gateway, but more exact information is lacking. The administrative documents indicate that Lugalanda's reign lasted for 6 years and 1 month.

By and large, it seems that no major works were carried out within the confines of the Tell K sanctuary for a period of about fifty years after Enmetena's extensive renovations were completed. One small caveat is that the subsequent wholesale razing of the sacred site by Lugalzagesi means there is no way of knowing whether any significant changes were made to the temple itself (the Enmetena temple, as it then was) before Urukagina ascended to the throne, though the complete absence of any positive circumstantial evidence makes it extremely doubtful.

The Reign of Urukagina

The series of shifting titles by which Urukagina is known expressively illustrates the tumultuous nature of the reign of the last ruler of the First Dynasty of Lagash. Following in the footsteps of his predecessors, Urukagina was first styled ruler of Lagash, but this was later changed to 'king' of Lagash and finally, in the last three years of his reign, to 'king of Girsu'. Urukagina's origins are obscure, and his filiation is unknown, and for these reasons he was formerly considered to be a usurper. He also made an exception of himself by choosing Ninshubur as his personal god, thereby differentiating himself from previous Lagash I rulers, who had favoured Šul-MUŠ×PA (see, for example, RIME 1.9.9.6). More recently, however, evidence has emerged to indicate his familiarity or intimacy with the circle that formed around Lugalanda, suggesting that Urukagina could indeed have been Lugalanda's legitimate successor. To cite one relevant text, a commander (gal.ug₃) named URU.KA, who appears in some administrative documents (AO13267; DP59, for example), has been identified as Urukagina.

His reign, which lasted a little more than nine years according to the preserved sources, is remembered mainly for its beginnings and its unhappy end—the doubts that surround his origins and the legitimacy of his ascent to the throne, eventually followed by the fall of Lagash that brought an end to a long period of relative peace and prosperity. Less well known are the royal inscriptions of Urukagina that record his proclaimed reforms and temple building activities. A text known as the Reforms of Urukagina mainly deals with the administration of lands and burials, but it also includes a pledge to protect widows and orphans, and the declaration of a pardon that was granted to criminals (RIME 1.9.9.1). In political terms, the stated policies seem designed to present Urukagina as a righteous ruler who is eager to establish new rules for the people of Lagash in order to redress past wrongs. It is a projected persona that was developed more fully by the compilers of later law codes, including that of Urnamma, which was drawn up at the end of the third millennium BCE, and most saliently in the famous code of Hammurabi that was published in the eighteenth century BCE.

Urukagina's work as a builder of religious structures includes changes to the brewery area on Tell K and the Eadda temple of Enlil in Girsu, but he is also mentioned as the 'king of Lagash, who built the Eninnu', which is probably a reference to the more comprehensive work he carried out in the sacred precinct. His royal inscriptions were found on a stone tablet, some door sockets and some bricks, but most were exhumed in indeterminate archaeological contexts, and some certainly did not originate on Tell K. One of them deserves serious attention, however: the Urukagina foundation tablet (AO22934), which was found on the upper level of Tell K in the area between the Ur-Nanshe Building (or the Enmetena restoration as it would then have been) and the Enmetena block (Heuzey 1900, p. 81), though unfortunately with no clear archaeological context because Heuzey only records that it was retrieved by the workers in Sarzec's absence, as discussed further below. Significantly, the inscription (RIME 1.9.9.6) commemorates the refurbishment of Ningirsu's 'coach house' and 'brewery', two buildings that had previously been mentioned together in Enmetena texts that were found close together in the same area (detailed previously). The very fact that the Urukagina inscription was incised on a foundation tablet indicates that it must have been ritually interred before his renovations were carried out. It is also reasonable to assume that the earlier texts in the name of Enmetena and the later Urukagina inscription refer to the same double installation: two buildings that were placed close together on the Enmetena Esplanade. The location of the brewery or brewhouse is well known, and the particular reference to it in the Urukagina inscription surely confirms that the post-Enmetena elevation of the ground in that area, together with the construction of a new Oval Reservoir, can be attributed to Urukagina with a reasonably high degree of confidence.

The exact details of Urukagina's raising of the summit of Tell K are not without complications. The evidence for a general elevation derives from Sarzec's discovery that the Oval Reservoir was built on an earthen bed, with inclusions of ash, fragments of bitumen and potsherds, which was 0.7 m thick to the south-west, but reduced to 0.3 m in the north-east. The reason for the differential can probably be accounted for by the complex way in which the reservoir was constructed in order to facilitate the inward flow of fresh water and the outward flow of fermented beer. In all likelihood, water poured into the Oval Reservoir via the inlet on the NW side of the T-shaped junction that was found at the reservoir's NE end, where the installation was generally at its lowest point and the foundation layer was thinnest. The reservoir was higher on its SW side, where the underlying ground was built up to 0.7 m, but its internal floor had a carefully designed dual slope that was seemingly calculated to exploit the hydrostatic properties of the fermenting liquid and to encourage thermal circulation (mentioned above). As Heuzey records (Sarzec and Heuzey 1912, p. 421), the NE–SW element of this overall slope was achieved not by varying the installation's brickwork but with the aid of the varying thickness of the foundation layer of ash and other ingredients. It should therefore probably be assumed that the Urukagina floor level was associated with the higher underlying level, and that the lower end of the fermenter towards the north-east was partly built into the ground. It was certainly the case that the bituminated compartments of the three adjacent cisterns (probably conditioning tanks previously installed by Enmetena, as discussed in Chapter 19) were below ground level, and certainly lower than the NE end of the fermenter, as can be seen on Sarzec's photo (Pl. 55 (2); Fig. 42). The broader inference is presumably that the ground was generally raised by some 0.7 m, not only around the brewhouse and the area of the Enmetena Esplanade, but across the summit of the mound.

A further difficulty is presented by the absence of any traces of an Urukagina pavement in the vicinity of the brewhouse, but the lack is offset by the greatest anomaly of all, which is the very fact that the Oval Reservoir not only survived but that it was so well preserved. Was it buried beneath rubble when the site was razed and subsequently brought back into service by the Akkad occupiers? Were the tiles and bricks of which it was formed—unlike those that were used to build the recovered pavement—made in such a specialised way that it would have been pointless to try to reclaim them? Did its role in the brewing process make it an object of special import? The answers to these questions cannot be known, but the surviving inscriptions and other finds, together with the raising of the base level under the Oval Reservoir, point to the fact that Urukagina oversaw a substantial project on Tell K, perhaps on a similar scale to that previously completed by Enmetena. Indeed, as well as the reference to the brewery and coach house on the Urukagina foundation tablet, the similarities in the amount by which the mound's summit was raised by the two rulers—0.8 m by Enmetena and 0.7 m by Urukagina—might suggest that Urukagina was consciously following in his predecessor's footsteps. Other than the Oval Reservoir, no trace of Urukagina's work has survived because the site was soon wiped out by Lugalzagesi and then reoccupied by the Akkad conquerors, but the fact that Urukagina repeated Enmetena's inscribed declaration more or less verbatim, and that he used the important word Eninnu in the climactic position at the end of the inscription, are expressive indicators that seem to acknowledge a kinship between the architectural ambitions of the two rulers (RIME 1.9.9.6):

> For Ningirsu, warrior of the god Enlil, Urukagina, king of Lagash, built his temple, built his 'palace' of Tirash, and built the Antasura. He built a coach house for him, a building whose awesome splendour overwhelms all lands, and he built for him a beer and wine house, which provides (him with) great vats from the mountains. For Shulshaga he built his Kitushakkile, and for Igalim he built the Emehushgalanki. He built the temple of Bau for her. For the god Enlil he built his Eada of Imsag, and built him a pantry, the room where his divine regular offerings are delivered. Urukagina, king of Lagash, who built the Eninnu—may his personal god, Ninshubur, forever pray for his life to Ningirsu!

Sarzec was informed by his local workers that the Urukagina foundation tablet was dug up in a spot south of the Enmetena Block between 1881 and 1888, while he was unable to visit the site (see Heuzey 1900, p. 81). Little more is known, except that it was sold in Baghdad along with some other pieces found nearby and later absorbed into a collection that eventually found its way to the Louvre, where the tablet is now kept. The object was clearly picked up by looters, and the story of its discovery is fraught with uncertainty, but the presumed find location might nevertheless be important because of some other suggestive artefacts that were found in the same area: the silver Vase of Enmetena, the plaque of Dudu and perhaps (though with more caveats) a pair of finds that were excavated by Sarzec to the north-east of the block, namely a stone Enmetena door socket inside which was a carved lion's head from the reign of Ur-Nanshe.

The Silver Vase of Enmetena, the Plaque of Dudu and the Onyx Lion of Ur-Nanshe

Two of the important objects that were found in close proximity to each other belonged to two of the most prominent Lagash I figures of the century or so before Urukagina's reign: the ruler Enmetena and Dudu, the high priest (sanga) of Ningirsu. Both artefacts must originally have been located within the holiest confines of the Ningirsu temple's inner sanctum, and they were surely regarded as some of the most noteworthy of the votive and cultic objects that made up the inventory of the god's possessions.

The silver Vase of Enmetena (AO2674; Fig. 23) is a large cult vessel with a straight high neck and an ovoid body, made of silver, that is set on a circular copper support that has feet in the shape of four lions' paws. The copper base, which was made using the lost-wax casting technique, has unfortunately suffered greatly from oxidation. The vase itself was made from a single sheet of hammered silver foil, except at the neck, where the foil is doubled for reinforcement, and at the rim, where the doubled foil is soldered with copper. The incised decorative imagery and patterns, together with the inscriptions, are extraordinarily clear. The vase measures 0.35 m (h) overall, but 0.28 m without the copper support, while the diameters of the rim and ovoid body are 0.1 m and 0.18 m, respectively. Its cubic capacity is 4.15 litres. An example of the artistry of a Sumerian silversmith, the vase shows a remarkable degree of technical sophistication. Arranged in fifteen cases that run all the way around the top of the neck, the inscription (RIME 1.9.5.7) records that the vase, which was dedicated by Enmetena to Ningirsu, was intended to contain a monthly offering of oil (or fat), and it notes that the administrator of the Ningirsu temple at that period was Dudu:

> For the god Ningirsu, warrior of the god Enlil, Enmetena, ruler of Lagash, chosen in the heart by the goddess Nanshe, chief executive for the god Ningirsu, son of Enanatum, ruler of Lagash, for his master who loves him, the god, made (this) *gurgur* vessel of refined silver, whose monthly fat (offering) the god Ningirsu consumes and set it up for his own life for the god Ningirsu of Eninnu. At that time, Dudu was the temple administrator (*sanga*) for the god Ningirsu.

The decorations are arranged in two bands. The upper register that encircles the shoulder of the vase depicts seven bovids seated on the ground, each with three legs folded beneath its body, while the fourth (the right forepaw) is bent at the knee, as though the animals might be about to stand up. Facing in the same direction (leftwards as we look), they all have raised heads on which can be seen protuberances that represent horns that have not yet emerged from beneath the skin. Complementing the animals' physical proportions, this suggests that they are bullocks, young cows or heifers. Their almond-shaped eyes (slightly pointed on top in a way that echoes the points on the tops of the heads) are accentuated with a double arch, while the descending contour from the shoulder to the upper part of the leg is described with a narrow pair of lines, and their lower legs are enlivened with pairs

FIGURE 103. The Plaque of Dudu. Musée du Louvre AO2354.

of parallel lines. The tails, which fall behind the animals' bodies, seem to emerge from above their hind legs, where a neat tuft of wavy hair is laid downwards across the animals' hindquarters. Recumbent cattle with raised forepaws also appear on the Plaque of Dudu (Fig. 103), and they might generally be associated with the deity or with a particular aspect of the divine being, perhaps fertility. This again recalls Ningirsu's dual identity as the warrior god, and also the patron deity of irrigation and agriculture. The animals might furthermore be suggestive of the god's herds (belonging to the temple estates), and they could additionally be associated with sacrificial offerings and banquets.

The cattle are placed on a narrow twofold divider that is decorated with a herringbone pattern, below which is the taller register on which are shown four similarly composed groups of creatures: four frontal representations of Imdugud, the Thunderbird, with outstretched wings, and scenes below and between every two adjacent birds that show a lion attacking either a mountain goat or a deer. The sequences of Imdugud birds above and lions attacking goats or deer below are alternated so that the claws of each bird grasp the backs of two adjacent, opposite-facing goats, lions, deer and then lions again. In this way, the Thunderbirds act as linking devices to connect the four self-contained scenes of animal combat below with their neighbours on either side (expressly coupling the same kinds of animals), and also to join the upper and lower sequences. The composition as a whole is brilliantly thought out and wonderfully executed: strikingly simple and direct, but also deceptively intricate and well worked. The lions are shown attacking the heads of the goats (doubtless intended to be ibexes) and the heads of the deer, which might be stags. The flanks of the lions' victims are articulated with short dashes, which, in the case of the deer, might be meant to show that they are still fawns, but the fact that the ibexes are given the same markings perhaps rather indicates that the marks were applied to add texture to the bodies. Below the successive pairs of lions with ibexes or deer is another twofold band decorated with a herringbone pattern that represents the ground on which they stand. The ratio of the heights of the pictorial bands from the top to the bottom of the vase's bulging belly is approximately 3:8:5, which means that the register containing the Thunderbirds and lions is almost exactly the same height as the combined heights of the blank band that runs around the bottom of the vase plus the register with resting bovids at its shoulder. This adds to an overall sense of harmony and artistic control that is further emphasised by the blank bands, which demonstrate a high degree of compositional finesse and confidence.

Imdugud, who appears four times, is depicted with rounded, elongated ears that project upwards above his pointed head, the top of which is adorned with four doubly arched tufts of hair that are perhaps extremely stylised indicators of a lion's mane. The creature, who was believed to be a bird with a lion's head, has eyes with arching brows that are slightly upturned at the sides, while the tops of the eyes themselves (or perhaps the eyelids) are extended downwards to form the sweep of the mythical beast's wide nose, on either side of which are rounded, elongated cheeks that feature stubby, upward-pointing whiskers. The feathers that cover the drop-shaped body have rounded ends and thick shafts (or rachides) from which diverging lines emanate to represent the vanes. Towards the bottom of the creature's body is a large, almost circular navel that is inscribed with a double outline. The uplifted and widespread wings have an upper double band that is decorated with a herringbone pattern. The tops of the wings bend down and inwards at the creature's neck, while their undersides are formed as smooth arcs that could almost be parts of a large circle that is interrupted by the lines of the slightly flared tail feathers. The wings are formed of four angled rows of feathers, with four or five rows close to the body that are laid out vertically. The tail, which has horizontal rows of feathers, flares out slightly towards the bottom. It is difficult to make out whether the slightly bent feet are intended to be talons or paws, but they are shown with long curving claws, while double lines like those on the legs of the bovids and other animals suggest the anatomy of the lower legs. Close to the body, the upper parts of the legs are covered with two rows of feathers. The fact that there are five claws and not four, as on a bird's foot, might be an anthropomorphic characteristic (as indeed might the navel) that was applied to connect Imdugud with Ningirsu as his avatar, but lions also have five claws on their front feet so this might also be a further leonine feature.

The heads of the lions are shown frontally and from above, and though this strains the anatomy it stresses the likeness between the lions' heads and that of the Thunderbird. The lions' long manes (contrasting with the Thunderbird's hair) are formed as series of arcs (or perhaps segments) with outlines and inner lines, and their slender tails curve downwards to touch the ground. The stags' antlers, which point upwards, include varying numbers of curving branches or points that have a flamelike appearance. The ibexes have extravagantly turned-back horns that include the ridges or rings that are produced on real animals as the horns grow. The undersides of the ibexes' jaws feature pointed beards, and curling tufts of hair can be seen on the upper parts of their legs. As indicated previously, the short strokes along the sides of the bodies of the lions' victims add texture to their coats. Otherwise, the bodies of the stags and wild goats are drawn like those of the bovids on the register above, with eyes and shoulders marked by double lines, and additional strokes applied to the limbs to suggest anatomical features and articulations.

The exact meanings ascribed to the vase's decorations by its ancient Sumerian makers, viewers and users are elusive, but some hypotheses can be advanced. Since Imdugud is an embodiment of Ningirsu, his image defines the vase as the property of the god, as is also stated in the inscription. In terms of heraldry, the grouping of the Thunderbird with his claws on the backs of lions is commonly interpreted as an emblem of the city-state of Lagash (the motif is prominently used on Ningirsu's net on the Stele of the Vultures, for example), and the device might confirm that the vase was intended as a gift from the community at large, represented by the ruler. The heraldic significance of the ibexes and stags might refer to other communities, possibly in far-off mountainous regions in the case of the mountain goats, and they might also conceivably suggest the origins of the silver that was used to make the vessel. The fact that the lions are shown seizing the other animals perhaps refers to the power that Lagash wielded over those other localities, with the dominant Thunderbird stressing that the exercise of such power is subject to the god's favour, as is the city-state's ongoing prosperity.

A more general level of meaning might also be detected, however. The groups of wild lions and their prey are organised compositionally by the four Thunderbirds, with a crowning band of calmly seated bovids above. This constitutes a progression from brute nature to domesticated animals that presumably recalls and celebrates the transformational power of the god, whose taming of the Thunderbird symbolises his role as the divine instigator of irrigation and agriculture. The thematic strands evoke an association between wild animals and farming that is also present in the inscriptions on the much earlier Feathered Figure (described in Chapter 13), where the agricultural order is symbolised by the laying out of the ground with the surveyor's rope, and the bison and the gazelle are created or born in grass-filled meadows. The congruence between the lyre and the bull that is a common feature of the way prestige versions of the instrument were built communicates another aspect of the same theme: the transformational harnessing of the raw power of nature to create harmony, whether musical or more generally cultural (see Chapter 19). These are aspects of human civilisation, but nothing can be achieved without a firm reliance upon the deity, so the vase as an object embodies the shaping power of human hands as an expression of the order that was infused into the cosmos by Ningirsu.

Many of the same themes and motifs are present on the Dudu Plaque (AO2354), which was excavated by Sarzec, but badly damaged shortly after its discovery, possibly while it was being transported from Tello to Paris. Fortunately, Sarzec took an impression of it (an estampage) as soon as it was found (Sarzec and Heuzey 1912, p. 205), and that image forms the basis of the following description. The plaque, which was commissioned and dedicated by Dudu, the chief priest (sanga) of Ningirsu during Enmetena's reign, measures 0.25 m (h) × 0.23 m (w) × 0.08 m (t). It is decorated in relief and perforated in its centre with a circular hole that has a diameter of 0.08 m and a depth of 0.1 m (the depth of the hole reflecting the fact that the back of the plaque is convex in shape). The perforation is framed with an irregular squarish protrusion all the way round. According to Heuzey (Sarzec and Heuzey 1912, p. 204), it is made of a bituminous stone that might have been produced artificially by mixing clay and bitumen. The inscription records that the material came from a city that was located probably in the western part of Elam (URU×A), and Heuzey further surmises that the applied decorations might have been partly stamped onto the bituminous block, after which further details were added by carving.

The inscription, which is placed on the background around the Thunderbird and on the body of the calf in a box in the middle register, includes Dudu's dedication to Ningirsu (RIME 1.9.5.28), while more details of the commission and the provenance of the material are added in the rest of the text, especially close to Dudu's back, where he is again named:

For the god Ningirsu of the Eninnu, Dudu, the temple administrator of the god Ningirsu, had (this stone) brought down from (the city of) URU×A and had it made (to be fixed by) a peg beam. Dudu, the exalted temple administrator of the god Ningirsu.

The design is placed inside a frame that runs all the way around the outside of the plaque, and it is arranged in three registers divided by horizontal relief bands. On the upper register Imdugud, the Thunderbird, grasps the backs of two opposite-facing lions, who turn their heads and strain their necks to bite his outstretched wings on either side of his body. On the left of the central hole is a seated or recumbent calf with three of its legs beneath its body and a raised right leg that is bent at the knee. The way the mythical beast and the animals are represented recalls the way they are incised on the Vase of Enmetena. Their forms are more robust and stockier on the plaque, but that is probably partly to do with the techniques used respectively on the different materials. Unlike on the Vase of Enmetena, the Thunderbird has triangular ears with internal hollows, while his forehead shows no traces of hair, and his head generally is compressed, lacking the elongated cheeks of the representation on the silver vessel. The lions' heads, which face upwards, are viewed from above, and their tails cross each other on the ground, unlike the lions' tails on the vase, which meet to form a U-shape below Imdugud's tail feathers. The calf differs from the bovids that are incised around the shoulder of the Vase of Enmetena on account of its contracted proportions and the absence of descriptive lines on its forelegs. To the right of the Thunderbird and the calf is the standing figure of Dudu, who faces to the right, and occupies the upper two registers. Despite the losses to the top of his head and his left hand, it is clear that his head and face were fully shaved. His right ear is extremely large and characterised by a pointed lobe. Only part of the lower lid of his eye is preserved, and his nose is missing, while his closed lips and chin, which were intact when the object was found, cannot be made out clearly in the estampage. He is bare chested, with prominent nipples and defined clavicles, and two of his lower ribs can be seen. He wears a kaunakes with four rows of flounces, and his arms are thick with sharply pointed elbows; his right arm is bent at his chest, where his hand is closed. His left arm is also bent, and although his left hand is missing, it is clear that he was shown holding a staff, of which two lengths of the bottom section survive, close to the preserved parts of the frame on the right of the plaque (by Dudu's forearm and next to his front foot). It is possible that the staff might have been the support for an emblematic standard, but the top is sadly missing so this must remain conjectural.

A guilloche of braided ropes or ribbons that is formed with three bands of intertwining relief, arranged to create four loops, occupies the lower register. The guilloche motif is common in Early Dynastic art, and in the Dudu Plaque it might perhaps be intended to represent a whirlwind or a storm. This draws attention to the fact that, as on the Vase of Enmetena, the carving invokes a contrast between the wild forces of nature (the storm and the biting lions) and the domesticated calf, with the Thunderbird again acting as the divine intermediary that tames the ferocious lions, ensuring order and prosperity. The figure of Dudu is separated from these symbolic elements, but he was probably shown as the intercessor who leads the community in the worship of Ningirsu. The turbulent guilloche is presumably an emblem of Ningirsu in his role as the god of the storm, but it should also be recalled that, while Ningirsu fights with the force of an irresistible tempest, he also subdues the stormy powers of destructive chaos, for example in the epic poem Lugale, where he defeats the monstrous Asag who howls like an 'accursed storm' (ETCSL, 168–86).

The damage to the plaque (Fig. 103) is mostly confined to the right-hand side, especially the top and bottom corners. The upper right corner, which contained the top of Dudu's head, his eye and nose, as well as his left hand and the tip of the stick with its surmised standard, is missing entirely. Below that, the right edge of the middle part of the plaque is broken, and the break has removed the frame and part of Dudu's staff. The angle of the bottom right corner is also missing, so that the plaque follows the curve of the guilloche at this point. The bottom left corner is slightly chipped, and further small breaks can be seen in the middle of the frame that runs across the top of the carving and on Dudu's cheek. His skirt is abraded towards the centre of his body, around the navel area. The softness and instability of the material has led to further cracking all across the surface, and in its present state all its four corners are broken. An irregular fracture along the upper edge has led to the loss of the Thunderbird's right ear, and Dudu's head is missing altogether. More of Dudu's staff has been lost in this area, and the lower register is so badly damaged that half of the guilloche has been lost. A broken piece of the bottom left corner has been reattached. The inherent fragility of the bituminous mixture means that the damage recorded on the estampage was probably mostly unintentional and that the plaque was generally well preserved when Sarzec unearthed it. The details that might give pause for thought are the sharp chip in Dudu's cheek, the abrasion on his skirt (which recalls passages of probably intentional damage on the Ur-Nanshe Plaques) and the loss of the inferred standard (echoing the possibly deliberate removal of a conjectural standard from the Feathered Figure). Since none of this can by any stretch of the imagination be confirmed, however, it is perhaps safest simply to say that the original damage was accidental.

The small onyx protome of a lion from the reign of Ur-Nanshe (AO3281), which is 0.075 m (h) × 0.92 m (l), was found in an Enmetena door socket that bears an inscription commemorating the building of the 'reed shrine' of Ningirsu (RIME 1.5.9.10): 'Enmetena, ruler of Lagash, who built the "reed shrine" of the god Ningirsu's giguna (Multi-coloured Reeds), his personal god is the god Šul-MUŠ×PA'. The Onyx Lion has a hole in its back that was designed to take a lost additional element, meaning that the animal sculpture was probably the base of a composite votive object. Its mane is represented as pointed, or V-shaped incised tufts, each of which has a centrally incised vertical line. Its ears are round and flattened against its head, while its flattened circular snout with oblique whiskers recalls the Ur-Nanshe Stone Heads of Lions discussed in Chapter 19. A fragmentary inscription on the body records the fact that the Onyx Lion was dedicated to Ningirsu, thereby confirming that it formed part of a votive object (RIME 1.9.1.24a): 'For the god Ningirsu, Ur-Nanshe, king of Lagash, son of Gu-NI.DU . . .'

The contexts of the silver Vase of Enmetena, the Dudu Plaque and the Enmetena door socket with its Ur-Nanshe leonine protome are not well described in the texts, but it is safe to say that the vase and the plaque, which were found in excellent condition, were in all likelihood ritually buried and therefore preserved from harm. Made of precious metal and stunningly worked, the Enmetena Vase in particular was an exceptional object that could not possibly have survived the devastating attack on the temple that was carried out by Lugalzagesi. It was almost certainly displayed in the cella, and since the invading army were especially concerned to destroy and mutilate the mound's holiest spaces and its most potent symbolic objects, it is inconceivable that the silver vase would not have been stolen or at the very least defaced (though the value of the precious metal might make mere defacement unlikely). These objects, with the telling exception of the Onyx Lion, belonged to the reign of Enmetena, who ritually buried his predecessor Ur-Nanshe's ex-votos when he ordered the renovation of the Ningirsu temple (as argued in Chapter 19). The Onyx Lion might also therefore have every claim to be associated with the group because of the relationship between the two rulers that Enmetena declared when he interred Ur-Nanshe's relics.

The Urukagina Temple and the Razing of Early Dynastic Tell K

The possibility that these temple artefacts were deliberately buried alongside, or near, Urukagina's foundation tablet might well signal another instance of a successor–predecessor connection, this time between Urukagina and Enmetena. The further inference is that Urukagina ritually interred the objects when he carried out refurbishment works on the temple in the same way as Enmetena had done. Neither rebuilt the temple entirely in the comprehensive manner of Ur-Nanshe, who decommissioned the Lower Construction and dramatically reshaped the religious landscape not only of Tell K but of Girsu as a whole, together with the state of Lagash at large. Instead, they both created reworked buildings on the same ground plan that might be described as derivative structures, as long as the word is stripped of all negative implications, because the later temples were not inferior copies of an untouchable original, but respectful inheritors of the tradition. That is why, in addition to the foundation tablets that commemorated every temple built on Tell K, relics of previous rulers were also buried in the fabric of the raised platform. Symbolic artefacts associated with successive generations of rulers were interred to pay tribute to them as the illustrious forebears of later architect kings. As previously noted, building works of this kind, which were executed periodically (in Urukagina's case practically within living memory of the recent overhaul by Enmetena), must have been governed by well-established protocols.

There is nevertheless a difference between the work carried out by Enmetena and that undertaken by Urukagina. Whereas Enmetena ritually sealed the old Ur-Nanshe Building, there is no reason to believe that Urukagina exhaustively rebuilt or replaced Enmetena's temple, and it seems far more likely that he simply renovated the structure, retaining the same foundations, while raising the floors and thresholds. In this regard, it should also be recalled that the Enmetena temple already stood a little higher than the average elevation of the top of the tell. The reference height to which the summit was raised by Enmetena was 13.63 m, but the height at which he capped the walls of the Ur-Nanshe Building was a little above this, as outlined in Chapter 19. The truncated Ur-Nanshe walls were 1.12 m tall, and on top of that was a bed of bricks (0.05 m) and a layer of bitumen (also 0.05 m) that together added a further 0.1 m. That means that the older temple was sealed at a Sarzec height of approximately 14.05 m, and it can be surmised with a reasonably high degree of confidence that Enmetena must have added a further structural deposit of mud-bricks on top of the bitumen sealing. As indicated by the bed of earth mixed with ashes found under the Oval Reservoir, Urukagina subsequently added a further 0.7 m to the average level of the summit, raising it to the benchmark Sarzec height of 14.33 m (13.63 m + 0.7 m). In the central area, therefore, the renewed temple did not necessarily stand much taller than its predecessor, and unlike the Enmetena temple, which was almost certainly raised on a podium, as is indicated by the differential between the sealing height of the capped Ur-Nanshe Building (14.05 m) and the general Enmetena levelling height (13.63 m), the Urukagina installation might well have been situated at approximately the same ground level as the rest of the raised mound (14.33 m). Perhaps the key point to emphasise in this respect is that the capped walls of the Ur-Nanshe Building were buried at least 0.28 m (14.33 m – 14.05 m) beneath the mudbrick foundations of the Enmetena and Urukagina derivations. Accordingly, they were protected from harm when the mound was finally razed, such that the building destroyed by Lugalzagesi at the very end of the Early Dynastic period was the renovation overseen by Urukagina, with its foundations at the representative Sarzec height of at least 14.33 m. The exact height cannot be known, but what is certain is that the base of the Urukagina temple lay between minimum and maximum heights of 14.33 m and 14.5 m, because it was situated in the portion of the Sarzec gap towards the top of the tell that cannot be accounted for by comparing the stratigraphy in the central area with the archaeological evidence from elsewhere on the mound, notably the Urukagina deposits under the Oval Reservoir in the Enmetena Esplanade. It is also unequivocally the case that the base height of the Urukagina walls lay in the destruction horizon that is evidenced across the tell's summit.

On account of the magnitude and speed of the events, the epigraphic record is unsurprisingly almost entirely silent about the date and perpetrators of the catastrophe that befell Tell K because Girsu in its entirety was destroyed with one fatal blow. Consequently, with one miraculous exception, nothing survived. And yet, the conquest of the state of Lagash was foreshadowed on a single clay tablet that dates to the final years of Urukagina's reign, two years before the invasion that brought the Presargonic era to a close. Found somewhere along the NE slopes of Tell K, it contains a lamentation bewailing events that were already taking place just outside Girsu's walls and announcing with a high degree of poetic pathos the fate that was soon inevitably to engulf the city. Many later examples of the lament genre have survived, notably the Lament over the Destruction of Ur, and the genre remained current in the culture of ancient Mesopotamia for centuries, if not millennia. It was later adopted by the Jews and is widely familiar today thanks to the Book of Lamentations in the Old Testament, which grieves for the destruction of Jerusalem in 586 BCE.

The Lamentation over the Destruction of Lagash (AO4162; RIME 1.9.9.5; Fig. 104) was written in response to the deteriorating situation in Lagash that developed under Urukagina, when the gradual weakening of the state was followed by its ultimate fall and loss of independence. The age-old conflict with Umma was never finally resolved; in addition, inscriptions from Urukagina's third, fifth and sixth regnal years record that Lagash was repeatedly attacked by a 'man of Uruk', probably Enshakushana (see AO13753; DP545). Administrative documents also illustrate the strains placed on the economy of Lagash by the ongoing hostilities. Increasingly, the texts relate to the procurement and supply of military equipment, and, for example, the fact that full rations were distributed to corvée troops in year six of Urukagina's reign—meaning that additional forces were co-opted into the army for the whole year. Following the Uruk assaults came the attack led by the formidable Lugalzagesi, who besieged and sacked the city of Lagash in the eighth year of Urukagina's reign. This is the context for the Lagash lamentation, but the historical fall of the city, with the consequent contraction of the state, is also reflected in a significant change to Urukagina's title. At the beginning of his reign, Urukagina is styled ruler (ensí) of Lagash in the preserved texts; thereafter, through to his seventh regnal year, he is known as king (lugal) of Lagash. Following the conquest of Lugalzagesi and the annexation of Lagash, however, he is reduced to being the king (lugal) of Girsu alone. Texts dating to the reign of Urukagina break off in his tenth regnal year, probably because Lugalzagesi also finally seized Girsu, bringing the First Dynasty of Lagash to a close.

Lugalzagesi (c.2316–2292 BCE), the ruler of Umma, subjugated a number of previously independent cities, including Uruk, Eridu, Larsa and Adab, and his overriding aim seems to have been to transform Sumer from a federation of city-states into a unified political entity under his sole authority. Accordingly, he subsequently styled himself 'king of Uruk' and 'king of Sumer' (lugal kalam.ma, or 'king of the land'), and he reigned for about twenty-five years before eventually being defeated by Sargon of Akkad. His claims to sovereignty over various Sumerian city-states are recorded in a royal inscription that was reconstructed from about a hundred fragments of a stone vessel found in Nippur, which represents the only text securely attributed to Lugalzagesi as king of Uruk (RIME 1.14.20.1). The inscription, which styles him 'king of Uruk' and 'king of Sumer', states that he is owed allegiance by city-states including Ur, Larsa and Nippur. The noteworthy absence of Lagash and Girsu from the

FIGURE 104. Tablet containing the Lament over the Destruction of Lagash. Musée du Louvre AO 4162.

list might suggest that Lugalzagesi conquered Lagash after the inscription was made, but this is possibly contradicted by the Lamentation over the Destruction of Lagash, in which Lugalzagesi is referred to only as the ruler of Umma. Conversely, therefore, this might mean that he invaded Lagash towards the beginning of his career, but there could be several reasons why his other titles were omitted. Their absence might reflect the predominating importance in the mind of the Lagash poet of the immemorial conflict with Umma, or it could simply be a way of slightly denigrating Lugalzagesi's status.

The Lamentation over the Destruction of Lagash is charged with exceptional immediacy. With inconsolable sadness the piece chronicles Lugalzagesi's attack on the heartlands of Girsu, narrating in vivid detail the impious chain of violent devastations that he carried out in the territories of the state of Lagash, where he annihilated sanctuaries and boundary shrines. His actions were, the poem states, a 'sin against the god Ningirsu'. The poet recounts how, temporarily sparing the holy city of Girsu, Lugalzagesi led his forces through the Gu'edena borderlands, where he systematically uprooted the steles that demarcated the state's limits, targeting the sanctuaries, temples and shrines that were devoted to the gods of Lagash and other important figures in the Sumerian pantheon. The term Gu'edena means the 'edge of the plains', and after the boundaries of the state had been ruptured, three successive waves of destruction were unleashed: first, around the Lagash–Umma border; secondly, in the regions crossed on the march from the frontier to the environs of the city of Lagash; and finally inside Lagash's city walls. One of the first places of high symbolic importance that was attacked by Lugalzagesi's phalanx in the Gu'edena region was Antasura, the rural sanctuary of Ningirsu in the extreme north-west of the territory. Similarly, many of the border chapels that had been established by Lagash I rulers along the dyke that marked the division between the two states were plundered and torched. As recorded in the lament, Lugalzagesi's soldiers flattened all the important cult places as they progressed inexorably towards the city of Lagash itself.

Finally, the verses chronicle how Lugalzagesi seized the metropolis of Lagash, where he perpetrated unprecedented sacrilegious mayhem by plundering a series of cardinal sites, including the Bagara temple of Ningirsu, the shrine of Gatumdug (é.^{d}Gá.tùm.du$_{10}$, the tutelary goddess of Lagash), the Ibgal of Inanna (ib.é.an.na.^{d}Inanna) and the temple of Nanshe (šà.pà.da). The poet deplores the desecration and looting of precious votive artefacts made of bronze and lapis lazuli, and the smashing of the holy statues. Some of Lugalzagesi's troops were dispatched to set fire to Lagash's urban sanctuaries, while others ravaged the countryside, where they destroyed auxiliary temples in neighbouring towns (é.^{d}Nin.dar at Ki.èš^{ki}, é.^{d}Dumu.zi.abzu at Ki.nu.nir^{ki} and Lugal.Uru$_{11}$^{ki} at Uru$_{11}$^{ki}), as well as rural chapels (abzu.e and é.engur.ra.^{d}Nanše). They also torched the cultivated land, in particular the fields of barley that were considered to be the property of Ningirsu. All that then remained of Urukagina's domain was the sacred city of Girsu and the immediately surrounding countryside, which is presumably why Urukagina is referred to in the text not as the ruler of Lagash, but only as the king of Girsu (lugal Gír.su^{ki}).

The events inscribed on the Urukagina clay tablet represent the last-known instalment of the Lagash–Umma border conflict, but in terms of literary history, the Lament over the Destruction of Lagash is the earliest surviving example of the lament genre that later flourished (if that word can be used for such a melancholy topic) in the Ur III period, when the destruction of one after another important city was mourned in verse: Ur, Nippur, Eridu and Uruk were all commemorated in this way. The Destruction of Lagash is the precursor of the later laments, but in some ways the most vivid of them all, for one reason because it recounts events almost in real time, but also because it is the lone voice that miraculously speaks across the intervening millennia about the impending end of the state. In its closing lines the poet declares that, by entering and ransacking the territory of Ningirsu, Lugalzagesi has committed an irredeemable act of blasphemy against the god, and that the people of Umma will be made to pay for his crimes for all eternity. In a last vicious and ironic swipe, the poet asserts that it is Nisaba herself, goddess of the harvest and writing, and the personal goddess of Lugalzagesi, who will wreak vengeance on the miscreants: 'May Nisaba, the goddess of Lugalzagesi ... make them bear this sin on their necks!' This is a generational curse, and since Nisaba was the goddess of writing, which was conceived of in Sumerian culture as a means of recording things for all time, it implies that the offence against Ningirsu will be acknowledged and paid for by his descendants forevermore. Despite the prayers, invocations and stinging curses uttered by the poet on behalf of Urukagina and the priests and people of Lagash, however, Lugalzagesi remorselessly continued his assault, which was not complete until he had overrun and destroyed the jewel in Lagash's crown: the abode of Ningirsu himself—the sacred city of Girsu with its chief temple on Tell K.

The very end of the story, which could not, by definition, have been inscribed on the tablet, was instead written in the archaeological record. The sacred complex was plundered and razed to the ground, creating a destruction horizon across Tell K that contained some of the defaced and shattered fragments of objects that were formerly the supreme emblems of Girsu's power and prestige. Of paramount importance were the artefacts that celebrated historically important victories that had been inflicted by the rulers of Lagash on the state of Umma, and chief among these was the Stele of the Vultures: the victory stele of Eanatum that had presumably been transferred from the trophy room in the temple built by Enmetena to the latest iteration of the shrine to Ningirsu that was renovated by Urukagina. There can be little doubt that this was Lugalzagesi's key target because it spectacularly encapsulated the former triumph of Eanatum. As described in detail in Chapter 18, the carving depicts the ruler of Girsu–Lagash at the head of his troops, inspired and supported by Ningirsu, who is also shown entrapping and killing enemy soldiers with his divine mace and net. Enthroned in the sanctuary's trophy room, the famous testament to the glory of Ningirsu and his earthly nominee, Eanatum, represented a monumental affront to the state of Umma, its warrior god Sharra and the neighbouring territory's ancestral rulers. As the text on the Stele of the Vultures records, the defeated leader of Umma was forced to swear numerous oaths of repentance on weapons belonging to the great gods Enlil, Enki, Inanna and others to atone for the fact that the people of Umma had irreligiously insulted Ningirsu by crossing the sacred borders of his state, appropriating his lands and disrupting water supplies. Fragments of the stele were found in more than one place on Tell K, in the destruction horizon at the top of the mound and lower down on the tell's NE side, close to the Tell J reservoir. The fact that no other commemorative objects from Early Dynastic Girsu seem to have been desecrated to the same calamitous degree suggests a determination to eradicate forever the actual and symbolic history that was carved on the stone. This is evident in the way the carving was smashed, but also in the systematic way the imagery was defiled.

The Stele of the Vultures: Patterns of Effacement

Ever since the surviving pieces were excavated by Sarzec, it has been clear that the Stele of the Vultures (Fig. 94) was forcibly removed from the Ningirsu temple on Tell K and deliberately damaged when the sacred precinct was ransacked by the army of Umma after the fall of Girsu in the reign of Urukagina. The excavated fragments bear witness to the brutal manner in which the temple was razed to the ground, but a thorough analysis of their condition also reveals that the memorial stone was subjected to intentional patterns of destruction, including the systematic defacement of specific symbols at key points in its visual narrative. A greater understanding of the targeted procedures employed by the ransackers helps to give some insight into the significance of the broken pieces that were found. This does not mean that the surviving pieces were the only sherds of the stele that were not completely obliterated, and it is still possible that more remains might be found in the future, but it does demonstrate an awareness of the meaning of the carving on the part of those who destroyed it.

Though the stele has been the focus of a plethora of iconographic and epigraphic studies, little attention has been paid to its physical condition. In select cases it has been noted in the literature that certain features of the carving were mutilated at some past moment, but the implications of presumably purposeful acts of effacement have not been explored, and the breakages have not therefore been subjected to close study. As is clear from the descriptions laid out below, the condition of the surviving pieces of the memorial is testimony to the fact that it was not accidentally broken but deliberately vandalised when the Temple of Ningirsu and Tell K generally were ravaged by invaders. Furthermore, the systematic nature of the damage indicates that it was the result of a calculated programme and not just the work of an indiscriminate, rampaging mob. Since the time of Eanatum, the Stele of the Vultures—an object with constitutional significance—had been at the centre of the networks of political and religious authority in Girsu–Lagash. Once it was disfigured, the empowering symbolism and prestige of its narrative and iconic reliefs, along with the inscribed myths, historical events and sworn oaths that firmly and seemingly irrevocably re-established the state's borders, were categorically rendered null and void. Most importantly, the effacement was carried out by descendants of the very enemies whose utter humiliation was flaunted in the stele's pictorial and literary programmes, and there is bitter irony in the fact that, in its inscriptions, the ancestral ruler of Umma, whose defeat the monument was made to commemorate, is forced by Eanatum to swear that he will not pulverise the newly re-established border steles, as he had previously destroyed the boundary stone erected by Mesilim of Kish when Mesilim famously brokered an earlier resolution of the border issues.

In general and with a high degree of caution, it is possible to identify several stages in the destructive process. A number of major blows were struck (perhaps with maces, axes, heavy hammers and bolster chisels), and the stone was split into relatively large chunks. The most important of these strikes, at the top of the carving's obverse, is treated in detail immediately below, and another affected the ritual scene at the bottom of Fragment G (between B and F), where the bottom of the heap of sacrificed animals and the lower part of the body of the tethered sacrificial bull were shown on the ground in front of Eanatum's feet. In addition, a series of more subtle defacements can be observed on the fractured pieces. They included the abrasion and hammering of particular details, together with further chipping and repeated striking (perhaps with smaller chisels or similar sharp implements). The key question of whether the initial blows were struck on the stone's mythological or historical side is extremely difficult to answer, and any theory is necessarily fraught with speculation. The difficulties are further augmented by the fact that (as seen in the discussion of the monument's contents) the obverse and reverse of the carvings expressed clear correspondences between the mythological framework and the representation of historical events. With those caveats stated, it would seem likely that the mythological side was struck first, and that the initial blow was aimed at the upper right edge, at the top of Ningirsu's casting-net, between the Thunderbird fastener and the netful of captives and corpses below. The fact that this was probably a measured or controlled blow can be seen in the clean horizontal break that resulted, extending across the carving towards the left and splitting the long handle of the god's mace. Albeit with a high degree of caution, it should be recalled that the monument might well have been displayed in the position that seems to have been traditional for such victory steles: inside the doorway of the Ningirsu temple's treasury room, acting as a kind of monumental screen, presumably with the obverse facing outwards. If that were the case, and if the smashing had been the work of mindless vandals, including if the stone had simply been pushed over before the invaders set to work with their hammers, it might reasonably be assumed that the damage would have been more indiscriminate, perhaps generally aimed at the colossal form of the god's head in particular, but that clearly was not the case because Ningirsu's head survived relatively intact. The probable reason for this, as is outlined in the following paragraph, is that the first blow was intended to deliver the state of Umma once and for all from the mortifying degradations imposed on it after the victory of Eanatum, which was the stele's principal subject.

There is a clear correspondence in the passages of carving on the two sides of the stele between Fragments D and E: with the captured and killed Umma soldiers filling the bulging net on the obverse, and the dead and mutilated soldiers of Umma being trampled by the Lagash phalanx on the reverse. The exact line of the presumed initial break indicates that whoever inflicted it might well have paid attention to the scenes shown on both sides in order to make the cut both clean and meaningful. That being the case, the horizontal break achieved two things: it severed the god's Thunderbird emblem from his net and split his divine mace (carried in his right hand and acting as the emblem of his individual might) laterally in two; in the process, by releasing the casting-net from the sealing talons of the Thunderbird, the break metaphorically liberated the figures caught inside the net, and at the same time delivered the fallen warriors of Umma from under the marching feet of their Lagash enemies on the stele's historical reverse. Ningirsu's control over Umma was thereby terminated, and the citizens of Umma were symbolically emancipated. The reason why the casting-net was in all likelihood struck first (rather than the fairly well-preserved face of the god, for example) is clear when the stele's inscriptions are taken into account. In the text, the defeated ruler of Umma is made to swear on the casting-nets of a host of important deities, including Enlil and Ninhursag (Ningirsu's parents), Enki and many more, but notably not that of Ningirsu himself (at least not in the preserved text). The repeated oath signals the ruler of Umma's enforced acceptance of a peace treaty, ratified by the divine great powers (as they might be called), whose terms are imposed on the state of Umma in perpetuity. This was national humiliation on the grandest and most enduring scale, but the shame of legal bondage could not be dispelled simply by defacing Ningirsu because, although the treaty categorically upheld his claim to the disputed territories, he personally was not its originator. Instead, he was the agent or divine instrument who was authorised to give effect to its provisions and restore justice (terrestrial and cosmic) on behalf of the pantheon of signatories. Accordingly, the carved symbol of the long-standing and extremely complicated conflict between Umma and Lagash is not the god, but the casting-net that stands for the combined power of the consortium of deities who support Ningirsu's (and Lagash's) claims, acknowledging them as supremely right. To break Ningirsu's hold on the net, therefore, was to liberate Umma from the detested age-old treaty and simultaneously to rebalance the scales of cosmic justice.

More broadly, with respect to the observable and recorded damage on the seven surviving fragments of the stele, a distinction must be drawn between, on the one hand, damage that could be called accidental, such as the corrosive effects of naturally occurring chemicals or the harm that the pieces suffered after they were found by Sarzec, and the defacements that were deliberately caused when Tell K was razed by the army of Umma on the other. In his initial analyses, Heuzey (Sarzec and Heuzey 1912, p. 194) noted that deposits of saltpetre (potassium nitrate) were found, particularly on the mythological sides of Fragments B and C (both showing Ninhursag), and it can safely be assumed that these were laid down naturally while the stone was buried. Heuzey (Sarzec and Heuzey 1912, p. 176) also maintains that the circular holes drilled in Fragments E and G show that the sherds were reused as door sockets in the Hellenistic period, but this incorrect idea should be discarded for the following reasons. Most importantly, if Fragments E and G had been salvaged in this way then they would both have been found at the same stratigraphic level as Fragment B, which was found on Tell A and therefore probably recycled when the Hellenistic shrine was constructed; on the contrary, however, Fragment E in particular was excavated on Tell K at the same height as the destruction horizon associated with the temple. Furthermore, the drilled cavities were clearly never used for this purpose because they show no signs of the radiating abrasion that is characteristic of door sockets. Consequently, as is argued below, the circular cuts must have been targeted damage, even if the reasons for that remain elusive. Other significant losses were caused after the fragments were excavated, as can be shown by comparing the photo of Ningirsu's face on Fragment D, which was taken after the fragment's accession into the Louvre, with the same passage of carving in the cast or squeeze (the estampage) made by Sarzec himself, presumably shortly after the piece was found (see Sarzec and Heuzey 1912, Pl. 4 bis, for the later Louvre photo and p. 195 for Sarzec's cast). Between the time of Sarzec's impression and the date of the photo that was taken when Fragment D was added to the Louvre collections, the upper part of Ningirsu's head, including his eye and nose, were broken off and lost. In addition, a large swathe of the inscription between the god's face and the head of the Thunderbird was rendered largely illegible, though the original text can be seen in Sarzec's estampage.

As regards the stele's mythological symbolism, the leonine head of the Thunderbird, which is not visible anywhere on the fragments, was apparently targeted when Girsu fell. This contrasts with the heads of the vultures on the reverse of Fragment A, which remained untouched. Similarly, the horned crowns of Ningirsu and Ninhursag—emblems of their divinity—seem to have been detached from their heads in every preserved instance. Ningirsu's crown and the upper part of his chignon on the mythological side of Fragment D were chipped off (with additional accidental damage happening later, as detailed above), while Imdugud's head was markedly removed above the god's casting-net. Ningirsu's arm (above the elbow) is slightly chipped, as is part of the head of the right-facing protome of the lion (also above the net), but these might perhaps be secondary marks that were caused when the main horizontal break was made that released the casting-net from the feet of the Thunderbird and split Ningirsu's mace in two. The surface of the mythological side of Fragment C, showing Ninhursag with the bird-topped standard (Imdugud or an eagle) behind her, is badly abraded. The bird's head was decisively mutilated, while the head of the goddess was severed from her body below the diagonal line that runs down from her ear and to her mouth. The horn of divinity and the Imdugud feathers on the right side of her crown are not preserved. The inscription to the right of Ninhursag's face is also badly broken.

As noted above, the principal horizontal fracture between Fragments D and E separated the feet of the marching Lagash soldiers from the Umma dead on the reverse. The soldiers themselves are generally extremely well preserved, however, though some of them have lost their noses, notably the man at the very front of the phalanx. In stark contrast, the face of Eanatum, who leads the army into battle, was completely eliminated, along with his left arm and his feet (the break between Fragments D and E cuts through his ankles), and it seems likely that the ruler's features were erased on purpose. The soldiers in the register below (Fragment E) are almost intact, apart from the circular cavity that was drilled into the surface of the carving. Though it was almost certainly not drilled in order to allow the slab to be reused as a door socket, it is difficult to understand why the depression took this deliberately circular form. If it was aimed at some components of the carved scene, it must have been intended to remove the pictorial elements between Eanatum, who stands at the front of the chariot, and the infantrymen behind him. It seems that, behind the ruler, there was a figure holding a spear, the shaft of which can be seen pointing down towards the ground in Fragment E (below the ruler's forearm). Was that figure especially significant? Was he also holding the reins that controlled the animals that pulled the vehicle, with the possible further implication being that these were metaphorically the reins of power? Was the head of state thereby shown symbolically cut off from its engine—the source of its dynamic energy—leaving Lagash like a driverless runaway chariot inevitably careering towards disaster? It is impossible to know, but it is curious that Eanatum himself was left more or less unscathed on this fragment, with only marginal damage to his eye, nose and right shoulder.

The historical side of Fragment A, which contains the flying vultures carrying body parts, presents a deep fracture below the birds, near to the right edge of the monument's curving top, that destroyed two or more adjacent text boxes. Above the horizontal dividing line that separates the top row of text boxes from the ones below, the fracture continues upwards, forking off in two thin lines (to create an overall Y shape), one cutting through the bodies of the birds, though without causing great harm. These slender ruptures do not run all the way through the thickness of the stone, and it might be presumed that they were secondary effects of the deeper cut below. The surface of the mythological side of Fragment A contains no representational content, only inscriptions, and the main body of the text, though lightly abraded, is otherwise unaffected—the main damage being around the left side of the monument's upper curve.

The reverse of Fragment C, which mainly shows the heap of enemy corpses, is particularly abraded, with the details of the dead soldiers' eyes and ears having seemingly been rubbed out. Was this done in order to abate the humiliation they suffered in defeat, as it were? Without further evidence it is impossible to say. The middle part of the inscription on the narrow divider between the top register and the one below is broken away above a shape that probably represented the helmeted head of a standing soldier, but the head is so badly eroded that no details of the facial features can be made out. This section is under the abraded corpses, but significantly to the left of the stele's upper right curve, which is worn away and irregular.

Ningirsu's severed foot on the mythological side of Fragment G is chipped above the heel, but above that there is an irregular bulge that is almost certainly the remnant of a carved ankle bone, as can be seen by comparison with Eanatum's front foot on the reverse of Fragment F, where the ankle bone and the depression between it and the Achilles tendon at the back of the leg is delicately modelled. There is another small circular cavity on the reverse of Fragment G, at the centre of the ritual scene that, as argued in Chapter 18, might represent the burial rites performed in honour of the fallen Lagash soldiers who are being interred in a tumulus to the left (in Fragment B). The lower part of the leg of the celebrant (a naked priest) is obliterated by it, along with a small section of the heap of sacrificed animals and some of the palm fronds that can be seen hanging over the side of the plant pot. The priest's headless body is damaged, with chips on his upper leg, hip and the upper part of his arm, and the tip of the folded plant (below) is chipped away. As noted above, the fracture at this point seems to have been caused by a significant impact at the bottom of Fragment G (between B and F), where the lower body of the sacrificial bull is completely missing.

The obverse of Fragment F, showing the arched shaft of Ningirsu's chariot, contains reasonably well-preserved relief and cuneiform characters. The god's skirt and the section of the arched shaft on the bottom left are both slightly chipped, and the lion that decorates the joined hoops through which the reins are threaded is severely abraded, but not otherwise cut or marked. The carving and the inscription on the reverse are deep and very well preserved, with the exception of a chip below the middle of the spear shaft to the left of the surviving tops of the line of heads, and some

slight gouges that disfigure the body of the bull. Only the feet and the bottom of the skirt of the seated form of the ruler have survived, but (as noted above) the front foot in particular is extremely well carved and in excellent condition. The bird motif on the obverse of Fragment C, close to Ninhursag's head, is badly abraded, as is Ninhursag's crown on Fragment B. These pieces were both damaged by saltpetre, and it seems that the cleaning that was carried out when the fragments were restored might have further eroded the already damaged surfaces.

The End of Early Dynastic Tell K

Three pieces of the Stele of the Vultures were found around the level of the razed Urukagina temple, together with an ex-voto in the name of Enanatum I. This was a mortar that had also been smashed, though its dedicatory incipit can still be made out: it was created to celebrate Ningirsu and his royal representative as they subjugated 'foreign lands' (RIME 1.9.4.4). Perhaps the most extraordinary survival, however, was the border stone dedicated to Ningirsu that recorded Eanatum's reconquest of the frontier territory of Gu'edena on behalf of the god and the state of Girsu. It contains the following inscription (RIME 1.9.3.4):

> For the god Ningirsu, warrior of the god Enlil, Eanatum, ruler of Lagash, chosen in the pure heart by the goddess Nanshe, the powerful mistress, who subjugates the foreign lands for the god Ningirsu, son of Akurgal, ruler of Lagash. When he crushed the ruler of Gisha (Umma) who had marched on Gu'edena, he restored to Ningirsu's control his beloved field, the Gu'edena. The territory in the region of Girsu, which he restored to Ningirsu's control, he named it LUM.ma.girnunta.šakuge.pada (LUM.ma has been chosen from the 'Princely Way' by the pure heart). He dedicated (this monument) to (the god Ningirsu).

Border monuments played a highly significant role in the long-running Lagash–Umma dispute, as they presumably did in similar conflicts elsewhere in the region. After battle, the victors pulled the old stones down and replaced them with their own. The pillar found on Tell K, which was probably typical, was made of extremely hard limestone, so that the proclamations inscribed on it were nearly impossible to erase, and the pillar itself was practically indestructible. It would once have been prominently installed on a pedestal on the raised embankment that contained the dyke that separated the two states, where its polished white surface communicated an unmistakable message of hostile defiance. Most significantly, this particular stone, which was found on Tell K next to a fragment of the Stele of the Vultures, was actually mentioned by name in the text that was carved on the stele. Its symbolic importance must therefore have been supreme.

The stone was found close to the spot occupied by the temple on Tell K, but it must previously have been displayed in the no man's land on the extreme edge of Lagash by the frontier with Umma. The really interesting question is: how did it get from the Gu'edena borderlands to the holy city of Girsu? The explanation must almost certainly be that it was taken there by Lugalzagesi, who removed it when his rampaging army crossed the border into Lagash. It must then have been carried all the way to the sanctuary of Ningirsu on Tell K, where it was placed on the ruined temple as an act of vengeance, but also symbolically to transplant the long-contested borderline from Girsu's self-declared periphery to its sacred centre on Tell K, from which the god had in some absolute sense been shockingly expelled. It was an act that notionally obliterated the god's domain, intending to extirpate Girsu from the record once and for all. Together with the razing of the Ningirsu temple and the defacement of the Stele of the Vultures—one of the shrine's most potent religious, legal and military symbols—the final transfer and erasure of Lagash's border post confirmed to the world, and before heaven, as it were, that Lugalzagesi's victory was total and seemingly irrevocable.

CHAPTER 21

Darkness and Renaissance: Tell K in the Akkad, Lagash II and Ur III Eras

AFTER BEING OBLITERATED BY THE FORCES OF Lugalzagesi, Girsu underwent a period of darkness—the dark ages of Lagash, so to speak, though the interval was in fact relatively brief. Lugalzagesi was soon defeated by Sargon of Akkad, at which point Girsu–Lagash was integrated as a single entity into Sargon's Akkad state, where it became a province that was ruled by local governors who were directly controlled by the Akkad kings. The era of Sargonic control was the first time the region had been gathered together under what is considered to be an imperial power. The Sargonic period, when formerly independent Sumerian city-states were subjected to unified Akkad rule, marks a major shift in the dominant narratives of Mesopotamian history, but Sargon's methods of control also fostered continuity. The territorial networks and spheres of influence of the existing Mesopotamian city-states were preserved during the Akkad regime, when governors were installed in the ancient capitals to act as provincial representatives of the central administration. Spanning more than four generations, the Sargonic era endured for about 150 years, from the time of Sargon himself to that of Sharkalisharri, the last king of Akkad. Administrative texts, which form the main preserved corpus of documents that shed light on the history of Girsu–Lagash under Akkad rule, include approximately 3,800 Sargonic tablets dating from the last part of the reign of Naram-Sin through to the reign of Sharkalisharri. In addition, about 800 Late Akkadian texts have survived (see Sallaberger 2015, pp. 237–48). The Sargonic tablets from Girsu, which are rarely explicitly dated, are mostly written in Sumerian, even though the official language of the empire was Akkadian, and the sheer volume of preserved administrative documents suggests that the city was a strategic provincial centre in the imperial period. The theory is further supported by texts that show that the local governor travelled frequently to the Akkad capital, while the reigning Akkad king regularly paid visits to the province (Sommerfeld 2006, pp. 9–10; and Sallaberger et al. 2015, p. 238). Unfortunately, unlike the documents preserved from the previous Lagash I period, the available Sargonic sources say little about any religious constructions that might have been commissioned in Girsu under Akkad rule.

Almost nothing is known about the state of affairs in Girsu–Lagash during the reign of Sargon (c.2316–2277 BCE). The initial destruction (which should probably more accurately be termed the conquest) of Girsu is attributed to Sargon, as the ruler (ensí) of Akkad, and the overthrow of Lagash 'to the sea' is recorded in a number of royal inscriptions. The addition of the phrase 'to the sea' is doubtless Sargon's shorthand way of proclaiming the comprehensiveness of his victory. One such royal inscription names the defeated ruler of Lagash as a certain Meszi, who is otherwise unknown (RIME 2.1.1.12). Sargon was succeeded by two of his sons, Rimush and Manishtusu (c.2276–2254 BCE), but no concrete information has survived to confirm the order of their respective reigns. Following the Sumerian King List, it is nevertheless generally accepted that Rimush preceded Manishtusu, even though the Ur Sumerian King List (Steinkeller 2003) and the Cruciform Monument record that Manishtusu ruled before Rimush (BM91022). As indicated by the approximate date range of their periods in office, it is estimated that the combined reigns of the two brothers lasted twenty-three years (Sallaberger and Schrakamp 2015, p. 136). Royal inscriptions from the time of Rimush record that Lagash, under the local governor Kitushid, led a coalition of Sumerian cities in a failed military revolt against Akkad imperial rule, during which Kitushid was captured and the city walls of Lagash (or Girsu—the text is unclear) were destroyed (RIME 2.1.2.2 and RIME 2.1.2.3). Since there are no recorded mentions of the names of any governors of Lagash under Manishtusu, no comparative timeline can be established to correlate events in Girsu–Lagash with the reigns of the kings of Akkad between the time of Rimush and the advent of Naram-Sin (c.2253–2198 BCE).

Another major revolt, this time including Lagash as a key member of a group of cities that was led by Ipurkishi of Kish and Amargirid of Uruk, occurred during the reign of Naram-Sin (see Grayson and Sollberger 1976, pp. 112–31). Lagash took part in the uprising, alongside the cities of Umma, Adab, Isin, Nippur, and Shuruppak (RIME 2.1.4.2), but the action, which was again unsuccessful, was ruthlessly repressed. Having subdued Girsu–Lagash, Naram-Sin installed Lugalushumgal as city governor, and he retained the position under Naram-Sin's successor, Sharkalisharri (RIME 2.1.4.2004). Some slight and disputed evidence suggests that Lugalushumgal might have been preceded by a certain Ure, who is mentioned in an inscription on a tablet relating to a border dispute (AO2694; RTC83). Whereas the appointment of Lugalushumgal is securely attested, however, the transcription and dating of the Ure text are much contested (Michalowski 1993, p. 20; and Sallaberger et al. 2015, pp. 272–3). Sharkalisharri (c.2197–2193 BCE), the last king of Akkad, controlled Lagash for at least the first half of his twenty-five-year reign, as is corroborated by the fact that twelve of his regnal years are named on documents from Girsu (Sallaberger 1999, p. 56, n. 217). Thereafter, Girsu–Lagash seems finally to have been liberated from Akkad rule.

The Akkad Layers on Tell K

Some slight clues about the fate of Tell K during the Akkad period can be gleaned from the upper layers of the mound, but much remains conjectural. One thing that can be stated with a high degree of certainty is the depth of the deposit between the final levelling horizon of the Early Dynastic sanctuary and the summit of the mound. As detailed in Chapter 19, the additions to the mound made by Urukagina raised the ground level to an indicative Sarzec height of 14.33 m, while the summit of the mound when Sarzec first surveyed the site in the later part of the nineteenth century lay at a Sarzec height of 17 m. The differential was only about 2.67 m, and that relatively shallow increase, in which few remains were found, would suggests that no large-scale construction projects were carried out after the time of Urukagina—at least none that required the systematic raising of the entire mound. Indeed, as is now well known, the most momentous architectural event on Tell K after the end of the Early Dynastic period was not an Ur-Nanshe-style construction of a replacement temple to Ningirsu, but the transfer of the god's principal shrine from Tell K to Tell A under Ur-Bau. The situation in the central area of Tell K between the top of the sealed Ur-Nanshe Building at a Sarzec height of 14.05 m and the recorded base of a construction at about 14.5 m is complicated by the fact that Sarzec unquestionably ignored important mud-brick remains that existed in these strata (referred to as the Sarzec gap). Nonetheless, some archaeological traces of structures that postdated the Early Dynastic buildings were reported by Sarzec, and they help to provide a sketchy overview of later events. In addition, a few important objects and inscriptions were excavated, admittedly of mostly uncertain stratigraphic provenance, but some can be fairly accurately dated, and their contexts also contribute to the general reconstruction.

Accordingly, above the sealed Ur-Nanshe Building, Sarzec found a wall made of fired bricks that is marked *Mur* on the section on Plan C (2) (Fig. 33), but not otherwise indicated as an independent structure on the plan. Sarzec chose not to regard this fragment, which probably derived from the corner of a building, as part of an autonomous construction phase because he and Heuzey preferred to attribute all vestiges of structures built after Ur-Nanshe to Gudea and Shulgi. This was certainly incorrect, however, because the wall marked *Mur* on Plan C (2) is shown noticeably below the level of the two foundation boxes (*Logettes*) on the left and right of the section, which were ascribed to Gudea and Shulgi, respectively (the one on the right being a fraction higher). The wall marked *Mur* must therefore date from a time between the reign of Gudea in the Lagash II period and that of the final Lagash I ruler, Urukagina, whose renovated temple, which was destroyed by Lugalzagesi, was based in the Sarzec gap between the bottom of wall *Mur* and the top of the sealed Ur-Nanshe Building on the section on Plan C (2). Found at a Sarzec height of 14.5 m, wall *Mur*, which was almost certainly built during the Akkad period, was positioned approximately 0.45 m above the SW wall of the preserved section of the Ur-Nanshe Building (about 0.17 m above the indicative Sarzec height of the destroyed Urukagina temple). No information is given about its measurements (see Heuzey 1900, p. 3), but on Plan C (2) it has overall dimensions of about 1 m (w) × 1 m (h). It is described as a corner, but no lateral outline was recorded, and its return is not indicated on the section, though it would have been conventional to describe it. Nor did Sarzec or Heuzey give any idea of the size or other characteristics of the bricks that were used to build it, except to say that they were square—which is significant.

As just noted, the external façade of *Mur* (the low side on the left on Plan C (2)) seems to have been at least partly aligned with the SW wall of the buried Ur-Nanshe Building below it. This could be nothing more than a coincidence, and since the profile of wall *Mur* is not shown on any of the plans, it is not possible to confirm whether its lateral outline and positioning actually did follow the lines of the Ur-Nanshe walls. Nevertheless, it could also imply that the Akkad temple followed the same outlines as the earlier sequence of temples built by Ur-Nanshe, Enmetena and Urukagina, and perhaps also that discernible vestiges of the Urukagina building provided a guide for the Akkad architects. Indeed, it is surely likely that some slight remains of the base of the Urukagina walls survived the onslaught of Lugalzagesi because the eradication of the Girsu temple from the record was categorically achieved by the destruction and desecration of its holiest artefacts (as described in Chapter 20). Though it was clearly important to see the building razed to the ground, the objects that symbolised the ascendancy of the state of Lagash over Umma were the invaders' primary target. Moreover, the distance between the indicative Sarzec height of the base of the Urukagina walls and the bottom of the Akkad *Mur* was a mere 0.17 m, and since the Early Dynastic temple must unquestionably have been made of mud-bricks, there is every reason to assume that Sarzec might have overlooked traces of the bottom section of its walls.

Any construction work carried out during the Akkad period was presumably on a reduced scale, with only the sanctum sanctorum at the top of Tell K being rebuilt, not the whole complex. Nonetheless, the existence of an Akkad temple is practically indisputable thanks to the British Museum team's discovery in a spoil heap to the south of Tell K of an exceptional fragment of a votive bowl that was dedicated to Ningirsu by the Akkad king Rimush (Fig. 105).

FIGURE 105. Fragment of a vase dedicated to Ningirsu by the Akkad king Rimush (TG3545).

A few imperial objects inscribed in the names of Akkad kings had previously been found in Girsu, but this was the first artefact that was expressly dedicated by an Akkad king to Ningirsu as the local Sumerian supreme deity. The presentation of a sacred bowl of this kind implies the ongoing existence of a shrine or chapel to Ningirsu, and it seems reasonable to conclude that the fragment *Mur* was the final remnant of that Akkad temple.

As noted above, two Sumerian rebellions of significant proportions took place during the reigns of Rimush, whose votive bowl was offered to Ningirsu, and Naram-Sin, but they were ferociously suppressed, using the full might of the Akkad forces. In the aftermath of the Sumerian defeat, the Akkad victors implemented a policy of retaliation and severe punishments that were inflicted on the rebel leaders, including those of Girsu–Lagash. These events were recorded on the Akkad Stele, which was found broken into pieces that were scattered along the slopes of Tell K, and like the Stele of the Vultures, it exhibited signs of having been purposely mutilated. The fact that it was found on Tell K probably indicates that it was originally erected on a pedestal in a commanding position, presumably close to the Akkad-era Ningirsu temple, where it menacingly cast the shadow of imperial dominance over the temple and by extension the whole city. That said, the extremely negative connotations of the stele contrast starkly and perhaps strangely with the dedication to Ningirsu of the Rimush votive bowl, which both complicates and enriches the picture of Akkad rule.

The Akkad Stele

As with so many other objects from Tell K, it is again unfortunate that the provenance and archaeological context of the exceptional Akkad Stele are so problematic because a detailed record of the circumstances of its discovery could have shed a great deal of light on an obscure chapter in the history of Girsu. It was apparently retrieved on Tell K by Sarzec in 1894, but no information about its find location is recorded in the published report (Sarzec and Heuzey 1912, pp. 198–202). Despite that, it is stated by the Louvre that it was found 27 m from the Ur-Nanshe Building on the slopes of the mound, close to the Large Stairway (referred to by the Louvre as the Gudea stairway), and this information is repeated by Huh (2008, pp. 85, 290 and 382). The stairs alluded to are the Large Stairway near the Pillar of Gudea, as marked on Cros's Plan B (Fig. 36). It is not clear where the additional information comes from, or whether it can be verified, but further confusion surrounds early discussions of the exact nature of the recovered object. Heuzey (Sarzec and Heuzey 1912, p. 198) refers his readers to Pl. 5 bis, Fig. 3 (a, b and c), where three photos are printed: two (a and b) showing the two sides (A and B) of a roughly triangular piece of the Akkad Stele (AO2678; Fig. 106), which Heuzey incorrectly regards as two distinct fragments, and another piece of stone (c) that is inscribed with cuneiform text, but which almost certainly did not form part of the monument (AO2679). Heuzey, who was indubitably working solely from the photos when he wrote his text, describes the pictorial content of the single fragment that actually did derive from the stele as though it represents two separate pieces, both of which (according to him) show scenes from the same face. In reality, just one fragment was retrieved that has carved imagery on both sides, though which is the front and which is the back is uncertain. Heuzey then goes on to say (Sarzec and Heuzey 1912, p. 200) that the cuneiform-inscribed piece (AO2679) was from the 'reverse' of the same monument, thereby implying that the total thickness of the monument was made up of the thickness of the pictorial fragment (or fragments as Heuzey thinks) plus the thickness of the textual piece. This would in any case be impossible because the thickness of AO2678 (between 0.1 m and 0.12 m), which represents the full thickness of the original stele, is almost exactly the same as that of the inscribed fragment (0.109 m). Furthermore, as is now well known, both sides of the cuneiform fragment contain text. Accordingly, the fact that Heuzey makes these categorically implausible assumptions provides secure confirmation that he did not have the objects in front of him when he wrote the published description, but was working from the photos. Another cuneiform-inscribed stone that was circulating in the art market before 1915 and is now in the Yale Babylonian Collection in New Haven (YBC2409) has also been ascribed to the Akkad Stele (Foster 1985). Somewhat similar to Heuzey's Pl. 5 bis, Fig. 3 (c), it too was almost certainly not part of the Akkad monument, as has been forcefully argued by Gelb et al. (1989–91, pp. 88–9).

The widely accepted attribution of the stele to Rimush (Foster 1985; and Sallaberger and Westenholz 1999, p. 42), which should be treated with a high degree of scepticism, presupposes that AO2679 (Heuzey's Pl. 5 bis, Fig. 3 (c))

FIGURE 106. Fragment of the Akkad Stele from Girsu. Musée du Louvre AO2678.

and YBC 2409 (the Yale fragment) were indeed parts of the Akkad Stele, but this is extremely unlikely, as can be demonstrated by looking in detail at AO2679 and the two sides of AO2678. The figurative fragment, AO2678, measures 0.345 m (h) × 0.275 m (w) and its thickness ranges between 0.1 m and 0.12 m. It contains three preserved horizontal registers, each 0.16 m tall, that are separated by plain bands in quite high relief on the fragment's two sides (Fig. 106). The figures are carved in low relief on a plain background, and the details are incised. This imagery has usually been read from top to bottom, but the traditional Mesopotamian reading order proceeds in the opposite direction, and the main scenes on such monuments are usually placed towards the top, as is the case for a series of highly significant Sumerian artworks, including the Uruk Vase, the Standard of Ur and the Gudea Steles (see Chapter 41 below). For this reason, the figures on the upper register on both sides are probably not shown marching into battle, as they are usually said to be (see Foster 1985, p. 22; and Nigro 2001–3, p. 77), but rather standing beside their victorious king after the battle has been won. It is also likely that divine symbols were carved on the stone above the head of the triumphant king on the upper register on one or both sides, as is also the case on Naram-Sin's Victory Stele (Nigro 2001–3, p. 74). The missing lower registers probably showed a parade of the victorious soldiers with degraded prisoners of war and a display of looted booty (Nigro 2001–3, p. 92). It is also possible that corpses being eaten by animals were depicted.

On both sides of the fragment, the Akkad soldiers, who are portrayed with their torsos shown frontally and their legs in profile, face in the direction of the missing side of the stele (Fig. 107). They seem generally to have been pictured wearing pointed helmets (though only one clearly survives in the middle register of Side A, along with obliquely hemmed skirts (shorter at the knees) that are wrapped over their legs, and long fringed stoles covering one side of their chests. As is again clearest on the well-preserved figure in the middle register of Side A, the garments are secured with belts. In a possible sign of the way the troops were deployed, they generally carry three different types of weapons: bows, axes and spears. Their Sumerian enemies are all unarmed, naked and in some cases (notably the prisoner on

312 The Mound of the House of the Fruits

FIGURE 107. Reconstruction of the Akkad Stele, showing the obverse (left) and the reverse (right).

the right side of the middle register of Side B) significantly smaller than the Akkad soldiers. This is not the case for the well-muscled Sumerian soldier who is shown being murdered in the middle register of Side A, however, so it may be that the intention was partly to show the enemies as formidable opponents who were decisively beaten and diminished by their Akkad vanquishers. The Sumerian soldiers feature a bowl-cut hairstyle, with wavy locks falling from the crowns of their heads, and short pointed beards that are formed of vertical strands. Their appearance can best be seen in the figure of the soldier on the ground on the left of the middle register of Side A. The preserved depictions of the enemies of Akkad are probably intended to be Sumerian leaders, since their appearance recalls individuals portrayed on fragments of some of the Gudea Steles (AO4582, for example) or the statue of Ur-Ningirsu II (VA8790). Consequently, the way the vanquished armies are illustrated might have allowed the original viewers of the Akkad Stele to situate the events in a historical time frame as a particular rather than a generic scene of victory that recorded the decisive defeat of the coalition of Sumerian forces from the cities of the south.

On the lower register of Side A an Akkad soldier can be seen stabbing a Sumerian enemy with a long spear, and perhaps grasping his foe's now missing head in his outstretched left hand. To the right of this vignette is an axe that was doubtless being wielded by a lost Akkad soldier, while still further to the right can be made out the remains of what might have been a raised hand holding a spear (Nigro 2001–3, p. 85), though it might also be a pointed Akkad helmet. The central register of Side A shows an Akkad soldier on the extreme left who is aiming his drawn bow towards the unpreserved figures of enemies on the right of the carving. Beneath his feet is a wounded Sumerian (with bent legs partly hidden by the lower part of the archer), who might be raising his right hand to his face in a gesture of surrender. In addition to his pointed helmet and the quiver that he carries on his back, the Akkad archer, who has a bracer or arm guard on his wrist, wears a long tunic formed of vertical wavy folds that is open at the front, where a short skirt and his bare leg are just about visible. The robe, which recalls garments worn by some of the divine standard bearers on the Naram-Sin Victory Stele, is often found on carvings showing Mesopotamian warriors (including gods) through to the Neo-Assyrian period. The soldier's height fills the register (as, apparently, does that of the partly preserved figure directly below him on the bottom register), and this might indicate that he was meant to represent the king, a high-ranking officer or some other high-status person.

The well-preserved Akkad soldier to the right of the archer carries what looks like a club in his outstretched right hand, and he seems to be on the point of using it to strike a Sumerian enemy. The Akkad warrior, who might again be the king, since multiple representations of particularly important individuals are common on monuments of this kind, is shown grasping the Sumerian by his long beard—a sign of the vanquished soldier's diminished virility. Alternatively, the club-like weapon might be a long blade, in which case the Akkad soldier is shown just as he is about to decapitate his Sumerian foe (Westenholz 2012, p. 97). The Sumerian has his arms by his sides (pointing slightly away from his body), with his palms open, in an attitude of surrender—the same iconography as is used in the portrayal of heroes and warrior gods and their vanquished enemies on contemporary Akkad cylinder seals. Towards the right of the same register can be seen the scant remains of another Akkad soldier, with another Sumerian enemy (whose bent knees are partly obscured by the Akkad warrior) lying on the ground at his feet. On the upper register of Side A are two Akkad archers, whose right arms hold the remains of horizontal arrows that they are presumably in the process of fitting into the bows that they carry by their chests. Their quivers are held behind their shoulders, and the quiver of the leftmost soldier seems to contain three arrows. As is also the case for the archer on the middle register, their quivers are fitted with lanceolate tassels that hang down from pommelled tops. To the right of the archers only the right lower leg of an Akkad figure is preserved, together with the handle of his weapon (possibly a mace), and the outstretched legs of a fallen enemy. Since this scene is on the climactic top register, it might depict the king's ultimate triumph, as he perhaps treads on one or more enemy corpses.

On the lower register of Side B nothing is preserved except the head of a figure that might represent an Akkad officer carrying a bow, or perhaps a Sumerian with his characteristic hairstyle. Directly above that, on the middle register, an Akkad soldier is shown pushing a prisoner of war, whose upper arms are tied behind his back. The Akkad victor drives the naked prisoner forward with his right hand, while in his left he carries a tall spear that reaches up beyond the dividing band between the middle and upper registers. To the left, a slightly larger figure, who again might be the Akkad king, can be seen smashing the head of a pleading enemy with a club or a mace that might have been fitted with a pyriform head. The vanquisher has his foot on the leg of the defeated Sumerian. The Akkad warrior, who possibly held an axe in his left hand, which was at about the level of his waist, seemingly has a pointed beard. Apart from the familiar short skirt and fringed stole, he wears a pointed helmet that is fitted with a neck guard, and it is noteworthy that the same kind of protective head and neck cover is also worn by Naram-Sin on his victory monument. The enemy is seated on the ground, with his torso raised, his legs stretched out in front of him, and his two hands lifted in a sign of submission. His beard, which is long and pointed, hangs down on his chest, and his loose hair falls down onto his shoulders. The way the hair is seemingly depicted might indicate that he has humiliatingly been deprived of his chignon, the emblem of royalty, as is the case for the defeated enemy king (possibly Lugalzagesi) on the victory stele of Sargon that includes Ishtar holding a netful of captives (Nigro 2001–3, p. 90). Foster (1985, pp. 23 and 26) surmises that the pleading Sumerian might be the ensi of Lagash, and the standing captive to the right might be his son, while Nigro (2001–3, p. 91) interprets the figures as the pleading ensi of Ur, the leader of the insurrectionary cities of the south, and the captive ensi of Lagash. The portrayal of the inferred Akkad king can be likened to the iconography of the triumphant god who tramples on his enemies while using a mace on their heads that is found on cylinder seals from the same period. To the left of the defeated Sumerian, only the upper part of the pommelled tassel of another Akkad quiver is preserved. On the upper register, an Akkad soldier, who has his left arm by his side, is holding an axe in a horizontal position, with its metal head facing upwards; his uplifted right arm probably holds another weapon, of which only the handle is preserved. To the left of that, just the lower body of another Akkad soldier can be made out.

In terms of its overall shape, the top of the stele was probably cut into a flattened arch, comparable with the arched top of the Stele of the Vultures, while its slightly curving profile might have narrowed towards the bottom. The tapering form might have been applied to allow it to fit into a slot in a pedestal or even just so that it could be erected in the ground. If the smiting figures in the middle registers on both sides of the fragment are correctly interpreted as being portrayals of the Akkad king, and if it is also assumed that he was placed at the centre of the respective scenes, that would imply that the width of the stele was about 0.33 m. Furthermore, if it is assumed that the monument had a low curving top, as is usual for Mesopotamian steles, then there is not enough space for an additional register above the preserved upper one. As far as the bottom section of the carving is concerned, it can be perhaps surmised that the narrative was completed with two further registers that have been lost. The most likely subject for at least one of the sides would have been depictions of prisoners of war and enemy corpses, with a bottom register showing Sumerian dead lying on the ground. Since the graphics were read from bottom to top, it is surely also likely that the lower side of the obverse (whichever that was) might have shown the king of Akkad and his army making preparations for battle. If these inferences are correct, the illustrated portion of the stele probably had a height of about 0.7 m.

This relatively small monument is so badly damaged that only a very small part (perhaps as little as a ninth or a tenth) of the original stone has been preserved. Moreover, the bodies and faces of the Akkad soldiers in particular are heavily abraded and also show signs of having been systematically defaced. Some facial features have been pounded into oblivion, for example, while others seem to have been cut repeatedly with a chisel, and some of the Akkad soldiers' arms have been amputated. In the case of the archer on the left of the middle register of Side A, his bowstaff and string—symbols of the might of the Akkad victors—have both been broken and rather carefully removed. By contrast, some of the bodies of the defeated Sumerians are much better preserved, with the exception of the group that includes the trampled and pleading enemy of Akkad and the standing, bound captive, whose faces have both been slightly chipped. The nature of the damage makes it probable that the stele was disfigured in antiquity, sometime after the fall of the Akkad regime. As noted above, in a celebration of the Akkad king's triumph, the dynamic battle scenes arguably culminated on the upper register in a static tableau illustrating the end of the conflict, in which the king was surrounded by his army, and all were probably shown trampling on the bodies of the vanquished and the dead, as on Naram-Sin's Victory Stele.

Unlike the Naram-Sin monument, where the king is an unmatched, even supernatural figure, the ruler on the Akkad Stele appears much more as a *primus inter pares*—the first among equals. He can possibly be distinguished by his size, his central position in the various scenes, the actions in which he is engaged (crushing the enemy underfoot, for example) and his weapons, particularly the mace. Though he fights heroically in his own personal capacity, he is also slightly oversized compared to the other figures, and in a sense therefore almost endowed with extrahuman powers, as is suggested the analogy between his iconography and the representations of gods and heroes in the contemporary Akkad glyptic tradition. On the one hand, his status is founded on and legitimised by his superior strength, but on the other hand, he is not depicted as isolated or detached from the action, his troops and the enemy, as is Naram-Sin on his Victory Stele. On the Akkad Stele, the decisive role played by the army in the triumph is celebrated alongside the individual power of the ruler, such that both contribute to the renown that is accorded to his reign. Despite the smallness of the surviving fragment, the outstanding quality of the carving and the care taken with its composition can still be appreciated. The work is also remarkable as one of the earliest representatives of images that were used repeatedly during the Akkad period and thereafter, enduring for centuries as generic elements in the depiction of warfare. In particular, the motif of the triumphant individual warrior emphatically crushing an enemy soldier underfoot was very widely adopted.

Finally, who was the Akkad king who is represented on the stele? Despite some clear iconographic differences between the Akkad Stele and the Naram-Sin Victory Stele, there are nevertheless a number of striking parallels between the two that are not found on other Akkad monuments depicting kings. Stylistically, the Akkad Stele's combination of a realistic attention to the details of human anatomy and other pictorial elements, set in the context of an idealised narrative of historical events that also incorporates traditional imagery and a particular set of compositional rules, fits well with the idea that the Akkad Stele was probably another Naram-Sin commission. The commonly accepted view is that the differences between the two monuments heavily outweigh their similarities, especially in the changing modes of representation that are applied to the two figures of the king, who is shown as a relatively straightforward *primus inter pares* on the Akkad Stele, but as a supreme, even quasi-divine ruler on the Naram-Sin carving. There can be no doubt that the two works display clear differences, but for the reasons outlined below it is nonetheless methodologically questionable to conclude that they are from the reigns of different rulers solely on the basis of their iconographic content, without reference to the imagery's associated historical contexts and settings.

A common problem with the art-historical approach to ancient artworks is the disconnect between stylistic issues and historical contexts, such that all works of art commissioned by a named king tend to be considered as characteristic examples of one particular style or school of art that is defined by an unchanging set of iconographic modes. The approach results in a sweeping enumeration of styles: the Sargon style, the Naram-Sin style and so forth. It oversimplifies and flattens the works, so to speak, overlooking important events and developments that might have taken place during a ruler's reign that would surely have been reflected in the changing aesthetic practices that were applied to monumental and state-authorised representations. A small instance of such a change was noted in Chapter 16 with regard to the differences between Ur-Nanshe Plaque A and Ur-Nanshe Plaque D, where the altered portrayal of the inferred crown prince, from the enigmatic figure on Plaque A to the almost certainly later toned-down depiction of Lugalezem on Plaque D, was presumably a response to actual events, namely the surmised death of Ur-Nanshe's originally chosen successor. If the iconography of the enigmatic figure on Plaque A were treated in isolation from the deducible historical context, and without comparing Plaques A and D, then the significance of the changing nature of the portrayals could very easily be overlooked. For a king of Naram-Sin's exceptional charisma, who made a brilliant success of his reign, the art that he commissioned should surely reflect the meteoric trajectory of his career and the seemingly inexorable growth of his power and prestige. Nor would Naram-Sin be the only great ruler in history for whom a changing iconography might have been required to express the altered way they saw themselves and were viewed by others at different times in their lives. On the contrary, it is a very familiar phenomenon in the history of art. Accordingly, the problem with using the exceptional Naram-Sin stele as a fixed point of comparison—as an example of the representative Naram-Sin style—is flawed from the outset precisely because the Naram-Sin Victory Stele is in every way an outstanding work. More to the point, assuming they were both commissioned by Naram-Sin, the Akkad Stele and the Victory Stele must have been created at two different moments in the king's reign: the first at the start of his tenure, when the Sumerian revolt took place, and the second at the end of his reign, in the wake of some extremely portentous events, including Naram-Sin's self-deification and his conquest of the mountainous regions at the edges of the known world. With this developing historical context in mind, it should not be surprising that the two steles, which were both in all likelihood commissioned by Naram-Sin, display stylistic differences, but also more nuanced, yet fundamental similarities that bear witness to their common lineage. Placed side by side, they mark and encapsulate the two ends of Naram-Sin's reign, plotting his career from his time as an exceptional warrior with the elevated status of a first among equals to his ultimate exaltation as a peerless monarch who exuded a godlike aura.

The Akkad fragment (AO2679), which was taken by Heuzey to be another piece of the Akkad Stele, measures 0.285 m (h) × 0.295 m (w) × 0.109 m (t). It was created as a record of the distribution of some large tracts of fields in the state of Lagash, under the authority of an Akkad king whose name has been hammered with a punch tool (notably in the middle of the lower register of Side A) and deliberately erased. The plots were donated to a group of royal dependants or retainers, including some military officials, all of whom are listed along with their titles (Foster 1985; and Gelb et al. 1989–91, pp. 88–90 and 115–16). In the context of the allocation of lands (specifically said to be in the province of Girsu), the inscription speaks of the creation of a 'royal' domain. The text records one of the largest single land transactions that is contained in any preserved official Mesopotamian document, though it should be stressed that the total, which was previously calculated as 15,684 km² by Gelb et al. (1989–91, pp. 68 and 88–90), was in reality much closer to 1,600 km² (the area of a square with sides of about 40 km). In all likelihood, the land was distributed on a prebendal system as payment for services provided for the crown, and it seems likely that most or all of it represented the confiscated temple estates of Girsu–Lagash.

If the land distribution text had formed part of the Akkad Stele, it would suggest that the monument performed two functions: a) as an admonitory celebration of the Akkad victory over the Sumerian rebels; and b) as the record of a legal arrangement, performing the function of an ancient *kudurru* (a border stone and confirmation of land rights). The idea that two such disparate aims could have been achieved through pictures and words on the same carving is improbable, not least because the juxtaposition of violent scenes of warfare and a text recording the allocation of confiscated lands on a monument that was intended for public display is otherwise unheard of (Gelb et al. 1989–91). The Akkad Stele and the land distribution inscription were nonetheless almost certainly made at around the same time, and both were perhaps commissioned to mark the same event, namely the crushing of the Sumerian revolt, followed by the seizure and redistribution of large areas of lands in the state of Lagash—the estates being handed out to Akkad officials and probably also to some locals who remained loyal to the regime. The thesis is partly confirmed by the fact that, on the basis of its epigraphy, the inscription can be dated to the classical Sargonic period that includes the reigns of Naram-Sin and his followers (Gelb et al. 1989–91, pp. 88–9).

The Akkad Stele and the land distribution inscription were therefore presumably two distinct carvings that were both produced in the early part of the reign of Naram-Sin to memorialise his quashing of the insurrection in the south of Sumer, including Girsu–Lagash. The Akkad Stele shows in graphic detail the defeat of the rebels and their subsequent fate, with those who were not killed on the battlefield being captured and brutally murdered, while the land allocation inscription records the retributive confiscation and redistribution of lands. They were both apparently found on Tell K, but it should again be stressed that no information whatsoever is given in the published report about their find locations, and Heuzey's confusion about the number of pieces, together with his incorrect ideas about how they fitted together, indicates that he either did not have, or did not recall, any first-hand information about them that might have come from Sarzec, but also that he did not have the stones in front of him when he was preparing his published account. If they were indeed found on the slopes of Tell K, they were presumably originally erected on pedestals in commanding positions, conceivably quite close to the Akkad Ningirsu temple (if not within its confines), where they cast the shadow of imperial dominance over the holy site and by extension over the city and the state of Lagash generally. That being the case, it would represent a remarkable historical irony that the two Akkad memorials might have been sited together in the holiest spot on Tell K because it is a curious reversal of the way such monuments had been juxtaposed in the temple (or its close environs) over many centuries, all the way back to the era of the Lower Construction. The assumed placement of the Akkad carvings was intended to proclaim to the world that Akkad imperial authority in Girsu–Lagash emanated from the very heart of Tell K. Once they were defaced, the empowering symbolism of the narrative victory reliefs and the retributive land redistribution inscriptions was rendered null and void.

Tell K from the Second Dynasty of Lagash to the Third Dynasty of Ur

After the fall of Akkad, Girsu–Lagash enjoyed a renaissance under the Second Dynasty of Lagash. The rebirth was initiated by Puzurmama and driven forward with revolutionary energy by Ur-Bau, who was the author of a seismic event: the relocation of the Temple of Ningirsu from its ancestral home on Tell K to its new site on Tell A. The big move was crowned by Ur-Bau's son-in-law and successor, Gudea, who soon rebuilt the entire Tell A temple complex—the New Eninnu—on a stupendous scale. Very little is known about Ur-Bau's predecessor, Puzurmama, except that he was a high-ranking military official of the Akkad empire. He is known to have become the ruler (ensí) of Lagash after the reign of Sharkalishari, and thereafter he adopted the more elevated title of king (lugal) of Lagash (RIME 2.12.5.1). This is not a mere matter of nomenclature because the reappearance of the office of king in the state suggests that Girsu–Lagash enjoyed a renewed period of independence in the late Sargonic period. The sequence of events after Puzurmama is obscure. A reconstruction of a royal inscription in the name of Dudu, king of Akkad (known only from a later copy), seemingly mentions an attack on Girsu, but the text is too poorly preserved to inspire much confidence (RIME 2.1.10.2). Subsequently, with the advent of the Second Dynasty of Lagash (Lagash II), followed by the rise of the Third Dynasty of Ur (Ur III), the historical narrative becomes much more distinct.

The epoch-making relocation of the Ningirsu temple, which shifted the focus of worship in Girsu to Tell A, involved the remodelling of Tell K so that it could continue to function in a subsidiary capacity. In the central area, the Akkad shrine to Ningirsu (probably including wall *Mur*, as previously argued), which was by now surely a mere shadow of the illustrious temples that had previously occupied the site, was levelled, and a new building was constructed on the foundations. Dating to the time of Gudea, it was apparently rather small, as evidenced by the extent of the recorded remains, and it was not intended to be another instantiation of the temple. The discoveries attributed to Gudea include a foundation box containing a figurine and a tablet that were found above wall *Mur* in the mound at a Sarzec height of about 15.1 m. This deposition might have been connected with a wall that is marked O on Plan C (1), and that in turn was directly associated with a door socket inscribed in the name of Gudea. Made of fired bricks, wall O was offset to the north of the plot that was occupied by the long succession temples, and its location is strongly suggestive of the changed use of the sacred summit under Gudea.

In the peripheral areas, on the SE side of Tell K's middle terrace (at a Sarzec height of about 10.8 m), there is evidence that a platform was fully or partially rebuilt. This is the fired-brick block adjacent to the curved drain (marked on Sarzec's Plan D; Fig. 34) that can be seen in the photo taken by Sarzec (Pl. 58 bis (2); Fig. 50). Unlike the drain, the block was not marked on Plan D, and as previously noted the curving water channel was wrongly labelled on the plan as a 'more recent' wall, a description that should have been attached to the omitted Gudea construction. It is also clear that the Early Dynastic Large Stairway, at a lower level, on the NE side of the tell (also shown on Sarzec's Plan D), was rebuilt by Gudea, who repaved it and installed foundation boxes on both sides of the surviving upper flight of steps (at a Sarzec height of 8.8 m). Two metres below, where the stairway began at a Sarzec height of 6.8 m, was the Pillar of Gudea (illustrated on Plan D), which took the form of a composite pedestal made up of four adjoining circular columns (detailed in Chapter 9) that was in all likelihood a podium for a large votive object, perhaps a stele or the Cylinders of Gudea (though they were probably displayed elsewhere, as is explained below). The Small Staircase on the SE side of Tell K (shown on Plan D) was also rebuilt by Gudea, and it was again flanked by two foundation boxes.

The evidence suggests that Gudea refurbished Tell K as a more limited staged platform, with a monumental ascent on its NE side (the renovated Large Stairway) that was fronted by a podium (the Pillar of Gudea), and a smaller (perhaps service) access point on its SE side. The summit was crowned with a rather modest commemorative building that was built with the same NW–SE alignment as the long series of previous temples that had stood on the mound, but situated to the north of the spot previously occupied by the older temples, and therefore not referencing their traditional ground plan. The Gudea inscriptions found on Tell K commemorate the reconstruction of the transferred complex—Gudea's New Eninnu—in its replacement home on Tell A, and this should in all likelihood be regarded as Gudea's way of paying tribute to the Ningirsu temple's age-old location, even as he was constructing its latest iteration elsewhere. There could not, of course, be two Eninnus because the sacred centre of worship was the house of the god, which had been moved to Tell A, so perhaps the commemorative structure on Tell K acted like a cenotaph—a memorial shrine that was intended to acknowledge the ineradicable importance of the ancient sacred locus, even though it no longer contained the god's cult statue, which had been removed to Tell A.

It is appropriate here to highlight a fundamental point about the locations of certain kinds of brick-built constructions and other architectural elements that were inscribed with commemorative texts because a commonly held misconception about inscriptions of this kind has previously proven to be misleading. Structures made of inscribed bricks (or structures that incorporate dedicatory artefacts such as foundation deposits) that explicitly commemorate a temple or another key building do not necessarily mark the spot on which the celebrated edifice itself stood. Though this is most often the case, and can usually be relatively easily confirmed, it is also apparent that there are some notable exceptions—instances in which the erection of a temple, to take the most obvious example, was memorialised on inscriptions that were not located in its architectural fabric. The only way to be certain about the meaning of structures and texts of this nature is therefore to recontextualise them. A case in point is the Pillar of Gudea, which was made of bricks inscribed with the standard Gudea formula celebrating the building of the New Eninnu, though some of them were marked with texts commemorating the construction of a cedar porch that is described as the place in which Ningirsu pronounces judgement (RIME 3.1.1.7.44):

> For Ningirsu, Enlil's mighty warrior, his masters, Gudea, ruler of Lagash, built his House, the White Thunderbird. There he installed for him a ... with cedar (ceiling), (Ningirsu's) place where he gives judgement.

Though this is commonly taken at face value to mean that the god's court of justice was situated on Tell I, where it was somehow physically linked to the Pillar of Gudea, which might even have been the actual seat of divine judgement, this was almost certainly not the case. As the British Museum team's excavations have conclusively shown, the cedar porch of judgement was located on Tell A, where it was of course placed inside the sacred precinct of the New Eninnu. The composite Pillar of Gudea was formed of a base that supported four adjoining columns that occupied a square with sides of about 1.6 m (overall), while the diameter of each of the four individual columns was approximately 0.8 m, and the entire structure was about 1.8 m high (see the detailed description in Chapter 9). It probably functioned as a podium or an elaborate pedestal for an important cult object. As Heuzey rightly pointed out, the starlike and roseate forms of the individual columns perhaps had symbolic associations with divinity, but no overarching symbolism can be detected in the way the four circles were placed. For example, there is no perceptible geometric relationship between them and a larger concentric circle that could contain them all. Indeed, as noted above with respect to Sarzec's photos (Figs. 51, 52 and 54), their proportions seem to have been pragmatically derived from the measurement of the sides of a standard Gudea square brick rather than from any underlying theories about the philosophical meaning of circles. The Pillar of Gudea was by no means the only construction of its kind that was commissioned by Gudea. Numerous bricks belonging to cylindrical or rounded pilaster-like structures were found on Tell A, and it is almost certainly the case that similar commemorative pillars must have been installed within the sacred precinct of the New Eninnu, especially in the ceremonial courtyard, as is mentioned in Chapter 41. What should be noted, however, is that brick-built columns, which were made up of several different kinds of expertly formed shapes, were seemingly an innovative feature of Girsu architecture under Gudea, and no such constructions were found in the Early Dynastic layers of Tell K.

One especially interesting discovery made during the British Museum team's excavations further confirms that brick pillars of the kind exemplified by the composite Pillar of Gudea were indeed used as supports for the display of votive artefacts. An inscribed Lagash II brick that must have come from a rounded upright (TG2266) records the fact it was part of a pedestal that held a divine weapon belonging to Ningirsu. Inscribed in the name of Nammahni, the text reads: 'For Ningirsu, mighty warrior of Enlil, his lord—Nammahni, ruler of Lagash, made his weapon, the 50-headed mace'. The curved brick indicates that the support was almost certainly a pillar-type structure, while the inscription further shows that the divine mace was not held in the god's hand as an appurtenance of the cult statue, but was displayed separately on a brick installation.

The Display Setting and Provenance of the Cylinders of Gudea

The Cylinders of Gudea, which were apparently found in the vicinity of the Pillar of Gudea, suggestively add to an understanding of the changed character of Tell K under Gudea. Narrating and explaining the reasons behind the building of the New Eninnu on Tell A, they were conceivably displayed either on the Pillar of Gudea at the bottom of the Large Stairway, which was the ceremonial approach to the upper part of the mound, or most likely inside the newly built cenotaph in the former sacred precinct, thereby reinforcing the idea that the relocation of the temple to Tell A and the shrine's subsequent enlargement were sanctioned by the god himself. There were seemingly three cylinders in total (including an inferred Lost Cylinder of which only fragments have been preserved), and the diameters of all three (based on the measurements of the two that were found) were between 0.32 m and 0.33 m. The relative lengths of the diameters of the cylinders and that of the four brick columns that formed the Pillar of Gudea make it highly improbable, both practically and as a well-conceived design, that the composite installation supported the cylinders. Furthermore, the way the cylinders were fabricated, with a relatively thin outer shell of terracotta and an internal filling of plaster, would have made them highly unsuitable for outdoor display, where they would have been subject to natural processes of erosion. Indeed, the very sharpness of the preserved cuneiform inscriptions bears witness to the fact that they were well protected, both during their active lives and after they were eventually decommissioned. It is therefore altogether more likely that the Cylinders of Gudea were displayed on a podium (or podiums) elsewhere, and that they were kept inside a building. In addition, the fact that they were covered with a continuous cuneiform narrative that was doubtless designed to be read by some of their viewers (and maybe read aloud to audiences), makes it a fair surmise that they were shown singly and in the round, such that visitors or readers could move around them. Alternatively, they might have stood on turntables of some kind. Whether all of this means that they were displayed in the inferred cenotaph on the summit of Tell K is a matter of conjecture, but it seems highly plausible.

With regard to the provenance of the Cylinders of Gudea, it should be stressed that, while there is little doubt that they were unearthed in the vicinity of Tell K, and certainly within the confines of the extended sacred precinct of Girsu (the Urukug), their precise archaeological context is unexpectedly obscure and has not formerly been considered with the attention it deserves—a fact that is even more surprising in view of the immense importance of these icons of ancient Sumerian literacy. The first uncertainty is whether Sarzec actually discovered the Gudea Cylinders during his first season or second season (1877 or 1878), when his main focus was unquestionably on Tell A, where he first came across some of the spectacular Gudea statues that made his name. The opening of the published account (Sarzec and Heuzey 1912, pp. 5–6) would seem to suggest that he unearthed them in Season 2 (1878), when he is known to have cut a series of long soundings in the general area of the Urukug that included Tells A and K:

> I wished, however, to uncover the archaeological riches that might be contained in the surrounding plain and the smaller tells, which, at varying distances, surrounded the main mound (Tell A). I spaced out my workers in long lines, ordering them to open, metre by metre, using their pickaxes, soundings of sufficient depth. By this expeditious means I succeeded in discovering a fairly large number of precious objects. This is how I uncovered several stone thresholds, then a whole series of brick-built boxes containing bronze statuettes and inscribed tablets, but the most important result of this rapid reconnaissance was the discovery of the two large barrels made of terracotta that I found buried at the foot of one of the tells: the one that I mark on my general plan with the letter I', and that I will describe in the continuation of my work.

True to his word, in the more detailed discussion of his excavations in the environs of Tell K that follows (Sarzec and Heuzey 1912, p. 66), Sarzec describes the moment when he unearthed the two Cylinders of Gudea in the vicinity of Tell I' (also called the Mound of the Turning Path), which was one of the much smaller mounds (hardly more than humps) that made up the associated tells (I and I'), south-east of the Pillar of Gudea. The problem is that his later account contradicts the one given above:

> An important discovery, which dates from my first trip, contributed to my decision to carry out deeper excavations at this point. I mean the two large terracotta cylinders, sixty and fifty-six centimetres long, and thirty-two and thirty-three centimetres in diameter, entirely covered with long columns of inscriptions. It was in the very interior of the turning path that I chanced upon them during my first surveys. I suppose they rolled down there when the buildings on the tell burned down. When I discovered them, the openings with which they are pierced along their axes were closed with conical terracotta plugs. The interior was filled with a compact mass of plaster that had been poured in, doubtless to make them heavier and more solid. Thinking that the plaster filling might contain some interesting objects, I carefully removed it, but without finding anything. These exceptional documents are perhaps not unrelated to the important constructions whose remains I have discovered on the site of Tells I and I′.

The 'important constructions' found in the vicinity of Tells I and I′ that are referred to in the last sentence is the four-part Pillar of Gudea (fully uncovered eleven years later in 1889), and it is of interest that Sarzec believed that the 'ancient monuments of Tello', as he describes them a few lines before the quoted passage, were destroyed by fire. He is doubtless referring to the important buildings that he discovered in the upper layers of Tell K, where his systematic excavations began in 1888, and it is revealing that, from the outset, he seems to have been convinced that they were finally consumed in a general conflagration—a mistaken idea that subsequently misled generations of scholars. Of the greatest significance, however, is the fact that in this paragraph he clearly states that the Cylinders of Gudea were found by chance in his first season (1877), and not uncovered by his workers in 1878, as previously reported. His belief that they must have rolled down from the upper part of the tell when the buildings there burned down must be taken to mean that they descended (in his opinion) not from Tells I and I′, but from the summit of Tell K. In this passage he also recalls that they were found intact, with two holes on their flat tops and bottoms that were sealed (again, according to Sarzec's interpretation) with conical terracotta plugs, and their interiors were filled with plaster.

In general, Sarzec must be considered a reasonably reliable witness, and some of the information he relates suggests that he might have compiled the contradictory reports some years after the events, so his memory might have been faulty, but the inconsistencies in his two accounts open the possibility that he did not in actuality stumble across the objects, but perhaps rather acquired them from local tribespeople, who might have informed him where they had been found. In this regard, it should be recalled that the provenance of some of the important artefacts seemingly chanced upon in 1877, including the upper part of the Gudea Colossus, has been questioned, and it is feasible (if not, indeed, probable) that some of the items supposedly found in his first one or two seasons were either presented to him by local people or bought from them. Despite the precision with which the find location of the cylinders is described, further doubt is cast upon his recollections by the fact that the Gudea Cylinders and the upper part of the Gudea Colossus are both said to have 'rolled down' from the top of adjacent mounds: Tells I and I′ in the case of the cylinders and Tell A in the case of the statue. Not only is the coincidence suspect, it is also extraordinarily unlikely that any of these objects rolled down the side of a hill in the straightforward way Sarzec implies: the statue, which is an extremely heavy object, would not have moved without being propelled, while the terracotta cylinders would unquestionably have been broken or very badly damaged if they had tumbled down the side of a bumpy mud-brick mound from the top of Tell K to the comparatively low-lying drain or conduit in which they were apparently found. Furthermore, is it credible that the two cylinders could have accidentally rolled down a slope and landed side by side in a spot where they then remained undisturbed for thousands of years? And if Sarzec came across them (and the statue) so readily, why were they not found earlier by locals, who must have been extremely familiar with the site? Finally and alternatively, therefore, it is maybe more conceivable that Sarzec's workers located the Gudea Cylinders in the vicinity of Tells I and I′ during his first or second season, but while he was absent from the site, and that they pointed them out to him on his return, or during one of his daily inspections. Or, in a similar manner, Sarzec could have acquired the cylinders upon his arrival at the start of his first season, and the locals could have directed him to the place where they might have originated (the area of Tells I and I').

A further point that is often forgotten or misunderstood is that Sarzec's account would suggest that he actually found the two cylinders in a well-preserved state. That being the case, they must presumably have been carefully deposited, hidden away and protected before they were subsequently rediscovered. This again does not fit well with the declared provenance and find location offered by Sarzec. Although he refrains from mentioning it in his reports, and indeed stresses the care that he took with the objects, it is surely probable that the two cylinders were broken into pieces when Sarzec, in search of hidden treasures, removed the terracotta plugs from their ends and dug out the plaster with which they had been filled. No explanation is recorded about the breakage, and it might be that they were damaged while being transported from Tello to the Louvre, but since they were apparently preserved unharmed when Sarzec found them, and he freely admits that he tampered with them, the first explanation seems more likely. Lastly, no mention is made at any point of the fragments of the lost third cylinder that is known to have existed, and the provenances of some inscribed pieces that derived from it therefore remain unknown.

What conclusions can be drawn from this discussion? First, in view of the excellent condition in which the Gudea Cylinders were found, it is probable that they were deliberately and painstakingly interred in antiquity. Secondly, and despite the inherent uncertainties, the different possible scenarios outlined above indicate a general find location in the vicinity of Tells I and I', but the idea that they were picked up at a precisely defined point, such as the 'very interior of the turning path', as stated by Sarzec, is doubtful. Thirdly, does the possibility that they were secreted in antiquity mean that they were ritually buried in a favissa pit somewhere near the place where they were displayed, either close to the Pillar of Gudea, or possibly elsewhere? This is not in any way improbable, but unfortunately it cannot be verified.

After Gudea

Among the kings of the Third Dynasty of Ur who came after Gudea, Shulgi in particular is known to have renovated the relocated spectacular New Eninnu that Gudea constructed on Tell A. Gudea was deified after his death, and Shulgi is known to have worshipped his newly divine predecessor with special devotion, treating his statues as sacred relics. He also continued the work of remembrance and commemoration on Tell K that Gudea had initiated when he refounded the Ningirsu temple that had been transferred by Ur-Bau. This is demonstrated by the foundation box in his name that was found in the topmost layer of Tell K (marked on the right of the section on Plan C (2)). There is no suggestion that Shulgi built an entirely new memorial, but he might have repaired or refurbished the walls of the inferred Gudea cenotaph, as he did with the New Eninnu on Tell A, and marked his work by installing a foundation box. The Gudea box and the Shulgi box were found at more or less the same Sarzec heights of 15.1 m and 15.2 m, respectively, and they were both aligned along a NE–SW axis. As previously suggested, it is probable that wall O on Plan C (1) and the two foundation boxes marked the edges of the plot occupied by the inferred cenotaph—the memorial to the old Temple of Ningirsu, the former sanctum sanctorum on the summit of Tell K. Remarkably, several ex-votos dedicated to Ningirsu dating to the Lagash II and Ur III periods were recorded that could also be associated with the shrine that was built in memory of the mound's former glories.